MW00606951

WORLD CAPITALS:

Toward Guided Urbanization

WORLD CAPITALS:

Toward Guided Urbanization

Edited by

H. Wentworth Eldredge

ANCHOR PRESS/DOUBLEDAY
GARDEN CITY, NEW YORK
1975

Anchor Books edition: 1975

Library of Congress Cataloging in Publication Data

Eldredge, Hanford Wentworth, 1909–
World capitals.

Includes bibliographical references.
1. Capitals (Cities) 2. Urbanization. I. Title.
HT153.E46 301.36′3
ISBN 0-385-05323-1
Library of Congress Catalog Card Number 73–79661

Printed in the United States of America

To Diana, Jamie and Alan
who once again survived—just

Preface

A national capital is a multifunctional city of a rather special sort. Despite world communism and a number of powerful international religions, the still ruling ideology in the closing decades of the twentieth century remains *nationalism*—state worship in slightly varying modes. Thus the capital bears high the symbolic torch for the entire nation—the image the chosen city creates is a powerful factor in national status and internal self-conception. In addition, the capital must perform the normal urban functions of caring for its own generally numerous citizenry, earning its own keep and continued existence as a system by producing goods and performing services (including its national governing function). As a result of these complicating factors, it is not surprising that nation states have lavished scarce resources on the quality of life of their capitals—especially in urban physical design and grandiose architectural furnishings. From absolutist Pharaohs and Bourbons through mature (and immature) "democracies" to contemporary dictatorships, this zeroing in of public wealth on the capital has been clearly evidenced from ancient Thebes through Alexandria, St. Petersburg and Paris on to Washington, Moscow, Ankara, Brasilia and Chandigarh.

It should be noted immediately that of the eleven "capital" cities chosen for detailed exploration here, two (Chandigarh and Toronto) are not *national* capitals but *provincial* capitals. Chandigarh, originally designed as the government center for India's Punjab, was conceived by Nehru as the symbol of the new India—little spectacular could be done to revamp imperial Delhi, designed by and for the British Raj. Well-studied Toronto, as the wealthiest and most powerful city in the wealthiest and most powerful Canadian province, pioneered on the North American continent in the thrust for metropolitan government, and was included here as being possibly of more present significance for Canada's image than the national capital of Ottawa.

If it be true that capitals are of such considerable importance in holding high the old nation's flag and raising the new nation's banner for all to see, then treasure and brains heaped on such cities should have produced something rather fine. If man fails in his capital city production, then can he be expected to produce in the foreseeable future a glorious city anywhere—rich in varied options for rewarding human living?

The process of *urbanization* is first explored as an introduction, followed by the eleven test cases chosen. It was heart-rending to leave out, for example, Delhi, Peking, Rome, Canberra, Cairo and Buenos Aires, but in book production structure often dictates function. A final section of three chapters attempts to assess capabilities for managing in a human fashion both the urbanization process and the resultant *urbanism*—given late twentieth-century techniques of physical and societal design and the ability to *deliver* outstanding political, economic and social goods and services to expectant societies—both sophisticated and unsophisticated.

Grateful thanks are due to my esteemed contributors who have suffered overtime in hammering this book together. From varied backgrounds, each has looked at his or her city from a different viewpoint varying from that of practicing planner to architectural historian. There was never a thought of dictating a format—which would have been patently impossible in any case. Like the proverbial elephant described by the blind men, each specialist sees his or her city from a special—often divergent—viewpoint. The result is not a scientific picture but it is a well-informed practitioner's view.

Both cities and books take a longer time than one thinks to build. (Major L'Enfant's Washington New Town, designed in the eighteenth century, is still not finished.) Four complicated years went by in bringing this task to fruition.

Without the noble efforts of Donna Musgrove who struggled through numerous versions of chapter manuscripts, and the excellent support of Elsie Sniffin and Judy Jones, who assisted in holding the entire circus together, there would never have been a book. My heartfelt thanks to them and to Dartmouth College which generously supported my research. David Harrop at Doubleday produced the final book. Obviously, any faults and errors are mine.

H. Wentworth Eldredge

Tarn House
Norwich, Vermont
1975

Contents

List of Illustrations

PART I

Western: Old World

CHAPTER 1

Urbanization: A Never-ending Process

H. Wentworth Eldredge

URBAN SOCIETY: THE STATE OF URBANISM

According to a poll taken by the metropolitan government of Tokyo in the summer of 1970, half of the nearly twelve million citizens of that city, the world's largest, disliked living there "because of air pollution, traffic and the lack of playgrounds for children."[1] Eleven disparate mayors of important American cities in solemn confab after viewing the rubble and gutted buildings of the Brownsville section of Brooklyn—so reminiscent of a bomb-damage site—under the guidance of the beseiged and cornered Mayor Lindsay of New York, warned of the immanent collapse of U.S. cities.[2] The mayor of New Orleans said his city "was going down the drain"; Kevin White of Boston found that Brownsville "may be the first tangible sign of the collapse of our civilization" and stated his own city was "a tinderbox . . . an armed camp." Wilmington's Harry G. Haskell predicted some American cities would soon go bankrupt.[3]

If this be a reliable collective judgment on the urban place, "man's noblest creation," there is still some progress to be made before the utopian city can be enjoyed by humankind. It would seem that man as yet is hardly a very successful city-building animal. Perhaps he just lacks experience. Given the now generally accepted one-million-year, twenty-four-hour time clock of man's existence on earth, only the last fourteen minutes have been spent in settled villages—with the last seven in what may be termed true towns and cities—and the final ten seconds in the industrial city of today. The domestication of this most intelligent primate is thus a very recent thing, and it clearly has been difficult to tame the predatory hunter and to sophisticate the simple early agriculturist to live even reasonably well, tightly packed together in huge man heaps.

With empty deserts, deserted Arctic tundra, and the sparsely-peopled rain forests of the tropics, as well as the seemingly sparsely-settled and muddled land in use in readily habitable areas, it would appear that there remains ample room (excluding the sea) into which the 3,500,000,000 persons now on earth could, using some ingenuity, expand with elbow room. Whether the 7,000,000,000 predicted for the year A.D. 2000 could do so is a much more chancy question. But whatever gross square mileage of the earth's water-free or ice-free surface remains, the optimum areas for human habitation available are clearly lessening. The "good earth" is increasingly covered by settlement (leaving the "bad earth" still empty) and increasingly these settlements are becoming denser, more numerous and more sprawling, carelessly sealing the planet's surface under streets and buildings by the process of *urbanization* into the increasingly universal human state of *urbanism*.

Perhaps this dichotomizing of the process of urbanization versus the state of urbanism is a fictitious intellectual device merely useful for understanding the city-making human proclivity. Clearly urbanization still goes on apace on a global scale and no *fixed state* of urbanism has yet been reached anywhere—nor does it appear likely for the foreseeable future that one will be.

Louis Wirth, University of Chicago sociologist of the pre-World War II decades, in his classic "Urbanism as a Way of Life,"[4] has distilled the essence of the modern city. Although his sweeping characterization on a macroscale has been sniped at by various hairsplitting intellects, it still serves as a cogent, synoptic map to guide us in the urban present. It may be roughly summarized under five headings.

1. Urban society is characterized by a large, dense, heterogeneous mass of people with the city proper radiating its influence widely.

2. It tends to be ecologically subdivided into diverse populations by class/income, ethnicity, color (where applicable). The urban area is generally divided by function: industrial, business, shopping, education, various levels of residence, recreation, etc. This occurs both by chance and by design.

3. There is an increasingly elaborate division of labor operating an increasingly complex technology.

4. The formal institutions of political, economic and social life (secondary groups) tend to take over human interaction from the primary or family/community groupings of the simpler past. Individuals tend to interact with each other in highly segmental roles not as "full" or "complete" human beings.

5. Moreover, the individual, sometimes suffering from anomie and even alienation, is often buffeted by the irrational currents of crowd or collective (emotional) behavior. The broad sense of felt community is replaced by "a spirit of competition, aggrandizement and mutual exploitation" leaving this social being open to severe stresses. There is ample evidence of conflict and disjunction within contemporary pluralistic society. To many the conjugal family appears as the only haven.

Some reasonably precise—at least operationally valid definitions—are in order to proceed further in our exploration of the vital question as to whether this urban/urbanizing world can in fact be guided by its creator. Urbanization is, as stated above, the process by which men gather in settled villages developing gradually into towns, preindustrial cities, industrial cities, metropolises, megalopolises, world urbanized regions, on to the predicted ecumenopolis or world city[5] of Constantinos Doxiadis, the Greek city planner and theoretician.

Man's controlling technologies for managing his own fate—intellectual, technical, biological, behavioral and organizational—appear condemned to be still inadequate for the stupendous task of guiding on a macro-, holistic or comprehensive scale his societal destinies. Man's "shining alabaster cities," unfortunately, are now hard to glimpse through the smog and in any case it might not be rewarding to peer too closely into filthy slums, traffic jams, with too many frenetic multihued citizens disliking each other, brawling, stealing, killing, fornicating or lulled by the idiot box and moronic professional sports' spectacles in huge colisea! For whatever the complex reasons, it would appear that humans everywhere are crawling over each other with turtle-like callousness in the "urban jungle" or should one say "behavioral sink."

Contrary to these trumpeted portents of a horrid future is the presently obscured fact that the cities are where man has produced *civilization*—the life of the mind in theatre, literature, architecture, philosophy, education, the visual arts, the dance and all those multiplicity of incredible feats of the human psyche which have together lifted their possessors far above the other beasts. But we now appear to have arrived at the present contradictory stage where the question must be posed as to whether in conquering the planet man has merely elaborated means for the eventual suicide of his own species as the colorful study *The Limits to Growth*[6] suggests.

Despite the generally perceived horrors of these great modern man heaps, the world's inhabitants continue to flood swiftly into urban places "where the action is." Country dwellers pile into Stockholm from the emptying barren north; leave the fruitless agriculture of the Indian countryside for the bustees of Delhi; crowd Tokyo and Caracas; and rush in to man the bureaucracy of federal Washington or simply to escape the racial inequalities of the American rural Southland. Cities remain as powerful magnets or huge sponges.

The United Nations foresees a "crisis" in *Human Settlements*.[7] By the year 2000 with the world's population doubling, the world urban population will increase three times to three billion, or about half the world's people will be city dwellers. The dimensions of the housing and public infrastructure needs are staggering since "between 1970 and the year 2000 over 1,000 million new urban and rural dwellings will be required in addition to 2,000 million new modernized work places with accompanying public facilities and public service areas." The United Nations Economic and Social Council's Advisory Committee on the Application of Science and Technology to Development noted that around 90,000 people a day are moving into the urban areas of Latin America, Asia and Africa—a form of "over-urbanization" with which neither job opportunities nor city physical and political infrastructures seems remotely ready to cope.

If contemporary man shows some unease in dealing with his present industrial city life, one can only hope for a rapid increase in his capacities for managing urban society in order to face the exponential increase in complexity promised for the posturban, "postindustrial" (Daniel Bell), "postcivilized" (Kenneth Boulding), "superindustrial" (Alvin Toffler), or "information" (as the Japanese planners term it) societies promised ahead.

ETHOLOGY: BIOLOGICAL MAN

As the social and behavioral sciences, especially the former, attempted to establish themselves as separate disciplines in the late nineteenth and the first half of the twentieth century, they emphasized that they were dealing with a unique sort of creation: man. This creature, although admittedly a primate mammal, was so bright that he had constructed over the millennia a nonbiological shield as protector against and as exploiter of the natural environment; this was dubbed *culture* by the anthropologists, but popularly known in its advanced stages as civilization. The fact that man was an animal was for almost thirty years pushed under the rug as social scientists acted "as if" man was a *tabula rasa* on which experience—usually the social experience of living in groups using a common culture—wrote large and firmly. Behavioral scientists often tended to follow Pavlov in the socialist world and John Watson's behaviorism and the rat-research school in the non-socialist.[8] In that age-old controversy, at least during recent times, *environment* seemed to win out over *heredity;* it is only within the past decade or so that the pendulum has swung ever so slightly the other way. More certain of their identity as students of the human animal and his society and culture, the behavioral and social scientists are now commencing to pay heed to the siren songs of the biologists and zoologists who are interested in the comparative behavior of living things. Man may be a naked ape! This most tentative, comparative biological study of behavior is dubbed *ethology*. These researchers and their popularizers have refurbished the temporarily forgotten thesis that man is quite simply the human animal species and (a) that he does inherit physiological patterns along with his cousins, the present fauna of the earth, and (b) that there were and are pre- and protohuman societies with learned "customs" as well as biologically influenced proclivities.

What does all this have to do with guiding urbanization and urbanism?[9] Just this: If man has certain biological propensities as well as pre- and protohuman social patterning, it behooves us to design and structure huge human agglomerations in a fashion to fit *with* and not work *against* these behavioral sets.

> When the pressures of modern living become heavy, the harassed city-dweller often refers to his teeming world as a concrete jungle. This is a colourful way of describing the pattern of life in a dense urban community, but it is also grossly inaccurate, as anyone who has studied a real jungle will confirm.
>
> Under normal conditions, in their natural habitats, wild animals do not mutilate themselves, masturbate, attack their offspring, develop stomach ulcers, become fetishists, suffer from obesity, form homo-sexual pair-bonds, or commit murder. Among city-dwellers, needless to say, all these things occur. Does this, then, reveal a basic difference between the human species and other animals? At first glance it seems to be so. But this is deceptive. Other animals do behave in these ways under certain circumstances, namely when they are confined in the unnatural conditions

> of captivity. The zoo animal in a cage exhibits all these abnormalities that we know so well from our human companions. Clearly, then, the city is not a concrete jungle, it is a human zoo.[10]

It is conceded that man is clearly the most malleable, most generalized and most intelligent of all earthly living matter, but that merely underlines the necessity of maximizing his potential in physical/societal structures that nurture rather than minimize capabilities. Uncertain though it is, ethology has posited a number of behavior patterns to which societal and physical planners must pay heed. Here are tentative findings in seven behavioral areas to be considered below relevant to the task at hand of understanding urbanization and urbanism:

(a) the territorial imperative
(b) status orders
(c) in groups versus out groups
(d) aggression
(e) space/distance
(f) behavioral sink
(g) stimulus levels.

(a) *The territorial imperative* has been popularized by the writings of Robert Ardrey,[11] based on the scientific investigations of Konrad Lorenz and others. Each living group in order to obtain adequate nourishment and *Lebensraum* must develop and hold territory inviolate from outsiders. Without this group, space, the basis for survival, is lost. "To have and to hold" territory for group maintenance (both psychic and physical) might be "an iron law of nature" evidenced all the way from the nesting robin through the Uganda kob (antelope), or from a hippie pad onto the "inviolable" frontier of "sovereign" nations. In a more gentle sense, private family living space seems to be the necessary nourishment for both the family institution and for the adequate nurture of its young. This in no way implies that the monogamous conjugal family is the end point of human evolutionary development.

(b) *Status orders:* All animals tend to rank themselves as group members. The pecking order of chickens is a well-known biological phenomenon brilliantly portrayed in that flinty story, *Lord of the Flies*.[12] Armies, where the stakes are very high—life itself—have found pecking orders valuable; and the ranking of every navy ship's company was—at least until recently—one of the stiffest hierarchical systems on earth. There is little need to belabor the fact that class and caste (with the individual's status concomitant) have been well nigh universal in human societal experience.[13] This indicates undoubtedly that the benefits of a status order have tended to outweigh the costs for societal survival despite the vociferous contentions of the New Left. Even the idealist Russian revolutionary army found it had to scrap "togetherness" between officers and men and return to the strict traditional military class structure (anti-Marxian revisionism!) in ordering the huge tough machine which stopped the highly hierarchical Nazi armies at the gates of Moscow.[14] Today one hears much about "participatory democracy" and "one man, one vote" (shades of Rousseau). But to the cynical sophisticated urbanist, it must appear odd that in an increasingly complex world—inundated by rapid social change which demands new intellectual, technical, biological, behavioral and organizational technologies—expert leadership should be subordinated, even scrapped.

(c) *In groups versus out groups:* perhaps group identity and group morale come close to the crisis we have heard so much about recently from complaining youth. Their passionate search for identity and their seeming failure to discover it, except in odd Woodstocks, does suggest that the great impersonal man heaps of the urban megalopolis are not understandable to human beings and that the time may have come to attempt to build a truly warm multigroup or pluralistic society. That time seems immediate in the United States with its warring ethnic, color and income groups continuously at each other's throats. The out-group concept, however, introduces a troublesome complexity akin to the difficult conflict management so needed in international relations. Multigroup cities seem designed to produce a machine-gun tattoo of veto actions; every plan gets shot down! How then to build the reality of rewarding multiple in groups without eternal, often purposeless, strife with other out groups where opposing vectors tend to produce stagnation. It seems patent that the urban experience with its loss of community needs some tinkering as our ethologists have cogently pointed out.[15]

(d) *Aggression:* The debate swirls and will continue on undoubtedly as to whether man is a gentle agriculturist with a fundamental benign love of all his fellows. Or whether he is a predatory hunter designed and constructed by Nature and/or God to battle fiercely in the eternal struggle to survive as the most complexly aggressive and violent living thing? Is he basically a herbivore or is he basically a carnivore? The fact obviously is that he is omnivorous with rudimentary canines and serviceable lettuce-crunching grinders; this may indicate that he is both the Dr. Jekyl and the Mr. Hyde of protoplasm. Ethologists, despite the Eskimo who never knew war, the gentle Christus (see modern Israel!), the peaceful Quakers and Seventh-Day Adventists as well as benign Buddhism (see imperial Japan, both state Shinto and Buddhist of World War II!), have tended to uphold the thesis that man has the basic behavioral tendencies of an aggressive, restless carnivore.[16] This portends, if even partially true, trouble within the frustrating impacted cities among diverse groups, and on a much larger scale apocalyptic prospects for mankind in conflict between states and ideologies. With pressures to maintain territory, facing the *behavioral sinks* predicated below, as well as the implications of constricted space and a mindless burgeoning of population masses, there may well be an unhappy future of continuing conflict in store for us all—developed or undeveloped. This depends of course on whether the ethologists are correct in their quantum jump from animal biological/behavior patterns to human biological/cultural patterns.[17] This is not an unworthy question which has in recent times been brilliantly treated by Hannah Arendt in exploring the relationship between violence and power in a study[18] "provoked by the events and debates of the last few years as seen against the background of the twentieth century, which has become, indeed, as Lenin predicted, a century of wars and revolutions, hence a century of that violence which is currently believed to be their common denominator." She accepts no innate aggression but blames the current near chaos, both internal and external, on the failure of modern society to use adequate power/force in maintaining order.

(e) *Space/distance:* Seemingly man carries a surrounding bubble of personal space in which he is included. Anyone who trespasses these invisible boundaries is invading privacy—unless specifically invited as are lovers and children generally speaking. This bubble varies from culture to culture and from class to subclass, but all societies appear to define a "respectable" or "normal" distance between persons. To come closer is to threaten![19] Latin Americans rapidly back North Americans into a corner in heated conversation; *latino* space is less large than *norte Americano.* An English aristocrat shudders at Cockney chumminess; while Anglo-Saxons tend to cringe at the visual, olfactory, auditory, thermal and tactile invasions "common" to the behavior patterns of South Europeans. Although in certain culturally defined situations—for example, the subway—multipronged invasions of personal space (by "nonpersons") are tolerated, these would bring on explosive scenes, for example, even on a tight movie stand-by line. Apparently all this has prehuman roots in animal social patterning.[20] Also it is tangled up with group territoriality; in addition to the personal buffer zone each animal maintains as proper distance between individuals. Some animals are contact species (pig, parakeet, hedgehog, etc.), others, like the horse, dog, cat, muskrat, are noncontact species. But for man space cannot be seen as simply *physical space;* it is important as to how this space is conceived. The biologist Calhoun, applying this thought to increasing population densities, believes that rewarding societal high density situations are still possible.[21]

Thus, *proxemics,* or the understanding and design of space (from residence to region) in order to maximize behavioral returns to humanity and to individual humans, is a vital if barely understood knowledge and skill.[22] We simply are aware now that space affects individual humans and individual human behavior and that it further affects group processes, but precious little exact knowledge exists, much less planning know-how. No one could argue for spatial determinism as do some benighted architects, whose enthusiasms exceed their wisdom. Inflating these ideas to the level of urban design the argument holds even less water as a modified version of ingenuous nineteenth-century geographic determinism—or the more derived materialistic determinism fallacy of the simplistic Marxists. Perhaps at the roots of contemporary city planning is the naiveté evidenced in the beliefs held by some eminent practitioners that the physical framework *makes* the quality of life and determines *action patterns.* Nothing could be further from the truth; but to backtrack quickly, undoubtedly the physical framework (a) offers opportunities and (b) limits options to humanity. The thesis here, of course, is that societal planning (economic, political and social) must accompany physical, territorial and general environmental design, but why make societal planning harder by erecting or countenancing damaging spatial frames?

To drive the argument to the negative pole, in cases of extraordinary space constriction among animals, behavioral sinks (see below) of erratic, counterproductive actions develop. There are twelve square miles of Hong Kong that house 2,000,000 people; while one square mile of Calcutta—perhaps the first great human behavioral sink—contains over 450,000 pullulating "humans" existing in their own excreta.[23] Whether normal behavior can be anticipated under such conditions seems unlikely and the deadly trilogy of frustration, tension and aggression can flower there as it has in the hot fetid black ghettos of America during the summers of recent years.

(f) *Behavioral sink:* the soaring crime rate, drug addiction and flamboyant abnormal sexual patterning of the slums in Western cities and in worse slums in developing areas (although not always perceived as such—they are often slums of "hope" not Western "despair") can be approximated to the purposely created behavioral sinks of the animal researcher. Unchecked propagation with maximized availability of food, including Sika deer on an island in Chesapeake Bay, caribou uncontrolled by wolf predation in the Canadian Arctic, and Norway rats in a constricted room, resulted in (a) Malthusian population checks, seemingly induced by endocrine changes brought on by stress or (b) in the last case abnormal behavior patterns damaging to the survival of the species. Calhoun, who coined the phrase "'behavioral' sink, a receptacle for foul or waste things"[24] to designate gross distortions of behavior, researched the rats. Apparently these rodents can tolerate considerable disorder but like man must be alone at times. The sexual behavior patterns of the rats became disorganized (pansexuality and sadism were endemic); male social behavior broke down into extreme cruelty; a high mortality rate for females unbalanced the sex ratio and led to further harassment of the surviving females. Predictably, offspring had little chance in such a turmoil. The experiment was not pushed to crisis; hopefully, the human experiment in dense city living will not be pushed that far either. In short, overpopulation is quite possibly the greatest threat to humankind as the twenty-first century dawns, as shortages in food, energy and other resources develop.

(g) *Stimulus levels:* If man *is* a social animal then interaction is "his thing." Alone on the prairie frontier, lost on the tundra or buried in the forest seems to offer slight possibility for fruitful (or nonfruitful) interaction. Civilization is the product of *urbs* (the city); the higher culture and human development do not flourish outback in the bush. Thus there must be a maximizing point for interaction potentialities needed to forward human culture; Otis Dudley Duncan has searched years for the optimal city size which would maximize opportunities and minimize the polar twin sterilities of overcrowding and of lack of contact.[25] Ebenezer Howard, who invented in the late nineteenth century the modern British garden city/new town, hypothesized with no evident induction from empirical data that 30,000 was the ideal town population (if not too far from London). Britain's newest New Towns are to reach 250,000; roughly evaluated experience, mainly economic, suggests that given available space with contemporary Western society and technology, optimized human returns demand at least such a magnitude of people in one articulated group. The mathematically *potential* contacts among the inhabitants of a village, town or city rise exponentially with size. It would be nice to know whether all such contacts could be meaningful or rewarding; patently they are not, as current "crime in the streets" and acerbic confrontation make clear. The key factor in population density isn't merely how close people live together physically but the frequency of meaningful interaction influenced by cultural and technological factors.[26] Does high density lead to *stress?* Unquestionably, the human animal is a tough and resourceful beast. As a result, René Dubos considers this a possible Achilles heel for species man since the quality to survive almost any deleterious environment may destroy the *qualities* of human social life called civilization.[27]

Yet great visual art, great literature, great music developed in the urban caldron as did the best governmental and economic systems mankind has yet to forge. Big city means big civilization, however weighed. And finally, contact can be geometrically expanded by technological quasi-contact where telephone calls equal at least 30 per cent of a contact credit; and the video phone may promise a still higher return as part of the projected "wired city."[28] If both massive "good" and massive "evil" did not emerge from this bubbling city stew, it would be most surprising; how to make the good predominate is our task.

ECOLOGY: HABITAT

This small planet, as part of a complex universe of many universes billions of years in forming, sets the demanding stage on which has been and is being played man's emergence and development. But while the stage setting influences, molds and conditions, it is the actor who now enhances the production (or conversely ruins it). Having only recently learned to push the natural environment about with his powerful technologies, man seems driven to destroy the viability of the physical base on which his species' role must be lived out. Like a blind Samson he appears to be pulling the temple walls down on his head; while this has been evident to thoughtful people—including the planning profession—for decades, the contemporary public hue and cry about the environment is a very recent thing.

Traditionally the city planning profession—design oriented—has seen itself directly related to the earth's surface, although given its aesthetic roots and pretensions, it has not always dealt in an empathetic fashion with the natural environment both inorganic and organic. The current concern about ecological imbalance and massive pollution due to industrial civilization may be just another of the passing fads disturbing our agitated society. William Wheaton[29] has observed about the new environmentalism: "One of the questions hanging over the ecology movement is the persistent view that concern over the environment was "turned-on" [originally] to divert attention from the far more serious issues of poverty, civil rights and the Vietnam war"—not to mention the youth cultures' noisy rejection of the establishment-run traditional society. Hopefully not—the situation already is too serious.

Developing nations do not seem to share this present concern; they are ready to trade increased pollution at home for increased GNP and in any case wish to leave it up to the highly industrialized nations to shoulder the costs of a global cleanup since pollution in its varied forms is largely the product of high technology societies.

The chief polluting agent on earth is quite simply man himself; he is already too numerous, filling with careless crudity the available space, messing up the limited optimal living areas with his own wastes, and not only gobbling up the stored resources of countless eons produced by solar energy but returning them disaggregated and reaggregated by his fabulous physical technology as indigestible detritus. Thus more and more waste tends to take the form of impossible monster products; for example, plastics or atomic leavings. Human civilization thus makes unpleasant, useless and even destroys the land and the sea and the air in a seemingly irreversible process. Only within the past five years has the notion percolated both into the understanding of the power elite and into mass consciousness in the advanced nations that humanity is committing collective suicide on a global scale within a quasi-predictable future. Credence must be given to a neo-Malthusian position that while we may not all collectively starve—artificial foods are not too far distant in any case—we may suffocate in our self-induced air, water and land pollution.[30] While Hiroshima was patently more spectacular, this environmental destruction could be more complete with casualties multiplied ten thousandfold! With a frightening projected global population growth and an exponentially expanded technological growth based on pure natural science, man is quite likely to smother the earth and exhaust its resources as a livable habitat for the human species.[31] Cannot society wisely sophisticate its behavior beyond mere technical technology to include planning, operational and managing skills employing intellectual, biological, behavioral and organizational technologies and use all these to treat spaceship earth, especially in the clotted urban areas, to the end of optimizing human returns (however defined)? Unless something like this is done, man may prove to be an unsuccessful species, a ripe candidate for organic *extinction* as the biologists succinctly express it.[32]

For a moment look backward over several million years to a helpless, not too bright, protohuman battling in his small numbers. He is without any but the simplest chance tools in an often cold, unpredictable habitat and is attacked from within by those efficient viruses and bacteria and from without by numerous huge and dangerous beasts. Close to starvation puny groups searched for favorable spots to eke out their short harsh survival. High mountains, tropical rain jungles, arid deserts were shunned (unless pursued there by fiercer men) for the salubrious river valleys, gentle plains, sheltering forests and fertile sea littorals. The environment was omnipresent and omnipowerful. Here first man commenced to stake out his "arena" with possibly several million years of protohuman bare survival. The complex tale of multiracial origins and the great migrations from a Middle Eastern heartland (or was it Asiatic or African or all three?) has been as yet only faintly sketched. Humanoid and human waves of various sizes and shapes, and presumably colors and intelligences, chased preceding waves across land bridges and on and on to people the entire globe. Some wild animals were slowly tamed (the initial hanger-on dog and pig); vegetables, grains and fruits were collected in one spot to nurture; and the foundations were built for the beginning of *settled* village life after millennia of a brutish wandering existence. Mankind "progressed" with glacial speed from the Old to the New Stone Age; agriculture with settled village life finally was achieved. A new level of foresight was required to plan the husbandry cycle and order the larger number of men concentrated in the first Neolithic villages. Still relatively helpless before storm, drought, flood and plague, the beginnings of town life (civilization) were soon guided by religious practices tangled up with reliable empirical knowledge.[33]

The essential point to grasp here is that human material culture enabled human society to end immediate slavery to the natural environment. Culture cushions man from the *direct,* all powerful impact of nature, but it never can allow him to ignore the ultimate reality of the surrounding physical world of land, water, air and climate—nor of the resources that the earth has stored.

As the great civilizations of the Middle East, North Africa, the Orient and much later the Americas grew, human vainglory did unquestionably increase as is evidenced by the grandiose and magnificent cities of ancient Egypt, the Middle East, India, China, classical Greece and imperial Rome. Alternately punctuated by natural disasters and exploited-resource crises, the paranoid human delusion of grandeur survived over centuries of continuous warfare. It weathered the catastrophic European feudal period while continuing to blossom meanwhile in the innovative Arab civilization of North Africa and the Iberian Peninsula. Only later did city life re-emerge in Western Europe with the growth of the medieval towns and free cities. Finally the entire West grew up during the Renaissance when preindustrial cities of great sophistication once again appeared, especially in the Mediterranean basin. From the growth of objective empirical science evolved the necessary first agricultural revolution and the resultant paleotechnic industrial cities[34] based on and bound by iron and coal, and finally to the rapid emergence of the powerful Industrial Revolution. Here Western man did become greedy indeed and truly paranoid, as he made the whole world his oyster and wantonly destroyed the oyster beds—literally by his despoliation of the surrounding surface riches, rape of the underground resources and befouling of the air, water and land as restless amoebalike movements of individuals and groups (kept alive by the new agricultural efficiency and medical skills) scuttled across the globe, while clustering in increasingly huge chaotic messes in the great urban wens. It is not surprising that Anglo-Saxon intellectuals, having viewed urban turmoil, have tended to detest the city[35] with a wistful and romantic over-the-shoulder look back to man's "innocence in unspoiled nature." Not so with French or German thinkers—even after Rousseau spread his mythology; continental Europeans tend to praise the urban way of life.

We have been brought up to a sharp halt in the past decade. The realization that the earth's bounty is finite and that especially in the United States a primitive frontier attitude toward the living environment is not only incredibly naive but also downright dangerous. Man must manage his numbers, his waste, his habitations, his movements and his technology to deal wisely with his benefactor and master, Nature. From Rachel Carson to Buckminster Fuller, publicists have alerted public opinion to the fact that urban civilization "fouls its nest" and must direct itself in harmony with and not in opposition to its habitat. The destructive effect on the environment, it would appear, is directly proportional to population density and size, and level of technology. The challenge grows with civilization and it cannot be avoided except by civilized behavior.

This new environmentalism as applied to man's physical habitat so far has been considered in the United States as primarily a negative cleanup process including hopefully increased foresight in the applications of technical technology. Symptomatic of a concerned U.S. governmental interest are some ninety-seven official technological assessment studies (of varied worth) undertaken recently, attempting to weigh in advance the effects of secondary and tertiary environmental and societal results of major technological steps.[36]

In addition, there is a very considerable development in transeconomic cost benefit analysis—in planning and in monitoring planning success—going on in the multipronged research into social (better societal) indicators[37] attempting to get at quantifying the quality of life (health, behavior, "culture," amenity, etc.).

If we move in the direction of a more positive attitude toward expanding the options made available by the physical environment in terms of both resources and amenities we move in the first case into maximizing resource mapping, analysis and development (economic geography) and in the second case into a hybrid area of "humanized" geography and environmental psychology, environmental sociology (just born) and that dramatic hybrid, the bio-ecology of which the leading prophet is Ian McHarg.[38] This bio-ecology appears to be a combination of the "naturalist's" approach with an aesthetic-design orientation to the physical world that deliberately searches to relate warmly to the enormous variety of habitats. While there are some intellectual quirks in all of this new probing, there remains little doubt that the once symbiotic relationship of simpler cultures with Nature may be recaptured—at least partially—in a planful way by the increasingly sophisticated intellectual technologies of increasingly sophisticated societies.

Thus the settled life of advanced civilization has in fact turned out to be counterproductive in many ways—or at least somewhat less certain in its "benefits"—as now the "costs" are coming up for payment. Our species, which has already fully populated the globe, will probably double in the next three decades. The fantastic technological expansion has made each of these individuals an exponentially more damaging destroyer of our habitat. And the focus of the major human/technological threat is patently the city. But perhaps it will be possible to solve our human ecological problems in a rewarding fashion as a species, by a responsible strategy, anticipation and design. The thesis of this book is, of course, that such a wise, planful guidance of our collective destinies is just possible, but much optimism seems out of place.[39]

URBANIZATION: ORIGINAL

The slow movement from the life of nomadic tribal hunters to settled villages with a considerable increase in population must be a fascinating story. It is now only partially glimpsed through the foggy archaeological re-creation of the initial civilizing steps from Paleolithic crudity to Neolithic "refinement." The year 10,000 B.C. still serves as a useful proximate date to set the beginning for town life. With foresight shown to husband quasi-tamed animal resources (rather than chase them in the hunt) and with grains, fruits and vegetables held over to plant and nurture rather than collected by the chancy search, one senses the forward-looking "civilized," rational man speeding up the creeping development made possible by the tiny store of Old Stone Age culture. Walls or better stockades shielded the life of communal villagers from wild beasts and wild men, and as the division of labor increased freeing some individuals from the eternal pressure of the food quest, enabling them to elaborate, to think and to delve and to plan. As metals replaced stone in tools and weapons, the dual role of technology—so helpful and yet so dangerous—soon became evident. What percentage of the earth's early populations was put to the sword in the eternal warring of early man? To the crude power of animals and man himself—often as slave—was added the power of the winds so important for the early distant exchange of goods by sailing ship.

Through governmental coercion on a large scale—often "divinely" assisted—populations were welded together in the great early civilizations, and collective planned action resulted in the first preindustrial cities (both power and trade oriented) of the Old World. Over five thousand years later the story was repeated in the New. Perhaps not true cities, these early attempts have been likened to "massed villages." The most striking feature of this original urbanization seems in retrospect to be the length of time involved, which was clearly enormous and which allowed for the slow domestication in the most literal sense of nomadic hunters into a settled village life. Not only were walled towns built, which in due course elaborated the pomp and panoply of first theocratic and later secular imperial rule, but men's minds were built to plan ahead and to contain the skills needed personally and societally to adjust to tens of thousands of others living in dense masses. Although cities of one hundred thousand did exist, they were unusual; the first cities seemed to run around twenty thousand to fifty thousand in size. This was all that the early urban and agricultural technology could manage to serve.

The mainstream of Western civilization (city life) flows—with some interruption—in a somewhat similar pattern from Babylon and Sumer through Luxor to Minos, Athens, Alexandria and on to Rome to Chartres—from the ancient Near Orient to late Medieval Europe. While each people involved added something to the growing store of human knowledge and city living, the basic pattern of the preindustrial city continued on; there was no systems break. Certainly from 3000 to 2500 B.C. it would seem that—added to grain cultivated by the plow and a variety of domestic animals—the sailing ship, the simple loom, copper metallurgy and eventually the calendar, writing, astronomical observation and abstract mathematics were all in constant use. This pattern of new skills, all city based, gave an exponential lift to human capabilities. Gordon V. Childe named this "the urban revolution."[40]

Without becoming involved in a typically vacuous chicken vs. egg controversy, it would seem that technology, society and urbanism are three interrelated, reciprocally acting variables along mankind's long rough road—a trek by no means ended yet.

The most quoted and discussed student of the preindustrial city is the sociologist Gideon Sjoberg, who places this early city type as the next step following primitive folk society as described by anthropologist Robert Redfield.[41] Sjoberg, with a skillful broad brush, treats many disparate towns and cities under the single heading of "preindustrial." He lumps examples from varied times, places and cultures, claiming their *structural* characteristics have remained more or less the same.[42] He posits this ten-point fundamental typology of "first urbanism":

1. Primarily government and religious centers.
2. Elites have lived near the center with the lower classes fanning out toward the periphery. Peasants often remain outside the city proper. Typically, occupational groups live and work in a particular street or quarter.
3. The effects of social class tend to be all pervasive—a small upper class readily identifiable by distinctive dress, speech and behavior controls the vast bulk of commoners.
4. The family is the primary socializing agency; kinship serves as a basis for occupational enrollment.
5. The technology and economic organization are simple compared to modern industrial standards.
6. The main economic unit is the guild with a relatively slight division of labor.
7. Commerce is characterized by a modicum of standardization in prices, currency, weights, measures and the grading of commodities—plus the widespread adulteration of goods (!).

8. Political power rests in the hands of the elite, as do religion and education with some considerable lack of enthusiasm on the part of this select group to delve in commerce or much less work with their hands. There is a tendency toward a despotic rule accruing to one individual.
9. The bureaucracy is a potent integrative and stabilizing mechanism resting as it does on religious sanctions.
10. The magico-religious heritage does slowly mesh with the embryonic experimental science—reflecting the growing base of reliable practical knowledge.[43]

With the advent of the absolute monarchies of the Tudor/Stuart/Hanover, Hapsburg, Bourbon dynasties the preindustrial city moved in Sjoberg's terms to a transitional form and in Mumford's to the Renaissance, eventually, Baroque. While hardly a change in kind, the stepping up of order, elegance and form under the great monarchies of the sixteenth to eighteenth centuries was of such a degree as to merit special treatment in the march toward the Industrial City.

With regular paid armies to keep the *canaille* in check, with navies to conquer and to guard shipping (or plunder) and with far-flung trading empires held under mercantilist theories, these wealthy rulers could afford to adorn their capitals with organized physical and societal forms. The capital city, as we see in London, Paris, even planned Washington, and as echoed in twentieth-century Stalinist Moscow, was regarded as an adjunct of the palace, and grandeur was built into the urban framework. Medieval bourgs and cathedrals did, of course, symbolize the townsites of importance of the preceding epoch, but the long vistas, controlled facades, elegant kings' palaces (Versailles and the Louvre) and private royal gardens (Luxembourg, St. James's Park) with zoos, museums and concert halls to amuse the court provided a new sophisticated level of life—even if they just were marking time for the ominous first hisses and clanks of the age of steam and iron soon to come. Typically it would seem that the first mass production was to outfit with regularized equipment the king's soldiers. Then by trapping the power of burning fossil fuel in steam engines, man sealed his rural doom and moved inexorably into the all-embracing world pattern of industrial urbanism.

There is a special spatial pattern for the flowering of the industrial city as it moves toward the metropolis, particularly in its American form, which needs here to be briefly sketched. With the advent of scientific agriculture and the opening of new crop lands available through advancing transportation technology, the ratio of agriculturists to city dwellers was steadily reduced. Now 3 per cent of the population produces approximately 98 per cent of the United States food supply. Powerful centripetal forces moved farm populations to city jobs; the place where the capital, power, markets, entrepreneurial skills, transport nodes and action were concentrated. These pulls and pushes accounted for the tight pattern of the traditional industrial city. Next came three recognizable centrifugal phases in the industrial city's history. Phase One: With the advent of the local steam railroad, but more especially local electric traction at the turn of the twentieth century, the first burst of inner suburban expansion occurred in the "streetcar suburbs." Sometimes these were outside the boundaries of the political city. While there was considerable early annexation of surrounding areas into this original political city, the independent suburb as a taxing entity with its own feeble caretaker government early became all too common.[44] Phase Two: After World War I the first great burst of automobile suburbs occurred, surrounding every city of reasonable size as the middle-class city dwellers rushed to escape urban ills. The great conurbations were now well under way. Phase Three: As World War II ended, the cheap technology of septic tank and electric pump, the automobile explosion aided and abetted by the FHA/VA easy mortgage and the superhighway (the latter compounded by the originally titled "Interstate Defense Highway System") led to the scatteration (East Coast) and slurbs (West Coast) pattern so unrewardingly familiar today. Chaotic, varied land uses filled the interstitial residual spaces in the explosive movement into the loosely knit interaction framework of late twentieth-century America. Concerned Europeans make fearful pilgrimages to this country to stare at the portents of things to come for them—unless they show considerably more wisdom *and* determination than now is evident. Hopefully there will be a Phase Four leading to a more idyllic postindustrial city.

Urbanism as understood today is a state of society characteristic primarily of industrial Europe, North America, Japan and some portions of the rest of the globe. Obviously some preindustrial city remnants do still exist here and there. But, rightly or wrongly, the industrial city is equated with "modernization" by *all* the developing nations (including the socialist/communist world) who seemingly aspire to reach this presumed paradise of technological prowess. Their hectic march toward such a goal seems almost inevitable. Conversely, those nations that have already attained the dizzy heights of advanced industrial society are busy wondering if they have not created a Frankenstein.

First, what has industrial society created?

1. Huge populations in functional interlinked cities: Metropolitan New York of seventeen million as part of the American East Coast megalopolis, BOSHWASH, extending twelve hundred miles from southern New Hampshire to northern Virginia, containing upward of thirty million persons, is the prize exhibit.
2. The most advanced production system in history spewing out goods in ever increasing amounts.
3. The highest level of living (reality) in human history—always under tension with ever higher aspirations (standard of living).
4. Various dimensions of popular rule—some more democratic than others!
5. Transportation and communication networks of unparalleled complexity (microefficiency and macrodisorganization).
6. Unparalleled opportunities for recreation and the creation, display/performance, and consumption of the higher culture.

It does look grand to the eyes of the black African, wandering Bedouin, Asian peasant or rain forest Amazon Indian—as portrayed by film, shiny aircraft and car, slick paper magazines, by errant tourist, resident diplomat or dispatched soldier or sailor on his awe-inspiring "battle wagon." But the actual reality of the great modern metropolis is not so wondrous. In fact, Western man is sorely troubled at "the long laundry list of urban ills" (of potential unrealized and perhaps the inability ever to build physical and societal "shining alabaster cities undimmed by human tears!").

Second, let's look critically at the actual record:

1. Destruction of the good earth, clean air and water.
2. High population densities without adequate housing still after five thousand urban years.
3. Disorganized governments with curious taxation systems unable to marshal the resources to fund and build urban "public furniture" adequate even for ordinary city housekeeping, much less sufficient for expanding human horizons.
4. Poor ecological integration of living, playing and working.
5. Choked transportation facilities.
6. Loss of the human community of the preindustrial era town and the, as yet imperfect, understanding of whether subcommunities within a huge urban man heap can actually be formed.[45]
7. Large numbers of "uncivilized lower class" (culture of the poor or "outcasts"!) citizens, not sharing the common culture, who are inept and—many drug laden in the United States—prey on the other city dwellers. The real, not imagined, violence and "fear in the streets" of modern America, where the laundry list is at its worst in Western society.[46]

It is not a pretty picture and frankly one wonders if the developing countries actually know what they are rushing toward with undeliberate speed.

URBANIZATION: CONTEMPORARY AND FUTURE

But there is a second question which affects the future of the planet as much or more. Gerald Breese has explored the urbanization of developing peoples and finds that the massive urbanization that occurred over the past five thousand years *will be matched in scale within the next fifty years*[47]; the past is merely the prologue to this inescapable future. A quite alarming prospect!

Can this new giant wave of urbanization reaching the two thirds not yet industrialized peoples of the globe—the so-called Third World which quite probably will constitute four fifths of the world's population by the year 2000—be guided? The determined, if disorganized, drive for modernization undoubtedly has a necessary concomitant of urbanization.[48] Will the world's burgeoning cities in the developing areas be condemned to repeat the same mistakes in exacerbated form of the Western urban stew? Can new nations profit from the hard-won two-hundred-fifty-year experience of the present industrial cities? Need they repeat America's worst mistakes (Europe still has a chance) neatly capsulized by Wilfred Owen: "Abandonment of the center city, the uncontrolled commercialization of urban roadsides, the neglect of public transport, the absence of community planning, and lack of concern for the environment."[49] Or can the emergent nations by deliberate and shrewd national urbanization policies and planning skip the industrial city's present sorry state and glide quickly across into a postindustrial Nirvana? This appears very doubtful. Is there a way to modernize, urbanize, industrialize, organize or institutionalize, and (sadly) populate without wrecking their own futures and quite possibly pulling the globe down on both their and our collective heads? Hopelessly crowded cities may be a possible cause for world revolution pitting the have-nots against the haves. The developing states, as Lloyd Rodwin has pointed out,[50] have discovered that these highly urbanized nodes (usually their capital cities) are the centers for GNP growth (so necessary for have-not peoples) with the highest life expectancy, largest school populations, most favorable doctor-to-patient ratios, largest per capita income, etc., and thus tend to encourage movement to the city.[51]

Following approximately the Marxist "Law of Combined Development"[52]:

> Developing countries might move more rapidly from the preindustrial, or transitional, stage into the industrial or even mass-consumption era (threshold of the postindustrial era) by concentrating on productive cities as they have on productive farms. Following the green revolution that is modernizing agriculture, the gray revolution that is urbanizing large areas of the developing world should be creating acceptable destinations for those leaving the farms and villages. It is essential to begin now to focus investments that are going to take place anyway—in housing, education and industrial development—to create new growth points and to reinforce existing moderate-sized cities.[53]

Let us examine these assertions more closely. The "green revolution" is proving not to be an unmixed blessing; for example, in the Indian countryside. The capital, entrepreneurial organizational ability and the trained skills to use chemical fertilizer, irrigation and special seeds with rigorous care are limited to a relatively few superior landowning farmers. Chemical fertilizers and the energy to pump irrigation water became increasingly scarce and expensive. These fortunate few oust tenants from the land as a powerful push, driving hordes of poverty-stricken, ignorant peasants to "overurbanize" (large populations with *no* jobs or *quasi* jobs) the entire country. The external diseconomies (not dissimilar to the effect of the mechanical cotton picker in our own rural South) are frankly exacerbating India's urban/national problems as well as possibly improving the economic situation: The actual benefit/cost trade-off in economic and transeconomic or social indicator terms is by no means clear. Assuming for the moment that massive cityward migrations do occur to potential growth nodes, does anyone believe (a) that sufficient capital is available either for private enterprise or public infrastructure, (b) that adequate private economic sector entrepreneurial expertise can be found and (c) that governmental political/managerial/bureaucratic skills (not to mention simple honesty) are available in sufficient dollops to profit from this double jump potential—without massive First and Second World aid and direction? Which, as all are now aware, seems bitterly resented unless in the form of largesse with "no strings attached," which would undoubtedly lead to a large percentage being wasted in inefficient "frictions" and pure graft in both the public and private sectors. These are quite simply lacking in the Third World: government capabilities, adequate capital and trained human resources. Without mincing words, global disaster—even without atomic warfare—awaits us unless mankind can move the vast untutored masses of the earth toward a level of living (reality) satisfactory to the exaggerated standard of living (aspiration) now mankind's nigh universal expectation.

How well is the contemporary wave of urbanization going? In a word: poorly. Not only, it would seem, are the old mistakes being repeated but some splendid new ones are being discovered as military/totalitarian regimes of spectacular incompetency pop up all over Africa, Latin America and Asia. Is there sufficient time to tutor world citizenry to live tightly compressed into an urban globe?

Again, it took the West five hundred years "to manage"—no matter how poorly—the industrial city. Can the generally nonwhite, largely embittered backward masses manage the much touted double jump to the socialist ideal city in fifty years or less? It seems improbable with population growth universally outstripping crude GNP gains (much less the selective sort of economic development so needed for such a remote possibility as an urbanism of style and quality). In the foreseeable future the pressures of overurbanization in the cluttered urban places of backward nations will become worse rather than better.

It is transparent that the huge metropolises of developing areas are only part of broad societal change which must be coped with in a holistic planning fashion on the scale of:

(a) the national (or better, international) territory;
(b) the physical structure;
(c) a societal plan including a reordering of government, economic, social life structuring;
(d) long-range or "futures" planning, but with rapid recognizable changes fed back in a cybernetic fashion.

Unless there is a national economic development plan, with a national territorial urbanization policy including adequate funding as noted above—and who can run such a scheme—there is room for little optimism about that trinity of modernization/urbanization/industrialization. It should be noted that in 1975 the "advanced" United States is not remotely capable of national planning on such a scale with only France, Japan and possibly the USSR (under different auspices) possibly showing such macromanagerial skills.

From the four capital cities in developing areas examined below one should not presume to lay down any hard and fast conclusions. But nothing in the stark visual glories of Brasilia, the now almost completely nonfunctional monumentality of Chandigarh or the free-swinging concentration of Dakar, or increasingly affluent Caracas suggest such sophisticated holistic planning skills in large supply. Even Tokyo, which is considered to have passed rapidly through the transitional city, can claim some of the most spectacular housing lacks, transportation inadequacies, horrendous pollution, social welfare gaps and general urban muddle. Only now the Japanese National Plans of 1970 and 1971 are coming to grips with these problems on a realistic scale facing their special energy crisis. And no one today doubts Japanese skills and capabilities.

The following eleven case studies may encourage or discourage. It is, no doubt, unfortunate that a giant cross-cultural study of the thousands of world cities, precisely quantified both by economic and transeconomic (societal) indicators, is not available, with sequential stages nicely projected into alternate possible urban futures on a world scale.[54] It seems one must unquestionably wait a bit for that. The eleven city studies that follow may, however, help to illumine both the advanced and developing capital cities' tribulations in their strivings to form "good places in which to live and to work" for their local citizenry, and as proud symbols for their respective nations. If the capital can't make it, what city can? Quite possibly capital cities are in fact "Potemkin Villages"[55] in the finest tradition—as was Imperial New Delhi and Stalin's Moscow—not to mention Washington, D.C., in conception.

NOTES

[1] The New York *Times,* November 5, 1970.

[2] The New York *Times,* April 22, 1971.

[3] In November 1972, Newark was investigating just how a municipality could declare bankruptcy to the loudly expressed horror of the "sovereign" state of New Jersey.

[4] Louis Wirth, "Urbanism as a Way of Life," *American Journal of Sociology,* Vol. 44 (July 1938), 1–24.

[5] John G. Papaioannou, "Environmental Changes: Time and Space," manuscript prepared for presentation at the International Future Research Conference, Kyoto, Japan, 1970.

[6] Dennis L. Meadows and Associates, for the Club of Rome. Washington, D.C., a Potomac Associates book, Universe Books, 1972.

[7] A publication by the United Nations in the field of housing, building and planning on a global scale. Center for Housing, Building and Planning (United Nations, New York, 1970). Foreword to the inaugural issue.

[8] Cf. B. F. Skinner, *Beyond Freedom and Dignity.* New York, Alfred A. Knopf, 1971.

[9] Robert M. Griffin, Jr., "Ethological Concepts for Planning," *Journal of the American Institute of Planners,* January 1969, pp. 54–69. See Wolfgang F. E. Preiser, "Environment and Spatial Behavior," *Council of Planning Librarians, Exchange Bibliography* #235, November 1971.

[10] Desmond Morris, *The Human Zoo.* New York, McGraw-Hill, 1969, p. 8.

[11] Robert Ardrey, *The Territorial Imperative.* New York, Dell Publishing Co., 1966.

[12] W. G. Golding, *Lord of the Flies.* New York, Putnam, 1959.

[13] H. Wentworth Eldredge, *The Second American Revolution.* New York, Wm. Morrow, 1966, Chap. IV.

[14] Apparently the Chinese Peoples Republic is experimenting with heavy doses of egalitarianism today for its huge three-million-man Red Army, at least during peacetime.

[15] Desmond Morris, op. cit., Chap. IV, "In-Groups and Out-Groups." "The Dangers in Pluralism" by Norton Ginsburg, *The Center Magazine,* Vol. VI, No. 5 (September/October 1973), p. 55.

[16] Konrad Lorenz, *On Aggression.* New York, Harcourt, Brace and World, 1966. Actually Ardrey's *The Territorial Imperative* and Desmond Morris' *The Naked Ape* (New York, McGraw-Hill, 1967) imply a basically violent position. Cf. the excellent "Aggression among Nonhuman Primates" by Charles H. Southwick (Reading, Mass., Addison-Wesley Module in Anthropology, #23, 1972) for a treatment of *agonism* which links *aggression* with *escape* in a complete pattern for behavior involving physical conflict between members of the same species.

[17] G. Goren (anthropologist), "Man Has No Killer Instinct," *The New York Times Magazine,* November 27, 1966, pp. 47ff., and "Ardrey on Human Nature," *Encounter* 28:66–71, 1967. Also Margaret Mead (anthropologist), "Warfare: Only an Invention—Not a Biological Necessity," *Asia* 40:402–5, 1940.

[18] Hannah Arendt, *On Violence.* New York, Harcourt, Brace and World, Inc., 1970, p. 3.

[19] Robert Sommer, *Personal Space.* Englewood Cliffs, N.J., Prentice-Hall, a Spectrum Book, 1969, Chap. 3, "Spatial Invasion." Robert M. Petty, "Crowding," *Council of Planning Librarians Exchange Bibliography* #240, November 1971.

[20] Edward T. Hall, *The Hidden Dimension.* New York, Prentice-Hall, 1966, Chaps. II and III especially. He employs the useful term "proxemics."

[21] John B. Calhoun, "Space and the Strategy of Life," mimeographed supplementary document supplied by The World Future Society adapted from his "Frontiers of Science" address to the American Association for the Advancement of Science, at the Dallas meeting in December 1968.

[22] Lawrence Mann and George Hagevik, review article, "The 'New' Environmentalism: Behaviorism and Design," *AIP Journal* (September 1971), 344–47. Cf. Robert Sommer, op. cit.

[23] Exacerbated in 1971 by the estimated ten million, mainly Hindu Bengali, refugees flooding from East Pakistan (now Bangladesh) into the provinces of India's East Bengal in which Calcutta festers.

[24] John Calhoun, "A 'Behavioral' Sink," *Roots of Behavior*, E. L. Bliss (ed.). New York, Harper, Hoeber, 1962.

[25] Cf. William A. Howard, *Concept of an Optimum City Size,* Council of Planning Librarians Exchange Bibliography #52, 1968.

[26] Hugo Engelmann of Northern Illinois University posits that as interaction frequency increases "violence increases and changes from directed to non-directed violence" and that "experience becomes more stereotyped and we are less and less able to perceive unique individuals," *Behavior Today,* Vol. 2, No. 15 (April 12, 1971).

[27] René Dubos, *So Human an Animal.* New York, Charles Scribner's Sons, 1968, p. 167.

[28] *See* Chap. 14.

[29] William Wheaton, dean of the College of Environmental Design, University of California (Berkeley), "After the Ecology Teach-In or Whatever Happened to Labor Day," AIP *Newsletter* (June 1970), p. 8.

[30] Cf. the strongly worded *Population Resources Environments: Issues in Human Ecology* (San Francisco: W. H. Freeman and Co., 1970), by Paul R. and Anne H. Ehrlich.

[31] Dennis L. Meadows and Associates. op. cit.

[32] Gerhard Lenski, *Human Societies*. New York, McGraw-Hill Book Co., 1970, Chap. 3, "An Introduction to Evolutionary Theory."

[33] Lewis Mumford, *The City in History*. New York, Harcourt, Brace and World, Inc., 1961, especially Chaps. I and II.

[34] Ibid., Chap. XI.

[35] G. Morton and Lucia White, *The Intellectual versus the City*. Cambridge, Mass., Harvard University Press, 1962.

[36] Vary T. Coates, *Technology and Public Policy,* Summary Report. Washington, D.C., George Washington University, University Program of Policy Studies in Science and Technology, 1972, p. 5.

[37] Cf. Chap. 15. There are a number of excellent publications in the area but a useful start can be made with Leslie D. Wilcox and Associates, *Social Indicators and Societal Monitoring: An International Annotated Bibliography*. San Francisco, Jossey-Bass, Inc., 1972.

[38] Ian McHarg, *Design with Nature*. Philadelphia, Natural History Press, 1969.

[39] John R. Platt, "Life Where Science Flows," pp. 69–80 in William R. Ewald, Jr. (ed.), *Environment and Change: The Next Fifty Years*. Bloomington, Ind., Indiana University Press, 1968.

[40] Gordon V. Childe, *Man Makes Himself*. New York, Mentor edition, 1951. Lewis Mumford criticizes Childe for too much attention to technology and too little to societal features such as religion and the polity.

[41] Cf. Robert Redfield, *The Primitive World and Its Transformation*. Ithaca, N.Y., Cornell University Press, 1953. There has been much anthropological debate over Redfield's characterization as much too sweeping.

[42] Gideon Sjoberg, *The Pre-Industrial City*. Glencoe, Ill., The Free Press, 1960. Cf. also his "Cities in Developing and Industrial Societies," in H. Wentworth Eldredge (ed.), *Taming Megalopolis*. New York: Doubleday/Anchor, 1967, pp. 103–55.

[43] Adapted from pp. 106–11 in *Taming Megalopolis*.

[44] Robert C. Wood, *Suburbia*. Boston, Houghton Mifflin Company, 1959.

[45] A readable "pop" sociology tract on this phenomenon is Vance Packard, *A Nation of Strangers*. New York, David McKay Company, Inc., 1972.

[46] According to the Tokyo Metropolitan Police there were in that city of 11,400,000 three murders with handguns in 1970—in New York City (7,900,000), 538; New York had a total of 1,117 reported murders compared to Tokyo's 230. There were 74,102 reported robberies in New York City, Tokyo, 474; New York's 1970 narcotics cases totaled 52,479, rape victims, 2,141 and assaults, 18,410 with respective Tokyo figures 292; 400; and 7,268. The New York *Times,* October 3, 1971.

[47] Gerald Breese, *Urbanization in Newly Developing Countries*. Englewood Cliffs,

N.J., Prentice-Hall, 1966. Cf. also his *The City in Newly Developing Countries: Readings on Urbanism and Urbanization.* Englewood Cliffs, N.J., 1969.

[48] For a perceptive general social science analysis, beyond mere urban concentration, of the "Modernization of Traditional Societies" see that series by Prentice-Hall and especially S. N. Eisenstadt's contribution, *Modernization: Protest and Change* (Englewood Cliffs, N.J., Prentice-Hall, 1966), which concentrates on the political turmoil of emerging nationhood. S. J. Udy contributed "Work in Traditional and Modern Society" to the series exploring the work ethic a *sine qua non* of the urban industrial society and hardly that of less technical cultures. David McClelland, a psychologist, sees economic growth as the foundation of modernization dependent on the development of the need for achievement among simple peoples in his important study *The Achieving Society* (Princeton, N.J., Van Nostrand, 1961).

[49] Wilfred Owen, *The Accessible City.* Washington, D.C., Brookings Institution, 1972, p. 122.

[50] Lloyd Rodwin, *Nations and Cities.* New York, Houghton Mifflin, 1970, especially Chap. VIII.

[51] United Nations: *Urbanization, Development Policies and Planning, International Social Development Review,* No. 1 (1968), pp. 21–35.

[52] Leon Trotsky, *The History of the Russian Revolution.* Ann Arbor, Mich., University of Michigan Press, 1964, Vol. 1. Lenin later borrowed certain of these ideas in essence, suggesting that late-comers can jump over preliminary original steps in societal evolution.

[53] Wilfred Owen, op. cit., p. 126.

[54] The New York *Times,* November 4, 1972. The United Nations Statistical Office is just now starting a "quality-of-life" statistics to add to the excellent job it has done on comparative economic data.

[55] B. M. Frolic's happy phrase fittingly applied to Moscow. Cf. Chap. 8.

CHAPTER 2

Stockholm: Three Hundred Years of Planning

Göran Sidenbladh*

A little more than fifty years ago the city of Stockholm had an area of just over thirteen square miles. About 400,000 inhabitants lived within the city limits. At the beginning of 1972, the city had almost twice as many inhabitants on five and one-half times as large an area; another 400,000 were living outside in other municipalities within the Greater Stockholm area. As of 1960, three quarters of all dwellings in the city of Stockholm had been built after 1920; by European standards such structures are young. In the older parts of the city there had been only minor changes up to 1950 when the reconstruction of the Central Business District (CBD) commenced. One reason for the continuity in the growth of Stockholm was the fact that no enemy troops have been in sight for more than

* Director of City Planning in Stockholm from 1955 to 1973, where he joined the master planning team in 1944. Graduated in 1934 as an architect, specializing in city planning at the Royal Polytechnical Institute of Stockholm. He worked for different public planning authorities in Sweden for the next ten years. He has traveled four times to the USA: in 1938 on a Swedish scholarship, 1956 sent by the city of Stockholm, 1961, visiting lecturer at MIT and 1967, visiting lecturer at University of California, Berkeley. Served as member of juries in city planning competitions, several times in Stockholm, in Copenhagen and in Adilswyl near Zürich, and on the United Nations' panel of consultants for the Singapore State and City Planning in 1970.

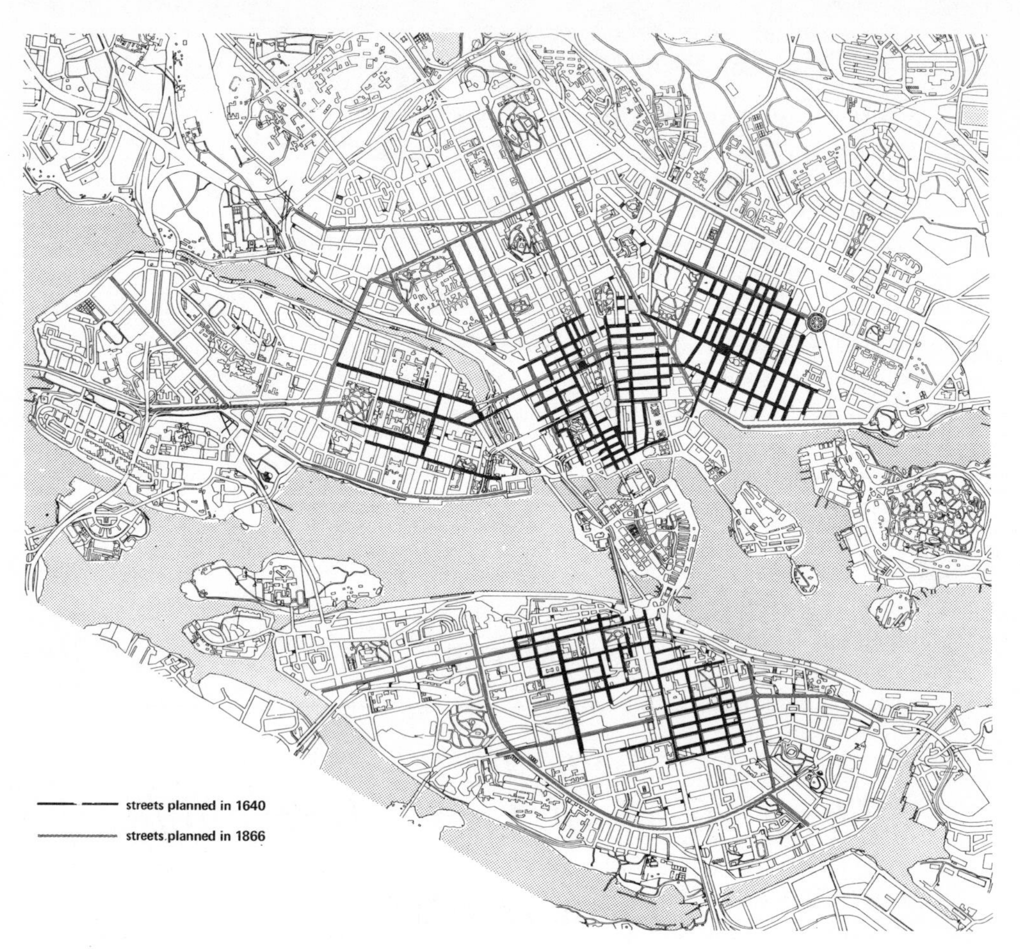

FIG. 1 The inner city of Stockholm.

four hundred years and that coups d'états and revolutions have been very "civilized" for an even longer period.

Stockholm today has this general form: In the center there are three small islands which contain the historical core. There one finds not only the Royal Castle, the Parliament and the seat of government but also narrow streets with curiosity shops, some offices of shipping companies and dwellings (Fig. 1). North and south of these islands, within a circle of easy walking distance is a part of the city which had developed up to 1900. This entire area is called "the inner city" or "the Stone City." Here the modern CBD with dwellings for 300,000 in the peripheral parts is located. Outside the Stone City there is a ring of suburbs built during the first half of this century dominated by free-standing houses with gardens and a rather open development with walk-up apartments. Still farther out, six to ten miles from the center, there are a number of modern semisatellite "new towns"—as well as some suburban sprawl—built after 1950. To this over-all picture of Stockholm must be added large numbers of summer houses or "second homes" spread over the vast archipelago to the east.

Among the contemporary great cities in this part of Europe, Stockholm has a long history. It became a royal city—but not capital in the modern sense of the word—some seven hundred years ago. Leningrad (St. Petersburg) was founded in 1703. Helsinki was made the capital in 1812; Oslo, which took its name in 1924, had been a city and royal residence since the early Middle Ages and became the official capital in 1814, but was not the largest city in Norway until 1830. During its early history, Stockholm was an important fortress protecting the single inlet to an extensive navigable inland water system and became an important port and trading place. In the middle of the seventeenth century, it was made the royal capital—the permanent seat of the national government. An era of rapid expansion started, and in 1636 a city planning office was organized. Within a few years it produced the first set of master plans which served as the formal physical guidelines for more than three centuries. The political and economic conditions during the middle of the seventeenth century made this an era of active city founding and expansion in many parts of Europe. Worthy of note was the city planning during the reign of Christian IV, King of Denmark 1596–1648, who in 1617 extended Copenhagen to join Christianshavn, in 1614 founded Christianstad (now in South Sweden) and in 1624 planned a city by the Akershus fortress and named it Christiania, which now is the center of Oslo. Gothenburg on the west coast of Sweden was founded in 1623 and with a city planning office right from the start. In the Low Countries, Amsterdam had a planning authority which produced a wonderful master plan in 1617.

Early planning in Stockholm from 1640 to 1840 was done by a branch of the administrative bureaucracy under the city governor, who was appointed by the national government and who, as a rule, was a member of it. The relation between the planning activity and the City Council, the body elected by the citizens, varied from time to time. To understand and value the planning of this period one must recognize that it was a national goal to remodel and extend Stockholm into a capital that would mirror the important political role of Sweden. Conflicts with the citizens, who had less vision and money to spend, were inevitable. These tensions became part of the local tradition.

Most of the early city planners, who were subordinate to the aristocrats, the "establishment" of the seventeenth century, had been trained as officers in the fortification corps, and brought with them the military tradition of discipline. At that time there was no strict limit between civilian and military authority. These ruling circles had a much more international outlook than the citizens of Stockholm whose experience was limited to dealing with the towns on the coasts of the Baltic, where some of them were born and most of them had their trading partners. The aristocratic national government had more interest in geometric regularity, the latest fashion in city planning, than the citizens, accustomed to irregularity, and now forcefully regulated. Another important period of improvements in addition to the initial seventeenth-century beginnings occurred during the middle part of the eighteenth century when the king's power was almost nil. At other times, however, kings with absolute power ordered splendid projects, but did not live long enough to see essential parts of them built.

As in so many other national capitals, the people in Stockholm have had to struggle long to get full rights to govern their own city. During the period when the national government and the governor had the dominating role, the burghers could influence only by disobedience. All land for expansion was publicly owned: part of the northern "suburbs" by the Crown, the rest by the city. To get a building permit one had to follow the rules given by the landowning authority—even if there was a certain amount of "wild" building without permits by squatters.

Most houses were built of timber and frequent big fires leveling an entire parish in a day or two—gave opportunities to implement improved plans. One part of the city alone suffered eight such conflagrations; the regulated building sites were let for an annual fee and under the condition that a masonry (!) building was to be completed within three years. If the builder failed, his rights to the land could be sold to someone more capable of building.

With few alterations and some additions, the master plans from the 1640s were adequate for the city up to the middle of the nineteenth century. Then two new factors came to influence the growth of the city: industrialism and private ownership of land. With the factories came the need for dwellings built specially for the workers; the guilds were abandoned and the new economic system needed capital which was raised by mortgaging urban property. This called for private ownership of land and those who paid ground fees could acquire full title to the property by paying a sum which entitled them to freehold.

During the remainder of the nineteenth century Stockholm remained a city for pedestrians. With the approximate limits of the 1640 plans extended in 1866, the population grew from 86,000 in 1840 to 300,000 in 1900 and 460,000 in 1940. The sparsely settled detached housing areas—often with large gardens behind—were replaced by tenements in five stories along the streets and four stories in the courtyards.

By 1863, all Swedish municipalities had been granted new legislative powers that enabled them to govern their own affairs more effectively. However, for the city of Stockholm certain restrictions remained until 1904. The new law of 1863 made the city responsible for city planning, and at that time a city planning committee was set up with members elected by and among the Council. This committee published a set of master plans for the city in 1866. By 1875, planning and building controls were essentially a municipal responsibility. The city authorities found, however, that when they started the implementation of the plans of 1866, land, needed for new or widened streets, had to be paid for at the full market price. A generation earlier, large parts of that land had been city property leased to the owners of the buildings. Some of the proposed boulevards, Parisian style, were never laid out because of this high land cost. The lesson learned was that it was far preferable for the city to buy the land early before it was needed for public construction. Thus, at the beginning of the twentieth century, Stockholm started a new policy to buy land even outside its limits. It was clear that the population was growing rapidly, and that good urban life was possible only when building and population densities were lowered. The first municipal garden suburbs were started in 1908. Halted during World War I—which gave time for preparing master plans—this development accelerated in the 1920s.

The garden suburb program had three parts: (1) acquisition of land, (2) planning for development with single family houses, and (3) incorporation of entire rural districts with the city. Two such incorporations took place in 1913 and 1916 by which the city territory grew from thirteen to fifty-four square miles. After World War I when normal activities were resumed, members of the City Council were anxious that this would not place heavy financial burdens on the city. They concluded that the area already incorporated would be large enough for any probable growth; that they were wrong did not become obvious until some twenty years later. By then it was too late to solve the problems of metropolitan Stockholm under *one* municipal unit. The lack of vision and foresight in the twenties made necessary the complex agreement forming a Greater Stockholm Council in the 1960s.

For the inner parts of the city, a master plan was published in 1928. By 1930, a new design style and new policy changed the patterns to a more open development in a kind of domestic Bauhaus fashion. Looking back on this century, 1840–1940, it would appear that industrialism came so late and planning came so early that Stockholm almost escaped the chaotic development which destroyed so many of the fine old cities of Europe.

POST-WORLD WAR II PLANNING

Under the pressure of World War II conditions, the traditional system for financing and building dwellings almost collapsed. As in most other Western countries, the national government took over and offered the necessary legal and financial supports for "public housing." This help enabled the city of Stockholm to plan and build—on city-owned land—an extensive new system of suburban units. This has been one of the three large planning tasks of this postwar period. The other two, dealt with below, are the rebuilding of the Central Business District and the construction of an adequate transport system.

New Suburbs

The traditional structure of Stockholm was simple and very conventional: a single nucleus or core surrounded by dense multifamily housing and farther out, somewhat scattered, areas with single-family housing. By the end of World War II, the increase in population proved to be much greater than previously anticipated. As there was insufficient land for multifamily housing in the inner parts of the region, the city had to meet this demand by building suburbs with relatively high density outside the prewar low density areas.

The new suburbs of the late 1940s were planned as neighborhood units, strongly influenced by British and American planning theories. With modifications—some of them of major proportion—this way of planning and building has been followed during the past twenty years. By 1970, twenty-seven such units have been completed, based on the 1952 master plan for Stockholm, prepared by a team led by Sven Markelius, director of planning from 1944–54.[1] Three general conditions were essential for this development to occur[2]:

a. that the city owned sufficient undeveloped land;
b. that the neighborhood planning concept was accepted;
c. that the 1943 National Housing Act provided adequate national government financial support.

The first two points will be dealt with in some detail immediately below, the third will be discussed under "Housing Policies."

Land

In 1904, when liberal politicians were gaining influence in city politics, the city started to buy farms and forest land outside the then city limits, and some years later the city incorporated rural districts to the south and the west. This acquisition of land continued and after sixty years the city owned approximately 70 per cent of the land in the suburban areas inside the present city boundaries. In most cases the city bought the land early when it was at a reasonable price and long before the city would have been forced to buy for needed development. The land was kept in good order as farm and forest until it was required for building; in many cases land was held as long as twenty years, even more. For most of this period, there was no special legislation to support or make easy this activity and all land was bought by free negotiations. But in 1953, a national law was passed giving any municipality the right to expropriate unbuilt land within its boundaries that could be proved needed for housing.[3] This land may not be sold but must be leased to the builders. This law is practically never used by the city of Stockholm, but, of course, its very existence makes it far easier for the city and a landowner to reach an agreement and to close a deal. In 1967, another national law was passed favoring the municipal acquisition of land.[4] When any private land is being sold, under certain conditions the city may purchase it before the intended buyer. The land must be needed for future housing or buildings that belong to such domestic uses and could be in another municipality. The city must give notice within three months' time and pay the price agreed upon.

FIG. 2 Vällingby Center. Planned in 1951, opened in 1954. The principal layout plan by Sven Markelius, director of city planning, together with architects Backström and Reinius who also designed most of the buildings seen. To the left, shops with restaurant above. To the right, shops with social service facilities above. Tall building to the right dwellings, to the left headquarters of Svenska Bostäder, municipal building corporation which built it all. *Photograph by Cogg Bildbyrå*

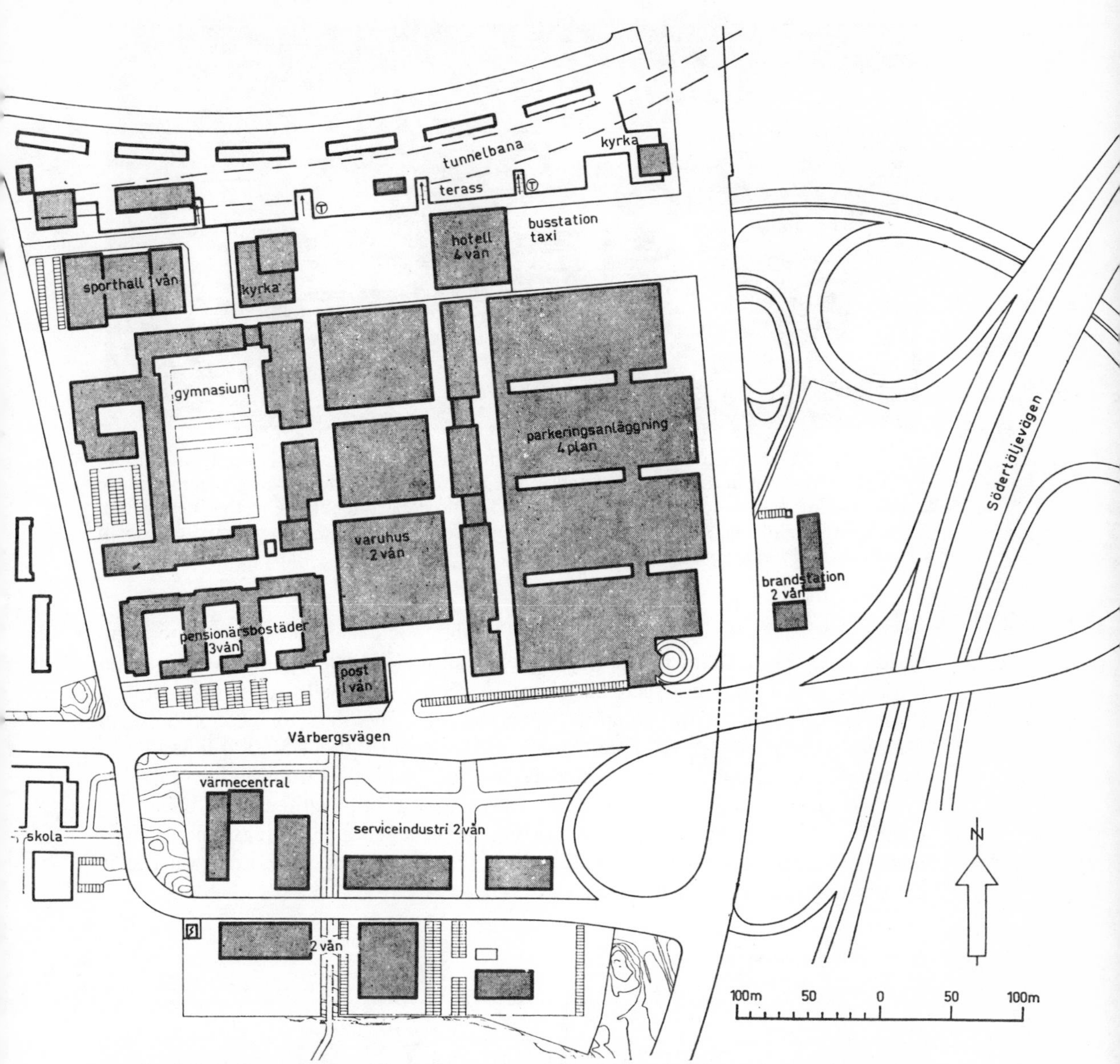

FIG. 3A Skärholmen Center. The subway (*tunnelbana*) station is at the northern edge. Four hundred parking spaces in four levels (*parkeringsanläggningar 4 plan*) are in the eastern third; department stores (*varuhus 2 våningar*) in the middle; senior high school (*gymnasium*), old persons' home (*pensionärsbostäder*), and hall for indoor sports (*sporthall*) in the western third. Service industry and district heating (*service industri, värmecentral*) are at the southern fringe.

Ideas

The neighborhood planning concept broke through into Swedish thought and practice when Lewis Mumford's *Culture of Cities* was translated into Swedish in 1942. Abercrombie's *Greater London Plan* came in 1943 with its satellite new town concept. The time was ripe for such thinking.

Up to 1950, the goal was to plan each neighborhood for about ten thousand inhabitants. There were many difficulties getting the civic and commercial centers built; in fact, in the early years there was very little success at all (Fig. 2). With

FIG. 3B The Skärholmen Center area. In the lower right-hand corner is the town symbol by Aston Forsberg and the control tower for the four thousand parking places. In the center, the low commercial buildings with the Tempo department store in the foreground. To the left, an old persons' home. Apartments are built on the hill immediately north of the center. *Photograph by Cogg Bildbyrå*

experience it became evident that 10,000 people could neither support good and varied shopping facilities nor justify the expenditures of public monies for certain forms of social services, such as assembly rooms and halls for indoor sports. From about 1950 on, the planning principles were modified to build *clusters of neighborhood units* (semisatellite towns) with a total of about 50,000 inhabitants, with each unit containing approximately twenty thousand persons (Figs. 3a, 3b). This last figure was reached after studies made jointly with experts from the Chamber of Commerce of the then existing suburban shopping areas. Increasingly more and more of both commercial and noncommercial services are gathered in the one main center in each cluster.

New Suburbs of Stockholm.

Name of cluster and main center	Land bought	Main center opened	Master plan		Dwellings built	Neighbourhoods planned			Additional population served by the main center Jan. 72	Present administrative areas corresponding to	
			approved	changed or extended		#	Population aimed at	Jan. 72		units in col. 7	areas in col. 10
1	2	3	4	5	6	7	8	9	10	11	12
VÄLLINGBY	1927 1931	1954	1950	1954 1959	1951-56	6	44,000	45,400	27,000	Blackeberg, Råcksta, Grimsta, Vällingby, Hasselby Gård & Strand.	Norra & Södra Ängby, Beckomberga, Flysta, Nälsta, Solhem, Kälvesta, Vinsta, Hässelby Villastad.
HÖGDALEN	1930 1950	1959	–	1956	1950-61	2	20,000	18,000	36,000	Bandhagen, Högdalen.	Rågsved, Hagsätra, Älvsjö, Örby, Stureby.
FARSTA	1912	1961	1953	1956	1956-60	3	35,000	21,800	29,000	Farsta, Larsboda, Farsta Strand.	Fagersjö, Hökarängen, Gubbängen, Sköndal.
SKÄRHOLMEN	1931 1945 1961	1968	1961 1963	–	1962-69	4	45,000	36,000	7,000	Bredäng, Sätra, Skarholmen, Vårberg.	Vårby Gård, Masmo, Segeltorp.
TENSTA	1966	1970	1964	–	1966-70	3	35,500	28,800	1,600	Tensta, Rinkeby, Hjulsta.	Tensta Hage, Spånga Garde.
N. JÄRVA	1966	not before 1977	1969	1969-75	1972-79	another planning concept, about 80,000				11,000 acre former military training grounds. The housing will be in Stockholm and Sollentuna mainly, places on work also in Solna and Sundbyberg.	
Akalla Husby Kista Hasta				1971		32,000		80			

The first cluster, Vällingby, planned in 1950, was called an ABC town, where *A* stood for work (*arbete*), *B* for dwellings (*bostäder*), and *C* for center with culture and commerce (*centrum*). The procedure for building dwellings has become a routine made more easy by the fact that housing constantly has been a sellers' market. To build a center is more complicated as there are many parties involved with different ways of financing. To build places of work requires, indeed, quite other methods. Anyone who wants and is able to build a factory or an office is offered suburban land by municipalities under favorable terms trying to attract good sources of tax revenue. Commercial building is thus constantly a buyers' market.

This last problem of providing places of work in the new suburbs is also apt to conflict with national planning policies. In most cases the relocation of industrial/ commercial enterprises to the new suburbs is simply decentralization within the Stockholm region. Most frequently, they are industries that are doing well and want to expand without losing their various contacts with the Stockholm market. Since 1946, industrial buildings have generally needed a permit from the National Labor Board. This authority has tried to persuade those enterprises that are willing to move 10 to 15 miles out of central Stockholm to move farther (100 or 150 miles) to areas where there is a surplus labor force. If an industry will accept a relocation that far away to the north, it could not only have an instant building permit but might even obtain a relocation grant from the national government.

The problem of locating places of work within the Stockholm region—as in many other metropolitan regions—has become one of the prime issues in planning. To offer the suburbanites an opportunity to work near to where they live is the ambition of many planners. However, in existing Swedish suburbs, people do not live the way the planners thought they would. In a society where so many have the time, the money and the vehicles that enable them to travel long distances within the metropolitan area, less than half of the employed work nearby even when such possibilities exist. To guide actual planning, the traffic patterns have been studied for 1960 and 1965. How many commute within, into and out from different areas outside the central part of the city? The following areas have been chosen: the entire southern suburban sector (SS), the entire northern suburban sector (NS), two old and well-established suburban towns, Solna (So) and Sundbyberg (Su), the new clusters of Vällingby (V) and Farsta (F).

The 1965 figures for gainfully occupied night population are compared with the total number of jobs in the same areas. These are the "job opportunity quotients": SS 52 per cent, NS 69 per cent, So 76 per cent, Su 125 per cent (that is more jobs than workers), V 55 per cent, F 36 per cent.

How many jobs offered are taken by local residents? SS 80 per cent, NS 80 per cent, So 43 per cent, Su 35 per cent (there were not enough residents?), V 48 per cent, F 45 per cent. In spite of that there were many more workers living within walking distance, less than half of the jobs in Vällingby and Farsta were taken by residents.

How many of the workers of all kinds living in an area worked there? SS 41 per cent, NS 55 per cent, So 33 per cent, Su 43 per cent, V 26 per cent, F 16 per cent. That is, only one sixth of the working population in Farsta worked there, but one third could have done so.

How many living in the areas went to work in central Stockholm? SS 51 per cent, NS 41 per cent, So 29 per cent, Su 38 per cent, V 45 per cent, F 57 per cent.

There are not so many commuters in the older areas as in the newer ones. This gives us hope that as time goes by, more suburbanites will accept work opportunities near where they live. However, this may be a rather slow process. In Vällingby, which is about fifteen years old, a little less than one half of the workers commute to the city center and only one quarter work locally. The other one quarter commutes to work elsewhere. Even if we are bold and successful planners, in Stockholm we do not expect to reach better results than that one third of the employed residents work in a suburban area, one third commute to the central parts of the city, and one third commute elsewhere. If a suburban area is built for 100,000 people, it should have a 48,000 working population of which 16,000 will be locally employed, 16,000 go "downtown" and 16,000 elsewhere. This is the Stockholm planner's rule of thumb, at least for the near future. How it will be, or could be changed, is discussed further on. This rule has been at the root of one of the basic discussions in planning the large area of Järva. This plan is, in many respects, different in scale from the other suburban developments of Stockholm.

Järva New Town

The development of Järva is of such dimensions and incorporates such quasi-new principles that it is worth presenting separately. The planning has been done jointly by five municipalities: the city of Stockholm, the towns of Solna (56,000 inhabitants), Sundbyberg (29,000) and Sollentuna (34,000), and the "rural district" of Järfälla (39,000). These five have together bought the main parts of the training grounds that the Stockholm garrison has used since 1905. This consists of more than 13,000 acres formed like a green wedge with its point only five miles from the center of Stockholm and stretching to the northwest to the still rural areas on the periphery of Greater Stockholm. As housing on adjoining land was closing in and military technics required more space, the grounds became no longer suitable for their military purpose. The Army was willing to sell in exchange for better training fields farther away, and the Parliament agreed that each municipality could buy what was inside its limit. However, an airfield and some land for national, mostly nonmilitary purposes, was not sold. The five municipalities formed a planning committee which has been responsible for the development plan for the entire area. Today the Järva grounds offer a very attractive landscape of open fields, woods and several lakes to which a manor house and some ancient farms give character. The area is well served by transport facilities as two motorways—E4 and E18—run along the edges and two parallel railways are not far away.

The primary aim of the municipalities in buying the land was to construct dwellings. The national government, which only kept what it needed of Järva for its own use, refrained from entering the housing market itself. From the very start of discussions about the planning program, it was obvious to everyone involved that this was a unique opportunity. Never before—or after—would such a vast, central, virgin area be available for planning. If ever any locational alternative to the center of Stockholm were to be offered to commerce, industry, science and recreation, according to thoughts on the regional plan, it had to be on the Järva grounds.

In 1966, the joint planning committee wrote the program for an inter-Nordic competition for a plan with dwellings for 100,000 and places of work for 70,000. Late in 1968, it approved a development plan, which the five municipal councils have accepted to serve as a base for further planning.

To a foreign reader, the most remarkable thing about the Järva plan may be that the national government has not done the planning itself but let the five local authorities prepare the plan, not only for the land sold but also for the parts of the area that will remain national property. Indeed, this is according to the planning laws of Sweden; in many other countries the national government would have done the planning as with the British new town corporations. There are two reasons why the administrative solution chosen at Järva is expected to work. The first is that since 1952, a regional planning body exists formed by all municipalities within Greater Stockholm with the task of settling intermunicipal planning problems. The second reason is that the five municipalities bought the land together, and they must decide later among themselves what portion of the total purchase money each will have to pay.

One third of the total planned area will be "regional open green space." Almost the entire area inside Järfälla will be kept that way. The contemporary interest in "clean nature" supported the advocates for green space.

The possibilities of offering the expanding economy of the private sector as well as the public, an alternative to the Central Business District, was explored in more detail. It is probable that there will be large offices or officelike industries moving into the area. The Swedish planners have investigated and compared the Järva with Hamburg Nord—three and one half miles north of the Hamburg downtown area—and with La Défense—two miles from the Étoile in Paris—and have come to the conclusion that office areas should be planned to suit sizable commercial units that want possibilities for future expansion and too should have access to the external economies of a large concentration of offices. To begin with, the national government reserved land for technical science institutions and an annex to the Stockholm University. In early 1971, however, the plan was changed to contain conventional suburban development. The main reason seems to be that the Parliament recently approved a proposal to decentralize public offices and institutions with more than 6,000 employees to places outside the Stockholm region.[5]

The combination of dwellings and work places within short distances of each other—in some of the discussed alternative plans formed as parallel ribbons—would affect the need for traffic capacities. As already mentioned, the rule of thumb is that one third of the working population will work locally, one third will go to the CBD, and one third will work elsewhere in the region. The traffic plan for Järva assumes that during rush hours travel to points of attraction within the area would be 60 per cent by car, 40 per cent by rail and bus. The probability of this will be discussed below under the heading "A Balanced Traffic System?" The densely built areas will be served by two branches of the Stockholm subway system.

The Development Plan of 1968 would permit housing for 110,000 to 140,000 people, most of them in multifamily, multistoried apartment buildings, but recent surveys prove that the figure will stop at below 80,000. The administrative and financial mechanism for implementing these portions of the plan offers some problems yet to be solved. The plans show no neighborhood units; most of the dwellings will be concentrated in two solid blocks, each with about 40,000 inhabitants. The calculated figure for work places is about 50,000. That is, the plan gives room for more places of work than for workers to live. About 10,000 will work in different services dispersed throughout the area; and 40,000 in areas planned and built by the national government, Stockholm and Sollentuna. Will that be possible?

In the discussion about building on Järva, some have argued for a "city satellite"—almost a second city center—advocating that such a thing should be built there. To do so, they say it would not be necessary to reconstruct extensively the Stockholm CBD, the lower Norrmalm area, to fit modern needs. On the contrary, the argument goes, it would open up an opportunity to preserve what is left of the existing buildings there. Whether that is possible or not will be dealt with in a following section.

Housing Policies

The extensive development of new semisatellite suburbs has been possible not only because the city owned sufficient land, but also because there were national and municipal housing policies that channeled the flow of enough money at controlled interest rates, approximately at the right times. As part of national social policy, forward-looking housing legislation had existed since the 1930s, but the economic conditions during World War II made necessary more comprehensive schemes for financing the greater part of the housing industry. During the last twenty years, the rules have been based on the general principle that national and municipal housing efforts should be combined. The National Housing Authority has economic resources to give loans, grants and reduction of interest and rents. The municipal authorities must prepare building programs to take the initiative in promoting construction, to inspect the buildings produced with any kind of public aid and to exercise rent control. First mortgages and the reduction of interest on secondary loans have been given to public bodies and co-ops as well as private builders. The last category must accept rent control until the loans are paid back—usually after thirty years. Municipally owned building organizations are given first mortgage loans between 70 and 100 per cent of the calculated capital value; co-ops between 70 and 95 per cent; privately built, one-family houses up to 90 per cent and multifamily dwellings between 70 and 85 per cent. The National Housing Authority tries to brake the increase in building costs by keeping the "calculated capital values" low. Building costs above this limit must, of course, be paid by the builder or the future tenants. A condition for public help in financing dwellings is that they are built according to standards issued by the National Housing Authority.

Rent subsidies are given to families—mostly those with two or more children or elderly people—who otherwise would not be able to pay for a dwelling of good quality. The rules have been changed from time to time but approximately 90 per cent of all dwellings produced in Stockholm since 1946 have had some sort of public financial help including all dwellings built on city land. Any family can live in such housing; there is no upper income limit that excludes them from such a possibility. The stability of policy has, of course, been due to the fact that Sweden since 1932 has had practically a continuous social-democratic government. Changes in the Stockholm City Council between a majority of the combined left parties or of a combined liberal and conservative coalition (lately the latter call themselves "moderate") have had little influence. The accumulating economic burden has caused some concern in national politics; at present, interest reduction is not as generous as earlier and thus rents have been allowed to rise. This in turn has made necessary rent reduction (social subsidy) for a rising number of families. Such consequences have been accepted and preferred, as there is little need to keep low rents for those who are able to pay.

Lower Norrmalm: the Central Business District

A little more than one hundred years ago the main business district began to move from the island Gamla Stan (the Old Town) to its present location on Lower Norrmalm, an area which was first planned and redeveloped from 1636 to 1660. A gravel ridge originally more than one hundred feet high ran through the area from north to south. The main streets which were laid out parallel to the slopes in the 1640 plans, were forty feet wide, and the minor streets, perpendicular to the former, were twenty-four feet and sometimes very steep. By 1890, 36,000 people lived in an area which in 1865 had only 4,400. With limited legal and economic resources, the planning before 1900 could do almost nothing to the area. The first east-west cut through the ridge Kungsgatan was opened in 1911, and was for its time a daring enterprise. What was south of it remained unchanged by the vivid planning debates. About 1930, new initiatives were taken and after eighteen years of proposals and counterproposals the City Council decided in 1945 to widen streets to form a new east-west boulevard and extend an already existing boulevard north of the area to meet it.

Demolition had not even begun when it was discovered that rebuilding a CBD had far more to it than deciding "which streets should be made how wide." The boulevards would neither be efficient traffic arteries nor good shopping streets. In 1945, a new planning team, gathered by Sven Markelius, was given the task of amending the plan just decided upon. The boulevards had to remain, but separation of traffic was introduced and the through traffic moved outside or below the surface of the CBD. The forms and functions of buildings were studied to meet modern conditions. These amendments were accepted in the 1946 plan, which served as the basic document for redevelopment up to 1962.

There were two factors that affected the actual start of work on the Lower Norrmalm site. The construction of the new subway line had to be made in an open cut. The desire to improve conditions in the city center for traffic to and from the suburbs made it urgent for an early start. However, the problem of obtaining legal possession of the land was difficult and tended to delay operations.

By the beginning of the twentieth century the city knew that this area with its steep and narrow streets had to be rebuilt eventually, and thus commenced to buy property on Lower Norrmalm when such was offered for sale. By 1951, when work on the site was actually started, the city owned some fifty pieces of property there. In 1953, at the request of the city the rules in the (national) Building Act regulating condemnation of land for redevelopment purposes were changed. With the new rules the city—any city—could ask the national government for authorization to buy land by compulsory purchase *before* a plan for a thorough recon-

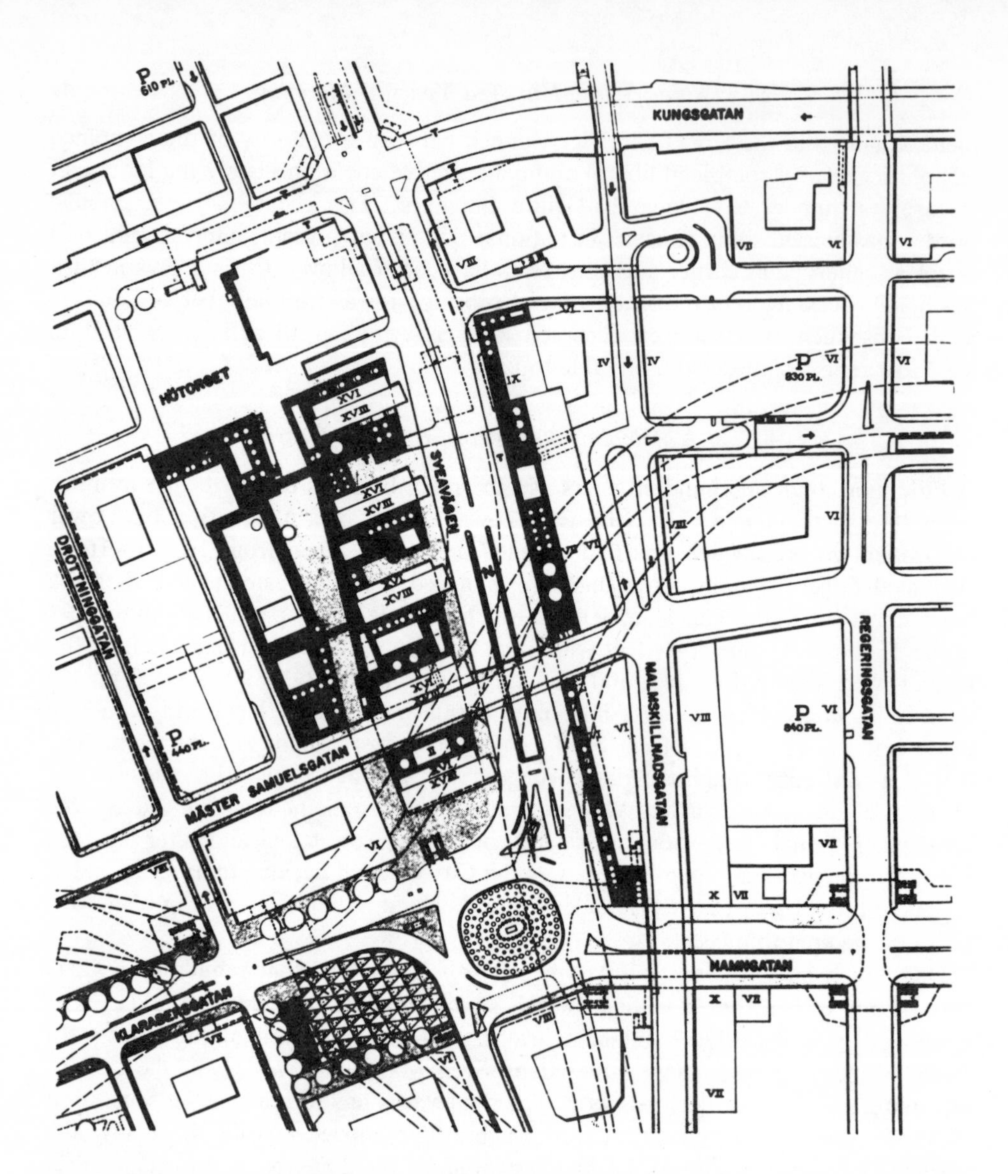

FIG. 4A Stockholm's CBD Mall. From the Haymarket (Hötorget) the mall (Sergelgatan) runs parallel to the boulevard (Sveavägen) to the split level open place (Sergelstorg) where two more boulevards (Hamngatan and Klarabersgatan) meet. The dark areas are the platforms twenty feet above street level.

struction or redevelopment is completed or even published. The conditions of the law are that if the properties are within an area that the city has decided to renew radically but has not yet decided exactly how this will be done, they can be taken by eminent domain. As court procedures may take years, the city could ask for the right to take over the land to proceed at once.[6] Given this, the properties may be used, even for the construction of streets or buildings—in spite of the fact that court proceedings have not come to an end, that the definite price of the land is not known, and that the extra compensation the city may have to pay is not settled (Figs. 4a, 4b).

The land that, according to the new plans, is to be used for building sites is leased to various builders and investors. The ground rent is normally fixed for a first period of ten years, but the lease cannot come to an end before sixty years.

FIG. 4B The Haymarket area from the Southwest. The Haymarket itself with the concert hall is at the upper left edge. The mall in front of the five tall buildings cannot be seen, but the platform with connecting bridges for pedestrians is visible. *Photograph by Erik Claesson*

Thus a leaseholder is able to mortgage his contract almost as if he owned the land. The leasehold gives the city the capability of controlling the builders and saying when, how and for what purpose they may build. Connections to district heating and underground service streets are also guaranteed through the leasehold contract. Some such contracts are combined with an obligation on the part of the owner of the building to let space to certain tenants.

Solutions

The core of the 1946 plan was the area south of the ancient Hötorget (Haymarket). The first stage of redevelopment was a new mall, Sergelgatan, with five, eighteen-storied office blocks on its east side and low buildings on its west side containing shops, a motion picture theatre and a food market. On the lower buildings, there is a platform or pediment level with roof gardens and places for out-of-door eating connected with all year-round restaurants inside. With bridges over the conventional streets, this platform level has been extended to form an open-air and car-free space about twenty feet above ground level for casual recreation to be used as weather permits.

To the south, the street-level pedestrian mall opens into a new square, Sergelstorg, where the boulevard extended from the north meets the new east-west boulevard. This square is built with two levels. On the upper, there is a large fountain that is a roundabout for vehicles in the form of a superellipse. The lower level is for pedestrians only and has direct connection with the entrance hall of the subway. This lower level is connected throughout with the conventional sidewalks and with the mall by escalators. The surfaces for pedestrians are heated so as to keep feet dry even when it is snowing.

It is obvious that the scheme of the Hötorget area has similarities with the famous Lijnbaan in Rotterdam, which in the same way as Sergelgatan runs parallel to an existing wide boulevard. The Rotterdam planning office under Van Traa and the Stockholm planners communicated during the period of conception. While the Lijnbaan lies rather close to the water table making solutions with two or more levels difficult, the gravel ridge in Stockholm is cut through and the street level lowered in some parts as much as thirty feet. But the lower level of the Sergelstorg still remains almost twenty feet above water. There are three basements under Sergelgatan mainly used for loading, unloading and for parking.

The CBD plan of 1946 has been revised twice, in 1962 and 1967, partly to adjust it to the regional planning done since 1952, partly to profit by experience. Approximately one thousand of the original buildings in the 1967 renewal area, by the summer of 1972, have been demolished, thirty new and much larger units have been constructed, and in June 1972 ten more were being built. About twenty new sites lie vacant, many temporarily in use for traffic purposes. On the average, about six old buildings have been replaced by one new. All buildings except one have been built on city land under leasehold contract. The first age of renewal comprised thirty acres of which twenty-two acres were building sites and some seven acres were allocated to streets and parking. The sites for buildings have shrunk to one half of the original area, but the space for traffic has increased six and one half times what it was when reconstruction started, although not all is on the ground level. This traffic area includes not only the fewer but much wider conventional streets, but also all off-street parking, the underground service streets and space for pedestrians on the platform and the underground level. The floor space index was 2.23 and is now 2.52, an increase of only 11 per cent. The first stage of reconstruction resulted in little less than 3.2 million square feet of floor space. The second stage, to be completed by 1975, will hold 4.4 million square feet. By 1969, the annual investments in buildings was calculated to be 200 million Sw.Kr. and other investments about the same. The national government holds some property and plans to acquire more and use it for its own purposes. Up to 1969 the total investment in new buildings is 900 million Sw.Kr. (approximately $180,000,000). The city has invested about the same amount in buying land, evacuating tenants, demolishing and building streets, service ducts, etc., excluding the cost of the subway. The city built one tall and one low building because in the initial period it was difficult to attract interested private money. Two buildings were built by the national government; all the others by private builders.

As is true in most other countries, there is a growing opposition to such large-scale, complete urban-renewal operations. According to the 1967 plan, about one half of all buildings within the renewal area were to be demolished and replaced by new ones. Many present property owners have said they want to pull down existing structures and build anew, in spite of the fact that the city's plan does not force them to do so. In the end probably only one third of all buildings would be left untouched. Under the 1962 plan, buildings have been classified by the city antiquarian, and only about seventy are listed as of "historic interest." Less than ten of these have to be demolished. Many of the others are privately owned and the chances that they will be preserved are not very bright. The public debate about historic conservation seems always to hang onto the tail of the renewal procedure.

Those who object to such planning schemes do it along two lines, seemingly unaware that the two are self-contradictory. One is that more of the old buildings ought to be saved; the other that in the new environment cars dominate with their noise and fumes. Stockholm citizens claim that the city could function better with public transport only—including taxis—and that in the CBD private cars should be prohibited or at least heavily restricted. If the old city structure is to remain, there is no realistic alternative to letting the combustion-motored traffic congest the conventional streets. Only with a thorough reconstruction can cars be hidden below or behind so that the pedestrians will neither see, smell nor hear them. And how could modern city activities function in a structure planned three hundred years ago primarily for dwellings in any case? It may be that traffic space in relation to floor space need not be six times larger than before, but pedestrians, buses, taxis and private cars delivering goods and customers need much more traffic space than what existed in the past.

The renewal of the Stockholm CBD is often compared with similar planning elsewhere. Conventry in England, Bremen and Munich in West Germany, Rotterdam in Holland, Montreal in Canada, Baltimore's Charles Center and San Francisco's Golden Gate Center in the United States are such examples. In some cities the core is surrounded with a ring road, which makes it possible to exclude almost all through traffic and to have the essential central streets or squares reserved for pedestrians only. One reason why this system cannot be used in Stockholm is that on the south side of the CBD along Strömmen (the Stream) and on the east side no ring—or tangent road—has proved to be possible. Many have tried to discover a feasible solution, and there will probably be more proposals in the future as the renewal of the eastern fringe of the CBD lies a decade ahead. It is impossible to say at this point how much money will be available to meet goals formulated in the late 1970s. Secondly, in Stockholm all the derelict buildings were in the center and the good, dignified, public buildings at the periphery of the CBD. Before 1950, the CBD proper had a structure like a ring around this central core area with its steep, narrow streets and badly used or badly built buildings. Prior to 1960, all people in responsible positions were anxious to start changing these very unsatisfactory core conditions. So the Planning Department started to rebuild at the center. Prior to the 1960s, very few were prepared to argue that it was a bad thing to provide more space for traffic.

Experience

The renewal of the Stockholm CBD has been going on for over two decades. What experiences of value for the future and for other cities could be gained from this effort:

1. The legal system functions satisfactorily. The city experts and the lawyers representing owners of private property all know the rules of the game and in most cases both parties seem to be content. A large number of builders and investors has accepted the leasehold system.

2. What happened to the old shops in the renewal zone?[7] In the area completed by 1966, there had been 174 shops of different kinds which were replaced by 138 new ones—20 per cent less. The floor space, however, is more than double, and the turnover—in fixed prices—three times what it was before. The number employed grew by 26 per cent, the turnover per square foot by al-

most 50 per cent. Of the old shops, about 27 per cent have disappeared, 36 per cent have moved to permanent locations outside the area, only 11 per cent returned to the new buildings. The rest (26 per cent) survived in buildings that were not affected by the renewal. Not every shop in the new buildings is doing well, but most of them are successful.

3. Different methods to separate traffic have been tried. Most often the cars have access to the first basement for loading and unloading and to parking farther down. During the sixties, multilevel overstreet parking garages were preferred; but now it seems as if basement parking is in favor again, as it is more flexible. The underground levels can be used for different purposes. An overstreet parking garage, specially if it has sloping floors, cannot be used for anything but storing cars. All new buildings have access to underground delivery streets; each such street serves five to ten buildings.

4. The space exclusively reserved for pedestrians is, of course, an essential element in the plan. From the ticket halls of the subway there are walkways at the first basement level. Shops open into these areas. At Sergelstorg such an area opens to the sky. At the conventional street level there is one mall. Two old streets are reserved for pedestrians from 11 A.M. until midnight. Since spring 1970, all of the main thoroughfare, Kungsgatan, is reserved for pedestrians, buses, taxis and delivery trucks. The platform, or pediment, level, twenty feet above the street, has practically no commercial value in itself, but in fine weather has proved more popular than expected. Unfortunately, hippies have used it as a meeting place, which has created problems.

With the three subway lines crossing each other and the Central railway station on the west side, the CBD clearly should remain the most effective location for commercial activity in the city. This requires that people can reach it from every part of the region, even if they travel by road and not by rail. Is there a possible solution for balanced metropolitan traffic in the Stockholm area?

A Balanced Traffic System?

Each day about two million journeys are made within Greater Stockholm. Half of them are journeys to work and are repeated at least five days a week at the same time, along the same route, in the same way. Considerably more than half of all travelers have several possibilities to choose from as to how and what way they wish to go. Some can even choose when and where they want to go.

To balance traffic in Stockholm would be to influence the million daily commuter decisions in such a way that the traffic load would correspond with the existing capacities, which in turn are presumed to be in accordance with the traffic policy goals set by the responsible local authority. In a very simplified fashion these goals could be expressed in one sentence: "More journeys from the suburbs to the central parts of the region should be done by collective (public) means of travel, by rail or by bus." Could those who have private cars be prevented from using them to reach certain parts of the region? How does one "plan traffic" as part of a general transportation system? What mechanisms exist or could be introduced to implement such policies using both the "carrot and the stick" techniques?

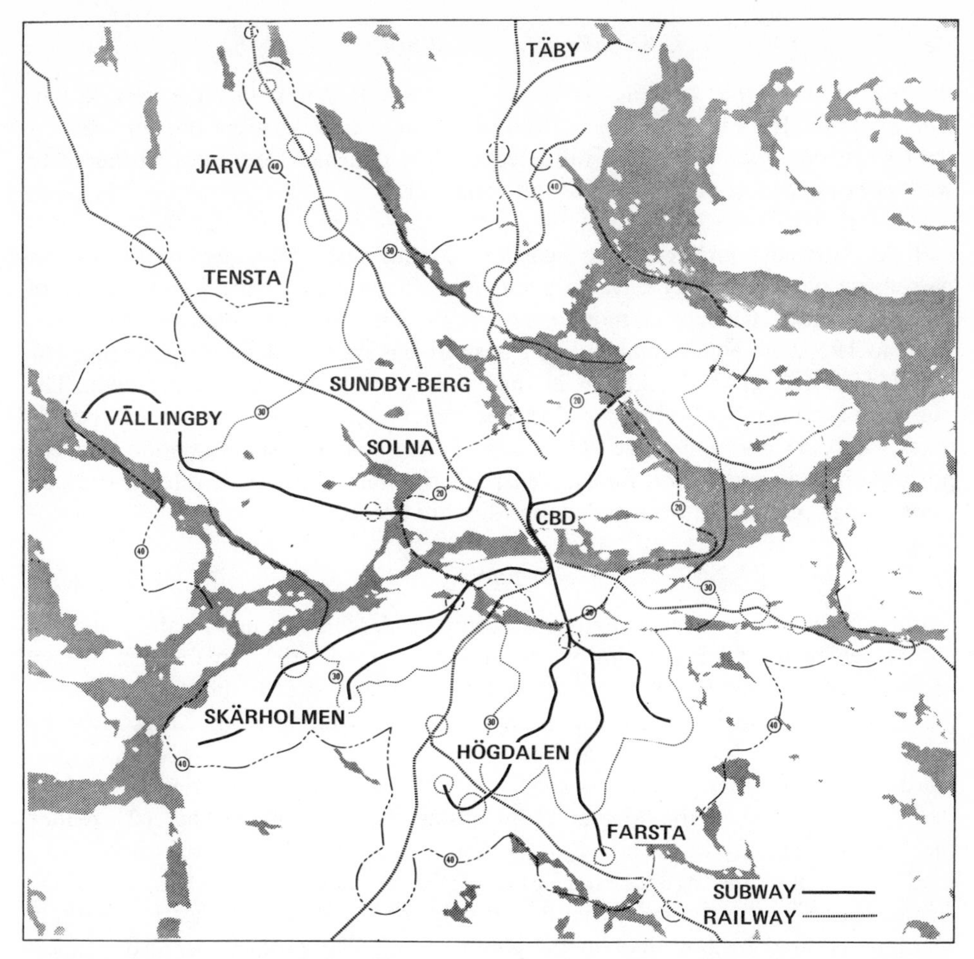

FIG. 5 Subway and railway lines now in operation. Figures indicate approximate traveling time in minutes from CBD, including walking time at both ends of the journey. Location of suburban "clusters" mentioned in Table shown on page 32, plus the suburban center of Täby and the towns of Solna and Sundbyberg outside the city of Stockholm.

"Carrot"

Public transport in Stockholm, as elsewhere, is made more attractive by improving quality and quantity (Fig. 5). Quality is related to price, regularity, comfort and accessibility. The fares are kept low by design, the basic fare price—until October 1971—was one Sw.Kr. (about 20 cents), which was introduced several years ago. The total income covers about four fifths of the total expenditures of the traffic organization; the rest is paid by local income taxes. The balance of fares versus subsidies offers a perpetual political issue. As the living standard rises, it will be increasingly difficult to keep the customers on public transport by offering low fares; "zero fare" (no charge) has been discussed repeatedly. After a period of "zero fare," the situation could be expected to stabilize. Presumably the load on public transport would not be much heavier than today, as very few people now refrain from travel during peak hours because of the fare. Those who go by car already pay more. "On the minute" arrival on rail commuter lines is expected as normal. More bus lines will have reserved lanes so they can move when the rest of the traffic becomes congested, but speed still favors the private car. The total time from door to door (1966) is 20 per cent less when one goes by car than when one goes by bus or rail except when one has very short distances to walk at both ends from public transport terminals.

Comfort is to have both the station within easy reach—external accessibility—and the internal comfort of the vehicles. During rush hours two thirds of the passengers on the subway have to stand up.[8] Automobile seats, at least most of them, are much wider and more comfortable than those in the subway. From 1945 to 1965, the capacity of public transport has increased by 67 per cent. The population of Greater Stockholm in that period has grown by 50 per cent. The number of "seat miles" offered is 155 per cent more, but the number of "person miles," only 55 per cent more. That is, to keep about the same relation between population and travelers on public transport, the number of seats offered has had to be 67 per cent more. No wonder subsidies are needed.

"Stick"

During the last twenty years there has been considerable discussion about how to reduce vehicular traffic and improve conditions for pedestrians in the central part of the region. What has been done in the CBD has already been told. Traffic planning has a goal to limit the number of persons coming from the suburbs by personal vehicle to 25 per cent, and that only 10 per cent of those who work permanently in the CBD should do so. Three methods have been tried to achieve this: (1) reduction of the "demand" by raising the price of parking, (2) reduce the "supply" of parking facilities and—now being debated—(3) introduce some kind of "rationing" as well as "road pricing" (users charges). There is no parking free of charge in the central areas; in centrally located new buildings less parking space is required by law than in peripheral areas. The problem is further complicated by the 300,000 people with 50,000 cars living in the inner city who demand the right to use their cars under about the same conditions as the suburbanites.

Could parking fees be so high that they would effectively deter people from driving their cars downtown? Certainly not so long as parking fees are tax deductible for business people! Could not illegal parking be fought more effectively? Nightly counts have shown that in some areas there are 50 per cent more cars parked than there are legal places to do so. Should the city prohibit the building of more garages in the city center? This is done for "cultural" reasons in the historic Old Town. In the CBD there are about 8,000 parking places. The 1967 plan says that there should be room for three times as many. This figure is fiercely attacked by the young and by the preservationists, and in July 1970 a Traffic Policy Committee suggested that the number should be maximized at 12,000 or 15,000. The owners of department stores and shopkeepers say: "Our customers must be able to park, or we will die." The battle is in full swing and undoubtedly will continue!

The Subway Story

The great cities of the world could be divided into those who built an off-street, rapid transit rail system early, before private cars congested their streets, and those who did not even seriously talk about it until the cars were there. In 1941, when Stockholm had less than 600,000 inhabitants with not more than 30,000 cars, the City Council decided to build a subway—a rail transport system running entirely off street, partially at or above grade, but in the central areas in tunnels. Ever since, this decision has governed transportation planning and the discussions about traffic policies. This is still the basic controlling policy even now when Sweden has the highest car ownership ratio in Europe: in 1968, 3.7 persons per car; the United States had 2.0, and the United Kingdom, 4.0.

Stockholm City, sometimes named the "Venice of the North," is laced with water. The widest east-west direction was bridged at only one point up until 1934, when a second bridge was opened, with a third in 1966. The city is built on three stretches of mainland and on fifteen islands. Traffic from the suburbs to the city center thus has to pass over one or more bridges; very early it was obvious there was not room or capacity enough for surface public transport on the bridges. Thus the three subway lines have been built from one suburb through the center of the city in tunnels and on to a suburb on the other side.

The first through line (System I) was built from 1945–57 and serves 150,000 people in the west, branching in three lines to the south where it serves 210,000. Only 20 per cent of the total length is in tunnels. The second line (System II), built from 1958–64, with 60 per cent in tunnels, serves 150,000 inhabitants in the southwest and runs to the city limits in the northeast. Here an interchange station was opened in 1967 to which bus and tramlines bring people from outside the city limits. Since the end of 1965, a total of thirty-six miles of line has been in operation with sixty-three stations. The third main line (System III) is under construction and is planned to open in 1975, connecting the northwestern suburbs with the CBD; after 1985, it may be extended to the southeastern sector where one of the southern existing branch lines of System I will be connected to it. The newer part of System III will be built with an even higher percentage of underground trackage than System II.

Investments in subway Systems I and II have been made either directly or indirectly by the city. From 1945 to 1964, $340,000,000 at varying price levels have been invested. The 1965 subway plan proposes extensions to be built up to 1980 that would cost in 1964 prices an additional $350,000,000.[9]

Up to July 1965, planning, constructing and running the subway system was done entirely by Stockholm City, even if the operation was handled by the city-owned "Streetcar Company" (ABSS=Aktiebolaget Stockholms Sporvägar). The subway planning was treated as part of city planning and was done by the Traffic Section at the City Planning Department, aided by experts from other departments, and was done *for* the Master Planning Committee, composed of twelve prominent politicians representing all parties. This guaranteed that traffic planning, land use planning and suburban development were co-ordinated. The substructure of the subway was built by the Public Works Department with its own labor force or by contractors. The ABSS itself built the rest and could use the substructure free of charge.

So far Stockholm is the only Swedish city that has a subway or a local rail transportation system separated from street traffic. So long as the system was within the city limits only, naturally the city paid all costs. However, as one line was about to reach out to the city limits where it would meet local buses and trams from neighboring towns, and as other future lines would have to pass through two other towns to reach land that Stockholm was going to develop, the question arose as to who was going to pay for the construction of the substructure under these circumstances. The other municipalities said definitely they would not. In 1963, after lengthy discussions, the national government was asked to co-ordinate Stockholm metropolitan public passenger transport. In December 1964, an agreement was signed by the Executive Committee of the city of Stockholm (Stadskollegiet) and the Administrative Committee of the Stockholm County Council (Landstingets Förvaltningsutskott) and by the national railroads (Statens Järnvägar).[10] The agreement stipulated that the County Council was entering a new field of activity—public passenger transport—and together with the city of Stockholm formed a "body" that until the end of 1970 owned the transport company, AB Stor-Stockholms Lokaltrafik (SL). From 1971 the Stockholm County Council became the sole owner of the SL. The SL has successively bought existing private and municipal railways, boat lines and bus lines and taken over the national railway regional bus system. The national railroads consented to run local trains according to a schedule, annually agreed upon with the SL, charging it the costs for these services and paying it the fares collected.

In most towns and rural districts major highways are financed by the national government with taxes collected on cars and gasoline. The agreement of December 1964 further stipulated that 95 per cent of the costs of the substructure of the subways would be entitled to be financed in the same manner as such highways. The national government introduced such a bill to the Parliament (Riksdag), and the national budget for the fiscal year 1965/66 supported the principle of such national grants to local passenger transport, as *inter alia* subways are able to transport people at lower costs than highways. However, this was accepted only under the condition that the total amount of "traffic money" given to the Stockholm metropolitan area would not be higher than it would be without such grants. In addition, the budget included capital investments for the national railroads in order to facilitate local traffic within the metropolitan area.

In the parliamentary debates on these matters, members from the provincial parts of the country saw the proposal as exclusively favoring the capital and possibly two more cities. However, the Lower House accepted the bill without voting; in the Senate about 10 per cent of the votes were against the proposal. The Act on National Grants to Building of Subways has been in force since July 1965.[11] The subways and the local trains are from a political viewpoint the most essential elements in Stockholm traffic planning, but construction of new arterial highways absorb the larger part of the investment capacity. The National Organization for Building Roads (Statens Vägverk) is firmly turned toward highways, especially since it is financed by taxes on cars and gasoline. It is such a startlingly new idea to spend taxes collected in this fashion on both roads *and* rails that the latter gets less than the local politicians demand, but more than national government officials are willing to give.

The modes of travel for people *working* in these zones were studied in 1961, and a projection for 1990 has been done based on the regional plan of 1960. Here are the figures included in the provisional goals for traffic planning: during the 1970s the population within the region will grow from 1.3 million to 1.7 million but there will be twice as much traffic. During these ten years people will

TABLE A JOURNEYS TO WORK IN STOCKHOLM

Places of Work area	1961 (public transport) % collective	% cars	1990 (public transport) % collective	% cars
CBD	87	13	90	10
I	71	29	50	50
S	52	48	15	85
P	35	65	15	85

I=the rest of the inner city, S=suburbs within nine miles from the center and P=the peripheral suburbs.

spread and many will live outside a forty-five-minute ride on the subway. To offer a viable alternative to the single city core in the present Stockholm CBD, the regional plan discusses a restructuring of places of work.

THE STOCKHOLM REGIONAL PLAN

> The city of Stockholm depends on its region. The region of Stockholm depends on the city.

The Stockholm region consists primarily of the eastern part of middle Sweden that juts out into the Baltic. The location of the capital was favorable when traffic and transport went by sea; Stockholm fortified Lake Mälar, the only natural inlet to navigable water that stretches ninety miles to the west and forty-five miles to the north. Sailing voyages to Finland were protected by the group of Åland Islands, which were especially important as Sweden and Finland were parts of one kingdom up to 1809. The provinces around the Mälar basin once produced most of the food consumed in Stockholm; they have now become the area where the major part of Swedish manufacturing has developed and is continuing to develop. This area looks upon Stockholm as the main center, and thus the entire Mälar valley is developing into one economic region. There is already talk about making one plan for the whole region; and the four provincial governmental offices have published common inventories to tackle two problems: (a) water pollution and (b) resources for recreation of various kinds. So far, a proper and legal regional plan exists only for Stockholm, its suburbs and some of its nearby vacation land.

In 1949, the national government ordered forty-six municipalities—including Stockholm—to form an association to prepare a regional plan. The legal background was the Building Law of 1947.[12] The various municipal councils appointed an assembly that elected the governing board who in turn hired the staff that prepared the plan. A plan was approved by the assembly in 1958 and by the national government in 1960. Unfortunately the real value of this planning did not match expectations; thus, only two years later—in 1962—the work on a new edition of the plan was started which resulted in the Outline Regional Plan of 1966. This in turn was reviewed, and revised it was called Outline Plan 70. In the spring of 1969, regional planning merged with the Greater Stockholm administration, which will be dealt with in more detail below.

The plan of 1958, which had access to some of the 1950 data, had as its goal the making of basic projections up to 1990. The 1966 edition was intended to be more of a program with illustrations than merely conventional land-use maps; in April 1968, a condensed edition of the 1966 outline plan was published in English, in which some of the most essential problems were discussed beyond the 1966 stage. The 1970 edition includes a land-use map for 1985 and alternative plans for the development thereafter up until 2000. The revised Outline Plan 1970 starts with an analysis, and how far and how current investment planning is directing future development. Predictions about conditions in the year 2000 are given less attention than methods of how to get there. Once again the plan has been revised and will reappear as Regional Plan 73.

What interest does current regional planning within Greater Stockholm offer to observers elsewhere? Most important is that there exists a live regional plan for the Stockholm area.[13] The Ministry of the Interior could and did order all municipalities within an area that needed a regional plan to co-operate, and to have a plan prepared with the national government paying half the costs. The plan is to be approved finally by the ministry and will guide the member municipalities in their master planning, as well as the provincial Highway Department in planning major highways. Regional planning in Stockholm is probably no more successful than corresponding planning in many other metropolitan areas. It has been based on a political administrative mechanism designed almost twenty-five years ago, before there was any experience either with large-scale, publicly financed housing or from post-World War II automobile traffic. Regional planning today does not fulfill the needs and expectations of most parties involved: A principal weakness seems to be that the linkage is feeble between regional planning and detailed planning and building. It is easy for the regional planners to paint with a wide brush without enough contact with the real conditions. Thus, those who are responsible for further hard planning and hard decisions on investment for actual construction may look upon the regional plan as too theoretical. Evidence of these shortcomings in the official regional planning mechanism is that by 1958 a special Board of Planning for Greater Stockholm had to be created for voluntary co-operation between the nineteen municipalities in the central part of the region. The purpose is "to further a purposeful and well-planned expansion of Greater Stockholm." Apparently, the regional planning authority had not had capacity enough for this. Twenty-five years ago physical planning in Sweden was basically permissive; it made possible certain actions by others. Regional planning still is, but more and more municipal planning has become "project planning" with housing, schools and parks as principal items. The more capable of the municipal authorities are now attempting to produce economic planning for the next decade. And the highway authorities have draft plans for ten years and capital budgets for the next five years that are revised every three. So far there has been considerable difficulty in making permissive planning and project planning meet. One hypothetical question that may be asked is: Could the regional plan have power enough to halt development in one municipality so as to make possible the concentration of resources in another? It seems obvious that regional plans themselves with the administrative mechanism until 1971 could not. Possibly this can be done now when Stockholm's regional planning has been made a responsibility of the Greater Stockholm County Council (see below). Such physical planning might now be co-ordinated better with social and economic planning.

A considerable amount of debate has been concentrated on the regional traffic models. The preliminary goal is that journeys from the periphery of the metropolitan area to the existing core should not take more than forty-five minutes from door-to-door, which means in effect thirty minutes by train or bus. Thus the subway, with its present speed, could only serve areas up to ten to fifteen miles from the center and that areas farther out should be served by more rapid trains or express buses. In spite of that, the plan shows one third of all dwelling areas in the region outside the reach of the subway system and that one half of the population in the year 2000 will be more than forty-five minutes away from the central core. Under the very low densities proposed, Stockholm with only 2.5 million inhabitants will stretch out so far that many will have to travel about two hours a day. Probably the region will function as one labor market for people with rare and highly paid skills, but for those with medium or low income in trades found almost everywhere the region will probably split into more local labor markets.[14]

Are the problems of planning in the Stockholm region difficult? There are about one hundred cities in the world with a larger population than Stockholm and a lot of them are growing more rapidly. However, Stockholm is more spread out than many cities of the same size, and distances always create problems; in addition, there are the island topography with water everywhere, the irregular rocky (granite!) terrain, as well as the Swedish proclivity to sprawl over the countryside. This is especially true if the second homes for vacation use (several months a year) are taken into account; their number has tripled in the last twenty years. If such new houses are not to block off recreational green space needed for those who have no summer houses, they must be pushed farther and farther away from the permanently occupied dwelling areas. Distances between fifty and one hundred thirty miles between winter home and summer home are now normal. This is a quality that the Stockholm region can still offer as it is situated on the periphery of Europe. Such reasonable availability of fine open space in many other urban regions is becoming very rare indeed.

RESOURCES FOR THE FUTURE

By the end of the century one million more persons may be living in the Greater Stockholm area. And each one will ask for more space, not only indoors at home and on the job, but also out of doors for vehicles—probably three times as many as today—and for life in the open, many in a "second home."

The task ahead may be shown in probable figures:

	1970	2000
Population (millions)	1.3	2.3
Person per room	0.78	0.45
Rooms (millions)	1.7	5.1
Rooms to build (millions)		3.4

The dwelling volume by the year 2000 will be three times the present. As dwelling and building densities fall, each person and each room require more land and the total urban area grows much faster than the population figures. Will there be enough land available for building? In addition, the land must be furnished with the necessary communication networks. The problem is to supply capital not only for dwellings but also for transportation systems as they extend out over boundaries of several autonomous poor municipalities. Will present administrative mechanism be adequate to secure the implementation of plans for the expansion of Greater Stockholm?

Land

The method used by the city of Stockholm and some of its neighboring municipalities to make certain an orderly urban process is to buy the land early, as has been described at the beginning of this chapter. This activity has been continued and Stockholm owns outside its border (January 1971) more than two hundred square miles of land, which is twice the present city area; on this land alone a million people could be housed. But of course a large part of new development will occur on land that is not owned publicly. The development of such land will be regulated by approved plans and contracts between the landowners and the appropriate municipal board. These boards have capabilities to influence where and how, but hardly when new urban development should come. Similar contracts must be drawn, too, when the city of Stockholm builds on its land in other municipalities. Through an amendment to the Housing Act made in 1959, a municipality is given certain rights to develop land for housing in other communities, under condition that the two municipal authorities agree; Stockholm has made ten such contracts with four neighboring communities. In most cases, the land was already owned by the city; in some others, however, the land was sold to Stockholm by the other municipality.

Money

Dwellings make up half of the total capital costs for building a new neighborhood or a cluster of neighborhoods; the other half of capital expenditure consists of public infrastructure such as streets, utilities, parks, schools, shops, etc. The future rents paid by the tenants, in multifamily dwellings and in shops, cover the capital costs of the buildings themselves, the local streets and playgrounds. The charges for consuming water and electricity cover interest and amortization of the capital costs for these utilities. All the rest must be paid by local income taxes. The problem is that rents can be collected as soon as the tenants move in while the first income taxes—according to Swedish law—not until two years later. This means that a small community cannot start suddenly to develop land to meet the production program of the Greater Stockholm Council. The half of the total investment that cannot be covered by income from the dwellings represents much more money than the community is allowed to borrow under law.

Why not let private enterprise raise money and develop the land? Some municipalities have no objections to this at all. However, in the present era of housing, about 90 per cent of all dwellings built in Sweden have some sort of public economic support. And the burden of financing schools, day nurseries, main roads and sewage systems still has to be carried by the municipalities.

This financing is a very serious problem in several of the peripheral communities around Stockholm. The right to levy income tax is used primarily to raise money for education and social welfare. If a community, following the regional plan and according to the plan for production of dwellings, wants to increase its population threefold in ten years' time, it could only do so with special support—partly as "expansion loans"—from the Greater Stockholm Council, a key part of the evolving holistic planning mechanism.

The Greater Stockholm County Council

During the 1940s, twenty years after the city had abandoned the scheme of extending the city in all directions, it became obvious that an effective form of metropolitan government would be necessary. The city boundaries formed a very real obstacle as the capital city had somewhat different legislation than the surrounding small municipalities. The capital formed a "national province" of its own, while the rest of the metropolitan area formed another. Not until 1964 was a solution found; the two "national provinces" were merged; the differences in law were thus evened out. And the city accepted fusion with the county of Stockholm which so far has been formed only by the surrounding municipalities. By January 1, 1971, the Greater Stockholm County Council started functioning.

The new county will continue to be responsible for hospitals, public dentistry, some special homes for children and professional schools, etc. It has taken over regional planning, is the metropolitan traffic authority, and acts as housing authority (but only supplementary to the existing municipal authorities). It co-ordinates the building of water works and sewage disposal plants in order to develop a sound regional water supply, plans schools from the tenth to the twelfth grade and supervises the preservation of areas for open-air life.

Since 1967, twenty-eight municipalities in the central part of the region have had a common housing agency through which 30 per cent of the new flats, built with the aid of government loans in any of the municipalities, are let to those registered at the agency. It may be that this organization will be taken over by the Greater Stockholm County Council.

The formation of the Greater Stockholm County is, of course, an economic operation of large dimensions. It has the right to levy income tax, but only within "political limits." The number of employees has been raised from six thousand to thirty thousand. Half of them are now on city payrolls. The agreement was reached under condition that the total tax burden on the citizens inside and outside the city limits remain as is. However, it is uncertain for how long.

The Greater Stockholm Council has taken over some governmental responsibilities that for one hundred years have been closely linked to the life of the central city. Is this a political-psychological problem for all the citizens in common or only for those who have enjoyed political power?

A PLANNED CITY?

To what extent have efforts during three centuries resulted in a truly planned modern city? What balance is there between different private interests and the public interest as understood and expressed by the city authorities? And what about the citizens? Do they like to be planned for?

Of course, planning reflects the sociopolitical conditions of the society it is intended to serve; the Stockholm plans mirror a mixed economy society. The proportion between the public and private sectors varies widely among different industries. Public transportion is 98 per cent governmentally owned; taxis, however, are run by an "owner society" (strictly private enterprise). Of all dwellings built, almost 90 per cent have some sort of governmental economic support. Between 40 per cent and 50 per cent have been built by municipal corporations, even if some of them use private contractors. In the CBD, however, only three (!) buildings have been built by public enterprise, all the rest by private. Every day half a million people decide how they will journey—whether to use public or private transport and in what mix—a momentous private decision.

Even if the shell of the city is constructed by the joint action of public and private enterprise, a large and dominating part of city life is based on and led by private initiative. For the year 1963, some national figures are available illustrating the proportions between public and private. Over 90 per cent of the industrial labor force worked for private independent enterprise and only 4 per cent for consumers and producers co-operatives. The rest (6 per cent) worked for national or municipal industries. The co-ops transacted 10 per cent of wholesale and 14 per cent of retail business. Forty-three per cent of total investments, and 21 per cent of consumption were public. In Sweden, the private building industry, as well as the commercial interests centered in the Chamber of Commerce, have found a *modus vivendi* and co-existence possible with the various public bodies.

It may seem that planning in Stockholm—and in the rest of Sweden—is concentrated very much on the buildings and less on the people living in them. This is true. There is almost no legal mechanism that secures the connection among social planning and land use and other physical planning. But the municipal authorities are free to construct such connections if they want to. In Stockholm there is a growing interest in reconstructing the "gray areas" and helping the people there to attain a more decent life. Both the buildings and the people are registered in computers in such a way that a full picture can be presented, enabling the Planning Commission, the Housing Authority and the Social Care Commission to act jointly.

During the past few years the relation between the planners and the planned for has changed markedly. Earlier the debate was kept mainly within City Hall, between the planners and those elected by the people, to decide about goals and about plans. Big plans, of course, raised public debates, and the newspapers aired contributions editorially and from others. Lately groups of citizens have organized themselves with the main purpose of influencing public decision making in planning. They demand to be consulted on all new projects and loudly they question the goals of the already established plans. Two groups, Alternative City and Guardians of Environment, cover the entire city, but most groups are interested in their neighborhood only. More than fifty "village community" organizations have sprung up all over the city and act as pressure groups using all possible methods. They have demanded and got large public hearings, some of which have been very stormy. Some older and more dignified organizations have had to choose between being pushed aside or accepting these modern techniques of direct participatory democracy.

What do these people seem to want? Some are only rebels against the Establishment with little constructive criticism to offer. Argument runs along two lines: Save more of the existing buildings and banish the private cars from the city center. Even for the new parts of the suburban belt, the people demand that private cars be pushed out of the picture, while the bus-and-rail system be improved and—say many—made free of charge. They object loudly to being the "victims" of planning, but curse when playgrounds and day nurseries are not ready when they move into the newly built dwellings. How common are such opinions? Probably it is only a vociferous minority that expresses its discontent, sometimes very noisily, but also very cleverly; while all those who do not care or are positively satisfied never let the planners know; at least, this is a satisfying theory for the planners.

The new and the unknown have always irritated or frightened people, causing them to react in a chaotic fashion. The problem is to inform the citizens how better to use their centuries-old town; a house lives longer than most men and a street has a lifetime twice as long. And how very thoroughly do people change during their lifetime: their habits, needs, ideas, taboos, misconceptions, ambitions—all change! Man adapts himself to the city with less difficulty than the city can be replanned and rebuilt to suit him.

NOTES

[1] *General Plan för Stockholm, 1952,* with a summary of twenty-eight pages and subtitles in English, Stockholm, 1952.

[2] "Municipal Land Reserves in Sweden: Key to Planning Success" by Shirley S. Passow (mimeographed; Columbia University, May 1969).

[3] SFS ("Swedish Collected Publication of Acts") 329/1953.

[4] SFS 863/1967.

[5] These problems will be dealt with by the government and probably also the Parliament during the coming years.

[6] This legal mechanism ("prior admittance") is explained by W. G. Westman, "Zone Expropriation on Lower Norrmalm in Stockholm" in *Stockholm, City and Regional Planning* (Stockholm, 1964).

[7] Research by Lars Fröjd and Rolf Karlsson, Royal Institute of Technology, Stockholm, 1969.

[8] The proportion of passengers standing is worse in most other subways. In Paris 83 per cent, Moscow and London, 75 per cent, Toronto, 68 per cent. BART in San Francisco is exceptional with the *claim* that all may sit.

[9] *Tunnelbanaplan för Stor-Stockholm, Bihang* 85/1965.

[10] See *Stadskollegiets utlatande* 69/1965.

[11] SFS 138/1965.

[12] *Byggnadslagen* which has a national code added—*Byggnadsstadgan*—that was changed in 1959. Both are now being revised by a governmental committee, *"Bygglagutredningen."*

[13] There are only three more areas in Sweden that have live regional planning.

[14] Folke Kristensson: *Människor, företag och regioner,* Stockholm, 1967. Compare also: Roland Artle: *Studies in the Stockholm Economy,* Stockholm, 1959.

CHAPTER 3

Paris: Baroque Elegance and Agglomeration

Jean Bastié*

THE OLD CITY

The original site of Paris is the Île de la Cité in the Seine, and the slopes of the Ste. Geneviève hill on the left bank in the present area of Lutèce. During the Middle Ages the city developed on both banks of the Seine, but in a special fashion on each: on the Right Bank, the active and expanding Paris of the merchants and artisans; on the Left Bank, the quieter area of the abbeys and the university; while on the Île de la Cité lived the monarch and the bishop. The placing of the royal residence during the fourteenth century at the Louvre on the Right Bank was the point of departure for the most prestigious axis of all Paris—

* Professor of geography of the *Faculté des Lettres et Sciences Humaines* of the University of Paris (Nanterre); since 1954, he has concentrated on the Parisian agglomeration and its problems. Author of *La croissance de la banlieue parisienne* (Growth of the Paris Suburbs), 1964; *Paris en l'an 2000* (Paris in the year 2000), 1965; *Paris, ville industrielle* (Paris, Industrial City) as well as numerous articles. He directed with Professor J. Beaujeu-Garnier the completion of *L'Atlas de Paris et de la Région Parisienne* (Atlas of Paris and the Paris Region), 1967. He has conducted a number of research projects for various urban services and planning departments in the Paris metropolitan regions.

Translation by David and Susan Kinsey.

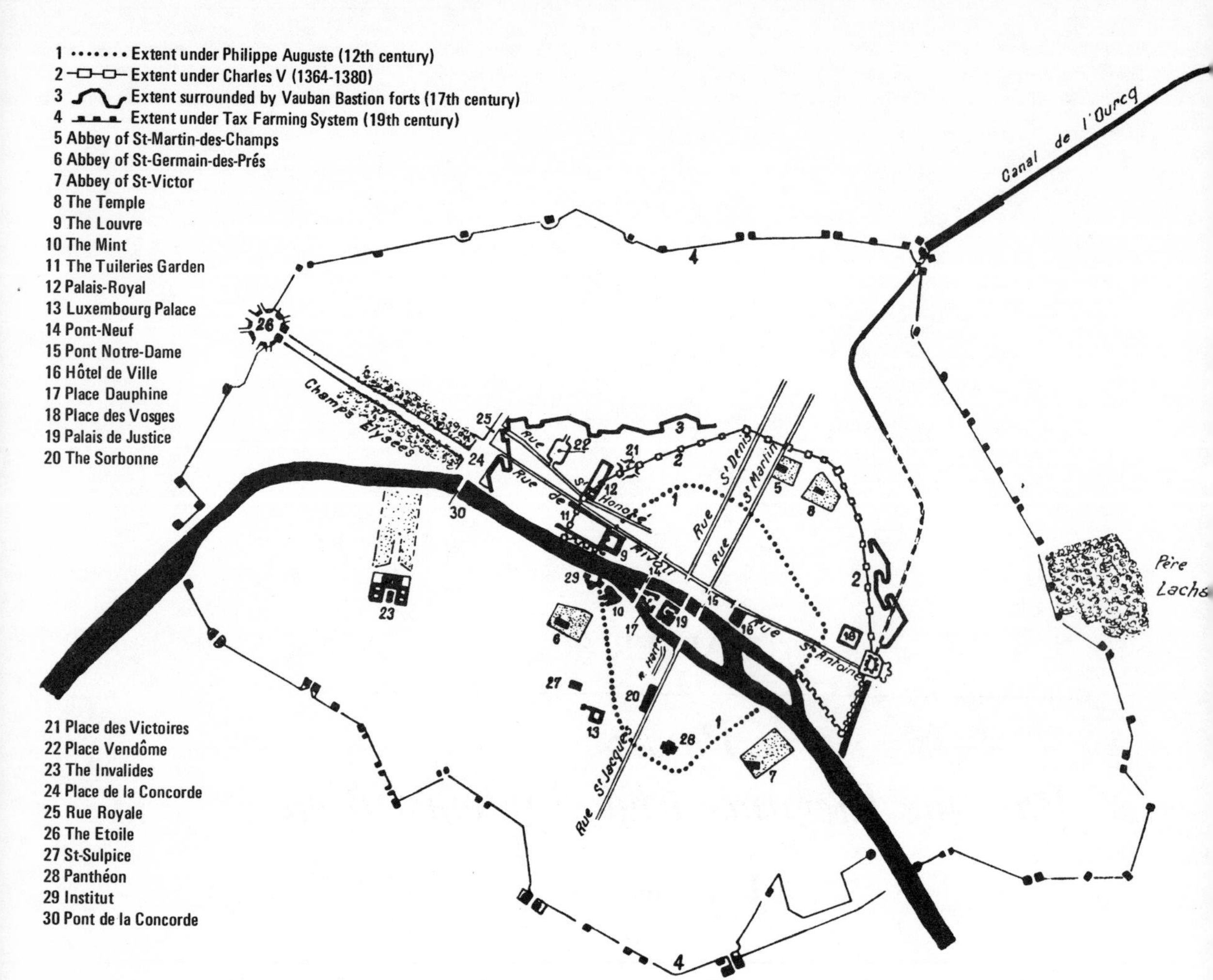

FIG. 1 Paris from the XII to the XIX century. *Jean Bastié, map*

that of the Louvre-Concorde-Étoile which ornaments the western part of the capital (Fig. 1). The absolute monarchy of the Bourbons left behind some magnificent additions: squares such as Place des Vosges, Place Vendôme, Place Louis XV, which became the Place de la Concorde; splendid perspectives such as the esplanade of the Invalides with the fine building of the same name, the Champ de Mars (present site of the Eiffel Tower) with the École Militaire (Fig. 2), and the promenade at Vincennes. But the ancient regime did not open up clear spaces on the periphery of the city. Finally Paris "within the walls" was surrounded by a general farming area, which when the actual farms had disappeared offered room for the interior boulevards. The first Empire of Napoleon (1804–14) did not last long enough to make any important additions, but did leave the Arc de Triomphe at the Étoile and the Arc de Carrousel, the columns at the Vendôme and Chatelet and the two fine Seine bridges: Austerlitz and Iéna.

At the beginning of the second half of the nineteenth century, the impressive system of boulevards built by Baron Haussmann modified the face of the capital. Although subjected to numerous and violent criticisms during construction and since, the boulevards remain nonetheless indispensable to the city and beneficial today. Haussmann was primarily interested in the central city and his conception

FIG. 2 The Champ de Mars and the École Militaire, looking south from the Eiffel Tower. The new UNESCO building constructed in 1955 in Y shape blends well with the traditional design of the École Militaire to the rear left. *Photograph by Jean Bastié:* Encyclopédie Visuelle, *Armand Colin-Véronèse, "Régions Françaises: Agglomération parisienne."*

of urbanism was only partial and concerned primarily with prestige. He destroyed not only the urban tissue remaining from the Middle Ages based on tiny cut-up plots—for example, portions of Rue St. Denis—but also the extended gardens of the suburbs, such as at Belleville. New apartments on geometric plots walled the new boulevards such as Sébastopol or Belleville. But the general urban "mess" was not touched; the land plotting remained incoherent, density remained very high, buildings very old, dwellings very uncomfortable. Under such conditions existed the less affluent and the poor, while the better off lived in the new apartment buildings lining the new boulevards.

The city increased in size, and the total area rose from about thirteen square miles to close to thirty-five square miles by the annexation of the surrounding communes, still largely rural, which fell between the circling city walls of 1784–91 and the circumferential fortifications of 1841–45. This circular enclosure urbanized rapidly in a completely anarchic fashion. The number of *arrondissements*† rose from twelve to twenty and within these limits, the population increased to 1,650,000 by 1870.

The plan adopted was generally radial concentric, the classic result for a city which has had a series of encircling walls. There are two axes at right angles to each other: from the north to the south—Boulevard Sébastopol prolonged by

† Local government sectors inside the city (similar to wards). They are generally referred to by their numerical designation, e.g., XVII, X, etc. (Translators' note.)

the Boulevard St.-Michel; from east to west Rue de Rivoli continued by the Champs Élysées. The concentric circles are made up by the inner *grands boulevards,* the exterior boulevards and the military boulevards. The left bank also has two supplementary military roadways. Finally on this general canvas there are the *places,* or circles (from which extend the radials), such as the Étoile, Place de la République, Bastille, la Nation, d'Italie, Denfert-Rochereau. The west of Paris contains most of the wide new streets.

During this period of horse-drawn traffic when in the wealthy *quartiers* (districts or neighborhoods) rolled elegant and varied carriages, these *étoiles* (stars) or circular *places* with radiating avenues were patterned on the *rond-point* (assembly circle) in the long wooded avenues of the hunting forests. Star-shaped forms were considered then the most elegant urban design. Everything was conceived in a grandiose fashion at the time: a 125-foot-wide boulevard with the dome of some imposing edifice at the end of the vista.

The cost of all this road building rose to almost double what had been anticipated, leading to a disbursement by the city itself of 500 million gold francs. The State Council, the court of condemnation and the juries of expropriation were most generous to the landholders. A considerable number of these suddenly made their fortune through being expropriated, and many others were able to hold part of their land not needed for road building or public works, thus benefiting with a considerable "unearned" increment. But the high cost to the city of expropriation and construction limited Haussmann to only a portion of his projected boulevard building.

The urban development of the Second Empire of Napoleon III (1852–70) did not consist solely of piercing the city with new traffic routes, but also the establishment of a system of public gas street lighting (over 10,000 lampposts); a water supply system brought to Paris from a source 110 miles from the capital and the construction of some 310 miles of water supply pipes within the city. Numerous parks and gardens were developed such as the Bois de Boulogne (west) and the Bois de Vincennes (east), the parks at Buttes-Chaumont, Monceau and Montsouris as well as numerous squares. Over 100,000 trees were planted in the parks and along the new boulevards. Various imposing monuments and public buildings were constructed including the Opéra, les Halles (the former great food market) and military barracks placed at strategic points such as the Place de la République, Boulevard Henri IV, and Place Monge. There were few urban functions into which Haussmann did not intervene. For example, the fifteen omnibus companies were fused into one, *la Companie Générale,* and in 1860, new lines were created and others extended to the city limits.

The transformation of Paris carried out during the Second Empire has had important consequences for the citizens of the capital. Some of the poorer classes were driven out from the center by the great new apartments, which were priced beyond their means, and emigrated to the recently annexed zones or even to the far suburbs, whereas the affluent concentrated by preference in the western *quartiers* of the city.

The work of Haussmann was not simply an accident in the history of Paris—a portion of the new great boulevards through the city were already in the plans of the *ancien régime* of the Bourbons and in the plans of the *artistes* of 1795. The erection of the 1845 circumferential fortifications made the extension of the urban area into the newly annexed zones inevitable. The work of Haussmann continued to influence the Third Republic (1871–1940). Haussmann's "right arm," engineer Alphand, director of works for the city, continued in office up to 1891, thus presiding over nearly forty years of the capital's transformation. A remarkable example of administrative continuity which explains much!

The works of Haussmann were chiefly financed by loans; by the end of the Third Empire approximately 60 per cent of their costs, or about 1,500,000,000 gold francs, were still to be paid off; annual payments on these continued until 1929. The debates and polemics around Haussmann's methods of financing did much harm to the investment in future urban infrastructure. In the forty-three years from 1871 to 1914, for a much more numerous population, with the need for the most necessary public works of great importance and cost and at higher prices, the city of Paris did not borrow more than Haussmann had in eighteen years. The half century, 1870 to 1920, did much less for the quality of Parisian urbanism than the preceding fifty years, 1820 to 1870, despite the enormous increase in population, which rose from two to four million during the latter period.

TODAY

With almost 8,500,000 inhabitants in 1970, the present Paris agglomeration has a population greater than that of Switzerland, Austria or even Sweden, and almost equal to that of Bulgaria, Greece, Portugal or Belgium. The second and third largest French metropolitan region, Lyon and Marseille, have only 10 per cent of this population. Parisians by themselves are four fifths of the total population of the fifty French agglomerations with more than 100,000 inhabitants. They constitute almost one fourth of the urban French population and one sixth of the entire country. One Frenchman out of six is a Parisian. Paris is the fourth largest metropolitan area in the world, after Tokyo and New York, which have twice as many people, and after the urban region of London, which has half again as many people.

A new administrative system for Paris was instituted by the law of July 10, 1964, and the decree of February 25, 1965, changing the number of *départements*‡ in the Paris region from three to eight. The Seine-et-Marne stayed the same; eighty *communes*** of the old Seine *département,* except for Paris, were added to about forty *communes* of the old Seine-et-Oise *département,* and then divided into three *départements* (Table A, Fig. 3a). The city of Paris became a *département* by itself.

The Paris region covers an area of 4,630 square miles, which is roughly 2 per cent of France. Outside of the Paris agglomeration proper, the region includes a population of 700,000, distributed in seventy-four towns or agglomerations with 2,000 to 60,000 inhabitants; the most important of these towns are Mantes and Melun. There are also 350,000 rural inhabitants who belong to 830 communes. The combined total for the region is 18.5 per cent of the French population.

‡ An administrative district. Metropolitan (the European mainland) France is divided into 95 *départements,* administered by nationally appointed civil servants known as *préfets,* and by locally elected assemblies known as *conseils généraux.* (Translators' note.)

** A district of local government, similar to a township or municipality, with an elected mayor and local council (*le conseil municipal*). (Translators' note.)

TABLE A

THE EIGHT NEW *DÉPARTEMENTS* IN THE PARIS REGION[1]

County Seat	*Department Number*	*Department*	*Area in Square Miles*	*Population in 1962*	*Population in 1968*	*Population Estimates (made in 1965) 1975*	*1985*	*Number of Communes*
	75	Paris	40.5	2,790,000	2,590,000	2,600,000	2,500,000	1
Nanterre	92	Hauts-de-Seine	67.5	1,382,000	1,462,000	1,704,000	1,761,000	36
Bobigny	93	Seine-St.-Denis	90.6	1,084,000	1,252,000	1,347,000	1,462,000	40
Créteil	94	Val-de-Marne	94.5	975,000	1,121,000	1,399,000	1,560,000	47
Versailles	78	Yvelines	825	687,000	853,000	945,000	1,355,000	262
Evry	91	Essonne	695	479,000	674,000	1,080,000	1,422,000	198
Pontoise	95	Val-d'Oise	484	548,000	693,000	869,000	1,110,000	187
Melun	77	Seine-et-Marne	2,280	524,000	604,000	656,000	830,000	532
			4,577	8,469,000	9,249,000	10,600,000	12,000,000	1,303

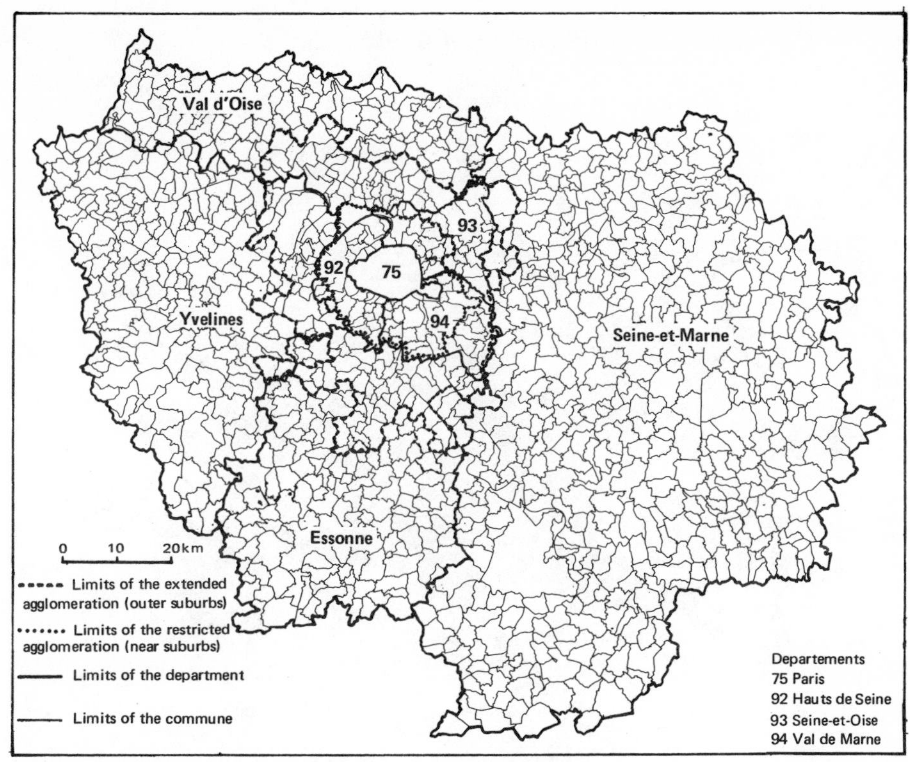

FIG. 3A The limits of the Paris region. *Jean Bastié, map*

The Paris urbanized area has been continuously expanding geographically (Fig. 3b). Although in 1850 it included scarcely that part of Paris in the first eleven *arrondissements* or 13.5 square miles, in a little more than a century (1850–1970), its area has grown to 695 square miles, and its population has gone from a little more than 2 million inhabitants to 8½ million. However, while the population of the city of Paris increased 65 per cent from 1.7 million to 2.6 million inhabitants, the population of the suburbs has multiplied by 14 per cent: from 400,000 it has increased to 5.6 million. For the entire agglomeration, the successive million population levels were reached in approximately the following years: the first in 1835, the second in 1860, the third in 1886, the fourth in 1900, the fifth in 1920, the sixth in 1936, the seventh in 1954 and the eighth in 1965. Between the 1962 and 1968 censuses, the average annual growth has been 100,000, or 1.3 per cent per year. Three fifths of this growth is due to a natural growth surplus; the remaining two fifths is the result of a positive migration balance.

Land use varies greatly. The average density of the region, including the 695 square miles of undeveloped open spaces—rural areas, forests, parks and airports—is 11,750 people per square mile. But the density of the developed and essentially residential area can also vary greatly: from 250,000 people per square mile in old *arrondissements* with dilapidated housing in the center of Paris to only 7,500 per square mile in the suburbs with beautiful middle-class homes such as Le Vésinet. In areas with single-family homes, the average density is 9,650 per mile; in the newer mass apartment complexes, the density ranges from 50,000 per square mile to 86,500 per square mile. On the fringes of this extended agglom-

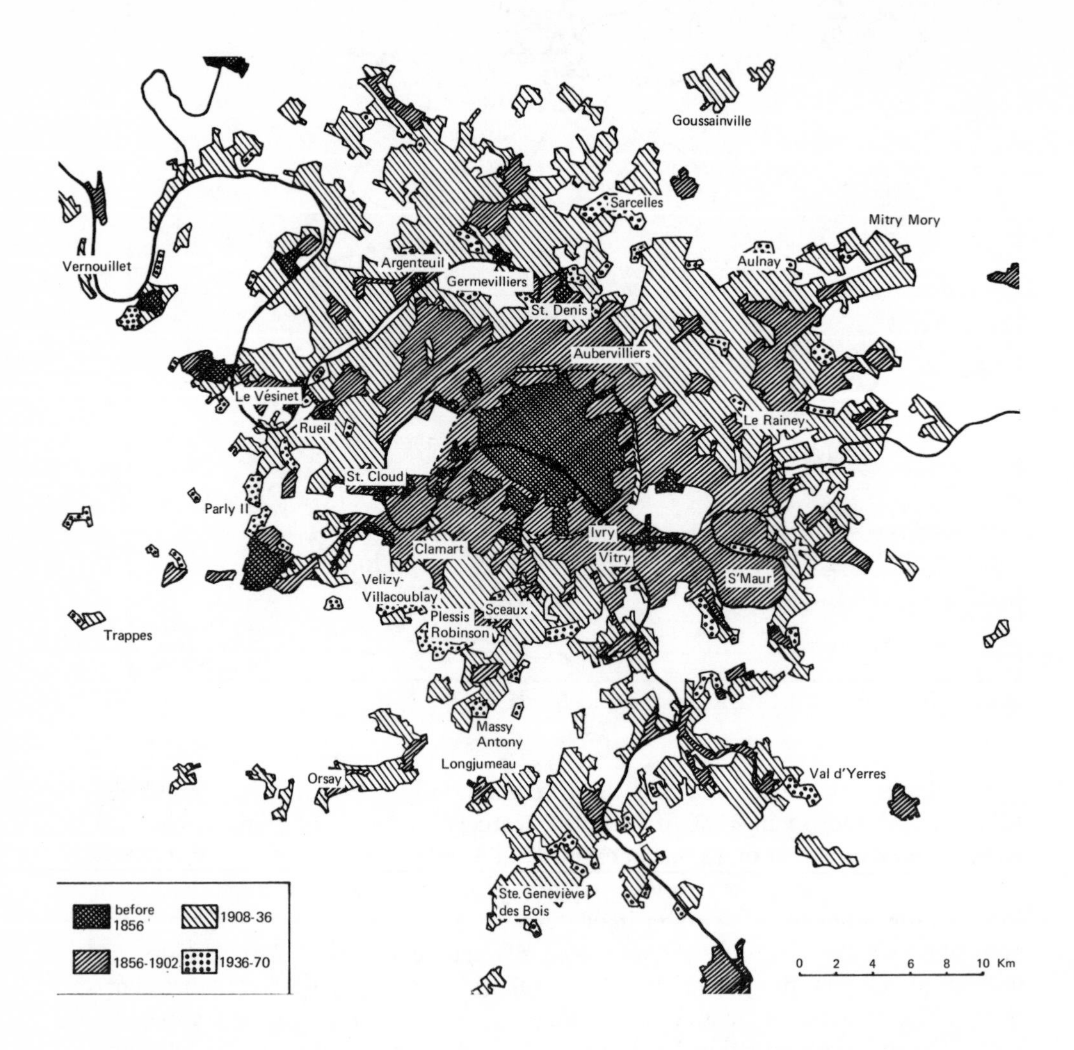

FIG. 3B Stages in the growth of the Paris agglomeration. *Jean Bastié, map*

eration, in *communes* where most of the land is still farmed, the average density is barely 1,250 people per square mile.

Table B shows how industry and commerce use relatively little land, as does housing; however, roads and public services demand a great deal of land. As for large open spaces, farm lands, and undeveloped land, they occupy one third of the land. This extreme diversity in land use and in densities explains why the word "Paris" suggests at least three images:

(1) *Beautiful Paris,* the best known or often the only one known by foreign or provincial visitors. This is historic and monumental Paris, the sacred quadrilateral spread along both sides of the Seine, from Notre Dame to the Étoile and from Montmartre to Montparnasse for 7.7 square miles. This part of Paris equals less than 2 per cent of the total area of the agglomeration, but its density testifies to the vast amount of past and present activities (Fig. 4)! Here are the monuments,

TABLE B

LAND USE IN THE PARIS AGGLOMERATION[2]

	Limited Agglomeration (1962 definition) 187,000 acres 5.7 million inhabitants Density: 2,930/square mile		*Extended Agglomeration (1962 definition)* 362,000 acres 8.0 million inhabitants Density: 2,125/square mile	
	Acres	% of total acres	Acres	% of total acres
Green open space	30,200	16%	61,200	17%
Other undeveloped open space (farms)	32,000	17	110,500	30.5
Industry	16,510	9	22,500	6.2
Housing with commerce and industry	54,400	29	154,000	40
Roads and major public services‡‡	54,250	29	23,200	6.2

‡‡ Plus major public facilities.

FIG. 4 Beautiful Paris: View to the north from Notre Dame toward Montmartre. *Photograph by Jean Bastié:* Encyclopédie Visuelle, *Armand Colin-Véronèse, "Régions Françaises: Agglomération parisienne."*

museums, theatres, shops and offices without which there would be no need for dwellings; here are more than 600,000 inhabitants and over 1,000,000 jobs. It is this heart of 7.7 square miles that makes Paris one of the great metropolises of the world, but this heart would not beat without the flesh that surrounds it: the mass of 8.5 million Parisians who live and work on the 695 square miles of the extended agglomeration.

(2) *The City of Paris,* bounded by both the Marshals' boulevards, which followed the 1840 fortifications, and by today's peripheral boulevards. It extends over 34.8 square miles or 40.5 square miles if the forests of Boulogne and Vincennes are included. Each night this city shelters 2.6 million inhabitants, but each day it contains more than 3.6 million people. The so-called peripheral *arrondissements* of the city of Paris, those numbered XI to XX, are even less well known to those who do not live there, but they still contain many craft and industrial activities.

(3) *Greater Paris,* or the Paris agglomeration, is the functional or metropolitan area in the largest sense and adds to the city everything that constitutes the near and far suburbs: 280 communes, 655 square miles and 6 million suburbanites. The image and the boundaries become very fuzzy because the administrative jurisdictions (*communes, cantons, arrondissements* and *départements*) do not correspond to any physical reality. Furthermore, these jurisdictions continue to grow because of the continuing spatial growth of the agglomeration.

Statisticians and geographers have differentiated two distinct areas in the suburbs by applying the essential criteria of population density and daily movements to 1968 census data (see Fig. 3).

1. *Near suburbs* that form a first urban ring or internal zone with 3.1 million inhabitants who, along with those of the city of Paris, constitute the limited agglomeration of 5.7 million inhabitants. This area extends over 135 square miles and is 6.2 miles wide. These near suburbs embrace the largest part of the *départements* of this first ring: Hauts-de-Seine, Seine-St.-Denis, and Val-de-Marne, for a total of 70 *communes.*

2. *Outer suburbs* that form a second, more suburban ring, or external zone, with 208 communes, 2.7 million inhabitants, and which, when combined with the limited agglomeration, constitutes the extended agglomeration. This second ring extends over 530 square miles, is 21 miles wide, and spreads over the *départements* of the second ring: Val-d'Oise, Yvelines, Essonne and even the Seine-et-Marne.

The entire extended agglomeration, or urbanized region, includes 279 *communes,* 0.4 per cent of the national territory, and 8.5 million inhabitants. In 1970, it included twenty-nine *communes* with more than 50,000 inhabitants, or one third of the French towns of this size, eighty-two *communes* with 20,000 to 50,000 inhabitants, and seventy *communes* with 10,000 to 20,000, or a total of 181 towns near Paris with more than 10,000 inhabitants.

POSITION, SITE AND GROWTH

The Paris agglomeration is relatively near the *nord* (north) region of the country with its coal and industries, and these two regions are linked together by the Oise River and canals. Paris is near Normandy with its ports at Le Havre and Rouen where the navigable Seine empties into the English Channel. The Seine acts as Paris' lungs, connecting her with the sea and justifying the exaggerated claim that Paris is a seaport.

The capital is also not far from the confluences of the Marne-Seine, and the Oise-Seine, whose valleys open routes to the east and north. At its bend at Orléans, the Loire is also nearby.

Although not the geometric center of French territory, Paris, because of its transportation connections, belongs to northwest Europe, one of the most industrialized and urbanized regions in the world.

Depending upon one's definition, the Paris basin covers from 25 per cent to 35 per cent of France, and includes between 16 and 20 million inhabitants, or between 35 per cent and 40 per cent of the population.

The advantages of the original site are well known: There was an easy crossing of the Seine River because of the islands which were also helpful for defense purposes, and there were many hills on the edges of the major plains of the Île de France (Fig. 5). To the north there is a pass between the knoll at Montmartre and the knolls at Buttes-Chaumont; to the south there is the Bièvre Valley between Ste.-Geneviève's hill and Butte-aux-Cailles. This axis with the Seine Valley constituted a crossing at Paris which was deforested a long time ago. The abundance and variety of construction materials due to the multiplicity of Tertiary layers also facilitated the development of the agglomeration.

FIG. 5 Geographical site of the Paris agglomeration. *Jean Bastié, map*

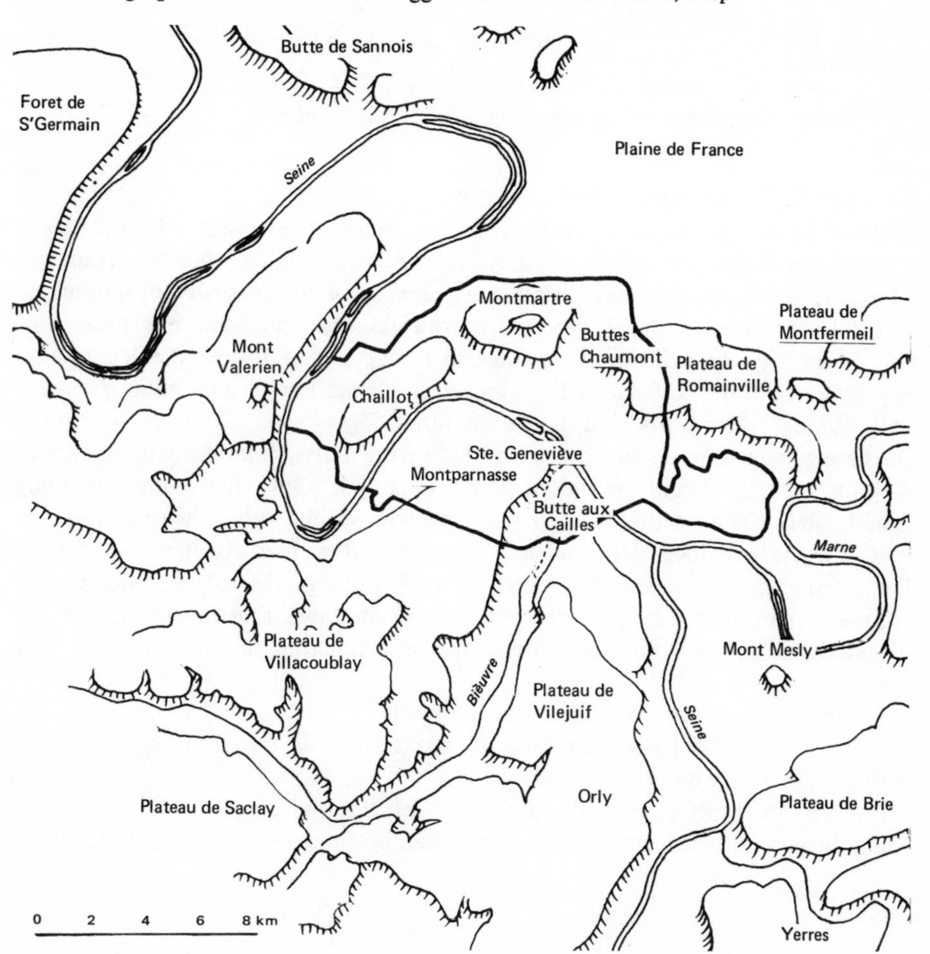

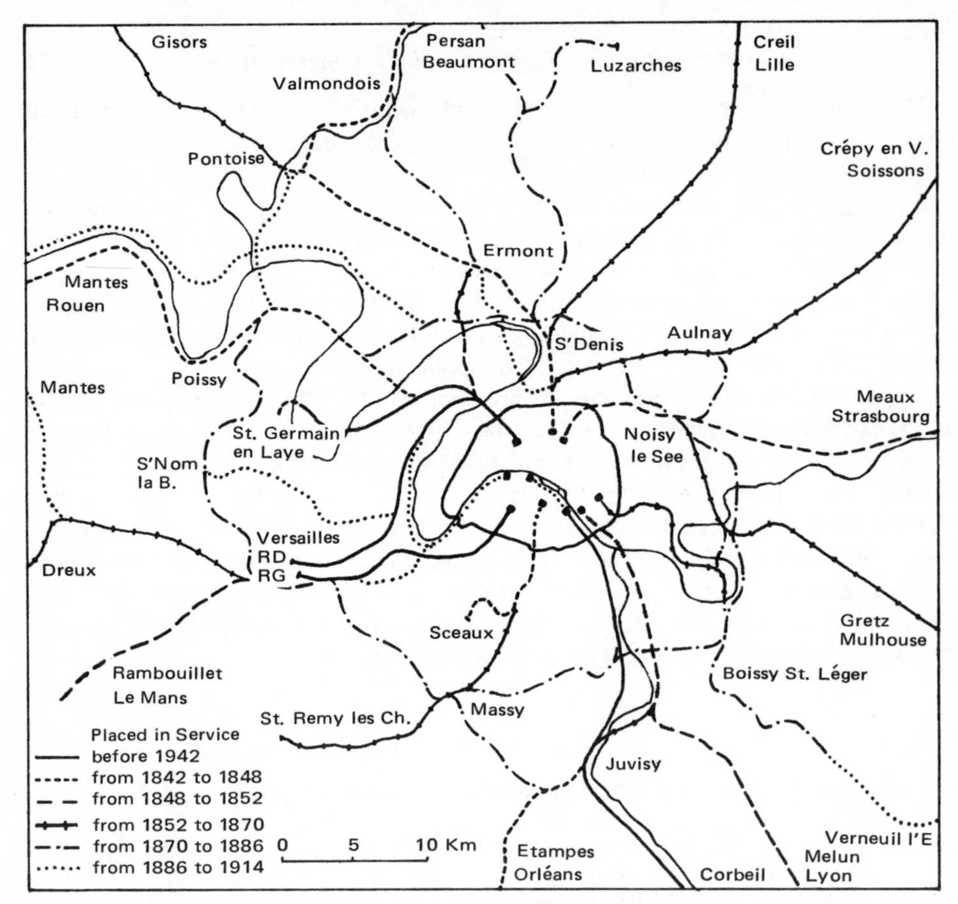

FIG. 6 Railway construction in the Paris region. *Jean Bastié, map*

Since the beginnings of the Industrial Revolution in the nineteenth century, the agglomeration has extended downstream in the convex lobes created by the meanderings of the Seine for two reasons: because these plains offered advantages for industry and for urban expansion, and because of the intensity of commerce with the lower Seine and the Nord. Nevertheless, the extension has been concentric, (see Fig. 3) principally in fingerlike shapes that follow the location of transportation arteries, especially the suburban railroad lines which allow a variety of bulk shipments, transfers, and daily commuting.

Of the eighteen railroad lines which radiate from Paris, four were in service in 1842, nine in 1852, and twelve in 1870 (Fig. 6). Only five were originally designed solely to serve the suburbs. The purpose of the others was to link the capital and the provinces. It was only later that they had significant suburban traffic and that many local stations were built. A study of the stages and forms of the spatial expansion in the past century and a half shows that the expansion has been essentially carried out characteristically as a function of transportation (see Fig. 7):

(1) linear along highways prior to the railroads,

(2) clusters around local railroad stations as soon as the suburban rail lines permitted daily commuting,

(3) diffuse in empty areas with only motor vehicles and buses.

The influence of these means of transportation, however, was far from immediate.

For example, in the case of the railroads, trains had to become more rapid and more frequent, the stations more numerous, and the cost of daily trips more reasonable. All this required between one half and three quarters of a century.

Since World War II, the spatial expansion of the agglomeration has shown three stages. During the first stage, until 1954, individual homes were built on vacant lots left in subdivisions from between the two World Wars, often far from Paris. During the second stage, mass apartment complexes (*les grandes ensembles*) filled the available remaining, sufficiently large sites in the interior of the agglomeration. They were often situated on plateaus, far from train stations, but relatively close to the center of Paris by car. Finally today since such sites are very rare, construction takes place more and more on the fringes of the extended agglomeration at distances farther and farther from Paris (see Fig. 3).

The growth in urbanized land is not only due to the needs of housing and industry. Spatial urban expansion proceeds in many ways, by everything that a

FIG. 7 Principal quarternary activities in Paris (defined as tertiary in French). *Jean Bastié, map*

Principal Concentrations

Public and quasi-public services

Headquarters for Social Insurance Agencies

Other Social Service Headquarters

University

Headquarters for Social Service Banks

FIG. 8 The Louvre and the Tuileries Garden. *Photograph by Jean Bastié:* Encyclopédie Visuelle, *Armand Colin-Véronèse, "Régions Françaises: Agglomération parisienne."*

city downgrades, rejects or has need of. Activities and services multiply and diversify spontaneously: quarries and sandpits; forts with free fire zones without buildings; freight stations and switching yards; expressways; airports with longer and longer runways (Orly's area is six square miles while the new Paris-Nord is eleven square miles); drinking water and waste treatment plants; gas and steam-generating plants; garbage disposal; junkyards; coal, oil and wood storage; workhouses and homes for the retired; asylums; hospitals; cemeteries; stadia and playing fields; race tracks; zones and service corridors for high tension electricity and radio installations; and, finally, the suburban truck farms (important because of their proximity to the city, but whose importance will also diminish). Other than providing the space necessary for housing, commerce, industry and the transportation network, one of the major problems of urban planning today is how to reserve enough space in the most functional location for each of the above (and other) necessary land uses.

THE MAJOR GEOGRAPHIC SECTORS

Each sector of the agglomeration, both in Paris and in the suburbs, owes its uniqueness to several factors: physical relief, land use, the nature and importance of its activities, traffic network, age, density and characteristics of construction, to which are tied population density and social structure. Often the boundary between sectors with different aspects and functions is not clear, but a transition zone can be identified. This urban sociological mosaic differs obviously from the administrative mosaic.

The central core (I to VI *arrondissements*) includes almost all the historic buildings and monuments. It is arranged around the great traditional north-south and east-west cross: Boulevards de Sébastopol and St.-Michel parallel the old north-south axis of Rue St.-Martin and Rue St.-Jacques. On the Right Bank, the Rue de Rivoli parallels the embankments, and the Rue St.-Antoine makes the east-west connection with the Bastille and the Place de la Concorde. On the Left Bank, the Boulevard St.-Germain serves the same role. Numerous narrow streets lined with old buildings still exist, such as in les Halles (until recently) and Marais areas on the right bank, in spite of many clearings. Even in the neighborhoods that have remained working class, ribbons of middle-class housing follow the new streets. Their densities reach 480 people per acre.

The two banks of the Seine have clashed since the Middle Ages. As noted above, the Right Bank had crafts and commerce, while the Left Bank was occupied by the university and religious edifices. One finds remnants of this conflict even in today's organization of the center of Paris and the location of various activities. Commercial activities are infinitely more numerous in the 138 acres of the first four *arrondissements* on the Right Bank than in the 118 acres of the V and VI on the Left Bank. Moreover, the last royal residences, the Louvre and the Tuileries (Fig. 8), both located along the Seine, have played essential roles in determining the urban structure of Paris since the seventeenth century. In the long run, they have contributed to a better arrangement of the east-west axis in relation to the north-south axis, even though parts of the palaces had to be torn down.

The entire center city and western sections were rearranged, beginning in the middle of the nineteenth century. The Préfect Haussmann, who was largely responsible, had an incontestably large vision and cleared paths for traffic up to 125 feet in width as on the Champs Élysées.

The west is planned around a radial system of twelve handsome avenues that begin at the Étoile. It includes most of the bourgeois apartments and the mansions with private parks, spacious rooms and apartments, that are increasingly occupied by the offices of ministries, embassies and corporation headquarters. There is a growing tendency to demolish these old apartments and to replace them with functional office buildings. The old villages in the center of Paris are the most popular residential areas and the busiest commercial sectors; for example, Passy. The buildings on the edges of the Bois de Boulogne are new and the most recent construction has been in the XVI *arrondissement* where the upper class is concentrated. There the density is, in places, as low as forty people per acre.

The east, north and south periphery consists largely of old, uncomfortable apartment buildings with small dwelling units; this area still includes many warehouses and industries and a very large number of dilapidated blocks. The density in some neighborhoods reaches 340 people per acre; the population is mixed: workers, clerks and the lower middle class. The first ring of the entirely urbanized suburban *communes* is not very different from the area inside the exterior boulevards and the peripheral roads (the zone of the 1840 fortifications).

The old industrial suburbs in this first ring become especially important to the north along the downstream bends in the Seine up to Argenteuil, and upstream to Ivry and Vitry. Cumbersome and disagreeable industries have grouped together there, as in the St. Denis plain where there are gas factories and heavy chemical plants. The old village centers have become blighted areas and the workers live in numerous clusters of public housing (H.L.M.).‡‡

The residential suburbs pushed truck farming and fruit growing farther away from the center. These suburbs are predominantly middle class on the better sites with a very explicit hierarchy: The very rich live on the St. Cloud hill, at Vésinet and close by the park at Sceaux; the middle class live in Clamart, St. Maur, Le Raincy; and the masses live the farthest away. Subdivisions of little houses with small gardens stretch away from train stations, joining arteries along the axes up to eighteen miles from the center. These subdivisions have very poor transportation connections and are underdeveloped in terms of public services; they are increasingly dominated and crushed, at distances farther and farther from Paris, by groups of multiple-family housing known as "mass apartment complexes" (*les grands ensembles*). Today 300 of these complexes have more than 500 dwelling units, and twelve have more than 3,000. The most important are: Sarcelles (12,000 dwellings), Massy-Antony (8,500 dwellings), and in the luxury category, Parly 2, near Versailles (more than 5,000 dwellings). More are being constructed farther and farther from Paris.

HOUSING

According to the 1968 census, the Paris region contained 1.1 million buildings with 3.6 million dwelling units, of which 820,000 buildings and 3.2 million dwellings were in the agglomeration. Paris proper contained 80,000 buildings and 1.2 million dwellings, including 100,000 furnished hotel rooms. About 4 per cent of the region's dwellings, or 140,000, are second (or summer) homes, and one third are occupied by their owners. Joint ownership* has increased in the metropolitan area since the end of World II; today 25 per cent of Paris' dwellings are owned according to this formula.

This housing is old, especially in Paris and even more so in its center, as Table C demonstrates.

TABLE C

PERCENTAGE OF DWELLINGS
ACCORDING TO DATE OF CONSTRUCTION[3]
(1968 Census)

	Agglomeration	*Paris*	*Center of Paris*
Before 1915	42%	70%	90%
From 1915 to 1948	27.5%	20%	9%
Since 1948	30%	10%	1%

Since 1959, an average of 80,000 to 100,000 dwellings have been constructed in the metropolitan area annually for a total of 1.2 million, or one third of the present total supply.

Approximately 1,500 dwellings have been destroyed each year in Paris since 1960, while 10,000 have been constructed. Paris is becoming more dense; each

‡‡ H.L.M.—*habitation à loyer modéré* or moderate rental housing. (Translators' note.)

* *à copropriété*—a French system, similar to the American condominium, in which the residents of a building own their particular apartment and a share of the common areas of the building. (Translators' note.)

time that one square yard of floor space is demolished, 2.5 square yards are constructed, and in the last fifteen years the gain has certainly been more than 108 million square feet of floor space, including 21.4 million square feet of office space, principally in the business areas, but also at Maine-Montparnasse and along the Seine. The total floor area of the dwellings built is nine times greater than that of the buildings demolished. The ratio for offices and shops is 3 to 1; and the ratio for industry and warehouses is 1 to 4. One finds an extension of built-up land and a rise in height. Often buildings with eight to twelve floors replace those with from one to six floors.

As for urban renewal, in 1960, seventeen areas in Paris were designated as blighted areas; they cover 645 acres and now contain 180,000 people. Today, it is estimated that the renewal program should, in the long run, be extended to at least 3,750 acres. But the process is very slow. In Paris only 15,000 dwellings have been demolished by redevelopment and roughly the same number constructed. In the entire agglomeration, more than three fourths of a minimum program established in 1955, calling for the demolition of 60,000 dwellings and the construction of 100,000, remains to be achieved.

The public authorities have reduced the density of the east and southeast of Paris by renewal operations that produce financial deficits, while private enterprise has increased the density of the west and southwest by diffuse, spontaneous and largely profitable operations. The public authority responsible for half of the demolitions controls only a slight amount of the construction.

THE PEOPLE OF PARIS

Sixty per cent of all Parisians were not born in the agglomeration. The attraction of Paris to people in the provinces is a direct function of its proximity, but Paris' influence is great even in the most rural regions that are far from Paris such as Brittany and the Massif Central. Nevertheless, the Nord furnishes a numerous contingent, because of its large population. The foreign population is smaller than before World War II, because of an increase in naturalization, but it has commenced to mount again since 1962. The capital also contains a large, fluctuating population at certain times of the year, such as around the Auto Show and the Paris Fair.

There has been a complete change in the pattern of in-migration since 1962. The positive migration balance during the recent past of 80,000 per year has been cut in half to 40,000 per year, especially by the growth of out-migration toward the provinces. But the number of migrants to Paris has kept the same absolute value, and exchanges with countries abroad have increased greatly in both directions.

The age composition of the Paris population, in comparison to the total French population, has a surplus of middle-aged adults, with a deficit of the young and the older. This can be explained by the attraction of the Paris labor market. Many people arrive between the ages of fifteen and thirty-four and leave at retirement age. Thus, the region can only maintain its age composition by continuing migrations in opposite directions, depending upon age. The composition by sex has a distinctly feminine predominance, which grows higher as the social level of a neighborhood rises. There are ten women for every ten men in Aubervilliers, but there are fifteen women to ten men in the chic XVI; the feminine population growth rate in the past century is the result primarily of the growth of office activities.

The birth rate below the French average is explained by the conditions of life in Paris: females work, much time consumed in commuting and inadequate housing. The Paris population is not particularly fertile, in spite of the large percentage of adults. The marriage rate is, on the contrary, quite high, but divorces are also numerous (a rate double the French average). The death rate is lower than the French average because of the age structure and the availability of medical facilities. Infant mortality rates are particularly low. The Paris population grows naturally less quickly than that of France in general, and even this natural growth is due to the effects of migration. Internal urban movements also characterize this population, consisting of numerous moves between homes, generally back toward the center. The housing crisis and its consequences drive the underprivileged from the central city; arrivals in the center from the exterior play a compensatory role.

Daily commuting trips regulate the life of the agglomeration. Each week day more than four million people, including two and a half million salaried employees, commute. By midday Paris becomes as populated as its suburbs, which contain many dormitory *communes*. The social structure of the agglomeration is very heterogeneous. It strongly reinforces class differences between social extremes. There is a clear conflict between the west of Paris and the rest of the city. The former is middle class; the latter contains the masses. This split is well reflected in the voting percentages for different parties. The suburbs tend to be increasingly better educated.

The working population includes about 4.3 million people, of whom 90 per cent are wage earners—a 2 per cent increase between 1962 and 1968. This involves a greater proportion of women (40 per cent) than in the rest of France (35 per cent). Between the ages of twenty-five and thirty-nine, women have relatively less of a tendency to work than do men of that age, but they have a greater tendency to work before twenty-five and after thirty-nine. Women largely take service jobs: 460,000 in comparison with 250,000 men employed. It is only in Paris that the number of jobs is greater than the working resident population, by more than 700,000. In all of the other *départements* of the region there are clearly more potential workers than jobs.

The total rate of labor force participation is clearly stronger in the Paris region (47.1 per cent) than in France as a whole (41.1 per cent). This is true for all age groups, except for those under eighteen years because of the high rate of participation in education in this age group.

The most numerous socioprofessional category is that of workers, 35.2 per cent (France, 37.7 per cent). High-level staff represents 8.7 per cent (France, 4.9 per cent). The agglomeration contains relatively fewer employers and workers than the rest of France, but more staff and office employees.

INDUSTRY

The Paris agglomeration is by far the most important and most complete French industrial region. It represents one fourth of France's industry not only in manpower, 1,650,000 workers, but also by the value of its production, by its power of innovation and by its influence. All of the major branches of industrial activity,

TABLE D

LABOR FORCE BY ECONOMIC ACTIVITY IN THE PARIS REGION[4]

Economic Activity	*Labor Force*	*% Change: 1962–68*
Fishing, forestry, agriculture	56,500	— 16%
Mining	6,500	— 2%
Construction and public works	394,200	+ 25%
Steel	656,000	— 10%
Mechanical repairs	41,940	+ 8%
Glass, chemicals, oil	174,480	— 5%
Other industries	463,340	— 5%
Transportation	247,520	+ 10%
Commerce	514,660	
Banking and insurance	199,760	+ 9%
Other commerce	189,360	
Services	704,160	+ 18%
Water, gas, electricity	58,120	+ 25%
Communications	110,320	+ 24%
Administration	457,760	+ 17%
Total	4,274,620	+ 7%
Unemployed	124,000	

TABLE E

LABOR FORCE BY OCCUPATIONAL CATEGORY IN THE PARIS REGION[5]

Occupational Category	*Labor Force*	*% Change: 1962–68*
Farmers	23,940	— 17%
Salaried laborers	26,980	— 19%
Employers	340,780	— 6%
High-level staff	381,920	+ 27%
Medium-level staff	630,500	+ 26%
Office employees	980,860	+ 16%
Industrial workers	1,555,720	+ 2%
Service workers	369,100	+ 6%
Others	107,920	— 4%
Total	4,417,720	+ 8.9%

with the exception of mining, are represented, from steel mills to textiles.

It is a model of the old urban and metropolitan industrial region that still retains numerous advantages: (1) heavy infrastructure and installations already amortized, (2) inexpensive energy sources, (3) numerous raw materials available due to the concentration of transportation facilities and the strong demand for these materials, (4) coexistence with a rich hinterland of activities, (5) the supportive role of subcontractors, (6) transportation time reduced to a minimum because of the proximity of varied manufacturers, (7) all kinds of qualified manpower, of both sexes, trained in the old work habits, (8) flexibility of the labor market, (9) a very important consumer market with great purchasing power and (10) traditions of scientific and technical research and invention: One result is the presence next to a colossus, such as the Rénault factory at Billancourt with 35,000 workers, of innumerable dynamic and small businesses, that are often at the frontiers of the stage of the art in their industry. In brief, the agglomeration is a crucible, made of many complex relationships, that brings industries together with themselves and with other activities.

The industries of the Paris region represent important but unequal parts of French industry as measured by comparing the number of Parisian wage earners with the number of the other French wage earners, according to the *Institut National de la Statistique et des Études Économiques* (INSEE) seven major industry classification scheme. In all, 28 per cent of French industrial manpower works in the Paris region.

TABLE F

IMPORTANCE OF MANPOWER IN MAJOR INDUSTRIES IN PARIS REGION IN COMPARISON WITH FRENCH INDUSTRY[6]

Percentage of French Manpower in Industry	*Industry*	*Wage Earners*	*Percentage of Paris Region Wage Earners*
55%	Reproduction	100,000	6%
37%	Chemicals	150,000	9%
35%	Steel	739,000	44.2%
28%	Miscellaneous	150,000	9%
22.5%	Construction and public works	290,000	17.5%
18%	Foods	70,000	4.2%
16%	Textiles and garments	165,000	10%
28%	Of French Industry	1,655,000	100%

The manpower (both directly and indirectly productive) employed by all these industries represents about 44 per cent of the working population of the agglomeration.

The sector known in France as the "tertiary sector of the secondary sector" ("nonproductive" industrial jobs) is better developed in the Paris region than elsewhere. These are the innumerable positions in corporation headquarters, offices, warehouses, sales and accounting, laboratories and research groups. The proportion of manpower that is directly involved in production is smaller in Paris, 60 per cent, than in the provinces where it is 70 per cent. Production manpower in Paris concentrates on the most advanced and delicate stages of manufacturing; the proportion of staff, technicians and skilled workers is for these reasons higher than in the provinces. This manpower, all other factors held constant (such as qualifications and seniority), often earns salaries far superior to those in the provinces. Thus, the total wages distributed is much higher than Table F seems to indicate, because of these relationships with the provinces and major industries.

The industrial development of the Paris agglomeration is definitely the result of the last two thirds of the nineteenth century.[7] The railroad, by lowering transportation costs and by the radial pattern of its lines (Paris is the center of the cobweb), reinforced the polarizing power of the capital, thus accentuating the already existing pattern of the road system. This industrialization, prepared by the development of the old luxury industries which were a function of the centuries-old capital, and by the chemical industry which was born partially from the utilization of abundant urban wastes, commenced to accelerate at the beginning of the nineteenth century. The growth of steel works was due largely to the extension of the rail network from Paris. The electrical, automobile and airplane industries began to play essential roles at the beginning of the twentieth century. The enemy occupation of France's industrial North and East in World War I made Paris the principal French arsenal and definitely assured its industrial predominance.

Since then this pre-eminence has not been challenged; neither by the economic crises between the world wars, especially in 1930, nor by World War II and the Occupation, nor the decentralization incentives given since 1954, nor by the decentralization policy of the *métropoles d'équilibre*[8] and regional planning (*aménagement du territoire*),[9] nor by the acceleration of technical progress and the take-off in the level of industrial production (1960s level being 3.5 times that of 1938).

Steel can be distinguished as the most important industry by its number of wage earners (730,000). Steel represents the largest proportion, 42.7 per cent, of the added value by the same industrial sector in France. The industrial pre-eminence and polarizing power of the Paris region depends upon the steel industry and the associated automobile industry.

Industrial location has evolved principally under two forms, which are both characterized by a slow but inescapable deindustrialization from the central part of the agglomeration (Paris and the older suburbs):

(1) Outward dispersal or shifting of the center of the agglomeration toward its periphery. This old and spontaneous slipping-away process has taken a new form with the creation of industrial zones in the suburbs.

(2) Decentralization or departure toward the provinces, a process whose results vary greatly, depending upon the sector involved, the size of the business and the stage in the manufacturing process.

Public authorities have intervened by both prohibitions and incentives to push businesses to move slightly outward from the center or to decentralize. Industry needs more space and more modern and functional plants. Businesses can find it more profitable to build elsewhere than in the Paris agglomeration, whether their activities were there before or not. Furthermore, progress in transportation methods have lowered costs; progress in communications, in spite of the French delay in producing and distributing telephones, will shorten distances. The inconvenience of distance and dispersion will decrease even though transportation will still be a cost; diverse functions or even different stages of manufacturing no longer have any need to be near to each other. This is equally true for suppliers and clients, as for competitors.

From 1962 to 1966, the region's level of industrial manpower remained constant, while it increased by 12 per cent for all of France. On the other hand, secondary employment increased by a huge percentage. However, the industrial complex of the Paris agglomeration still represents considerable power. It combines with its volume of activities a great inertial thrust and a formidable power for self-renewal.

The preponderant position of Paris in the French economy was pointed out for the first time in 1947 by J. F. Gravier in his work *Paris et le désert francais.*[10] Since then the policy of industrial decentralization inaugurated in the middle fifties, and later the regional planning schemes for balanced urbanization (*métropoles d'équilibre*), inaugurated about 1962, attempted a better distribution of all activities including economic and population over all France. Since 1964, the annual budget for capital expenditures by the national government following the successive national plans for modernization and public investment (VIth Plan: 1971–75) have given rise to the establishment of regional statistics for the twenty-one regions in the program. The portion received by the Paris region varies considerably according to the nature of the public expenditure; however, the Paris region received 25 per cent of the national total for economic investment in 1967.

Most industry in Paris is in mixed zones, along with housing and other activities. Exclusively industrial zones are rare, not very large, or pushed toward the periphery. The most important one is in the Villette area (XIX). The east differs from the west, which is much less industrialized, especially on the Right Bank. The southern peripheral *arrondissements* differ from those of the less industrialized north. These asymmetries in Paris obviously result from ancient factors as noted above.

In the course of the second half of the nineteenth century open and cheap sites were most numerous in the peripheral *arrondissements* of the south and east. These areas were urbanized the last, which facilitated the installation of factories and warehouses.

The Right Bank in Paris presents the greatest number and the largest variety of generally light industries. By excluding as many as possible of the headquarters and office employees, there are approximately 300,000 wage earners producing goods on the Right Bank while there are only 100,000 on the Left Bank. Beginning in the center, the most important industries are clothing, textiles, fancy leather goods, followed by newspapers and publishing. Specifically Parisian industries (jewelry, souvenirs, perfume) are centered there too. Moving toward the east (X and XI), clothing, newspapers and publishing fall back as specialized metalwork, electrical machines and electronics become more and more important.

Toward the north, printing, leather and foods industries are added to fine metalworking, while to the south specialized metalwork, notably automobile parts, retains practically exclusive control. Left Bank industry is on the whole less varied than on the Right Bank. The automobile and aircraft industries dominate with their associated precise metalworking shops.

The industrial location pattern of the near suburbs is the opposite to that of Paris. The west and especially the northwest is much more industrial than the center east; the northeast is more so than the south. However, this asymmetry disappears when one moves to the middle and outer suburbs. This occurs because of the industrialization of the southern sector. The industrial take-off of the southern middle suburbs is one of the most striking features of the recent past.

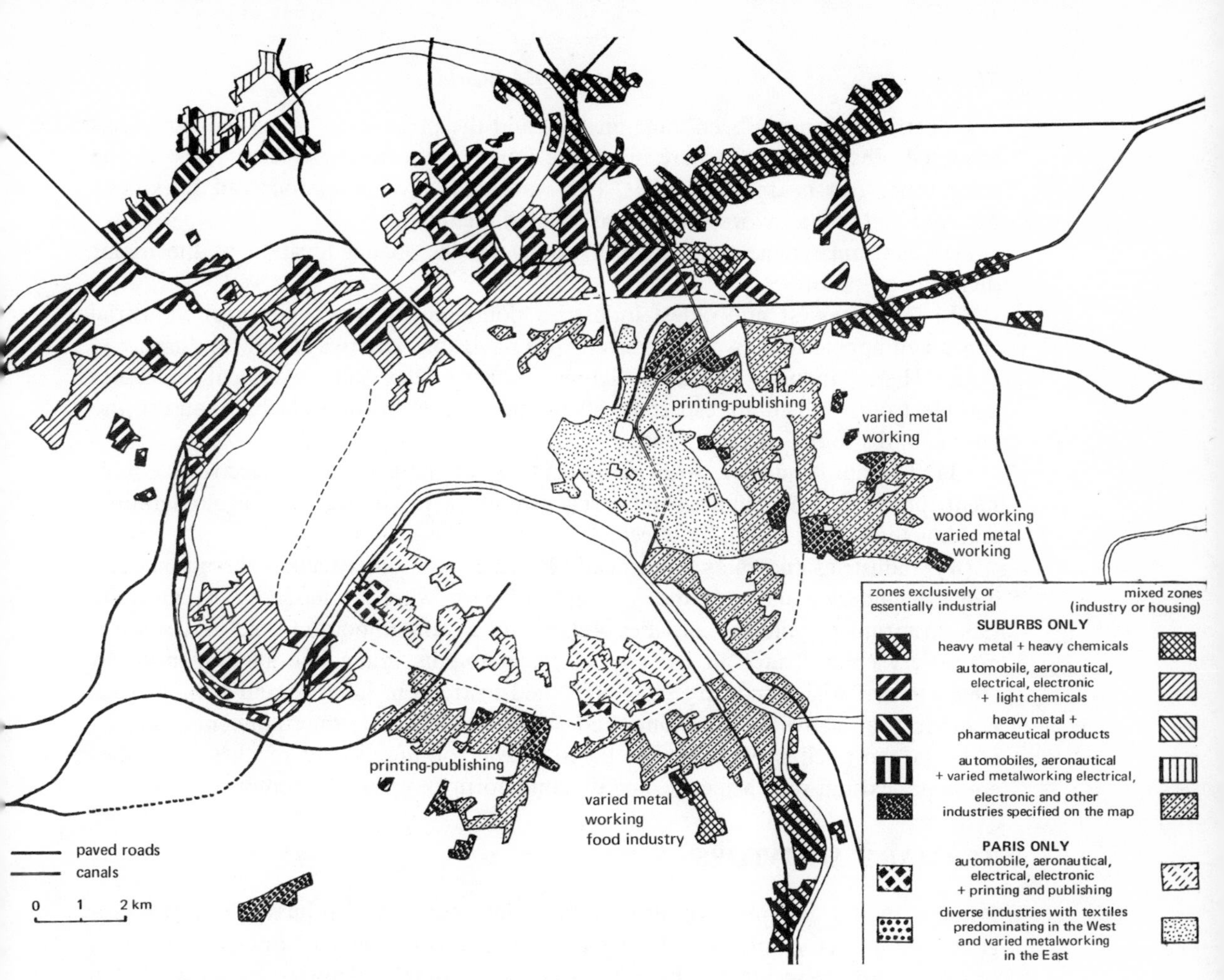

FIG. 9 Types of industrial zones in Paris and the inner suburbs. *Jean Bastié, map, based on the* Atlas of Paris and the Paris Region

To the north, chemicals, especially pharmaceuticals at Romainville and Noisy-le-Sec, and foods at Pantin have displaced the woodworking of the south. To the south, heavy steel mills and chemicals are strong only at Vitry between the Seine and the Orléans rail line. Everywhere there is some specialized metalwork and even more electrical machines and electronics. In the remainder of the suburbs, to the west and north, two major industries dominate: metals and chemicals. Here metals almost always mean the automobile and aircraft industries and their related subcontractors. There this metal industry becomes mixed with heavy chemicals.

Some important industrial zones are even farther from Paris. To the west there is the Poissy industrial zone, followed by all of the Seine valley to Mantes with Renault at Flins. To the northwest there is the Montmorency valley zone. To the south along the Seine one finds the industrial zones at various points.

Planned new industrial zones are more numerous to the north and east than to the west and south. More than seventy of these one hundred zones have a promoter-developer and comprise at least five thousand acres which are at best half developed or reserved for development. They are as well connected with waterways as with rail lines.

Industrialization has been most intense, and the presence of some industries has attracted others in areas where all of the important locational factors exist at the same time: (1) nearness to Paris, (2) waterways, (3) numerous rail lines, (4) flat land and (5) a favorable regional industrial climate.

One can make some general observations on the spatial location of the major divisions of industry:

(1) The heaviest and oldest industries dominate the most powerful industrial zones and appear to be well connected with navigable waterways and rail lines.

(2) Heavy industry excludes lighter industry, especially electrical machines and electronics which are especially strong to the east of the right bank and in the near suburbs to the east and south.

(3) The auto industry, with its associated suppliers (motors, electrical equipment, parts) is the dominant industrial activity in the entire Paris agglomeration, and has the largest multiplier effect.

(4) Industries known as "specifically Parisian"—if one excludes the automobile industry and one includes the garment industry with its subdivisions, and the rich spectrum of cultural activities—also play a very important role and still remain very concentrated in the city of Paris and its immediate surroundings. In effect, this "Parisian industry" is greatly tied to trade in luxuries and to numerous nonindustrial activities: teaching and research, tourists, entertainment and the arts—in short, all aspects of the Parisian way of life. Many of these activities could not exist in such a specific and dynamic form except in the context of Paris.

TERTIARY ACTIVITIES

Paris is by far the primary French financial center, the primary industrial region, the primary intellectual, scientific and artistic center, but all of these primacies are concentrated here more than in other countries because of the city's lengthy role as the political and administrative capital.

The national government employs roughly 350,000 people in the region (including the military); local government employs 150,000 and the semipublic sector employs 400,000 for a grand total of 900,000. The national level of government per se (ministries, central administrative offices, various national services) employs 220,000 people or 25 per cent of this total; 10 per cent are concerned with the specific needs of the people of the region. The ministries themselves do not employ more than 26,000 people; adding all the national services together brings the total to 60,000. The intellectual and scientific functions of the capital add another 70,000 jobs; the national tasks of the semipublic sector, another 80,000. Education (85,000) and the Post Office, including telecommunications (80,000) employ the most workers. Between 1956 and 1962 the number of national civil service workers increased by 70,000 and in the last ten years the total number of public and semipublic jobs increased by an average of 4.5 per cent a year.

The semipublic (industrial or commercial as well as administrative) sector, from the railroads (SNCF), metropolitan transportation (RATP) and gas and electricity (EDF) to the national coal company, Air France, the Paris airport, the HAVAS agency (news service) and others represent nearly 400,000 people, which means that public authorities control directly or indirectly slightly more than 20 per cent of employment in the metropolis.

Finally, more and more international institutions and organizations (more than 400)—intergovernmental and private—for Europe, for France or for the entire world are locating in Paris. Their number tends to multiply: they create jobs as well as attract foreigners and foreign currency. UNESCO alone has 1,700 Paris employees.

There is a large concentration of endowed institutions and cultural activities in Paris: 70 theatres, 80 museums, 170 large libraries, and the great majority of France's institutes and research centers. To this must be added the numerous meetings, congresses, colloquia and exhibitions. In spite of recent efforts to utilize the resources of the provinces and to encourage activities there, Paris retains a majority (60 per cent) of those employed in entertainment and a semiexclusivity in the field of the press and modern publishing: 81 per cent of the evening newspapers, 78 per cent of the weeklies, 73 per cent of the monthlies, and 260 out of the 300 most important French publishers. Today, great reputations in literature, in painting, in music, in all the arts and entertainment fields result from the lively interaction in this concentration rather than by yesterday's more imperial organized means. From this complex, Parisian influence extends inordinately to the nation and to the world.

Cultural and artistic, in addition to economic, decentralization has made some progress compared to the situation prior to the last war. Evidence for this is to be found especially in the theatre with the creation of repertory troupes in certain provinicial cities, for example: Lyon, St. Étienne, Toulouse and in the Parisian suburban towns (St. Denis, Nanterre, Villejuif), and finally with *Maisons de la Culture* (Houses of Culture) in Le Havre, Bourges and elsewhere. But the clustering at the center of Paris of so many diverse activities requiring a multiplicity of contacts and a continuous flow of information; the presence of numerous establishments of higher education and research; the presence of all the principal decision-making centers of the nation, private as well as public international organizations; the continuous passage of people from the entire world, of important personages, high officials, scholars, big businessmen, artists and tourists—all this in a setting so rich in evidence of the historic past—create still the most propitious climate for invention and innovation especially in the artistic, literary and scientific domains.

The University of Paris with the *grandes écoles* (Polytechnique, Normale Supérieure, Centrale, École Nationale d'Administration) give training to nearly 200,000 students, one third of them from the provinces and abroad. A revealing fact is that this percentage increases as one examines the advanced levels of the university. And to the extent that higher education becomes stratified and more specialized, at the very top levels this education can only be offered in France under such favorable conditions as those found in Paris. And these intellectual, scientific and artistic activities are basic to important industries that produce cultural goods: presses for newspapers, magazines and books, and facilities for producing records, photographs and movies.

The historical and artistic riches of the capital, as well as various new projects and other activities, attract numerous tourists from the provinces and abroad. Certain places are heavily visited: the Orly Airport (four million visits annually), the Eiffel Tower (two million), the Louvre (one million), Notre Dame, the Panthéon, the Invalides, the Arc de Triomphe, the Sainte-Chapelle, in addition to several chateaux around Paris: Versailles, Fontainebleau, Rambouillet, Compiègne and St. Germain. The multiplicity of colloquia and congresses also develops tourism; at the international level there are more than three hundred of them each year in Paris.

Tourists feed an important but under-equipped hotel industry (more than 130,000 people are employed in hotels, cafés and restaurants), even though the region's hotels handle half of foreign stays in France. Tourists are a very sizable fraction of the clientele of luxury shops (fashions) and entertainment spots. North Americans are more than half of the clientele of the de luxe hotels, followed by English and European businessmen, especially Germans, Belgians and Swiss. The Japanese tourist is moving in. Foreigners' trips to Paris have become increasingly middle class at the same time that the average length of stay has decreased. But Paris permanently contains tens of thousands of traveling foreigners at Christmas and Easter and in the summer months. From June to August some merchants exist only on sales to foreign visitors. In effect, by their ties with the influx of tourists, the luxury shops, travel agencies, great hotels, restaurants and cafés give several neighborhoods in the center of Paris from Notre Dame to the Étoile and from Montmartre to Montparnasse an incomparable appearance with their display cases and the women of fashion who give these quartiers their reputation.

However, it is the concentration of banking, insurance and commercial houses, headquarters of huge industrial or other businesses, their administrative, sales and research offices that perhaps most affirms the power of Paris. Of course, just as accentuated is the Paris preponderance in the service sector (55 per cent of the national manpower in services for businesses, 45 per cent of commercial and industrial suppliers and agents).

All of these tertiary activities are still very concentrated geographically in the central business district: the Bourse, Opéra, Madeleine, St. Lazare and Champs Élysées. However, these activites have for a long time been slipping to the west; north in the XVI (Chaillot), south in the XVII (Ternes), along the Avenue de Neuilly, toward the Défense sector and on to Rueil. But this does not stop them from either multiplying where they are, especially in the VIII where the construction of modern, functional buildings expands office space, or from creating strong new clusters in several places in Paris, such as the Maine-Montparnasse and Front de Seine projects or the planned Avenue d'Italie, de Bercy and Rapée projects.

Furthermore, the distribution of goods and services to the Paris population requires a vast commercial complex, very diversified because of the high average standard of living of the population, whose life style as well as spatial distribution changes quickly—which means that ever changing forms of distribution such as department stores, drug stores, self-service stores and suburban shopping centers must be established.

This quick portrait can only give a slight idea of the variety, movement and life which gives the central business sections of the capital this excessive overlapping of secondary and tertiary activities that are so varied in importance, appearance and clientele. These activities include many tasks of organization, decision making, public relations and change. In spite of all the inconveniences of excessive concentration, especially traffic, these functions can nowhere else take place in France with as much dynamism and efficiency as in the heart of Paris. This concentration, however, poses increasingly difficult spatial planning problems.

For example, les Halles, the storied and colorful wholesale produce market of Paris, constructed during the Second Empire of Napoleon III (1852 to 1870) by the architect Baltar on the site of the ancient Marché des Champeau ("Market of the Fields"), dating from the twelfth century, became simply too small for a metropolis comprising more than eight million inhabitants. The handling of such vast quantities of foodstuffs destroyed the quality of life in that entire district and generated traffic tie-ups throughout central Paris. Les Halles has been closed down, and since 1968 the wholesale market for most food products has been transferred to Rungis in the southern suburbs, just under three miles from Paris in modern functional installations covering nearly five hundred acres. This area is linked with the city by the southern express highway (Autoroute du Sud) and is also served by railway connections; it is near the Orly Airport.

PLANNING THE PARIS METROPOLIS

Between 1910 and 1911 the first commission, The Commission on the Extension of Paris, charged with considering the physical planning problems of the Paris agglomeration deliberated. They left an excellent report, but the 1914 war followed too soon for these ideas to have any real consequences. After hostilities ceased, the Parisian administration became practically helpless before a veritable explosion of defective and chaotic land plotting. This continued until the creation in 1928 of the *Comité supérieur d'aménagement et d'organisation générale de la région Parisienne* (CARP—Higher Committee for Planning and Administration of the Paris Region) which finally obtained legislative approval in 1932 for a law establishing a planning program. This was generally called the Plan Prost-Dausset, ready in 1934 and finally approved in 1939. Since the early 1950s the absence of a metropolitan administration charged with planning for the functional urbanized area became more and more apparent. The Regional Planning Service of the national government, created in 1945, was charged by a resolution of 1956 and a decree of 1958 with establishing a Paris Regional Plan and adequate administrative structure. After the work of the Maspetiol Commission, which sat between 1958 and 1961, the *Délégation générale au district de la région de Paris,* a special administrative agency for the Paris district, was created in August 1961.[11] PADOG,[12] the regional plan attempting to limit the growth of Paris and create a polycentric city with several growth nodes, was approved in 1961.

All this activity at first had only psychological effects which were developed by numerous publications and through numerous meetings creating four general attitudes in the minds of the general population:

(1) The unity of the Paris region and the necessity for a common organization to study its general planning problems and to prepare future solutions on a regional scale.

(2) The inescapable character of the demographic growth of the agglomeration; even if everything planned was accomplished and succeeded for the maximum growth of provincial cities and the so-called *métropoles d'équilibre.*

(3) The need to see the large picture and especially to foresee an important spatial extension of the city. Urban land requirements grow rapidly and increased density within existing boundaries becomes impossible; furthermore, one must supply numerous public facilities to catch up with past delays and to meet current needs.

(4) The need to break the radial-concentric pattern and to lower the overwhelming predominance of the center of Paris, to revive the development of secondary nodes, and to avoid the obligatory passage through the center of Paris of all internal metropolitan interconnections.

From 1962 to 1965, following the directives of the *Délégué Général au District* and the general principles enunciated in the *Livre Blanc* (White Paper),[13] several studies were undertaken and the *Schéma Directeur d'aménagement et d'urbanisme de la région de Paris* (Strategic Plan for the Paris Region) (Fig. 10), which responded to the previously explained four attitudes, was prepared replacing the 1961 PADOG plan. It is conceived in long-term perspectives of a quarter of a century toward the year 2000 and of important growth: first, demographic, with an increase of six million inhabitants (75 per cent of today's population), and, second, spatial, with about 386 square miles added. Commencing in 1967, in each year some of the postwar baby-boom generation become adults, including an average of 200,000 people more annually than for the generations born between 1931 and 1945. These new adults are now responsible for today's current births. Except for an unforeseen and rapid change in the behavior of those recently married, the annual number of births should rapidly increase over an extended period of time. Starting in about 1976, when most of those between the ages of twenty and thirty (the most fertile years) will be from those populous generations born after 1946, if all other factors remain constant, the birth rate should increase by one third and the natural annual net increase should increase from today's 300,000 to 550,000 or even more. This also counts on a decrease in the death rate which does not appear to be slowing down despite the increased percentage of older persons in the population.

Making estimates for 1980 and beyond is still very risky. One can only imagine numerous unknowns which will be influential in both directions, accelerating or decelerating the growth of the French population from now to the end of the century:

(1) The birth rate: the pattern of a rising standard of living; the discovery and distribution of convenient contraceptives and their use by the population; the self-image of young adults and their idea of the ideal family.

(2) The death rate: the discovery of cures and new methods to combat the most widespread fatal illnesses—cancer and cardiovascular diseases. It seems certain that the average life span, which in France is now sixty-seven for men and seventy-three and one-half for women, can be increased to eighty and beyond for both sexes.

(3) Migration: France has the least dense population of all Western European countries—a fact which is not explained by natural physical conditions. With Italy's average density, France would have 100 million inhabitants, or with the density of Great Britain or West Germany, France would have 130 million. The trends breaking down the national boundaries of Western Europe lead one to foresee an increasing uniformity of density.

Therefore, France seems likely to remain for some time a country of immigration, not only for Europeans, but also for peoples from underdeveloped countries who seek work.

One must note the tendency, since the end of World War II, to minimize, even in the short run, the French demographic growth by an underestimate of the birth and immigration rates and an overestimate of the death rate. The total population of 46.5 million reached in 1962, even without the returnees from North Africa, was not expected until 1971, according to the experts in 1950 and 1956.

For all of the above reasons and with the stated reservations, one might think that up to 1980 the net annual growth should progressively rise from 450,000 to 700,000 and then stabilize itself at this level, but until when? By this reasoning, the French population in the year 2000 could reach 70 million and even more. This will occur in a Europe, not including the U.S.S.R., with 570 million inhabitants, instead of 425 million today, and in a world that will have 6 to 7 billion people.

At the same time the urban percentage of the population, now 62 per cent of France, will sharply increase. In comparison with the British rate of 80 per cent or the West German 75 per cent rate, the French rate is slightly lower. By the end of the century, it is possible that it could reach 80 per cent and perhaps higher, which would mean a doubling in the number of urban citizens, or 28 million more people than today.

This French and urban growth accompanied by an increasingly youthful population is, furthermore, a powerful evolving and renewing factor, as Alfred Sauvy has demonstrated.[14] Whether we care for it or not, we are condemned to very strong urban growth. This great thrust of urbanization, which France cannot escape, will determine the future of the Paris agglomeration. Today the agglomeration contains 27 per cent of France's urban population. Consequently, it appears difficult for the rest of the French cities to absorb this total projected French population, which would, in effect, mean more than doubling in size, an actual increase of 140 per cent!

All French cities and metropolitan areas, small, medium and large, must double their populations in forty years in order that the Paris agglomeration will merely double. Thus, with the most predictable growth rates under the most plausible hypotheses, the Marseille, Lyon, and Lille agglomerations could have one and a half million inhabitants by the year 2000; Bordeaux could reach one million; and Toulouse, Rouen, Nice, Nantes and Strasbourg could exceed one half million. These increases could take place without stopping the urban Paris region's population from reaching fifteen million, or 21.5 per cent of the French population foreseen for the end of the century (16.5 per cent for today), but still 27 per cent of France's city dwelling population.

As part of past attempts to regulate population densities and Paris, note should be taken of height and plot control legislation. The regulations of 1859, 1884 and 1902 essentially limited the height of buildings by the width of the street; this permitted (since 1902) the construction of six floors plus the roof and superstructure which led to buildings rarely higher than sixty-five feet. Since 1958, the maximum authorized height has been held at 103 feet including roofs and superstructure, and in the peripheral *arrondissements,* up to 115 feet could be constructed on the sides of broad avenues. In 1959, the CUS (Coefficient of Plot Usage), which is the relationship between the area of the building base and the total area of the plot, was fixed between 2.5 and 3.5 according to zones; it should, little by little, liberate more and more of the earth's surface from construction and lead to high-rise construction, especially on the inner fringes of the City of Paris.[15]

The estimates of potential urban growth in Paris are staggering, but it is unreasonable not to consider them.

Thus, the *Schéma Directeur* proposes to organize and locate the inevitable growth of the Parisian metropolis which is the entity responsible for this unique urban region, served by a dense system of radiating common carriers and expressways that link the center of Paris with other important metropolitan areas. This spatial unity should permit the maintenance of the unity of the labor market, of the cultural and recreational possibilities and should also guarantee freedom of choice for its citizens. Furthermore, from an economic point of view, the relative proximity of numerous and diverse activities at such a busy international crossroads maintains for everyone the maximum in external economies and the largest possible multiplier effect. The urban spatial expansion will not be in spontaneous small clusters tending to perpetuate the radial-concentric structure which (as noted above) is due primarily to the main transportation arteries—especially rail lines—and is the principal cause of the congestion at the center of Paris. Instead, it will be directed into two long urbanization axes, tangential to the existing agglomeration: essentially the two parallel axes are oriented southeast and northwest, the northern one is 46.6 miles long and the southern one is longer, 56 miles (Fig. 10).

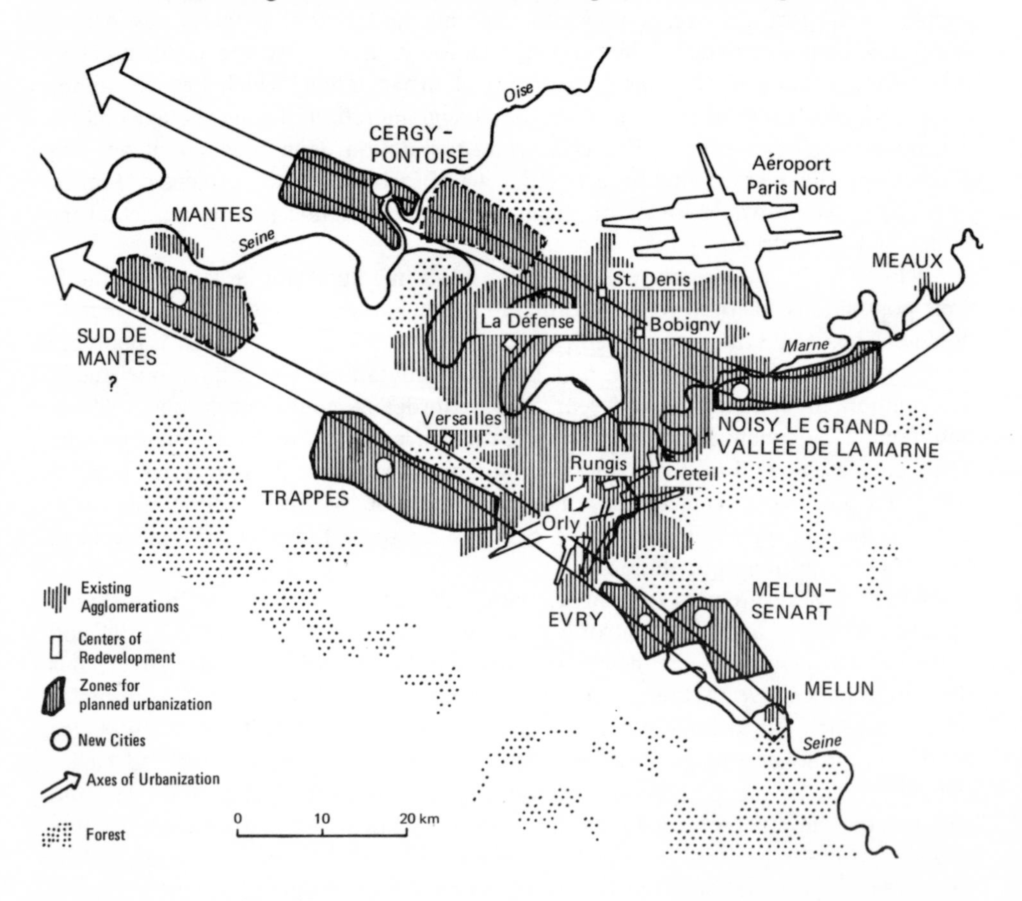

FIG. 10 Schéma Directeur: The twin axes proposed for the growth of the Paris region showing the five new cities. *Jean Bastié, map*

There are multiple advantages to these axes tangential to the agglomeration:

(1) the separation of traffic along these axes from their connections with either the center of the agglomeration or outside it, which now become perpendicular to the axes;

(2) the construction at the least cost of profitable investments in transportation;

(3) relative proximity both to urbanized and to green zones.

Spatial expansion is foreseen in various places in the valleys and on the plateaus. The intention is to protect the flood plains and river banks, as well as scenic landscapes, and to use them for recreational areas.

Five new urban centers or cities with at least 100,000 inhabitants and up to 500,000 will be located along the urbanization axes (see Fig. 10). Two of these cities will be to the west, or going from north to south, Cergy-Pontoise and Trappes; two are to the south, Evry-Courcouronnes and Melun-Senart; and one is to the east, Noisy-le-Grand-Vallée de la Marne. The northern tangential axis unites the remaining three.

These five urban centers and their surroundings should only absorb two thirds of the expected growth, or four million people, while the remaining third, or two million people, should locate in the existing suburbs, on one hand by spread-out density and on the other hand by the creation of five additional important urban subcenters:

(1) one to the west: La Défense-Nanterre,

(2) two to the north: Seine-St.-Denis, Bobigny,

(3) two to the south: Créteil, Rungis-Choisy-le-Roi.

Each of the ten new centers or each "restored" center is designed to serve a population between 300,000 and one million inhabitants. These new "cities" or subcenters have an area of at least 750 to 1,250 acres and contain all of the public facilities and services that correspond to the size of its population, or the equivalent of those of a large provincial metropolis. Secondary centers are also planned. The success of these new urban downtown areas—their surroundings, access, division of activities and housing, variety of functions, attractiveness, intensity of the life style—is an essential condition of the completion of the *Schéma* itself, because the already existing centers of the average cities do not seem able to adapt to their expanded tasks.

The *Schéma Directeur* accentuates the need to create and organize a complex system of heavily used mass transit, reaching out to the distant suburbs. The principal transportation arteries represented by the 162 miles of a new Regional Express System (R.E.R.) will constitute the backbone of the urbanization axes. This is the first time that the mass transit lines which cross Paris will continue out to the far suburbs. This major innovation is perhaps the most important part of the *Schéma,* the one that will contribute the most to maintaining the unity of this urban region. Also it will finally achieve the old project of joining the major railroad stations already existing in the heart of Paris. This plan was defeated in the middle of the nineteenth century; although not adopted when the first Métro lines were constructed, it was discussed in the PADOG plan in 1961.

Unfortunately, the *Schéma* did not call for several 2.5 mile extensions into the suburbs of several lines of today's Métro. The Métro finished essentially between 1898 and 1914 has evolved little since. But with about seventy miles of track and 353 stations with frequent service, it represents an exceptionally practical mode of public transportation. But the suburbs are not so well served, which is why the R.E.R. was conceived. The R.E.R. will not consist entirely of new rights-of-way; at least 37.2 miles will use existing trackage. But on both the Métro and the R.E.R. tracks the average traveling speed using cars of large carrying capacity and less frequent stops should be twice that of today's Métro, 31 m.p.h. instead of 15.5 m.p.h. and the hourly demand is expected to reach 50,000 passengers instead of 25,000. One of these R.E.R. routes, the first to be completed, will cut Paris from the east to the west and will connect St. Germain-en-Laye and Montesson with Boissy St.-Leger and Lagny via the Défense, the Étoile, Auber, Chatelet and and Lyon Railway station. It is already in operation between the Étoile and the Défense and between the Nation and Boissy-St. Leger. Two other lines will cross Paris from the north to south and will extend north to Cergy-Pontoise, Valmondois and the Paris Nord Airport, and south to Trappes and Tigery-Lievsaint. They will cross the east-west line at Auber (St. Lazare Railway Station) and at the Lyon Railway Station.

Further, five hundred miles of expressways are also planned. Two beltways will be from 6.2–9.3 miles and 12.4 miles from the center of Paris. The first is the fifty-mile suburban beltway (R.B.) which consists partially of the old national highway N. 186; the second is the sixty-five-mile Interurban Seine-et-Oise Expressway. The two come together in the west. When added to the peripheral boulevard (Fig. 11), there will be three automobile beltways, although there will be none for mass transit; the so-called small and large railroad "belts" are not used.[16] Seven expressways radiate in all directions. In Paris, traffic will be improved by the completion of the peripheral boulevard (22.4 miles), the express lanes along the embankment of the Right Bank, the completion of the north-south axis from the north and east railroad stations to the Bastille and its extensions, the Maine-Montparnasse and Denfert-Rochereau connections with the southern peripheral boulevard, and the penetration into Paris by the Bagnolet loop.

Automobile traffic, and especially parking, has become more and more difficult in all of Paris and most acutely in the central part, the *zone bleue* (the blue zone) where parking is limited to one hour. To cope with the problem a vast program of subterranean parking garages has been undertaken; many of these are already in service at prominent places such as on the Champs-Élysées, at the Bourse and by Napoleon's Tomb, Les Invalides.

As for the old Métro, plans call for lengthening its platforms, completing the transformation to wheels with pneumatic tires and switching to automatic control. But nevertheless, road improvements have three times as much investment as mass transit. Eventually, the completed rail and road systems should sketch a sort of steel mesh with large octagonal sections, instead of today's radial-concentric plan.

The *Schéma Directeur* correctly insists on building in flexibility for the future structure of Parisian activities and land use with consequences in the location of employment thus controlling most of the volume and intensity of daily commuting. The suggestion is to give maximum help to loosening the concentration of secondary and tertiary industries that need not be located in the center of Paris. One must encourage the creation outside of Paris, and as far away as possible, of powerful centers of such activities (with a complete range of businesses, offices

FIG. 11 The peripheral boulevard on the south of Paris. *Photograph by Jean Bastié:* Encyclopédie Visuelle, *Armand Colin-Véronèse, "Régions Françaises: Agglomération parisienne."*

and headquarters, capable of integrating with the downtowns of existing cities and creating new industrial zones. This is necessary to reduce massive commuting, harmful to individuals as well as to the profitability of business and requiring excessively costly investments.

The increase in the number of jobs, at least two million between now and the end of the century, should permit the creation of these new centers, without detracting too much from Parisian central areas because substitutions will take place and because tertiary jobs will replace industrial jobs. In the long run one is moving toward the inescapable deindustrialization of the city of Paris. Paris still today contains the major portion of specifically Parisian industries, namely, souvenirs, jewelry, goldsmithing, ironwork, perfume, cosmetics, toys and games, musical instruments and precision goods. One can only wonder what will be the consequences of moving for these industries.

The *Schéma Directeur* is equally concerned, as noted above, with the location of recreational facilities, the creation of flood plains (Jablines on the Marne, Cergy on the Oise, Moissant on the Seine), the protection of forests and the landscape. The land and technical agency (*l'Agence foncière et technique*)[17] is charged with buying vast private forests, often poorly maintained and transforming them into delightful woods. Thus is an attempt at reversing an old evolutionary practice: in effect, more than 37,500 acres of forests have disappeared within 12.4 miles of Paris in recent times.

The *Schéma Directeur* is designed to serve as a framework for fifty detailed structural planning directives, which will be integrated with (a) the intercommunal urban plans (P.D.U.I.) numbering one hundred or so for the entire region, (b) the communal plans and (c) at last the detailed urban plans. In reality, the give-and-take between the differently scaled plans should be unremitting during their formulation. These are the plans that will locate the necessary public facilities. This inventory of intrastructure has already been largely completed by numerous working groups of experts who have worked for the *Délégation Générale au District,* in conjunction with the civil servants of the interested public agencies.

The Board of Directors of the national district and the advisory economic and social council[18] have approved the major strategies of the *Schéma Directeur*. Nevertheless, they have requested a more narrow blending of the *Schéma's* ideas with those of the national French regional planners; especially in the case of the Paris Basin they hope for more attention to urban development by taking the Marne and Oise valleys as axes, as well as the development of other towns in the Basin: Amiens, Rouen-le-Havre, le Mans, Orléans, Troyes and Reims. Furthermore, they requested an absolute priority for mass transit and housing construction, a more rapid dispersal of the activities of the interior of the agglomeration, the definition of a land policy, the progressive construction of new cities—which will under no circumstances be dormitory towns, the gathering of the necessary funds to fulfill the *Schéma Directeur* and the establishment of a schedule for fulfilling various aspects of the plan!

The *Schéma Directeur d'aménagement et d'urbanisme de la région de Paris* thus clearly marks a very important date in the history of Parisian urban planning. For the first time, long-term growth estimates have been made while maintaining the unity of the urban region; a spatial expansion is assumed, expected and located in connection with a road and rail system. Powerful secondary centers of activity are chosen to counterbalance the attractive power of the center of Paris, the irreplaceable heart of the system, but also the factor responsible for the radial-concentric pattern and congestion in the agglomeration.

At the end of five years of life, the *Délégation Générale au District* has been, in effect, transformed into a prefecture for the Paris region and, as a result, its responsibilities at the regional scale have become reinforced.

Five planning task forces (*missions d'aménagement*) have already completed enormous preparatory work for the five new cities. The land agency has already acquired 12,500 acres within its perimeter and it should have acquired 25,000 acres by the end of 1970; infrastructure construction has begun, the Val-d'Oise prefecture at Cergy-Pontoise is under construction, two legs of the R.E.R. are in service, 60,000 dwellings have been begun and 200,000 are programmed. In spite of the competition of spontaneous urban development such as at Parly 2, the movement is irreversible.

But the fulfillment of the *Schéma Directeur* depends largely, in the early stages, on the financial restrictions relating to investments in the Paris region that are included in the Sixth Plan (1971–75) and on the priority given to the construction of new cities. Up to the present, $4 billion per year had been invested in the Paris region, one half for housing construction. Some of this construction will take half a century, other projects for a century; to program and locate them obviously means difficult choices and represents a heavy responsibility.

It can only be hoped that the 1966 *Schéma Directeur* does not meet the fate of its two predecessors: the 1934–39 Prost plan and the 1960 PADOG plan. The living conditions of the twelve to fifteen million Parisians in the year 2000 depend on it.

NOTES

[1] *Direction régionale de l'INSEE* (*Institut National de la Statistique et des Études Économiques*) and *Où va Paris,*" "*Les grandes enquêtes,*" 1967, p. 21.

[2] *Atlas de Paris et de la Région Parisienne,* p. 183, and *Cahiers IAURP* (*Institut d'Aménagement et d'Urbanisme de la Région Parisienne*), No. 3, 1965.

[3] *Direction régionale de l'INSEE: notes rapides sur les résultats du recensement de 1968, No. 5, Octobre 1969,* p. 3.

[4] *Direction régionale de l'INSEE: notes rapides sur les résultats du recensement de 1968, No. 5, Octobre 1969,* p. 9.

[5] *Direction régionale de l'INSEE: notes rapides sur les résultats du recensement de 1968, No. 3, Octobre 1969,* p. 5.

[6] *Paris ville industrielle, La Documentation Française,* 1970, p. 6.

[7] Jean Bastié, *La croissance de la banlieue parisienne.* Paris, Presses Universitaires de France, 1965, pp. 137–60.

[8] See *Urbanisme,* No. 89 (1965), a special issue devoted to the *métropoles d'équilibre.*

[9] See Niles M. Hanse, "French Regional Planning Experience," *Journal of the American Institute of Planners,* XXXV, No. 6, November 1969, pp. 362–68.

[10] "Paris and the French Desert," Paris: Flammarian.

[11] General sources: *Réflexions pour 1985, La Documentation Française,* 1964, and *Schéma Directeur d'aménagement et d'urbanisme de la région de Paris, Avis et rapport, Tome III, La Documentation Française,* 1966, pp. 54–69.

[12] *Plan d'Aménagement et d'Organisation Générale de la Région Parisienne.*

[13] *Livre Blanc* (White Paper) was the title given to *l'Avant-project de programme duodeconnal pour la Région de Paris.* Paris, Imprimerie Municipal, 1963.

[14] Alfred Sauvy, *De Malthus à Mao Tse-Toung.* Paris, Denoël, 1958, p. 117.

[15] (Editor's note.)

[16] Differing from both Tokyo and London. (Editor's note.)

[17] Purchases land for the nation or for local government. *Plans directeurs d'urbanisme inter-communaux* (P.D.U.I.). (Translators' note.)

[18] F.D.E.S.—*Fonds de Développement Économique et Social*—the French Government finances through this intermediary needed local and regional physical infrastructure. (Translators' note.)

CHAPTER 4

London: Metropolitan Evolution and Planning Response

John W. Shepherd*

THE HISTORIC CITY

It seems certain that there was a Celtic settlement on the site of what was to become Roman Londinium, perhaps inhabited by a tribe whose name was prefixed by the adjective "londo-" meaning wild or bold. However, it was the Roman conquerors of ancient Britain who were the first to recognise the immense strategic value of the place where the lowest bridging point on the River Thames coincides with an outcropping of two low gravel hills on the northern bank. Having constructed the first London Bridge, the military occupation ran straight paved roads across the rest of the country, establishing once and for all London's commercial dominance in Britain. Next to the bridge on the drier ground to the north was

* Received undergraduate and graduate education at the London School of Economics and Political Science. From 1966 to 1968, he worked with the research section of the Royal Commission on Local Government in England (the Redcliffe-Mand Commission), thereafter spent a year with the Greater London Group (London School of Economics) on an evaluation of the new planning system in London. From 1969 to 1971, he was Visiting Assistant Professor of Geography at Queen's University, Kingston, Ontario, and is currently at the London School of Economics pursuing research on the London scene.

laid out a fortified settlement with a regular street pattern. Though these earliest lines have gone, the former position of the Roman wall still traces out the single square mile of the City of London, the financial and commercial core of the sterling area and Britain's overseas trade.

It was not until much later that London became the *de facto* political and administrative capital of Britain. In 1050, Edward the Confessor established a royal palace and an abbey at Thorney Island about one mile up river from the mercantile City of London. On this site there now stand the Palace of Westminster, the Houses of Parliament and Westminster Abbey. Then, in 1066, William the Conqueror attempted to unify London under the Crown and extend royal control over the city merchants. This he did by building the White Tower, nucleus of the Tower of London, hard against the eastern wall of the city near Aldgate. It was from this point in time that London developed—spreading outwards from dual centres at Westminster and the city and continually absorbing the scattered villages in its path.[1]

The first official plan for London, in the sense that it was actually written down, is generally considered to be that contained in a proclamation of Elizabeth the First of 1580. Its purpose was to control the exploding growth of the metropolis, especially the suburbs of Clerkenwell, Finsbury, Rotherhithe and Southwark. Its method was crude: all new building was forbidden "where no former House hath bene knowen to have bene in the memorie of such as are now living. . . ."[2] Ostensibly aimed at relieving the pressures of overcrowding on the poor, London's earliest "Green Belt" was also an attempt to control unrest among the masses and preserve the manufacturing monopoly of the City Livery Companies at a time when neither the Crown nor the City Corporation could agree on how to govern London's unincorporated suburbs.[3]

Continuing the theme of ideas and ideology in a broad concept of city planning, four short vignettes follow which describe later aspects of the growth of London and the main reaction on the part of different sorts of planners toward the problems and opportunities presented. The first sketch describes the work of private enterprise planners, the aristocratic landlords who developed the West End and Bloomsbury in the seventeenth and eighteenth centuries. Their work remains today as part of the architectural heritage of London that statutory planning seeks to preserve against unsympathetic re-development and the effects of motorized traffic. The themes of the second and third vignettes are modern British town planning. This grew out of two great nineteenth-century movements, the one to improve the public health of cities and the other the housing of the urban working classes and poor.[4] Here we describe first the achievements of those unlikely planners, the medical doctors who, in the 1830s, found the vital causal link between environment and disease. Then comes the work of the far-seeing planners of the late nineteenth century who by practical example helped set the standards for subsequent public housing development and also generated the movement for a regional solution to London's problems. The final vignette deals with the massive suburbanisation of London in the 1920s and 1930s which provoked a decisive intellectual input into city-regional planning and formed the basis of the bold schemes for directing London's growth from the end of the Second World War until the middle of the 1960s.

A VISION OF THE CITY OF LONDON, CONSTRUCTED ON THE PLAN LEFT BY SIR CHRISTOPHER WREN.

Drawn and Engraved by MR. WORTHINGTON G. SMITH, *under the Direction of* MR. GODWIN.

Streets.

A A A. Old London Wall. B. Cheapside. C. Cannon-street. D. Farringdon-street. F. Barbican. E. Bishopsgate-street. G. Cripplegate. H. Moorgate-street. I. Holborn. J. Leadenhall-street. K. Tower-hill. L. London-bridge. M. Ludgate-hill. N. Fleet-street. O. Newgate-st. P. Aldgate.

Public Buildings, &c.

Q. Tower. R. Trinity House. S. Custom House. T. Billingsgate. U. Bank. V. Mint. W. Post Office. X. Goldsmiths' Hall. Y. Post Office. Z. Excise. 1. Insurance. 2. Royal Exchange. 3. Monument. 4. Guildhall. 5. Market. 6. Wood-market. 7. Public Halls. 8. Newgate Prison. 9. Bridewell Dock. 10. Queenhithe.

Churches.

11. St. Paul's Cathedral. 12. St. Benet's. 13. St. Clement's. 14. St. Margaret's, Fenchurch-st. 15. St. Michael's, Cornhill. 16. St. Mary Woolnoth. 17. St. Botolph's. 18. St. Stephen's, Walbrook. 19. St. Mildred the Virgin. 20. St. Margaret's. 21. St. Stephen's, Coleman-st. 22. St. Alban's, Wood-st. 23 St. Lawrence, Jewry. 24. St. Mary-le-bow. 25. St. Martin's, Ludgate-hill.

THE EVOLUTION OF MODERN PLANNING

Discovering Urbanism

The imperial grandeur of the wide boulevards and imposing rond-points that dominate many European cities was rejected as a ground plan for London when Christopher Wren's scheme for the reconstruction of the city after the Fire of 1666 proved impossible to implement (Fig. 1). Yet for two centuries the expansion of London between Westminster and the city owed much to an innovation in townscape brought from continental Europe. The *town square,* which first appeared as a grand piazza at Covent Garden in 1630, was shaped into intimate residential neighbourhoods that spread through Soho, St. James's and Mayfair in the remainder of the seventeenth century; into Georgian Bloomsbury and, in the early nineteenth century, to Pimlico, Camden Town and Islington.

These districts were developed by London's aristocrat planners, among them the Dukes of Westminster, Bedford and Northampton, whose family estates were situated on the fringes of built-up London. A design formula of various sized squares interconnected by short, wide streets suited both the commercial aims of the landlords and the pretensions of London's growing elite class. This basic pattern could be manipulated to fit a coherent scheme for a continuous area of land, keeping land holdings intact during a period of rapid conversion from rural to urban use, and making estate management more efficient. It was also the cheapest way of putting many dwellings on a single site by keeping down the cost of frontages and road making.[5]

To the tenant, the town square offered privacy and the illusion of rurality close to the sophisticated life of the capital. The elegant three-storey houses faced onto an open space planted with a lawn, trees and ornamental shrubs. The "therapeutic value of the circulating air" in the square thus became a highly valued feature in the malodorous atmosphere of pre-public sanitation London.[6] Coach-houses and stables were situated in the mews at the rear of the houses, while the tone and character of an entire estate were maintained by conditions in the leases which prohibited the conversion or use of premises for commercial purposes.

Part of the intention of the street layout connecting the squares was to permit easy interaction among the residents and with the fashionable parts of London, while minimizing contact with the "lower orders" of the city. Where an estate issued out upon London at large, gates and gatekeepers were installed to keep out unwanted traffic and the town mob. Thus, Taviton Street Gate (Fig. 2) deflected south-bound traffic around the Duke of Southampton's estate and guarded Gordon Square from the slum-dwellers of St. Pancras. As bastions of privileged

FIG. 1 Sir Christopher Wren's plan for the City of London, 1666. Wren's plan for rebuilding the city after the Great Fire involved scrapping the tortuous mediaeval street layout and the substitution of the straight lines and focal points of the Renaissance. The principal streets were to be ninety feet wide, others, sixty. Narrow alleys were banned; noxious trades were to be disallowed. A Royal Commission and the City Surveyors considered it impracticable for the business life of the City and it was rejected. *The Guildhall Library, City of London*

FIG. 2 Planned physical segregation: Taviton Street Gate looking into Gordon Square on the Bedford Estate, 1893. *Trustees, the Bedford Settled Estates*

amenity, the gates were fervently defended by the residents of the squares, and, despite their hindrance to general circulation, it was as late as 1893 when Parliament gave powers to local authorities to remove the last of them.

The Industrial Environment and Public Health

Between 1801 and 1841 the population of London as a whole doubled to two million, but that of its main industrial districts around Whitechapel and Stepney quadrupled. The development of these "East End" parishes contrasted horrifically with those to the west of the City of London. Here the builder's and the landlord's objective was the quickest return on the minimum investment. Streets were therefore narrow, irregular and undrained. The tiny houses were packed around dark, suffocating courts, their cellars providing additional rentable living space. The basic means for the removal of human waste were the cesspool and the communal refuse heap.

Town planning as a function of public authorities has its origins in the period 1837–44 when a series of official reports, like that of the *Select Committee on the Health of Towns* (1840) and the *Inquiry into the Sanitary Conditions of the*

Labouring Population (1842), made clear the social cost of these conditions. The significance of their findings was twofold. First, they showed that the epidemics of cholera and typhoid that broke out in unsanitary urban areas were taking their toll not only of paupers (whose elimination was justified by Malthusian economics), but also of skilled artisans, shopkeepers and able-bodied labourers.[7] It was this erosion of the nation's work force which eventually persuaded politicians of the need for state intervention against the evils of uninhibited industrialism and town growth.

Secondly, the reports proved that ill health was directly related to the condition of the physical environment and that much of the sickness was preventable if the city was properly drained and if minimum standards were set for the housing of the labouring classes. It was the doctors with first-hand experience of the fever wards who, by observing the geographical regularities in, and co-variants of, disease, made the deductions that showed how to prevent future outbreaks.

The numerous reforms to London's government, public health and housing, which evolved over the remainder of the nineteenth century, shared an origin in these discoveries. In 1855, a Metropolitan Board of Works, whose authority extended over all of built-up London, was set up to plan and construct a drainage system for the whole urban area and to coordinate this task with road building and slum clearance. *Model by-laws* contained in the Public Health Acts and the London Building Acts at first imposed minimum sanitary and structural standards on individual dwellings. Gradually the impact of these regulations was generalized to control the layout of houses in streets, the relationship of streets to each other and, in the early part of this century, to the design of entire suburbs.[8]

Housing and Social Reform

Concern for the less easily defined objectives of modern planning gathered under the heading of *amenity* or *quality of life* arose in the late nineteenth and early twentieth centuries as a direct reaction to the sort of development encouraged by the first housing by-laws. By 1901, the transition to the railway age had sent London sprawling for eight or nine miles into the surrounding countryside and its population to a total of 4.5 million. The area of the London County Council (which replaced the Metropolitan Board of Works in 1888) was now almost completely built over, mostly with monotonous rows of "back-to-back" terraced houses of the working classes or with the larger, more ornate but equally uninspired rows of "villas" for city clerks and businessmen.

Two groups of reformers led the protest for more creativity and humanity in town development. Ebenezer Howard, clerk, lay preacher and inventor, promulgated his vision of the *Garden City* as the cure for metropolitan overgrowth.[9] Mrs. Henrietta Barnett, on the other hand, a charity worker among the poor of Whitechapel, saw her *Garden Suburb* as a planned method of saving Hampstead Heath from urban sprawl. Thus in one sense the objectives of these two approaches clashed. Howard's scheme was incorporated as part of a larger plan for halting London's growth and decanting excess population into a surrounding ring of garden cities while the garden suburb meant actually extending the existing built-up area. Nevertheless, their humanitarian goals were identical, namely to re-unite metropolitan man with Nature and to re-establish a community of social classes that was alleged to have been destroyed by the excesses of specialisation and industrialism.

The essence of Howard's thinking is in his analogy of three magnets, each representing the attractions of the metropolis, the country and the garden city. Only the latter combined the advantages of the other two without their disadvantages. A "socially-balanced" town of thirty thousand people could combine the benefits of open-air and proximity to work with opportunities for employment, culture and social relationships. The Garden Cities Association therefore raised the capital to build two such towns at Letchworth (1903) and Welwyn (1920), some thirty miles north of London. The land upon which the towns were built was owned communally and profits from increases in land values were eventually used to develop the public services of the town. Gradually the ideas contained in Howard's work were elaborated and integrated to produce the first recognisable regional strategy for London, including a prototype for the modern green belt.[10]

Design for the London Region

Acts of Parliament passed in 1919 and 1932 extended the scope of town planning by making it compulsory for local authorities to draw up plans for suburban development and redevelopment in existing built-up areas. However, neither the scale at which they operated nor the scope of the powers available were adequate to the emerging task in the London region, namely, the shaping of metropolitan-scale physical growth. From 1920 to 1939, the built-up area of London multiplied no less than fourfold, thrusting low density suburbs ten to twelve miles into the neighbouring counties. A number of factors were responsible. One was the sheer size that London had already attained. As the largest concentration of labour and buying power in the country, it was an ideal location for the new growth industries freed from coal-field sites by electrical power. Another factor was the revolution in personal mobility. The extension of London's underground railways, electrification of surface rail lines and rising private car ownership encouraged nearly half a million people to leave the inner parts of London for homes in the suburbs between 1920 and 1939. Finally, the example of Hampstead Garden Suburb itself encouraged new space standards for suburban developments, especially those undertaken by the London County Council outside its administrative confines.[11]

Improvements in transportation also tied developments in towns well beyond the metropolis to changes at the centre. Some, such as Luton, Dunstable and Slough, to the west and northwest, grew by attracting industries of their own, benefitting from nearness to London's consumers and the growing industrial areas in Middlesex, a county bordering London. Others, quiet country towns in rural counties around London, namely Buckinghamshire, Sussex, Surrey and Kent, saw commuter suburbs flourish on their outskirts as electrified railways brought them within an hour of the offices of Westminster and the city. In towns like these, residential growth was almost completely uncontrolled, with their modish "semi-detached" mock Tudor villas either strung along the main highways or dotted in unrelated clusters lacking amenities and requiring the costly extension of sewerage, water, gas and electricity lines.

Concern over the rate at which agricultural land was being urbanized and the cost of servicing sporadic residential development with public utilities brought numerous local authorities together in 1927 to form the Greater London Regional Planning Committee. Significantly, for the conceptual course that regional planning was to take, this committee appointed Raymond Unwin as its Chief Technical Adviser.

Unwin naturally brought the architect's insight to bear on the problem. Starting from the assumption that the existing urban form of London and its environs was "chaotic," he proposed that it be reshaped by securing a "harmonious relationship" among the three major land-use categories of residences, industry and open space. Thus, regional, like existing local planning, depended less on an understanding of the economics of employment location or the forces generating suburbanization, in short, on how London *worked* than on how it *looked* on the architect's drawing board. The guiding principle of "unity of design," Unwin wrote, was equally applicable to

> the grouping of walls, roofs and windows into a facade, to the disposition of buildings and openings around a civic centre, or to the laying down of a pattern for distributing urban development over the undulating background of hill and dale, field and forest forming the region.[12]

Unwin also expounded the geometric advantages of the circular city, the shape to which he wanted London to conform more closely and of the need to perceive undeveloped land in a completely different way to that encouraged in the planning acts. Thus the fact that the radius of a circle increased less than in proportion to its area suggested that overcrowding at the centre of a city might be lessened by "decanting" population beyond the built-up limits since aggregate distances to the city centre and hence total travel would not be increased by as great a factor as densities could be lowered. Again, instead of assuming all open land was building land, planners should set down their cities on a background of open space preserved for agricultural and recreational purposes.

In his final report to the Greater London Planning Committee,[13] Unwin therefore recommended a halt to London's further outward spread, the preservation of its immediate hinterland by means of a Green Belt ring and the decentralization of surplus population to a series of new "satellite" towns. To the social and metaphysical arguments of the Garden Cities Association, which had first proposed such a solution for London's problems, was therefore added the "objectivity" of science and design in a comprehensive regional planning scheme.

THE BARLOW REPORT AND ABERCROMBIE PLANS

Thus, prior to the Second World War the style and methodology of town and regional planning were evolving. However, statutory town planning was mainly local in scale and restricted in technique to the design and sanitary engineering aspects of suburban development. For the most part physical planning was irrelevant to the pressing issues of the period such as regional disparities in income, unemployment and social welfare.[14] Three documents were responsible for a revolutionary change in this situation and the birth of town and country planning as an important part of national economic and social policy. These were the reports of the *Royal Commission on the Distribution of the Industrial Population* (the Barlow Report), presented in 1940; Patrick Abercrombie's *County of London Plan* (1943) and his *Greater London Plan* (1944).

Regional Urban Planning: the early synthesis

The important contribution of the Barlow Report was that it showed how physical planning could make more effective the regional economic policies then being pursued by central government. The Special Areas Act of 1934 had designated areas of high structural unemployment in Scotland, northeast England, west Cumberland and South Wales, to receive financial and other assistance for the diversification of their industrial base. The government's early measures brought only marginal relief however, and by 1937 the Commissioner for the Special Areas was suggesting that any attempt to divert jobs to the older industrial areas must simultaneously *restrict* the magnetic influence of the centres of rapid employment growth in the West Midlands and South East England and Greater London in particular.[15]

The Barlow Commission combined the arguments concerning regional imbalance with those relating directly to London's internal problems to provide a powerful rationale for a halt to further expansion of the capital. Within London, it noted, the *economic* benefits deriving from urban agglomeration were outweighed by the costs of traffic congestion, high rents, long journeys to work and loss of agricultural land. On the *social* side, the Commission singled out the scale of the slum clearance problem and the overcrowding in, and immediately surrounding, central London. Finally, the report pointed out that a dense concentration of population and industry was *strategically* extremely vulnerable to aerial bombardment, a consideration which weighed heavily on policy-makers in 1939. The Commission felt that strong government intervention was needed to influence the geographical distribution of both population and industry and check the growth of London. For this purpose a Central Authority should be set up to coordinate local planning schemes and also the work of other government departments within the framework of a national plan for urbanization.

Barlow's recommendations were not officially endorsed by the government until 1944, but the destruction of war and the vision of a better environment for a victorious army following the pace urged politicians at both the local and central levels into action. In 1941, the London County Council commissioned Professor Patrick Abercrombie, a leading architect-planner, to devise a scheme for rebuilding the bomb-damaged and obsolescent parts of the core of built-up London. He had barely been at work on this a year when the Minister of Works and Buildings asked him to prepare a plan for the whole London region bearing the Barlow recommendations in mind.

The resulting complementary plans for the County of London and the Greater London Region were remarkable for the way in which they welded into a comprehensive whole a number of hitherto unrelated physical planning ideas combined with distinct social policies for improving the living conditions of Londoners. Abercrombie seized what he saw as the perfect opportunity to carry out a complete, once-for-all reconstruction of the physical pattern of London and its region. Two crucial assumptions underpinned both plans. The first was that following government enforcement of Barlow's recommendations, no further employment growth would take place in the London area. Secondly, Abercrombie accepted official projections of a static, perhaps declining, population in postwar Britain. These two assumptions, coupled with the wartime evacuation of thousands of Londoners, government direction of resources and labour and the licensing of the building industry, appeared to provide a unique moment in history to redirect the "unplanned" growth of centuries.

The Greater London Plan of 1944 covered over 2,600 square miles of country within a radius of thirty miles from Charing Cross. The total population of the area was over ten millions. Taking the geometric simplicity of Unwin's earlier efforts and fusing it with the biological analogies of urban growth suggested by Patrick Geddes,[16] the foundation of the plan was the organic nature of metropolitan growth depicted in "a tendency towards concentric rings which can be measured in terms of housing density."[17] The aim was to impose upon this underlying pattern some semblance of ordered design for population grouping, land-use, transport and public services,[18] the assumption being that an orderly arrangement of land-uses would simultaneously promote the functional efficiency of the entire region.

Thus the Greater London Region was divided into four concentric zones (Fig. 3). An *Inner Urban Ring* covered the County of London and certain neighbouring districts with the similar characteristics of high population density, a large proportion of obsolescent nineteenth-century housing often intermingled with industrial land-uses and a lack of open space. Decentralization of over a million people and jobs, and urban renewal on an unprecedented scale, was proposed for this zone. Next came the *Suburban Ring* of interwar housing where ordinarily no further increase in population would be permitted but where steps would be taken to create greater community identity. Enclosing the whole of the built-up area, Abercrombie proposed a *Green Belt Ring* some ten miles wide to halt the outward spread of London at the limits it had attained in 1939.

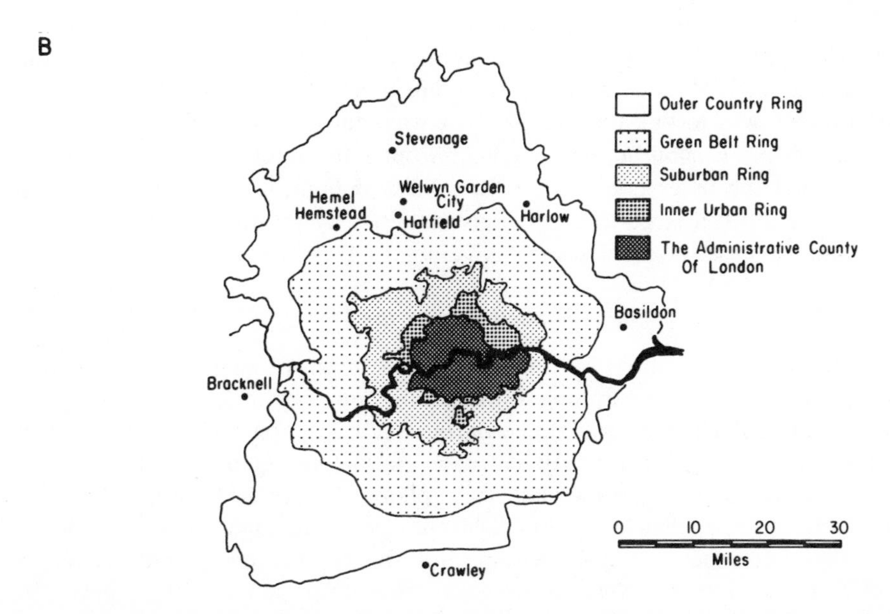

FIG. 3 The familiar "organic" view of London, the concentric zone pattern of Abercrombie's Greater London Plan of 1944. The new towns shown are those actually built after 1946. Abercrombie chose more sites to the south of London.

It would also serve as an agricultural and recreational area for London and preserve the character and distinctiveness of the small towns and villages located within it. The fourth, or *Outer Country Ring,* was to receive most of the population decanted from London. Over 400,000 people would go into eight completely New Towns and a further 300,000 into expansions to existing centres. The remainder of the decentralized population was to go outside the Abercrombie Region altogether.

Proposals for the reconstruction of the inner parts of London, contained in the *County of London Plan,* were based on a reduction of population densities and, comparable to the methodology of the Greater London Plan itself, on redefining a land-use pattern obscured by uncontrolled urban growth. The rational for Abercrombie's scheme of internal redevelopment was that unlike the other major urban areas of Britain such as Manchester or Birmingham, London had not developed by the growing together of a number of distinct, sizable towns but by the gradual envelopment of numerous villages in the outward spread from the centre. Abercrombie proposed a redefinition of this structure in terms of territorially defined communities, often based on the ancient villages of London, to be used for the planning of new neighbourhoods, roads, open space and work places. Borrowing Clarence Perry's ideas from the New York Regional Survey of 1929, Abercrombie suggested a remodelling of each community in terms of six or seven "neighbourhoods" whose size (about 10,000 people) and location were determined by the minimum pupil threshold and catchment area of an elementary school. A sense of identity would not only be fostered by being a "native" of Bermondsey or Poplar or Southwark, but also by planning each community in relation to physical barriers to pedestrian communication such as roads, railways and zones of regrouped industry.

Finally, this overall physical pattern for London and its region was to be bound together and articulated by a series of "ring and radial" highways which would, Abercrombie theorized, separate traffic travelling across and beyond London from that circulating or terminating within it. Of the four ring roads, one in central London was to link the main-line railway stations; one tightly surrounded the inner, Victorian suburbs; another cut through the interwar, low density development and the outer one orbited the whole of built-up London. There was to be a minimal disturbance to existing communities by locating new roads where possible through areas of obsolescence and along railway lines and canals.

The Administration of the Plan

The newly-elected Labour Government of 1945 accepted the main recommendations of Barlow and Abercrombie on directing new jobs to less fortunate parts of Britain, the containment and decentralization of London and the building of New Towns; and it enacted a battery of legislation to equip central and local authorities with the means to realize their plans. A central Ministry of Town and Country Planning had been established in 1943, and the "blitz and blight" Act of 1944 introduced special measures for the comprehensive redevelopment of central cities. *The Distribution of Industry Act,* passed in 1945, gave the Board of Trade power to restrict industrial expansion in the London region while giving incentives to industrialists willing to locate in the Development Areas of Scotland, the North and Wales. In 1946, the *New Towns Act* set up a number of Development Corporations, public bodies quite separate from local government, whose purpose was to buy land and make plans for a series of New Towns to be built wherever the Minister of Planning felt it "expedient in the national interest to do so."

The foundation for a more effective physical planning system was laid in the key document of planning legislation, the *Town and Country Planning Act,* 1947. In one stroke it reduced the number of planning authorities in England and Wales from 1,500 to 150 and within the area covered by the Greater London Plan from over 130 to 10. Each administrative county and county borough (the major units of rural and urban local government respectively) became obliged to produce a twenty-year *development plan* showing the allocation of land among the main uses by 1951 followed by a five-yearly review. Every plan was to be referred to the Ministry of Town and Country Planning (renamed Housing and Local Government in 1951) for approval, supposedly in the context of a national plan for urbanisation. All private development then had to be undertaken in accordance with the development plan and this was regulated by a process of *development control* whereby anyone proposing to build on or change the use of land had to obtain planning permission from his local authority.

Undoubtedly the most controversial section of the 1947 act was that which attempted to resolve the basic financial problem of land-use planning in a democracy; namely, how to compensate those denied the right to develop their land and how to secure a tax from those who gained by the communal planning effort ("the unearned increment"). The Labour Government's solution was to nationalize the right to develop land (not the land itself), and to pay compensation in cases of hardship on a once-for-all basis. However, after the return of a Conservative Government in 1951 these financial provisions were repealed on the ground that they were unworkable and dried up the supply of land brought forward for development.[19]

Few governments in the West have gone so far so quickly to establish control over the location of industry and the use of land in the national interest. But in one respect observers considered it had not gone far enough. Their criticisms related to the administrative machinery needed specifically to bring the Greater London Plan to fruition. The 1947 legislation had divided the Abercrombie Region into no less than ten separate local planning authorities—seven counties and three county boroughs. There were also hundreds of small authorities (urban and rural districts) responsible for the provision of public housing, sewerage and other services and, in addition, a number of large public corporations such as the Port of London Authority, the London Passenger Transport Board, British Railways and the Gas and Electricity boards taking key investment decisions on the vital transportation and other infrastructure aspects of regional development.

Abercrombie himself had considered that nothing less than a Regional Planning Board with powers to control the use of land and coordinate all large-scale investment decisions affecting the London region was needed to realize the basic strategy. In 1949, a London Planning Administration Committee reporting directly on the problem of implementing the London plans also found that some form of regional coordination was necessary, but could not agree on its exact constitutional nature. In the event, no regional machinery was set up beyond the creation of a virtually powerless London Division of the Ministry of Housing.

The Achievements and Lessons of London Planning 1950–65

The importance of the Greater London Plan in the immediate postwar period lay in the masterly combination of the promise it held out for a better existence for the people of London and the apparent technical competence of its supporting arguments. As such it presented an appealing political platform for the new Labour Government and a focus of expertise for the young profession of town and country planning. Paradoxically, the shortcomings of the plan also lay in precisely these areas. As a utopian blueprint it was to meet the harsh realities of the postwar world. Successive balance-of-payment crises meant financial retrenchment at home and a lack of money for its major, but uncosted, proposals. The new towns program was delayed and the road scheme for London virtually abandoned. Political and legal realities meant long battles over specific aspects of the plan[20] and the nationalization of development rights virtually froze the supply of land coming to the market. Consequently, the aspects of the plan which were to make most headway relative to the goals were those in which local government already had considerable powers for action, namely housing, or where the outcomes were generally favourable to property and other interests, namely in the institution of a Green Belt around London. Once the New Town Development Corporations were given adequate resources there was to be considerable activity in this sphere also.

On the technical side, the plan suffered from a heavy reliance on the architectonics of plans and an ignorance of the social and economic forces shaping the urban structure. Thus, the Greater London Plan assumed that postwar natural increase in population would be insignificant and that migration into the region would cease with rigid controls over the growth of industrial employment. In fact the excess of births over deaths in the London region during the 1950s and early 1960s was substantial and net gains by migration at least until 1962 when the Commonwealth Immigrants Act reduced the flow from overseas were very high. As the following table shows, between 1951 and 1966 the *increase* in population in South East England was no less than 1.8 million, consisting of a decline in the Greater London area of 300,000, and growth in the Outer Metropolitan Area of 1.5 million and in the rest of the South East of 650,000.[21]

TABLE 1

POPULATION GROWTH IN SOUTH EAST ENGLAND 1951–66

	Total Pop. (000s)			*Annual Average Percent*	*Change*
	1951	*1961*	*1966*	*1951–61*	*1961–66*
Greater London	8,208	7,985	7,914	—0.27	—0.18
Outer Metropolitan Area	3,505	4,518	5,009	2.89	2.2
Outer South East	3,501	3,848	4,149	1.0	1.6
Total South East	15,215	16,351	17,072	0.75	0.90
England and Wales	43,800	46,200	47,400	5.5	2.6

Source: South East Economic Planning Council, *A Strategy for the South East* (1967), p. 85.

Only a half million of the 1951–66 increase was actually located in accordance with the Greater London Plan. The massive growth in the Outer Metropolitan

Area was "unplanned" in that it was accommodated in additions to existing towns and villages without an overall regional strategy. By the mid 1960s, therefore, serious shortages of land for residential development were building up in the zone between the outer edge of the Green Belt and the Outer Metropolitan Area.

Total employment in the South East also followed a powerful upward trend contrary to the plan aims. In the decade 1951–1961, three quarters of a million new jobs were created—half of the increase for England and Wales as a whole. Some 250,000 were manufacturing jobs located in towns beyond the Green Belt, many of them slipping through the Board of Trade controls.[22] But although *manufacturing* employment declined in the Greater London area, the planners completely failed to predict the enormous growth in *service* employment in central London and its consequences for population distribution and the demand for travel. In Greater London the expansion of service jobs of all kinds—professional, clerical and distributive—amounted to no less than 42,000 a year between 1955 and 1962, more than matching the decline in manufacturing employment. Fifteen thousand new workers every year were commuting into Westminster, the West End and the City of London. It was not until 1964 and the re-election of a Labour Government that control of office development was put on a similar footing to that for industrial building and embodied in the Control of Offices and Industrial Development Act, 1965.

Housing in Inner London

It was against this background of wrong forecasts and inadequate resources, coupled with rather hazy policy guidelines emanating occasionally from Central Government[23] that local planning authorities attempted to implement their responsibilities in the regional plan. By far the greatest problems were faced by the London County Council (LCC) covering the central and most congested of the Abercrombie zones. The LCC development plan of 1951 and the review of 1960 set out targets for the reduction of population and industry in the area in order to improve the living and working conditions of those that remained. In fact the target population for the area of 3.15 million people by 1971 was almost reached by 1960. Once again the planners were surprised by events for the voluntary migration, mostly of young families with children who were financially able to move to the suburbs, and the wider London region took place much faster than had been forecast. Even so, out of an annual average of 35,000 people leaving the County of London between 1951 and 1961, some 21,000 went in planned moves to the New and the Expanding Towns.[24]

Since families were not moved without the firm prospect of a job to go to, an important factor in planned decentralization became the rate at which the LCC could persuade the small manufacturers of inner London to move to a New or Expanding Town and buy out "non-conforming" industrial land designated in the plan. On the first point a direct clash soon appeared between London regional policy and national development policy, for the Board of Trade was concerned to grant Industrial Development Certificates only to those firms which located or relocated in the development areas in the North and Wales. Only grudgingly did it recognise the "second-in-line" status of London's New Towns.[25] As for the second point, there was always too little cash for the LCC to buy up unsightly industrial land.

FIG. 4 Construction of the Pepys Estate, South London, 1966. Renewal is a familiar sight on the periphery of the inner city. Here construction is taking place on the site of the Royal Victoria Yard, Deptford. To the left and right are two of the three twenty-five storey tower blocks; in the middle ground, conversion of the rum warehouses is in progress. Across the Thames lies the Isle of Dogs, the Millwall Docks and on the left of the picture, an example of postwar LCC housing. *Greater London Council*

Within the LCC area the impact on housing standards of a declining population and the building activities of public and private agencies varied widely from one part of inner London to another.[26] Overall, the crude net deficiency of dwellings (surplus of households over dwelling spaces) almost halved between 1951 and 1961 and the degree of statutorily defined overcrowding declined by 7 percent. In that decade over 120,000 new dwellings were built, two-thirds of them provided by public authorities at subsidized rents for working people. The largest and perhaps the best of these schemes took place in a part of London's East End that had been devastated during the blitz. Stretching for two miles along the Commercial Road between the City of London and the East India Docks is the Stepney-Poplar Comprehensive Development Area.[27] Here, in the closest approximation to the principles of community planning set out in Abercrombie's County of London Plan some 100,000 people have been rehoused in relatively low density, low rise conditions. Shops, schools, pubs and other social facilities have fairly successfully created new neighbourhoods within the traditional community structure of Stepney, Poplar and Bromley-by-Bow.[28] In more recent large-scale rehousing developments such as the Pepys Estate at Deptford about four miles down river from London Bridge on the south side of the Thames, earlier planning standards have been re-appraised in line with the realities of rising land costs in London. Here, on land that was the main victualling yard of the Royal Navy in the days of Samuel Pepys, are some 2,000 homes, 12.5 acres of open space, shopping and other facilities on a total area of fifty-five acres. Over 400 homes are provided in three twenty-five storey blocks, an increasingly familiar aspect of the London housing scene, but one whose sociological ramifications have not been fully explored (Fig. 4).

However, the figures on increases in housing supply quoted above are to some extent mere statistical artifacts. Thus, it has been estimated that it requires a fall of about 5 percent in Greater London's population to reduce the number of households by 1 percent, since the average size of a household has declined steadily since the war. Add to this the problem of households sharing accommodation (almost 350,000 within inner London alone in 1966) and the 15 percent of the total housing stock which became obsolescent within the last ten years, and the dynamic nature of the housing problem facing London can be seen.

The Metropolitan Green Belt

The London Green Belt as approved by the Ministry of Housing ranges from eight to fifteen miles in width, tightly enclosing the interwar suburbs. Population growth within it has not been completely halted. In the immediate postwar years especially, the aim of a complete ban on building close to London could not be met since the LCC had to carry through pre-existing plans for thirteen out-country rehousing schemes—"rather more than housing estates but a good deal less than towns."[29] By 1957, this program was completed and the Green Belt began to achieve what came to be its main purpose, that of halting the outward sprawl of London and preserving the identity of smaller towns.

However, given the evolving nature of the London region, debate has arisen on the precise purpose of the Green Belt, for in designating such land in their development plans the county authorities hope to extend its present area, in some cases up to twenty-five miles from the edge of built-up London. This is because Green Belt controls, which also apply to this "proposed" Green Belt land, have been found to be a useful method for controlling the influx of population into specific areas and for raising the value of existing property. Also, according to original theory, a Green Belt was to serve as a recreational area for townsmen, particularly those from inner city districts lacking open space. But as the following table shows, only a small proportion of the total area is given over to specifically recreational use.[30]

Thus, while agriculture is the clearly dominant category, almost a quarter of the total area is taken up with what can be termed "non-conforming" uses—houses, factories, transport installations and mineral workings. Even some valuable agricultural land is in a derelict condition, as, for example, in the large areas of formerly market gardening land in the Lee Valley in North London.[31] Again, a substantial proportion of the woodland category is not directly accessible to the public at large, though it makes a vital landscape feature.

The London New Towns

Few other aspects of British town planning have received such critical attention as the New Towns, especially the eight designated for London between 1946 and 1949. The reason for this interest is not hard to find. They represent a large-

TABLE 2

LAND USE IN LONDON'S APPROVED GREEN BELT, 1960

Land Use	*Percent Total*
Agriculture	62.3
Residential, commercial, Manufacturing	15.0
Woodland	10.3
Recreational	5.4
Transport and extractive	3.7
Institutions and public services	2.6
Water and unused	0.7
Total	100.0

Source: D. Thomas, op. cit., p. 130.

scale positive attempt to solve the problems of overcrowding in the metropolis and in the idea of a virtually autonomous Development Corporation they embody all the stages of planning from the securing of land to the settlement of industrialists, workers and their families.

As Table 3 below shows, by 1970, the eight London New Towns had easily exceeded the population total of 400,000 allocated in the Abercrombie plan, though they have not achieved the *annual* growth rates set in their subsequent

TABLE 3

ORIGINAL, CURRENTLY PROPOSED AND 1970 POPULATION OF LONDON'S NEW TOWNS

	Date of Designation	*Population (thousands)* Original	Proposed	Dec. 1970
Basildon	1949	25.0	134	83.0
Bracknell	1949	5.1	60	37.3
Crawley	1949	9.0	79	67.8
Harlow	1947	4.5	not decided	76.5
Hatfield	1948	8.5	29	26.3
Hemel Hempstead	1947	21.2	80	70.0
Stevenage	1946	6.7	105	66.3
Welwyn Gdn. City	1948	18.5	50	43.6
Total		98.5	537+Harlow,	470.8

Source: Town and Country Planning, Vol. 39, No. 1 (January 1971), p. 46.

individual plans. Hence in the current terminology they have become Mark I or First Generation new towns to distinguish them from those of more recent designation which, as we shall see, serve a different set of planning goals.

Two questions often asked of London's New Towns are: Have they succeeded in developing as self-sufficient settlements with an existence independent of London and are they socially balanced communities? Recent research has provided some first answers. On the self-containment issue, for example, it has been found that despite their proximity to London (they are all located well within daily commuting range), the New Towns have indeed developed viable economies of their own.[32] The actual degree of New Town dependence on either central London or on the rest of Greater London varies but is generally quite low. Thus Basildon, which was partly planned as a London dormitory centre has the highest proportion of its workers employed in the Greater London area while Stevenage, which has been highly successful in attracting industry of its own, has the lowest.

TABLE 4

COMMUTING FROM THE LONDON NEW TOWNS

	Distance to Central London		Percent Resident Workers Commuting	
New Town	*Miles*	*Average Rail Time (Mins.)*	*Greater London*	*Central London*
Basildon	25	33	13.9	6.2
Bracknell	30	55	3.6	1.3
Crawley	28	54	6.4	3.4
Harlow	20	33	9.4	3.8
Hemel Hempstead	24	31	6.1	2.7
Stevenage	27	45	2.8	1.3
Welwyn Gdn. City (and Hatfield)	22	31	6.4	3.8

Source: Thomas (1969), p. 379, and Census 1966.

A consideration of the question of social balance in the New Towns obviously depends on how the concept of a "balanced" community is defined. One view, as we have seen, can be traced to the utopian idealism of the garden city planners and envisages the mixing of people from different backgrounds in close residential proximity to each other. This was the policy adopted by the égalitarian Labour ideologists of the 1940s and by the first land-use planners of the New Towns. However, it emerged that this was not in accordance with what higher income groups in New Towns wanted, and in order to attract them the Development Corporations have had to provide more differentiated and socially segregated neighbourhoods. This has resulted in a social pattern typical of other English towns. As a sample survey of Crawley New Town found, "neighbourhoods built in the early stages of the New Town's growth, and clustering around the town centre, have more manual workers . . . than the newer neighbourhoods away from the centre."[33]

A rather broader concept of social balance involves a comparison of the socio-economic composition of the New Town population with that of the nation as a whole. Data from the 1968 Census show that while the social compositions of the individual New Towns are rather similar, there are systematic differences compared to the average for England and Wales. Thus, the New Towns taken together have a higher proportion of managers and professionals than the country as a whole (16.1 percent compared to 14.6 percent), more middle-ranking white collar workers (20.5 percent against 18.2 percent) and a much higher proportion of *higher income manual* workers (54.3 percent to 49.8 percent).[34] This is one important result of the Industrial Selection Scheme which operates in London matching people to jobs available in New Towns: The fact that they have fewer unskilled manual workers than England and Wales as a whole (5.3 percent compared to 8.1 percent) has therefore laid the New Towns open to the charge that they have not performed one of their original functions, that of helping in the solution to the housing and social problems of the most deprived areas of inner London.

Lessons, Innovations and the Reform of Planning

The two most important lessons learned from attempting to implement the Abercrombie plan have been, first, the necessity of keeping development plans as *flexible* as possible in order to accommodate short-term changes and, second, to integrate policies on land-use and transportation more closely.

Transport and Land Use

One predictable outcome of population growth and dispersal, the concentration of office jobs in Central London and the establishment of the Green Belt was more and longer journeys to work. In London's case these took place mostly by public transport, particularly by surface and underground railway. By the mid 1960s, therefore, London's commuting hinterland stretched for at least twenty-five miles around Charing Cross,[35] with almost 1.2 million people traveling daily into Central London. At the same time, however, the number of private cars in the London Region more than trebled to over three million, and by 1966 every third household in inner London and every second in the suburbs owned at least one car. Public transport, especially London's buses, was thus caught in a downward spiral. Passengers were lost to the private car, fares were raised and services cut to increase revenue and reduce costs. Thus, public transport became even less competitive with the car. The results of this cycle can be seen in the following table.

TABLE 5

PASSENGERS ENTERING LONDON EACH MORNING (000s)

	1957	*1962*	*1965*	*1967*
Public transport	1,043	1,097	1,041	1,032
Railways	785	883	861	860
Buses and coaches	258	215	180	172
Private transport	89	123	117	111
Cars	69	94	99	98
Motorcycles	20	29	18	13
Total	1,132	1,220	1,158	1,143

Source: P. G. Hall, *London 2000* (London: Faber and Faber, 1969), p. 159.

But the private individual who insists on driving into the centre of London has not done so without cost to himself and other motorists. Average traffic speeds in Central London were down to ten to twelve miles per hour by 1965 and conditions were only marginally eased by short-term palliatives like parking restrictions and one-way streets. The problem is that London's streets and roads lack the capacity for the amount of traffic that uses them. Hence the choice has become one of which sort of city Londoners want to pay for—a familiar and historic environment or a motorized city with motorways (expressways) cut through the existing urban fabric.

This was the essential question put by the Buchanan Report, *Traffic in Towns,* published in 1963.[36] Buchanan's solution depended on just that understanding of the relationships between land-use and transportation that had been lacking in the first development plans. The technique consisted of delimiting whole environmental areas within cities and assessing their capacity to bear traffic intrusion. In the short-run, traffic could be restricted and canalized along existing networks away from environmental precincts while a re-ordering of land uses coupled with highway building could secure longer term objectives. However, in 1961, the London County Council had already commissioned a costly *land-use transportation* study on the model of those carried out for Detroit and Chicago in the 1950s covering a Greater London area extending well beyond the Green Belt.

Predicting from known relationships between income growth and car ownership and from trip volumes between different land uses the London Traffic Survey, not surprisingly, foresaw huge future increases in travel demands. By 1981, there would be half as many cars in Greater London as in 1961, with proportionately more in the inner suburbs, resulting in a doubling of trips for optional purposes like journeys for personal business and social life, school and shopping. After assigning these demands to theoretical primary road networks the study concluded that a highway pattern, not unlike that of the Greater London Plan 1944, could best cope with expected flows.

Two of the main arguments eventually to be used by antagonists of these motorway proposals were that not enough consideration had been given to the *restraint* of motorists by charging them the full economic and social cost of driving in Central London and that the effects of new investments in public transport, especially the London underground, had not been taken into account. A report published in 1964 by the Ministry of Transport showed that the technical difficulties of *road pricing,* the direct charging of motorists for the use of congested roads, had been ironed out.[37] It has also been found that traditional accounting methods of assessing the viability of investment in public transport do not reveal the total situation. For example, the construction of London's newest tube, the Victoria Line (opened in 1969), running from Walthamstow in the northwest via Oxford Circus to Victoria Station and Brixton, was economically justified by making allowances for savings in surface traffic congestion and other social costs. Yet in normal accounting terms it will eventually "lose" some £3 million each year in maintenance and interest charges alone.[38]

Revised Development Plans

These social, economic and methodological changes affecting planning therefore warranted a new look being taken at the nature of the statutory system that had been operating since 1947. Reporting in 1965, a Planning Advisory Group showed how existing county and county borough development plans were so detailed and rigid that they soon became out of date.[39] Neither could they adequately show the interrelationship of traffic and land use. The group, therefore, suggested a completely new hierarchy of plans and the administrative decentralization of certain responsibilities for them. For the bigger urban centers and the counties there were to be *structure plans,* strategic in nature and much less detailed than existing development plans, allowing the Ministry of Housing to process them more efficiently. Then there would be detailed *local* plans for development control purposes and *action area* plans showing the programming of comprehensive development. Neither of these detailed plans would be submitted to central government. The Advisory Group also pointed out that in the biggest urban centres of all, the conurbations like Greater London, structure plans could not be prepared by numerous separate planning authorities but needed much more territorial coordination. In 1968, a new Town and Country Planning Act implemented most of the Group's recommendations on the nature and status of development plans.

LONDON GOVERNMENT AND PLANNING SINCE 1965

In April 1965, a complete reorganization of London's local government took place which had a profound impact on the way London is planned and on the assumptions that have guided planning policy. Out of a fragmented and confused pattern of local authorities of various shapes, sizes and status, emerged a two-tiered metropolitan government consisting of the Greater London Council with almost eight million inhabitants and thirty-two London boroughs ranging in population size from 146,000 to 340,000. This section traces the evolution of the new system from the report of the Royal Commission on Local Government in Greater London (1960), chaired by Sir Edwin (now Lord) Herbert; through the modifications made to its proposals by central government in the London Government Act 1963, to a description of how the new planning system works and a consideration of the Greater London Development Plan, published in 1969.

The Herbert Commission Model

The Royal Commission was to ". . . examine the present system and working of local government in the Greater London area; to recommend whether any and if so what changes in the local government structure and the distribution of local authority functions in the area would better secure effective and convenient local government. . . ."[40] The functions of London local government that the commission examined were extensive, ranging from education, housing, planning, welfare services, refuse collection and disposal and fire protection to relatively minor tasks such as licensing and weights and measures inspection. Three important metropolitan services—police, water supply and public transport—fell outside the commission's terms of reference since they were not performed by local authorities in London. But in 1970, control over them was in fact transferred from the London Transport Executive to the Greater London Council.

The *Review Area* of London, which the commission was given to deal with, proved more restrictive and often involved the commission in a rather tortuous logic to support its case for a metropolitan planning authority. The boundary ran roughly midway through the approved Green Belt, enclosing some 840 square miles of virtually continuously built-up territory whose population had been in absolute decline since the early 1950s.[41] Thus, although the commission succeeded well in showing the illogicality of the existing planning *structure* in London, it did not adequately analyse the nature of London's planning *needs* largely because it glossed over many of the implications of an inadequate socio-economic definition of its proposed new London-wide planning authority.

The territorial requirements of regional planning probably did not bulk large in the government's decision on the review area. The political impetus for the commission's inquiry stemmed from the need to find a solution to the demands for autonomous local government status of certain large, second-tier municipalities in the County of Middlesex.[42] This being an entirely urbanized county adjoining London to the northwest, a local government review had to take in a wider territory than Middlesex alone. Extending the review area to London within the Green Belt and no farther had two advantages so far as the Conservative Government, which set up the commission, was concerned. First, it provided an opportunity to include both the London County Council (a Labour Party stronghold and the greatest prize in English local politics) and the Conservative-voting suburbs of Greater London within the review territory. Secondly, the continuously built-up area provided a relatively clear-cut definition of London, unlike one based on patterns of social and economic interaction. This undoubtedly helped to reduce the antagonism toward reform of the counties surrounding the LCC and Middlesex whose metropolitan sectors, representing valuable population and taxable resources, were to be lost to a revised London local government.

The Herbert Commission advanced three main reasons why a Greater London Council should become the new planning authority for London. First, the population, employment and other projections upon which the Greater London Plan was based had been completely overtaken by events and no permanent body had been set up to monitor the effects of change on the underlying strategy. Secondly, while the whole review area was bound together by the retail, entertainment and employment attractions of Central London, it was, for purposes of town planning and main highways administration, fragmented among either authorities, and for housing into a bewildering ninety or more. There were also certain problems facing London that required area-wide coordination. One was the new and expanded towns program. Another was the housing redevelopment situation in the districts fringing the central area where obsolescence and overcrowding were most critical yet land for rebuilding most scarce. Finally, the commission explained the need for the integration of land use and major transportation planning powers in a single planning authority. The question remained as to whether the commission's review area was appropriate to the solution of these planning problems. Could a Greater London authority with a total area less than one-third the size of the Abercrombie Region draw up a new Greater London Plan? How would it plan the location of new housing in relation to investment in transportation links when the most important bulk carriers of travelers, British Railways and London Transport, would be outside its control? How would it reconcile the fact that most of the population growth in the southeast of England was taking place well beyond its boundaries (Fig. 5)?

The commission recognized its dilemma but stuck firmly to the principle that town and country planning was a vital function for a directly elected local authority for London to carry out. If land use planning passed to a Joint Board or to Central Government it would "fatally weaken" local government since control over land use underlay the provision of so many other local services. According to the commission there would be a *single* master plan for Greater London drawn up by the GLC alone. The GLC would also be the final arbiter of applications which conflicted with its plan or which related to the crucial central area of London.

The London Government Act 1963

The London Government Bill became law in 1963 after fierce, sustained opposition from the Labour Party, which accused the government of gerrymandering its power base in the LCC and of breaking up established and respected local

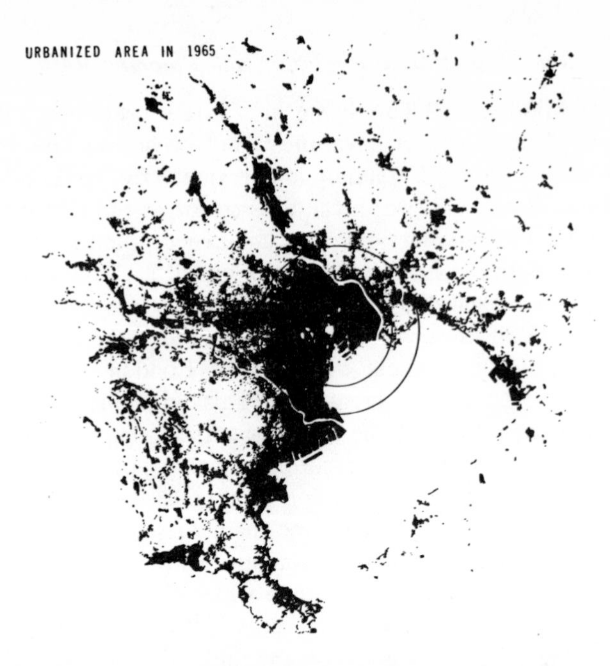

authority services. However, two important changes were made by the Conservatives to the commission's original proposals. First, the number of Boroughs was reduced from fifty-two to thirty-two and their average population thus raised to almost 250,000. The reason for this lay largely in the criticisms of educationists, led by the Ministry of Education itself, that the Herbert Commission's boroughs would be too small to carry out their suggested duties effectively. Also the education service of the LCC was to be preserved and in the centre of Greater London there was to be a single huge education authority, a special committee of the new GLC covering twelve London Boroughs to be known as the Inner London Education Authority (ILEA).[43]

This increased size and potential of the London Boroughs also persuaded the government to give them other powers not envisaged by the Herbert Commission. The most important of these entailed granting to each Borough the *full* status of a "local planning authority." Thus the responsibility for producing the new Greater London Development Plan (GLPD) was therefore divided between the GLC, the thirty-two London Boroughs and the City of London (as a borough). The GLC was to prepare the plan for London as a whole showing the general future patterns of population densities, employment location, amenity provision, areas of comprehensive redevelopment, and in particular the location of major road schemes. Once this plan had been approved by the Minister of Housing each Borough would draw up its Local Development Plan within the context of the sections of the GLDP relating to its area. But, and this represented yet another curb on the GLC's leadership in the planning sphere, the Minister and not the GLC was to judge whether Borough plans conformed to that for London as a whole. Arrangements for development control were much more complex than envisaged in the Herbert Report. No special provision was made for the crucial central area of London.[44]

The Context of Strategic and Local Planning in London

The authority of the Greater London Council extends over an area of some 620 square miles with an estimated population of 7.6 millions in 1970. In 1966, for which the latest census figures are available, the total population of 7.7 millions resided in 2.6 million households and there were some 4.6 million jobs located within the GLC boundaries. These figures are crude indicators of the *scale* of the responsibilities of the GLC which, in 1970, itself employed almost 37,000 people (not including 22,000 teachers working for the ILEA).

The council consists of one hundred directly elected members and sixteen aldermen appointed by the party winning at the polls. At the first election in 1964 the Labour Party, to its own surprise, won control of the GLC but lost it heavily to the Conservatives in 1967. The Conservatives won again in 1970 though with a less spectacular majority of seats.

If the comparison be made between the London Boroughs and their nearest equivalent in British local government, the county boroughs, then they are also exceptionally large and powerful bodies. Croydon and Lambeth (Fig. 6) are the largest with 1970 populations over 320,000, a level exceeded by only six urban authorities outside London. Labour won twenty of the thirty-two boroughs in 1964 but was stripped of power in all but the four in its core area of support (Southwark, Tower Hamlets, Newham and Barking) in 1967. In 1972, Labour regained control in an additional seventeen boroughs.

Thus, in terms of at least two parameters influencing the planning process, namely *size,* which broadly reflects ability to set up effective organisations for planning, and *politics,* which will influence planning policy, the London situation is characterized by powerful authorities at *both* levels of government and also a good deal of volatility in the sphere of political control. This division of functions between GLC and boroughs is most succinctly shown in table form:

A. Functions Shared by the GLC and the London Boroughs

Function	*GLC*	*Boroughs*
Town Planning	Structure plan; strategic development control	Local plans; local development control
Housing	Overspill; interborough transfers; record of housing needs	Housing authorities in own areas
Highways and Traffic Management	Authority for defined metropolitan roads; major traffic management	Authority for all except trunk and Metropolitan roads; local parking schemes
Environmental, Health	Refuse disposal; main sewers	Refuse collection; local drainage
Open Space	Large parks; sports centres	Local parks

B. Functions Under Exclusive Control of the GLC or the Boroughs

Function	*Control*	
Public transport (buses and underground)	GLC	
Education	ILEA in 12 inner boroughs	20 outer boroughs

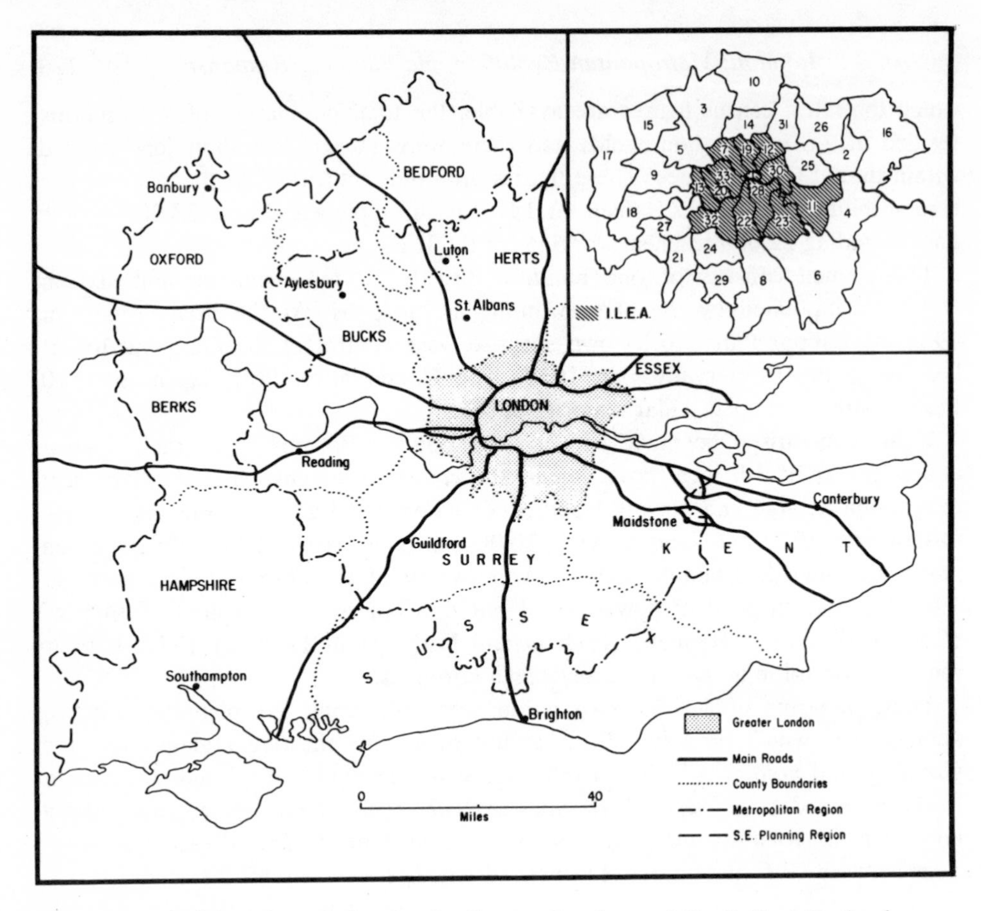

FIG. 6 The administration of planning in Greater London and South East England.

1. City of London
2. Barking
3. Barnet
4. Bexley
5. Brent
6. Bromley
7. Camden
8. Croydon
9. Ealing
10. Enfield
11. Greenwich
12. Hackney
13. Hammersmith
14. Haringey
15. Harrow
16. Havering
17. Hillingdon
18. Hounslow
19. Islington
20. Kensington and Chelsea
21. Kingston Upon Thames
22. Lambeth
23. Lewisham
24. Merton
25. Newham
26. Redbridge
27. Richmond
28. Southwark
29. Sutton
30. Tower Hamlets
31. Waltham Forest
32. Wandsworth
33. Westminster

Function	*Control*	
Ambulance Service	GLC	
Fire Service	GLC	
Building control	GLC: inner London	20 outer boroughs
Research and Intelligence	GLC	
Personal Health		32 boroughs
Welfare		32 boroughs
Child Care		32 boroughs
Libraries		32 boroughs

Thus to the GLC went the strategic or metropolitan-wide functions like land-use and transportation planning and also major spending powers in highways and, to a lesser extent, housing. In 1970, the GLC's direct financial responsibilities were considerably enhanced when it took control of the £117 million ($292,-000,000) per year revenue account of London Transport. The London Boroughs on the other hand are *social welfare* and *housing* authorities, but they are also statutory *town planning* authorities with duties to draw up *local* development plans and decide on certain classes of planning applications.

Several interpretations of strategic and local planning have been made. Within the GLC there was the fusion of the town planning and highways departments into the Department of Planning and Transportation in October 1969, and it is still too early to tell whether a workable synthesis of the approaches of town planners, architects and traffic and highway engineers will evolve. There is also a current attempt to extend the scope of planning with the introduction of PPBS (Planning Programming and Budgeting Systems). Perhaps the most promising step toward broadening the range of concern of traditional town planning was taken in 1969 with the appointment of an economic historian with expertise in demography, to the position of Chief Planner, Strategy.

At the local level there have also been some isolated attempts to integrate the Boroughs' particular package of responsibilities into a broader concept of planning. This has taken the form of Corporate Planning or long-range matching of resources to needs or the coordination of information systems on housing, social welfare and town planning.

Strategic planning was first defined in terms of development plans. The GLC was to prepare a *metropolitan structure map* showing the main physical and economic characteristics of its area, the principal uses to which land would be put, the distribution of population and the proposed communications system. After the GLDP had been approved by the Minister, each of the London Boroughs and the City of London would prepare development plans for their areas. Each local plan was to be drawn within the framework of the GLDP, forwarded to the GLC for its observations and passed to the Minister for final approval. Both the GLC and the Boroughs were empowered to make *action area plans,* the new terminology for maps relating to comprehensive development areas.

The second definition of strategic planning worked through the development control regulations. Here the London Government Act defined two sorts of relationship between the GLC and the Boroughs. Applications for development relating to the following sorts of area were to be decided by the GLC:

(i) those relating to specified Comprehensive Development Areas, among them Stepney-Poplar, Bermondsey, the South Bank and Knightsbridge Green, Kensington.
(ii) those relating to the GLC's transportation responsibilities including development within 220 feet of a metropolitan road; shopping centres over 250,000 square feet and places of public assembly (sports arenas, etc.), with a capacity over 2,500 people.
(iii) applications to extract minerals on a large scale.[45] In all other cases the Boroughs were generally empowered to make decisions. The development control system is now operated by a form of "gentleman's agreement" between GLC and Boroughs as a result both of early experience in practice and pressure from the boroughs for more local discretion.

The London Boroughs have to some extent also influenced the method and the content of the Greater London Development Plan itself. In March 1966, the GLC, after consultations with the boroughs, issued a preliminary plan report entitled "The Purpose and Nature of the Greater London Development Plan." The London Boroughs Association was successful in getting references to the testing of the economic viability of the GLDP deleted on the grounds that they were time consuming and it also disagreed with the proposed use of mathematical planning models as being too experimental.

The Greater London Development Plan

The statutory Greater London Development Plan (GLDP) actually consists of a written statement and a large-scale map of proposals. Figure 6 shows a generalised draft version of this map. An accompanying essay entitled *Tomorrow's London* provides a non-technical background to the GLDP and a weighty *Report of Studies* presents the research that went into the plan.

The GLDP has been the object of considerable controversy and criticism. It has been attacked both for its vagueness on some issues, namely homes, and its definitiveness on others, like roads and office development, as not providing a sufficiently long-term, imaginative new structure for London that the boroughs can work towards; and as favouring isolationist solutions to London's problems in relation to the rest of southeast England.[46] Then as a *coup de grâce* in late 1969, the Labour Minister of Housing, responding to protests over the road proposals in the plan, took the unusual step of setting up an independent statutory inquiry to examine over 22,000 separate objections to the GLDP and, if necessary, to recommend alternative strategies. The London Government Act states this GLDP is in effect an interim plan. It is not complete until the Boroughs have produced local plans within its approved strategic framework. But whether the GLC has provided a sufficiently strong lead and whether it can persuade the Boroughs to accept its vision of London is still in doubt.

It can be seen from Figure 6 that in many respects the GLC do not propose any bold restructuring of London as was contained in the wartime plans. A strong focus on the centre is maintained, the relationship between residences and work places will remain broadly the same and the Green Belt stands inviolable. A number of diverse "Areas of Special Character," ranging from the Government Precinct in Whitehall, the Central London parks and the Bloomsbury Squares to Thames-side reaches, historic Greenwich and Epping Forest are listed as being "essential to preserve." The statement notes, however, that the GLC can only set out policy guidelines for such areas as the detailed decisions in most of them will be taken by the London Borough Councils.[47] A theory of accessibility to public open space is described in the statement but there are no firm proposals for areas chronically deprived of neighbourhood parks and amenities like north Southwark, Hackney and Tower Hamlets; and the statement merely notes the GLC's part in three ad hoc schemes of regional recreation.

The firmest proposals in the whole plan are those for new motorways and shopping complexes, though the two are not clearly integrated. Arguing that when schemes currently in progress are completed London will be well served by a number of major *radial* routes, the GLC sees an immediate need for three encircling urban *Ringwcys* to facilitate suburb to suburb movement and divert traffic away from the centre. Ringway I cuts through the residential areas of inner London, Ringway 2 at about seven miles from the centre passes through the interwar suburbs, and Ringway 3 circles the built-up area about twelve miles from Central London. Originally programmed for completion by the early 1980s, this vast and disruptive undertaking, costing at least £2,000 million ($5 billion) at 1970 prices, is now planned over a thirty-year period following public outcry over the proposals.[48] In addition to concern over the destruction of homes and the deterioration of environmental standards that the Ringways will entail, there has been considerable indignation at the failure of the GLDP to put forward a considered statement on London's great asset, its public transport infrastructure, as a complement or alternative to private motorisation.

Population and Employment

Reversing decades, even centuries of thinking on the optimum size for London, the main objective of the GLDP is now *to slow down* the rate of decline of London's population. If current trends continue the planners find that the population of the GLC area, which stood at 7.9 million in 1966, could be down to 7.0 million by 1981. If this were allowed to happen London's resident labour force would fall by 700,000, most of the outflow consisting of skilled, better educated and more productive workers. The strategy, therefore, is to provide for a population "which is not so great as to militate against good living conditions nor so small that it gives rise to difficulties in the maintenance of the labour force."[49] The target population is thus put at between 7.1 and 7.3 million people by 1981, consisting of a population decline of 600,000 in inner London and a stable population in the suburbs.

This projection is made on the basis of an assessment of future housing capacity in Greater London until 1981 and a calculation of the population that can be thereby accommodated. The assumption is that planning can do little to change the amount of housing that will be available since the statement nowhere indicates what proportion of the finite amount of land within the GLC area should be allocated for residential purposes among all competing uses.[50] Such an approach requires, of course, a firm statement of priorities for the plan based on a policy commitment to adequate housing and not merely a quantification of the inevitable.

The GLC is equally concerned at the outflow of workers of a certain sort from London which causes labour shortages in some sectors and the employment of inefficient workers in others. In contrast to the housing situation the Council proposes to do more toward a solution to this problem, namely allocating more space for office development. Two justifications are given for this policy. One is that the planners believe they have shown that enterprises are more efficient in Greater London due to advantages of concentration, and thus a worker in London adds more to national output than elsewhere. The other is that the continuing outflow of resident workers could increase the volume of commuting into London.

Central London

Central London is defined as the area bound by the main line railway stations of Victoria, Paddington, King's Cross and Waterloo. It is in many ways the key to the GLC's role as strategic planning authority. Most of the 1.3 million jobs in the

FIG. 7 The City of London from Westminster Bridge. *B. Lessware*

area are classified as serving national or head office interests. Its importance to the national economy is shown by the contributions of the City of London and tourist services to the balance of payments. The banking, insurance and brokerage institutions of the city earn over £200 million ($500 million) in "invisible exports," ninety percent of Britain's four million overseas visitors go to London and three-quarters of them stay at the centre close to London's rich collection of theatres, concert halls, art galleries, museums and historic buildings.[51] All but a tiny proportion of the central area labour force commutes to work each day, 300,000 of them coming from beyond the GLC boundary altogether. Nevertheless, of the quarter of a million people who do live in the central area, many exist on low incomes in sub-standard public housing or in high-rent private accommodation only because they are within walking distance, or a cheap public transport fare, of their jobs.

Conflicts among competing land uses and different activities are therefore at their most acute in Central London and it is the main task of strategic planning to decide which activities and services have a vital need for a central location and which could be moved out altogether, either to London suburbs or further afield. However, the lack of an agreed *regional* framework for development, the paucity of research on linkages among activities in Central London and the division of responsibilities for the area between the GLC and six other planning authorities all appear to have contributed to the weakness of proposals for the centre contained in the GLDP. Following the ban on office development in 1964 and the granting of a government subsidy for hotels, residential and university precincts such as Bloomsbury were invaded by offices and hotels. The GLDP now allocates about 4 percent more office space for Central London, a move facilitated

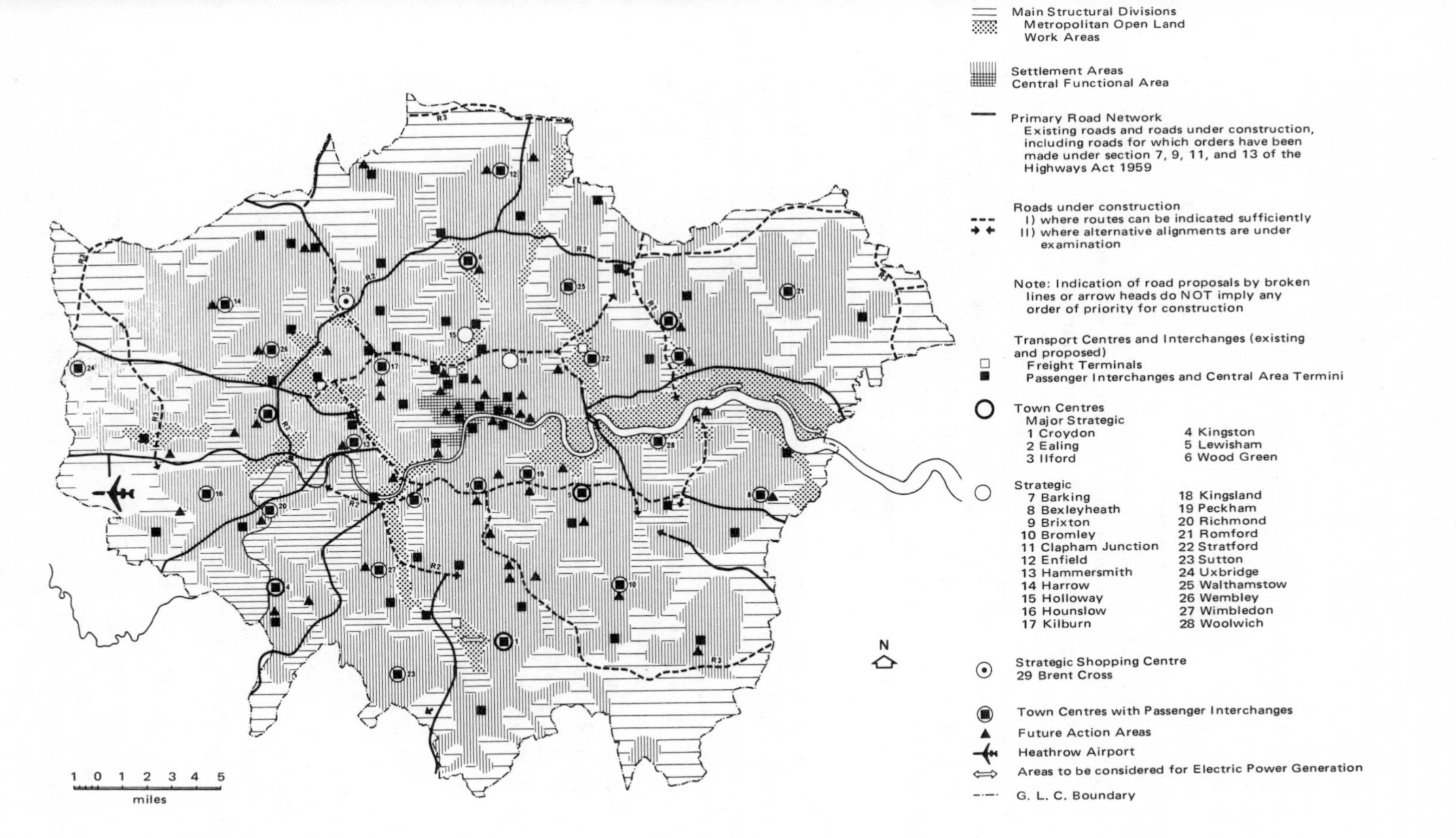

FIG. 8 A simplified version of the Metropolitan Structure Map produced for the Greater London Development Plan, March 1969. This was the stage at which the draft plan was sent to the London borough councils before its submission to the Minister of Housing for final approval. In December 1969, the government announced its intention of setting up a statutory inquiry to hear public objections to the plan. *Greater London Council Planning Department*

by the raising of the exemption limits of the 1964 office building controls on the return of a Conservative Government in 1970.[52] Yet nowhere in the GLDP are the detailed consequences of this proposal spelled out. The City of London skyline is already despoiled by "spotty" office buildings (Fig. 7) and Piccadilly Circus and Covent Garden, landmarks for the overseas tourist, are threatened with total redevelopment. A policy of office location clearly related to the current modernisation of main line railway stations is also a necessary part of a strategic plan for Central London.

Firmer plans do exist for particular parts of Central London but again the GLDP lacks an imaginative and integrated approach to each area as part of the whole Central London system. For example, of the fifty-six *Action Areas* scheduled in the GLDP, fifteen are located in the centre (Fig. 8). Included are the redevelopment of Piccadilly Circus for improved vehicular movement and the segregation of pedestrians from traffic; plans for the commercial, cultural and luxury residential development of the Covent Garden site when the fruit and vegetable market completes its move to Vauxhall, South London; and a new transportation interchange at Victoria Station linking Heathrow and Gatwick airports. The GLDP also designates seven *Areas of Special Character* where care must be taken to preserve the environment and certain buildings of historical and architectural value. These include the Whitehall-Trafalgar square area, the Royal parks, the Tower of London area, the Bloomsbury squares and the London University quarters.

Finally, on the disturbing question of housing and employment for the lower paid and working class residents of Central London, the GLDP is totally inadequate, offering only the suggestion of "multiple purpose" buildings to the boroughs who must grapple with an acute housing problem. The Borough of Westminster, for example, views the situation in terms of the decision to rehouse people on its own astronomically expensive land or whether to encourage them to move out of the centre altogether. The likely consequence of the latter course is one of worsening employment problems in the low wage service jobs that are vital to the functioning of Central London such as those in restaurants, theatres, hotels and office cleaning. The people doing these jobs need to live in or close to the centre because they are dependent on public transport to get them to work.

The Borough of Southwark has clashed with the GLC over the redevelopment of dock land at King's Reach and Hay's Wharf near London Bridge. As the port activities of London move down river, valuable land is becoming available for redevelopment and manual employment is disappearing. Offices, hotels and luxury apartments command the highest return and the GLC has approved private applications for major speculations of this kind. Such developments do nothing to help solve the chronic housing problems of boroughs like Southwark, nor will the high priced accommodation that will result be within the incomes of the teachers, nurses and social workers needed in inner London.

Housing and Social Stress in Inner London

The GLDP recognizes two aspects of London's housing situation as lying within its strategic responsibility. These are the stark contrasts in housing needs and opportunities that exist between the crowded inner boroughs and the suburban ones, and the concentration of chronic housing and social stress into four large districts within the inner area.

Over two-fifths of London's population live on one-fifth of the residential land surface represented by the ILEA area and the boroughs of Haringey and Newham. Land shortage is the critical problem and since the redevelopment of schools, roads and other facilities alongside homes means that only one family in three can be rehoused in the inner area, the GLC accepts the inevitability of substantial population decline. Where the families who are moved out will go to is barely considered in the GLDP. About 60,000 people will go to Thamesmead, a form of "new-town-in-town" on a Thames-side site on Plumpstead Marshes some nine miles east of Central London. This joint Greenwich/Bexley Borough and GLC scheme will provide work for one-third of its work force and the rest will travel elsewhere, mostly to the centre. Once again an attempt is being made to encourage a socially mixed population with possibilities for home ownership and water sports facilities. The general problem of population decentralization remains, yet the GLDP contains no clear directions to the suburban boroughs to raise their residential densities in the interest of inner London nor does it commit itself to the new generation of new towns like Milton Keynes and Peterborough.

Undoubtedly the most urgent problem facing London at present concerns four "Housing Stress Areas" which lie close to the centre of the city. To the west, spreading across the borough boundaries of Brent, Kensington and Chelsea, Hammersmith and Westminster and to the north in Islington, Camden, Haringey and Hackney are the areas of working class and immigrant settlement. The people here mostly live in large, crowded Victorian dwellings subdivided and rented furnished by the landlord.[53] The other two areas—the northern parts of Tower Hamlets and Newham and of Southwark and Lambeth south of the Thames—are different. For the most part, these are stable, working-class districts where people work locally in the declining manufacturing industries. Physical dilapidation of homes is on the whole greatest here with large numbers lacking basic amenities like a bath or inside lavatory. In all four areas are found London's pockets of poverty, deprivation and homelessness.

The GLDP calls for the greatest housing effort to be directed toward these areas, if necessary with Central Government support while the Report of Studies emphasises that different strategies are required in each zone. In the northern and western areas the main objective is the relief of overcrowding and the conversion and rehabilitation of existing dwellings. In the zone east of the city wholesale redevelopment is necessary while in the south combinations of all these actions are needed.

A physical solution to housing problems of this scale will inevitably take time and it is therefore important to take a strategic view of the social stresses which correlate with poor standards of built environment. Thousands of young children, for example, are destined to spend all their formative years in substandard conditions. Unemployment among adolescents, particularly West Indian youths, is currently creating a sense of aimlessness and alienation which expresses itself in crime. The Plowden Report pointed out the educational inequalities that have arisen in these inner city areas as a result of the priorities of postwar town planning:

> Some of these neighbourhoods have for generations been starved of new schools, new houses and new investment of every kind. Everyone knows this, but for year after year priority has been given to the new towns and new suburbs, because if new schools do not keep pace with the new houses some children will be unable to go to school at all.[54]

Following the Plowden recommendations and government provision of a limited amount of extra resources for such schools, the Inner London Education Authority has successfully defined 150 "Education Priority Areas" in inner London[55] as eligible for extra funds for buildings and teaching staff to provide a "compensatory environment."

Participation, Inquiry and Protest

Following the publication of the Skeffington Report on public involvement in the planning process,[56] the GLC held a number of public meetings in different parts of London to explain the GLDP and elicit local response. As they presented the public with something of a fait accompli these meetings were inevitably little more than a public relations exercise, though they did raise practical issues such as what is actually meant by public participation in planning and how, if at all, it can be achieved within existing administrative structures.[57] More pertinently, the localised and detailed nature of public concern over the GLDP raised the question of how the interested, but non-expert layman can relate to the conceptual structures of a strategic metropolitan plan.

These questions were brought into sharper focus when the nature and procedures of the statutory inquiry into the GLDP, which began work late in 1970, became clearer. In place of the usual inquiry by a planning inspector, a five-man *panel* was appointed under the chairmanship of Mr. Frank Layfield, Q.C. Despite the support of expert "assessors," the panel conducted the inquiry in legalistic style. The GLC briefed counsel to defend its plan against all comers. Those who opposed the plan or elements in it and could not afford representation were often subjected to aggressive cross-questioning from the "defence." Once again, the main problem was the concept of strategic planning for, if an objection could be interpreted as raising local issues, it was then more easily dismissed. However, it was often impossible to disentangle the local from the wider issues and the law proved scarcely more adept at this than the planners had previously been.

By March 1972, over 400 proofs of evidence, 1,300 support papers and nearly 600 background papers had been submitted to the panel. Transcript of the daily proceedings to that point covered some 150,000 pages. And, in the course of the probing by the panel and expert witnesses, there has been a substantial revision by the GLC of its proposals on general strategy, population size and dispersal, housing and employment.[58]

Early in the proceedings the GLC came under fire from two opposing directions on its proposal for a 1981 Greater London population of 7.3 millions. A number of inner London boroughs and the City of London objected that the GLC was accepting decline too readily and that the statement did not contain enough positive proposals for restraining out-migration. In complete contrast the South East Economic Planning Council, the Town and Country Planning Association and certain outer Boroughs contended that the current rate of decline should be maintained or even increased. By early 1972, however, it appeared that population trends were confirming the opinions of the population decline group, for preliminary analyses of the 1971 census showed that net out-migration had been higher than expected and that the GLC planners might have to accept a 1981 population as low as 6.8 millions. The GLC planner's case for restraint has emerged in the inquiry as resting on three main hypotheses. First, London is a highly efficient production centre with lower average costs than other parts of the country. An indiscriminate decline in its labour force would not be in the national interest. Secondly, since those who are leaving London are mostly from the younger, more skilled, middle income groups, a "social polarization" of inner London neighbourhoods is likely to occur, manifesting itself in residential enclaves of the very rich and the very poor. Thirdly, the GLC considers that if London's population were to decline too far the per capita cost of providing essential city services will rise or the quality of service will decline. But as the inquiry proceeded, the GLC witnesses were forced to admit that available evidence on the first two assumptions was at present either inadequate or was capable of an opposite interpretation. The GLC has therefore rested its case on the third hypothesis and that of the future problems of a crude labour shortage. Yet even here it is still not clear to what extent the costs in terms of loss of local revenues might be matched by the benefits of less congestion and less pressure on land resources that is purported to follow a decline in population.

Almost nine out of every ten of the 20,000 objections to the GLDP concerned its transport proposals, more particularly the Ringways scheme. The most sophisticated and successful opposition to the proposals has come from two highly organised and expert voluntary groups, the London Motorway Action Group and the London Amenity and Transport Association, which have challenged the GLC's assumptions, documented the strategic consequences of its proposals and presented alternative solutions to London's transport problems.[59] Their case rests not on outright opposition to the total roads package but more specifically to Ringway 1, and the neglect of public transport. The choice as they see it is between spending at least £1,000 million ($2,500,000,000) on Ringway 1 and high capacity for Ringway 2 or investment in an improved public transport system including more buses, new underground lines and improvements to the suburban surface rail system.

THE REGIONAL FRAMEWORK

According to the Royal Commission on London Government an important argument for a Greater London authority was that it would draw up the successor to the Greater London Plan of 1944; neither its geography nor its powers have permitted the GLC to do that. The real successors in scale and status (for they too are advisory not statutory plans) are *The South East Study* (1964), the *Strategy for the South East* (1967) and the *Strategic Plan for the South East* (1970). These three represent a decade of dialogue and dispute on the nature of plans and planning to be carried out at the regional level, the part that London should play within the South East and the best physical urban form to accommodate the huge population growth envisaged for the region down to 1991.

The South East Study

The South East Study was the work of a team of planners within the Ministry of Housing and Local Government. Done with the express purpose of re-examining the Abercrombie assumptions, it both continued one line of thinking contained in the earlier regional plan and abandoned part of it. It still saw the need to hold employment growth down within London (particularly in the services sector), to decentralise jobs that did not need a London location and to overspill at least one million people from the conurbation in order to relieve the housing shortage. But the study also considered that the tide of economic growth in the South East generally was so strong that a realistic plan had to accommodate that growth within the London region, since it was taking place *despite* government efforts to steer manufacturing employment to the development areas.

The task was therefore to find land for homes for an extra 3.5 million people by 1981.[60] The Ministry planners made the bold proposal that roughly one-third of this growth should go into a "second generation" of new and expanded towns, of a sufficient size and distance from London to generate growth of their own and thereby actually reduce the attractive force of the capital within the South East and the country as a whole. Accordingly the Study proposed three "counter magnets" to London at Southampton-Portsmouth, Newbury and Bletchley, each to expand eventually by 150–250,000 people. Smaller scale town expansions were recommended to take place at Stansted, Ashford, Ipswich, Northampton, Peterborough and Swindon. Despite criticisms from the development areas which saw the Study proposals as enhancing the prosperity of the south at their expense, the new Labour Government of 1964 designated three new growth points under the New Towns Act—Milton Keynes (renamed for Bletchley),[61] Northampton and Peterborough. Each was to receive an additional 70,000 people by 1981. Newbury is expanding on a much smaller scale in conjunction with the Greater London Council's own overspill program while the biggest proposal of all for a "Solent City" has been the subject of a detailed plan.

Economic Planning Council and Standing Conference

The renewed interest in regional planning generated by *The South East Study* engendered a response from both Central Government and the local planning authorities. On assuming power the Labour Government devolved some of the responsibility for the initiation of national development policy onto eight Regional Economic Planning Councils and Boards under the aegis of a new central department for national economic planning, the Department of Economic Affairs. At the same time the local planning authorities in the South East strengthened their own machinery for coordinating physical planning across their boundaries and renamed it the Standing Conference on London and South East Regional Planning.

The South East Economic Planning Council, a purely advisory body, is one of the eight regional arms of the Department of Economic Affairs. It consists of individuals chosen not as regional representatives but for their knowledge of regional life in industry, labour relations, commerce and the universities. Its official role is to advise a regional board of civil servants from a number of Ministries in Whitehall on regional planning matters.

In 1967, the Economic Planning Council offered nothing less than a complete strategic physical plan of its area of 10,600 square miles and population of 17 million. Significantly, the emphasis in its *Strategy for the South East* had shifted even further from earlier restrictionist policies for the development of the London region. At a time when the national economy remained depressed the Council

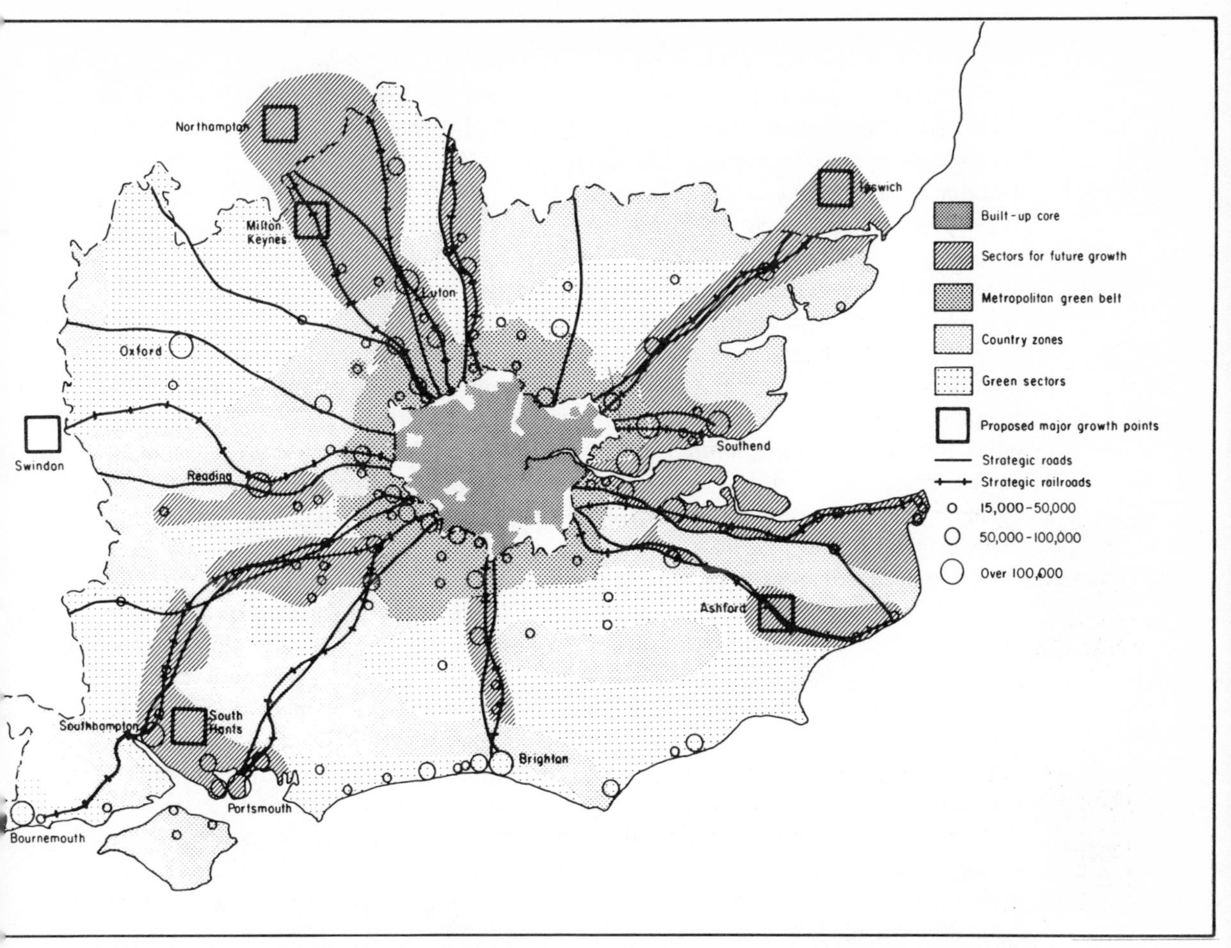

FIG. 9 The Strategy for the South East of the South East Economic Planning Council. Existing and firmly planned elements of regional structure are combined with a new emphasis on six centres of sectoral growth along transport routes to break out of the traditional concentric basis of regional plans.

called its strategy "a sober assessment of what needs to be done if the region is to continue to make its major contribution to the country's economy."[62]

The objective of its plan was twofold. First, to make provision for an additional 2.14 million people expected in the region by 1981 which it projected would be distributed as follows:

	1964		1971		1981	
	No.	*Percent*	*No.*	*Percent*	*No.*	*Percent*
Greater London	7.99	47.5	7.94	44.9	8.01	42.2
Outer Metropolitan Area	4.82	28.6	5.36	30.3	5.90	31.0
Outer South East	4.02	23.9	4.40	24.9	5.60	29.5
South East Region	16.83		17.69		18.97	

Figures in millions.
Source: Strategy for the South East, p. 4.

Secondly, the Council predicted a growing need to economise on scarce labour in the region since projections of demographic structure showed a rising proportion of dependent age groups in the population, namely the very young and the aged. Labour shortages would be particularly acute within Greater London where a decline of 9 percent (500,000) in the working age population was forecast for 1981. As a result, a number of contingencies had to be planned for. Among them was the prospect of serious problems in providing essential services in the inner London area; the likelihood that demand for labour in London could result in a renewed "drift to the South" from other parts of Britain; and that long-distance commuting to Central London would increase. Hence the Council produced a strategy which it felt would make "more efficient use of available manpower and . . . reduce employment pressures in London. . . ."[63]

In complete contrast to the traditionally perceived pattern of concentric rings, it proposed *sectors* of urban growth arrayed around London along the main transportation lines. Three major sectors were to terminate in the "counter-magnet" cities proposed in *The South East Study* and inter-sectoral county zones would be preserved between for agriculture and recreation. A concession to existing planning thought was that the Metropolitan Green Belt was still to be retained in its original form (Fig. 9).

The alleged advantages of this strategy were as follows: first, it built upon current public investment in the electrification of railways and the motorway program. Secondly, it recognised current planning policy on the containment of Greater London and the dispersal of population to the second generation of new towns, but in addition, unlike *The South East Study,* it also made provision for the "unplanned" growth that was expected to take place in the Outer Metropolitan Area. Finally, rapid mobility along the urbanised sectors both to London and the terminal cities would both widen the range of job opportunities to workers and enhance accessibility to London upon which a good deal of the growth potential of the South East was based. The Council drew extensively on the experience of plans for other world capitals including Copenhagen, Paris, Stockholm and Washington.[64]

The Council's report drew a quick reaction from the local planning authorities across the South East. They considered that the Planning Council represented nobody but itself, had not done regional economic planning at all but had infringed upon their physical planning responsibilities and had moved too quickly to establish a single "best" plan for the London region.

The progress of the Standing Conference (SC) of planning authorities, on the other hand, had been slower and more exploratory. Since 1962, the Conference had issued an impressive series of trend reports on the region culminating in July 1967 in three "hypothesised sketches" for a regional plan.[65] The Conference Technical Panel explicitly rejected the idea of radials of growth focused on London. It contended that such a plan would further accelerate the dominance of London and was not sensitive enough to the needs of agriculture and settlement between the radials. Instead the strategies offered by the SC were variants on a different theme. These involved several distinct clusters of growth located at various distances from Greater London (Fig. 10).

Evaluation

Faced with radically conflicting plans and hypotheses on how the South East should develop over the next few decades, the Secretary of State for Economic Affairs sought a means to satisfy the honor of both the Planning Council and the Standing Conference. He did so by calling for an evaluation of work done to

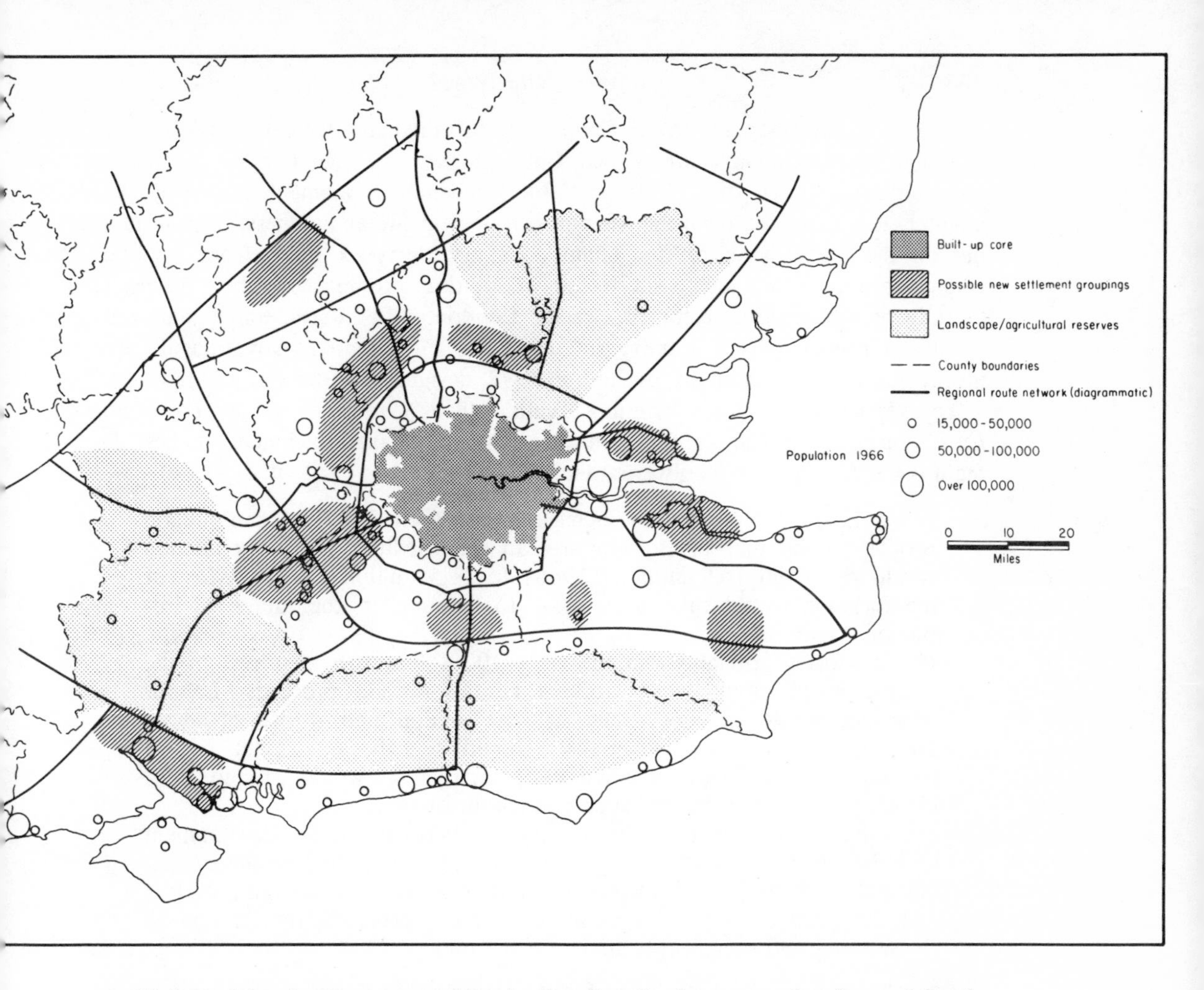

FIG. 10 One of the sketches prepared by the Standing Conference on London and South East Regional Planning to accommodate a population of twenty-three million in the Conference area by the year 2000. Settlement is here grouped very close to London, much of it within the approved Green Belt. Other sketches experimented with clusters of growth of various sizes, but all large enough to develop high levels of specialisation and functional linkage within them.

date with the object of providing an agreed regional framework for local authority planning and government decisions on investment and economic and social policies for the region. In May 1968, therefore, a South East Joint Planning Team was called together representing the Department of Economic Affairs, the Ministry of Housing, the SEEPC and the SC. Included in the Joint Team was the widest range of planning talent ever assembled in Britain—economists, geographers, architects, sociologists, engineers and town planners from the departments and organisations concerned.

Quite separately from these issues of regional strategy an intense controversy had blown up over the location of the Third London Airport to relieve Heathrow, and after protests from agricultural and residential interests the Labour Government in 1968 abandoned the long-standing plans to expand Stansted Airport in Essex.

A Commission (the Roskill Commission) was set up to investigate alternative sites from a social, economic and civil aviation point of view. At the risk of engendering a "megalopolis" from London to Birmingham the Commission chose a village in Buckinghamshire named Cublington as the location for an airport and supporting town of 100,000.[66] Colin Buchanan, a member of the Roskill Commission, dissented from this view in favour of a site at Foulness, a bleak mud flat on the north bank of the Thames estuary thirty-six miles from London. Buchanan argued that such a site would, in addition, promote growth in the traditionally poorer eastern sector of Greater London. After considerable and well-organised pressure from country interests, the Conservative Government gave up the quest for an inland airport and, in 1972, designated Foulness.

The report of the Joint Planning Team, called *Strategic Plan for the South East,* appeared in June 1970.[67] In the light of detailed technical studies the main issues facing the region were found to be:

> (a) a long-term population increase of between four and five million people by the end of the century. In the medium range, population would rise from 16.9 million (1966) to 21.5 million (2001). Most of the increase would take place near to London in the Outer Metropolitan Area;
> (b) a shortage of labour in the early 1970s but with an arrest in the decline in the number of workers as the decade proceeds. Labour shortages would be most acute within London and a rise of about 100,000 workers travelling in daily should be expected. In the rest of the region it could be assumed that employment would expand sufficiently to meet the increased supply of labour there;
> (c) conflicts in the region's countryside between urban development and the need to conserve large tracts of open country, promote agricultural productivity and safeguard mineral resources (sands and gravels);
> (d) the need to resolve regional inequalities, especially in relation to the housing and social problems of inner London.

Two alternative spatial strategies for accommodating these changes and objectives were evaluated. One was based on the "corridor and counter-magnet" proposals of the South East Economic Planning Council. The other placed population and employment growth closer to London, rather like the strategies suggested by the Standing Conference. Evaluation was based in part on a quantitative computer model which assigned and worked out the costs of road traffic flows among different population patterns, but also important in the selection of the eventual strategy were the results of a study on the mobility of industrial establishments in the London region. This showed that while the movement of manufacturing firms had been surprisingly extensive, over 60 percent of such moves had taken place within less than twenty miles of existing urban centres, including London.

The plan adopted therefore bore more resemblance to the predilections of the Standing Conference, clustering most of the growth within the London Metropolitan Region. Five major growth centres were chosen; the two other areas of big increases were suggested (Milton Keynes-Northampton, and the twin centered counter-magnet of Southampton-Portsmouth), and eight medium scale growth areas were also singled out—five close to London and three in the outer region.

Despite a projected doubling of private vehicles in South East England between 1966 and 1981 (from 3.1 million cars to 7.1 million), and a 50 percent rise in trip-making of all kinds, this strategy represented a confirmation of the traditional faith of British planners in concentrated urban forms over the more dispersed types which attempt to accommodate maximum locational choice and individual mobility. Urban concentration was found to favour the growth of large labour markets with diverse skills and wide-ranging job opportunities, promote the development of specialist service activities and social/welfare facilities, provide an adequate threshold for efficient public transport systems and reduce the impact of urban growth on the existing tracts of open countryside in the region.

CONCLUSION: THE LAYFIELD REPORT

The Report of the Panel of Inquiry on the Greater London Development Plan (the Layfield Report) was published late in February 1973 and received considerable attention from both national and local media. The substantive planning recommendations made in the report commanded most publicity, especially the road and transport proposals. The Panel accepted, and the government in a statement to the House of Commons, supported the principle of the inner motorway box (Ringway 1) for London with important changes of line to the original route and recommendations for additional tunneling in attractive residential areas. Other significant policy proposals made in the report include the improvement of public transport and further restrictions on car parking in Central London; the greater use of compulsory purchase and large-scale rehabilitation of private residential property in the housing stress areas; more control over the scale and bulk of office developments in Central London and the rezoning of suitable Green Belt land for residential purposes. Finally, the Panel found that Greater London's population will decline to between 6.37 and 6.55 millions by 1981 (compared to the GLC planned figure of 7.3 million), but was not convinced that the socio-economic implications of this trend would be as serious as envisaged in some quarters.

These specific elements of planning strategy naturally aroused immediate interest but the Panel also made searching criticisms of the administration of planning in London, paying particular attention to the nature of *Structure Plans* in the metropolitan context. Its observations in this sphere have considerable relevance for the future of urban and regional planning in Britain, for in 1974 new metropolitan planning authorities for major urban areas, based on the London model, and new county planning authorities elsewhere will supersede the old ones as a consequence of the Local Government Act 1972.

After reviewing the generally uncoordinated elements in the recent history of planning legislation, the Panel came to the conclusion that *Structure Planning* was, if not entirely impossible, an exceedingly difficult concept to apply in the unique situation of Greater London. Three reasons were given. The first was the size and complexity of London which made it "impossible to obtain information about its problems, to analyze them and to make proposals in a manner similar to that for any other urban area in the country."[68] The Panel acknowledged the considerable resources of planning manpower and skill that have been built up in Greater London since 1965 and suggests that if ". . . the G.L.C. could only, with the greatest difficulty, and after extensions of time, produce a plan containing relatively limited information, diffuse aims and vague policies, the chances of success for those structure plans presented by local authorities lacking the resources and skilled manpower of the G.L.C. must be open to doubt."[69] Are we to conclude from this that metropolitan planning is impossible? At several places in the body of the report, particularly in connection with the private house-building and the location of industry, the Panel suggests *that the planning authorities' ability to influence the situation in the face of powerful market forces is minimal.* (Editor's italics.)

Secondly, *Structure Planning* in London has lacked success because the division of powers over metropolitan services has prevented the inclusion in the GLDP of a detailed consideration of all the elements that the PAG report felt was within the competence of a strategic plan. Thus the London Government Act of 1963 emphasized the role of the Boroughs as the primary units of local government with substantial responsibilities in the fields of planning, housing and other relevant services. By inference this stricture also includes the bodies responsible for public transport operating within and across the GLC boundary—London Transport (up to 1970), British Rail and the National Bus Company. Therefore, as an immediate contribution to the problems of coordination that currently exist, the Panel recommended the setting up of two new over-arching authorities for housing and transportation.

Thirdly, wrote the Panel, *Structure Planning* for the metropolis was made difficult by the fact of "the importance of London in the national economy" which ensures that "basic decisions about major interests in London will be the concern of the national Government."[70] Indeed, the interest of Parliament and government in the causes and consequences of the problems of Greater London appeared to be growing in the weeks leading up to the publication of the Layfield Report. Significantly, on 15 December 1972 Parliament debated an Opposition motion on the inflation of prices in the London land and housing markets and the decline in industrial employment. On the government side, too, there are indications that it is disturbed at the way resources for industrial development have, in a period of rapid inflation, poured instead into property investment, mostly offices in London, and at the extremely unfavourable level of office rents in London compared to those of the capitals of Britain's new partners in the European Economic Community.

The Layfield Report must therefore be seen as a considerable indictment of the idea of Structure Planning, at least as applied in the Greater London context, though, as the Panel notes, there were certain mitigating circumstances in this case such as the lack of an agreed regional planning strategy for South East England as a whole. But while it recognises the need for structure planners with technical expertise in economics and sociology, the report does not openly acknowledge the basis of the contradictions in the working of the metropolitan system, against which the planners are powerless to struggle: contradictions not only in the policies currently in operation but also in the market forces outside their control.

Some of these contradictions have been mentioned already. Certain types of unskilled labour are scarce in Central London because people can no longer pay rents that have been inflated through competition for land by the very concerns that require their services—offices and hotels. Young married teachers and social workers, essential to the welfare of Londoners, are finding it increasingly difficult to set up home anywhere in Greater London. Again, an acute housing problem exists side by side with empty, speculative office blocks or with land, complete with planning permission, that remains undeveloped in the expectation of inflationary rent increases.

Central Government also adds to the confusion over policy for, while it appears to support the movement of offices out of London, it is itself the single most important customer of the office developers. Finally, the Metropolitan Green Belt stands as a symbolic reminder of the two guiding principles of London planning since Abercrombie—containment and decentralisation. However, it is now becoming apparent that the material conditions, at least for a substantial proportion of Londoners, are now very different from those which prevailed when the planners recommended that London's dynamism should be curbed in the interest of the nation as a whole. Disappointing rates of *national* economic growth, the rationalisation of manufacturing and ports industries and, not least, policies on the regional location of employment have all contributed to a situation where the Londoner's average income from labour is now well below those in other, once less favoured, parts of the country.[71] The situation in certain sectors of London's economy (facing the Common Market) is already giving rise to serious concern and will call for rethinking on more than just the nature of development plans.

NOTES

[1] S. E. Rasmussen, *London the Unique City*. London, Jonathan Cape, 1937.

[2] N. G. Brett-James, *The Growth of Stuart London*. London, Allen and Unwin, 1935, p. 69.

[3] V. Pearl, *London and the Outbreak of the Puritan Revolution*. London, Oxford University Press, 1961, Chap. 1.

[4] W. Ashworth, *The Genesis of Modern British Town Planning*. London, Routledge and Kegan Paul, 1954, Chap. VII.

[5] Sir John Summerson, *Georgian London*. London, Penguin Books, 1962, Chap. 5.

[6] D. J. Olsen, *Town Planning in London, the Eighteenth and Nineteenth Centuries*. New Haven, Yale University Press, 1964, p. 19.

[7] R. A. Lewis, *Edwin Chadwick and the Public Health Movement* 1832–1854. London, Longman's, 1952, p. 42.

[8] L. Benevolo, *The Origins of Modern Town Planning*. London, Routledge and Kegan Paul, 1967, p. 89.

[9] E. Howard (F. J. Osborn, ed.), *Garden Cities of Tomorrow*. London, Faber, 1946.

[10] Lord Meath, "The Green Circle Around London," *The Sphere*, 6, 1901, p. 64.

[11] Peter Willmott's book *The Evolution of a Community, A Study of Dagenham Forty Years On* (London, Routledge and Kegan Paul, 1963), is a pioneering study in the sociological aspects of planning, clearing away some illusions about the relationship between physical design and social interaction and seeking to provide empirical justification for mixed communities.

[12] Quoted in W. L. Creese (ed.), *The Legacy of Raymond Unwin: A Human Pattern for Planning*. Cambridge, Mass., M.I.T. Press, 1967, p. 157.

[13] Greater London Regional Planning Committee, *Second Report*, London, 1933.

[14] Ashworth, op. cit., Chap. VIII.

[15] For a wider view of urban growth strategy in Britain than we are concerned with here and the details of fiscal and other policy tools of regional planning, see L. Rodin, *Nations and Cities* (Boston, Houghton Mifflin, 1970), and A. McCrone, *Regional Policy in Britain* (London, Allen and Unwin, 1969).

[16] P. Geddes, *Cities in Evolution.* London, Williams and Norgate, 1949.

[17] *Greater London Plan, 1944* (London, H.M.S.O., 1945), par. 13.

[18] Ibid., par. 26.

[19] Details on the theory of land values and the British experience of attempts to manipulate them for the public good can be found in P. Hall, *Land Values* (London, Sweet and Maxwell, 1965).

[20] See, for example, H. Orlans, *Utopia Limited* (London, Routledge and Kegan Paul, 1953), for an entertaining, if somewhat unbalanced, account of the development of Stevenage New Town.

[21] The territorial divisions used here are not directly comparable to Abercrombie's concentric rings but they do illustrate the zonal distribution of population growth. The South East region relates to the regional planning machinery set up in 1964; the Outer Metropolitan Area to a region of 40 miles' radius from Central London defined by the Ministry of Housing and Greater London to the area of the Greater London Council set up in 1965. Figure 6 shows the main administrative subdivisions of South East England.

[22] A. E. Holmans, "Industrial Development Certificates and Control of Employment in South East England," *Urban Studies* (1964), p. 138.

[23] See J. A. G. Griffith, *Central Departments and Local Authorities* (London, Allen and Unwin, 1966), Chap. 5, for a detailed discussion of how policy filtered down from the Ministry of Housing to local planning authorities. In the absence of a regional authority for London the "normal channels" were the only way in which local authority ascertained whether in fact it was conforming to the Abercrombie strategy.

[24] As was previously noted, progress in New Town building was slow at first. Therefore, in 1952 the Town Development Act provided for the movement of people and jobs from big urban areas to *existing* country towns by means of agreements involving Central Government, the "exporting" and the "importing" local authorities. The benefits were meant to be reciprocal—the large towns gaining elbow room and the rural ones an impetus for growth.

[25] P. Self, *Cities in Flood.* London, Faber and Faber, 1957, p. 139.

[26] Report, Committee on Housing in Greater London (Milner Holland Report), Cmnd. 2605 (London, H.M.S.O., 1965), Chap. 4.

[27] Redevelopment in a comprehensive development area was carried out according to a single, detailed master plan. In such an area the planning authority had special powers of finance and compulsory purchase of land and buildings. Among other parts of London developed successfully under CDA powers are the South Bank cultural centre which includes the Royal Festival Hall, Queen Elizabeth Hall and National Theatre and the Barbican scheme in the City of London.

[28] Centre for Urban Studies, *London, Aspects of Change.* London, Macgibbon and Kee, 1961, Chap. VI.

[29] P. Self, op. cit., p. 63.

[30] D. Thomas, *London's Green Belt.* London, Faber and Faber, 1970.

[31] However, a Lee Valley Regional Park Authority has been formed and plans are in progress for turning this area which, unlike the Green Belt, is directly accessible to thousands of working-class East Enders into a 10,000-acre sports and recreational park.

[32] R. Thomas, *London's New Towns,* P. E. P. Broadsheet 510 (1969), p. 410.

[33] B. J. Heraud, "New Towns: The End of a Planned Dream," *New Society,* July 1968, p. 47.

[34] R. Thomas, op. cit., p. 420.

[35] Royal Commission on Local Government in England, Research Studies 1, *Local Government in South East England,* Greater London Group (1968), p. 434.

[36] Ministry of Transport, *Traffic in Towns* (London, H.M.S.O., 1963).

[37] Ministry of Transport, *Road Pricing: The Economic and Technical Possibilities* (London, H.M.S.O., 1964).

[38] C. D. Foster and M. E. Beesley, "Estimating and Social Benefit of Constructing an Underground Railway in London," *Journal of the Royal Statistical Society,* Series A, 126 (1963), pp. 46–92.

[39] Planning Advisory Group, *The Future of Development Plans* (London, H.M.S.O., 1965).

[40] *Report,* Royal Commission on Local Government in Greater London, 1957–60, Cmnd. 1164, H.M.S.O. (1960), p. 1.

[41] The area chosen appears to have been based, rather curiously, on the Metropolitan Police District. Its population in 1959 was 8.6 million (840 square miles), compared to 8.2 million (720 square miles) for the census-defined Greater London Conurbation.

[42] G. Rhodes and S. K. Ruck, *The Government of Greater London.* London, Allen and Unwin, 1970, p. 24.

[43] For detail on the political struggle in education in particular and over the whole reform in general, see F. Smallwood, *Greater London, The Politics of Metropolitan Reform* (New York, Bobbs-Merrill, 1965), and G. Rhodes, *The Government of London: The Struggle for Reform* (London, Weidenfeld & Nicolson, 1970).

[44] W. A. Robson, *The Heart of Greater London,* Greater London Paper No. 9, London School of Economics (1965).

[45] Town and Country Planning Regulations, 1965, S.1. 1965, No. 679, Reg. 3.

[46] For a detailed critique of the overall strategy of the GLDP and its systematic aspects, see Town and Country Planning Association, *London Under Stress* (London, 1970).

[47] Greater London Development Plan Statement, GLC (1969), Section 6.4.

[48] GLC Minutes, 27 January 1970, p. 45.

[49] GLDP Statement (1969), op. cit., p. 10. According to the 1971 Census, London's population of 7,452,346 is a drop of 6.8 percent from the 1961 figure and is now about equal to that of the 1920s.

[50] Thus, despite London's massive housing problem involving a minimum of 3,000 statutorily homeless people, a current shortfall of 325,000 houses due to families sharing accommodation and some 340,000 houses which

currently fail to meet minimum standards, consideration is given in only one instance to the possibility of rezoning land for residential purposes.

[51] GLDP Statement (1969), op. cit., p. 38.

[52] The contradiction remains, however, that while the demand for office space increases and London office rents soar above those of European capitals, several huge office blocks such as Centre Point in Tottenham Court Road, Space House in Kingsway and London Bridge House are deliberately kept *empty* by the developer. This is because their capital value is increasing much faster than their rental value.

[53] The distinction is important. Under the rent acts these tenants have less security than those in unfurnished accommodation.

[54] *Children and Their Primary Schools* (H.M.S.O., 1967), par. 132.

[55] ILEA Education Bulletin No. 106, July 1968.

[56] Committee on Public Participation in Planning, *People and Planning* (London, H.M.S.O., 1969).

[57] More recently the idea of a *statutory conference* has been evolving. This would be held before the planning authority has finalised its plan and would take the form of a dialogue between the authority and interested groups and individuals. The main issues would therefore be raised before the public inquiry took place. See *Town and Country Planning,* Vol. 39, No. 7–8.

[58] Greater London Council, *Statement Revisions,* February 1972.

[59] J. M. Thomson, *Motorways in London.* London, Duckworth, 1970.

[60] Ministry of Housing and Local Government, *The South East Study 1961–1981* (London, H.M.S.O., 1954), Chap. 5.

[61] Milton Keynes, some thirty-five miles northwest of London, was designated a new town in 1967 when the population of the area stood at 40,000. By 1981, it is projected that the population will be 121,000. One important difference between second-generation new towns like Milton Keynes and those of the immediate postwar years has already been noted, namely, they are to act as counter magnets to London's employment growth (as then projected). They are different in other respects also. Plans are more flexible and the urban structure is more dispersed with a mixture of land uses, a breakdown of employment concentration and a "cellular" rather than nodal pattern of population grouping. More provision is made for car ownership and use.

[62] South East Economic Planning Council, *Strategy for the South East* (London, H.M.S.O., 1967), p. vii.

[63] Ibid., Chap. 3.

[64] P. G. Hall, "Planning for Urban Growth: Metropolitan Area Plans and Their Implications for South East England," *Regional Studies,* Vol. 1, No. 2 (1967), 101–34.

[65] Standing Conference on London Regional Planning, *The Conference Area in the Long Term,* L.R.P. 680 (London, 1969).

[66] Report, Commission on the Third London Airport (London, H.M.S.O., 1970).

[67] South East Joint Planning Team, *Strategic Plan for the South East* (London, H.M.S.O., 1970).

[68] Greater London Development Plan—Report of the Panel of Inquiry (London, H.M.S.O., 1973), par. 2.11.

[69] Ibid., par. 2.13.

[70] Ibid., par. 2.11.

[71] David Eversley has written that "the London Docklands must be reckoned as belonging to the same category as the South Wales valleys, and other old coal, iron and heavy industrial areas." D. E. C. Eversley, "The Docklands—An Exercise in Geopolitics," *East London Papers,* Vol. 14, No. 1 (April 1972), 51–64.

PART II

Western: New World

CHAPTER 5

Washington, D.C.: Symbol and City

TODAY: A CRITIQUE OF THE PHYSICAL PLAN IN ITS SOCIOGEOGRAPHIC SETTING

Carl Feiss*

SYMBOLIC CAPITAL

Washington, the capital of the United States, has no precise boundaries; it has no normal central municipal government of its own. Functional Washington's population is unknown and unknowable; since the end of the 1929 Depression and through World War II, it has become the focal point of vast, still continuing inmigration. While the titular center of the federal government is found in the District of Columbia, decentralization of government agencies has moved into the two adjoining states of Maryland and Virginia, both of which now house major nodes of federal employment. The Baroque city of Washington, D.C., designed

* Planning and urban design consultant with a home office for many years in Washington, D.C., B.F.A. from the University of Pennsylvania and M.C.P. from Massachusetts Institute of Technology; past director of Denver Planning Commission, of American Institute of Planners, of American Society of Planning Officials. Fellow of the American Institute of Architects (Special Services Award), trustee of the National Trust for Historic Preservation and author of *The Future of Buffalo, Report on the Community Renewal Program for the City of Rochester, N.Y.;* coauthor of *A Report of the Renewal Possibilities of the Historic Triangle of the City of San Juan* and *With Heritage So Rich.* Contributor to professional journals.

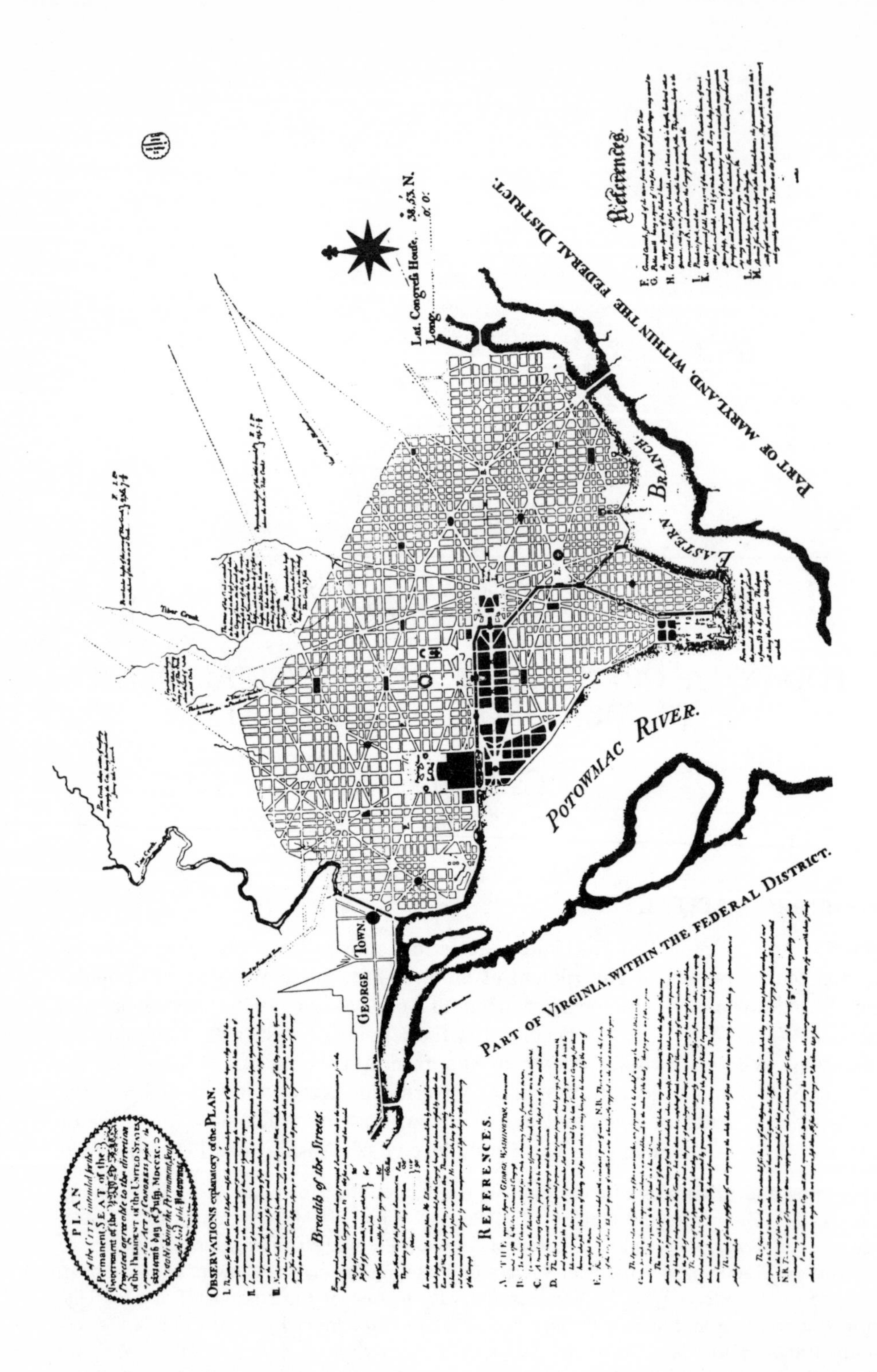

FIG. 1A Plan for Washington by L'Enfant, 1791. From *John Reps,* Monumental Washington, *Princeton, Princeton University Press, 1968*

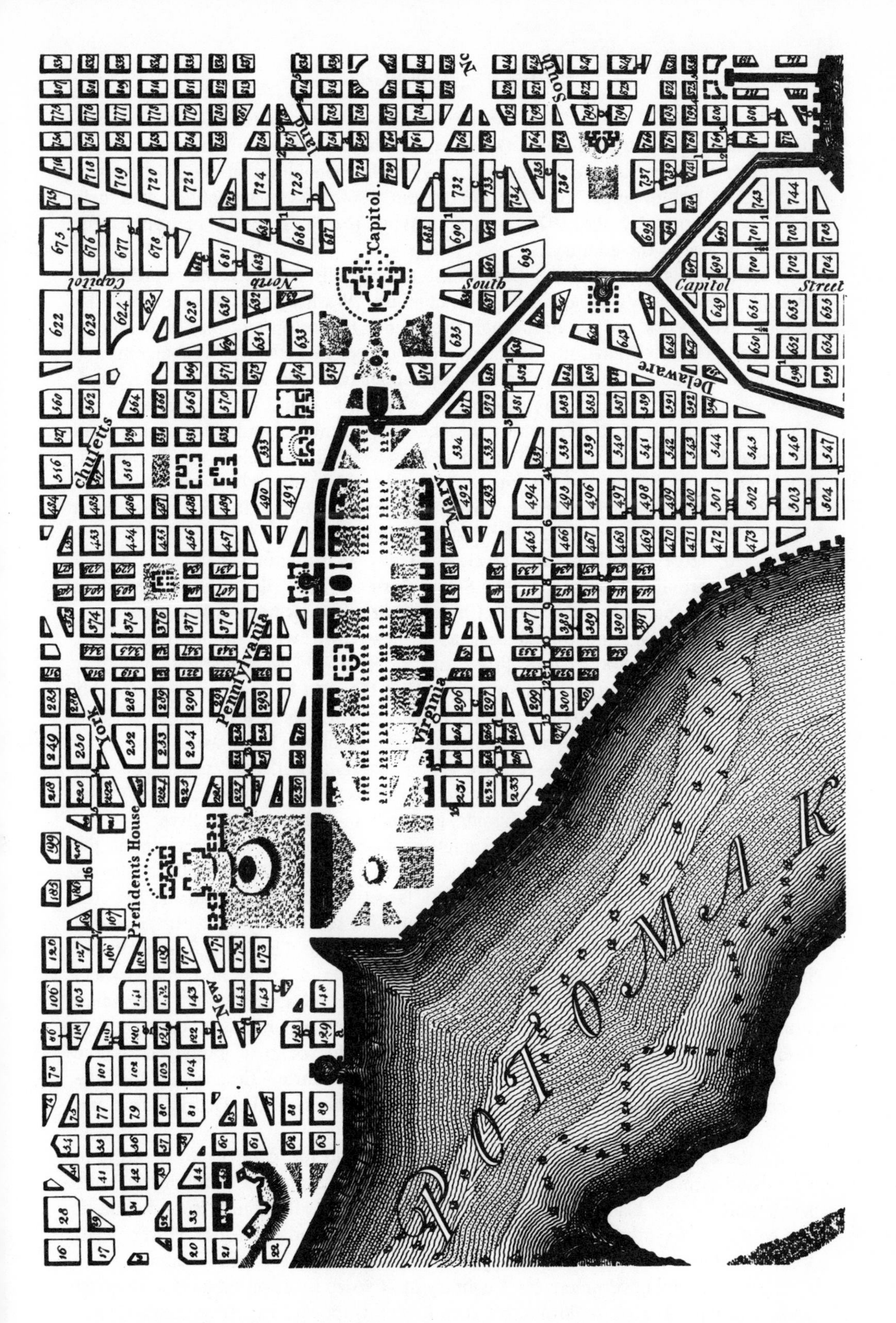

FIG. 1B Central portion of the Ellicott Plan of 1792. From *John Reps,* Monumental Washington, *Princeton, Princeton University Press, 1968*

by L'Enfant in 1791 as a "New Town" covers only ten square miles of the sixty-nine square miles of the federal District of Columbia, itself only a small part of greater or metropolitan Washington. In 1970, the population of the District was 756,500, a loss of approximately 7,400 from 1960; the metropolitan area held 2,900,000 people by the 1970 census, making the Washington metropolis the seventh largest in the country.

Washington is a part of the East Coast megalopolis that stretches north from Hampton Roads, Virginia, through Richmond, Washington, Baltimore, Philadelphia, New York and on up through Providence to Boston and into New Hampshire and Maine. There are no boundaries or edges between Washington and Baltimore on the north; its eastward sweep, about to engulf Annapolis, Maryland, stops at the Chesapeake Bay; it creeps westward about fifty miles and will ultimately extend to the foothills of the Appalachians and the Shenandoah National Park. Its extent to the south today is still lineal below the Rappahannock River and east of the Potomac, but northern Virginia with new bridge and highway connections is becoming a vast suburb of the capital city, just as southern Maryland has been for years. Now that the circumferential expressway has been completed, large suburban satellite cities—really Washington's new giant neighborhoods—are developing rapidly: Silver Springs, Rockville and Columbia in Maryland; Vienna, Alexandria, Falls Church, Fairfax and Reston in Virginia.

While historic Washington started as a new town with an approved plan, (Figs. 1a, 1b) by 1800, it took fifty years for it to achieve a population of fifty thousand. It was not until the end of World War II that it had become a reasonably sophisticated and cosmopolitan city. By that time it had only a few modern office buildings, other than those built under federal auspices. Even as late as 1950 there was only one legitimate theatre and a handful of decent restaurants and hotels. Washington simply was not thought to have a culture of its own either by its visitors or by its full-time inhabitants, generally in-migrants themselves.

The sprawling megalopolitan Washington of today has been a growth of the last twenty years; the Baroque central city seems to get smaller and smaller as the rest of Washington grows larger and larger. Through the late 1920s, the District of Columbia had the self-identification of a southern town with the added graces and foibles hung over from an era when Yankee Theodore Roosevelt and his handsome family combined Edwardian-Long Island social and high society graces with a whiff of far-West gusto. This was the ruling class that later sanctioned the imperial stage set of Roman architecture which this country's most fashionable architects of the first forty years of this century employed as the style for government offices and monuments. It was during these years that the creeping blight of the black slums in the geographic heart of the District grew and grew.

But the capital of the United States is too huge and too complex to describe in simplistic terms. Monumental, photogenic, historic Baroque Washington, one small part of the historic plan, is a national symbol. Buildings from within it are world-wide symbols, just as the Arc de Triomphe and the Eiffel Tower, well-known monuments of central Paris symbolize Paris and by reference, France.

The seat of any government for a country of any size takes on an aura of prestige which distinguishes it, regardless of location and appearance, from other cities. The capital cities of the Western world, stemming as they do conceptually from

Athens and Rome, instead of Isfahan or Peking, through many metamorphoses, still use the Mediterranean classical vernacular as the architectural symbolism of leadership, powerful government, the rule of law and the sepulchers of heroes and of art. The fact that Napoleon and Thomas Jefferson were honored in the same architectural form—one, a temple to his glory in the Invalides in Paris, and the other, a temple to democracy in his capitol in Virginia—is a case in point. This form appears in various guises and disguises in central Washington, for instance, both to house the Treasury and the Supreme Court, as easily designed pseudoclassic monumental artifacts suitable to any use. One should look at Washington's buildings, not so much as monuments, but as design conveniences.

Washington is now a very modern city with many of the amenities found in other capitals in the Western world. Without the deep historical antecedents of the European capitals, Washington's short 170 years cannot possibly match the built-in evidence of the thousand-year cultures to be found elsewhere. Nor is it the oldest seat of democracy, since the capitals of Iceland, San Marino and Switzerland take historic precedence.

The Constitution of the United States states very simply that "The Congress shall have Power . . . to exercise exclusive Legislation in all Cases whatsoever over such District (not exceeding ten miles square) as may, by Cession, of particular states, and the Acceptance of Congress, become the Seat of the Government of the United States, . . ." The residents of the District of Columbia today do have a shadow local government with a Mayor and Council appointed by the President and approved by a joint committee of the Congress.

Serious problems face the citizens (generally black), taxpayers and employees of the District of Columbia in their daily lives. Inadequate salaries for police and firemen, for teachers and other public servants, plus woefully inadequate public facilities of all kinds, are of little consequence to the millions of visitors to Baroque and monumental Washington. Poor public services mean little to the giant federal bureaucracy (generally white) which lives, in large part, outside the District. They mean nothing, also, to the hundreds of thousands of transient businessmen treating with the congressmen and the federal bureaucracy during the course of the year; hotels and restaurants have improved immeasurably; night clubs and bars abound, and the city provides the visitors, who are their best customers, with all the customary amenities.

The original settlement of eighteenth-century Georgetown and Baroque Washington, with their neighbor, eighteenth-century Alexandria across the river, is in a great bowl within low hills circling the confluence of the Anacostia River with the Potomac just below the fall line of the Potomac. Geologically, economically and socially, it is one of eastern America's most significant features because it separates the aquatic cultures of the watery coastal plains from the drier agricultural areas of the Piedmont, which in turn is replaced to the west by the mountain cultures of the Appalachians. The Potomac Gorge cuts back into the Piedmont from Georgetown. Much of northern Virginia and southwestern Maryland, including the northwestern and northern parts of the District of Columbia with all of the suburbs to the north, lie on this higher ground, above the swampy miasmas of the Potomac Basin. During the summer the northwest portion of the District, in the general vicinity of the Washington Cathedral, may be as much as five to ten degrees cooler on its hill than is the downtown and monumental part of the city. Before the advent of air conditioning and its almost universal use in the greater Washington area, a tour of diplomatic duty in the capital of the United States was always quite correctly considered by foreign governments as assignment to a tropical hardship post. As old Virginians, both George Washington and Thomas Jefferson should have known better than to select the present site of Washington, which even in those days was a fetid, swampy area ("Foggy Bottom"). Both of them built their own homes on the tops of high hills.

The suburban spread of the residential population of Washington out along the great diagonals into once beautiful northern Virginia and southern Maryland has followed the typical unplanned course of urban growth in the United States. The example of planned development set by the historic heart of the area was not followed, even within the District of Columbia, as urban growth spread beyond the limits of the L'Enfant Plan. One of the curious aspects of the Baroque plan is that it accepted the base of the Piedmont hills to the north as the determining edge of town. The only place where L'Enfant was willing to break this was at the eastern part of the city where he located the capitol buildings on the ridge and then spread the design to the east on the plateau above and back of the Anacostia River. It is thus primarily a flatlands plan; and as a flatlands plan, with the exception of certain sections of hilly northwest Washington, the extensions of the historic city outward have also largely been flatland grids, with occasional and very haphazard diagonals extending out from some of the earlier diagonals in the original Baroque plan.

Three years ago, the first great beltway was completed around the capital city through the surrounding suburban mess of both Virginia and Maryland. The beltway, an irregular oval, does not touch the District of Columbia although serving as a powerful new unifying force in the economics and culture of the whole urban region. The beltway has generated large shopping centers, new industrial parks, new federal centers of decentralized bureaucracy and vast new residential agglomerations, high-rise, high-density constructions. The Washington *Post* runs a column, "Around the Beltway," covering a variety of events along the highway in both Maryland and Virginia, announcing art festivals, flower shows, nature walks, concerts, special educational ventures and important sales. The beltway is fast becoming a major high-speed urban communications system for workers, shoppers and those simply in search of recreation. People in that part of the urban region served by the beltway and the highly charged local TV programs seemingly need never come into the heart of the city at all. The major central city department stores and specialty shops now have branches in the new giant shopping centers in the vicinity of the Beltway. During the rush hours, a reverse commuting movement out of the central city is beginning to balance movement into it.

A second beltway is being scheduled still farther out, to be completed within the next fifteen years. At the same time, the subway has just been started which will ultimately make contact via a high-speed rapid transit system with many of the new urban nodes and federal employment centers along the older diagonals and in contact with the first beltway itself.

During World War II and after, there was much discussion of planned decentralization of strategic government offices and schemes were made for this purpose. Decentralization has occurred but not in accordance with any clear plan and with little attempt to harmonize such decentralization with either available housing or transportation. It has taken place continuously during the past twenty years without evident impact on overcrowded federal space in the older government areas of the central city, since the federal government continues to increase.

During the early stages of World War II, the Department of Defense moved into the Pentagon across the Potomac in Virginia. The Central Intelligence Agency took command of a beautiful wooded site above the Potomac Gorge about ten miles west of town. These moves have been followed by numerous others, including the Atomic Energy Commission and the Bureau of Standards, involving thousands of employees. The United States Geological Survey will transfer two thousand employees to the new town of Reston, Virginia, some thirty-five miles from its present headquarters within three blocks of the White House. Whole new huge privately built office complexes are rising in the suburbs with the primary purpose of leasing to federal agencies. Since these agencies are staffed in large part by (generally white) white-collar workers who live now in middle-income suburbs, and since daily commuting into historic Washington is a horrendous experience, there is much theoretical logic behind decentralization of the giant federal complex. Presumably over a period of time those who formerly commuted from various parts of Virginia and Maryland into the heart of the city on the long diagonals will change their place of residence to be closer and more convenient to their employment centers.

Like most major cities of the world, the city center is the major white-collar employment area. New industrial parks are spreading out beyond the direct influence of a city center, all over the United States, replacing obsolete in-town industrial areas. However, the phenomenon of the deliberate move of office employment into the suburbs by the United States Government bears watching in terms of its effect, not only on the urban region, but also on the whole concept of decentralization. In scale it is a white-collar shift undoubtedly greater numerically than any other such selected actions elsewhere in the country.

Presumably, the decentralization of federal agencies, which, of course, is only partial, would have left a vacuum in the central city. The bureaucracy inflated by the giant federal aid programs, which first began developing during the 1929 Depression, has continued to enlarge, gobbling up more and more office space. Above all, the growing prestige of the capital city as a lobbying and communications center has developed new private business components on a massive scale.

The wealthy labor unions began the influx of private sector high commands. Shortly after World War II, using their massive pension funds, they commenced building marble palaces, as close to the capitol and the White House as they could get. The most bumptious of these, the AFL-CIO Building, rises ten stories above St. John's Episcopal Church to lord it over the handsome and traditional Lafayette Square and the White House itself.

Not to be outdone by the labor unions, a myriad of public interest groups (known as PIGS in official Washington) expanded existing headquarters, centralizing their operations. For the most part, these pressure groups (representing every conceivable national organization, professional group, lobby and all of the essential and unessential hangers-on) have grouped themselves in the northwest part of the central city and have constructed large office buildings, containing many hundreds of thousands of square feet of space for their own use and for rental purposes.

Finding that the city was modernizing in the early 1950s many big corporations, which had maintained rooms or suites in elegant hotels for the convenience of their top personnel engaged in lobbying with the Congress, the White House or federal agencies, found it wise in addition to open branch offices in Washington. Construction is at such a rate that it is no longer possible to keep tabs on the number of millions of square feet of office space that have been and are being built during the past several years. In 1968, *Downtown Progress* reported thirteen million square feet of new private office space since 1960 west of 16th Street, and three million east. Within one mile to the north and to the west of the White House there is a mighty push to fill the entire area with ten-story office buildings and an occasional service apartment complex.

Under Washington zoning, there is a 110-foot height limit so as to preserve the visual importance of key government structures, which is fortunate indeed for the entire city. Many architects argue against it, hoping for an opportunity to build spectacular skyscrapers. But since there is no limit to coverage and density for commercial structures and since many Washington streets are already overloaded with traffic, the city could quickly become completely paralyzed if the height limit were broken. The commercial and financial center of historic Washington has thus moved west from the older Pennsylvania Avenue and F Street triangle. Despite valiant efforts by downtown businessmen in that general area, a vacuum has been created, in part accelerated, by proximity to the vast north-central slum and black ghetto area and the influx into the eastern sections of that triangle by the low-income and lower middle-income black citizens. Despite the fact that integration in Washington is proceeding with a relative degree of success, the overwhelmingly black population, plus the disturbances of recent years and fear of crime in the streets have turned white customers away from the traditional older shopping sections of the city. These reasons coupled with the commuting time-distance factor and poor central parking facilities are negatives which are grist for the suburban centers.

All of the famous historic plans for Washington until *The Year 2000 Plan* prepared in 1961 by the National Capital Planning Commission and the National Capital Regional Council (Figs. 2a, 2b, 2c), completely neglected the commercial and residential center of the city. They expressed no concern for the spread of slum and blight throughout the central residential areas and the pitiful condition of many portions of the city. While the National Capital Planning Commission itself was given the responsibility of approving plans for slum clearance and urban redevelopment following the passage of the Housing Act of 1949, it took until the mid-1950s before its plans reflected an interest in other than the monumental center.

Recreation and open space planning concentrated on the appearance of the monumental areas, on lower portions of the Potomac shoreline and in Rock Creek Park. The 1901 McMillan Plan, which grew out of the city beautiful philosophy, did lay out the locus of open space development within the District of Columbia, and included the expansion to the north of open space along Rock Creek Park and along the Anacostia River (Fig. 3).

There were strong arguments among the classicist planners fifteen to twenty years ago that historic Washington was the nation's city and was thus only the nation's concern. The National Capital Planning Commission and the National Park Service, which are carrying out many of the elements of the formal plans, had

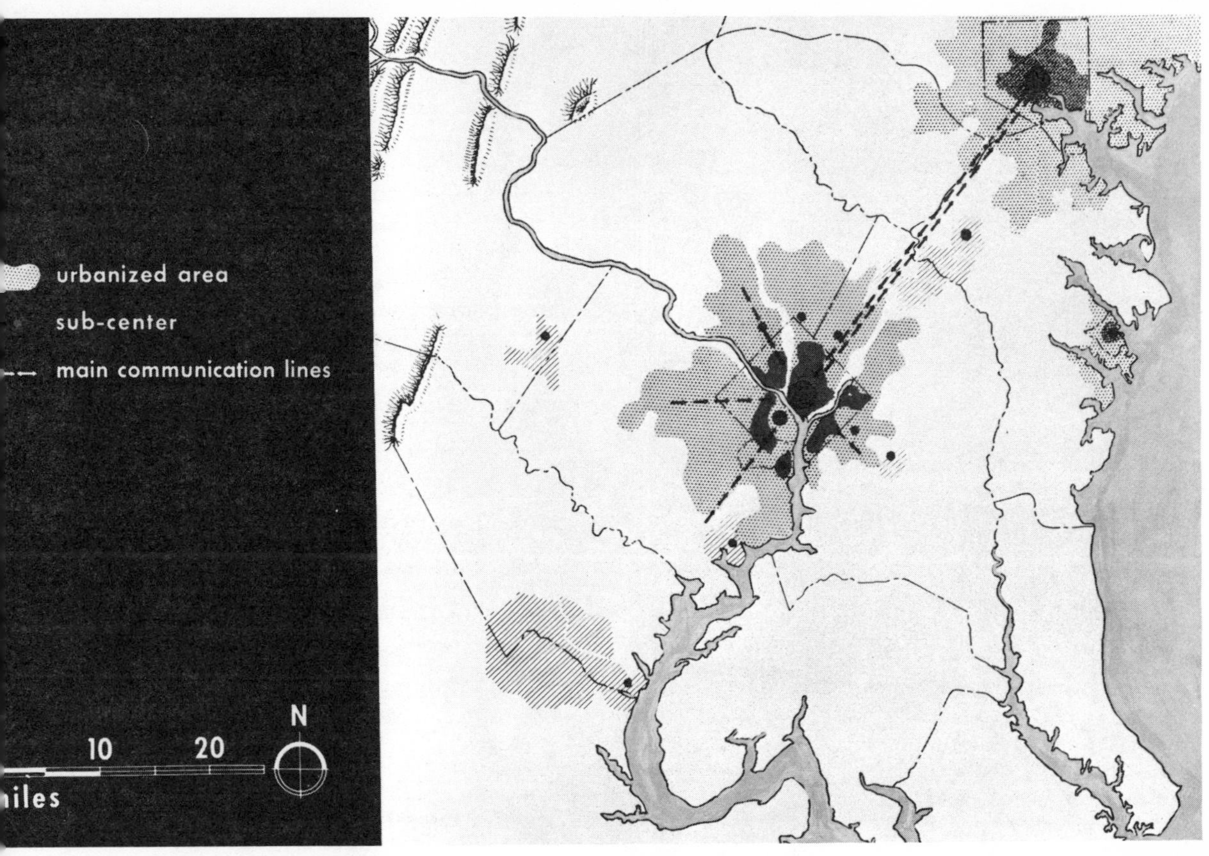

FIG. 2A The National Capital Region: *The Year 2000 Plan. National Capital Planning Commission*

FIG. 2B The Radial Corridor Plan: *The Year 2000 Plan. National Capital Planning Commission*

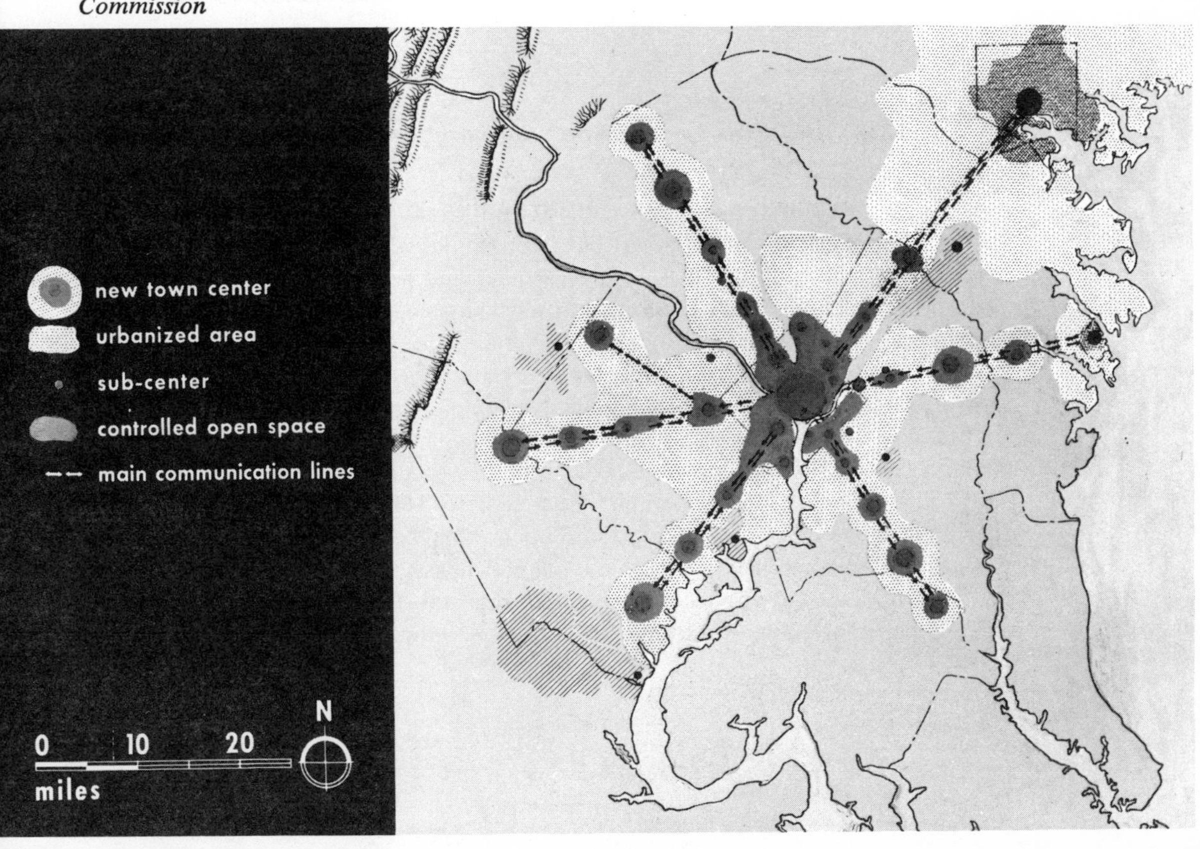

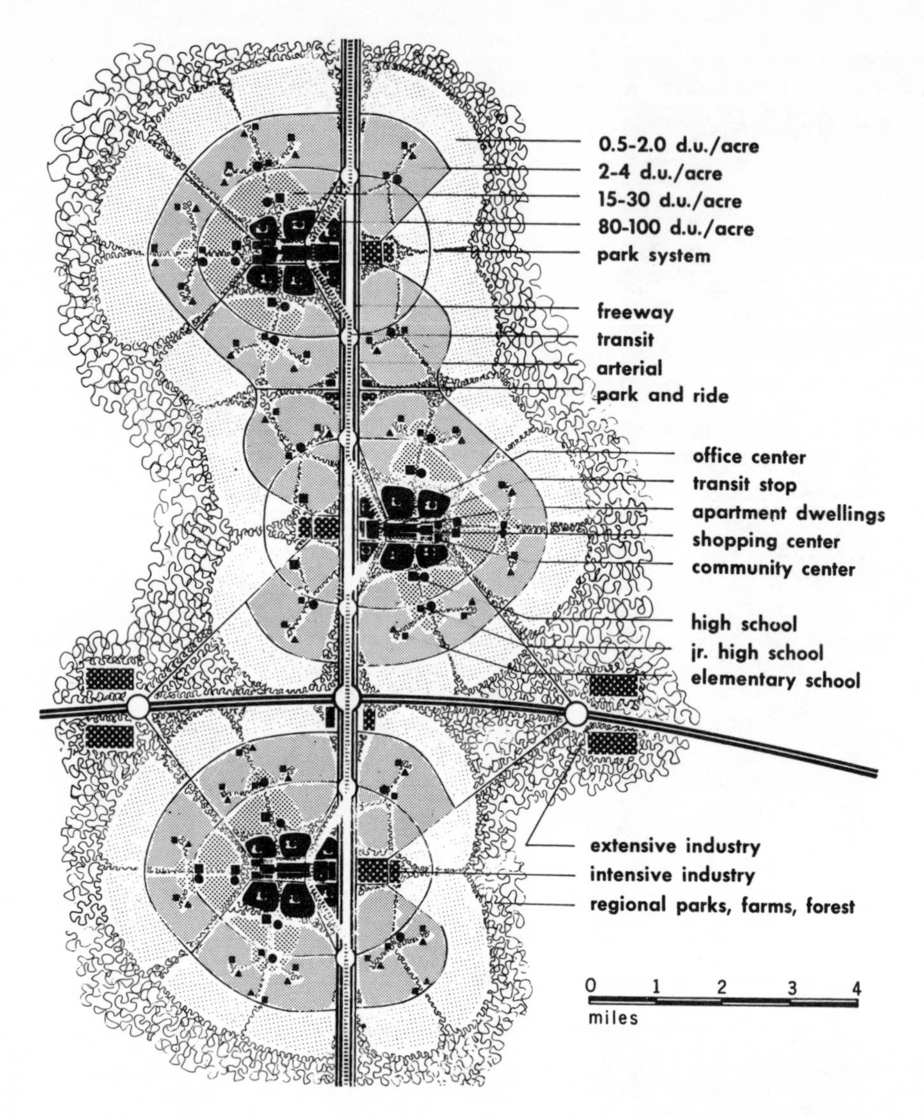

FIG. 2C Model Corridor: *The Year 2000 Plan. National Capital Planning Commission*

only the responsibility of seeing that the federal areas maintained at all times the quality of appearance which would be a continuous embellishment to the capital city as a national symbol. What went on behind and next door to these embellishments was somebody else's concern and to a large degree the situation still prevails. There is no municipal planning commission; members of the National Capital Planning Commission are chosen by the President of the United States and come from as far away as the Pacific Northwest.

The token city government with a "mayor" appointed by the president has no planning commission of its own, although the mayor sits in as an appointed member of the National Capital Planning Commission. This appointment is not mandatory under law. There is only a loose connection between the National Capital Planning Commission, the National Capital Housing Authority, the Redevelopment Land Agency, the Zoning Commission, the Highway Department and the Metropolitan Transportation Authority. In a nation which has prided itself on its

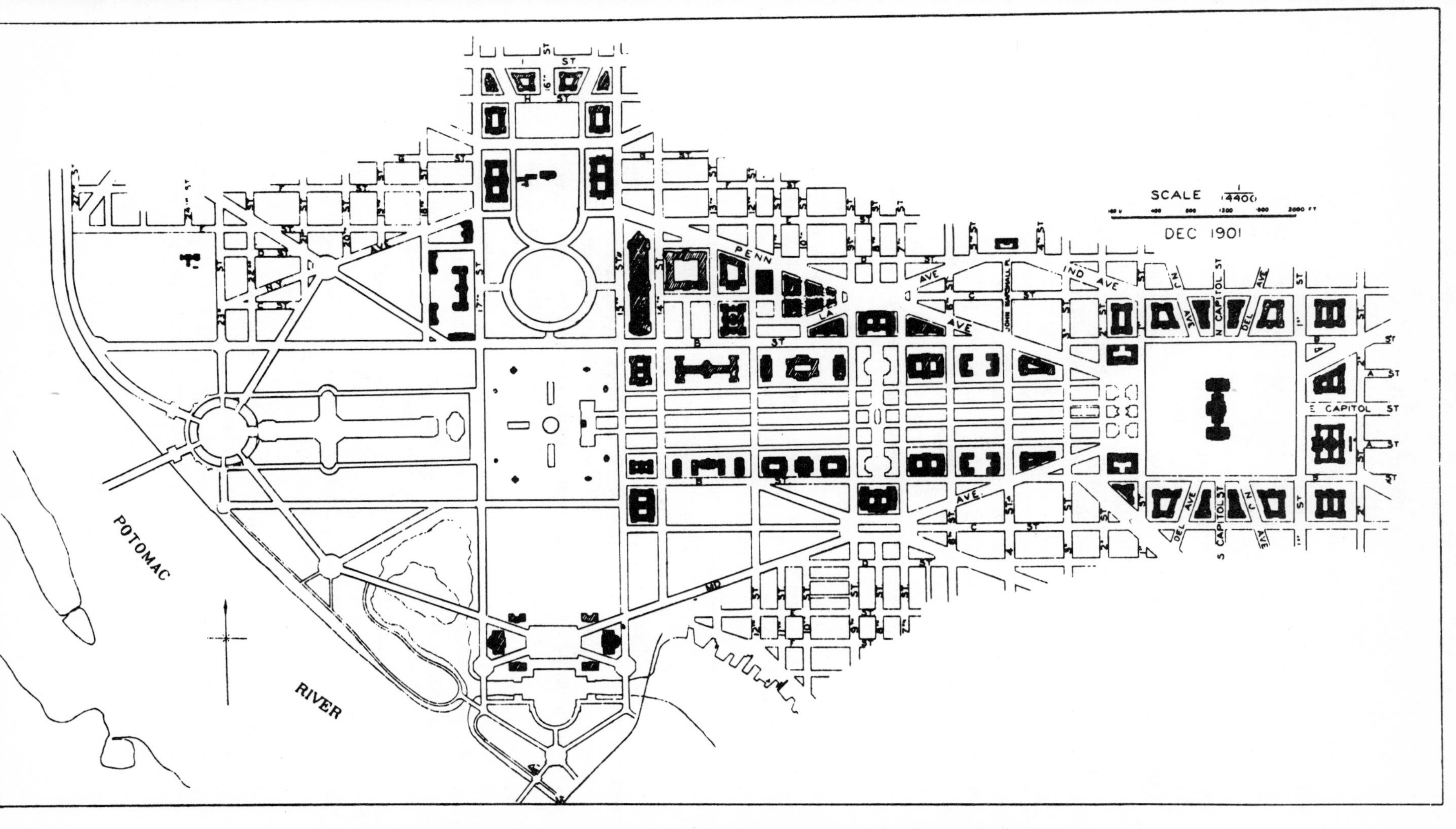

FIG. 3 Public building sites in central Washington, proposed by the Senate Park Commission, 1902. From *John Reps,* Monumental Washington, *Princeton, Princeton University Press, 1968*

efficiency and orderly development—at least in business—here is an example in the national capital of a lack of ability to develop a rational system for urban improvement.

The Year 2000 Plan was the first truly metropolitan plan for the Washington region; alas, it has fallen by the wayside. It was superseded in 1965 by a much less dynamic and imaginative version which in turn has been whittled away, so that today a headless planning operation performs its routines with little hope of getting a focus on the future. Currently, there is hope that the American Revolutionary War Bicentennial Celebration will somehow create for Washington a dynamic impulse for better planning so that by 1976 there will be something new to show.

The battle of the urban highway is being fought here as elsewhere; greater Washington is being torn up to make way for more and more ribbons of concrete. Members of the Congress, in their infinite wisdom, are actually designing the location and character of their pet highway proposals, despite objections from official planning agencies and citizens groups. At the same time, the giant renewal of southwest Washington, begun some fifteen years ago to clean up a large black slum area to the south of the Capitol, has successfully created a new-town-in-town for middle- and upper-income residents—generally white (Figs. 4a, 4b, 4c), and a well-designed low- and moderate-income new-town-in-town, scheduled for the Fort Lincoln area at the eastern side of the city, is slowly going ahead.

A substantial force for change has taken place in the living habits of the white population remaining in the District of Columbia, largely west of Rock Creek in a generally well-built and well-kept single family area. The bastions of the white, middle and upper classes are historic Georgetown, northwest Washington and parts of the Capitol Hill area behind the Supreme Court Building and the Library of Congress. The major change to the social structure west of Rock Creek since World War II has been the elimination of the black population from Georgetown and from several other sections where either new office buildings, new federal installations or higher land prices and absentee ownership have forced black rental occupancy out altogether. While the black population of the District of Columbia has increased many times over in the last thirty years, it still remains substantially in the low- and lower-middle-income and has been forced to remain in vast slum areas north of Massachusetts Avenue and east of Connecticut Avenue out to the eastern District line and beyond.

Howard University, founded in 1867 as a predominantly Negro university, has been the focal point for years for the black intellectual community. For upper income and educated blacks there have been the drawing cards of Howard University and of federal employment, but Washington became through the years one of the several meccas of the East Coast for the migrant poor black. For them unemployment has always been high, crime has become a serious problem, and education in the obsolete old school buildings scattered throughout the District has been a losing battle despite heroic efforts of the teachers and some members of the school board.

In Georgetown and other parts of the northwest there has been a heavy dependency on black domestic servants, largely middle-aged women, who now have to travel long distances by expensive, inadequate bus systems from the east and the northeast to the north and the northwest across the city. The residential

FIG. 4A Southwest Washington Redevelopment, original scheme: 10th Street Mall in foreground. *C. Feiss Collection*

FIG. 4B Southwest Urban Renewal: 10th Street Mall looking north. *C. Feiss Collection*

FIG. 4C Southwest Urban Renewal. *C. Feiss Collection*

segregation which has taken place throughout the city—contrary to the older urban tradition of the South—becomes a serious handicap to the worker and adds to many nasty traffic problems.

The most significant changes which have taken place in the white residential areas within the District of Columbia are the building up of large, multifamily dwelling concentrations in northwest Washington in the direction of American University out Massachusetts Avenue and the historic renewal of Old Georgetown. The multifamily residential growth is similar to what has occurred in many previously single family white residential areas in other parts of large cities throughout the country. The Georgetown historic renewal, however, is a rare phenomenon.

By the middle of the eighteenth century, Georgetown was a prosperous seaport, competing with Alexandria just a few miles down the river on the Virginia side for the Tidewater trade and the transshipment up the Potomac Valley across the Appalachians to Fort Pitt. There are few eighteenth-century communities in the United States which remain as intact and complete as Old Georgetown. It reached its economic apogee in the early part of the nineteenth century as the residential area for government officials since it was the only settled, urbane place in the great wastes of the new city. Most of its fine houses were built in the late Colonial and early Federalist periods; there was another later spurt of large home building in the 1880s and 1890s. During the early part of this century, Georgetown's shady streets were the home of a somewhat fading gentility—interspersed with black slums—and it was not until World War II that it commenced to be spruced up as the home of many individuals brought to Washington on war business. It continued to improve after the war, and today is one of the most attractive and expensive residential areas in town. Undoubtedly, air conditioning has had much to do with the Georgetown renaissance, since it was notorious for having a hot microclimate unrivaled by any other part of the city. Today, land values have skyrocketed; its houses and gardens are the focal point of tours, and the historic architecture of Old Georgetown is one of the acknowledged sights of Washington. A responsibility of the official Fine Arts Commission of Washington is the guardianship of Georgetown's historic architectural values, aided by citizen groups.

In southwest Washington, directly south of the government buildings on the mall, another major change has been effectuated over the past fifteen years. On the peninsula between the Anacostia and the Potomac and immediately west of South Capitol Street, a gigantic urban renewal project is now nearing completion. This area had been predominantly two-story brick row houses built over the past one hundred years. As evident from the L'Enfant-Ellicott Plan, it was an area which had very little interest to the early designers, and was largely laid out in an irregular grid; it had become a Negro slum and blighted area. In the early 1950s, it was designated a major urban renewal project and was cleared of practically all structures. After many false starts, a plan was finally approved which has completely altered every aspect of the area; southwest Washington has now become an urban show place. It is a lively example of the revitalization feasible under public urban renewal of a decrepit area. The solution to this problem of decay was to rebuild with high-rise expensive luxury apartments and town houses complete with shopping centers, churches and theatrical facilities; there was little attempt to rehouse the displaced black population in the area.

While the relocation of low-income blacks is a question that will always hang over the Southwest Renewal Area, from the livability, general design and appearance aspects as well as from the economic success of the several parts of the residential project, there cannot be any question that this is one of the most successful large urban renewal projects on the eastern seaboard. There are many imaginative architectural solutions to what is on the whole a dull plan; the privately developed town house and multifamily complexes are in garden settings, many of them beautifully landscaped, and those along the waterfront open onto a fine esplanade which will tie into a new waterfront shopping and restaurant center when completed. A major new shopping and office facility is under construction also in the center of the area. The southwest has, as a result, become a major attraction to middle- and upper-income white families with a good scattering of middle- and upper-income black families also.

The most spectacular part of the Southwest Renewal program is the nonresidential 10th Street Mall and L'Enfant Plaza area, including the huge office structures built for the Department of Housing and Urban Development, the Department of Transportation, the Navy and others. This giant new federal office complex is a leading example of contemporary architectural inhumanism. Vast, ponderous wastes of glass and masonry overwhelm anything remotely resembling human scale; the design is rigid and exudes a shameless egotism. Like the new Rayburn Building, just south and west of the Capitol, the sheer size of the masonry masses and their obvious intractability create a menacing mood that even the brightest sunlight does not dispel.

The lesson to be learned from the 10th Street Mall-L'Enfant Plaza debacle, the Rayburn Building, the gigantic new Kennedy Center for the Performing Arts and the new Smithsonian Museum of History and Technology is that today's architects do not know how to build monumental buildings and achieve beauty and dignity. One has the feeling that the domes, the pediments, the columns and all the classical vernacular have just been peeled off and there remains only a stark, classical coffin. The form is generally there, but nothing else. In those structures in which there has been an attempt to break away from the older vernaculars, the designer has not found adequate alternatives. He allows materials to overwhelm a building and substitutes none of the essential human elements of scale, texture or decorative design which bring buildings into focus and provide enjoyment and warm response from the viewer. Technology has further aggravated the problem by having devised air conditioning and lighting systems which make it unnecessary to have outside light and make it possible to provide either large areas of blank wall or large areas of blank glass, or both. Building bulk has been increased since light courts are no longer essential. In fact, interminable corridors and interminable interior spaces without light create a claustrophobic inner environment every bit as distressing as the exterior of the structures.

THE CULTURAL COMPLEX

While official architectural art seems to be retrogressing in Washington this cannot be said of culture as a whole: the District of Columbia has become a major cultural complex. Small institutions for higher learning which were nonentities on the national scene a few decades ago are now in fact attracting good faculty and students and are developing major campuses. Howard University and Catholic University are perhaps the best known nationally, with Georgetown University having pre-eminence in international and educational affairs. They have now been given keen competition by both American University and George Washington University. These five major private institutions have recently formed a consortium which makes it possible for students and faculty to take advantage of facilities at the different institutions. These universities have also added materially to the cultural life of the city through their musical events and theatre programs. This growth and strengthening of the five institutions have brought new life into several sections of the city, adding both young people and educators to the scene. Both Georgetown and George Washington universities have also added immeasurably to their facilities for medical education. Federal City College and the Washington Technical Institute have recently been established as the District's first public institutions of higher education.

The most spectacular cultural complex in Washington, comparable in area and conspicuous location to the Louvre in Paris, is the great Smithsonian museum assembly on the Mall. It consists of three major structures on the north side of the Mall and a mixture of large and small ones on the south. On the north are the

National Gallery of Art, the National Museum and the Museum of History and Technology. On the south are the Freer Gallery, the Old Smithsonian and a group of old and new buildings temporarily housing the Air Museum to be replaced by a new and very much larger structure adjacent to the Hirschhorn Art Gallery, which is across the Mall from the National Gallery of Art. This mammoth complex is supplemented by a newly developed large pair of museums housed in the early nineteenth-century Patent Office Building located several blocks to the north in the center of the old shopping district of the city: the National Portrait Gallery and the National Gallery of Fine Arts.

Unlike the Louvre, the museum complex on the Mall consists of a series of separate buildings. Although there is a tourmobile, there is no convenient way of getting from one to the next, particularly across the Mall. Despite the great formal plans, there is lack of adequate parking for private cars and buses which come by the thousands during the year. These are significant handicaps to the popular use and enjoyment of these cultural features. The museum structures that line both sides of the Mall fill in a number of the spaces on the McMillan Plan (1902), in which public buildings are indicated for each side of the Mall. They take the place of the foreign embassies, proposed to be on each side of a "Grande Promenade" in the L'Enfant-Ellicott Plan, and now primarily located on Massachusetts Avenue to the west.

The Smithsonian is only the public part of Washington's museum complex. The three major private art museums open to the public are the Corcoran, the Phillips Galleries and Dumbarton Oaks. The first two center their attention on contemporary art; the Corcoran also has attached to it an excellent school of art.

While Washington has only two major legitimate theatres handling touring productions, it has become a city of small theatres, theatre clubs and resident companies. The universities have theatres of their own. In addition, there is much good music in the city, particularly in chamber music, led by the Chamber Series at the Library of Congress, at the Phillips Gallery and at Dumbarton Oaks.

The greatest cultural unknown emerging on the Washington scene is the massive marble box, designed by Edward D. Stone, housing the Kennedy Center for the Performing Arts. Isolated in an almost inaccessible location, on the east bank of the Potomac just north of the Lincoln Memorial and south of Georgetown, appearing to be three times the size of the Lincoln Memorial and many times less attractive, it contains within its innards a theatre, a symphony hall, chamber music hall, opera hall and other facilities related to the performing arts. The one major cultural facility missing in Washington has always been adequate music and dance facilities. This center finally provides a solution even if almost impossible to reach except on foot.

PLANNING IN THE CAPITAL REGION

As discussed at length below by Donald Bozarth, planning in the capital region began with the L'Enfant Plan of 1791 and the 1792 L'Enfant-Ellicott Plan as finally approved. Unfortunately, the plans for the capital region, while they have magnitude in scale, do not match it in imagination or guts in attempting to control the nonpublic sector. No one has yet learned how to plan in advance of high-speed, large-scale, private development. The region has been urbanizing in the past three decades at an extraordinary rate, greater than ever in its history.

The Year 2000 Plan of 1961, while providing superb guidelines, has in turn failed to control development. Drastic action on the part of the National Park Service managed to prevent the destruction of the picturesque Potomac Gorge by walls of high-rise apartments, but the National Capital Planning Commission and the Regional Council, along with the planning commissions of the individual counties in the two states outside the District of Columbia, are not capable or legally strong enough to provide even the minimum mechanisms essential to prevent the misuse of land and its overcrowding. Nor can they control plans for highways and public facilities and services. The result is similar to the situation of many other major cities in the world: The Washington metro region is very much of a mess. However, there still are a number of handsome upper-income residential developments and some excellent new industrial parks. Here again the pattern of development results from plenty of private money to provide the quality of design that plenty of money can buy. The general public, particularly with respect to the mass medium-income housing shortage, are the victims of public policy, or lack thereof, and are the sufferers mainly of large-scale real estate operations. The centers of the surrounding suburban towns are worse than the older center of Washington; they are newly manufactured urban chaos. Though Baroque Washington was built in the absolute vernacular of a two-dimensional plan, it still was built within an orderly concept. The only relevance of the original Baroque plan for the central portion of the District of Columbia to the entire urbanizing region is the projection of main highways out and beyond its perimeter.

Curiously, no part of the urban region shows evidence that the L'Enfant Plan has had the slightest influence on suburban community layout; there are not even remote reflections of its essential form. While there is no question of the influence of this plan on the designs of Indianapolis, downtown Buffalo, early nineteenth-century plans for Cleveland and possibly on the Woodward Plan for Detroit, among others, it would seem that the historic geometric plan for the center of the capital has been all that the region can absorb. The sad and curious fact remains that the L'Enfant Plan was not a progenitor; it created nothing beyond itself and can be held responsible for neither order nor disorder in the historic growth of the region.

In 1889, building heights were first put under control with the establishment of a 130-foot maximum building height. A fifteen-story limit was levied in 1910 and then reduced to 110 feet. This has been strictly maintained with few exceptions ever since, although constantly under attack. A major purpose of the height limit has been to protect the appearance of the dome of the capitol and the top of the Washington Monument from all parts of the District. In the metropolitan region, there are no such restrictions in commercial areas or in high-rise residential areas leading to towering stalagmites of typical central city skyscrapers springing up all over the outskirts. While there are sporadic attempts to obtain uniform regulatory measures in planning incentives and controls throughout the metropolitan region through the new Council of Governments, it is not apparent that any of these efforts are succeeding as yet in accomplishing large scale design objectives. Only the handsome Potomac and Rock Creek parks, extending from the heart of the Washington complex out into the region, form a planned continuity that adds distinction to otherwise commonplace sprawl. In this respect, the 1902 plan has not been superseded. Fortunately, the Washington area has beautiful trees and there are a few remaining areas in the handsome horse country of Virginia and Maryland where the landscape retains the lush quality reminiscent of the English countryside.

THE BAROQUE PLAN

Despite its lack of influence on the metropolitan Washington scene, the original L'Enfant Plan designed in eleven months in 1791 has set the stage for the nation's capital. In the many changes which have taken place since the actual planning of the city during the early 1800s, none of the major Baroque elements of the original L'Enfant Plan were lost. This is as obvious today as it is in Karlsruhe, Germany, or in Versailles itself. Formed at that time, also, was the setting for the monumentality of this portion of the city leading to contemporary solutions for which the original planners cannot be held responsible. From the beginning the L'Enfant Plan seems to have been compelling and from the beginning it was criticized for its overwhelming scale and apparent irrationality. Still, in the more than one hundred years before the city grew to fit the plan, its scale was never reduced nor were its basic elements eliminated. Thomas Jefferson, thoroughly familiar with Versailles and a competent designer himself, apparently was at once caught up in the imagery of L'Enfant's Plan. And while the imagery was cast in the royal mold, the plan articulated clearly the separation of the executive and legislative functions of the special new form of democratic government, giving the President's house and executive offices and the congressional house or Capitol each distinct and prominent locations of their own. The Capitol on the top of its hill, as the seat of a democracy, was properly given the most prominent position. This was not a Versailles with a royal palace at the center of the design. The voice of the people to be heard in the people's capital located on its spectacular prominence in an otherwise flat landscape, facing down a broad esplanade to the Potomac River, was a concept of building location that had few peers in Europe and none in the United States.

The L'Enfant Plan was really nothing but a sketch plan (Fig. 5). The only details were suggestive floor plans of the President's House and the Capitol. With the exception of the area immediately in front of the Capitol and the White House and of the Mall itself, open spaces were largely blank. The squares and circles at the intersections of the long diagonals and their relationships to the underlying grid remained undefined. The plazas of Europe were demarcated by buildings and not by sidewalks, curbs and gutters or traffic lanes. Presumably, L'Enfant had in mind that the plazas of Washington would be lined by buildings and defined by them. The Washington plan in particular lacked architectural definition of the significant open spaces. It is true that L'Enfant lined the Mall with houses and gardens according to his "written references" on the plan. Unfortunately, that portion of the original plan of 1791 is so worn and indistinct that no structures are discernible, although they were placed by Ellicott in subsequent plans and appear in the final and approved design, along with other structures inserted in the design in various places not appearing in the original.

The major and traditional criticism of the L'Enfant Plan lies with the overlay of diagonals on a grid, or vice versa. The combination of diagonals and grid could not possibly provide good architectural treatment along such an important connec-

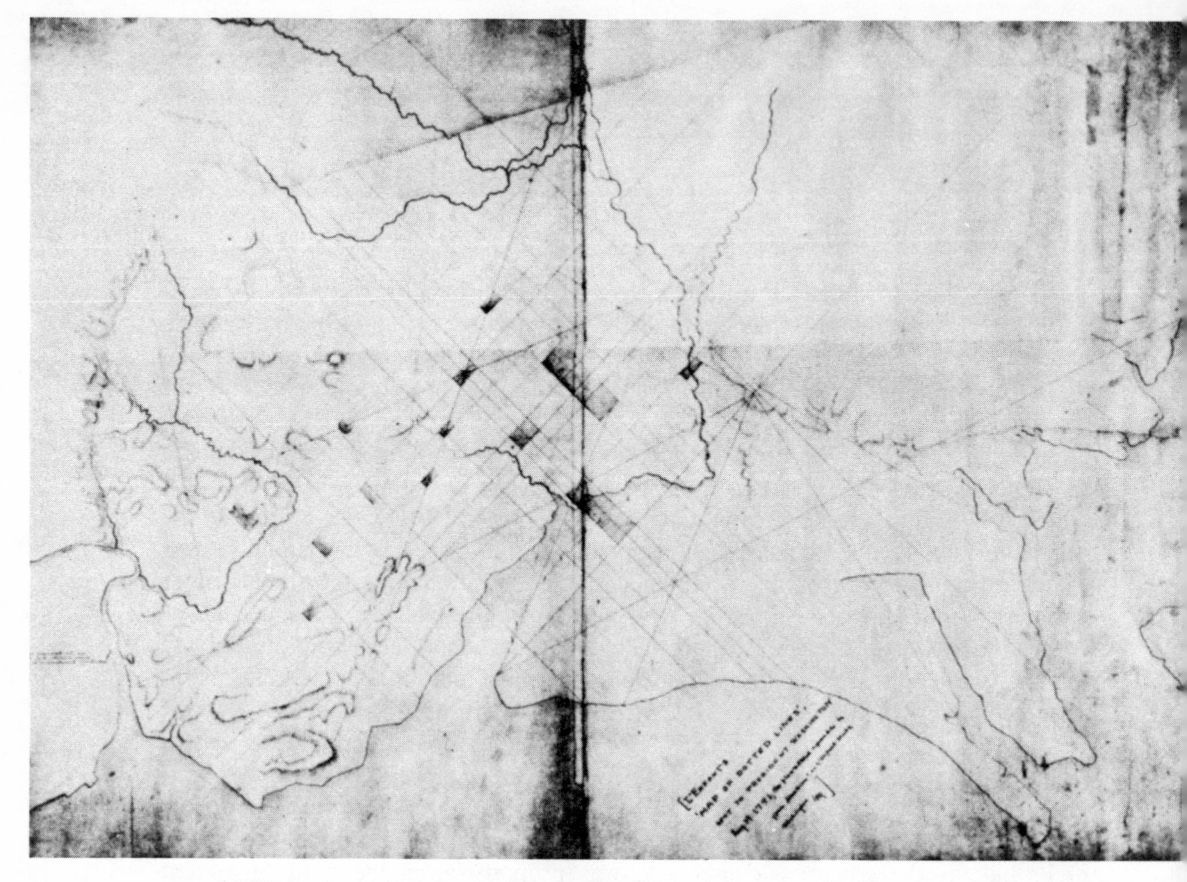

FIG. 5 L'Enfant's map of dotted lines, 1791. From *John Reps,* Monumental Washington, *Princeton, Princeton University Press, 1968*

tion as Pennsylvania Avenue, tying the President's house with Congress House. But this matter is really irrelevant to the original plan of L'Enfant; in his plan the avenue was broken by a number of open spaces and was not conceived of as a monumental connection between the executive and legislative buildings. About halfway between the two, he had plans for a square with a monumental "grand cascade." Otherwise, the street is not treated very much differently from many other of several diagonals. The Grande Avenue he had in mind and which appears also in the Ellicott Plan is a great parade running down the middle of the Mall from the Capitol to the great statue of President Washington to be located on an axis due west of the Capitol and due south of the President's house. This parade was to be four hundred feet wide and a mile in length, bordered by gardens, and was a much better idea than the present dreary monumental concept of converting Pennsylvania Avenue into another dreary monumental street of which Washington has an adequate number. The great parade down the Mall would have livened up the empty Mall and put the celebrations properly where they should be, in full view of the Capitol and the White House.† The present somewhat barren *tapisvert* (green carpet) of the Mall, which results from the beautifully designed, but humanly dead, concepts of the McMillan Plan of 1901, would not prevent a re-

† For example, the Champs Élysées in Paris, the Sieges Alleé in Berlin, even New Delhi's Rajphat, designed by Sir Edward Lytjens. (Editor's note.)

turn to the original L'Enfant concept, which is actually splendidly augmented by the Washington Monument and the distant Lincoln Memorial. Redesigned for parades and assemblies, the Great Mall could become one of the impressive gathering places of the world; recent demonstrations and marches on Washington have made natural and appropriate uses of this challenging open space. The Pennsylvania Avenue Plan of April 1964 for a triumphal boulevard tries to force the issue and proposes among other things a vast new paved open space, a "Red Square," on Pennsylvania Avenue in a city which has adequate other open spaces which could be used much more effectively.

The basic grid to which the Baroque diagonals were drawn, while regular in its north-south, east-west orientation, is extremely and curiously irregular in the spacing of the streets, resulting in a highly diversified block size throughout the historic area. At first glance it would appear that the diagonals were drawn across the grid, but actually this would have been impossible as the grid layout design is clearly related to the design of the intersections and the open spaces of the diagonals. A brief inspection of the original plan and of the 1792 Plan clearly indicates that the work on the drawing board was an ingenious attempt to integrate the static quality of the grid with the dynamics of the diagonals.

However, in 180 years the open space parts of the plan have failed to create good framing architecture. There is not one of the Washington squares, circles or other smaller open spaces that has generated anything remotely resembling the quality of architecture to be found on similar open spaces in eighteenth-century Europe, particularly Paris and London. In fact, they did not even generate as good an architecture as was to be found in Georgetown and Alexandria. Lafayette Square in front of the White House, with the most promising location and which had from time to time during the nineteenth century a number of good houses built on it, never achieved the architectural distinction of a square in London's Bloomsbury or for that matter Rittenhouse Square in Philadelphia or Louisburg Square in Boston.

The failure of the Baroque plan was that it was primarily two-dimensional. The only three-dimensional aspects related to the location of the Capitol Building itself on its hill, and to some degree the much less distinguished location of the President's house. A curious omission in the plan as originally conceived was a formal landing place for distinguished visitors as a major part of the river plan. The shoreline was lined with docks on both the Potomac and the Anacostia, and there were plenty of open spaces and squares which face the water and presumably could have been used for that purpose, but there was no one specifically and clearly designated. In a highly maritime-tidewater economy, it is surprising that Washington and Jefferson did not notice this. It has only been in recent years that the Potomac has been made a major decorative adjunct to the city. Unfortunately, it is now invisible from the Mall, since the banks were built up at the Lincoln Memorial as a dike to prevent the periodic flooding that used to plague the whole western end of the Mall below the White House and the Washington Monument.

The famous McMillan Plan of 1901 selected the Capitol and the White House area for special redesign considerations. Based on the Beaux Arts concepts of the day, it has remained a compelling plan for the formal part of the Baroque plan ever since. More than any other plan, it has been the responsible agent for the siting of public buildings in the Federal Triangle and along Constitution and Independence avenues which border the Mall to the north and the south respectively. It has in some degree been responsible for the siting of major buildings around the Capitol. In this latter instance, the McMillan Plan completely ignored topographical situations, and if it is ever completed as designed originally, would add to the unpleasant framework now achieved at the south side of the Capitol with the dominant Rayburn Building and the other House office buildings. The failure of the McMillan Plan to visualize a good continuous Mall facade for both its sides—the kind of facade to be found along the Rue de Rivoli in Paris or in Regents Park in London—was a serious one. Individual buildings centered on individual blocks, added from time to time with no basic design scheme, have not created a satisfactory lineal form, architectural relationships or satisfactory design interrelationships. If it were not for the unifying and also concealing strength of the trees along the Mall between the buildings, in summer, the unpleasant heterogeneity of the bordering buildings would be much more conspicuous. Recent Mall plans made in 1968 make no attempt to correct this approach, which will now have to remain the permanent solution.

Fiddling with the details of the Mall area will undoubtedly go on for generations to come. Superhighway schemes are now being designed to wind around and go under it, hopefully alleviating some of the heavy traffic through the center of the city. The subway plans for the central city possibly in time will relieve the intolerable parking situation which spills over into all the more formal decorative aspects of the design. None of the Mall museums provide for public parking, which undoubtedly some day will be accommodated under portions of the Mall. There would be nothing wrong with this since it could provide direct access underground to some of the museums and badly needed all-weather pedestrian communication transversely across the Mall. Current plans for the Mall, for completing the Federal Triangle and for embellishing Pennsylvania Avenue are in a confused state; they do not have the financial thrust of urban renewal behind them so that the dramatic events that have occurred in southwest Washington and along the 10th Street Mall are not being repeated north of the Mall's east-west axis.

The Mall is not the city, nor is it the entire Baroque plan. Like the Capitol Building itself, it is subject to all the whims of current architecture and planning. Nor are the Mall, the Baroque plan for the old city center, the plans for the big city and the metropolitan area of the city. Washington is the amalgam of all of these things which provide a special character and quality to the city. The capital today remains what it has been for many years in many parts: a remarkably beautiful and satisfactory place in which to live and work. For all of its difficulties as a new town, for all of its problems as a modern city, for all of its multiple populations, both resident and visitor, it is an excellent capital city with a dynamic, dramatic and distinctive ambiance.

TOMORROW: COMMUNITY DEVELOPMENT PLANNING

Donald F. Bozarth*

THE NATIONAL CAPITAL REGION

Early planning efforts were largely architectural in orientation and focused primarily on the monumental areas and other federal uses in the heart of the nation's capital. Today, the emphasis is on a more balanced consideration of the social, economic and political, as well as the urban-design-oriented physical aspects of over-all community planning and development. Although the monumental and symbolic signs of the seat of the federal government remain in the heart of the central city, the entire National Capital Region as a whole has become the setting for the headquarters functions of the government as Carl Feiss indicated.

The continuing population implosion into the area; the increased national attention being given to our "urban problems" and the "crisis of our cities"; the rising demands for attention to the needs and desires of the socially and economically deprived members of the urban community; the civil disorders of 1968; the inevitable selection of Washington as a "model" city or "demonstration area" for evolving national urban programs have all had their influence on planning for the nation's capital.

* Director of current planning and programming, National Capital Planning Commission, Washington, D.C., Mr. Bozarth has held various positions of responsibility with the Commission since 1959; he previously served as the assistant director of planning for the Redevelopment Authority of the city of Philadelphia, the assistant director of the Metropolitan Area Planning Commission in Little Rock, Arkansas, and the assistant director of slum clearance for the Housing Authority of the city of Little Rock. He received a master's degree in regional planning from the University of North Carolina at Chapel Hill and a B.A. in political science from Amherst College.

Although Washington is a planned city, it has had an official, comprehensive planning agency only since 1926. The National Capital Planning Commission (NCPC) is both the city planning commission for the District of Columbia government (city of Washington) and the central physical planning agency for the federal government in the National Capital Region. This unique combination (in American cities) of planning functions was intended to establish a planning framework for the balanced consideration of the sometimes conflicting local and federal interests in the development of the nation's capital. The Commission's basic functions are:

1. Preparation, adoption and periodic modification of the Comprehensive Plan for the National Capital. This long-range development plan includes, but is not limited to, generalized proposals for land uses, major thoroughfares, park, parkway and recreation systems, mass transportation and community facilities and services.
2. Reviewing proposed plans as programs. Each federal and District agency must consult with the Commission during preliminary and successive stages in preparing plans and programs for projects and developments paid for with federal or District funds.
3. Proposing amendments to the zoning regulations and maps to the separate Zoning Commission and reports on proposed amendments as to their relation or conformity with the Comprehensive Plan.
4. Approves proposed boundaries and urban renewal plans, new public housing projects or modifications to existing projects.
5. The Commission also acquires land for the park, parkways and playground system of the national capital, and makes grants to local park authorities in Maryland and Virginia for stream valley park acquisition.[1]

The membership of the Commission is unique in the United States; it is composed of five citizens, appointed by the President, who serve without compensation; five ex-officio members from executive agencies (the chief of engineers of the U. S. Army, the mayor, commissioner of the District of Columbia, the director of the National Park Service, the commissioner of Public Buildings, and the director of Public Roads), and the chairman of the committees on the District of Columbia of the Senate and the House of Representatives. The composition of its membership was intended to ensure a balanced consideration of plans for the nation's capital by: (a) the area's residents, (b) the citizens of the United States as a whole and (c) through the ex-officio members—the major federal agencies and the District of Columbia government that have land acquisition, construction and development programs in the Washington area.

Outside of the District of Columbia there are subregional and local planning agencies in each of the various political subdivisions—two in Maryland and seven in Virginia. The Maryland National Capital Park and Planning Commission includes representatives from the two counties in the suburban Maryland portion of the region. The Northern Virginia Planning District is the subregional planning body for seven jurisdictions in the northern Virginia portion of the National Capital Region.

All of these local governments, including the District of Columbia, are also members of the Metropolitan Washington Council of Governments (COG). This is a voluntary association of fifteen of the major local governments in the National

Capital Region established in 1957 to assist member governments in concerting their efforts to meet those area-wide needs which could not be met through separate unrelated programs by working through and strengthening existing local governments. The members of the governing bodies of the twelve member governments, plus the local members of the general assemblies of Maryland and Virginia, and of the United States Congress, are COG members. Its executive board, which meets monthly, and its five policy committees include members from each governing body. Fourteen advisory committees composed of local, state and national officials provide technical guidance to projects.[2]

COG has many varied programs in the Washington area ranging from environmental concerns to emergency region-wide snow removal plans. It was designated as the official metropolitan planning agency for the Washington area in 1966 when the National Capital Regional Planning Council (NCRPC) was abolished.

In the last four years, according to COG, it

> . . . has sought to bring together all relevant plans and policies of past and present planning efforts on the local, subregional, and regional levels. They are a valuable asset in the further development of regional policies and plans. In addition, they continue to serve as the basis for COG's review of regionally significant developments and as the foundation for decisions of immediate relevance.
>
> . . . has developed reports on regional statistics, health facilities and air facilities planning in the region; and the area's natural features, its governmental structure, and its programs of capital improvements.
>
> . . . has been developing metropolitan-wide functional plans and programs for open space and water and sewerage facilities. These preliminary plans and programs will help to guide development as the comprehensive planning process yields new data and regional policies are refined.[3]

Continued Rapid Growth

Like most other world capitals, the major factor influencing the planning of Washington is continued rapid population growth. The 1970 census shows that the Washington area has moved from tenth to seventh largest in the nation as a result of a population growth in the suburbs of about 800,000—an increase in ten years equal to the entire population of the District of Columbia. This rate of growth (38.4 per cent) was the second fastest growth rate in the country between 1960 and 1970. The population of the metropolitan area is now approximately 2,900,000 by these preliminary estimates. The 1970 census clearly revealed that this is now a nation in which the population of the suburbs is greater than in the central cities.[4]

COG recently reported on an economic base study that it had had prepared for the metropolitan area, including projections of the probable range of long-term population and employment growth as follows[5]:

> The findings from this study indicate that the region's economy and population may grow at a considerably faster rate between now and the year 2000 than is indicated by the above projections. The Hammer, Green, Silver Associates projections show a population range between 6.8 and 8.9 million by the year 2000 depending on various assumptions regarding

birth and death rates, in-migration patterns, and national population projections. This study suggests a "most probable" year 2000 figure is nearly half again greater than that assumed for the year 2000 when COG adopted its development policies in 1965.

Such predictions that the area's population will triple in the next thirty years does not appear to have surprised anyone. Although there have been some suggestions that nine million may be too many people, there has been little local public concern over these growth prospects; the concern has been how can this additional growth be more effectively planned.

In contrast with the region as a whole, the population of the District of Columbia actually decreased slightly in the last decade; the city's population appears to be stabilizing around 150,000.

NCPC's *Comprehensive Plan for the National Capital* is based upon a projected population of 800,000 in the District by 1985. This projected increase of approximately 54,000 between 1970 and 1985 would result from both proposed public and private actions—renewal and rebuilding of blighted areas, more intensive development at selected Metro subway stations and the predominantly residential redevelopment of two large relatively undeveloped federally-owned tracts of land.

In the last decade, there has been a marked change in both the age and the racial characteristics of the District's population. Washington's young and old people have increased in numbers while the most economically productive age groups have declined substantially. During this same period, the nonwhite population in the city has increased from about 54 per cent to almost 71 per cent. It is clear that the continued decline in the white population, resulting from movement to the suburbs, has been more than offset by the increases in the nonwhite population in the city.

In 1960, Washington was unique in having a black majority. By 1970, according to the U. S. Census, three other major U.S. urban centers had joined Washington in this category.[6]

In the region as a whole, the black population increased from 24.5 per cent to 25.7 per cent of the total population. This increase of 202,895 blacks largely took place in Washington (+123,108) and in Prince George's County, Maryland (+60,832), where the total black population tripled in the last decade. According to the census, the black population of the close-in suburbs grew by 80,000 in the last decade although the percentages of the population that are black changed only a little because of proportionate increases in the white population. This increase was reported as one of the country's larger movements of blacks to the suburbs.[7]

GOVERNMENTAL AND POLITICAL FRAMEWORK FOR PLANNING

The city of Washington, unique in the United States, is a municipal government, a state (for the purposes of many federal aid programs) and, most importantly, an arm of the Executive Branch of the federal government in the District of Columbia. Yet, the citizens of the District remained largely voteless for one hundred years until 1974. The first elections for mayor and the City Council took place in November under the Home Rule Act finally passed in 1973 with the newly elected government taking office in January 1975. The lack of some form of home rule and the many facets of that local issue have affected planning for the city; so have the current efforts to reorganize and streamline the new government of the District. These influences in the 1960s were so great that they lead to a presidential commitment at the end of the decade to reorganize planning in the nation's capital in order to give the District more planning resources and responsibilities—perhaps even its own planning agency which it is now finally getting.

Undoubtedly, the most significant local political issue in the District of Columbia in the last fifteen years has been home rule; the District's residents were not entitled to elect their own local government, or to have their own representatives (except in recent years one nonvoting member of the House) in the Congress. Although historically there have been various forms of local government in the District, all mayors since 1871 have been appointed. The District government is a part of the Executive Branch of the federal government. Its annual budget is subject to the control of both the White House and the Congress. But until very recently its citizens were not even able to vote in either local or national elections. In 1968, they were finally given the right to vote in presidential elections for the first time.

The fact remains, moreover, that the District is the seat of the federal government; this inevitably means that federal interests will always dictate that the city cannot have complete, unlimited home rule without some overview of federal interests by the federal government. This federal/local issue has had and continues to have a significant influence on the planning process and the organization for planning in the region.

Home rule proposals by the White House came near to passage in the Johnson administration, but the election of 1970 returned a Congress that was less sympathetic on this issue and recent efforts have focused on congressional representation. In regard to home rule, therefore, Washington still remains what many have termed "The Lost Colony."[8]

In 1967, the President reorganized the District government. The three-man commissioner form of government was replaced by a mayor-council form unique in the United States. The mayor, the deputy mayor, the chairman of the City Council and the other eight members of the Council are all appointed officials appointed by the President and subject to confirmation by the United States Senate.

Although far less than hoped for by home-rule interests, this was one of several moves by the federal government at that time to make the District government more effective and more sensitive to local needs (largely black). The names of candidates for the various council posts were solicited from the whole community and, once in office, the Council unofficially subdivided the city into four political districts with two councilmen assigned to work with interested groups and individuals in each area.

For the first mayor of Washington since 1871, President Johnson chose a Washington native and a housing expert, Mr. Walter E. Washington, the first black ever to head the local government of a major American city.

The new District government did prove to be more sensitive and more responsive to local needs and desires. It began a series of reorganizations aimed at improving the delivery of municipal services, started new programs in areas where none existed before and broadened other programs better to meet the communities needs. Although an improvement over the previous system, the new government did not satisfy the home-rule interests or the newly vocal black militants in the city. Undoubtedly, home rule and the organization of the District government will continue to be major issues in the 1970s. The Nelson Committee Report in 1972 on the District of Columbia government recommended many wide ranging steps to increase its power and efficiency.

Congress Permits Locally Elected Board of Education

The Board of Education was until recently made up of nine citizens who were appointed by the United States District Court for the District of Columbia with overlapping terms of three years each. The Board is autonomous in its operations except for its fiscal responsibility to the District of Columbia government. As one of many local efforts to improve and strengthen the local school system, Congress did, recently, abolish the old appointment system and replace it with popular election of all Board members. In 1969, the Board of Education became the first and the only elected local body in the District of Columbia.

This was a major milestone and gave District residents the first real opportunity in this century to organize and conduct city-wide election campaigns and exercise their right to vote. It is a beginning to more self-government. It may well be that the success or failure of the elected school board will have a significant influence on congressional attitudes about home rule in the 1970s.

Congressional Representation

For many years there have been efforts to give the District one or more representatives in the Senate and in the House of Representatives. Local interests and sympathetic congressmen have tried to get both a voice and a vote for the District in the Congress; others have argued that District representation should be limited to a nonvoting delegate similar to Puerto Rico's.

In 1970, the Congress finally approved a nonvoting delegate for the District in the House of Representatives. The new delegate was elected by May 1, 1971, and, like other congressmen, serves on committees, has an office, a staff and is able to introduce bills and offer amendments. Mayor Washington noted that the new delegate "will interpret the needs of the District" in the Congress and that it "gets us one step closer to home rule."

Proposed Reorganization of Planning in Washington

In the fall of 1968, President Nixon announced his intention to propose a reorganization of the National Capital Planning Commission that would give the District of Columbia government its own planning capabilities and abolish the dual planning responsibilities of the Commission. In effect, the concept was to split NCPC's functions into two pieces—with local District planning being transferred to the District of Columbia government and federal planning functions remaining with NCPC. In addition, the residual federal planning agency (NCPC or its successor) would be strengthened as the central physical planning arm of the executive branch in the national capital region.

This reorganization would reportedly contain provisions that would give the residual federal planning entity a planning overview role over District planning in order to ensure that local plans were, in fact, consistent with the continuing federal interests in the development and redevelopment of the City of Washington. The proposed redistribution of planning functions has its roots directly in the efforts to make both the District and the federal government more sensitive and responsive to local needs and wishes. It also reflected the desire of the city management types in the new District government to have a major planning and programming capability and be able to exercise some control over the planning function.

It has been NCPC's plight that its dual responsibilities as the planning agency for both governments usually results in failure to satisfy fully either of them. The federal agencies often have felt that NCPC was too District oriented; the District agencies, in turn, have usually felt that NCPC was too federally oriented.

The most significant proposal in the 1972 Nelson Committee Report affecting planning in the nation's capital was the recommendation that NCPC's local planning functions be transferred to the District of Columbia government. This recommendation was not carried out in full. After July 1, 1974, two planning agencies operated in the District area. A local planning agency (Office of Planning and Management) is concerned with "local affairs" while the National Capital Planning Commission (NCPC) deals with the "federal role" within the District and with general planning matters over the entire capital region. The latter body retains a veto power over the former's actions affecting federal interests. The awkwardness of such a situation is patent. In July 1975, the NCPC will have its two District members appointed by the elected mayor.[9]

TRANSPORTATION—A DECADE OF CRISIS

During the past ten years, the Washington area has been embroiled in a continuing debate and controversy over the transportation problems associated with rapid growth. Because of the issues involved and the fact that the ultimate solution will have a fundamental influence on regional and community planning in the 1970s, it warrants special consideration here.

Mass Transportation Study

In 1952, the Congress authorized a major transportation study of the metropolitan Washington area. The Mass Transportation Survey Report was prepared by the National Capital Planning Commission and the National Capital Regional Planning Council and transmitted to the President in July of 1959. The Transportation Plan recommended in this report was scaled to meet the needs of the region when the region's population had reached 3 million in 1980 (now projected at 4.3 million). The estimated cost of building and equipping the recommended new facilities was $2.5 billion.

The basic transportation system recommended included the following[10]:

1. A network of freeways and parkways—including thirteen radial routes—facilitating rapid travel between any two parts of the region, even at peak hours. A total of 329 miles of freeways and parkways was planned in the region (81 miles existed at that time, 178 miles were already planned, and 70 miles of new roads were proposed).
2. A new kind of fast, comfortable public transit service between the

suburbs and downtown Washington. This transit service was to take two forms:

Modern express buses on eight of the routes that lead to downtown, traveling on freeways and parkways at high speeds and making a limited number of stops until they reach the downtown street system. A total of 66 miles of express bus routes was proposed.

Modern rail transit service on four heavily traveled routes. The rail lines would be located in subways in the inner areas of the District of Columbia, and elsewhere would be in the median strips of freeways or on their own rights-of-way. A total of 33 miles of double track lines were proposed and three of the four lines were to extend as far as the Capital Beltway.

3. Arterial streets and highways extensively improved to carry automotive traffic not served by the freeways.

4. Expanded and improved local transit service on arterial and local streets to carry passengers not served by the new bus and rail routes.

The report also recommended the following:

1. The creation of an interstate compact agency to regulate transit in the area.

2. The creation of a temporary public corporation to acquire land, construct and operate the system, and

3. A second interstate compact creating a new interstate agency ultimately to succeed both of the above organizations.

It would have power to construct and own transit facilities, to operate them or provide for their operation by private firms, to review and consult upon highway construction plans as they might affect transit facilities, to assist the highway agencies in overcoming any deficit in funds, and to regulate and co-ordinate any private firms engaged in transit service.

In 1965, a basic twenty-five-mile mass transit system, scaled down from the eighty-three-mile system and largely within the District of Columbia boundaries, was authorized by the Congress under the National Capital Transportation Authority (NCTA). In September 1967, the NCTA was superseded and its functions and duties were taken over by the interstate regional body—the Washington Metropolitan Area Transit Authority. Under the compact, the agency is responsible to the people of the region through the makeup of its Board of Directors—two members and two alternates from each of the three participating jurisdictions.

Washington's Metro

When in 1960, the Congress created the National Capital Transportation Agency (NCTA) to initiate the development of a plan and program for a regional transit system, it also authorized the creation of an interstate authority empowered by Maryland, Virginia and the District of Columbia to act as a regional body.

In 1962, NCTA made its initial recommendations, proposing an eighty-three-mile system of rapid transit, fifteen miles of commuter railroad service and sixty-two miles of express bus routes serving primarily as extensions or feeders to the rapid transit system.[11]

In March of 1968, the new authority adopted the regional metro plan and program. The system provided for eight major radial lines extending from the

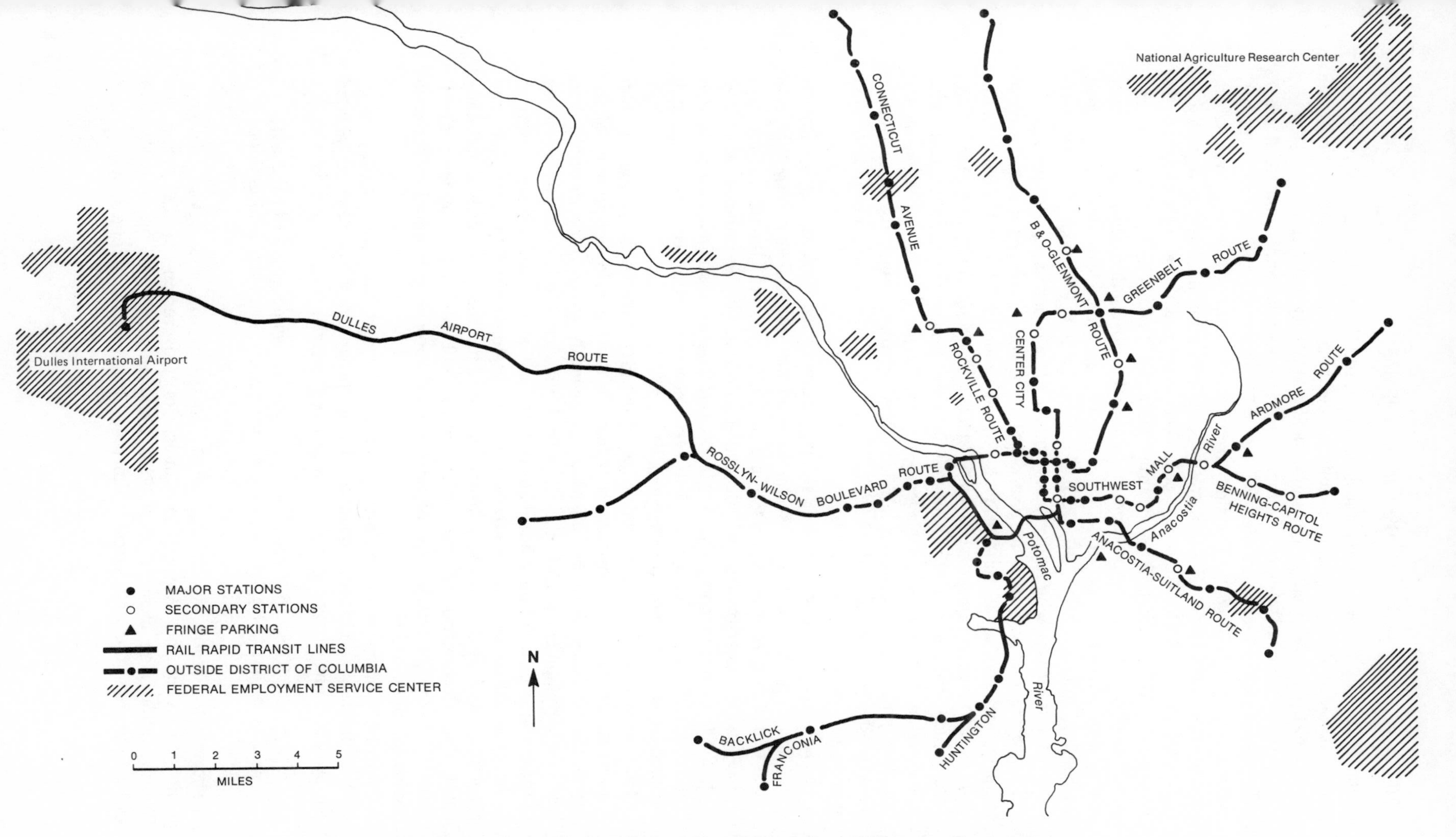

FIG. 6 NCPC Mass Transportation Plan, 1968. *National Capital Planning Commission*

center of the city to the beltway and including a total of 97.2 miles. As shown on Figure 6, the system will serve a total of eighty-six stations—forty-four in the District of Columbia, twenty-two in Maryland and twenty in Virginia.

Half of the system, primarily in high density residential and commercial areas, will be in subway. The remainder will be on or above the surface in a separate, single-purpose right-of-way. The first six miles of downtown service was scheduled for operation late in 1973 (it wasn't), the entire initial plan was expected to be completed by 1980 (it won't be). The system will be, according to the Washington Metropolitan Area Transit Authority (WMATA), "fast, safe, dependable all-weather transportation in comfortable air-conditioned cars . . . two-minute service during rush hours . . . bright, beautiful, clean stations designed for comfort and safety . . . 30,000 parking spaces at key stations . . . improved suburban bus service, with feeder buses running literally across transit lines . . ."[12]

The Metro was expected to cost $2,500,000,000 according to the original estimate, and was to be funded by a federal grant of $1,150,000,000, $850,-000,000 of revenue bonds issued by WMATA and $500,000,000 in local bond issues based upon a carefully allocated formula among the counties and cities in the region to be served. In November 1968, 72 per cent of the voters in the suburban jurisdictions requiring a referendum approved bond issues to finance the local shares of building the Metro. The entire regional plan was subsequently approved by the Congress in 1969.

The initial regional system will serve that portion of the National Capital Region within the Capital Beltway. As such, this step has disappointed those who had hoped that a truly regional system would be built to provide the needed leverage to support the development of the radial corridors in accordance with *The Year 2000 Plan* concepts. The WMATA's response to such criticism is that "future extensions of Metro routes, to serve new population centers burgeoning during the eighties are already projected."[13]

The reason given for the limited scope of the first stage of the regional system was the lack of projected revenue from fares in those developing portions of the region. On this basis, Washington's Metro is obviously going to follow rather than lead new development outside the Beltway. Unlike most other subway programs in the world, which consider adequate mass transit as an essential public service to be provided as needed in accordance with regional development plans and programs, the United States still insists on a revenue formula which significantly limits the effectiveness of the system as a tool for implementing regional planning. Instead, a certain level of ridership and revenue is required before such service will be provided.

WMATA's timetable for future projections beyond the first Beltway is to start in the 1980s. The consequences of such programming is clear, as pointed out by COG in its recent report, *The Changing Region*[14]:

> In the next 10 or 15 years highways alone will guide growth in the outlying areas of the Region. Rail transit will follow, not lead, land development.

The adopted Metro system is generally consistent with the regional development policies of the Washington Council of Governments (COG) and the Transportation Plan element of NCPC's *Comprehensive Plan for the National Capital.* In fact, the only current difference between the adopted system and

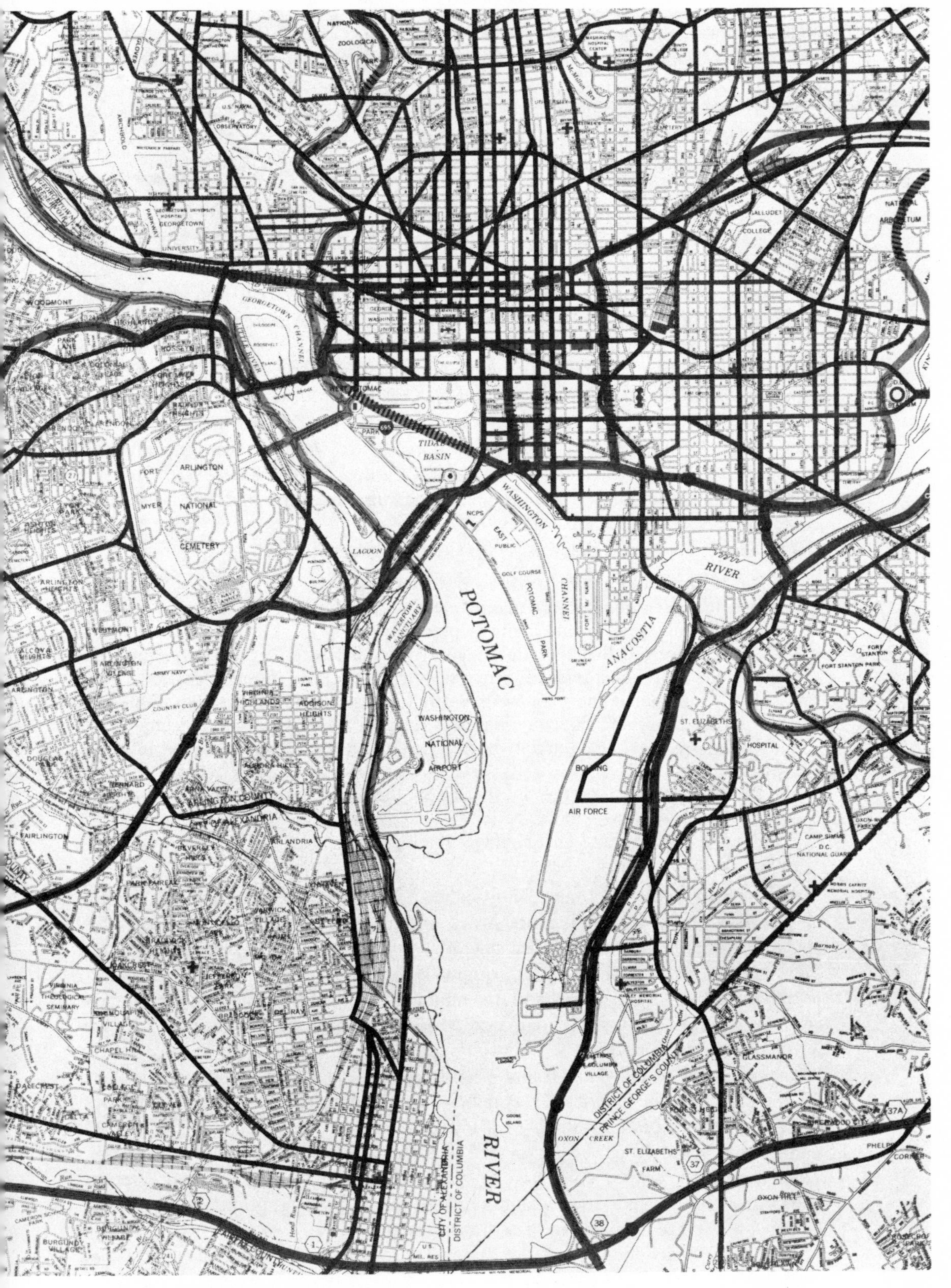

FIG. 7 NCPC Major Thoroughfare Plan, 1968. *National Capital Planning Commission*

NCPC's adopted Mass Transportation Plan is the Commission's proposal for a line to serve Dulles International Airport. This proposal is currently under study by WMATA.

Metro construction continues with signs that the funding crises on the Hill may be over. In 1972, the District of Columbia's annual share of Metro costs was appropriated and Metro bonding authority was approved by the Congress.

Major Thoroughfare Plan

The adoption and approval of the Major Thoroughfare Plan by NCPC and the District of Columbia Council in December 1968 (Fig. 7) was a major moment in the history of transportation planning in the nation's capital. It also represented a significant departure for the Commission from its earlier proposals of the 1959 Mass Transportation Study.

The adopted system contains a total of 36.3 miles of freeways, parkways and expressways in the District of Columbia. The system essentially comprises an inner loop in the old L'Enfant city—with a center leg crossing under the Mall west of the Capitol Building—with radial corridor freeways to the northwest (the Potomac River Freeway and the Palisades Parkway), the southeast (Suitland Parkway), and the south (part of the Anacostia Freeway) and northeast (the New York Avenue Industrial Boulevard).

The adopted system is noteworthy for the following reasons:

1) It did not contain the Three Sisters Bridge over the Potomac River which has been the subject of an intensive decade-long controversy between conservationists and highway planners.

2) It suggested that the equally controversial North Leg be given further study as a tunnel under K Street through the central business district.

3) It eliminated the proposed North Central Freeway (strongly supported by Maryland highway planners [largely white areas] and strongly opposed by the D.C. [largely black] neighborhoods that would be impacted by it).

4) It proposed that the South Leg of the Inner Loop be tunneled—for esthetic reasons—under the entire Lincoln Memorial-Jefferson Memorial area (an expense the highway engineers did not feel was justified on a dollar cost-benefit basis).

As noted, the adopted Major Thoroughfare Plan contains a total of 36.3 miles of freeways, parkways and expressways within the District of Columbia; this compares with the 42.5-mile system suggested in the 1967 Proposed Comprehensive Plan and the larger 74-mile system originally proposed in the 1959 Mass Transportation Study. On the other hand, the adopted rapid transit system in the District contains 38.4 miles of track compared with the 19-mile system proposed in the Mass Transportation Study.

The adopted highway and rapid transit systems contain a combined total of 74.7 miles within the District of Columbia—about evenly divided between the two. The Mass Transportation Study of 1959 had proposed a combined total of 93 miles—with about 80 per cent allocated to highways and 20 per cent to rapid rail. The increasingly greater emphasis on mass transit facilities reflects more recent approaches to transportation planning, and the increasing priority and federal financial assistance available to mass transit today.

As a basis for its adoption of the Major Thoroughfare Plan in December 1968, the Commission also approved a statement, *Policies and Principles for a Transportation System for the Nation's Capital,* setting forth its philosophy and a sophisticated rationale for the proposed plan. Because of the significance of this statement in comparing various approaches to transportation planning in the capital cities of the world, it seems appropriate to quote significant portions of the statement[15]:

> This Commission has clear and unmistakable planning responsibilities, both to assure the efficiency and to preserve the amenities of the Nation's Capital. This means that the transportation system it recommends must fully take both objectives into account. . . .
>
> The Commission believes that a policy that seeks to limit the flow of automobiles into the heart of the city is a practical and realistic approach to transportation planning. The Commission would go so far as to say that through no other approach can it meet its basic planning responsibilities. . . .
>
> This metropolitan community has already moved a long way toward adopting and implementing this precise approach. The people of Washington and the surrounding suburban communities in the region have set into motion the development of the largest and most comprehensive mass transit system ever planned at one time for an urban area. . . .
>
> This metropolitan area has also committed itself to a major freeway program. Already, however, this freeway system is generating traffic that the streets in the Nation's Capital cannot handle. Major improvements are yet needed in the heart of Washington to move this traffic to its destination and to protect the monumental character of the nation's city from the blight that traffic can produce.
>
> The Commission's major thoroughfare plan does not call for any new gateway arteries that would increase vehicular flow into the District, by bridge, tunnel or surface street. . . . They would generate traffic that would soon exceed the capacities of their own rights-of-way to handle it.
>
> The Commission's studies, utilizing precisely the same data employed to justify additional freeways into the District, clearly indicate that the projected mass transit system, coupled with the capacities of existing freeways and major streets, can carry the future traffic loads that are forecast for the heart of the Nation's capital. . . .
>
> Both plans tie transportation facilities directly into land use plans. They would provide the traffic-carrying capacity that would fully support the governmental activities of the federal establishment. They would fully serve the central business district and the office functions of downtown Washington, which comprise the greatest concentration of employment in the metropolitan region and represent one of the fastest growing and most viable central economic structures in the nation.
>
> The successful implementation of these plans will call for other supporting actions and policies on the part of the District Government. The location of new public buildings should be carefully planned to tie most efficiently into the transportation facilities that are provided. Through zoning and other control devices, private office and commercial space should also be located to take maximum advantage of available traffic capacities. The location of parking spaces should be carefully controlled and the number of parking spaces should as a matter of policy be limited in those areas directly served by mass transit.

However, the freeway debate in the nation's capital was not over. Despite the unanimity of NCPC and the Council's actions in adopting the Major Thoroughfare Plan, it was not acceptable to the Congress. In the 1968 Federal Aid Highway Act, the District government has been directed to build the Three Sisters Bridge, the Potomac River Freeway, a part of the East Leg of the Inner Loop and complete the Center Leg.[16]

Other sections of the interstate freeway system were to be studied and recommendations made to the Congress "with respect to such projects including any recommended routes or plans" within eighteen months. It was intended that the adoption of the Major Thoroughfare Plan would constitute the required recommendation. However, subsequent to the adoption of the plan the District of Columbia Council voted, in August 1969, to comply with the Act and commence construction of the Three Sisters Bridge. The recommendations regarding the other elements of the freeway system were made to the Congress largely in accordance with the Major Thoroughfare Plan. As evidence that this was not an acceptable recommendation, the Congress included in the 1970 Federal Aid Highway Act a reiteration of its direction to make recommendations on the controversial projects, this time within twelve months.

Both the District Council and the National Capital Planning Commission now agree on the main elements of the Major Thoroughfare Plan. However, construction of the Three Sisters Bridge had not commenced by late 1974 as it had been tied up with environmental suits involved with routing Interstate Highway 66 entering the elegant central governmental area from Arlington, Virginia.

HOUSING PROBLEMS AND PROGRAMS

The District's housing troubles, so evident to the members of Congress living in the capital, are just a part of the over-all housing situation in the metropolitan area (and in other U.S. metropolitan areas). In 1960, there were an estimated 101,327 housing units that were substandard and/or overcrowded in the National Capital Region. This was equivalent to 17.2 per cent of the total number of 590,621 occupied units reported by the census.[17] In addition to this replacement problem is the demand for new housing resulting from continued growth in the population. In 1970, there were almost 2.7 million people in the area. By 1985, a population of at least 4.0 million is projected. To house only this population increase, it has been estimated that 540,000 additional housing units will be required—an average of 27,000 units per year.[18]

According to a recent COG report, the principal housing problems in the region typically are substandard housing, overcrowding and the high cost of housing for families of low and moderate income. Housing opportunities for nonwhites is described as "a critical issue." The reason for this is that "nonwhites in all income ranges are located disproportionately in the District of Columbia. Income patterns indicate that housing opportunities for nonwhites are constrained by racial attitudes. Eighty-eight per cent of nonwhite households in Metropolitan Washington were in the District of Columbia compared with 42.6 per cent of all households in metropolitan Washington in 1960. Forty-four per cent of households in the District of Columbia in 1960 were nonwhite."[19]

The principal housing issues in such a program are identified as the location of multifamily housing and housing opportunities for nonwhites. Melvin F. Levine projects that 144,000 nonwhite households will be added to metropolitan Washington between 1965 and 1985 and that "under varying assumptions, 80,000 to 180,000 nonwhite households could be absorbed by suburban areas."[20]

The housing needs of the city were explored in depth by NCPC in mid-1966. Its special report on the *Problems of Housing People in Washington, D.C.* described how the people of Washington live, as follows[21]:

> A total of 148,800 households—comprising a population of 422,300 persons, 59% of Washington's total population—live in *Adequate* housing.
>
> A total of 103,300 households—comprising a population of 299,900 persons, 41% of Washington's total population—live in *Inadequate* housing. This category can be divided into three groups:
>
> a. 36,400 renter and home owner households—comprising 15% of Washington's total population—that live in structurally substandard units or in structurally sound units that lack essential facilities. Many of these households live in overcrowded units and pay more rent than they can afford.
>
> b. 21,800 renter and home owner households—comprising 11% of Washington's total population—that live in overcrowded units which are structurally sound and have all essential facilities. Many of these households pay more rent than they can afford.
>
> c. 45,100 renter households—comprising 16% of Washington's total population—that live in uncrowded structurally sound housing units with all the essential facilities. However, these households pay more rent than they can afford.

According to NCFC's report, "Washington's housing shortage is not an absolute shortage, but it is a shortage relative to housing unit sizes, rising rental and other living costs, and insufficient incomes of people living in the central city, and relative to suburban racial obstacles and other artificial housing restraints".[22]

In order to meet these housing problems, the District of Columbia government has a low-rent public housing program and a private moderate-income housing program aimed at increasing the supply of housing to these two income groups.

Low-income Public Housing in the District

In 1970, the National Capital Housing Authority managed a total of 10,778 housing units. An additional 2,000 units were either under construction or in development. Combined, this represents approximately 4.2 per cent of the city's total housing stock in that year. Between 1960 and 1970, the Authority had added a total of 5,026 housing units to its program in the city.[23] However, in the same decade, a total of 1,190 of the Authority's housing units were lost (removal of temporaries, displacement caused by public works, etc.)—for a net gain of 3,836, which is equivalent to an annual average increase of less than 400 units.

In the last decade, the emphasis of Washington's low-rent public housing program has shifted dramatically from direct land acquisition, construction and management of projects to rent supplement programs, "turnkey" new housing,** scattered site acquisition and the leasing of existing private housing in the city.

** Private construction then sold to local public housing authority.

The objective of these new programs has been to avoid the large institutional projects of the past where low-income and deprived families and individuals are concentrated.

Of particular interest is the fact that almost 40 per cent of the units added in the last decade developed under these new programs. This has been particularly true in the last five years; in fact, the Authority has added no new conventional units since 1968.

The low-rent public housing program has fallen short of meeting the low-income housing needs of the people in the District. It also seems quite clear that these same needs cannot be met solely within the geographic limits of the city. However, the National Capital Housing Authority has no legal authority to build or buy housing units outside of the District of Columbia. Although there are a handful of local housing authorities in other jurisdictions outside of the District, they are primarily concerned with providing housing for their own poor and inadequately housed. The lack of any regional housing program is a major void in regional planning and intergovernmental operation.

Moderate-income Housing

Under this program, the federal Department of Housing and Urban Development provides mortgage insurance on a nation-wide basis for financing construction or rehabilitation of rental and co-operative housing of modest design for families of low and moderate income. The principal program is based on below-market interest rates, providing insured mortgages at 3 per cent interest, which are eligible for, and are generally purchased by, the Federal National Mortgage Association under its special assistance functions.

The low interest rates and relatively modest designs permit rents which are significantly below market rentals. Eligibility for occupancy is governed by specific income limits established separately for each locality according to family size; families displaced by government action are given priority for initial occupancy and are placed on waiting lists. Private nonprofit, co-operative, limited dividend and public sponsors are usually the developers of such projects.[24] HUD's maximum income and rent limitations for Section 221(d)(3) projects in Washington in 1968 ranged from $6,200 for one person to $11,500 for a family of seven persons or more. Since 1964, when this program was established, approximately 3,200 housing units have been privately built for moderate-income families in the city. An additional 1,900 units have been proposed or are under construction.

Six-year Housing Program

The first city-wide housing program ever prepared for the District was part of NCPC's 1967 Proposed Comprehensive Plan (Fig. 8). It identified program needs and both long- and short-range program objectives for the District of Columbia.

Based upon NCPC's earlier housing study, the plan stated that:

> A variety of governmental programs will be needed to provide the large amount of good housing required in the District during the next 20 years. Although most of the city's residents will be able to afford private-market housing, many will require governmental assistance. At present, approxi-

FIG. 8 NCPC General Land Use Objectives, 1970–85. *National Capital Planning Comsion, 1968*

mately 92,000 households, containing 270,000 persons, or 37 per cent of the population, cannot afford adequate housing. Government agencies now assist only 9,000 households, leaving more than 80,000 that need, but do not receive, housing assistance. Of these, about one-third are eligible for and could afford public housing; but at least 40 per cent cannot afford even the low rents charged for public housing. In addition, some 36,000 moderate-income families are eligible for Section 221(d)(3) below-market interest rate housing. Although average incomes can be expected to rise considerably during the next two decades, a substantial number of households will still need governmental assistance. In particular, governmental action of a special kind will be necessary to help approximately 20,000 low-income families displaced by renewal programs and public works during the next 20 years.[25]

The plan proposed an "initial housing program" and recommended that the District of Columbia prepare a six-year housing program that could be co-ordinated with the over-all six-year public improvements program. Specifically, the housing program proposed a net increase of 65,000 housing units by 1985—from 280,000 to 345,000.

> Approximately 110,000 units will be built through both public and private actions, while about 45,000 existing units should be removed. There will thus be a net increment of 65,000 units. In addition, another 40,000 units in renewal and conservation areas will undergo major rehabilitation, as will many additional units in the rest of the city. About 100,000 housing units will be subjected to intensive code enforcement.[26]

Washington's "Housing Crisis"

In 1969, Washington's new City Council held a series of public hearings and concluded that "The District of Columbia today faces a severe housing crisis, a crisis that grows in magnitude, intensity and danger every day it is ignored." More specifically, the report of the Council's Housing and Urban Development Committee estimated that 100,000 District families lived in inadequate housing and that a total of 102,000 units must be built during the next decade. The committee's recommendation for the first stage action program involved: (1) a comprehensive attack on housing problems in the District; (2) proposed DC regulations on the tenants' rights, the licensing of rental dwelling managers, the management of rental properties, and (3) requiring the owner of an occupied residence that is to be demolished to make every reasonable attempt to find decent relocation housing for the occupants at a price they can afford.[27]

With slowdown in public housing construction in the Nixon administration throughout the entire nation, the District's massive program never got off the ground. None is proposed and none is in preparation. While "good housing" remains in short supply, there are large derelict dwelling areas in the capital.

In the 1960s, housing problems and housing programs were one of the most debated issues in the community. However, as the 1970s began, city officials became increasingly aware of other trends that would apparently shift the focus of attention away from concerns about increasing the supply of low-income public housing. First, was the realization that in some areas of the city—particularly in the Anacostia area—new housing starts had outpaced such necessary supporting public facilities as schools, playgrounds, libraries, etc. This had resulted in overcrowded and inadequate public services for both the old residents and the occupants of the new projects. Secondly, there was a rising trend of foreclosures and boarding up of some of the older rental apartment developments there. At the same time, there was a movement out of these areas by those relatively more affluent black and white residents to the suburbs to escape such conditions. Perhaps more importantly were the economic effects of the civil disorders of 1968, the overpublicized crime problem in the city, the national economic inflation and slowdown, the cutbacks locally in federal employment and the relocation of certain federal offices from temporaries in the city to leased space in the suburbs. All these combined to cause many city officials to believe that the city's number-one priority was to stabilize and revitalize its economic base, expanding job opportunities for its residents in the city.

URBAN RENEWAL

By the beginning of the 1970s, federal urban renewal legislation was being used by several local governments in the metropolitan area—in addition to the District of Columbia which has had a program since 1946. The most significant programs outside of the central city are in Alexandria and Rockville: Alexandria's program is largely oriented to the old city near the Potomac River; Rockville is a suburban center that is replanning its core as one of the corridor cities in the radial northwest of Washington.

By 1970, the District of Columbia had nine officially designed urban renewal areas embracing approximately 5.4 square miles. The most widely known of Washington's renewal efforts is the "New Southwest" described above by Carl Feiss where, since 1956, a total of 5,405 new housing units, four new federal office buildings, several new private office buildings and two shopping centers have been completed. Despite the fact that 57 per cent of the New Southwest is tax exempt public land and redevelopment is not fully completed, the city's annual tax revenues in the area have risen from $592,016 in 1953 to $2,833,486.48 in 1969.[28]

In 1965, "in recognition of an important architectural design which encompasses buildings, open spaces and the entire physical environment," the American Institute of Architects awarded the citizens of the city, the District government, the RLA and NCPC a citation for excellence in community architecture. This reward was given "for their vision, perseverance and judgment in producing a comprehensive solution to many of the problems of Southwest Washington, thus reasserting and enhancing the role of the central city as a cultural and commercial center and as a rewarding place to live."

The local urban renewal program has had both good and lean years in the last decade. The first major renewal actions were initiated in the three Southwest projects in the mid-fifties. Northeast No. 1 (for industrial and commercial reuse) and Columbia Plaza (for unsubsidized high-density apartments) were begun in 1959 and 1960 respectively. Northwest No. 1 (for low- and moderate-income housing) was approved in 1962. Between 1963 and 1968, the program showed little new initiatives.

However, the local program was revitalized in the late 1960s by: 1) the desire of the Shaw community for renewal help, 2) the impetus of the Neighborhood Development Program authorized by the 1968 Housing Act, and 3) the decision to use the urban renewal process as the framework for the replanning and rebuilding of the three areas in the city most heavily damaged by the civil disorders of April 1968.

The scope of the District's current renewal efforts can, perhaps, best be summarized by a brief review of the present six major projects, as follows[29]:

Downtown Urban Renewal Area

The objective of this project is to revitalize downtown Washington—the square mile between the Capitol and the White House, from Pennsylvania Avenue to M Street, N.W., which is the traditional commercial and employment center of the Washington region. Approximately 90,000 people now work downtown. In January 1969, the National Capital Planning Commission and the City Council approved the Urban Renewal Plan for Downtown, calling for the creation of a new residential neighborhood north of Massachusetts Avenue, including new apartments suitable for low- and moderate-income households, and the development of a revitalized retail shopping district, with twice as many offices and hotels.

Shaw School Area

This 675-acre urban renewal area is located just north of the downtown area. Since 1966 there has been extensive community participation in planning for the renewal of Shaw, provided by two community organizations under contract with RLA: the Model Inner City Community Organization, Inc. (MICCO), comprising over two hundred Shaw groups, and Uptown Progress, representing the Shaw business community. After numerous surveys, meetings, questionnaires, television and radio coverage, and widespread distribution of information materials within the community, MICCO prepared a conceptual plan proposal which in January 1969 was adopted by NCPC and approved by the City Council.

14th Street, N.W. Area

This 340-acre area, located immediately north of the Shaw area, contains a population of over 34,000 people and approximately 2,500 structures. The plan for the rebuilding of the area, damaged in the 1968 disturbances, was adopted by the Planning Commission and approved by the City Council on December 17, 1969.

The plan was initiated by community groups in the area through the 14th Street Community Planning Team, which consists of community organization leaders, residents and professional planners. It represented a unique degree of co-operative efforts by neighborhood groups, citizens and public agencies. The general objectives of the plan are to rebuild the damaged areas, to eliminate deficient housing conditions and other conditions now blighting the area, and to provide new and rehabilitated housing for low- and moderate-income families.

H Street, N.E. Area

H Street is a 284-acre area that had been the second largest retail corridor in the city. It was one of the three damaged areas in the 1968 civil disorders; over 18,000 people live in the renewal area. The plan was prepared in 1969 as a part of a co-operative effort between the community and the Government of the District of Columbia. In order to provide for citizen initiative in planning for the renewal of H Street, twelve community fellows who were residents or businessmen in the area, with the help of planning consultants, acted as a liaison to develop planning proposals and obtain neighborhood reaction to them. The plan was adopted by NCPC in April 1969 and approved by the City Council on June 17, 1969. Renewal actions began in 1970.

Anacostia-Bolling

Anacostia-Bolling is an example of the ability of the Congress, on occasion, to frustrate the plans of both the District government and the Executive Branch of the federal government. In the late 1950s, two military airfields along the east bank of the Potomac River in the District of Columbia were ordered closed down due to increasing air congestion in and around Washington's National Airport. As a result, the northern half of the site—about 432 acres—was indicated as surplus to the needs of the Department of Defense. It was subsequently designated an urban renewal area and preliminary planning studies were initiated by NCPC and RLA. A draft urban renewal plan was proposed providing for a "balanced community" of around 6,500 units or 25,000 people, one made up of the various family types and income groups living in the District. The breakdown finally chosen was one which maintained a balance of income groups in the school system while still concentrating on the housing needs existing in Washington.[30] The plan also provided for residentially related community facilities and public services, a riverfront park, a major shopping area and a site for a 10,000-man Defense office building.

However, the House Armed Services Committee did not feel that this land was, in fact, excess to the needs of the Department of Defense and was successful in adding a proviso to the 1967 Military Construction Authorization Act barring use of this area for other than military purposes until December 31, 1970. A five-year extension of this freeze was subsequently approved by the Congress in 1969. Despite these actions, it was still hoped that this land might yet be made available.

Fort Lincoln New Town in Town

A Fort Lincoln New Town was proposed on a 340-acre tract of land, made available by the federal government, in northeast Washington just north of the Anacostia River—originally a Civil War fort and later the site of the National Training School for Boys. The large size and underdeveloped character of this valuable in-town site and its outstanding natural features provided a unique and important resource for development to meet today's urban needs.

The objectives of this proposal, as described by NCPC, were[31]:

1. To create a balanced community in an attractive environment where persons of all social, economic and racial backgrounds can live together in a quality urban environment.
2. To help meet the District of Columbia's development needs, particularly in the area of low- and moderate-income housing.
3. To serve as a prototype for new urban communities to be developed

throughout the country by demonstrating that such an outstanding community can be created through the effective mobilization of public and private resources.

An exciting plan for the Fort Lincoln New Town was prepared by an experienced team of consultants headed by Edward Logue, the well-known development co-ordinator formerly of New Haven and Boston. The major features of the proposed plan included the following[32]:

1. 4,500 dwelling units for families and individuals in low-, moderate- and higher-income ranges.
2. An innovative public education system serving Fort Lincoln and the surrounding community.
3. An internal "minirail" system and adequate off-street parking.
4. Major highway construction to permit optimum development of Fort Lincoln and to provide proper connections with the surrounding community.
5. A campus for the Federal City College.
6. On-site employment opportunities for approximately 6,000 persons.
7. Public and private open space and recreational facilities.
8. A high level of community facilities and services.
9. A comprehensive approach to community design and use of new building technologies.
10. Creative involvement of government, business and the local community in planning and executing the project.

The final planning report was completed by the consultant in April of 1969 (Figs. 9a, 9b, 9c, 9d). It included a statement of objectives, a proposed site development plan and a program for the development of the entire site over a five-year period. It also recommended that (1) a Fort Lincoln Development Corporation be created to administer and manage further design and construction contracts; (2) an architectural organization be established whose responsibility "will help to achieve a sense of architectural quality, continuity, and innovation, and will provide a workable basis for implementing the social and design objectives of the plan"; and (3) a "services" entity which would, upon completion of construction, assume responsibility of management and maintenance as well as administer the school system and other community facilities.[33]

The three special authorities were a unique and controversial part of the proposed plan. It was based upon the consultants conviction that[34]

> Proper organization of the development process is essential to achieving the goals for Fort Lincoln. Reliance on the conventional approach involving a variety of public agencies, private developers, contractors, architects, and other interests would result in a lack of co-ordination, and would seriously jeopardize the desired design and environmental quality, as well as social and economic objectives.

The Fort Lincoln Urban Renewal Plan was adopted by NCPC on September 11, 1969. It was intentionally drawn as a general plan to guide subsequent more detailed site planning and development studies. It did not include any mention on how the plan would be carried out—thus clearly separating the planning issues from the unresolved questions surrounding the special corporations proposed by the consultants.

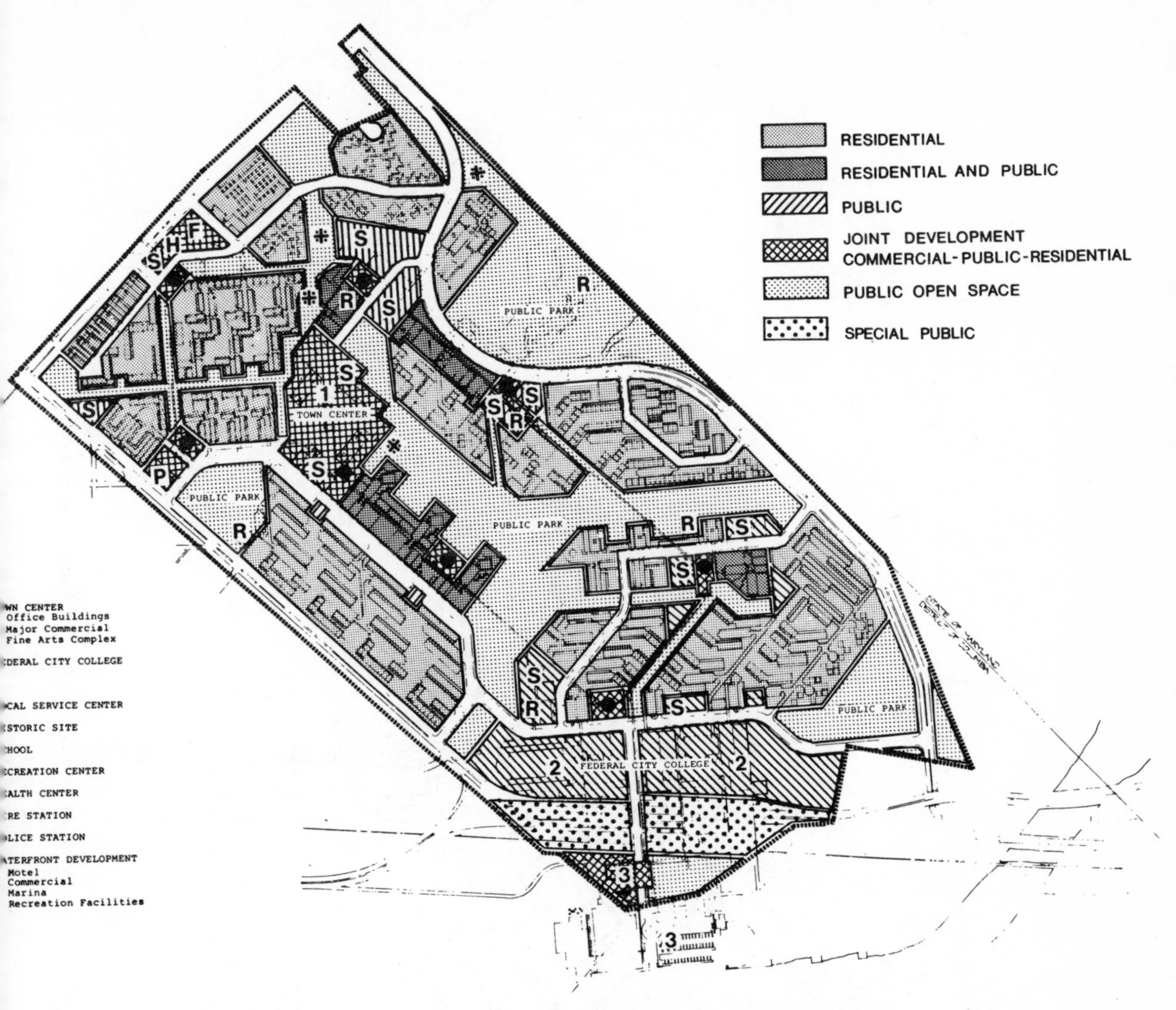

FIG. 9A Fort Lincoln proposed land use. *National Capital Planning Commission*

Fort Lincoln difficulties have been, in part, the result of a failure of an experiment in citizen participation. Since no one lived on the Fort Lincoln site, it was felt that the residents of the adjacent neighborhoods should participate in the planning of the area. Early attempts to organize a community of interests in the area broke down as individuals and newly formed organizations competed with each other for recognition by the mayor, and the money they expected someone would get to open an office in the area and pay for a staff of community organizers and planners for the citizens. Ultimately, the city had to break off its efforts to formalize citizen participation in this area. Instead, a city-wide advisory group of citizens was set up, which included some neighborhood representatives but was not dominated by the local interests.

HUD indicated that it was ready to fund additional feasibility studies. As a result, the RLA issued a Prospectus for a Feasibility Study and Development in September of 1970. A total of eight responses was received and evaluated by an interagency committee and the mayor's Advisory Committee on Fort Lincoln.

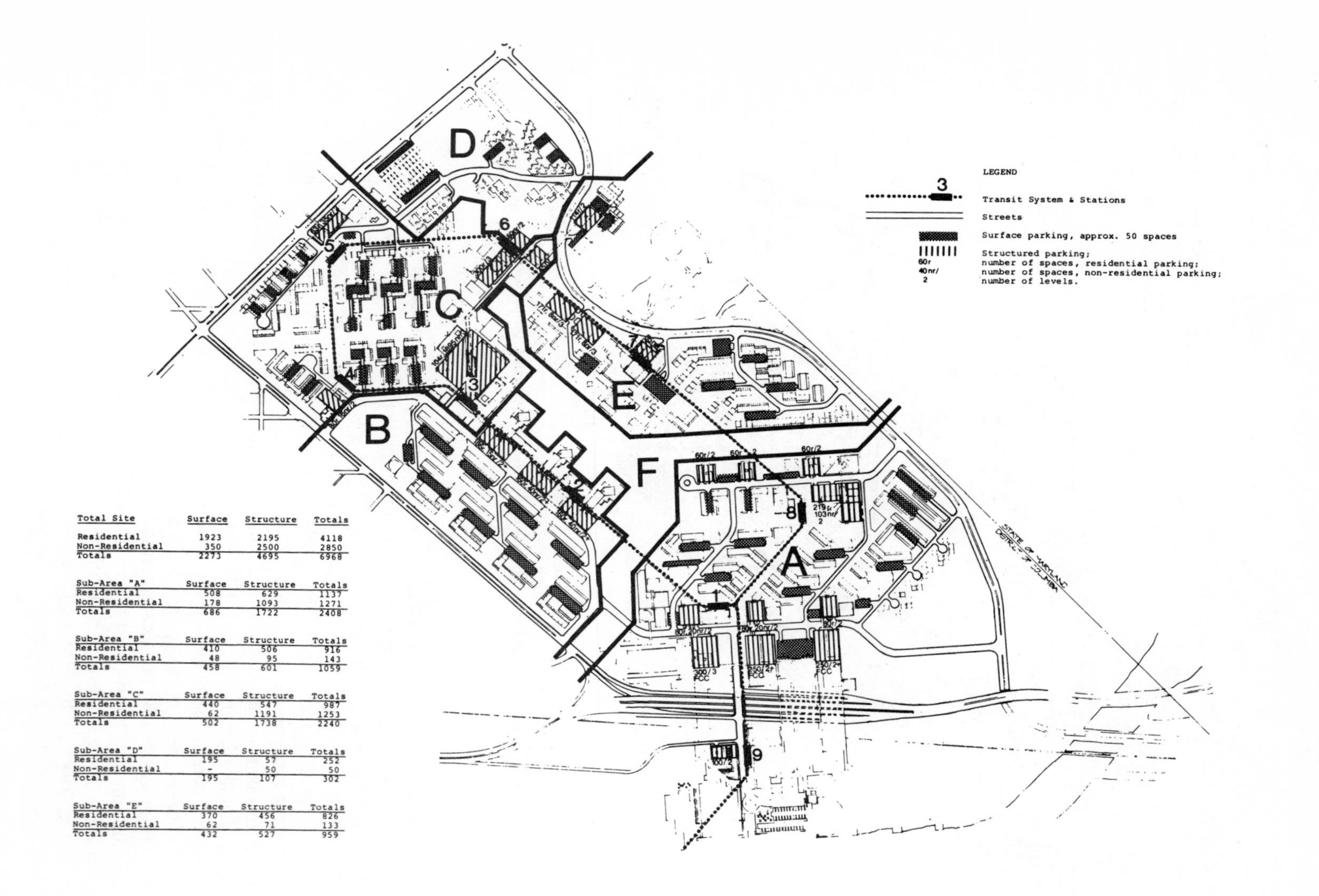

Total Site	Surface	Structure	Totals
Residential	1923	2195	4118
Non-Residential	350	2500	2850
Totals	2273	4695	6968

Sub-Area "A"	Surface	Structure	Totals
Residential	508	629	1137
Non-Residential	178	1093	1271
Totals	686	1722	2408

Sub-Area "B"	Surface	Structure	Totals
Residential	410	506	916
Non-Residential	48	95	143
Totals	458	601	1059

Sub-Area "C"	Surface	Structure	Totals
Residential	440	547	987
Non-Residential	62	1191	1253
Totals	502	1738	2240

Sub-Area "D"	Surface	Structure	Totals
Residential	195	57	252
Non-Residential	-	50	50
Totals	195	107	302

Sub-Area "E"	Surface	Structure	Totals
Residential	370	456	826
Non-Residential	62	71	133
Totals	432	527	959

FIG. 9B Fort Lincoln circulation and parking. *National Capital Planning Commission*

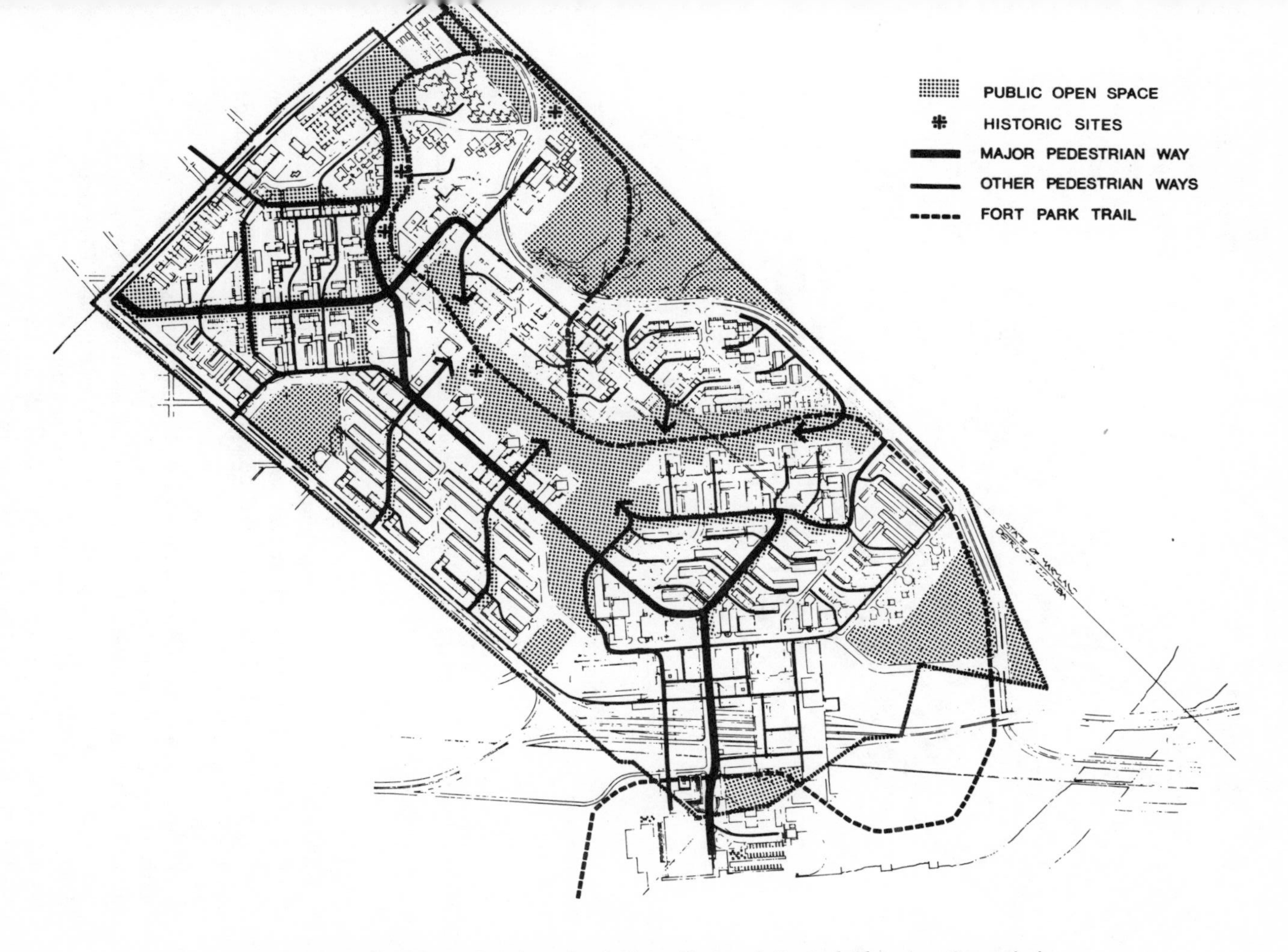

FIG. 9C Fort Lincoln pedestrian circulation. *National Capital Planning Commission*

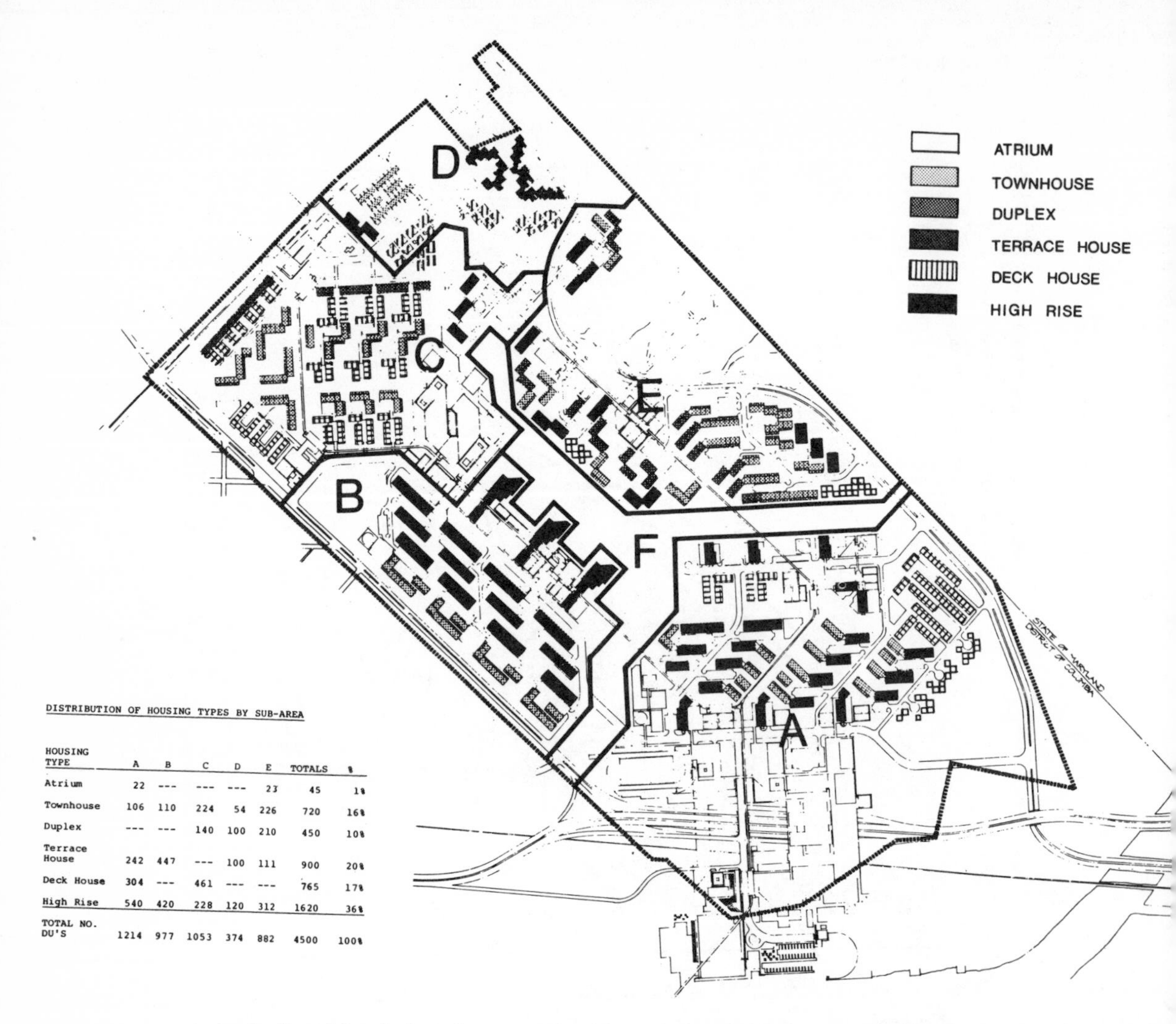

DISTRIBUTION OF HOUSING TYPES BY SUB-AREA

HOUSING TYPE	A	B	C	D	E	TOTALS	%
Atrium	22	---	---	---	23	45	1%
Townhouse	106	110	224	54	226	720	16%
Duplex	---	---	140	100	210	450	10%
Terrace House	242	447	---	100	111	900	20%
Deck House	304	---	461	---	---	765	17%
High Rise	540	420	228	120	312	1620	36%
TOTAL NO. DU'S	1214	977	1053	374	882	4500	100%

FIG. 9D Fort Lincoln housing-type distribution. *National Capital Planning Commission*

On November 19, 1970, the Westinghouse Electric Corporation/Building Systems, International, Inc., Consortium was selected as the contractor to perform the feasibility study and, if the plans are acceptable, undertake the actual development of the new town in town.

> The Westinghouse-BSI Consortium was viewed locally as a major commitment by one of the nation's largest corporations to undertake as complex an urban development task as could be envisioned. This commitment was from the top management of the Westinghouse Corporation down to operating levels of the various subsidiaries that would be involved. It was a commitment to bring to bear all the necessary corporate resources: managerial, technical, and financial, to produce at Fort Lincoln a community that would be a model for the Nation and that would offer the greatest likelihood of achieving the objectives of a socially, racially, and economically balanced community at this beautiful site.[35]

The reviewing committee also pointed out that[36]

> (1) The Consortium includes the American counterpart of the European Corporation that owns and produces the Balency system of industrialized building. The Balency system has been responsible for the production of over 30,000 dwelling units in England, France, Italy, Israel and South Africa. It is the housing system being utilized in the present development of the new community of Thamesmead at the edge of London, England, which is a planned community of about 60,000 people (15,000 dwelling units) on a site more than four times the size of Fort Lincoln. More than half of the community has been developed, and its architecture and planning have received international acclaim.
> (2) If Fort Lincoln were to proceed into construction, the Consortium was prepared to build a factory in the Washington area to produce the components needed for the Fort Lincoln housing. This facility would provide jobs for about 2,000 people, and would be capable of producing components to serve housing needs elsewhere in the District and the metropolitan area.

In 1972, the Commission adopted and the City Council approved, following a public hearing, an urban renewal plan for the Fort Lincoln Urban Renewal Area that was based on the Building Systems International/Westinghouse Joint Venture proposal. Following completion of the fifteen-month feasibility study, the Westinghouse Corporation indicated that BSI rather than the Joint Venture was prepared to be the redeveloper of Fort Lincoln with Westinghouse involvement to be limited to consulting support. On July 26, 1972, Council approval of the estimated $250 million project followed an announcement by the developer that 25 per cent of the project equity would be made available to local minority investors. HUD, which has already endorsed the plan in principle, is to provide approximately $28 million in federal grants. President Nixon gave high priority to Fort Lincoln in his Bicentennial program in Washington. At that time an estimated 40 per cent of Fort Lincoln was expected to be completed by 1976. Some building of governmental elements of the plan got under way in 1973.[37]

As of 1974, five years later, Building Systems International remains in the act. A school has been constructed by the District and some housing for the elderly put up by the Public Housing Authority. But plans are still under negotiation with the Redevelopment Agency and no actual construction of this promising New-Town-in-Town by the developers has begun.

Community Renewal Program

The legislation establishing the Community Renewal Programs (CRP) in the United States first appeared in 1959 as an amendment to the National Housing Act. It provided financial assistance through the Housing and Home Finance Agency (now HUD) to local communities for the preparation of a long-range program for housing, urban renewal and related activities.

These programs were required to include: 1) an analysis and evaluation of the problems, 2) definition of the needs and 3) formulation of a program to satisfy these needs consistent with the resources available in the community. The application for the District's program was approved in 1962 for a total budget of

$916,000, two thirds provided by federal grants and one third by the local community. The local program has since been extended and given additional funding.

The CRP report was submitted to the Board of Commissioners (since replaced by a mayor and council) in August of 1966. As described in the report,[38]

> The approach of the District's program was to examine the many facets of its complex social, economic and physical problems, from several points of view. By assigning various studies to agencies and consultants who represented different disciplines, it was possible to get not only a measure of the general magnitude of the problem, but also an insight into their many aspects and complex inter-relationships. In total, a dozen agencies and private consultants carried out assignments in their areas of specialization.

The report evaluated the physical, social and economic conditions found in the city, presented community goals and needs. It offered three alternative courses of action to the District of Columbia, as follows:

(A) A policy of limited action for holding the line.
(B) A policy of making substantial inroads into the problems.
(C) A policy of total action for solving the problems.

In explaining the ramifications of the three alternatives, the report states that[39]

> Although the alternatives are presented as three independent and free standing choices, each implicitly and explicitly includes many of the concepts and approaches advanced in the others. In this context, all three alternatives recognize the same set of goals, but only alternatives B and C are designed to purposefully and deliberately move the city toward these goals.

After a series of public presentations and hearings, the Board of Commissioners directed that the CRP staff prepare a detailed program along the lines of Alternative (C), a policy of total action for solving the problems. However, as time passed, it became clear that the total program needs and requirements for the entire city were: 1) too long range to interest some or to satisfy others; 2) too disruptive in terms of the displacement and relocation required, and 3) too costly when compared with the District government's likely available financial resources.

As the availability of federal funds for financial assistance to local governments tightened due to the Vietnam War, the inflation and the economic slowdown, urban renewal funds were rationed. It was clear that programs in the immediate future at least were to be shaped by limited congressional appropriations rather than the needs of the city as spelled out in the CRP. This was true even in Washington, despite White House and HUD preferences to use the nation's capital as a demonstration or model for other cities in the United States.

More recently, the District's CRP efforts and those of the Mayor's Economic Development Committee have been substantially combined since the broad goals, the scope and the operations of the two plans are similar. As a matter of fact, Alternative (C) of the CRP was initially authorized by the Department of Commerce as the Overall Economic Development Program (OEDP) for the District of Columbia.

The Office of Community Renewal, according to the City's Workable Program, is now proceeding to develop a detailed program of renewal, as follows[40]:

A. Physical Development
   1. Area Improvement Program
   2. Small Area Market Analysis
   3. Economic Development Studies
   4. Six-year Capital Improvements Program
   5. Anacostia River Development Program
   6. Urban Design Guidelines
   7. Information and Change Monitoring System

B. Housing
   1. Six-year Housing Program
   2. Housing Code Revision

C. Social Development
   1. Program for System of Urban Progress Centers
   2. Multiproblem Family Study
   3. Exploitation Study
   4. Social Improvement Program
   5. Employment Opportunity Study
   6. Employment Out-migration Study

Summary

The urban renewal program in the United States has been considered by many to be the major tool for revitalizing our cities and for co-ordinating all of the cities' development programs. However, by 1970, ideas about the future role of renewal were changing. In May of 1970, President Nixon's Task Force on Urban Renewal issued its report entitled, *Urban Renewal: One Tool Among Many.*[41] In describing the limitations of urban renewal, the report noted that it "is one instrument for meeting urban problems, but it is only one of the instruments. It cannot be expected to cure all of the ills of the cities, of which the most serious are poverty and racial discrimination." The changing times reflect a more sophisticated view of the role of renewal in American municipal government.

By 1970, it was clear that the days of the large-scale clearance projects in Washington—like Southwest—were over. The displacement and relocation problems were just too great to handle in a humane way in a short time. Gone also were the days when citizen participation was largely either showing up at a public hearing once a plan had been completed or just a matter of rhetoric.

Urban renewal planning in the 1970s promises to be significantly different than either the 1950s or 1960s. Gone was the old preplanning urban renewal process where planning always preceded project execution. The new Neighborhood Development Program brought a new system that unfortunately fostered piecemeal planning. The old familiar, somewhat detailed land-use plans were replaced with general land-use plans. Planning and execution became concurrent activities that were so operationally oriented to parcel-by-parcel interests that over-all planning for an entire urban renewal area was subordinated to concern about individual annual action area proposals. The new program was certainly flexible, as desired by renewal administrators, and certainly financing by each individual program has advantages. However, local experience to date has raised serious questions about the character and quality of the renewal planning that is likely to take place under the NDP program in the 1970s.

NEW DIMENSIONS IN COMMUNITY DEVELOPMENT PLANNING

There have been other significant changes in the approach to planning the nation's capital in the last several years; the earlier emphasis on architecture and physical planning still remains, but it has been joined by an increasing emphasis on the socioeconomic and environmental aspects and implications of planning. In the 1950s and in the early 1960s, there was growing demand for more consideration of, and better co-ordination of, social, economic and physical planning. There were complaints that there was little, if any, consideration of the social and economic consequences of various public physical improvement programs around the country—particularly urban renewal. Initially, such efforts at greater co-ordination were limited and uncertain. Many shared this concern but were not sure how to "plug in" some of the social science know-how into these programs.

Efforts were made to define social planning and, in some cases, separate social plans were prepared as part of the over-all planning for specific projects or programs. For a time, this new emphasis locally bred an artificial conceptual division between social planning and physical planning. It was not until the end of the decade that the Overall Economic Development Program reminded everyone of the "oneness of the problem."

> We cannot treat economic and related financial problems as separate and apart from social objectives, or vice versa. Each bears heavily upon the other. Major economic and social considerations should be integrated, toward one increasing purpose in our national life.[42]

The 1960s saw a veritable explosion of national and local concern for our society's social problems. The War on Poverty and other federal aid programs funneled money into such local efforts in an unprecedented way. In Washington, these concerns lead to the creation of the United Planning Organization, the Mayor's Economic Development Committee, the Model Cities Commission and many other new public and private groups. It led to new interest in the housing problem with increased demands for "citizen participation" and "advocacy planning."

Other factors which have added new dimensions to local development efforts are citizen participation in the actual preparation of plans and programs, and the growing concern among both professionals and the general public for more consideration of, and particularly better planning for, our total human environment.

Civil Disorders of 1968

In April of 1968, Washington and many other American cities were stricken by violence triggered by the assassination of the civil rights leader Dr. Martin Luther King, Jr. Extensive physical damage by fire was done in the city—primarily in the 7th, 14th and H street areas in the old city. These disturbances were followed by an air of despair, resentment, hostility, fear and uncertainty in the community.

From the city planning point of view, these disturbances were unprecedented in the city and raised a new and immediate challenge: planning to rebuild these areas. The District government, the Redevelopment Land Agency, NCPC and others, including the quickly appointed Reconstruction Development Corporation (RDC), began at once to assess the damage and to explore alternative ways and means of rebuilding. This was an unprecedented role for NCPC but one born out of an emergency; shortly thereafter, NCPC and the District Council approved urban renewal plans to guide the rebuilding efforts in all three damaged areas.

The disturbances in 1968 acted as a temporary deterrent to the tourists who usually flock to the nation's capital each summer and the suburban residents who shop downtown. The result was an economic setback to the city in retail and tourist business. Although this situation was significantly improved by 1970, its effect on the real estate market in the downtown area helped to bring about a new awareness in the District of the economic situation in the capital and new attitudes toward factors causing economic change.

It also brought out new leadership in the black community and a more militant style toward local issues, including citizen participation in planning.

United Planning Organization (UPO)

Washington's social planning agency is the United Planning Organization, a private corporation using several different public and private resources. It is governed by a large Board of Trustees that is representative of: (1) public officials, (2) major groups and interests in the community such as the Health and Welfare Council and the Metropolitan Washington Board of Trade, and (3) representatives of the poor.

As the city's antipoverty agency, the make-up of the Board of Trustees and other UPO-sponsored organizations have representatives of the poor who are the intended beneficiaries of those programs. UPO describes it this way[43]:

> From the neighborhood organizations, representatives of the poor are elected to serve on the Metropolitan Citizens Advisory Council (MCAC) which has the power to initiate and review program proposals. In addition, representatives of the poor are elected to fill one-third of the seats on the UPO Board of Trustees.
>
> In keeping with recent amendments to the Economic Opportunity Act, another one-third of the UPO Board of Trustees must be local public officials or their representatives. The remaining third must be representatives of concerned community agencies.
>
> Thus, while continuing as a private corporation, the United Planning Organization provides a working partnership of the poor, local government, and private organizations.

UPO's program is, perhaps, best described in *Alternatives, A Special Report on the United Planning Organization* issued in 1969, as follows:

> The United Planning Organization began seeking alternatives to lifelong poverty even before the advent of the Federal "War on Poverty." In 1961 a year-long study of the National Capital Area's social and human resource problems and institutions was financed by the Health and Welfare Council, the Washington Center for Metropolitan Studies, the Brookings Institution and Resources for the Future, Inc. After discussion of the findings and recommendations of this study group with representatives of the White House and the District Government, UPO was created as a non-

profit, private organization on December 10, 1962. UPO's mandate was to plan for human service needs throughout the National Capital Area and, in partnership with government and other private groups, to strengthen services and develop new approaches to the resolution of area problems.

After passage of the Economic Opportunity Act of 1964, which launched the War on Poverty, UPO was designated as the Community Action Agency for the Washington area.

Using several different public and private resources, UPO in the next four years initiated a variety of projects in the areas of education, health, employment, housing and economic development.

Some of the programs were demonstration projects, testing new means of dealing with problems such as juvenile delinquency or drug addiction. Many supplemented or extended the efforts of already existing agencies such as those dealing with school children, welfare recipients and the unemployed. Others served to stimulate self-help by individuals, families, neighborhoods or communities.

In education, Head Start, the Model School experiment, tutoring programs and education action teams sought to off-set the disadvantage of many ghetto residents.

In employment, training and job development programs concentrated on problems of youth and the hard core unemployed.

In housing, efforts focused on code enforcement and the shortage of decent housing at prices the poor can afford.

In the legal field, the Neighborhood Legal Service Project defended and enlarged the rights of the poor in their dealing with slumlords, gyp-merchants and others.

In economic development, programs were devised to assist small businessmen, to encourage the development of new businesses and cooperatives and to assist neighborhood residents with credit and budgeting problems.

In health and social service fields, mental health, family planning, drug addiction and other projects were made more accessible to those who needed them most.

Finally, the residents of poverty neighborhoods were encouraged to come together, to identify common problems and to work together toward constructive solutions to those problems. This has resulted in self-help projects ranging from clean-up campaigns to the formation of a housing cooperative to buy and rehabilitate an apartment complex.[44]

In a recent year, fiscal 1968, the UPO had a total budget of $31,237,977. Almost all of these funds were provided in the form of federal financial assistance, primarily from the Department of Labor and the Office of Economic Opportunity (the national antipoverty agency).

Almost half of these funds were allocated to various manpower programs while the remaining funds were allocated to a wide variety of program objectives, as follows[45]:

1. Manpower	50.3%
2. Education	10.7%
3. Community organization	9.6%
4. Summer programs	7.7%
5. Special services	5.4%

6. Metropolitan		4.2%
7. Legal		3.8%
8. Youth		3.7%
9. Administration		2.6%
10. Economic development		1+
11. Housing		1−
	Total	100.00%

UPO's own estimate of its activities to develop alternatives to some of the conditions that perpetrate poverty in the National Capital Area is that[46]:

> These programs, by themselves, obviously cannot meet the area's needs for jobs, education, housing, recreation, income, health care, transportation or justice. Those needs are too great in comparison to the resources available to UPO.
>
> However, such programs can serve, and have served, to point the way. The rest is up to the entire community, national and local, public and private, rich and poor.

The UPO, like other similar community action agencies in the war on poverty, was set up to be independent of the establishment, the local municipal government. This continues to be the case, although recent efforts have been made to co-ordinate more closely its activities and programs with those of the District of Columbia government. The independent status of the city's social planning agency has, perhaps, resulted merely in a deferral of the inevitable decision as to how best to organize the social planning function in the local municipal government.

Mayor's Economic Development Committee

On August 6, 1968, Mayor Walter E. Washington appointed the Mayor's Economic Development Committee (MEDCO) and charged it with responsibility for the development of an Overall Economic Development Plan (OEDP) for the District. The committee was appointed to represent a cross section of the District's racial, political, social and economic landscape. Members include militants and conservatives, Republicans and Democrats, representatives of the poor, the middle class and the wealthy. As stated in the Foreword of the OEDP[47]:

> MEDCO was appointed in the wake of the April, 1968 disturbances and Resurrection City. There was a pervasive air of despair, resentment, hostility, frustration, fear, and uncertainty throughout the community. Today, a great change is in process. Among our more affluent citizens, there is now a widespread realization of the needs of their less fortunate neighbors, and a new willingness to do what must be done to remove the inequities of our society. Among the poor, who have had to spend the past year living in the neighborhoods gutted during the 1968 violence, there is a first-hand appreciation of the futility of emotional rather than rational reactions to the problems they face.

In response to a recent question "Why MEDCO?," Joseph B. Danzansky, the chairman of MEDCO, replied that[48]

> Today, many of us have come to realize that the solution to our city's problems lies not in an expanding gross national product or in providing

better services for the poor, although both are important. The real secret in achieving a breakthrough is economic development. . . .

In the final analysis, the economic condition of a community reflects the economic state of its citizens. An economically viable city is impossible without an economically viable citizenry. . . .

That is why, as we proceed to develop Washington's first overall economic development program, we focused on the problem of adequate family incomes, flowing basically from job opportunities for all residents of our city.

Our goal was the development of a single, multifaceted program of economic and social goals, which would be supplemented each year by detailed action programs and expanded annually by one more year. Our 10-year overall program was completed last summer, discussed with the public in hearings, and then submitted to Mayor Washington, who adopted it as our city plan in February of this year. . . .

The main economic development policies and program objectives of MEDCO are incorporated into two documents—the ten-year OEDP and the First Year Action Program.

In referring to the ten-year OEDP, Mr. Danzansky observed that[49]

The time is long past when an economic development program, or any other great public endeavor, could be put into effect without broad involvement and participation by the citizens of the community. . . .

This document was drawn to give all the citizens of the District essential information about their city and a series of meaningful remedial goals for their consideration.

In approaching the question of economic development in the District, the Committee adopted an expanded interpretation of the subject. We decided not to produce a detailed physical blueprint for the construction of commercial and industrial enterprises in the District. Rather, we decided to interpret our mandate to promote "economic development" in its broader sense: creating self-sufficient families in self-sufficient neighborhoods within a self-sufficient community. . . . An economically viable Washington is impossible without an economically viable citizenry. That is why this study concentrates its attention on the problem of adequate incomes, flowing basically from job opportunity, for all residents of the District. . . . The study does contend that the solution of the jobs and income problem is the catalyst that can unlock the solutions to many of these other problems.

The ten-year OEDP recommended by the Mayor's Committee projects a total cost of $2,900,000,000, as follows[50]:

Program	*Expenditures Recommended*
1. Income advance, through income aid to those outside the employment stream	$236,200,000
2. Public school education	504,300,000
3. Higher public education	450,000,000
4. Health (public component)	307,000,000
5. Housing	164,700,000

6. Manpower training		260,000,000
7. Day care and child development		180,000,000
8. Transportation		800,000,000
	Total	$2,900,000,000

Public school and higher education in the District would together receive almost one third of the funds for improving the educational facilities of the city and raising the level of education of its citizens.

Improved transportation would receive almost 30 per cent of this total with the objective of solving the current problems of "workers and job seekers who depend primarily upon mass transit" and who "spend too much time getting where they want to go, and pay too much to get there."[51]

Approximately two thirds of this total cost would, as proposed, be paid by the federal government. The remaining one third was to be borne by the District government—with perhaps three quarters of this derived from additional tax revenues due to economic expansion within the District, without significant change in the tax rates, according to the committee.

MEDCO's ten-year OEDP pointed out the need for the city to take steps to avoid multiplying the number of agencies dealing with the city's problems. It complained that "every unsolved problem seems to have resulted in still another agency, or a redrafting of organizational charts."

In response to this situation, MEDCO concluded that "Today we have plans without a Plan: programs without a Program. The Overall Economic Development Plan will give the District a comprehensive development plan."[52]

The Mayor's Economic Development Committee has strong leadership and currently has significant federal funding and support. Its influence in the Washington community and on the planning of the City could be significant in the 1970s. However, the interrelationship between MEDCO and its ten-year OEDP, NCPC and its 1985 Comprehensive Plan and UPO's socioeconomic plans and programs are not clearly defined nor are they consistent in all respects. The necessary co-ordination of these programs remains a crucial agenda item for the District government in the 1970s.

Model City Program

The national Model Cities program was authorized by the Demonstration Cities and Metropolitan Development Act of 1966; it was announced as an experimental, innovative program, calling on localities to try new ideas and to evolve imaginative local ways to meet the most pressing local needs. It concentrates resources in planning, in housing construction and rehabilitation, in job training, health, welfare and educational programs, all to improve conditions of life in substandard neighborhoods. The aim was to demonstrate how a comprehensive improvement program in one neighborhood can contribute to the healthy growth of the entire city. The distinctive element of the Model Cities program is that the use of many federal financial assistance programs is co-ordinated at the federal and local levels, and concentrated on single "target" neighborhoods, using a single local "delivery" agency.[53]

Cities are required to work closely with neighborhood residents in the formulation and execution of Model Cities plans. The plans are intended to be responsive to residents' needs and recognize their competence as individuals and citizens. HUD has, however, recently emphasized that the elected officials of the locality are the ultimate arbiters of local policy with responsibility centered upon the mayor's office and a continued requirement for adequate citizen involvement.

In Washington, the Model Cities program is conducted for the District of Columbia government by an elected Model Cities Commission. According to this commission, the comprehensive goal of the local Model Cities program is to improve the quality of urban life through self-determination and self-fulfillment. The specific objectives of the Commission include such areas as economic development, employment, consumer affairs, social welfare, health, education, public safety, recreation, housing, neighborhood facilities and neighborhood environment. The Commission's First Year Action Program for the Model Cities area in Washington was assisted by a not inconsequential $9.7 million HUD grant.

The Model City area in the District of Columbia is approximately 1,600 acres in size and extends around the northern and eastern edges of the central business district. About two thirds is included within four officially designated urban renewal areas. It also includes two out of the three major predominantly commercial streets that were most heavily damaged during the 1968 civil disorders. The Model Cities Commission now reviews all proposed public improvement programs and projects within its area—as part of the official public review process within the District government.

The First Year Action Program has only recently been funded. It is, therefore, too early to speculate on the future prospects for the Commission or its program. However, it is known that the Nixon administration and HUD have been reevaluating the program and it has just been announced that the national Model Cities program will be continued but that the new objective will be to develop Model City programs for entire communities, not just certain sections of a city. The effect of this changing approach on Washington's Model city program is not clear at this time. The scope of the local program in the 1970s will, however, undoubtedly be largely shaped by HUD decisions affecting the entire country.

MICCO (*Model Inner City Community Organization*)

MICCO is the officially recognized community group in the Shaw Urban Renewal Area, a 500-acre project just north of the downtown area that has a population of approximately 40,000. It is an umbrella-type organization whose members represent over 200 separate community groups within the area. It is recognized by the District government and the Redevelopment Land Agency (RLA) as the citizen participation spokesman for the residents of the area. It has a large staff of community organizers and planners who work for the residents and with the public agencies working in the area. In other words, MICCO has its own planning capabilities and is an example of advocacy planning at the neighborhood or community level.

All of NCPC's and RLA's plans and programs in the Shaw area have been developed by MICCO or in conjunction with MICCO's staff and the community. In fact, MICCO prepared the conceptual plan which became the basis for the approved Urban Renewal Plan for the area. The funds to support MICCO's activities are provided by the RLA with funds advanced by HUD. Its current annual budget is approximately $440,000. MICCO's interests and activities span the total range of the problems facing the Shaw area—including both the preparation and the execution of neighborhood plans and programs.

To date, MICCO is the unique local example of an officially recognized, publicly funded, broad-based citizen participation organization. Since 1966, it has successfully represented the interests of its community in working with City Hall to eliminate conditions blighting the area and to renew Shaw as an attractive residential area, with new and rehabilitated housing for low- and moderate-income families, as well as good public and commercial services.

Although it has been reported that the scale of public funding of MICCO-type community activities will not be repeated in Washington and, possibly, in other cities, the experiment in Shaw has demonstrated that an effective partnership is possible in urban areas between an advocacy-planning citizen-participation type of organization and the local government.

Citizen Participation

"Citizen participation" has become a key slogan in planning circles in recent years. The objective of citizen participation is to insure more widespread involvement in the planning process and in decision-making on plans and programs. In fact, citizen participation has been a condition of many federal financial grant-in-aid programs in the past several years. For example, the Department of Housing and Urban Development requires "the creation of citizen project area committees" for all urban renewal projects in which rehabilitation activities are contemplated. These committees are required to represent a fair cross section of the residents of the area. The local renewal agency may provide technical assistance to these committees either by lending staff or by granting funds to enable the committees to hire their own staff and consultants.

In recent years, citizen participation has taken on new and different qualities. On some occasions, it has been used synonymously with community control—a term used by some neighborhood groups who want money from City Hall but who insist on local control over who gets it and how it is spent. In other situations, citizen participation in planning has meant little more than thinly disguised attempts at fighting City Hall or building a personal political power base in the community for a particular individual.

In voteless Washington, citizen participation has become something of a substitute for the normal political processes of local government; it is an integral part of the urban renewal, the Model Cities and the poverty programs. It is a relatively new but an evolving part of the District's public works planning and programming process. It is clear the citizen participation is well on its way toward becoming a permanent part of American local government. What is not clear—at least not yet in Washington—is how this will be done and who in City Hall will be responsible for and to it.

At present, citizen participation programs in the District of Columbia tend to be established by individual agencies on a single-purpose function basis. For example, the Board of Education has a Committee of twenty-one for each new school being planned. The Police Department has Citizen Police Advisory boards. Such groups rarely or never see their neighborhood problems in any city-wide and city-function perspective.

What is needed is a clearly defined and widely understood over-all city-wide system for citizen participation. The potential for such exists in embryonic form in the new "service area" concept described below. Hopefully, such a process for citizen participation in the 1970s will be set up and will prove to be less chaotic and frustrating for both the citizens and the public agencies.

The District's Innovative Service Area System

On April 20, 1970, Mayor Washington took what was described as "another major step to provide improved municipal services throughout the city". The city was divided into nine Service Areas as part of a system designed to offer co-ordinated city government services on a neighborhood level. The objective of this new system was to insure that the city made the best possible use of its existing resources and that the city's programs were really reaching and benefiting the people.

In announcing the new scheme, Mayor Washington said[54]:

> Different areas have different needs. Agencies now will be able to work together more effectively—to plan and to meet these varying requirements.
>
> Washington's problems in this connection are similar to those of most large cities in the nation, which are struggling with new programs—locally and federally funded—to meet the needs of people. Different city departments have identified various service regions, while the guidelines of federal programs have called for conflicting area boundaries.
>
> In Washington there are different regions for health, recreation, community renewal programs, sanitary engineering and other departments. There are overlapping and unmatched boundaries for such federal programs as Model Cities, the war on poverty, and neighborhood service programs. . . .
>
> The District's service area system will give agencies and federal program planners a firm base for effective joint planning and operations.

The new system is intended to require that city agencies utilize those same nine areas as a basis for:

1. Joint planning operations.
2. Collecting and evaluating data for identifying social, economic and physical problems.
3. Preparing more realistic budget and programming operations.
4. Co-ordinating agency activities to make services more readily available to people.
5. Insuring more effective joint use of facilities.
6. Reducing duplication and overlapping of activities and programs, and
7. Developing closer ties with citizens and citizen groups in order to make sure that planning and operations are increasingly responsive to the actual needs of citizens.

In order to carry out this new concept, a Community Services Advisory Committee, made up of ranking representatives of city service delivery departments, was established. The over-all committee was charged with assisting the director of the Office of Community Services (OCS) in the development and implementation of the new system. Nine Service Area Committees (SAC) were also established and charged with reviewing all city projects in that area and developing closer linkage with citizen and citizen groups. More specifically, each Service Area Committee is to have the following six tasks to perform[55]:

1. *Program Development and Project Review* will include initiating project ideas, identifying and reviewing new projects and proposals for renewal of existing projects.
2. *Special Projects* will be carried out by the SAC at the request of the Mayor.
3. *Periodic Reports* will be prepared for the Mayor at least bi-monthly to include Service Area needs and operational problems identified; actions taken since the previous report and additional recommendations for meeting identified needs.
4. *Service Delivery Report* will assess the delivery of government services at the neighborhood level and include recommendations for improvement. The report will be prepared on an annual basis.
5. *Service Delivery Procedures* will be developed by OCS with requested assistance from the SAC. The procedures will assure effective coordination of existing and new government services, appropriate location of essential government service delivery facilities, and appropriate service area evaluation procedures.
6. *Annual Report on the Social State of the District* will be prepared by the Director of the Department of Human Resources with requested assistance from the SAC.

In addition, each Service Area Committee will be responsible for holding public hearings within the Service Area to review proposed programs and reports and area problems so that each citizen group and area resident may have input into these activities. Furthermore, the SACs are also charged with "promoting in the Service Areas citizen organizations, or citizen organization co-ordinating groups, capable of influencing policy and operation."[56]

This innovation should, if carried out as proposed, clarify and simplify the way the city and its population is analyzed. It holds great promise for greater interagency co-ordination of services and, perhaps more significantly, for establishing a clear single city-wide framework for citizen participation at a community or neighborhood level. As part of the still evolving reorganization of the District of Columbia Government, it also may mean that all planning and programming activities will eventually be oriented by the nine Service Areas and the SAC Committees. This will undoubtedly influence planning in the 1970s. It could significantly improve planning data and information, insure more effective co-ordination of economic, physical and social planning and provide a framework for more meaningful citizen participation.

Preserving and Enhancing the Quality of the Environment in the National Capital Region

In the late 1960s, there was an upsurge of public concern over environmental pollution in the United States. The most notable legislative result was the National Environmental Policy Act of 1969. The increasing concern about, and support for total environmental planning in this country affects such diverse areas as air pollution, water pollution, health, aesthetics, population and land use among others. In fact, the concerns are so broad that there have been problems in conceptualizing and defining the limits of environmental concerns. Yet, at the same time, environmental planning potentially provides a much more wholistic frame of reference or umbrella for all kinds of planning—including community development planning. Many of the concerns and solutions offered by urban planners in the past have been accepted and are now put forward for public discussion under the environmental quality and environmental planning label.

The National Environmental Policy Act directed federal agencies to take "appropriate consideration" of environmental amenities and values in decision-making "along with the economic and technical considerations." President Nixon, in Executive Order 11514, went further and declared[57]:

> The Federal Government shall provide leadership in protecting and enhancing the quality of the Nation's environment to sustain and enrich human life. Federal agencies shall initiate measures needed to direct their policies, plans and programs so as to meet national environmental goals.

In the National Capital Region, NCPC adopted its "Policies and Procedures for Implementing the Goals and Policies of the National Environmental Policy Act of 1969, Executive Orders 11507 and 11514 for the Protection and Enhancement of Environmental Quality in the National Capital Region." By so doing, NCPC announced that all District and federal plans and programs for the national capital region would be reviewed and evaluated by the Commission in order to insure the objectives and policies of the Act were being carried out. The Commission further stated that "in view of the unique Federal presence at the seat of government, a special effort should be made by the Federal and the District of Columbia Governments in the National Capital Region to implement" these national goals and policies.

The long-range effect of the current attention being given to the environment by the public and the government is unclear at this time. It may prove to be one of those cycles of public attention that come and go—like the beautification period in the Johnson administration. On the other hand, it is also possible that the current popularity of environmental planning may prove long-lasting and provide a more wholistic base or frame of reference for our previous efforts at community, urban or metropolitan planning.

FUTURE PROSPECTS FOR COMMUNITY PLANNING AND DEVELOPMENT

If the 1970s prove to be as unpredictable as the 1960s, any speculation about future community planning and development trends in the Washington area is likely to be unreliable. However, it would appear that the 1970s are likely to witness the following fourteen characteristics:

> (1) *A continued sustained growth in the region's population.* Unless the nation adopts strong population control measures or some national urban settlement policy or even a policy intentionally to decentralize the headquarters function of the federal government outside of the national capital region, the continued population explosion in the area can be expected to continue. As in the 1960s, this growth is taking place almost entirely outside of the District of Columbia.

(2) *Completion of the initial regional rail rapid transit or Metro system.* The authorized ninety-five-mile system with eight major radial lines extending from the center of the city to approximately the Capital Beltway is scheduled to be in operation by the end of the decade; this is doubtful. Hopefully, the 1970s (or 1980s!) will also see: (1) the early approval of extensions to the initial system so that it will, in fact, serve the entire region, (2) more use of the Metro as a tool for leading or opening up new development, and (3) more adequate funding under the national program of financial assistance to urban mass transit systems (more comparable, perhaps, to the existing 90–10 per cent federal aid highway formula).

(3) *An increasing concern and public attention to the current relatively uncontrolled growth of the region.* This should lead to more and more demands for more effective regional planning and gradually more and more acceptance of the necessary planning controls on future developments. It may even lead to more deliberate consideration of suggestions for limiting the ultimate population of the area.

(4) *The unveiling and probable adoption of COG's long-awaited Regional Development Plan.* This is expected to take place early in the decade and should prove a major test of just how serious Americans actually are about making regional planning effective in a metropolitan urban context, and accepting and supporting the kind of development controls that are essential to effective regional planning. The new Regional Development Plan will either reconfirm the radial corridor concept of regional development first proposed by NCPC and the National Capital Regional Council in 1961 (abolished by President Johnson) in the proposed *Year 2,000 Plan* for the nation's capital or propose significantly different regional development policies. Interestingly enough, recent COG studies have indicated that despite the area's rapid growth and the relative ineffectiveness of regional planning in the last decade, the region has not yet entirely missed its chance to realize the basic features of the radial corridor plan in the National Capital Region.

As a result of an over-all comprehensive re-examination of *The Year 2000 Plan,* COG has found that[58]:

a. Most of the region's growth during the 1960s actually did approximate the radial corridor pattern envisioned in the original *Year 2000 Plan.*

b. The radial corridor patterns will break down after fifteen years. The net result will be urban sprawl.

c. In the year 2000, the low density wedges will no longer exist.

d. There is no way to guarantee that the new communities, vital to the radial corridor patterns, will be built.

e. In the year 2000, the region will become a "spread city" with over two thirds of the employment located outside the urban core.

f. Continuation of current trends will compound rather then resolve major urban problems.

However, COG's study also indicated that the concept of the radial corridor plan was still a valid alternative to urban sprawl. In its *Areawide Land Use Element—1972* report, COG concludes that "the Washington area now stands at a critical point; the stage is set for equally dramatic events in the future. If the area's local governments are to avoid a repetition of the problems of the past, and if they are to achieve the goals set forth in the original *Year 2000 Plan,* the time to act is now."

Current planning efforts of COG involve an emphasis upon methods and techniques for translating the plan's basic concepts into realities of development.

(5) *Strengthening the regional planning responsibilities of the Washington Council of Governments or its successor.* As a part of the area's efforts to make planning more effective in the 1970s, it can be anticipated that COG's planning responsibilities will be enlarged beyond its current advisory and recommendatory role. If, on the other hand, COG is succeeded by some more official area-wide governmental organization, it can be anticipated that it will be given more effective planning powers than now exist.

(6) *The formation of additional interstate compact agencies to carry out regional programs.* It is anticipated that the Washington Metropolitan Area Transit Authority will ultimately acquire and operate most if not all of the region's bus lines in the future. The proposed Potomac Basin Interstate Compact agency is expected to be created in the next year or two.

(7) Recently, increased attention has been given to the need for: *A regional or interstate agency to co-ordinate sewerage treatment plans and systems* throughout the entire Washington metropolitan area, and a regional body to operate the major airports serving the metropolitan area. It is possible that the regional planning function could also be combined with some regulatory powers in a compact-type agency. Regional housing and even new town agencies have also been suggested and may be given more serious consideration in the 1970s.

(8) *Strengthening the planning and programming functions of the federal government in the National Capital Region.* This is essential in order to ensure the continued effective operation of the headquarters functions at the seat of government. This will significantly effect NCPC's activities and will also enable the federal government to work more effectively with local planning agencies and a stronger regional planning program in this area.

(9) *Completion and adoption of all of the elements of the Comprehensive Plan for the National Capital.* With key planning elements in operation such as land use, mass transportation, parks and recreation, as well as a major thoroughfare plan reasonable control can be exercised over the capital. The grandiose concept of a Comprehensive Plan is becoming obsolete and it remains to be seen how the new dual planning system (local and the NCPC) works out in practice; nothing spectacular will be in evidence to celebrate in 1976 the bi-centennial of the Republic and the fiftieth anniversary of a planning agency in the city.

(10) *Approval of home rule for the District of Columbia.* Hopefully, the 1970s have seen the approval of at least a limited form of home rule allowing the election of the mayor and the council by the residents of the District (coming to fruition in 1975), and some form of financial relief from congressional review and approval of every penny the District spends and yet preserve the federal government's rights in matters affecting the federal interest at the seat of government.

(11) *Restructuring of the planning function in the District of Columbia.* This takes the form of a central planning and programming function in the office of the mayor in the District of Columbia Government—with NCPC having an overview of local plans and programs in order to insure that

local proposals are consistent with the federal interest in the development and redevelopment of the nation's capital.

(12) *Greater co-ordination of social, economic and physical plannings.* The 1960s was a period of increasing public attention and substantially greater funding of both social planning and economic development planning in the nation's capital. The 1970s should witness an even greater co-ordination of these activities with physical planning, as these newer functions are made more a part of the permanent operations of both the city and the federal government.

(13) *More systematic and responsive programs of citizen participation in planning and programming.* If the potential of the District's new Service Area system can be made a reality in the 1970s, it could mean an end to the various ad hoc, experimental and sometimes chaotic efforts at citizen participation in the 1960s.

(14) *Increasing emphasis on the quality of the human environment.* If current interest is sustained over the decade, these concerns could provide: a more holistic framework for social, economic and physical planning, and a more widespread public support for planning—particularly at the regional level—as a way of preserving and enhancing the environmental quality of the National Capital Region.

NOTES

[1] National Capital Planning Commission, *Justifications for Appropriations, Fiscal Year 1970,* Washington, D.C., p. 7.

[2] The Metropolitan Washington Council of Governments, *The Changing Region,* 1969, Washington, D.C., pp. 15–16.

[3] Ibid.

[4] Washington *Post,* September 4, 1970, pp. A–1 and A–10.

[5] *The Changing Region,* op. cit., p. 10.

[6] Washington *Star,* February 28, 1971, p. 1.

[7] Ibid.

[8] Andrew Kopkind and James Ridgeway, "Washington, The Lost Colony," *New Republic,* April 23, 1966.

[9] Washington *Post,* October 22, 1972, pp. D–1 and D–6.

[10] National Capital Planning Commission and National Capital Regional Planning Council, *Transportation Plan, National Capital Region,* 1959, Washington, D.C., p. 1.

[11] National Capital Transportation Agency, *Recommendations for Transportation in the Capital Region,* November 1, 1962.

[12] Citizens for Better Transportation, Inc., *It's Coming,* 1968, Washington, D.C.

[13] Washington Metropolitan Area Transit Authority, *Metro Groundbreaking, Dawn of a New Era,* 1969, Washington, D.C., p. 4.

[14] *The Changing Region,* op. cit., p. 7.

[15] National Capital Planning Commission, *Elements of the Comprehensive Plan for the National Capital,* 1969, p. 23.

[16] Federal Aid Highway Act of 1968 (PL90–495).

[17] Melvin F. Levine, *Housing in Metropolitan Washington: Today and Tomorrow,* 1968. Prepared for the Washington Council of Governments. Washington, D.C., p. 4.

[18] Ibid., p. 2.

[19] Ibid., p. III.

[20] Ibid., p. III.

[21] National Capital Planning Commission, *Problems of Housing People in Washington, D.C.,* July, 1966, Washington, D.C., p. 5.

[22] Ibid., p. 7.

[23] National Capital Housing Authority, Washington, D.C. Unpublished data.

[24] National Urban Coalition, *Guide to Federal Low- and Moderate-Income Housing and Community Development Programs,* March 1970, Washington, D.C., p. 6.

[25] *The Proposed Comprehensive Plan for the National Capital,* p. 62.

[26] Ibid., p. 63.

[27] District of Columbia City Council, *Housing Crisis in the District of Columbia,* 1969. *Findings and First State Action Program of the Housing and Urban Development Committee,* Washington, D.C., pp. 6–9.

[28] District of Columbia Redevelopment Land Agency, *Annual Report 1969,* December 31, 1969, Washington, D.C., p. ii.

[29] Ibid., pp. 3–19.

[30] National Capital Planning Commission, *The Anacostia-Bolling Urban Renewal Project,* March 1967, press release, Washington, D.C.

[31] National Capital Planning Commission, *Fort Lincoln New Town,* Undated pamphlet.

[32] Ibid.

[33] Edward J. Logue, Principal Development Consultant, *Fort Lincoln New Town. Final Planning Report,* April 1969, Washington, D.C., pp. 55–61.

[34] Ibid., p. 55.

[35] *The Fort Lincoln Selection Committee.* Letter dated November 16, 1970, to Mr. John Gunther, chairman, Board of Directors, D. C. Redevelopment Land Agency.

[36] Ibid.

[37] Housing and Community Development, *Newsletters* Vol. 1, No. 4, August 1972 and on-site reports.

[38] Government of the District of Columbia, Commissioner's Committee on Community Renewal, *Community Renewal in the District of Columbia. Three Alternative Courses of Action,* August 25, 1966, Washington, D.C., Preface.

[39] Ibid.

[40] Government of the District of Columbia, *Workable Program for Community Improvement, July 1, 1969–June 30, 1971.* Washington, D.C., p. 14.

[41] The Report of the President's Task Force on Urban Renewal. *Urban Renewal: One Tool Among Many,* May 1970, Washington, D.C., p. 2.

[42] The Mayor's Economic Development Committee, *Overall Economic Development Program for the District of Columbia,* 1969, Washington, D.C., pp. 1–7.

[43] United Planning Organization, *Alternatives, A Special Report on the United Planning Organization,* 1969, Washington, D.C., p. 3.

[44] Ibid.

[45] Ibid.

[46] Ibid.

[47] *Overall Economic Development Program for the District of Columbia,* op. cit., p. v.

[48] The Mayor's Economic Development Committee, *Memo from MEDCO,* August 1970, Vol. 1, No. 2.

[49] *Overall Economic Development Program for the District of Columbia,* op. cit., p. v.

[50] Ibid., pp. 1–2.

[51] Ibid., pp. 1–8.

[52] Ibid., pp. xvi–1.

[53] Model Cities Commission, District of Columbia Government, *First Year Action Program, Part II,* 1969–70. Washington, D.C.

[54] News Release, April 20, 1970, Public Affairs Office, District of Columbia Government.

[55] *Service Area Committee Procedures,* an undated memorandum, Office of Community Services, District of Columbia Government, pp. 3 and 4.

[56] *Statement of Goals,* an undated memorandum, Office of Community Services, District of Columbia Government, p. 5.

[57] *Protection and Enhancement of the Environment,* Executive Order 11514, March 5, 1970, Section 1.

[58] Metropolitan Washington Council of Governments, *Areawide Land Use Elements—1972,* July 1972.

CHAPTER 6

Toronto: A Federated Metro

John Dakin*

Toronto was the first urban area in the Western hemisphere to acknowledge in formal legislative and governmental structural terms that the most characteristic modern form of settlement is the metropolitan area. In achieving a new form of urban government in 1953 it attracted interest across the continent and throughout the world. Its claim to attention rests on this fact and the way in which it has sought to plan its growth through the new powers made available.

Toronto was founded at the end of the eighteenth century as a provincial governmental center. Incorporated in 1834, it prospered in the nineteenth century as a commercial and industrial city. Its population reached half a million by 1904, one million by 1947. Politically it expanded by annexation until 1912. After that

* Professor of Urban and Regional Planning and Department Chairman, University of Toronto (from 1961 to 1972). Educated in England (Bristol and London) in architecture and planning, he continued his education in South Africa in the social sciences, with a Ph.D. at the University of Natal. He had planning experience with Le Corbusier and Alfred Roth and in the provincial government of Natal, Africa. After private practice in England, he joined the University of Toronto in 1960. He has been a councilor of the Town Planning Institute of Canada and the Canadian Council for Urban and Regional Research and is a member of the Executive Committee of the University of Toronto's Centre for Urban and Community Studies and of the Executive Committee of the Institute of Environmental Studies. His chief research interests are metropolitan areas and telecommunications in relation to urban and regional planning processes.

date expansion of the central political unit did not keep pace with the spread of its urbanizing area. The Depression exposed serious weaknesses in government, taxation, and physical and social services. Serious thought about metropolitanization of government began in the mid-thirties.

After the war rapid development appeared in the municipalities adjacent to Toronto, and by the late 1940s the area was moving toward crisis in municipal finances. In 1953, the provincial government created the municipality of Metropolitan Toronto as an upper level government responsible for certain over-all matters, the original municipalities remaining as members in the new federation. The new government quickly and successfully tackled the major physical problems. Internal political modifications were made in 1967, by which time the population had reached approximately 1,800,000.

FIG. 1 The central business district from the northwest—approximately one mile square. *Lockwood Survey Corporation Limited, Toronto*

By 1970, the political jurisdictional area of Metro Toronto was nearly built up and once again spatial, governmental, financial and services pressures had become serious. In early 1969, the provincial government had expressed its desire for a new approach to government in the urbanizing area (suggesting a group of metros): a new phase was opening (Fig. 1).

In 1963, after ten years of Metro government, Frank Smallwood published his assessment of its performance: *Metro Toronto: A Decade Later*[1]; this study, abridged and updated in *Taming Megalopolis* (1967) reported on Metro largely, though not exclusively, from a political science point of view. It stressed the energy and success with which Metro had immediately addressed itself to financial and physical service problems but expressed the view that Metro was already in a changing situation and that it would

> have no choice but to pay increasing attention to some of the less glamorous problems of social accommodation that it has tended to subordinate to its higher priority public works goals of the past.[2]

This change was well in evidence by 1970 (Fig. 2).

FIG. 2 The Toronto New City Hall which accommodates the administrations of both the city of Toronto and Metropolitan Toronto. *Toronto Fire Department*

HISTORICAL PERSPECTIVES

Toronto was laid out in 1793 as ten small blocks along a spine road; the site was above a good harbor on Lake Ontario, protected by islands. The land rose away from the harbor in a series of slopes that had been the shores of a larger lake. On the east and west great ravines came down to the lake, cut by the water from the melting ice of the last ice age. In these ravines ran the two major rivers of the area—the Don and the Humber. The soil was deep and well drained. The new settlement would look to New York as well as to Montreal. It was a good location for a world city when its time should come.

South of an east-west line (Queen Street) John Graves Simcoe, the first Governor of Upper Canada,[3] reserved all land, except for the original ten blocks of settlement, to the Crown. This would allow the government to lay out urban extensions when appropriate. By 1797, plans showed two formal open spaces modeled on the domestic squares typical of the development of the great estates of London during the eighteenth century. North of the line plots of a hundred and two hundred acres were given to members of the government and others to induce them to settle. Land in subsequent concessions was granted to settlers as farm lots.

An important permanent result of laying out the concessions in this way was that they produced a grid of roads running at one mile and one quarter intervals in east-west and north-south directions. The resultant blocks of land contained a thousand acres. This grid became the basic pattern of road layout for the region and provided modern Toronto with ready-made rights of way for its arterial road system.

Early government was oligarchical, not democratic, in both temper and action. The legislature might propose a bill but the governor was under no obligation to endorse it. Later government was very proempire, more British than the Queen.

By 1834, pressure from Toronto persuaded the government to incorporate it as a city. Its area, including the liberties,† extended roughly two miles from the lake. It was by now a governmental center and commercial exchange for exports of chiefly lumber and farm products and for all those imports which a rising population in the province needed. Activity huddled round the harbor and business and residential land uses were intermixed (Figs. 3a, 3b, 3c).

Free-for-All

Like most commercial-industrial cities in the Western world, during the nineteenth century Toronto grew without much over-all public control. It got into trouble with water supply and sewage disposal and these remained a problem for most of the century. For the municipality there were frequent financial crises which arose directly from the city's rapid growth in a laissez-faire climate of values.

The City Council was forced to provide services by granting franchises to private companies; water, electricity and gas supplies, street lighting, public transportation and fire fighting were dealt with in this way—often in an unsatisfactory fashion. The refusal of the company running the streetcars to go beyond the area of their franchise as the city grew induced a desirable closeness of built-up area and eventually forced the city council to provide additional public transit. Gradually the city came to understand that it must itself be responsible for basic services.

† A political jurisdiction intermediate between urban and rural government; Philadelphia also had "liberties."

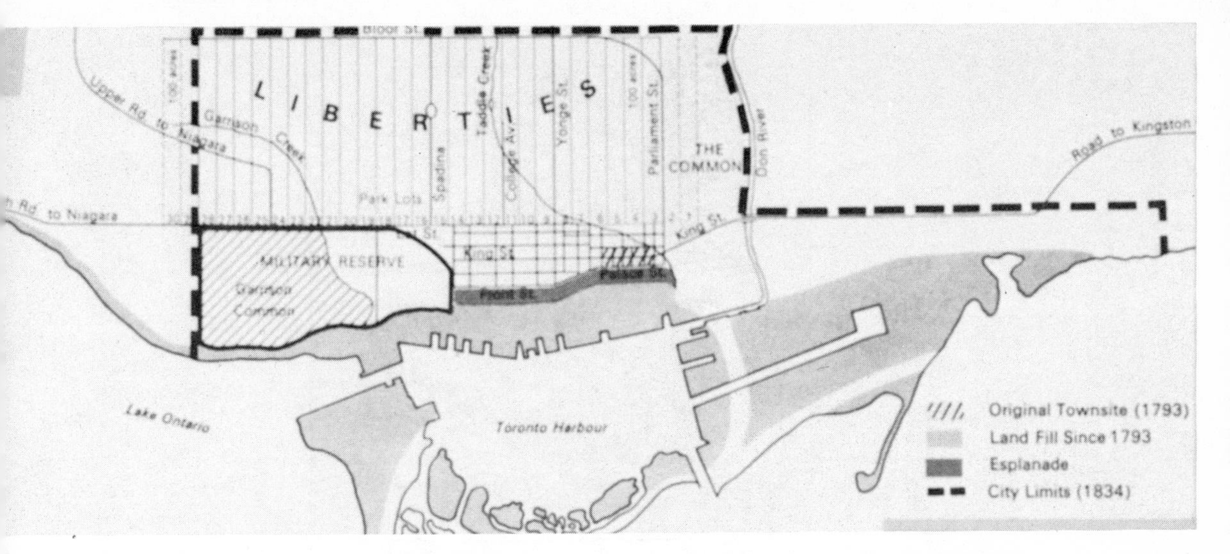

FIG. 3A City of Toronto, 1834. In earlier days Toronto attempted to solve its jurisdictional problems by the use of "liberties," whose residents had reduced rights and obligations. *Toronto Metropolitan Planning Board*

In 1853, the railway age was opened. It gave a great boost to the city, and the council, which apparently had had previously little money for anything, by 1862 had a debt of over one million dollars sunk in railways! The effects on the city's form were considerable. The esplanade along the waterfront, given by the provincial government "for the public use and benefit of the inhabitants of the City for ever," was in no time pre-empted by ambitious railway companies.[4]

The railways made possible the establishment of industry outside the traditional area of work located on the harbor. This was the first dispersal of manufacturing industry, which was now able to locate across the back of the city and up the Humber and Don valleys.

Wealthy citizens could now rescue their families from the discomfort and danger of living in Toronto and could set up establishments in the country around the city. As the dangers were considerable—cholera, typhoid and the other germ diseases of the period plus polluted air and water—the idea was attractive, and systematic commuting began.

In this free-for-all almost no planning in terms of phasing development or organizing layout took place. At the height of the esplanade chicanery one councilor did rise and call for "some general and comprehensive plan". A few relics of planned urban layout survived upon the ground, but the age had little ability to develop them to their three-dimensional urban potential and they remain, even today, as flat fossils in the strata of the city's growth.[5]

Yet the land use of the city was not without some order and reason. Below it lay the grid pattern of the eighteenth-century surveyors. The distribution of factories, offices, shops and various income levels of housing, although not a pattern to which we now aspire in planning, was nevertheless a functional pattern constantly evolving from the working of the market. It had the logic of a laissez-faire situation with strong value emphasis on the importance of money and material success. Respect for this kind of order continued down to 1966.[6]

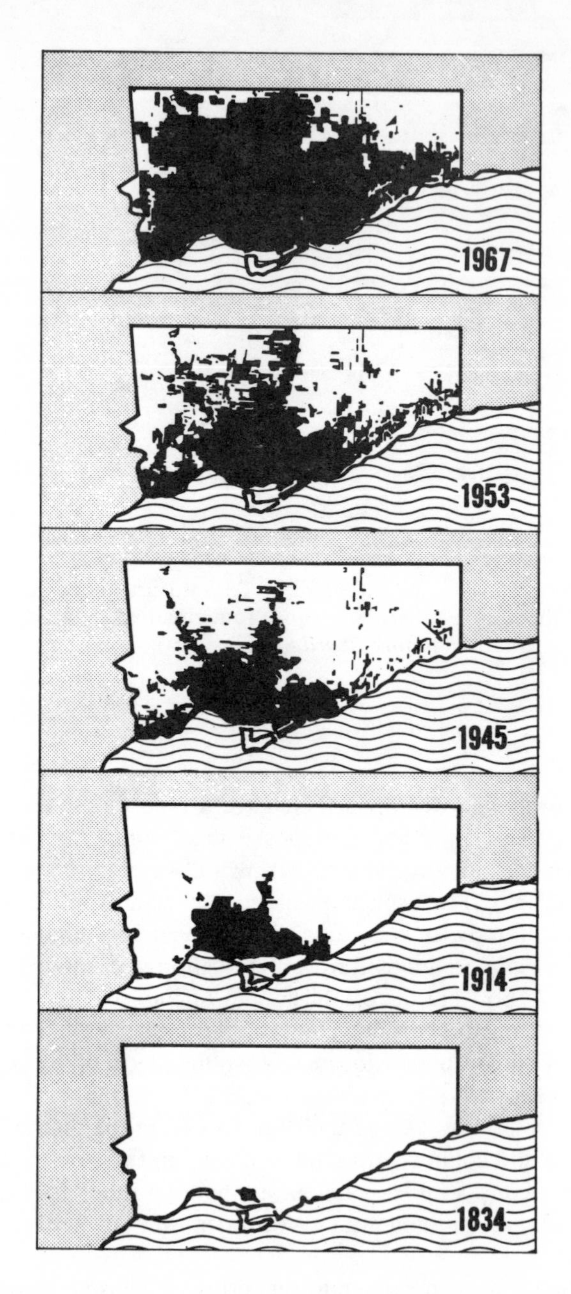

FIG. 3B The growth of the urban mass shown within the boundaries of the Metro Toronto political jurisdiction. *Toronto Metropolitan Planning Board*

Promises of a World City to Come

Just before the end of the century the Toronto Civic Guild, a private group, formed and eventually produced the city's first over-all plan since the end of the eighteenth century. This plan (1909) recommended two major diagonal thoroughfares to serve the downtown area, many new parks to help control tuberculosis and a new industrial estate to the east of the harbor.

Hard on the heels of the idea that thought should be taken for the city as a whole came cheap bulk electricity from the new hydroelectric plant at Niagara Falls (1912). This immediately opened up the possibility of major electric traction for public purposes including rapid transit.

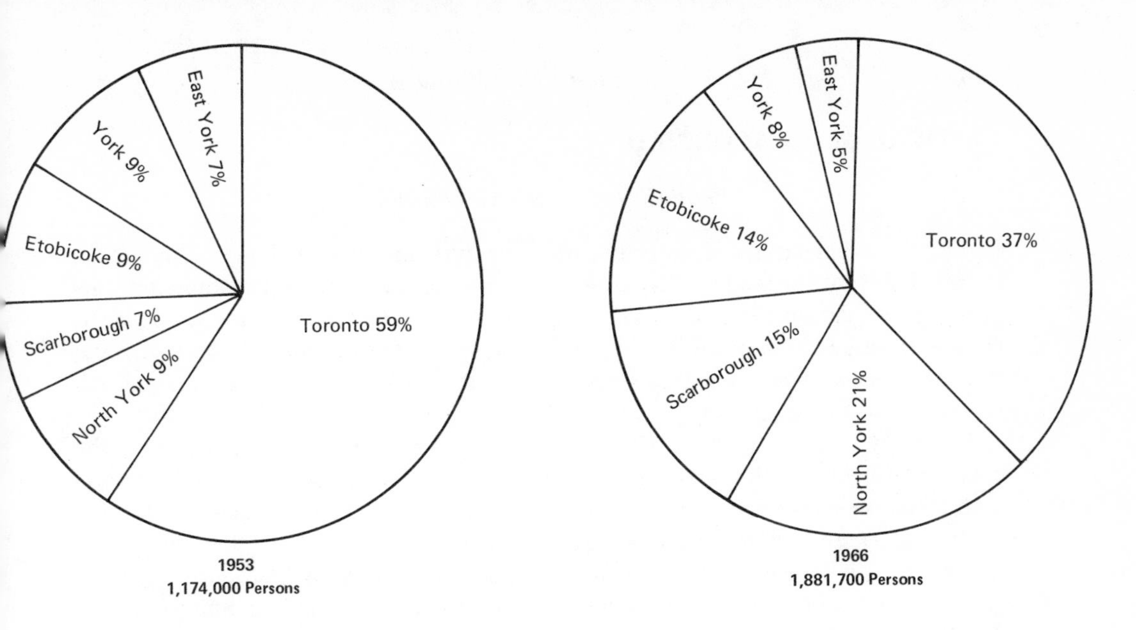

FIG. 3C Distribution of population, 1953 to 1966. The central city will accommodate a continuous diminished fraction of the total urban population. *Toronto Metropolitan Planning Board*

The opportunity for rapid transit was seized with vigor and imagination. Careful surveys of rider habits were made; the density and growth curves of the city were constructed and compared with those of other major cities. Most astonishing of all, two alternative plans for the future development of Toronto were made so that the rapid transit planning might be based on a wide examination of the possibilities. The alternatives represented the two hypotheses that the city would not spread across the Humber and Don rivers or would spread across them. Bridging costs were the problem. The resultant transportation proposals (1915) recommended a north-south line along Yonge Street (the central spine road), and a lake-shore route, the two meeting in a downtown loop.

The Toronto Harbor Commission, caught up in the conservation and landscape enthusiasm of the time, produced and proceeded to carry out a plan not only for the harbor but also for a considerable part of the western waterfront. What presentable waterfront Toronto had by the 1960s was mostly the result of that plan.

These attempts were the beginning of Toronto feeling itself a modern metropolis. It now rivaled Montreal in business and it had wide financial interests across Canada, out to the Pacific coast. It was rich, energetic, Protestant in ethic, Anglo-Saxon in origin, commercial in temper, laissez-faire in economic matters and conservative generally in government. Manufacturing industry had grown and its economic base had diversified.

The new transit proposals, the waterfront plan, and the Guild's plan for the city were evidence that Toronto was taking its metropolitan responsibilities seriously. But there was a difficulty: These efforts were the work of separate, largely independent agencies. They were not the voice of the Council or of the people. They were produced essentially by private, individual agencies—laissez-faire in a new shirt—with little comprehension of the need to plan holistically with regard for social as well as physical matters.

CRITICAL MASS ACHIEVED

Political-administrative Difficulties

During the nineteenth and early twentieth century the city of Toronto had been in the habit of expanding its boundaries by annexation to accommodate its growing population. The last annexation, which brought its boundaries to their present position, took place in 1912. Growth, however, did not halt on that date; the urban mass was forced to expand into the municipalities immediately adjacent.

The chief reason for the city's refusal to expand farther was its fear that the costs of bringing the adjacent areas up to its own level of services would be too high. The neighboring municipalities were forced to service their urbanizing areas, but often did not have adequate resources. As a result they were frequently driven to enter into agreements to buy service from Toronto. Thus the city came to supply water and other services to the surrounding municipalities. This was anything but satisfactory as Toronto had its own service problems and was in no position to raise finance for anything beyond its own needs.

The Depression of the late 1920s brought to light further difficulties: inequalities in welfare provisions (one municipality had 25 per cent of its population on welfare in 1932), education and inadequate police and fire-fighting services. Most important of all, the municipalities were bankrupt. Of the thirteen municipalities later to be covered by the jurisdiction of the Municipality of Metropolitan Toronto, ten were in such serious default to their debenture holders and the banks by 1932 that they had to be closely supervised by the provincial government.

In the early 1930s the provincial government set up the first over-all enquiry into the state of the Toronto area; the resultant report,[7] urging partial metropolitanization, was dated 1935; it took nineteen years more for the creation of Metropolitan Toronto to become fact.

During the latter part of the 1930s and the early 1940s the economic conditions improved but no major political or administrative changes were made that could relieve the difficulties exposed by the hard times.

On the physical planning side, however, some interesting attempts were made which showed that a critical size had been reached by Toronto. These were the 1943 plan for a greater Toronto, produced by the City of Toronto Planning Board, and the attempts to plan the area of the county of York in conjunction with the city of Toronto (1947–53). Their failure in effectuation indicated the urgent need to settle the political-administrative questions for a metropolitan population which by 1941 had reached 891,678—an increase of 352 per cent since 1901.

As the 1940s wore on it became increasingly evident that the political question would have to be faced fairly quickly. The provincial government did nothing and eventually the city of Toronto applied for annexation of the twelve surrounding municipalities. Simultaneously a small lake-shore municipality, Mimico, asked the provincial government for amalgamation of certain administrative functions across the entire urban area.

The applications were heard before the Ontario Municipal Board—an independent agency set up by the provincial government and having certain responsibilities in municipal and planning matters. After very lengthy hearings the

Board announced that it was unable to grant either application. The reasons for refusal were political. To break this deadlock the premier of the province requested the chairman of the board (L. R. Cumming) to suggest a solution. He pondered the nature of Canadian political institutions and in a most innovative fashion concluded *that as federation was used at national level it might be acceptable as a form of metropolitan government.* He reported along these lines in a model for all reports and the government brought the Municipality of Metropolitan Toronto into being with effect 1 January 1954.

The act made the "inhabitants of the Metropolitan Area a body corporate", with powers to be exercised by a Metropolitan Council. The council consisted of twelve members from the city of Toronto and one from each of the other municipalities with a chairman elected either from among the council members or from outside. The representatives from the adjoining municipalities were their mayors or reeves (townships). Operating under the provisions of the Municipal Act of Ontario, Metro was enabled to levy a rate (local property taxes), issue debentures, originate bylaws and set up programs involving the creation and operating of capital works. Like any other municipality it was to have departments for carrying out its functions: finance, assessment, works, roads, welfare and housing, planning, parks, traffic, police, etc.

As a result of a review of the working of Metro in the mid-1960s the twelve municipalities were amalgamated into five boroughs; thus making with the city of Toronto six major political jurisdictions in place of the original thirteen (Fig. 4). At the same time the composition of the Metro Council was changed to comprise thirty-three members plus the chairman. Each borough now had its mayor and between one and five controllers or aldermen on Metro Council. The city had its mayor, two controllers and nine aldermen. The chairman was elected as before. This was a more equitable arrangement than the original composition as the population of the city now represented a smaller fraction of the total urban population and the municipalities were by now better established as urban governments.

In terms of responsibilities the Metro Council was given the additional tasks of financing, school construction (through a Metro-wide tax), all welfare services, waste disposal (garbage), the Canadian National Exhibition, ambulance service, regional libraries and participation in urban renewal programs in conjunction with the municipalities. Experience of working Metro for over a decade had shown that both the political jurisdiction of the municipalities and the responsibilities of Metro needed revision.[8]

The original act (1953) had made Metro responsible for the wholesale supply and purification of water, the provision of major storm and sanitary sewers, basic education costs, public transportation, the major road network, regional planning (meaning Metro Area plus a fringe area), the administration of the jail and power courts, public housing, regional parks, houses for the aged and care of indigent hospital patients and neglected children. By 1957, it had amalgamated the thirteen police forces into a single Metro police department, assumed jurisdiction over municipal licensing and had undertaken pollution control. By 1962, it was moving toward consolidation of public housing activities and amalgamation of library services. Later in the 1960s pollution control and public housing became responsibilities of agencies of the provincial government.

The then areas of jurisdiction are political, 240 square miles, and planning,

720 square miles. The jurisdiction was made larger for planning so that the area into which urban growth would eventually take place would be safeguarded. This fringe consisted of a depth of one township—roughly ten miles—out beyond the boundaries of the political jurisdiction. The original idea, later de-emphasized, was that when a fringe municipality should become predominantly urban it would be taken into the political jurisdiction. Fringe control of subdivision had previously been exercised by the city of Toronto and, while not successful because of loopholes in the system, had convinced politicians and planners that some such powers were necessary.

A few other cities in the Western hemisphere had attempted metropolitan planning up to the early 1950s—notably New York in the late twenties and Philadelphia in the early thirties with no great success. Toronto claims it was the first to give official political recognition to the Metropolitan area as the newest form of urban settlement created by the modern industrial society.

Services Crisis

The 1940s brought the whole matter of services to a critical point; about the middle of the decade it became clear to many politicians and officials that the existing condition whereby each municipality had been independent would no longer work.

The symptoms of the difficulties were serious. Wells, hitherto relied on, could not meet the heavily increased demand for water. Streams, used for carrying effluents down to the lake, were becoming polluted beyond acceptable levels.

FIG. 4 Groupings of municipalities—1967 Metropolitan Toronto Planning Area. *Toronto Metropolitan Planning Board*

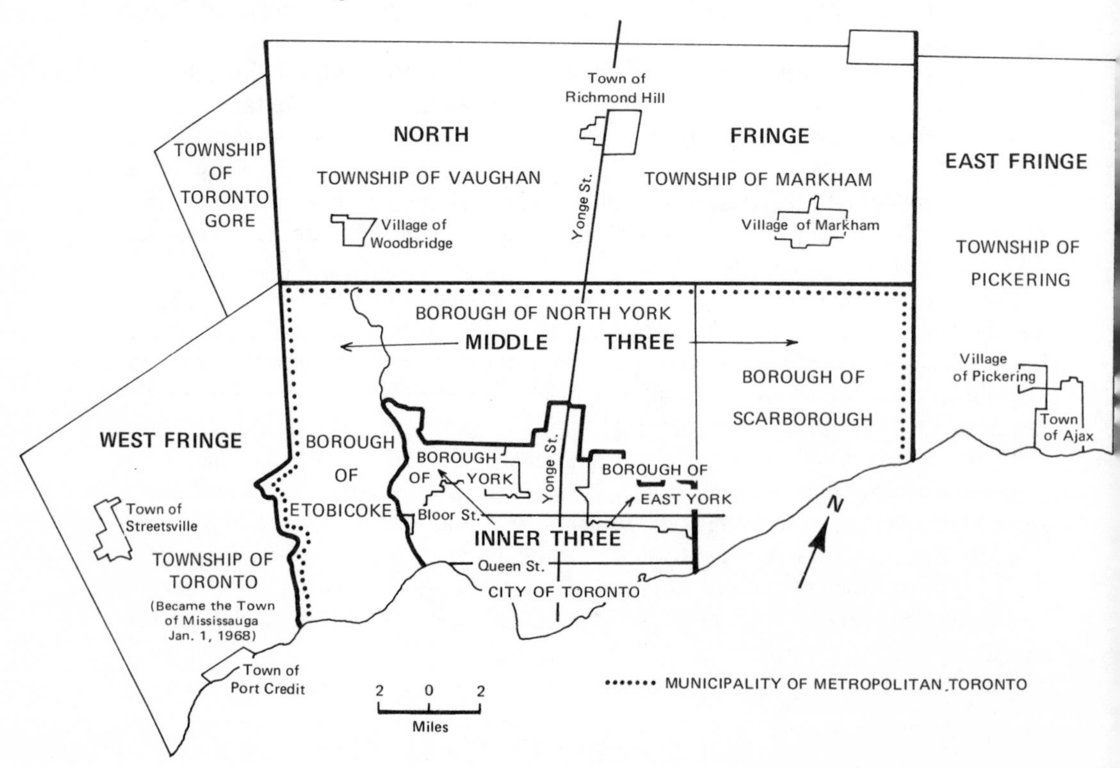

Agreements between the city and adjacent municipalities were unable to meet the situation; municipalities, like North York which was the fastest growing of them all, with no access to the lake, were particularly in bad shape; at one stage North York's water supply virtually failed.

Roads were generally overloaded in the Metro area; a superhighway system had appeared as a major proposal of the 1943 plan. Further, the roads of the one mile and one-quarter grid were often unimproved and because of the undulations of the terrain required large capital investment before they could be converted into an efficient arterial system adequate to support a superhighway network. Subways were also seen to be necessary and had appeared on the 1943 plan. Yonge Street was congested and its streetcar tracks and rolling stock were in very poor condition by the end of the war. The expanding suburbs were poorly served by public transportation and their low densities (almost entirely single family houses) made the provision of even limited services uneconomic.

The need was urgent—was predominantly for basic physical services. There were no trunk water mains or sewers except those serving the city. There were no expressways, the arterials were substandard, and there were no subways. As all municipalities, with the exception of the city, were under heavy growth pressure it was necessary to find ways of meeting these needs as quickly as possible.

In exerting pressure toward metropolitanization these needs interlocked with the facts of political jurisdictions and tax organization of the municipalities. Every municipality was under pressure to allow subdivision and grant building permits, especially for domestic construction. This meant services of all kinds had to be provided. But much residential property did not pay for itself in terms of its cost to the municipality being matched by the taxes it would pay; a municipality had to rely on the tax money it received from its industrial and commercial assessment for making up the difference. Municipalities typically did everything they could to attract new industry, including zoning large areas for the purpose. This eventually had excellent planning effects in that it assisted the distribution of industry across the whole Metro area, but in general the industry came more slowly than the houses and the municipalities were forced to restrict the rate of residential growth to match their financial capacities.

A most important reason for creating Metropolitan Toronto, therefore, was the alleviation of financial constraints on the municipalities so that services could be provided quickly. The solution worked very well; Metro has been able to raise loans when the municipalities could not and at cheaper rates. It has been able to use the money raised for directly financing trunk mains, water and sewage works, improving the arterial system, making good public transit deficits and helping to finance subway capital works, assisting in education costs, and for providing technical services of many kinds including over-all planning.

The focus of effort on physical services showed itself in the early budgets of Metro. F. G. Gardiner, the first Metro council chairman, "ran Metro like a giant construction company," it was said. Certainly he understood the physical needs, and the wisdom of his emphasis was borne out by the subsequent development of Toronto.

Toronto coped very well with its physical problems, but it did not grasp, however, that social results also flow from taking action on the city physical and that while costs may at first manifest themselves in dollars they may turn up later in human terms or societal costs. By early 1970, Toronto had achieved much physically, but the average price of a new home had risen by about $7,000 in the previous year to an all-time high of $42,805. Equally a record was the total of over 17,000 families (including 35,000 children) on the list for public housing.[9]

THE DRIVE TO PLAN

Early Municipal and Protometropolitan Planning

By the mid-1940s several municipalities, including the city of Toronto, had reached the conclusion that they should prepare plans to guide the physical expansion that was imminent. Some of these plans were rudimentary in the extreme. North York's, for example, simply designated the area intended for urban development for the succeeding twenty years and stipulated the broad land uses, paying particular attention to industry as this was the revenue producer.

Such plans, implemented by bylaws,[10] did the job reasonably well in the Toronto area. Councils were able to control the pace of development to something within their means to sustain; development was well serviced (almost always with piped water and sewage), and the quality of subdivision was steadily improved in terms of appearance, convenience, materials and construction.

On the metropolitan scale the city of Toronto prepared the first over-all modern plan (1943). This was inspired by the need to provide jobs for troops returning from the war. It was therefore essentially a capital works approach.

The planners took this need as point of departure and daringly produced a plan for the whole urban area and well beyond, although they had technically no mandate to go outside the boundaries of the city of Toronto.

The plan designated an urban area containing about as much room for future expansion—fifty square miles—as was already comprised in the built-up area. The intention was to draw the fangs of the development interests; it was thought they could hardly complain that the proposed outer green belt would restrict them if they had as much vacant land as all Toronto then comprised. The plan designated industrial land in a well-distributed pattern, provided an inner green belt, laid out a complete superhighway system (expressways), showed subways and suggested capital works.

Judged by the planning standards of Britain, the 1943 plan was not particularly remarkable. But Britain had enacted a useful planning act in 1932 and had acquired considerable experience in using its provisions during the 1930s. By the early 1940s, Britain was moving toward interim development control over the entire country (1943) and a New Towns Act (1946), and was shortly to blossom out into compulsory planning for the whole country (1947). Ontario, on the other hand, was not to achieve its first genuine planning act until 1946, spurred by this Toronto plan. Of its specific provisions, only one—the setting up of a parking authority—was achieved as an immediate result of the plan.

The second attempt at broad planning occurred toward the end of the 1940s. This was the work of the Toronto and Suburban Planning Board and its successor, the Toronto and York (County) Planning Board. The setting up of these boards to work in conjunction with the planning of the city of Toronto was new recognition of the needs brought to light by the 1943 plan. These boards successively carried on the thinking about broad area planning problems until the setting up of

Metropolitan planning in 1954. Some of the staff of the Toronto and York Planning Board became the first planners of Metro, two remaining with Metro planning to the present time and providing a very valuable continuity.

Planning in the Boroughs

The greatest growth pressure on the municipalities occurred in the 1950s. The fastest grower was North York, which was farthest from the lake and therefore in the most disadvantageous position from the point of view of piped services. Its population quadrupled between 1941 and 1951 and more than quadrupled again from 1951 to 1966. From 1941 to 1966, this represented an explosive growth from approximately 23,000 to 400,000.[11]

Various effective techniques were adopted during this period for helping control development. Scarborough, with other municipalities, insisted on the developers providing full services of pipes and roads in their subdivisions. Sewer levies were introduced and a technique of making agreements with developers was initiated by the councils. These methods proved their worth and became common practice in the area.

Two major characteristics of these typical master plans of the 1950s need emphasis. First, there was, and still remains, a very sharp split between the authority of the plan and the mode of its implementation. Second, by the end of the 1960s the plans were seriously dated in their approach.

The split between plan and implementation was evident in the fact that the plan does not include powers for its own implementation. The provisions of the plan are effected by means of zoning bylaws. The bylaw may be comprehensive in the sense of covering the whole municipality or several separate bylaws may be used to cover separate parts of the municipal area. Indeed, the plans of some municipalities were virtually lost to view by the mid-1960s while the bylaw was very much in evidence as it was generally recognized that nothing could be permitted in contravention of its stipulations.

The theory behind the use of the zoning bylaw technique for implementation had two major elements. One was the notion of providing certainty to an owner of property as to what he might or might not do with it (or his neighbor do with his). Secondly, there was the desire to avoid officials being in positions where they could grant or withhold favor and therefore might be open to corruption (of which there is little evidence).

As far as the certitude is concerned, the bylaw technique often failed to give the supposed assurance because councils hungry for assessment have been willing to listen to developers who have asked for amendments to the bylaws. Toronto has believed in its municipal planning up to a point but has not fully accepted its implications as a form of social-political control.

The plans in general strongly reflected the problems and values of the 1950s. The approach was largely to see the growth of Toronto as a straight enlargement of the 1930s' centralized city. It would expand with more of the same—single-family houses, schools, small shopping centers and local parks. In certain regards the image was basically that of the streetcar metropolis with improved communications. The municipalities, although they zoned land for industry, nevertheless were thought of as suburbs. Downtown was still the center.

Don Mills (about 30,000; commenced 1954) was the chief achieved attempt to organize expansion in some more coherent way than by creeping aggregation of subdivisions. Its promoters hired the best professional services they could find and set about producing a "balanced" community which would include all income groups, various kinds of work, a major shopping center, a variety of housing types including considerable use of apartments, and pedestrian ways to allow children to reach school with minimum contact with vehicular traffic. The venture was successful and, receiving considerable publicity, is today a flourishing community with some sense of entity and better than average appearance.

The concept of the single-family house as the "correct" type of development also had a binding effect. Until quite late in the period some municipalities would turn down subdivision applications because the "wrong" kind of dwelling unit was proposed. Semidetached units were objectionable to many councils, and apartments were difficult to finance because the mortgage interests did not think there would be any extensive demand for them in the suburbs.

By the end of the 1960s, many of these prejudices and preconceptions about housing had been broken down, although not all had disappeared. Yet the plans remained largely of the 1950s in approach to housing; councils swallowing apartments only because they imagined (often erroneously) that they were more financially satisfactory for the council than houses. By the end of the 1960s, some municipalities had come to realize that the detailed control and improvement of apartment development were a major planning task, but generally the improvement produced by planning in single-family development had not been matched by a similar improvement in apartment layout and design.

A third element, in which the plans were dated, was the political-social sphere. Whatever the plans might say, politicians put their stress on the usefulness of planning as a control on development and an improver of assessment. Planning was useful for helping municipal administration. It was not seen very clearly in its social objectives.

Toronto is a fairly conformist society; the plans were therefore not unexpectedly conventional. They became stereotyped to the immediate needs of the day; just how stereotyped did not emerge until toward the end of the 1960s when several incidents foreshadowed coming change.

One of these concerned the urban renewal of Trefann Court. The city of Toronto had prepared a renewal plan for this run-down area and as part of the process of putting it into effect had designated a social worker to assist the residents in understanding what was going on and to provide feedback to the city. The residents opposed the proposals with such vigor that the program had to be suspended. Other renewal areas also manifested similar indications that residents had serious objections to the city's renewal intentions. The public apathy of the forties had been replaced by an activism which was strong enough to bring about a major change in the attitude of the Metro Council by 1970.

A second incident concerned the building of the next leg of an expressway and rapid transit construction (Spadina) which had been started in the mid-1960s. Protests by some residents in the area through which the next new piece would pass were so vehement by 1969 that it appeared possible that the north-west part of the planned expressways and rapid transit system (planned in 1964 and incorporated in the Metro plan 1966) would be delayed or perhaps stopped.

By early 1971, the Ontario Municipal Board (which has the authority for granting permission for additional expenditure) had approved in a 2 to 1 vote Metro's request to be allowed to spend more money necessitated by rising costs on the Spadina part of the expressway network. The anti-Spadina groups immediately appealed to the provincial government against this approval. The Cabinet gave its decision against allowing further funds for the expressway but announced its intention to increase provincial government financial support for rapid transit in particular and public transit generally. It offered no feasible alternative and this decision rendered Metro unable to proceed with a basic expressway grid and left it with its transportation plan of over a decade substantially in chaos.

By early 1970, the city's development commissioner was pointing out that the increasing opposition of citizen groups to apartment building was a factor in the decline of construction in buildings of this type during the previous year. As between 1969 and 1968 there had been a decline of $24 million. The public's objections caused delays and this no doubt contributed. The commissioner was quoted as saying that "many developers are wary of building in the city of Toronto." Here was an important new element in the whole urban situation which could lead to a more social and human emphasis in planning.

City of Toronto Planning

Because of its age and its role as the center of the urban complex the city of Toronto has had different problems from those of the surrounding young and expanding municipalities. Its population has not changed in numbers a great deal over the last two decades, but there have been considerable changes in its fabric. A fact of major significance has been the health of the central business district. Little increase in employment has taken place (1969: 175,000), but many new buildings have appeared in the postwar period and by 1970 there was sign of still further increased tempo of building activity. In the late 1960s, several major developments, such as the Toronto Dominion Center, appeared and others were announced. Of these latter, two sponsored by public agencies were very important. The two railways—the Canadian National Railways and the Canadian Pacific Railway—announced that they were releasing 190 acres of land for development of various kinds in the area of Union Station (1968). This would include a transportation terminal, a telecommunication center, offices and residential accommodation for 20,000. The estimated value of this development was $1 billion at that time.

A second major project was proposed by the Toronto Harbor Commissioners. In addition to extensive harbor works, this proposal included residential development for 50,000 persons. A third—private development—proposed to build for 18,000 residents. With the railways, the harbor proposals and the private projects Toronto could apparently anticipate a new residential population of about 100,000 to the immediate south of its central business district and close to the lake. Meantime, office blocks were increasing in size and the tempo of renewal was high.

Some politicians, sniffing revenue, were ecstatic. By the end of the decade, however, businessmen were beginning to express concern about the deteriorating appearance of the central business district ("concrete jungle," "unco-ordinated development"); certainly the buildings were getting taller and in their aggregate not noticeably more orderly (see Fig. 1).

Increased traffic congestion and air pollution were further question marks hanging over the CBD. By 1963, the planners had reported on the traffic problems to the effect that perhaps some vehicular transportation would have to go below grade. By the end of the decade nothing had been done, and the Metro planned cross-town expressway, which by running well to the north of the CBD would take some load off downtown, was meeting public opposition as well as resistance by the city.

It cannot be said that the city's planning was able to cope effectively with all these matters. The pressure of development together with the manner in which developers—particularly public agencies—proceeded to prepare their proposals was such that planning was swamped.[12]

The considerations deciding development appeared almost entirely financial. Economic feasibility and financial return were effectively the only yardsticks. The prevailing greed was nicely exposed in the favorite form proposed by developers for large slabs of building near the lake. These were shown in open "V" formation with the opening of the V facing the lake. The idea was to win maximum view across the water for their tenants. As the slabs were 100 feet or more high they would totally exclude the possibility of buildings behind them having any view at all; the planners struggled and achieved some mitigation of such monstrosities.

By 1970, it was uncertain to what extent the planning process of the city would be able effectively to guide this splurge of development with some protection to public interests. There were serious weaknesses in the planning: public agencies were not compelled to collaborate and private developers did not necessarily inform the planners of their intentions in the preparation stage but simply presented their proposals fully worked out and ready for approval. If no amendment to the planning bylaw was required the planners might not even see the proposal at all until it appeared on the ground!

Perhaps the most serious weakness was the question of whether the city really wanted planning in the sense of safeguarding the public interest or whether it wanted it only when useful for certain short-term benefits such as avoiding expenditure on services or helping to increase revenue. The setting up of the Development Department in 1962 quite separate from the Planning Board underlined this ambiguity.

It was not clear that the society was firmly enough convinced of the merits of planning to give sufficient backing to the planners to allow them to deal effectively with the tasks appearing in the central business district. A very vigorous job of co-ordination and, where necessary, coercion was needed. The powers available were inadequate enough, but there was one ray of hope. In 1969, the planners produced a new policy approach to the downtown area. This depended on an appeal to voluntary collaboration by developers with the city authorities. It was well received.

To sum up, by the end of the 1960s planning in the municipalities and the city had achieved some success in ordering physical development in the growing edges. It had given scope for considerable experimentation in housing, although it had achieved little in dealing with the problem of providing shelter for those who could not meet market prices. It had been less successful in dealing with downtown redevelopment, and by the end of the decade the question of the extent of the suitability of the plans and planning already developed was bound to be raised. A new social emphasis was appearing and some responses to it being made. The city had learned something from its bitter renewal experiences and several municipalities were finding their planning boards and planners spending increasing time on the social implications of their work.

Professional expertise had grown, and at the beginning of the new decade Toronto had, at municipal level, the apparatus necessary for taking effective co-ordinating and innovative action in regard to the urban fabric. A more human emphasis had developed and it had a channel through which to work; the municipal planner formed the link between the planning at the Metropolitan Toronto level and the individual lives of people. The question was: Would it be possible to broaden the scope of local planning so that it might better cope with emerging social and human individual emphases? Could methods be evolved for effectively reconciling the local with the larger interests?

The Metropolitan Plan

Although Ontario had a planning act, the act which set up the municipality of Metropolitan Toronto (1953) specifically required Metro to undertake the planning of certain over-all aspects of the whole urban area (Fig. 5). These were:

(a) land uses and consideration generally of industrial, agricultural, residential and commercial areas,
(b) ways of communication,
(c) sanitation,
(d) green belts and parks,
(e) public transportation, and such other matters as the Minister of Municipal Affairs may define from time to time.

The jurisdiction set up for planning purposes was larger than the 240 square miles of the political jurisdiction. It included a fringe of 480 square miles (total 720 square miles) over which Metro was to plan at upper level, but for which it had only weak implementation powers. It was not enabled to spend money on capital works in the fringe unless it could show such works were for the benefit of the residents living within the boundaries of the Toronto political jurisdiction (the 240 square miles). At first the political jurisdiction contained thirteen local authorities. These were reduced to six in the 1966 reconstruction. The fringe contained thirteen and remained at that figure until 1971 when the north central fringe area was removed and became part of the regional municipality of York.

The Metro Planning Board after the 1966 reconstruction consisted of seven appointed members at large; six from Council; eleven from the fringe and subsidiary planning boards; and eleven from school boards.[13]

The planners prepared their first draft of the master plan in 1959. In its preamble it said: "The image of the Planning Area in 1980, presented in this plan, does not claim to be an exact prediction of what will be, nor is it intended to be a binding prescription of what shall be. It is an image of what is likely to be if the public and private individuals and organizations . . . pursue their interests in a rational way within the framework of existing institutions. It presents a working hypothesis of desirable future development which seems possible of achievement on the basis of presently known trends."[14] The plan was therefore no blueprint or straightjacket but tried to allow flexibility, within the limits of trends and realistic possibilities.

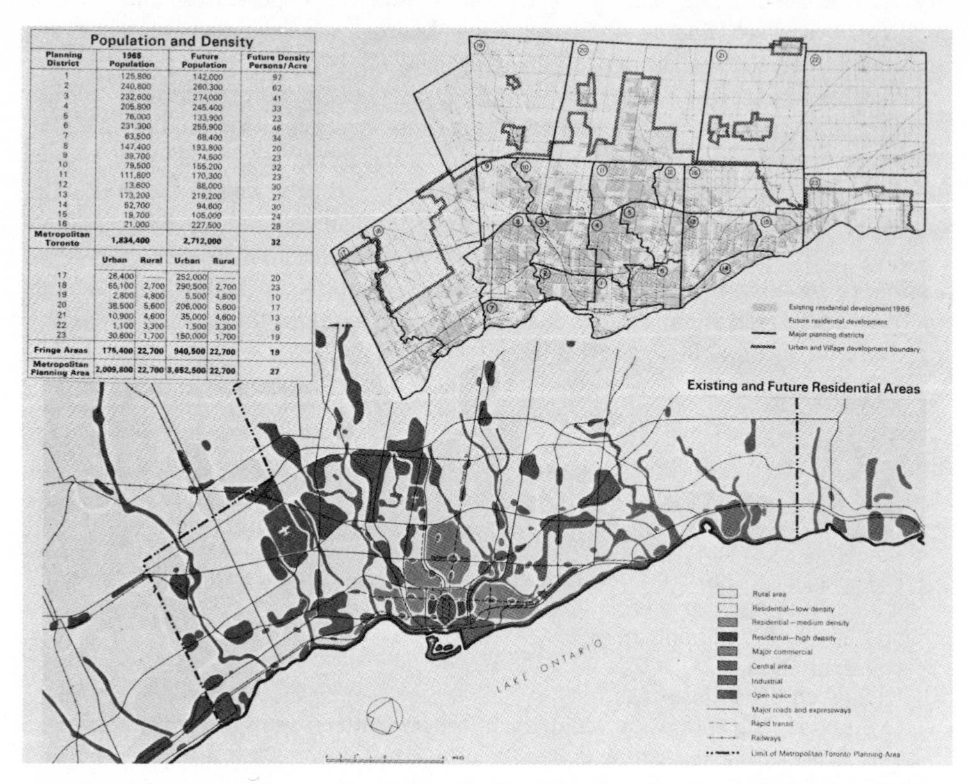

Population and Density

Planning District	1965 Population		Future Population		Future Density Persons/Acre
1	125,800		142,000		97
2	240,800		260,300		62
3	232,600		274,000		41
4	205,800		245,400		33
5	76,000		133,900		23
6	231,300		255,900		46
7	63,500		68,400		34
8	147,400		193,800		20
9	39,700		74,500		23
10	79,500		155,200		32
11	111,800		170,300		23
12	13,600		88,000		30
13	173,200		219,200		27
14	62,700		94,600		30
15	19,700		105,000		24
16	21,000		227,500		28
Metropolitan Toronto	**1,834,400**		**2,712,000**		**32**
	Urban	**Rural**	**Urban**	**Rural**	
17	26,400	——	252,000	——	20
18	65,100	2,700	290,500	2,700	23
19	2,800	4,800	5,500	4,800	10
20	38,500	5,600	206,000	5,600	17
21	10,900	4,600	35,000	4,600	13
22	1,100	3,300	1,500	3,300	6
23	30,600	1,700	150,000	1,700	19
Fringe Areas	**175,400**	**22,700**	**940,500**	**22,700**	**19**
Metropolitan Planning Area	**2,009,800**	**22,700**	**3,652,500**	**22,700**	**27**

FIG. 5 Development plan—general concept. By 1974, the planning jurisdiction of Metro Toronto over the fringe municipalities outside the political jurisdiction had been eliminated. *Toronto Metropolitan Planning Board*

A major planning technique was to designate urban and agricultural areas to stop sporadic development and ensure economy in public expenditures. Urban development has been reasonably well kept out of the area designated agricultural. The restriction of the area in which urban development may be permitted may have been a major cause of the rapid rise in land prices which took place in the second half of the 1960s. Certainly by 1970 the prices of land and buildings had become very high all across Toronto and some developers affirmed that it was no longer possible to develop land with single-family houses inside the political boundaries. Whatever price may have been paid for this policy it resulted in keeping the urban mass compact and assured full services to all new development. When eventual expansion into the nonurban area takes place at some future date it will benefit from a relatively uncluttered terrain capable of being coherently planned.

The planners' second major idea related to density. They observed that the curve of the area's population (residential) density fell very sharply at a distance of about four miles from the center. As the limit for piped services was to be ten miles from the center in the inland direction this implied that a considerable area had a low density of population—so low that services would be uneconomic and, in the case of public transportation, very difficult to provide at all. They hoped by planning along with the trends they would be able, by 1980, to raise the density at ten miles out from the center from a low of about one thousand persons per square mile (1951) to about eight thousand.

At the same time it would be necessary to discourage development in the north from pressing beyond the limit of the piped services ten miles. Opinion in the Toronto area was strongly in favor of allowing urban development of a major sort only on the basis of water and sewer services being available. Pressure could be taken off the north by planning for faster growth along the lake shore to east and west. The plan therefore hoped that the servicing of these areas would be much more economical than urbanizing beyond the ten-mile inland limit.

At the time of the making of the 1959 plan there was a good deal of undeveloped land well within the ten-mile limit (political jurisdiction line) to the north. This filled up rather more rapidly than was anticipated and by 1970 little was left. A cause of the unanticipated rate at which land had been consumed was the failure of development to take place at the increased rate hoped for in the east. Industry did not find the eastern area attractive and therefore residential development could not be permitted to the needed extent because of endangering the financial stability of the municipalities. Not until the proposal in the early seventies made to locate a second airport in Pickering did developmental interest in the eastern area become strong.

The western fringe, located near the international airport and adjacent to considerable concentrations of industry, had grown at a much faster rate and had been able to provide major services out of its own resources.

By 1968, it had become clear that the expectations of the plan in regard to the distribution of population were not being achieved in all respects. General densities had increased and the western fringe had worked out well, but the difficulty with the eastern fringe was serious, for here was good territory for urban development that could not grow in the political-administrative-work distribution conditions prevailing. Metro, unable to spend on capital works in the fringe for the fringe's own benefit, had not been able to give the needed assistance in providing piped services.

This experience made clear that to have a planning jurisdiction without the power to provide capital works (as was Metro's position on its fringe) is to be successful only when the trends make possible the achievement of the planning objectives. If the tendencies do not match the planning goals, success will be unlikely.

As with residential densities, the 1959 plan aimed at obtaining a more general job distribution across the whole Metro area. The municipalities, in their search for revenue, had already started this trend by a generous designation of land for industry in their plans. This dovetailed with the postwar desire of industry for larger sites than could be obtained in the already built-up area and for good access to expressways. The Metro planners systematized the industrial areas and aimed at very substantial increases in job opportunities outside the CBD. For example, the central urban area, which in 1956 had accounted for 84 per cent of the total employment, in 1980 would contain only 56 per cent. The suburban ring would increase from 11 per cent to 30 per cent of the total with about a fivefold absolute increase.

The distribution of jobs, particularly industrial jobs, was considered in conjunction with the distribution of residential population. The hope was that by distributing jobs fairly evenly in well-planned concentrations residents would have several choices of places to work within easy reach of home, and that commuting would be reduced. Not much is known for certain about this last expectation, but transportation surveys indicate that many workers live considerable distances from their places of work.

The planners also debated the location of white-collar work. This had traditionally been concentrated in the CBD, which has a regional, provincial and national role. They did not recommend specific major areas for commerce outside the CBD as new development; the reason given was that so to designate would force up land prices in those areas, which in turn would encourage commercial development to go elsewhere to cheaper land. The coming of major subcenters in Metro had to await the initiative of the boroughs in the late 1960s.

These matters have a vital reference to transportation. After all the research both plan and events ended up with a curious inequality between the factory worker and his counterpart in a downtown office. Because the CBD would accommodate about 200,000 workers and was regarded as likely to be stable (the center of Toronto is still a safe and attractive place for business) it was sensible to plan to focus rapid transit on it. Thus the WASP (White Anglo-Saxon Protestant) office workers living on the Yonge Street axis early were given an excellent rapid transit service; this in turn was followed by an east-west route also serving substantial white-collar populations.

The factory worker of miscellaneous ethnic backgrounds, however, was not so well served because industry was now dispersed and no public-service vehicles were allowed on the expressway system. Therefore the blue-collar worker was forced to a greater dependency on private cars than the white-collar worker. The dispersal of industry made its servicing by public transit much more difficult than the servicing of offices concentrated in downtown. If industry is to have access by public transit—there is good sense in planning this—then industry might be better organized in a few really large areas such as ten thousand acres, so that transit routes, especially rapid transit, could be run through them and beyond them connect well with residential areas. The sizes of the already planned industrial areas are difficult to categorize, but all are much smaller than ten thousand acres, some being even less than one thousand acres; they were located by the municipalities, not by Metro.

Transportation was the next most important aspect tackled by the Metro planners who were among the first to use simulation techniques systematically in conjunction with electronic data processing. The cost of this research beginning in the mid-1950s, has reached over two million dollars up to the present (Figs. 6a, 6b).[15]

Briefly, the technique of simulation, now familiar but then little known, was based on Newton's law concerning the attraction of masses (gravity models). Land uses in a city could be conceptualized as having mutual attraction. Thus the city could be divided into zones (Toronto's model used six hundred initially), generating and attracting traffic. As the zones would be connected by roads or other transportation links the traffic on any link could be simulated on the basis of whatever land uses, densities, routes and transportation modes might be assumed.[16] In the case of Toronto the model was fed the already planned arrangement of land uses and a tentative transportation plan that had to be produced before the transportation study could be completed. Various alternative plans for transportation with expressways and rapid transit were run. These ranged from extreme use of road to extreme use of transit, with four intermediate mixes. Certain major transportation links such as the Yonge subway (Fig. 7), the University subway, the lake shore expressway and the major east-west expressway to the

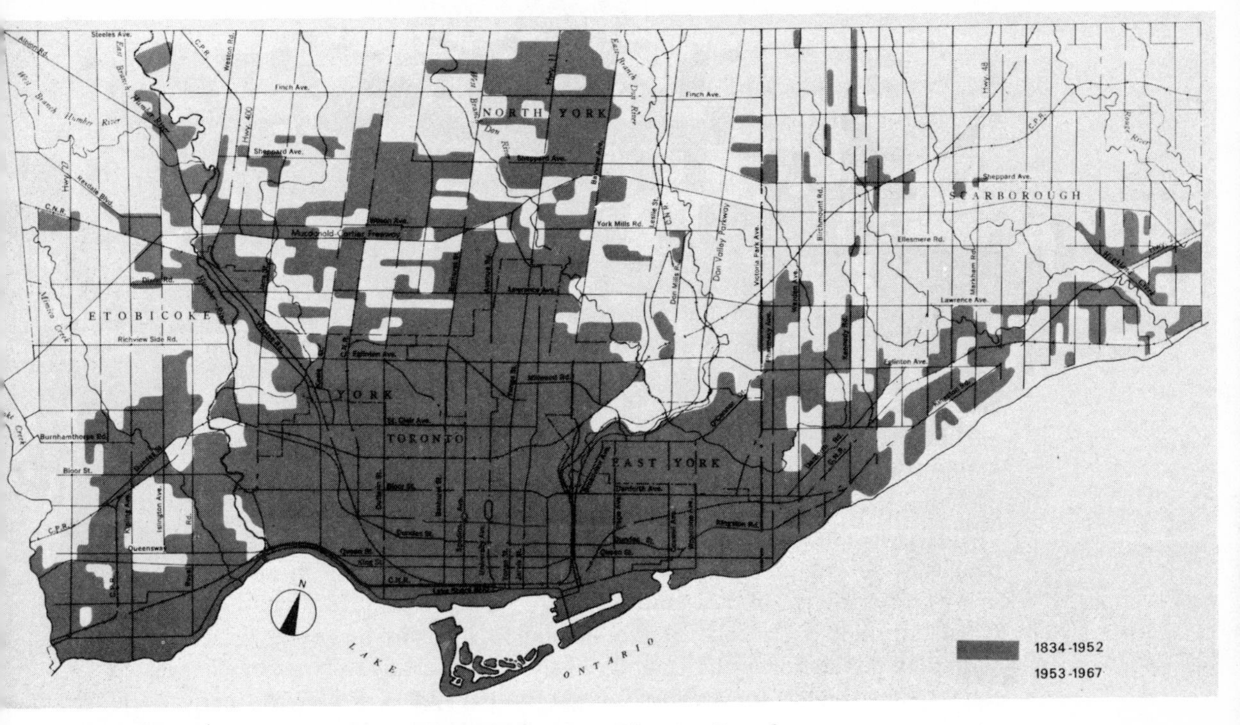

FIG. 6A Urban development. *Toronto Metropolitan Planning Board*

FIG. 6B Major transportation facilities. *Toronto Metropolitan Planning Board*

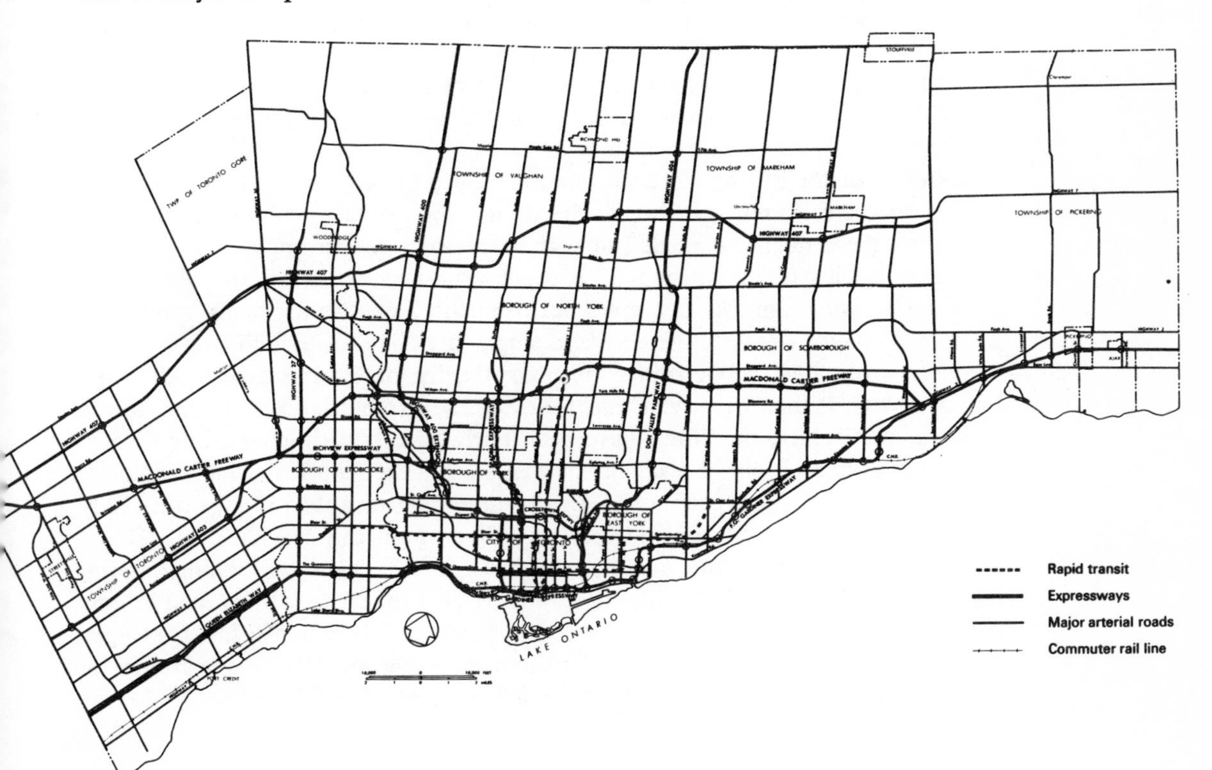

north (Highway 401) were either built or under construction by the time the study results were ready. The planners were not therefore able to start from scratch in either expressways or rapid transit. The plan eventually recommended expansion of both the expressway and the rapid transit systems.

This plan (175-mile expressway; 29-mile rapid transit) was based on a concept of balance. The notion was that any transportation system (including private and public modes) tends to come to a position of balance or equilibrium on the basis of travel desires, costs, habits, income levels, time-distance factors, etc. The Toronto model for the first time gave understanding of how the balancing process operates. It demonstrated that the position of the modal split oscillates according to the pressures on the various parts of the total system.[17] The model also showed that in the case of the Toronto public extreme types favoring heavily either private or public transportation have "only a modest effect on the operation of the system." Thus the modal split could not be shifted to any great extent by providing a very extensive public transit system.

This is a difficult idea for public and politicians to grasp. Why cannot more people be forced on to public transit simply by providing more public vehicles and public service routes and spending less on expressways? The planner's judgment, on the evidence of the simulation done in the early sixties, was that Toronto's population would not be likely to make any very great changes in its riding habits in the foreseeable future. By 1971, it was still too early to judge whether the provincial government's refusal to allow for the works on the partly built Spadina Expressway would constitute some evidence of major change of attitude.

There are several objections to attempting to force more riders on to public transit in Toronto: First, the road system is good and although congestion (technically defined) is present at certain localities it is not very serious and is accepted both by public and planners. The traffic of Toronto is not the traffic of New York, Los Angeles, London or Paris. People can use their cars comfortably; parking is neither very difficult nor expensive compared with many other cities. Banishing private cars from the CBD would be politically impossible; nor would high fees for parking be practical to implement.

A second factor is a public disinclination to use public transit. This is a multifaceted problem, familiar in many cities. In Toronto the inhibiting factors are many, but these might be singled out: the fare-zone system imposed a minimum fare of four trips for $1.00 or $.30 a trip by the end of the 1960s. The second zone started approximately five miles out from the center so for many commuters the minimum fare was effectively $.50 (a single fare zone was established in 1973); secondly, cross-town public routes are poor; thirdly, many trips take much longer by public transit than by private car; fourthly, the expressway system and arterial network, particularly the latter, have been fairly successful in channeling through traffic and keeping it out of residential areas, so that the motorcar while ubiquitous is not at the stage where people feel it to be more nuisance than it is worth; fifthly, the car gives choice and freedom which no public transit can provide.

By the end of 1969, the number of public transit riders was falling; during the first three weeks of 1970 the TTC lost over 1,300,000 subway and surface riders in comparison with the same period in 1969. In 1969, transit lost passengers in spite of 2.4 miles of increased service, but the early seventies saw a rise in the number of riders, approximately 492 million being carried in 1971.

FIG. 7 The present northern end of the north-south (Yonge Street) subway. Bus station and parking connected with the subway terminal are visible in the lower left quadrant. *Lockwood Survey Corporation Limited, Toronto*

The cost of a short run is excessive because of the fare-zone system; consequently many short-run riders are lost. As the system is supposed to be self-supporting the basic fare has constantly to be raised; in 1960, it was $.10 a single ticket against $.30 in 1970. The TTC has frequently had an operating deficit which the Metro Council has had to make good, which it has done on a year-to-year basis. In addition, Metro has taken over some construction costs for the subway rights of way. If it is desired to draw riders away from their cars and on to public transit it is necessary to subsidize the public system to keep down fares.

The general idea of the 1959 plan was to give an equal level of all kinds of transportation services to all areas and to arrange the phasing of capital works so that as the process went along, reasonable parity would be maintained.[18]

In the period 1965–70 feeling about cities underwent some change. A new emphasis appeared in concern for air pollution, quality of environment and public participation. Group protests caused some politicians in the Toronto area to express concern that the vociferous behavior of small groups was obstructing the achievement of action necessary or desirable for the benefit of the whole—referring to this as "mob rule." As the 1970s opened, it became clear that Toronto might have difficulty in carrying out some of its public works because of protests by ratepayers. This might very well mean the inability to hold to policies of fair shares to all sectors of the urban area and lead to an eventual imbalance in basic services. Already by 1969, the decision to continue the Yonge Subway, first from Eglinton (five miles north) to a point four miles out and later to Finch Avenue, a farther mile north, had been taken. This would mean a preferential emphasis once again to the old north-south axis. The very considerable claims of the northwest sector, which was a direction of traditionally strong growth, were not sufficient to bring along this part of the transportation system at an adequate speed, particularly as further construction in the Spadina Expressway was halted in 1971 and the rapid transit planned along its alignment works require some replanning, and the capacity of arterial roads would have to be much improved.

Although the transportation proposals appeared to give a good distribution of movement up to 1980, by 1969 it was clear that new studies would be required and the beginnings of a review was made. Generally speaking there are few cities of this size that have been as successful in dealing with their movement problems from the point of view of efficient structure for movement. The challenge of the 1970s is how to reconcile efficiency of movement with social aspirations including a mounting concern for the quality of the environment.

The provision of piped services was a very high priority for Metro at its inception; a major reason for setting up the Metro government was to help solve the services crisis. The Metro planners did not pay quite the attention to piped services they did to transportation but they made their contribution in this area and put forward specific plans in the 1959 document, which were successfully implemented.

The 1959 draft plan made proposals for housing, other land uses, schools, parks and open space, finance and administration. Because of the later housing crisis it is desirable to note that the proposed low-rental housing program calling for one thousand family units and five hundred units for elderly persons was not carried out. Belatedly (mid-sixties) Metro instituted a policy for apartments to meet the somewhat unusual conditions of Toronto. Apartments have appeared in all parts of the urban area in increasing numbers—even out on the growing edge. This had not been foreseen and control provisions were slow in appearing; by 1969, well over one third of all dwelling units were multiples.

The documentation of the 1959 plan was cumbersome, including survey material, explanations and discussions of issues, as well as proposals. In 1966, the Planning Board issued a new document with some modifications, but essentially both documents were different stages of the same plan. Toronto thus stayed with the planning intentions developed in the mid-1950s; in 1970, the Board and the planners felt that the plan was "still basically sound."

The 1966 document accepted some amendments in the first few years after its publication. The most notable of these was the proposal for the detailed planning of the waterfront along the fifty miles of Metro's lake shore.[19] This was one of the most extensive waterfront schemes to have been developed anywhere. Implementation was given to the Metropolitan Toronto and Region Conservation Authority, which already had responsibility for the inland valley systems. The annual planning budget for the lake edge was to be four million dollars.

Neither the 1959 nor the 1966 document became approved official plans! The ostensible reason was that the official procedures laid down by the planning act were considered unsuitable for plans at metropolitan level concerned with broad policies rather than detail. Among other difficulties was the unwillingness of the Metro Toronto Planning Board to act as surrogate planner for the fringe municipalities.

This is not to say the plan has suffered in effectiveness; it has been supported by the municipalities and the provincial government. It has also been given very solid support by the Ontario Municipal Board which is the authority through whose decisions much implementation has to be carried out. For the general planning of the urban area as a whole it has been useful, proving without a doubt the indispensability of an upper level over-all planning operation.

By the early 1970s, Metro planning had a number of emerging problems. Important among them were:

1. Housing costs were seriously out of line with incomes.
2. Planning jurisdiction over the fringe was not performing as required.
3. Little understanding had been achieved of how to deal with the growth dynamic generated by satisfying movement needs.
4. The physical efficiency-economic urgencies of the 1950s seemed about to be replaced by urgencies of a more human and social order. Public participation was becoming more important, raising problems of representation, bona fides of groups and individuals, etc.
5. Planning had given the appearance of having been captured by the dominant materialist ethos of Toronto; it was showing some lethargy in originating ideas and giving leadership in other values.
6. Some response to the need for planning the greater region was being made by the provincial government, but in this embryonic phase of genuine regional thinking Metro planning was finding itself largely excluded from participation. The provincial government or its agencies appeared likely to play an increasingly important role in the planning development of the greater region.

THE STRUGGLE FOR REGIONAL COHERENCE

Future Urban Shape

In the 1950s the planners applied theoretical concepts of pattern to the development of the urban area, concluding that it should grow as a linear development along the lake shore but with some fingers extending notably to the north. As growth did not appear in the lake-shore areas as anticipated (the east was particularly weak), and the growth rate of the northern finger was less than half that which was planned for up to 1965, developers bought up holdings in the agricultural area to the north, beyond the trunk mains, in the expectation that growth would have to go there.[20] This meant that in general the development industry disbelieved the plan in regard to the north, or at least thought its provisions would be changed and extensive urban development allowed. Some holdings thus assembled by 1970 were considerable—large enough for creating towns of thirty thousand inhabitants.

This situation suggested that the Metro plan was not entirely in accordance with the realities of the region. In the late sixties the position of the Metro Planning Board was that perforce they had to support their plan since to do otherwise might well cause a worsening of the whole situation. Both Board and planners therefore gave some impression of insensitivity to the real situation; in fact, the planners were fully aware of what had happened and by the end of the decade had the whole question under review.

The essential question that underlay the situation was that of whether or not to attempt to control the shape or pattern of the total urban mass. There might well be advantages in trying to do so: ensuring major "green fingers" within the urban development—there was still the possibility of providing two or three of these in 1970 since the land necessary was still unbuilt. Economies of services, particularly transportation, might be effected; corridor development of urban growth would help definition and differentiation of the urban mass; and phasing of growth in an orderly way in concentrated bursts would be encouraged.

Many cities have given thought to controlling the pattern of their growth. Some of those that have attempted a radial/finger form of growth, having attained a certain size, are Copenhagen, Hamburg and Sydney. In terms of trying to humanize the large urban mass there is much to be said for some kind of corridor development after the central mass has reached, say, two million.

The Toronto political and planning jurisdictions by the end of the sixties showed signs of producing satellite towns beyond the edge of the planning jurisdiction. One developer had assembled enough land to set up a sizable satellite in the 1970s, while another (Bramalea) had been developing reasonably well for a considerable time. The high cost of housing in Metro itself made such ventures by private enterprise possible since a market for cheaper housing existed even at the cost of long commuting distances. The alternative to thinking out and fixing the shape of urbanization was to allow the urban area to grow by steady edge accretion as it had always done—driving the open country ever farther away from more citizens and possibly involving some high costs in transportation facilities later.

Indication of new potentialities came from the Ontario government's institution of a rail commuter service along the lake shore, using the normal intercity tracks and financed by the province with subsidized fares. The service has been well patronized and by 1970 there was the possibility of some similar service to the north (experimental late 1972). Such a service suggests some kind of linear urban growth.

By 1970, all these matters pointed toward the conclusion that a great deal of thought was urgently necessary on the question of the shape, or pattern, of urban development throughout the greater Toronto region. By 1970, the Metro planning jurisdiction was no longer adequate for this purpose.

Tasks Beyond Metro's Capacity

As a greater region Metro's settlement areas stretch far beyond the boundaries of its 240 square miles *political jurisdiction*. Metro is powerless to assist the economic situation of any municipality outside this area; it cannot assist a small town in its hinterland to develop residentially as an overspill area as in Britain. Nor can it direct industry to such a town, thereby helping it to pay for its own expansion.

By the late 1960s the planning and providing of trunk services were showing signs of passing out of Metro's hands; the first indication of this appeared in 1965 when the Ontario Water Resources Commission (a provincial body) announced that it would put in mains from the lake to Brampton-Bramalea, fifteen miles inland to the northwest of Metro. The mains would pass through Mississauga, the western fringe of Metro under Metro's planning jurisdiction. A considerable portion of Mississauga, shown agricultural in the plan, would now be capable of being urbanized. This proposal was made largely without reference to Metro's planning.

In 1969, a similar situation arose to the north of Metro. A group of municipalities in difficulty with services requested the OWRC to examine the feasibility of providing a main sewer. The commission produced a plan at a then cost of sixty-two million dollars. While the plan showed only a slight increase in the area to be urbanized, the pipe, like those in Mississauga, would make urbanization possible for a large area designated agricultural in the Metro plan—a total in the north and east of 56,000 acres with a population of approximately one million.

The implication of both proposals by the OWRC would be the addition of another layer of fat all round Toronto. Theoretically, of course, it would be possible to refuse urbanization to areas through which the pipes passed but in the laissez-faire tradition of Toronto it was unrealistic to assume that the pressure for urbanizing such areas would be long resisted, especially in a society which has held urbanization under control by refusing it chiefly on the grounds of absence of services!

Another task seemingly beyond the ability of Metro was the ability to muster the political support of the fringe and of the provincial government necessary for the enlargement of its powers and jurisdictions to meet the next stage of urban growth.

The western fringe had virtually established its independence by 1970; the northern fringe had no great enthusiasm for joining Metro; and while the eastern fringe acknowledged its interest in job opportunities in Metro it also was ambiguous in its political wishes. Furthermore, Metro had not convinced the provincial government that the expansion of Metro's political and planning jurisdiction would be desirable. The task of winning friends to make a new Metro-based political creation required for the 1970s appeared likely to be beyond Metro's capacity by 1969. By 1972, it was clear that the provincial government would be responsible for upper level planning.

By the late sixties, a fourth task presenting great difficulty was appearing at the Metro level. This might be described as a growing demand for solutions to problems in the social-cultural sphere. Metro planning, while not by any means ignoring aesthetic matters, has stressed that the Metro plan was not "an exercise in civic design." This approach did not very well match the growing concern expressed by citizen action groups for visual and social effects (amenities).

This developing edge of public concern related in very clear terms to the friction between the public good as seen at the regional scale (expressways, subways, etc.) and the interests of local residents in preserving the quality of residential environments. The underlying conflict was, of course, that between centralized and localized decision making.

Politics Without Planning

By early 1969, the Ontario minister for Municipal Affairs, already embarked upon a policy of creating regional governments (several municipalities together), announced that he was going to eliminate Metro's fringe planning jurisdiction, drawing it back to coincide with the political jurisdiction (240 square miles).

Such action would cut Metro off from any say in the planning of the areas on its expanding edge unless some superplanning authority above Metro was created to look after the large scale planning matters of the greater region. That would require three tiers of planning jurisdiction. In short, the old problem re-emerged of how to reconcile the political boundaries and governmental and taxation structures with the hard reality that in economic and social terms the urban mass was a single functional entity.

The minister's notion in 1969 was that the western fringe should form a large area government. The eastern fringe would do the same and the north might also become a large governmental area. These proposals were curiously at variance with the policy being simultaneously followed by the provincial government in forming large governmental areas elsewhere.[21] The normal policy was to join rural and urban areas together into single jurisdictions.

That this was precisely what was *not* being proposed for Toronto aroused comment, especially as such a combination appeared very appropriate for the next stage of Metro. The reason seems to have been that this was thought politically undesirable by the provincial politicians. Metro was already large enough as a political entity and was seen as some threat to provincial government. At this time the minister did not appear to appreciate the planning significance of his proposals and he had no suggestions to offer as to how the physical growth of the area would be looked after under such an arrangement. There were protests from many directions, and as the year wore on, no definite decision emerged from the minister's office.

By early 1970, the Metro Toronto Planning Board had proposed a scheme for enlarging Metro's *political and planning jurisdictions.* It included taking in Pickering on the east and extending up to the watershed line, roughly seven miles beyond the limit of the then planning jurisdiction, on the north. The proposal discontinued the planning jurisdiction over the western fringe and indeed generally abandoned the idea of a planning fringe jurisdiction in favor of the two jurisdictions coinciding.

In very crude terms the question which now awaited answer was: Would there be found again a viable solution to the problems of how to plan for and administer the growth of the urban area as a whole? In 1953, affairs had reached a deadlock. Yet a very successful way was found. Could a second rabbit be produced out of the governmental hat?

The Toronto-centered Region Concept

A complication during the sixties was that agencies of the provincial government had been steadily moving into Metro to deal with various items in ad hoc ways. The lake-shore commuter rail service had been instituted without any over-all planning. Secondly, the proposals for trunk mains made by the OWRC were ad hoc solutions to so-called problems, offered without relevance to the planning of the region as a whole and without any regard to over-all priorities or budgetary considerations. Thirdly, the rapid rise in the cost of land and buildings coupled with a housing deficiency induced the provincial government to increase its activity in the field of public housing. This was done through one of its agencies—the Ontario Housing Corporation. By the end of the decade, this provincial agency was planning considerable housing areas (e.g., fifteen hundred acres in Scarborough). This activity proceeded largely without relationship to the municipal plans already in operation.

At the metropolitan and upward level the picture at the beginning of the present decade was an emerging free-for-all stimulated by agencies of the provincial government being forced to take on tasks which nobody else was able to do. It was urgently necessary that these operations should be co-ordinated with each other, co-ordinated with the planning of Metro, and that all should be co-ordinated in the planning of an area altogether larger than the jurisdictions then in operation.

Partly in response to this emerging situation, the provincial government had set up in 1962 a regional (fifty-mile radius based on Toronto) study of the area's transportation needs. The Metropolitan Toronto and Region Transportation Study (MTARTS) quickly came to realize that land uses were so intimately related to transportation that alternative patterns of urban development for the region should be prepared, which was done. Interested groups and individuals were invited to comment by the end of 1968; since then, as far as is known, little further work has been done on this project. Also during the 1960s the provincial government inaugurated studies leading to a regional plan with no public results. The fact that the control of municipal and metropolitan planning was in one provincial department, regional and economic planning (plus public housing) were in a second department, highway planning in a third, and conservation and resources planning in a fourth scarcely fostered efficiency in over-all planning by the province of Ontario for the Toronto region.

Both the MTARTS study and the regional planning efforts were important steps in the right direction. The setting up of a study jurisdiction over an area of this size (too small, however) was in itself a major achievement. The perception that some kind of regional planning was necessary was at a least realistic, if delayed, provincial response to the existing conditions. These efforts, however, by 1970 were feeble in light of the urgent need, which was for coherent structural planning statements about the future distribution of population and industry and connecting communications channels. In early 1970, the situation was fluid; there was *no* certainty that provincial government—the only agency which could effectively take any action—was going to give the necessary level of leadership and there hung over the area the very real possibility of another round of free-for-all. But this time it would be a free-for-all participated in both by provincial government departments and a medley of unrelated metropolitan style governments all acting independently and without effective co-ordination.[22]

In fact during the late sixties, the provincial government had been coming increasingly to realize the need for a regional plan for southern Ontario. In May 1970, the government produced a twenty-three-page conceptual statement for such a plan: *Design for Development: The Toronto-centred Region.* The area covered by the concept (which is not yet a plan) stretched approximately one hundred and twenty miles along the lake shore of Lake Ontario and one hundred miles inland covering eight thousand square miles (Fig. 8).

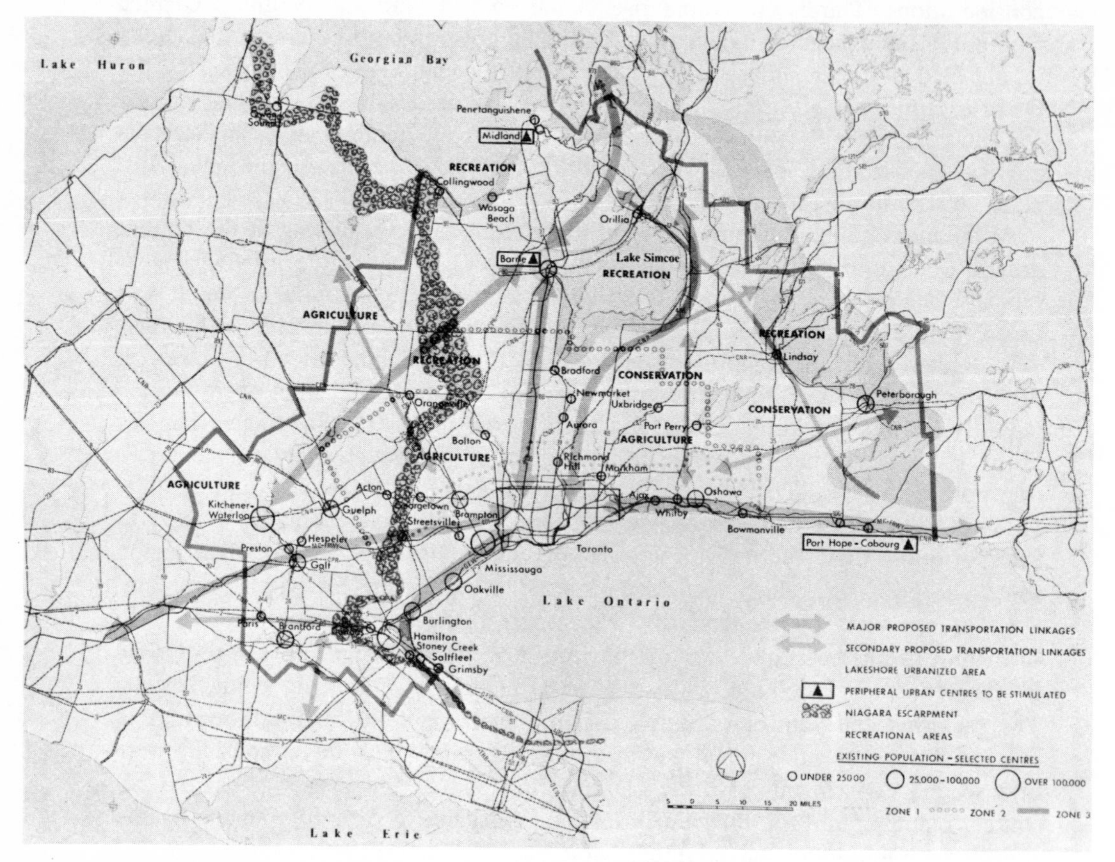

FIG. 8 Regional development concept, Toronto-centered Region. *Toronto Metropolitan Planning Board*

The concept indicated a settlement pattern of urban centers and linking corridors and divided the area into three zones:

Zone 1—Central lake shore based on Toronto.
Zone 2—The commutershed with limited growth permitted.
Zone 3—Hinterland in which growth points must become reasonably self-supporting.

The intentions of the concept are to slow the growth of the Metro Toronto area by diverting long-range urban development to the east of Metro and generally into Zone 3. The area will nevertheless be dominated by a strong urban corridor along the lake shore. The Metro Toronto planners consider the concept to be consistent with the intentions of the Metro Toronto plan, and estimate that Metro would be required to accommodate about three million population by the year 2000.

In 1972, the provincial government ministries were reorganized with benefit to the planning process. The old division between community planning and regional economic planning was eliminated by the creation of the Ministry of Treasury, Economics and Intergovernmental Affairs. This ministry has the responsibility of initiating and integrating general policies affecting all ministries of the government in such matters as planning, provincial-municipal relations, transportation, housing and environmental concerns.

Understanding the Urban Phenomena

Metro Toronto has made a contribution to our understanding of the middle-sized urban mass, particularly through its transportation studies. Because its planning has been systematized at two levels for the last decade and a half it has also generated considerable experiential knowledge of how such a mass can be guided during rapid growth. But it was clear that the knowledge gained was not sufficient for emerging needs, in two major respects. First, factual information at the crude data level was neither adequate in itself nor adequately processed. Not enough was known about many things, from the impacts of expressways to the attitudes and values of population groups, not to mention such basic items as the linkages between businesses and up-to-date transportation information.

Items under the second count were a much more serious deficiency. This was an understanding about how the physical city is structured and functions in relation to its cultural patterns of beliefs and behavior. The gaps in this area of knowledge were practically demonstrated by the new concern about expressway construction which had emerged in many cities of the United States during the 1960s and which had appeared in Toronto by 1969.

The values visible in this concern were: regard for the local social reactions to new expressways; concern for the dollar costs of expressways; anxiety about noise and pollution; fear that providing good access merely produces more travel and generates more congestion. Attempts were made in Toronto to apply pressure to stop work on a specific expressway already commenced and *then to halt all further expressway construction.*

These expressions of concern would scarcely be denied by anyone and the desirability of encouraging the values they represented was obvious. The problem, however, was not to be solved by being in favor of expressways because they favored economic growth or against them because they caused disruption of residential areas. The true discussion was at a much deeper value level. It had to do with such questions as: How much would Torontonians and the rest of the Ontario public be prepared to pay in taxes (building more subways, subsidizing public transit, increasing parking fees, etc.) in order to avoid the perceived disadvantages of having a completed expressway system?

At an even deeper level the question was more speculative but more horrifying in terms of the beliefs of Toronto. If expressways were not to be clogged by the traffic they attracted, very stringent control of building density and population density would have to be enforced. Expressways in the Toronto scheme of values enhance the price of land near them. This would have to be prevented, thereby thwarting what seems to Toronto to be a natural arrangement of the universe ("the unearned increment"). Or access to the expressway would have to be restricted. Expressway problems, given our present technology, may only be solvable in terms of very strict planning of land values. Such a situation would be totally unacceptable to the present sociocultural condition of Toronto.

By 1970, Toronto stood in the position where it would have to face moving toward coherence in regard to several incompatibilities of this kind. The application of technology exacts a price in terms of attitudes and behavior patterns; precisely what these prices are and would be under hypothecated conditions is the business of modern planning to discover. Toronto by 1970 lacked knowledge in this field, as indeed did most cities, but it stood in a not unfavorable position.

Values Emerging

The year 1969 felt like the end of an epoch. Was the provincial government about to take responsibility for producing and even implementing an over-all plan for the Toronto region? This would be an about face from 1953 when the province simply gave the area an enactment through which it could proceed to solve its *own* problems. During the fifteen years since Metro's establishment provincial government had become more involved with public issues and had shown itself less passive; public opinion had come to look for more active leadership from the province in many fields.

A second value shift was manifested in public protests against planning proposals or provisions, part of the general tendency toward an increase in direct action by interested groups. It was an eruption of direct democracy, reflecting some disenchantment with the normal workings of municipal government. To some this change appeared a revival of interest in local affairs after a long apathy and therefore was welcomed; to others it appeared as an irresponsible desire by small groups for getting their own way or a cynical use of the frustrations and confusions of the time by those who could make something out of it. By the early 1970s it was too soon to see clearly what this new participation emphasis would mean for the future planning of Toronto.

The value of public participation (democracy) should be held in high esteem; as a value, however, it has to be related to another value called the over-all public good. This is much of what planning is about—the weighing of the public good in relation to the good of some group or individual.[23] By the end of the decade there was some indication that in Toronto the values were changing in the direction of exalting the smaller group or individual good with some loss of vision for the larger public good.

A third change in values had occurred in relation to housing accommodation. By the end of the decade it was possible to envision apartments reaching 50 per cent of all units. Large numbers of the population, whether they liked it or not, were now not home owners, but tenants, the majority, apartment dwellers.

This was in part a reflection of the rising percentage of non-Anglo-Saxons in the population. In 1951, the percentage had been approximately 27 per cent. By 1961, it was approximately 39 per cent. White-Anglo-Saxon-Protestant Toronto was now considerably modified by increasing contact with other cultures. By 1970, it was multicultural with many ethnic groups (generally recent immigrants) living side by side, although it would be debatable whether Toronto could be called cosmopolitan. Certain it was that the old WASP culture was being rapidly changed and that this process would continue.

In planning, there was some change in values in that the emphasis of the 1950s on physical services was everywhere showing itself insufficient as the chief preoccupation. Municipalities were finding that social problems—welfare, education, young people's affairs—were taking more of their time and resources.

Planning boards were beginning to add social planners to their staffs by the end of the decade as one response to this change in values. Planning slowly commenced to respond to the increasing interest in the human aspects of planning proposals. Certain it was that by 1970 the planning authorities, including Metro, were anticipating a much stronger emphasis on social matters than there had been a decade before (Figs. 9a, 9b).

The end of the sixties also saw some indications of a rising interest in the aesthetic and "high cultural" aspects of the city. This was manifest in the new plan for the waterfront (long since largely lost to railways, harbors and expressways along the central portion), a general concern for the quality of appearance of the central business district, civic design, and the development of an entertainment nucleus with a major theatre and a center for the arts.

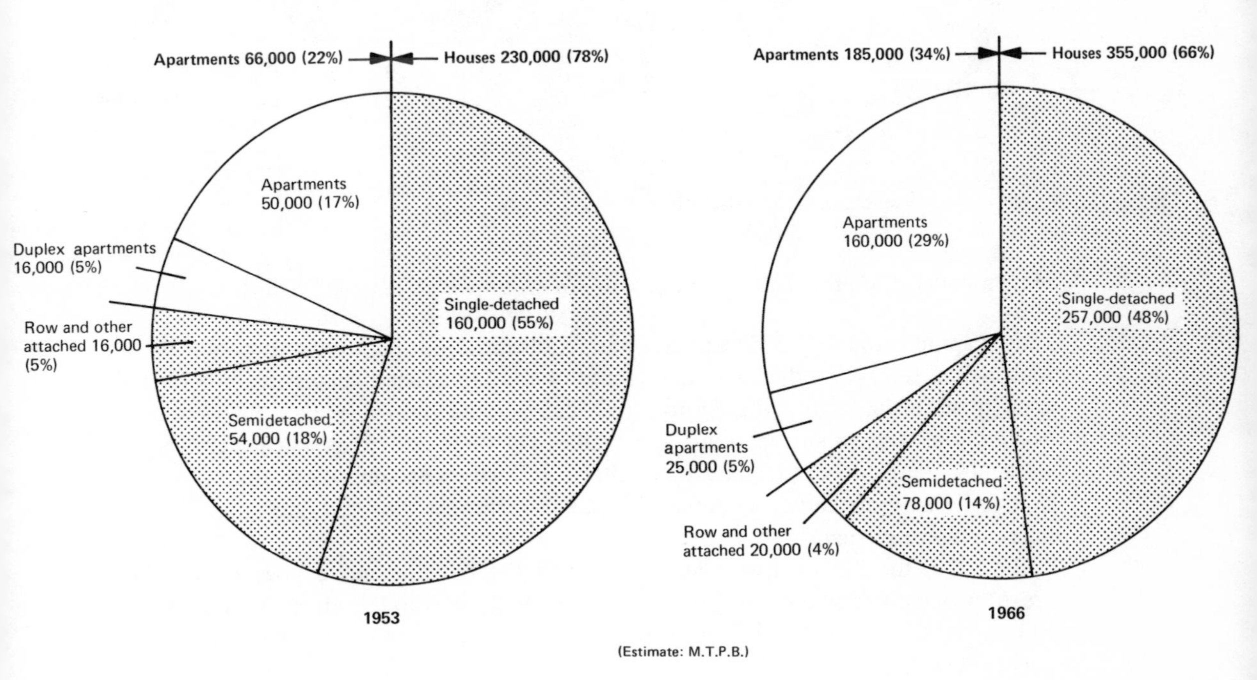

FIG. 9A Dwelling units by type, 1953 and 1966, Metropolitan Toronto. *Toronto Metropolitan Planning Board*

A NEW THRESHOLD

With the creation of the municipality of Metropolitan Toronto the political, financial and services crises of the late forties and early fifties were brought to an end. Means had to be found for providing the money to pay for services rapidly and for getting them on to or under the ground as fast as possible. Metro proved to be a suitable political instrument for this purpose.

Further, the experience of working the Metro system taught politicians, public and professionals concerned with urban growth a great deal in the first fifteen years. Much had been learned about financing, planning and carrying out large-

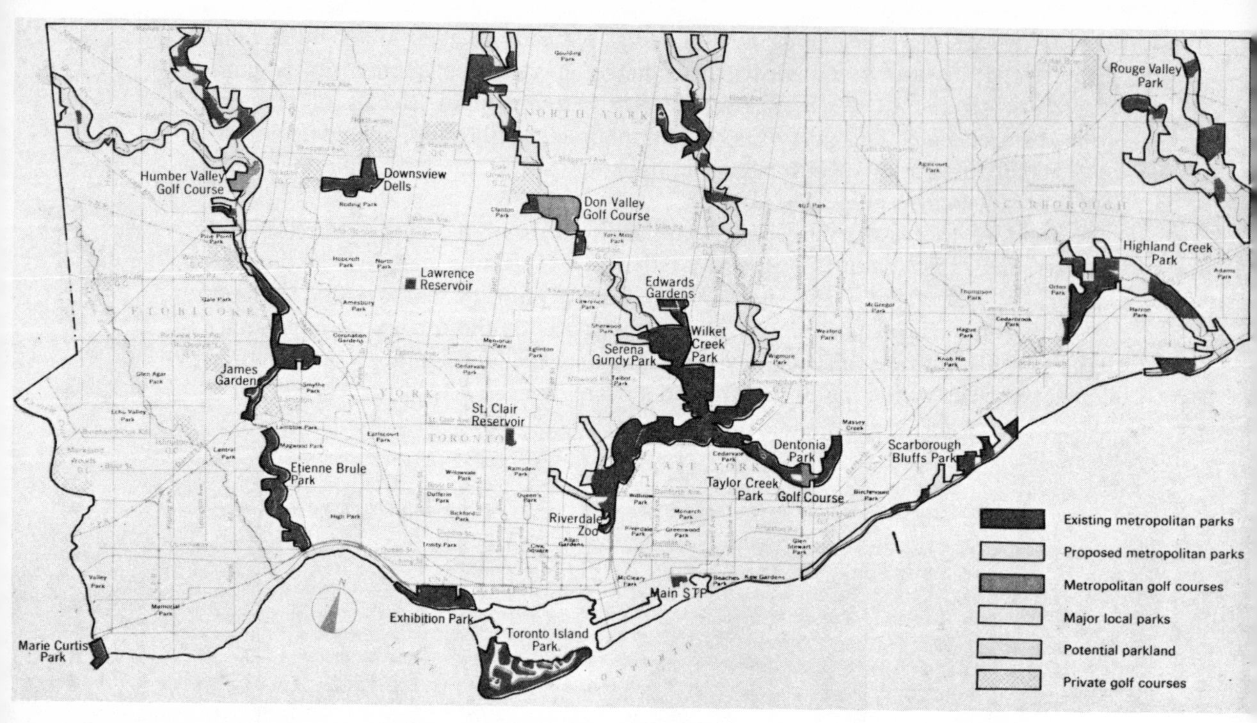

FIG. 9B Parks in Metropolitan Toronto. *Toronto Metropolitan Planning Board*

scale capital works. Piped services and transportation had been brought to a reasonable level of efficiency and there were established plans to guide the growth of the area into the future. It became clear by 1970 that the accepted assumptions and preoccupations—particularly with regard to physical services—were not going to be adequate indefinitely. It further became clear that whether or not Metro was satisfied, the provincial government was not and was set on making major changes.

By 1970, the Metro area had reaped well the benefits made possible by the creation of an upper level of government in 1953. It stood firm on its successes. But a new and more formidable collection of difficulties was now gathering in a darkening cloud:

1. The social problems connected with the excessively high cost of housing would cause increasing political difficulties.
2. Group opposition by the public was already considered a cause of falling off of investment in residential development in parts of the area. How could the housing difficulty be ameliorated if there was less investment? Apart from replacements, shelter for approximately sixty thousand new population per annum had to be found.
3. The future pattern of urban development was undecided especially in the northern fringe, despite anything the Toronto-centered Region statement might indicate. Would future shape be determined by succumbing to developmental pressure or could provincial government planning be strong enough to make significant contributions?
4. Very little had emerged by way of understanding certain significant relationships, such as the connection between expressways and the free market in land.

5. The planning jurisdiction over the fringe and consequently the distribution of population had not worked out as expected, and by 1971 the north fringe had been excised. A new technique would have to be found to ensure that as the urban mass expanded it could do so into areas adequately planned to accept the new growth. By the end of 1972 the provincial government had produced no firm proposals for co-ordinating the planning of the area governments.
6. The jurisdictions and the financial capacity of Metro showed clear signs of being unable to cope with some of the coming problems. The gaps were already being filled by unco-ordinated action by various agencies of the provincial government. If these agencies were to continue to do these jobs legally based co-ordination of action within the framework of some over-all plan would be imperative.
7. A new political solution to the emerging problems was due. If the provincial government should decide to withdraw Metro's planning jurisdiction back completely to its political boundaries and surround it with a cluster of new metropolitan areas the province itself would have to become the responsible planning authority for the co-ordination of the planning of this cluster of metros in accordance with an over-all regional plan.

In 1970, Metro Toronto was seen as standing on a new threshold, either about to be given new enabling powers to deal with the emerging situation, with the expectation that it would deal with it as well as it did with the old, or it might be seen as at the beginning of its degradation to the status of a superborough, about to be shorn of its ability to think and plan for the greater urban area Toronto must inevitably become.

By late 1972, it had become clear that the provincial Cabinet was going to act as the upper level planning authority determining the greater regional physical pattern and co-ordinating the activities of its own ministries and of municipalities to implement its intentions. At this stage it appeared that the method of achieving intergovernmental collaboration was to be by moral suasion. Hopefully the cabinet would be able to exact conformity to the provisions of the Toronto-centered Region statement not so much by reference to a legally approved plan rooted in the provisions of an enabling act as by willing agreement. The whole history of planning at municipal level has been that such hopes are inevitably frustrated; this reality, however, is not stopping governments all over the world proceeding along this path in their attempts to deal with greater metropolitan regions.

Metropolitan Toronto is now within sight of being responsible only for its own *political jurisdiction* (240 square miles). It is already subject to the specific plans of the upper level planning of the provincial government; a strongly hierarchical system of planning jurisdictions now has replaced the original partnership between the municipalities and Metro.

By 1972, Metropolitan Toronto was again revising its plan in light of its new role as middle member in this new hierarchy since new provincial policies were beginning to call for changes in the framework within which municipal planning operates and causing changes in intergovernmental relationships. In the new draft, however, the Metro planners felt the need to point out that the new policies "have once more omitted a clear definition of the specific planning functions for which each level of government is to be directly responsible." This weakness is serious; when provincial government reconstructions are complete it seems probable that the whole greater region will be covered by four subregional jurisdictions with Metropolitan Toronto at the center and still the dominant element because of the relative weakness of the adjacent subregions. In many ways the picture is reminiscent of the situation twenty years ago at municipal level, when the problem was how to achieve an upper level of metropolitan government.

The planning experience of the Toronto area during the last sixty years shows a sequence of events typical of many metropolitan areas in the world: A city perceives that it is more than an aggregation of its parts, therefore an over-all plan is needed (1909); planning legislation is required to achieve specific parts of the plan (1912, 1917, 1918); the city's physical expansion spills over into adjacent municipalities and a plan covering a group of municipalities is drawn up (1943); new legislation of a more detailed kind is necessary (1946); voluntary attempts to do metropolitan planning by agreement fail and special metropolitan-type legislation is placed in force with specific planning powers (1953); the metropolitan population spreads into the greater region beyond the effective range of metropolitan government and greater regional planning is required (1970); there is search for ways to achieve intergovernmental relationships adequate for the new tasks imposed by the identification of the greater region's present and emerging needs today.

Because of their indeterminate status, it has not been possible to mention certain important contemporary matters. In response to changing attitudes about movement in Metro in the early 1970s, the Transportation Plan Review was established, and is still reporting. The lengthy debates about a second major airport to be located to the east of Metro are still continuing. In the jurisdiction of the city of Toronto, prolonged discussion about the details of redevelopment of released railway land continues to attempt to bring Metro Center to birth—a very large development proposal between the CBD and the lake. The Ontario Municipal Board at present is holding hearings on the city's proposed bylaw to restrict building height in the downtown area to 45 feet (with exceptions permitted). In 1975, the Metropolitan Toronto Planning Board will be extinguished and the planning staff will become a department of Metro Government.[24]

NOTES

[1] F. Smallwood, *Metro Toronto: A Decade Later* (Toronto: Bureau of Municipal Research, 1963). Abridged and updated under the same title in *Taming Megalopolis,* ed., H. W. Eldredge, Anchor Books (2 vols., New York: Doubleday, 1967), p. 669. A quotation from Smallwood significant for our purpose might be:

> Ten years cumulative experience indicates that the Metropolitan Council has been consistently aggressive in tackling the so-called "hard core" problems where results are concrete and obvious, and considerably less assertive in meeting some of the "softer," more socially oriented issue areas where results are usually less tangible and even more controversial. An analysis of some of the particular fields where Metro's record of response has not been particularly aggressive indicates the true nature of this dichotomy. P. 668.

What Smallwood identified here is not merely a characteristic of Metro government, but is a cultural characteristic of Toronto.

[2] Ibid., p. 691.

[3] Emphasis was on Crown, aristocracy, Church and the armed services. He was to create in British North America a bulwark against "democratic" ideas prevalent in the thirteen original states of the United States.

[4] J. E. Middleton, *The Municipality of Toronto: A History*. (Toronto: Dominion, 1923). He gives a good sense of the culture of Toronto, bringing out well its British tradition blended with American business aggressiveness.

[5] E. Arthur, *Toronto No Mean City* (Toronto: University of Toronto Press, 1964). Contains many drawings and photographs of nineteenth-century Toronto.

[6] Metropolitan Toronto Planning Board, *The Official Plan of the Metropolitan Toronto Planning Area* (Toronto: 1959). Reiterated in: *Metropolitan Plan* (Toronto: 1966), Supplement, p. 5.

[7] A. F. W. Plumptre, "Report on the Government of the Metropolitan Toronto Area" (unpublished report to the provincial government of Ontario, Toronto, 1935).

[8] Smallwood pointed out the effects of population inequalities, financial inequalities, etc. on the Metro operation; these difficulties were more severe ten years after Metro's establishment than they had been in 1953.

[9] When looking at such figures it is necessary to remember that Toronto has a long history of high land and housing costs and has always had a housing problem.

[10] Implementation by bylaw was used in the expectation of giving certitude to the property owner and in order to avoid putting too much power in the hands of officials. Both the concept and the techniques of applying it have been prolific of confusion.

[11] For statistics of the Metro area see: Metropolitan Toronto Planning Board, *Metropolitan Toronto Key Facts* (Toronto: 1968).

[12] Somewhat belatedly the Ontario government, Metro, the city and the Harbor commissioners did come together to do a "conceptual" plan. At the time of writing this had not been made public and it was not known how much genuine collaboration had taken place.

[13] In 1963 H. C. Goldenberg headed a royal commission to report on "the structure and organization" of Metro. *Report of the Royal Commission on Metropolitan Toronto,* report to the Lieutenant Governor, Province of Ontario (Toronto: 1965).

[14] *Metro Official Plan 1959,* p. 1.

[15] See: Metropolitan Toronto Planning Board, *The Metropolitan Toronto Transportation Plan* (Toronto: 1964).

[16] For general discussion of the transportation planning and model techniques see: A. J. Dakin, "Metropolitan Toronto Planning," *Town Planning Review,* 40.1 (April 1969), p. 3.

[17] Modal split means the division between the various methods of transportation. For example, in the model research in Metro the modal split for the area as a whole for all trips was 61.5 per cent by car and 38.5 per cent by public transit (peak, 7–9 A.M., 1964). For the CBD in 1968 the figure for transit for the same peak was 67 per cent.

[18] As goals the transportation plan included: minimize total travel time; maximize average travel speed; minimize points of congestion; equalize accessibility and maximize accessibility to the central area; maximize use of public transportation especially rapid transit; maximize use of expressways. P. 30.

[19] Metropolitan Toronto Planning Board, *The Waterfront Plan* (Toronto: 1967).

[20] Over the period 1958–65 fringe growth was:

	Annual Increase	*Planned Annual Increase*	*Total Population 1965*	*Complete Developed Capacity*
West fringe	3,757	9,086	91,500	542,000
North fringe	2,129	4,441	67,200	246,500
East fringe	887	2,714	31,700	151,500

[21] For example, farther along the lake shore immediately east and west of Toronto.

[22] The danger did not go unnoticed. The Metro Planning Board was particularly sensitive to the relationship between the political jurisdictions and the problems of planning.

[23] One is aware of the refinements of argument which surround the phrase "the public good." When all the academic smoke has blown away there remains, in urban planning terms, the very real fact that there is often conflict between a local group and what the larger population may need. Frequently, these conflicts are within the total behavior patterns of the single individual—he wants quiet for his home but expressways to commute on.

[24] For bibliography on Metro, see: A. J. Dakin and P. M. Manson-Smith, *Toronto Urban Planning: A Selected Bibliography 1788–1970* (Monticello, Ill.: Council of Planning Librarians, 1974). For evaluation of Toronto plans 1793, 1915 (Transit), 1943, 1959–66 see: A. J. Dakin, "The Evaluation of Plans: A Study of Planning in Toronto," *Town Planning Review,* 44 (January 1973), pp. 3–30.

CHAPTER 7

Caracas: Focus of the New Venezuela

Francis Violich*

* Francis Violich has had many years of professional work and research in urban Latin America. In 1941–42 he spent a year studying the development problems of cities in most of the countries in Central and South America producing a pioneer work: *Cities of Latin America,* Reinhold, New York, 1944. Continuing to specialize in Latin American urban planning, he has been a professor of city planning and of landscape architecture at the University of California since 1951.

In recent years, Professor Violich has served in an educational capacity at universities and institutes in Venezuela, Colombia, Chile, and other Latin American countries and as a consultant in such cities as Caracas, Bogotá, Santiago, San Salvador and Saõ Paulo. He has worked with various international agencies concerned with Latin American urban development problems and, as an adviser at various times in the 1950s and 1960s, has been particularly involved in following the sudden and remarkable growth of Caracas, both with the national and municipal levels of government. Recently, in June 1969, he served as adviser to the Municipal Urban Planning Office (OMPU) of Caracas.

In preparing this chapter, Professor Violich drew on research carried out under the sponsorship of the Institute for Governmental Studies and the Center for Latin American Studies, both at the University of California, Berkeley. He wishes to acknowledge the valuable assistance in the form of critical review from colleagues experienced in urban planning in Caracas: Victor Fossi, Alberto Morales Tucker, Charles Boyce and David Fairchild, and is particularly grateful to Tomás Sanabria, architect, for the selection of illustrations.

URBAN PRIMACY AND CAPITAL CITIES IN LATIN AMERICA

Urban and Cultural Heritage: Spain and Portugal

The capital cities of Latin America form an integral part of the network of metropolitan areas that has grown directly out of the system of urban settlements established at the time of colonization by the Spanish and Portuguese during the sixteenth and seventeenth centuries. Virtually all of the leading colonial cities of each country became capitals. Furthermore, most of these today have evolved to become the principal metropolitan agglomerations of Latin America's total urbanization system. The first hundred years of urban growth were characterized by a quality of dynamic human activity, matched only by the urbanization that began slowly in the late nineteenth century and gained great momentum in the mid-twentieth century. Today, urban Latin America is undergoing the greatest change and expansion in its history and the capital cities are playing a key role in this process. Caracas, the capital of Venezuela, provides a particularly significant example, foreshadowing the "new urban era" in Latin America.[1]

Review of the regional location of the major cities of Latin America documents the colonial birth of today's metropolitan capitals. With the exception of Bogotá, La Paz, Asuncion and Mexico City, these are situated on or near the coast with an orientation to colonial overseas transport. This peripheral pattern of urbanization became difficult to break, as the single, strong regional focal points such as Buenos Aires, Lima and Caracas became attractive to hinterland populations by reason of cultural and political advantages and economic promise. Travel routes from the interior usually focused on the capital city and rarely connected inland cities with each other. Today's mobility of population has compulsively encouraged the further growth of already primate centers which are usually —though not always—the capitals and, year by year, these become more swollen with families from rural regions. In seeking the supposed advantage and stability of the capital, these people find themselves in a marginal situation, yet surrounded by the socially constructive stimulus of competition for betterment.

On the one hand, this concentration of population in single primate capitals of metropolitan scale is beneficial to over-all social and economic development since they concentrate at one point a great diversity of skills and resources. On the other hand, the relentless magnetism of these growing metropolitan capitals is an impediment to the establishment of new cities and new regional economies in those extensive inland areas of Latin America where regional economic development is greatly needed.[2]

These metropolitan capitals in Latin America have certain common characteristics: (a) the pattern of urbanization is continuous and relatively uninterrupted, extending into several municipalities, the central one of which may be the actual capital city; (b) the spatial distribution of social and economic activities forms a structured urban functional system that transcends jurisdictional boundaries in terms of the daily life patterns of the residents; (c) the capital area consists of a single center and a metropolitan-wide complex of services upon which the urbanized area as a whole depends; (d) it serves as a major focal point for the social and economic life of a surrounding microregion and, in most cases, of national social, economic and political life.

It is estimated that fourteen of the twenty-one Latin American capitals held in 1970 about 40,103,000 people or 14.9 per cent of the total Latin American population.[3] In addition there are eighteen more metropolitan areas which are not capitals and these hold about 23,708,000 people or 8.6 per cent. Thus, a total of 63,311,000 or roughly 23.5 per cent of the 274,000,000 people in Latin America live in metropolitan areas. Projections for the metropolitan capitals alone show that by 1990 they will hold 18.2 per cent of all Latin Americans. Thus, the present and future positions of the capital cities is a dominant one.

The dominance of the capital as a strong urban center is a cultural phenomenon that should be understood in historical and cultural terms. The early settlers from Spain emerged from an urban-oriented heritage caused by the harsh Iberian land that encouraged community-focused life in compact towns. These were most frequently the central city of small city-states. Furthermore, the unfriendly and unknown interior of the new continent and the need for water transportation between the new cities and the motherland prompted a coastal concentration for the system of urban settlements.

The Spaniards' preference for urban living also grew out of five centuries of indoctrination in city living by the Romans, who had played the same role in urbanizing the Iberian peninsula that Spain was to play in urbanizing much of the New World. In a subsequent period of urban development in Spain, this preference was contributed to by seven centuries of Moslem domination with an even greater emphasis on compact, enclosed city patterns. Even though Moslem culture—quite unlike the Roman—required virtually no public policy making and minimum administration in laying out and extending urban areas, Roman municipal institutions continued to prevail.

As a result of these fourteen centuries of urban experience the Christians of northern Spain had a direct influence on urban Latin America. Centuries of warfare with the Moslem invaders from the south had made them rugged and, in order to reconquer the entire peninsula, they were forced to turn their cities into functually effective citadels. Thus, the Spaniards—much more than the Portuguese—had developed a special capacity for building and managing cities as relatively autonomous and centralized city-states during the early Middle Ages. The need for unity among these states during the final century of Moslem domination—the fifteenth—and the century leading to the discovery of America, as well, led to highly developed skills in urbanizing and administering on a centralized, regional scale encompassing most of the Iberian peninsula.

A cultural tradition of centralization of population in strong, single urban focal points housing the social, economic and political leadership of each colony was transferred to the New World and later to the capitals of each of the new republics. As a final result of the unification that had been under way for centuries, Madrid itself had become the centralized, administrative capital of the Spanish empire in the seventeenth century. After independence this power was distributed among the various regional centers such as Lima, Bogotá and Mexico City. Decision making was clearly and firmly centralized within each capital with respect to development of the new republics. In this way, from the start, free initiative by cities of lesser status was discouraged in favor of assuring national political unification, an attitude that prevails even today in varying degrees.

The sixteenth-century planning of the thousands of Latin American towns and cities reflects a single grid model focused on a civil-religious center. It has been assumed that this was the result of direct centralized planning by Madrid, using the ideas of the Roman architect Vitruvius, whose writings were brought to light during the Renaissance. However, while the towns are virtually identical in many respects, Jorge Hardoy has pointed out after recent historical investigations that common sense, commonly known surveying techniques and accumulated experience handed down from one case to another tended to produce a standard type of town plan. He asserts, probably correctly, that there was little direct co-ordination between the various officials who laid out the towns and Madrid. As virtually all of the Latin American capitals and many of the lesser cities were laid out during the first fifty or sixty years after discovery, it would appear that the regulations contained in the Laws of the Indies are simply a compilation of accumulated standards and procedures.

The Portuguese were far less systematic and no consistent body of urban planning rules was developed. Brazilian cities have grown in an unstructured and, at times, organic fashion (except for several notable examples of the nineteenth and twentieth centuries, including Belo Horizonte and Brasilia), while the policies of building placement and regulations in Spanish America from California through Mexico and to the tip of Chile at Tierra del Fuego are highly consistent. Even today Brazil has no standard city planning law, although some kind of urban planning code is to be found at the national level in most of the countries that developed under Spanish rule. This consistency, in urban form and visual image among thousands of towns and cities from very small to very large distributed over two continents, has been a significant instrument in maintaining cultural unity from one Spanish-speaking country to another and a vehicle for contemporary cultural and professional communication that is not shared with Brazil.

After independence, a static legal and administrative tradition has proven to be an impediment to the kind of institutional evolution and experiment needed to adjust urban patterns of a past era to the vastly different technological and social requirements of today. The great wave of growth came to the Latin American capitals during the latter part of the nineteenth century when migration from Europe and industrialization of economies began in certain countries. Frequently in obvious imitation of European models of the period, ministries of Public Works were established, primarily concerned with development and embellishment of capital cities. This practice, which has a tendency to continue even today, contributed to attracting population to the capitals, furthering the cycle of primacy and laying the groundwork for today's metropolitan capitals in the larger countries.

Tremendous investments of public funds were made in these political centers which contrasted sharply with the neglect of smaller urban areas, especially in the hinterland. National governments did not concern themselves with the national scale of urbanization and the building of a national system of cities, such as the Spaniards had done on a continental scale. They tended rather to operate as local agents for creating an image of the nation as a whole within a monumental capital city. This practice has produced public works of European scale and monumentality. These are combined in Mexico City with indigenous elements, and in Rio de Janeiro with unique landscape character and, thus, each exemplify the basic image of the Latin American capital held by the foreign visitor in spite of an occasional overlay of contemporary architectural styles.

Demographic Growth and Urbanization Patterns

The over-all urbanization system has not changed essentially since colonial times. What has changed dramatically during the twentieth century—particularly in the case of the capitals—is the scale of individual cities, the over-all speed of urban growth and the basic urban structure. Within these, living habits have been transformed.

It is characteristic of most of the capitals that they contain extremely high percentages of the total population—a pattern more consistently predominant in Latin America than in other regions of the world. It is typical for the capital to be by far the leading city in size, while the second largest city is often as little as 10 to 15 per cent of the size of the primate capital. Buenos Aires, capital of Argentina, held for example, some 9,000,000 people in its metropolitan area in 1970. This represents about 38 per cent of the population of the country as a whole. Meanwhile, the next largest cities, Córdoba and Rosario, with 814,000 and 806,000 respectively, are less than 10 per cent of the size of the capital. Smaller cities in the next category, such as Tucumán or Santa Fe, are only half the size of Córdoba and Rosario. Similarly, Mexico City with 7,725,000 people holds about 15 per cent of the nation's population and is six to seven times the size of the second largest cities, Monterrey and Guadalajara with populations only recently reaching 1,000,000 and 1,300,000 respectively. The third largest cities, such as León and Puebla, are approaching 500,000.

Other examples of the primacy of capital cities are: Chile with 28.6 per cent of the population in the Santiago metropolitan area; Uruguay with 52.9 per cent in Montevideo, and Venezuela with 20 per cent of the population in Caracas. Exceptions to this pattern are Colombia and Brazil, where, for reasons of topography and scale, a more equable distribution of city size is to be found.

The capital cities of Latin America have also been among the fastest growing in the world. Highest among them, for obvious reasons, is Brasilia, which grew 11.2 per cent per year from 1960 to 1970, while Brazil grew about 3 per cent annually. Colombia's growth rate during 1962–67 was approximately 3.2 per cent, while Bogotá grew as much as 9.2 per cent. In the case of Venezuela, the national growth rate for 1961–66 was 3 per cent, while Caracas grew 6 per cent.

There is evidence that many smaller cities are now increasing at a faster rate than are the capitals, especially in Colombia, Venezuela and Mexico. For the moment, however, this growth is of less significance in view of the sheer magnitude of the metropolitan capitals. This new scale was unthinkable only a few decades ago and points, in an alarming way, at levels of growth of gigantic proportions in the decades ahead. For example, from 1940 to 1960 the Caracas urban area grew almost four times in size, increasing from 350,000 to 1,285,000 and in 1970 the area held over 2,000,000 people. According to current growth rates, the area will hold 6,696,000 by 1990 or 31.7 per cent of the projected population of the country as a whole. From 1950 to 1960, Bogotá's population doubled from 648,000 to 1,223,000 and in 1970 the urban area held an estimated 2,270,000. Applying the most recent growth rate, the 1990 population would be 7,718,000. Of all urban agglomerations in Latin America, São Paulo in Brazil demonstrates the most consistently rapid growth affecting the greatest volume of urban population in Latin America. Its position as a state capital gives it relevance as a possible prototype for the already large national capitals. From a population of 1,500,000 in 1940, the São Paulo metropolitan area grew to 3,670,000 by 1960 and doubled again by 1970, reaching approximately 7,864,000. Current projections estimate that São Paulo will be one of the largest metropolitan areas in the world with a population of 20,000,000 by 1990.

While some 63,311,000 people or roughly 30 per cent of the 1970 population of Latin America lived in metropolitan areas, according to estimates by 1990 there will be 145,247,000 persons in such areas or about 30 per cent.[4] Of these, 87,618,000, or more than half, will be living in the metropolitan capitals, should present trends continue. This will represent an increase of 24,200,000 residents of these capitals. It is obvious that the general problem of accommodation of increased urban population in Latin America in the future will place an unprecedented strain upon the capital cities. To see the enormity of this problem, it should be recognized that not only must the issues confronting each capital city be faced, but each will have to play a more positive role of national leader in dealing with the urban development problems of the country as a whole. A glance at the general question of population increase in Latin America sets the stage for pointing up critical problems facing the capitals.

The population of Latin America is increasing more rapidly than that of any other region in the world of comparable size. Just over a century ago there were only 33,000,000 people in all of Latin America. In 1950, there were 163,000,000, representing 4.2 per cent of the world's population. By the year 2000, according to estimates by the United Nations, the population of Latin America will comprise 10 per cent of the world's total, and will exceed that of any other major region in the world except Asia and Oceania. A demographic restructuring of the New World is taking place. As a result, by 2000, only a generation away, an estimated 550,000,000 people will be living south of the Rio Grande roughly twice that of the United States and Canada.

The tough, practical question is: Where will the greatly increased numbers of urban dwellers be placed and what will be the role of the capitals, already swollen beyond capacity? How can the accumulated problems of the past be solved to make way for the oncoming wave of population? Can or should this population increase be limited rather than merely accommodated?

In pondering the answers to these questions, it is necessary to recall the physical context of Latin America. For example, in 1950 more than one third of the population of South America was concentrated on less than one twentieth of its land surface. Yet only 29 per cent of the entire surface of Latin America is wasteland (as compared with 59 per cent in the Near East, 46 per cent in the Far East and 43 per cent in North America). The fact that 87.9 per cent of the land area of Latin America belongs to 9.14 per cent of the population suggests the crucial social and economic implications of this imbalance in population distribution.

Critical Issues: Social, Economic, Physical

The growth that has taken place in the metropolitan capitals of Latin America has failed to bring with it the progress inherent in the traditional leadership of capital cities. The capitals have had impressive economic growth and physical growth; however, as an urbanizing force and as an agent of human development in the broad social sense, their fundamental purpose has not been served. While cities in developed countries can be seen as abstract, statistical and impersonal expressions of economic and physical development, the Latin American city—and especially the metropolitan capital—can only be considered in terms of the human tragedy of illiteracy, sickness, apathy and suffering caused by the substandard urban condition.

The arrival of immigrants during the past two decades has brought a transfer of rural problems to the city. The move from rural to urban areas represents an expression of the desire for social development in that the city—and especially the capital city—symbolizes the twentieth century while rural areas represent the past. Thus, rural immigration into the capitals brings with it certain positive implications: The high birth rate of Latin America is producing a high percentage of younger population with greater mobility, a desire to live better and with fewer ties to the past. A new sense of self-organization has appeared among the younger element at the bottom of the social scale. The total effect is a trend toward breaking down the static quality of old social orders.

However, an estimated seventy to eighty million Latin Americans neither read nor write. In most countries public schools are provided for only the first six to eight grades and these are generally on double shifts with low teaching standards and high dropout rates. High school education is generally private and is achieved only by a small percentage of the school population.

In spite of the concentration of facilities in the capitals, health levels are extremely low. The tuberculosis rate is highest in the slum areas of the larger cities, due to substandard and overcrowded housing conditions. As a result of poor water and sewerage systems, the level of intestinal disease is high. Malnutrition is a prevalent and frequently undocumented problem among the poor, due to inadequate food supplies and dietary habits. The shortage of hospitals, clinics and doctors is enormous. These social problems are most visible in the spontaneously formed shack towns, the *barriadas* of Lima, the *poblaciones callampas* of Santiago, the *favelas* of Rio de Janeiro and the *ranchos* of Caracas.

The economic impact of increased urbanization of the Latin American capitals is of critical importance to metropolitan development as it offers a key to social change. Yet the present disparity is great between urban population growth and economic development. The massive migration to these urban centers has formed very large communities of families who live in a highly marginal state with relation to the development of supportive local economies. The end result is the creation of a large supply of labor with wages more identified with rural life than with skilled, urban pursuits.

Thus, industry is attracted to these concentrations of labor supply. For example, 80 per cent of El Salvador's industry is located in San Salvador, and almost one third of the economic product of Brazil is generated from São Paulo. Similarly, the greater the amount of industry located in a single urban center, the greater the attraction for new supplies of rural in-migrant labor. In turn, the unskilled nature of labor tends to encourage low productivity and inefficiencies that require maintaining low wages. Low per capita income—a chronic national condition throughout Latin America—produces low municipal income and impedes the provision of the whole range of community services that effective urban living requires. Inadequate revenues for public services are also due to inequitable fiscal systems. In numerous cases, and Caracas is typical, the building industry is a major one, reflecting explosive urban growth, and employment mirrors the fluctuations that come with speculative building practices. Irregularities in employment and income are consequences.

Furthermore, much of the economic activity of the Latin American urban areas is by nature nonessential and virtually nonproductive to national economies, yet is inherently a part of the cultural system and, therefore, of certain social value. Hidden unemployment can be found in the large numbers of street peddlers, tiny shops and similar types of enterprises to be found in Latin American capitals. Numerous handicraft activities occupy older residential sections, often near the downtown districts. These produce furniture and household equipment and perform various services. Little is known about these kinds of urban microeconomics and the role they play in providing psychological rewards and a provisional basis for existence by these semimarginal groups striving for upward mobility.

In general, very little attention has been given to the field of urban economics in Latin America, perhaps due to the pressure of the past decade to advance national economic development. The particular set of circumstances in Latin American capitals are complex ones that need sensitively to be taken apart to understand in a pragmatic and firsthand way the nature of the problem at the local urban level.

While the underlying social and economic issues are most critical to the Latin American capitals, the physical framework within which human activities operate becomes a very urgent issue. The day-to-day functioning of these cities is constantly threatened with failure of services, difficulty of movement, inaccessibility to facilities, as well as lack of essential facilities themselves. At the same time, the cumulative evolution of the over-all structural system of the Latin American capitals is generally consolidating in ways that are not conducive to social integration, but, rather, productive of increased isolation for an already overly separated class structure.

The activity systems of Latin American capitals are intricate and diverse, sensitively reflecting the transitional nature of social and economic development. While the simple grid pattern of the colonial period served the less complex needs of those early years, the urban structural systems that have developed through unbridled growth do not provide a suitable framework for the transitional social nature of today's cities. Latin American capitals need new models of urban and metropolitan structure directly related to the social and economic requirements of present residents and to their dynamic aspirations for the future; our review of the development and planning of Caracas will provide material to demonstrate this concept.

In contrast to the marked decentralization of cities in the United States, Latin American metropolitan areas tend to spread in less structured ways. The downtown cores are reinforcing themselves with increased high-density residential uses and related business, shops and entertainment, giving the downtown centers a more European kind of urban vitality. In contrast to the more homogeneous areas of cities in the United States, with zoned districts devoted to single functions, Latin American urban centers are guided more by a few large-scale economic forces and a vast number of freewheeling and small-scale enterprises. The cities tend to be characterized by sharply contrasting uses: high-quality residential areas next to squatter settlements of the most spontaneous character; single-family homes of stable quality next to skyscraper apartments; and industry indiscriminately invading older residential areas.

Transportation is perhaps the issue most critical to restructuring of Latin American capitals. Over the years the original grid system has been extended without attempting to structure districts or sort out traffic according to specialized street types. In those cities, such as Caracas, where the automobile has vastly increased in numbers, much more attention has been given to accommodating the street system to these needs rather than to mass transportation. The elementary streetcar systems built around the turn of the century have been replaced by uncoordinated bus lines, consistently poorly organized and rarely under public control. Upper classes tend to use their own cars while middle and lower classes use buses crowded beyond capacity. In some cities—Caracas is one—jitneys do a thriving business.

The combination of concentrated activities in the central areas for business, shopping and services and the sprawling suburbs out beyond requires a long journey to work for all classes. This situation is further complicated by the seemingly unchangeable lunching tradition of the Latin Americans which involves an entire return trip to the home and family at midday. In Caracas, this even includes the school children.

A rapid transit system has existed in Buenos Aires for decades. After many years of study, mass transit is a reality in Caracas and São Paulo. In Mexico City a first unit has been put into operation. Other mass transit systems in the construction stage include Santiago, Lima and Rio de Janeiro. While housing, schools and other facilities of social significance are urgently needed in the Latin American capitals, the development of modern urban transportation systems in those sprawling metropolitan areas is critical to social and economic advancement. Since automobile ownership rests with the small minority, transportation planning can be a more effective way of structuring the urban area. In the long run, and, more urgently, it can provide for large masses of the population a means of convenient and economic access to centers of education, health, employment and other facilities needed to advance the social changes now striving to take place.

The Urban Planning Process

In spite of the highly centralized authority of Latin American governments, the national role in local urban planning is not clearly defined. In most cases this legal and financial power has been directed primarily toward development of urban planning processes within the national capital. Only since the early 1950s have governments begun to deal at the national level with issues related to urbanization systems as a whole and their relationship to social and economic development. However, they have tended to place heavy emphasis on broad economic development goals with insufficient attention to urban growth and the local implications of public investment programming. While the earlier part of this century saw great emphasis on the planning and development of national capitals as political settings, at mid-century these urban centers were allowed to suffer the consequences of undirected national and regional growth. Yet, judging from the directions that the urban and regional planning field is taking in such countries as Chile, Brazil, Colombia and Venezuela, the latter part of this century could bring with it a greater balance and clarification of function among the three levels of planning essential to Latin America: national, regional and urban.

Comprehensive urban physical planning is provided for at the national level in various ways. In several countries—Nicaragua, Panama, Costa Rica and Peru—special offices for this function have been established. Chile, in 1966, created a separate Ministry of Housing and Urbanism for this purpose by removing the responsibility from the Ministry of Public Works. The Ministry of Public Works continues to play this role in El Salvador, Ecuador and on a grand scale in Venezuela, although legislation to create a new Ministry for Housing and Urban Planning activities is now in preparation. In Colombia and Mexico the planning function has been left to the municipalities, although with increasing national support. Argentina and Uruguay provide virtually no vehicle for urban planning at any level. Brazil has recently taken broad and promising steps to establish working relationships between the national and local governments.

Municipalities have limited authority for urban planning and development. History shows that while municipalities in Latin America have an early and cherished tradition of autonomy it is one that has weakened through centuries of neglect. This level of government is of increasingly critical importance with relation to the national capitals; for, as we have pointed out, metropolitanization has brought into a single agglomeration whole clusters of municipalities surrounding what is officially the capital city. Thus, planning for the national capitals simply cannot be done on other than an intermunicipal or metropolitan scale. This requirement is often further complicated politically as the national capital is often dominated by the party in power, while the surrounding municipalities hold majorities from opposing parties, the leaders of which might well be future national political aspirants.

It is also important to realize that in Latin America, unlike in the United States, a municipality is often a microregion in itself, in that it is a rural-urban territory—even region—dominated by a single major urban area. For this reason the clusters of municipalities that make up the metropolitan capitals of Latin American countries often cover very extensive areas comprising fairly solidly urbanized centers with outlying subcenters and still surrounded by rural land. While this is a condition favorable to regionally oriented planning, it is usually only the urban core of the region that is given the needed attention. However, the present trend in Latin America—as evidenced by recent metropolitan area studies in Santiago, San Salvador, São Paulo and, significantly, Caracas itself—is to look toward this broader framework for planning.

A key problem among the majority of the capitals is that present government at the national and municipal levels is geared to an urbanization pattern that no longer exists. Today, economic and social leadership in Latin America operates within a framework of metropolitan regions predominantly urban in character, for which there is no administrative format whereby these regions can fully and effectively express this leadership for the nation as a whole. New forms of government, particularly with relation to the unique nature of the metropolitan capitals, are necessary to unravel the present patterns of physical and social chaos and to guide future growth into more functional and constructive patterns. These should include greater professional efficiency and more continuity in the turnover of politics.

During the past several decades of urban planning in the major Latin American capitals, the emphasis has largely been upon physical development. However, such experiences as the widespread in-migration of rural population, the growth of diversified industry and the ineffectiveness of institutionalized low-cost housing programs have brought many leaders in the urban planning field to the realization that social and economic problems cannot necessarily be solved through physical development alone. They have also recognized that social and economic measures alone will not be effective. Urban planning is an integrated sequence of measures and actions leading to the improvement of political, social, economic and physical conditions seen as an interrelated whole. Indeed, on examining the more enlightened professional leadership of such countries as Chile, Colombia, Brazil and Venezuela, it appears that the urban planning movement in Latin America is on the threshold of a new period of transition. It is the urgency of crossing that threshold that is explored in reviewing the specific case of Caracas.

The traditional legal instrument for guiding the development of urban areas has been the *Plano Regulador,* roughly the equivalent of the General Plan or Master Plan of cities in the United States. However, it is a far more rigid and legalistic document, inadequate for dealing with long-range issues, for allowing flexible, continuous policy making and for offering a framework for co-ordinated and systematic program budgeting. Up to recently these urban plans have been highly architectural in nature and lacking in any social and economic analytical basis for the justification of physical decisions. Land use analysis has not been carried on in sufficient depth; nor have transportation studies been used as meaningful tools for determining future urban structural systems. However, promising changes are taking place in the conceptual and methodological basis for urban planning in the more progressive countries.

While a simpler and more arbitrary model was appropriate for the slower pace of urban development and the more homogeneous nature of the urban culture of the earlier decades of this century, attitudes symbolized in the *Plano Regulador* can hardly be expected to serve under the pressures of today's urban revolution. A central question is: In view of the homogeneous nature of the Spanish and Portuguese cultures that produced the great capitals of Latin America up to mid-century, can today's heterogeneous urban cultures produce models of consistency and relevance to our time? This is a major area of concern among those Latin American urban planners who are looking toward the richness of the barriadas (squatter slum colonies) of Lima and the similar ranchos of Caracas, in contrast to the sterility of many government housing projects, as a way of incorporating the dynamic quality of participatory social change into a more meaningful urban planning process.

In Latin American urban planning, public policy is rarely defined and subjected to public debate. Nor are development strategies to carry out policy objectively and systematically organized. A major deterrent to continuity in the planning process is the fact that—for political reasons inherent in Latin American culture—terms of authority tend to be finite. In the building of public works, there is a pronounced tendency in the capitals for the government in power to exhaust current funds in the interest of visible accomplishment. Monumentality, even veiled in contemporary design, is often given higher priority than socially oriented public need and serviceability. Public housing, typically programmed in large amounts in the capital cities, is too often simply direct construction by powerful national agencies that are often motivated more by the desire to safeguard investment of funds in solid construction than by sparking broad social and community benefits.

In spite of the vast amount of energy available in the community, little participation is brought into the implementation phase of the urban planning process. But in a few countries—Colombia, Peru, Chile, Brazil and notably Venezuela—the community development movement has evolved to a relatively active level in urban areas.[5] Accordingly, in determining priorities for schools, health centers, recreation facilities and similar urban equipment of social importance, the leadership and participation by the users of these facilities is incorporated in decisions as to timing, location and design. Thus, other long-range social benefits are generated in terms of community structure and further initiative.

Although Latin American capitals have a tradition of strong, centralized government, there is actually much less control over private land development than in the United States. Zoning operates more as very loose regulation for the size, shape and location of building, rather than as an effective guide for land-use decisions within the total urban system. Land subdivision control focuses only on those areas being urbanized for upper- and middle-income groups. Standards are inappropriately high to apply to the large masses of families who build their own *favelas* or ranchos with no controls or guidance whatsoever. While the outlying areas of the metropolitan capitals need revision of implementation systems adequately to reflect the economic and social gap between the landed and the landless, the aging central areas are desperately in need of legislative measures by which systematic redevelopment can be sought. Although much of the land in the central areas is being rebuilt, the process is a piecemeal one; for powers are not available by which whole urban sectors can be rebuilt by private financing under public direction. Thus, in many instances, the lack of legal and organizational frameworks for large-scale redevelopment is a greater obstacle than lack of funds.

The decisive split in social and economic levels in the Latin American capitals is reflected in the vast difference between the middle- and upper-class areas for business and residence, highly motivated by speculative goals and supported by government collaboration, and lower-class use areas identified by overcrowding, lack of services and given only marginal support by government. It is through establishing for these two groups a more rational and socially oriented set of priorities that implementation programs must be formulated in Latin America with some relevance to the present and the alarming shadow of the future.

To do this means basic changes in the Latin American cultural position: namely, the redistribution of political power from a small elite group to the larger, and as yet, passive community, together with the relinquishing of individual patronage by isolated, self-interested agencies. While these may be cultural changes too great to expect in a short period, there are already indications in enough of the Latin American capitals to believe that a new form of urban planning system is not only possible but actually beginning to take shape.

DEMOGRAPHIC AND PHYSICAL EVOLUTION OF METROPOLITAN CARACAS

Cordilleras, Llanos and Venezuelan Urbanization

Venezuela occupies a strategic geographic position for modernization. It lies in

FIG. 1 Administrative regions of Venezuela.

the extreme northeast corner of South America more directly oriented to Europe and the United States than any other country on the continent. This richly varied land stretches some eight hundred miles along the Caribbean from Trinidad and the northern tip of Guayana westward to the Colombian border; it spreads from three hundred to five hundred miles south to the northern limits of Brazil. To understand the role of Caracas, the capital, in this large and rapidly developing country, it is essential to know the regional structure of the country and the urbanizing forces that have been the basic determinants in the phenomenal creation of metropolitan Caracas (Fig. 1).

Spanning the northern region of the country and paralleling the Caribbean lies the rugged, extreme end of the Andes. In western Venezuela the Cordillera (mountain range) reaches heights of fifteen thousand feet in snow-capped peaks and then drops down precipitously to the fertile basin of oil-producing Lake Maracaibo. Eastward the range remains at six and seven thousand feet where the *Cerro del Avila* forms the barrier from the sea and provides the backdrop for the dramatic urbanization of the valley of Caracas (Fig. 2).

Even though this mountainous region comprises only about a quarter of the area of the country, the greater portion of the population lives here, and it is the most intensively urbanized. The Venezuelan Andes form the backbone of the urbanization system of the country. Here are located the cool, high valleys and plateaus where large towns like San Cristóbal, Mérida and Valera are rapidly growing into true cities, and the lower, warmer valleys where cities such as Barquisimeto, Valencia and Maracay, more accessible to the coast and to the sea, are growing

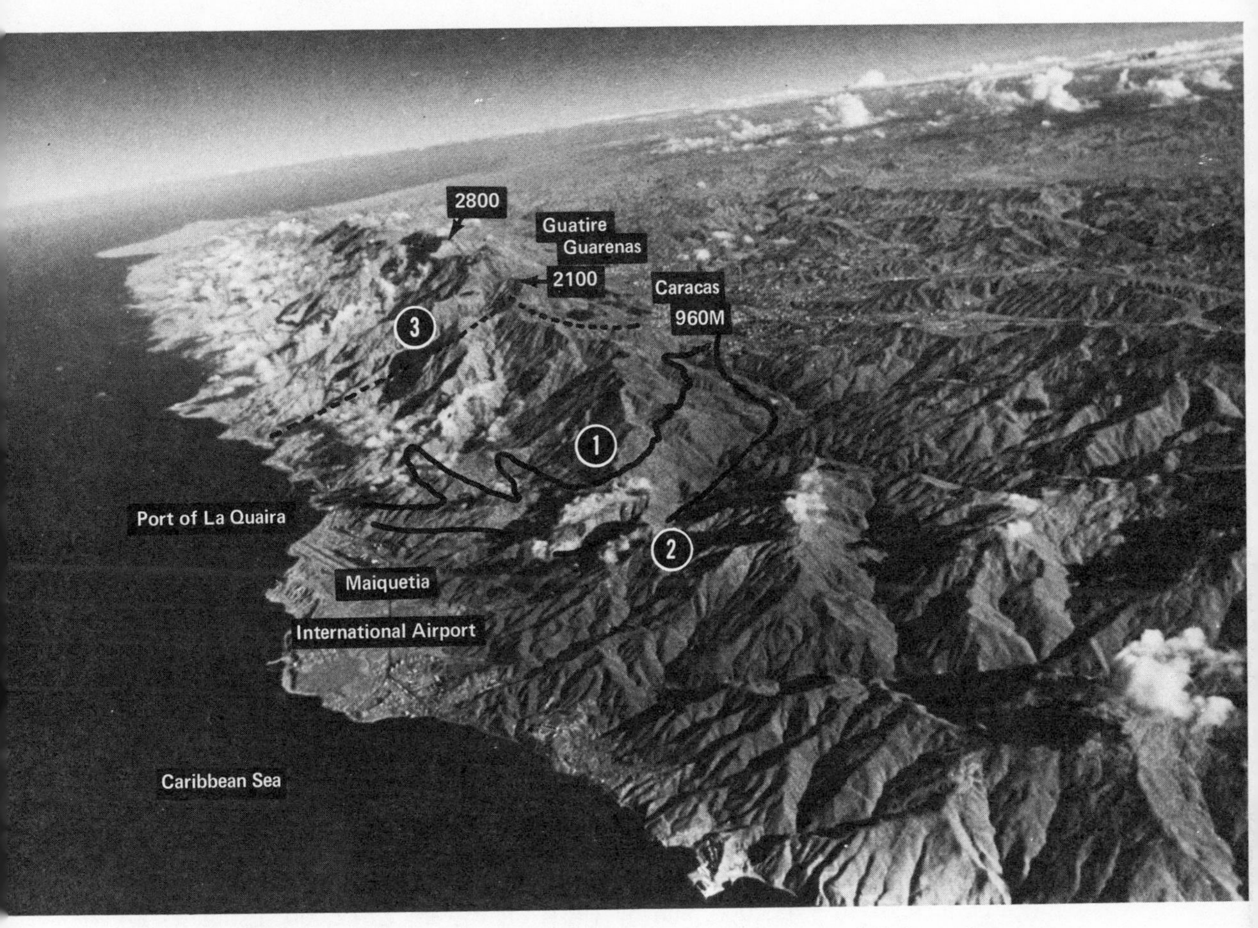

FIG. 2 Topography of the Caracas area. Methods of reaching the capital from the port area: 1. the old road, 2. the modern superhighway, 3. the cable railway which rises from sea level to a height of 2,100 meters at El Avila and descends to Caracas, 960 meters in altitude. *Photograph by Tomás José Sanabria*

together into a megalopolis, of which Caracas forms the major eastern element. While the continuous ridge of this *cordillera* provided a natural link for the early settlements and a logical route for the Andean invaders of Caracas of the 1900s, it has been outmoded by the construction of *autopistas* (express highways) along the lowlands of the Maracaibo basin on the north and the vast *llanos* (plains) on the south. These routes have cut travel time tremendously. Indeed, the system of highways built since the 1950s has contributed greatly to the *present* dominance of Caracas as the functional capital of the country.

The middle region of Venezuela contrasts vividly with these urbanized mountains of the north. Here we have the almost empty llanos of the extensive flat basin of the Orinoco, the one thousand-mile long river that drains a large portion of the undeveloped portions of Venezuela. These grazing lands are held in *haciendas* of great scale and, as yet, urbanization is confined to such small towns as Barinas and San Fernando de Apure which provide services to the primarily agricultural function of the region. Modern highways have given the frontierlike llanos new opportunities for contact with Caracas and the social and economic life of the country.

South of the Orinoco, the remaining major region plunges deeply into the relatively unexplored and almost totally undeveloped Guayana that reaches the northern limits of Brazil's Amazon basin. Topography rises abruptly to extensive plateau lands several thousand feet in elevation and to peaks and ridges of six thousand and seven thousand feet. These highlands, cut into gorges by rivers that drain north, cover about one half of the total area of the country and are Venezuela's natural frontier. They are also the setting of one of the world's most ambitious projects of regional development. This focuses the building of Ciudad Guayana at the juncture of the Orinoco and Caroni rivers, the extraction and processing of iron ore at Cerro Bolívar and the ultimate reclamation of the rich Orinoco Delta Area. This vast project, located at the threshold of the Guayana region, is paving the way for further penetration to the south and providing new economic stimulus to such existing cities as Ciudad Bolívar. On the completion of river dams of great scale, it will also provide Caracas with very large supplies of electric power.

About 10,035,000 people live in Venezuela, concentrated largely in about one quarter of the area of the country in the northwest. Population grew slowly up to about 1940 and development was at a minimum due to the restraints imposed by the forces of history. In 1873, Venezuela's population was only 1,784,000, or somewhat less than the population of metropolitan Caracas today. In the forty-seven years from that date to 1920, the country increased only by about 567,000, reaching 2,351,000.

While the national growth over the half century up to 1920 was only one third, that of the next twenty years up to 1941 was two thirds, reaching a total in that year of 3,850,000. During the next decade, up to 1950, about the same rate held with an increase to 5,035,000, and by 1961, there were 7,612,000. Estimates indicate that the latter figure will double by 1981, reaching 15,202,000.

Meanwhile, an almost complete reversal took place between urban and rural population. In 1936, the urban population (those in places over one thousand persons) was 34.7 per cent; rose to 53.8 per cent in 1950 and in 1961 to 67.3 per cent. The projection for 1981 is 82.7 per cent urban. In 1961, these were distributed over eighty cities from five thousand to twenty thousand, holding 9.7 per cent of the urban population, and in thirty-six cities, over twenty thousand which held 47.7 per cent. It is significant that the larger cities are growing far faster than the smaller towns; estimates for 1970 show that those in the first group will remain about the same—9.12 per cent—while those in the second group will increase to 57.3 per cent.[6]

The greater part of this growth has been in the larger cities and most dramatically in the capital. Between 1936 and 1959, a little more than two decades, the two largest cities, Maracaibo and Caracas, both increased by four times. Caracas grew from 234,000 to over 1,000,000 while Maracaibo grew from 110,000 to 400,000, reaching 635,000 in 1970. Barquisimeto, the third largest city, grew five times in that period from 36,400 to 150,000, and Valencia doubled in size, from 49,200 to 100,000. By 1970, Barquisimeto had 320,000 and Valencia, 261,000. These rates of growth have generally continued and many of the cities in the lesser categories are actually growing at a faster rate than the capital. However, estimates indicate that by 1980 only Maracaibo will have achieved the one million population level; with 1,500,000 by 1990, this growing metropolis will far exceed all other secondary cities. Among them, for example, Barquisimeto would lead with only 800,000 followed by Valencia and Maracaibo whose population would be about 640,000 and 610,000 respectively. Thus, it is clear that, while Venezuela's urban system will display active growth in a number of developing centers during the coming decades, Caracas, as the metropolitan capital, will continue to be the dominant urban center, far larger and more influential in social and economic life of the country than all others.

The Basic Landscape of Caracas

Although the site chosen for Caracas by the Spaniards ultimately became the closest major urban center to the motherland on the mainland of South America, it was until the middle of the present century one of the most inaccessible. Its magnificent physical setting is uniquely inappropriate for a major metropolis and its walled-in character seems to reflect certain qualities in the social make-up of the populace that may account for both its isolation over the centuries and its current dynamic vitality (see Fig. 2).

As the crow flies, the valley is only some eight miles from the Caribbean. Yet, the Cerro del Avila, and the Cordillera de la Costa (Coast Range) form a seven thousand-foot wall that has imposed both an obstacle and challenge to development. The Cordillera runs several hundred miles east and west almost without openings. On the sea side of the range, ledges running parallel to the range have provided harbors of questionable safety in past years and a major international airport in our time.

The safe haven provided by the valley in earlier times and its diversity and attractiveness today have motivated different stages of technological ingenuity in overcoming the barrier of the Andean wall. From La Guaira the colonial route for centuries was a system of trails for mules and horses through the tropical vegetation of the ravines and up and over the ridge using switchbacks. The second stage was the building of a vehicular route in the latter part of the last century—the narrow winding road clinging to the mountainside and following the natural contours with its reputed 365 curves—one for every day in the year. After the turn of the century this was augmented by a primitive rail line. Finally with the coming of the airplane, the old road was replaced with the magnificently engineered *Caracas-La Guaira Autopista,* reducing the curves to six by introducing the most impressive highway tunnels and bridges. The latest and most spectacular route over the Cerro del Avila is the *teleferico* system, built in the early 1950s at enormous cost from the sea near Macuto to the top of the ridge and down the south slope to the valley of Caracas.

This rugged and forbidding escarpment, often veiled handsomely with clouds and shifting fogs, gives way to an open valley, once gardenlike in character, stretching some ten to twelve miles east and west, and some three miles in width. Green slopes rise some three to four thousand feet above the valley on the north. To the south the elongated valley breaks out into several smaller valleys each separated by lower ranges of hills. The water flowing from these openings and from the steep mountainside of the Avila have created the main spine of the valley, the Guaire River, which from the beginning of urbanization has fixed a strong east-west direction for circulation and urban growth. It is this basic landscape that has laid the main lines for determining the urban system of Caracas today.

For almost 350 years Caracas remained a small town, hidden from ready access to the outside world and even to the remainder of the country. Just as the early colonial houses of Caracas that endured up to a few decades ago walled themselves in from the street, so the mountain-enclosed valley afforded privacy, delight and a sense of calm, urbane security. This introverted world was hardly one in which to prepare for the explosive social and political change of the mid-century. Yet, this was the major challenge that Caracas was called upon to face. As the enclosed colonial houses on the narrow grid streets were bulldozed away to make room for the automobile, the skyscraper office and apartment, the spacious and luxurious residential subdivisions of the elite leaders of the new economy symbolized a new position of exposure to the world. Side by side with the slum ranchos, these formed a clear statement of problems common to burgeoning metropolises. Today it is this sudden confrontation with wealth, produced by oil exploitation and the instant crystallization of staggering urban development problems, that has stimulated a new urban culture in Caracas. New ways of life and new challenges have come to this metropolitan center of decision making for what can become one of the most progressive and advanced countries in Latin America.

From Colony to Capital and Metropolis

Prior to the coming of the Europeans, the Caracas Valley was the serene home of Los Caracas—the Indians from whom today's capital of Venezuela takes its name. The site was chosen late in comparison with other settlements that grew into Latin American capital cities due to inaccessibility and an absence of exploitable resources. It was not until 1567 that a small town of twenty-five square blocks was founded by Diego de Losada at the westerly section of the valley at a point where a wedge of hills splits the valley into two subaxes (Fig. 3). Most of the other leading colonial centers had been established within the first three decades of the sixteenth century.

During the following centuries, this development was extended to comprise an area of about fifteen blocks in each direction. The remainder of the valley was planted with sugar cane as city dwellers took up hacienda holdings to the east in elongated strips of land running north and south from the central road paralleling the river. Each of these huge farms—some twenty-five to thirty in all—developed its own suburban center in due time, but each maintained a direct relationship with the town, which served as the focus of social life. This basic pattern of circulation routes, urbanized areas and property lines remained virtually unchanged for three centuries. Only in the latter part of the nineteenth century did Caracas begin to take on the first signs of becoming a modern city, as the full effect of independence from Spain began to be felt. By the end of the century, the enlightened, European-oriented administration of Antonio Guzmán Blanco made intensive efforts to introduce Parisian monumentality in the form of the Congressional Palace, the Presidential Palace, the Municipal Theatre and city parks. New residential areas of villas were built—El Paraíso—for elite families who were ready to break away from the traditional walled-in colonial dwellings that gave old Caracas its essential character.[7]

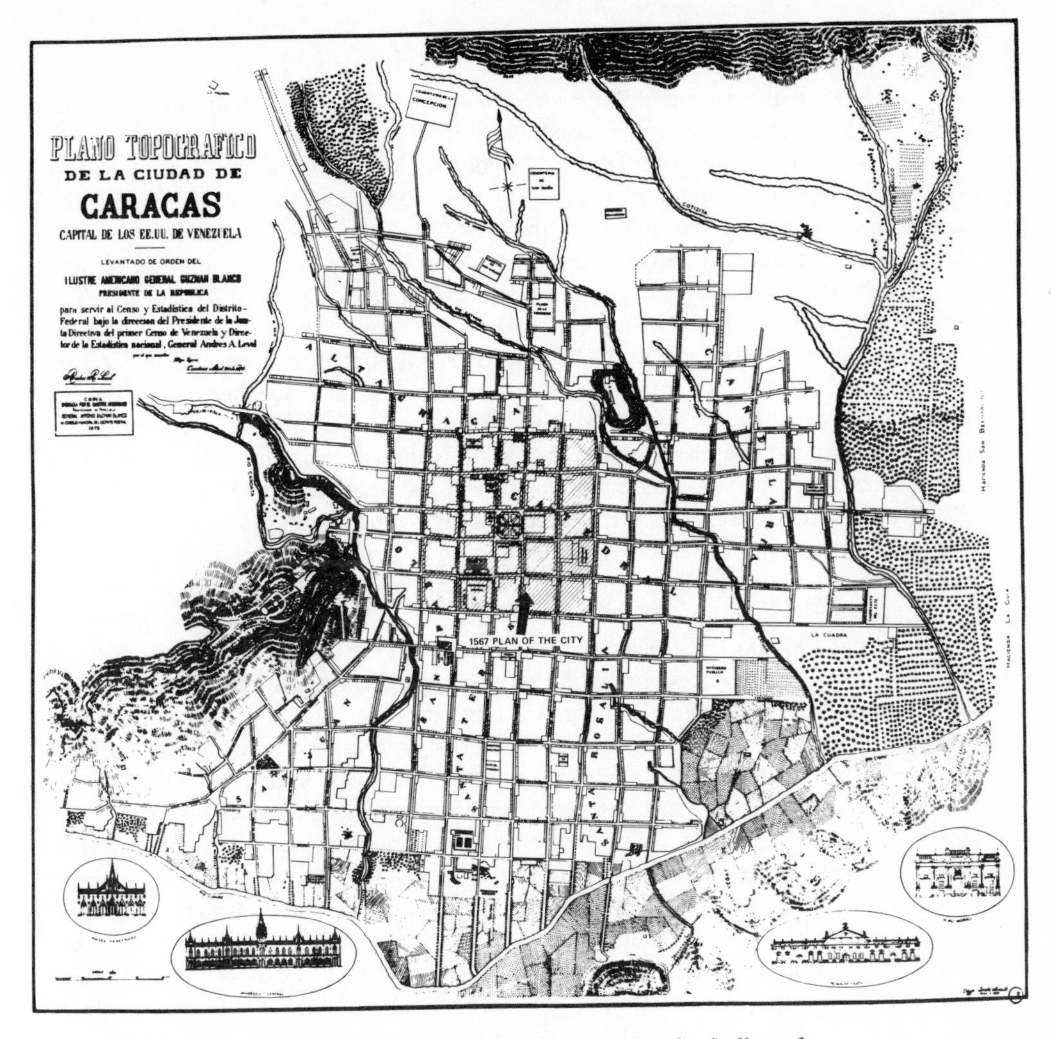

FIG. 3 Caracas in 1875 with the original 1567 Plan for the city indicated.

However, this was little more than an image of national leadership, for prior to 1900 Venezuela was far from a unified country. The liberal political ideals of the revered *Libertador* Simón Bolívar, born in Caracas late in the eighteenth century, were never achieved. Among his ambitions was the permanent unification of Venezuela, Colombia and Ecuador into a single republic—La Gran Colombia—whose capital would probably have been Bogotá, the center from which he campaigned for the liberation of these territories. Thus, Caracas might have missed becoming a capital city. Yet, it was not until a century after Bolívar's time that Venezuela, itself, was politically unified; during these years it remained a collection of states run essentially on an *ad hoc* basis by self-appointed chieftains, some of whom found support with the central government and some who did not. Caracas found it easier to reach Paris by sea than the interior of the country by land—especially the highly populated Andean area to the west. Without communication the government focused its limited resources on the capital and the surrounding region maintaining, in a sense, a colonial form of life.

Meanwhile, to the west a different mentality developed in the mountain towns of the high Andes near the Colombian border, one based on rule by self-imposed authority. In the late 1890s, one local chieftain, Cipriano Castro, gained dominance over lesser *jefes* in the region and began an historic march on the capital some five hundred miles to the east. With a band of only fifty men, he traversed the Andean ridge and by promises of material and political power reached Caracas in 1900 with an enlarged army of five thousand. These invading mountainmen, dressed in *ruanas* (short woolen capes) and wearing *alpargatas* (rope sandals) in place of shoes, had never seen European dress. They pitched camp in the Plaza Bolívar in the heart of the capital and the unification of Venezuela began. These rugged Andean people, strangers to the cultured *Caraqueños,* dominated the city and ran its affairs ruthlessly for thirty-six years, most of this time under the self-appointed dictatorship of General Juan Vincente Gómez. His was a barbaric record; yet, at the sacrifice of human life and individual freedom, he brought the country under a single government amassing personal fortune by the time of his death in 1936. However, his disdain for the people of Caracas and its European way of life was so great that he turned his back on the capital and chose Maracay, some sixty miles to the west, as the administrative headquarters where he focused public works expenditures on boulevards, parks, the elaborate Hotel Jardin and a home for himself.

While he and the many children he fathered as a bachelor chieftain profited enormously, he initiated the exploitation of petroleum and the opening of the country to foreign investment. At his death Caracas was in as backward a state as at the turn of the century. While other Latin American capitals had concentrated within their boundaries much of the fruit of the economic development of the early part of the century, Caracas remained with its outward colonial heritage of narrow streets, houses walled to the sidewalks, red roofs, scattered attempts at modernization from the regime of Guzmán Blanco and a few new residential suburbs. Yet, during the following decades it was to undergo more rapid and dramatic growth than any Latin American capital.

With the death of Gómez and the stimulus of a new reform government, the capital once more became the focus of political life. This time the new economic life breathed into Venezuela by the intensified exploitation of oil made possible programs of public works and private land development that touched off the physical transformation of Caracas. The valley site changed from a rural-urban town of a few hundred thousand persons to a highly urbanized metropolis of two million. Each of the haciendas became residential subdivisions during this period and their outlying subcenters formed the basis for the decentralization of the downtown area. The place names that identified each of the haciendas with the gardenlike landscape of the valley—Los Chaguaramos, Bello Monte, Altamira and Los Palos Grandes (The Palms, the Beautiful Hill, the High View and the Big Trees)—to name only a few examples, were all that was retained in the face of relentless speculative urbanization and massive public investments.

By the early 1950s, the valley had almost filled up by urban development with about 75 per cent of the population concentrated in the northwest third of the approximate thirty-square-mile site. The intensity of government construction and private apartment building in the capital under the government of Marcos Pérez Jiménez attracted immigrant families who augmented enormously the already existing and now well-known ranchos built of scrap materials in the *quebradas* (deep canyons) and on the hillsides. In 1953, there were 53,600 of these dwellings, housing 38 per cent of the population, or 310,000 people. The first apartment buildings appeared about 1940, as red-roofed buildings of soft, adobe brick. In the early 1950s, these sprang into being almost overnight, forming entire districts of multifamily dwellings and changing completely the previous way of living. Subdivisions designed for single-family homes could scarcely contain these apartment buildings, accommodate the traffic generated by them or provide the social services needed.

Those who tried desperately to relate the planning process to some recognizable model or some basic rationale during the 1950s were defeated by one of the most dynamic expressions of urban growth that Latin America has seen. During that period, the chaos and disorder were beyond belief. In spite of intensive congestion—in the new apartment areas and in the rancho colonies on the hills—almost half of the buildable land of the valley was still unoccupied into the latter part of the 1950s, much of it laid out with roads and services of high standard for a market that at that time was nonexistent. Pressed by the inflated values of land, speculative residential development located itself adjacent to industry, warehousing and transitional commercial areas, with the expectation that these would give way to new uses in a short time. Bottling plants, automobile sales—even assembly plants—and service buildings, all of certain architectural character were built for advertising purposes in the heart of residential subdivisions. Stores and shops representing a tremendous burst of highly individualized enterprise moved into older dwellings, garages in front of homes and temporary structures.

It was the cutting of the Avenida Simón Bolívar, begun in the late 1940s, that heralded the intensive rebuilding of Caracas. First conceived as a monumental boulevard to serve the central tier of blocks established in colonial times and to run from the El Calvario Hill on the west to the Parque Los Caobos, it underwent a series of design revisions throughout the 1940s and 1950s that have turned it into the largest and virtually the only major redevelopment project in the central core of any Latin American city. The first revision, about 1940, was the building of El Silencio, a housing project of neocolonial design on the six-block area at the foot of El Calvario where a monument to Simón Bolívar had been proposed. While this first ambitious effort of the new housing agency—the *Banco Obrero*—erased a slum and tenement area, the builders did not anticipate the considerably more intensive downtown uses to be generated by the growth to come. By the mid-1940s, the boulevard element had been converted to an elaborate underground expressway and parking facility at the base of Caracas' first two skyscrapers, twenty-two stories high.

The remaining ten blocks through the old center were to have been built by private enterprise with sites leased or purchased from the Centro Bolívar Development Corporation set up for the purpose. However, the very act of massive building demolishment, land clearance and excavation on this site and on the new Avenida Urdaneta running parallel a few blocks above the old colonial Plaza Bolívar tended to drive the largest private enterprise building projects out of the center to the new burgeoning residential subdivisions. The central area was virtually killed as a place for new building by the prolonged tearing up of streets, the noise, the dust and the uncertainties. Thus, the decentralization of the new Caracas came about almost as if a planner's strategy had so intended.

However, a trend toward recapturing downtown Caracas as a focal point of metropolitan life began about 1965 with building projects of both public and private nature. Generally these were designed at unusually high densities and ratios of land occupancy reflecting the highly inflated land values that had skyrocketed during these intervening years. One of the most exemplary of these is the Parque Central project, under construction in 1972 by the Centro Bolívar Development Corporation itself and located at the east end of the central district on some fifteen blocks of old, outmoded housing. Where formerly resided only a few thousand persons, some sixteen thousand will live in twelve towers of forty-two stories each and some eighteen thousand will work in three towers of fifty-six stories each. On the one hand, this daring effort represents an admirable attempt to reduce the metropolitan transportation problem by utilizing the central areas for combined purposes of residences and employment. On the other hand, it is highly possible that the official acceptance of population densities far exceeding those of virtually any other planned redevelopment project in the Americas lead only to paving the way for even greater concentrations of population in the national capital.

Population Explosion in Caracas

In relation to other capitals in Latin America, Caracas has grown during recent years more rapidly than any of the others. In 1926, it held only 146,900 people and by 1936 still had the general appearance of a quiet colonial city, even though it had reached 259,000. However, during the next quarter of a century—by 1961—Caracas reached the metropolitan proportions of 1,336,000, growing at an annual rate of 6 per cent. By 1966, there were 1,797,000 and 1970 figures indicated 2,171,000. The significance of this growth with relation to the country as a whole and its role of the capital is demonstrated by the fact that in 1936 only 7.7 per cent of the population lived in the capital, while by 1966, 19.3 per cent had concentrated their social and economic activities in this strategic and promising center of national life.[8]

Projections indicate that by 1980 the Caracas Metropolitan Area will hold 3,516,000, or 23.7 per cent of the national population, and by 1990, 5,458,000, or 27.4 per cent. Even assuming a declining rate of growth for Caracas it appears that the primacy of Caracas will continue at least until the early part of the twenty-first century.

This recent growth has been primarily due to in-migration although natural increase has been significant from the interior of the country and immigration from abroad. Population from the interior originated in the rural areas and smaller towns and reached its peak during the building boom of the 1950s, when conditions there were considerably worse than in more recent times. The availability of open hillsides and hidden *quebradas* in Caracas close to developed areas and readily found, cast-off building materials facilitated the spontaneous invasion of squatter settlements.

Immigration from abroad was particularly heavy during the 1950s when Italians, Portuguese and Spanish workers were encouraged to enter the country as temporary labor in the building programs; their skills were passed on to Venezuelan workmen. During the 1960s, very large numbers of these immigrants and others from Central Europe made Venezuela—and particularly Caracas—their permanent home. This immigration was not only large in numbers, but the social and cultural impact was great; whole districts were transformed into foreign colonies as newcomers prospered from various forms of entrepreneurship, business and professional activities, making permanent contributions to this metropolitan capital.

Demographic pressure on the restricted linear valley site dramatically increased the size of the urbanized area. In 1926, this area covered only some 2,000 hectares; by 1966, this urbanized area grew to 11,500 hectares. By that time, virtually all of the more or less level land and a substantial part of the hilly areas, especially to the south of the valley, were covered with urbanization. As a result, vertical expansion has become the predominant way of accommodating the population increase to the shortage of land within access of services and employment. While the 1950s saw the widespread construction of apartment buildings of ten and twelve stories, the period from 1960 to 1970 brought the twenty-two-story tower in profusion and a number of towers from thirty to forty stories. These new building forms are causing a major shift in demographic and social patterns, bringing with it the kind of *big city* anonymity that high density urban living allows, a pattern that is in sharp contrast with that of previous generations of *Caraqueños.*

Urban Physical Structure

The process of rapid and organic evolution of the urban structure of metropolitan Caracas is, when observed over several decades, of greater interest than the character of the structure itself today. The basic functional organization of Caracas was a simple one and, up to only a little more than a quarter of a century ago, conformed to the colonial model. That pattern changed in a short time to one of scattered decentralization; today there appears to be a marked trend to return to a centralized urban structural system supplemented with more clearly identified subcenters in the outlying areas. These changes in pattern are continually accompanied by changes in scale: from the early, pedestrian scale of the nineteenth century to the urban, vehicular scale of the mid-twentieth century, and now to the new, interurban scale that appears to be the direction for the remainder of this century. Growth is no longer confined to the valley, related hills and spur drainage basins, but is leapfrogging out to the more distant valleys thirty to forty miles away and to the coastal areas.

A frame of reference for the structure of the inner metropolitan area is the axis running east from Catia—at the head of the autopista from La Guaira and the airport at the sea—through the old center of the city out to Petare at the end of the main valley. This is the traditional route on which the lineal pattern of Caracas has developed and one that is critical to the future, since it is the axis along which the new rapid transit line, in advanced stages of design in 1972, will be built, thus reinforcing the basic structure (Fig. 4).

Up to 1960, this was an almost purely lineal pattern, with only minor circulation routes up the smaller tangential valleys; this has now changed to become somewhat circular and radial as tunnels and roads are built through and over the hills. The location and priority for the construction of what is Latin America's only urban freeway system has been basic in determining Caracas' urban structure. It is along these routes—especially the lineal ones—that the residential areas are strung in rather clearly marked development units, repeating the old pattern of

FIG. 4 Urban expressways with the El Pulpo (The Octopus) Interchange.

haciendas and ownership lines of colonial times. From Catia to the center, no such holdings had existed and the area tended to develop in warehousing, industry and lower income housing. The earlier "string" commercial development of the 1950s that grew rapidly to the east from the Parque Los Caobos in pursuit of the new residential suburbs has, in the 1960s, tended to shape itself into a major activity node of considerable scale, intensity and diversity. This has threatened to replace these functions in the old center. The university, strategically located in the 1940s close to this area, has grown to be a force favoring the concentration of activities in the Sabana Grande subcenter.

These new, eastern residential areas of increasingly high buildings and densities along the commercial thoroughfares have taken over many of the new single-family suburbs of the 1930s and 1940s. During the past decade this skyscraper development has pushed its way out to the eastern limit of the valley at Petare, whose now unique colonial character stands in striking contrast. This development was made possible by the construction of the autopista system which provides direct access to the end of the valley. Farther back toward the foot of the Cerro del

Avila, the single-family homes of the 1940s and 1950s are broken here and there with new high-rise apartments. Zoning has attempted, though failed, to contain these, except in such exclusive areas as the Country Club development, where private deed restrictions are firmly enforced. Office buildings of major importance, such as those of the oil companies, and at least one very large hotel, hold prestigious and conspicuous positions in spacious settings among these diverse and at times spectacular residential areas. The hills to the south of the valley, subdivided and ruthlessly graded in the 1950s for upper income single-family residences that took a decade to appear, are now finally heavily built upon, and even these areas are being invaded with hillside apartment buildings.

While most Latin American capitals are marked with a distinct cleavage between upper and lower income residential areas, the distribution of the ranchos and other forms of low-income housing is considerably mixed in Caracas. Although this eastern area is predominantly middle and upper income in character, the range downward to lower income is made possible by the extensive invasion of the hillsides with ranchos, especially at the east end. The pattern is also varied by pockets of older housing left in the wake of waves of speculative construction. A number of islands of public housing of considerable scale are scattered in the eastern area, although to the west of the center, toward Catia and the other portion of the "Y" configuration of the valley, a vast array of these superbloques, holding hundreds of thousands, produces a truly fantastic urban landscape. This is by far the largest concentration of public housing in any American capital, north or south. In seemingly limitless scale, the texture of ranchos covers the surrounding hills and forms an ironic backdrop to this overly institutionalized solution to the housing problem (Figs. 5a, 5b).

Fortunately, the function most critical to the effective operation of a capital—the basic governmental activities—still remains firmly in the old center. Numerous proposals to build new and more imposing facilities farther out, or at least on the periphery of the center, have been defeated in favor of capitalizing on the flavor of the past and contributing to the revitalizing of the downtown area by new construction. Thus, the old Capitol, the Plaza Bolívar, the Central Bank, Miraflores (the Presidential Palace and its related office building) and the Panteon (burial place of Bolívar and other heroes) form a series of interrelated functional and symbolic elements about which public and private redevelopment is proceeding according to a gradually evolving urban design plan whose main outlines appear to be agreed upon (Figs. 6a, 6b).

Through the decades prior to 1960, Caracas found it difficult to locate the great amount of diversified industry which sought close labor supplies and consumers; land parcels were limited and access difficult. As a result residential subdivisions were rapidly converted in the eastern area in Catia and toward Antimano. Due to limited zoning controls, scattered industries of many types were allowed. However, it is now generally recognized and particularly by industry that the national capital is inappropriate for industrial activity, and the marked trend is toward the outlying valleys beyond the inner metropolitan area. In addition, other urban centers with far greater advantages for industry, notably Valencia and Maracay, are becoming focal points in a trend toward a rational distribution of industry throughout the rapidly maturing urbanization system of Venezuela.

From the center of the capital, some five major transportation routes cut into the virtually unbuildable and extremely rugged mountains to the south, east

FIG. 5A Typical mixed land use.

and west. These go to Los Teques and the west, to the Tuy Valley with its established urban centers at Charallave, Ocumare del Tuy and Santa Teresa to the south, and to the smaller Guareña-Guatire Valley to the east. These points are all within twenty-five to forty-five minutes' travel on highways allowing maximum speed—which will, in the future, serve permanently as an outer ring of self-contained communities to absorb the growth yet to come. At Ocumare del Tuy and in the Guareña-Guatire Valley, a new town is being planned on a very large scale for this purpose. These areas, plus the *Litorral* (coast) to the north, combine to form the Greater Caracas Metropolitan Area and the basis for the planning of the recently formed Capital Region, discussed below.

FIG. 5B *Ranchos* above on the hillside.

CRITICAL URBAN ISSUES OF METROPOLITAN CARACAS

The Physical Plant and Social and Economic Problems

Metropolitan Caracas in a process of transformation for less than a generation is still maturing; its ultimate physical form cannot be forecast. Caracas appears to have a life of its own, confined only by the basic land form it occupies and stimulated by the economic and social pressures of the moment. How effectively has the physical form served to meet these pressures and satisfy the social aspirations of the residents?

FIG. 6A Former situation at the city center. *Tomás José Sanabria*

On the one hand, urban dwellers and planners alike, involved in these changes, praise the efforts that have brought about the building of a capital that is unique in its man-made chaotic character. On the other hand, they look with alarm at the social deprivation that exists side by side with economic well-being and wonder where Caracas truly stands in terms of its history, national goals and the foreshadowing images of future growth.

Caracas is a new Latin American capital—almost completely new—though not in the same sense as Brasilia. Yet, fruitful comparisons can be made with relation to the physical-social purposes of the planning of a national capital. The two capitals are vastly different in that the highly flexible framework of Caracas has permitted far greater individual and group initiative in making physical development decisions. This has brought about a type of urban design which richly expresses a wide variety of mutations at all social levels, albeit at certain social and economic costs. In contrast with Brasilia's predetermined form, the relatively unplanned growth of Caracas has served as a flexible mechanism for maximizing and releasing the forces of social change. Yet, there have been these costs, and many issues underlying physical development still await attention.

FIG. 6B Plan for redevelopment. *Tomás José Sanabria*

Social Issues of Caracas

In spite of the physical rebuilding of Caracas, visible to all and fascinating in its fluidity, the overriding theme has been social change. The critical issue is the unbalanced nature of this change, affecting in a highly beneficial way one sector of the population, leaving the remainder with aspirations unsatisfied. These goals lie in the components of the social system: education, health, public and family welfare, recreation and community organization.

Education, so basic to social change, has become an accumulated problem of major proportions in Caracas. From 1936 to 1954, the school population increased from 32,000 to 102,000, yet during that time there were 21,000 children, or 30 per cent, of the primary school age population for whom there were no facilities. By 1966, the same proportion of deficit persisted: The number of children registered in schools was 29 per cent less than the total facilities available for the age group or a shortage of 100,000 places, three times that of the earlier period. Even by 1970, over half of those attending school did so on double shift, a questionable device. This situation is especially critical in view of the low housing standards and the common need for both parents to be away from home at work during the day.[9] Even smaller ratios of teen-agers attend high school; yet the aspirations for education are high, as evidenced by the great pressures and high attendance at the numerous universities that have developed during the past decades.

Health is a critical problem in Caracas, not because of a lack of medical competence, but rather due to the prevalence of extremely low standards of housing and related environmental conditions. Intestinal diseases are common, produced by the insanitary environment of the ranchos. These conditions have a direct effect on the occupants, who represent an estimated third of the population, and indirectly on all of the residents of Caracas. The rancho settlements and general population growth have placed a severe strain on sewer and water systems, in spite of major investments in new facilities. Similarly, great advances have been made in the provision of hospital care and medical services; yet there remains a massive shortage of hospital facilities of all types, especially smaller clinics immediately accessible to the rancho population. This shortage is aggravated by the underlying social conditions that have both environmental and behavioral causes growing out of the marginal way of life of this third of the population.

Among this marginal population, crime and delinquency are factors of social importance that may be considered endemic to a situation where marked contrasts in income, living levels and culture stand side by side. In a sense, this phenomenon is one of social classes warring upon one another with material advantage the primary object.

The marginal social condition of the enormous lower income segment of the population of Caracas is further evidenced by extreme instability in family life. Unstructured household units lacking a consistent male head of the family are common, and women are called upon to fill the roles of family head, breadwinner and mother. Indeed, in view of these conditions, it is to the credit of the members of this deprived population, and further evidence of their deep-seated aspirations for betterment, that they maintain the minimum level they do. While an increasing number of studies[10] are being given to the rancho communities of this new metropolis, it remains a question whether it is the lack of adequate family structure and stability that primarily produces the antisocial environment, or whether the conditions of the environment tend to propagate social instability.

Recreation habits and requirements have undergone a sharp change in the shift from the enclosed colonial house to the more open single-family home in the *urbanizaciones* of the mid-century and now to apartment-house living with its demand for more organized use of the limited leisure time available and the greater competition for outdoor space. In one way or another this situation affects all age groups. The quiet stroll around the plaza in earlier times and even the ready access to the *Parque Infantil* (Children's Park) or the Country Club in more recent times are all patterns of the past that will have to be replaced by more structured and intensive forms of recreation. Little is known, as yet, as to what forms this might be in the changing cultural situation of Caracas, or how the patterns of use of leisure time should be directed to best serve the interests of social change among the widely diverse elements of that society. The field of socially oriented recreation is untouched in Caracas.

Perhaps the component most basic to social change is community structure. How is the resident of Caracas organized to deal collectively with his own problems of social change and a changing environment? At present most of the marginal or lower class community is quite inadequately structured objectively to participate in this process of change. Even the middle class lacks a group voice in development problems. A major shortcoming in the leadership of the urban development fields in Caracas has been the failure to draw upon the potentially great social advantages of the decision-making process. In spite of the obvious concern for urban betterment on the part of all levels of the community during the past decades, the lines of communication have been poor or almost nonexistent among the many geographic sectors, the various social levels and the often aloof officialdom responsible for guiding growth. This is a characteristic attitude brought on by the deep-seated, elite cultural attitudes of Latin America which, to be realistic, appear to be giving way under the pressure of the times. These need to be erased, if the urban planning field is to serve the social purpose that its effective application requires.

Economic Issues of Caracas

The problems of Caracas appear on the surface to be no more than social ones, judging from the fame of Venezuela's oil royalties, the general image of affluence attached to Caracas and the statistical fact that this country had, prior to the steep rise in oil income, the highest per capita income—about $850—of any Latin American country. This is far from the case; social problems are concentrated in the capital because of the host of economic problems and the economic opportunities that the capital symbolizes. The critical problem in Caracas is—unlike other capitals—not how to create economic underpinnings for national development, but rather how to channel the economic vitality that has been created into the building of a stable nation that is equitable in the social and economic sense. In examining economic issues critical to Caracas, both the national and the local purposes need to be considered.

At the national level it was estimated in 1961 that 28 per cent of the gross national product and 34 per cent of the national income had its origin in the capital. At that time Caracas held 27 per cent of the economically active population of the country and 26 per cent of the unemployed. In 1961, 71 per cent of this employment was in the form of commerce, transport and services with 26 per cent in manufacturing. The latter sector, once considerably higher, then consisted of largely light industry and artisan activities. While more reduced by 1970, it tends to hold itself at the same level due to the attraction of the ready consumers market in the capital.[11] Thus, the high percentage of service activities reflects the strong leadership role in public and private affairs pertinent to a capital. Indeed, a huge public bureaucracy has created the large mass of middle-class population that both contributes to the consumer economy and makes demands for public services. However, the lower figure indicates that the economy of metropolitan Caracas does not depend, as in Brasilia, entirely upon employment by government and major business headquarters.

The question is: How does one more clearly identify the nature of this economic concentration appropriate to the capital with relation to a more balanced distribution nationwide? Such balance might in turn alleviate the social pressures on the capital and give the various regions a fuller share of the economic entrepreneurship that Caracas has enjoyed. At the same time, how can the existing economic needs of the present population be met without continuing the cycle of in-migration to the supposed benefits of the capital?

This economic need in the capital is identified by a disproportionately high percentage of families in the lowest income levels and much smaller proportions in the middle and upper income ranges. For example, recent estimates of income distribution for Caracas show that 41 per cent of the population had monthly incomes of less than Bs. 500 (about $100 U.S.); 39 per cent had between Bs. 500 and Bs. 1,000; 10 per cent, Bs. 1,500; and 10 per cent, over Bs. 1,500. Thus, 80 per cent of the population of Caracas receives amounts less than Bs. 1,000 per month, a sum quite inadequate with which to maintain a level of living commensurate with any aspirations for social mobility. Compared with the nation as a whole, we find a similar ratio, an estimated 73.7 per cent.[12]

While there are indications that a gradual redistribution of income levels is taking place, the gap is still enormous. In that gap stands a good third or half of the population who are not yet integrated into the economy of Caracas, either as producers of services and goods or as consumers. Indeed, the reality is that a good segment of this marginal population may have no permanent role in the capital.

While accurate figures are not available, it is obvious that unemployment and underemployment is a critical problem which is hidden in the marginal occupations of great variety and inventiveness that prevail in the capital. These represent a level of persistent though not always rewarding entrepreneurship, worthy of exploitation and technical assistance. Furthermore, economic pressures and the limited period of schooling of those most in need of income require the employment of younger persons normally not part of the labor force. As much as 54.3 per cent of the males in the age group of fifteen to nineteen years were part of the economically active group in 1961 in Caracas. While this figure is high from a social point of view, it is even higher—62.1 per cent—for the country as a whole. Even in the age group ten to fourteen years, 4.1 per cent of the males were employed in Caracas, although the national figure was as high as 16.2 per cent.[13]

Little attention has been given in the past planning of Caracas to these aspects of urban micro- or self-help economics and their relation to land development policies and social betterment. However, a realization of these implications of physical planning is appearing in current work. It may well be that the broader regional basis for planning will provide a more complete framework for developing a balanced economic approach.

Physical Problems of Urban Development

We have attempted to clarify the development issues confronting Caracas that can be identified essentially in social and economic terms, in order to lay the basis for the main theme of this chapter: Urban physical planning is not an end in itself, but rather a means to maximize the achievement of nonphysical goals. These can be identified in social or economic terms and through nonphysical means, ultimately changing behavioral characteristics. Education can be improved by revising teaching curricula and health by introducing preventive medical practices, for example. However, each program requires a physical location and facility for the activity, the selection and design of which can work for or against maximizing the total solution.

Metropolitan Caracas is in the midst of massive physical change, and enormous investments of both public and private funds are being made in urban physical equipment. Therefore, it is critical to be able to sort out which problems are in the physical-functional realm, which in the social-economic, and how their interdependence can be used effectively. The urban planning process should do more than solve technical problems; it should also work toward systematically identifying and satisfying social aspirations. When urban problems are identified only in physical terms as they have been in Caracas with respect to certain phases of urban planning such as housing, the solutions are superficial and the planning effort is lost.

In this light, the three most urgent physical development problems of Caracas are: the massive problem of shelter for the vast marginal population; the provision of community services of social interest for residents in almost all categories; and the development of a transportation network that will facilitate access to all activity areas of the metropolis.

The squatter settlement problem of Caracas is probably the greatest of any Latin American capital, affecting an approximately one third of the population. It has been pointed out[14] that ". . . two different cities exist within the metropolitan area: on the one hand, the capital of the Republic with all the characteristics of a modern urban center in full process of growth and transformation, and on the other, the marginal city occupied by the *rancho* districts."

Caracas more than doubled its supply of dwellings in ten years, increasing from 120,000 in 1950 to 268,000 in 1961. In that year, 54,200, or 21 per cent, were ranchos with an average occupancy of five persons; estimates for 1965 indicated that the number had risen to 85,000. In 1961, some 74 per cent of all dwellings in Caracas were supplied with water; yet only 3.4 per cent of the ranchos were so supplied, and in addition, 17.1 per cent depended on public tanks and water trucks. About 79 per cent of the dwellings in Caracas had indoor toilets, yet 54.2 per cent of the ranchos used outdoor latrines.[15] While these conditions have improved considerably since that time, they are indicative of the basic nature of the problems that are produced by squatter settlements on a large scale in the midst of a modernizing metropolis.

In spite of the persistence of these conditions, ranchos and other forms of substandard housing continue to be a seemingly acceptable way of life for possibly a half million people in the metropolitan area, and year by year these communities become more permanent as dwellings are improved in a primitive way and basic utilities are made available. This is to a great extent due to the remarkable determination of the rancho dweller to involve his own efforts in seeking betterment, as well as to pressure, collectively, for the provision of services and community improvements from the official agencies. Indeed, his individual self-reliance has been forged into collective organization, a resource that has been tapped to a considerable extent by the community development movement of the government; more likely than not, he will shun the institutionalized public housing in favor of this position of independence.

Accumulatively, from one rancho dwelling to another and from one hillside community of ranchos to another, this spontaneous solution to the housing problem has taken over an estimated one fourth of the urbanized area of Caracas. The conversion of these areas into socially vital communities and the integration of the purposes they serve into the urban structure of Caracas is an issue of urgency, yet one for which present policies have not yet succeeded in finding a solution. Urgent as this immediate and collective problem of shelter may be, it takes second priority to the question of social services so profoundly lacking for the occupants of the ranchos. A few examples might suffice to indicate the enormity of the problem of supplying adequate physical facilities in light of present deficits, the oncoming population increases and the ever-rising social aspirations of the people.

About 40 per cent of the primary schools are at present in converted dwellings or other buildings not originally designed as schools, and 55 per cent of all schools are on double shift, most of them public. By 1990, the school population will triple, reaching more than 1,000,000 for whom 816,000 places will have to be added to the present supply of 235,000. This estimate is based on an anticipated standard of full attendance by that year, a complex goal to achieve in itself.[16]

In a similar way, the full range of physical facilities needed by each component of the social system could be reviewed in terms of present deficits and future needs, with respect to amounts to be supplied, locations selected for maximum effectiveness and resources for both construction and management. These would include hospitals, clinics, recreation areas of many kinds, public markets, police stations, fire stations, and community centers. It is the sensitive provision of these services that could give community structure to the Caracas metropolitan area of the future and build the basis for a kind of modernization that will go deeper than the present emphasis on mere physical improvement.

Finally, transportation stands forth as a facility of greater immediate urgency than the other two for it underlies the effectiveness of both the social and economic activity systems of the whole metropolitan area. When the capital was poised on the brink of tremendous expansion, its transportation system was of a most primitive nature. Yet, within little more than a decade, an almost complete conversion to the automobile age was made as a result of the sudden arrival of purchasing power, foreign automobiles (in due time locally assembled) and the urgent demand for urban circulation.

While in 1936[17] there were 9,000 vehicles, by 1948 there were 37,000. The archaic, though picturesque streetcar system had been replaced by 533 buses and 6,000 taxis called *libres*. These had to accommodate themselves to the still narrow colonial streets. By 1955, 100,000 vehicles were in operation in Caracas and by 1967, an estimated 200,000, a ratio of about one car per nine persons. It is further estimated that 400,000 to 600,000 vehicles will be needed by 1990 to meet expected population growth.

During the 1950s, the circulation system of Caracas was in a continual state of construction and reconstruction of major thoroughfares, autopistas, overpasses and underpasses. The monumental traffic circle at the Plaza Venezuela, built in the early 1950s at the doorstep of the new districts to the east, with its neoclassic, muscular sculpture and serene fountains, had to give way to an elaborate underpass, as uncontrolled thirty-story skyscrapers rose nearby. Close to the university entrance, the traffic interchange for the new autopista of the mid-1950s had to be replaced with another, so involved in its tentacle-like turning movements that it came to be known as *El Pulpo* (the Octopus). By the early 1960s, what is the most complex multilevel traffic interchange anywhere in Latin America, even rivaling those of Los Angeles, was built on the completion of the Catia-El Paraiso tunnel, only to be immediately caricatured by the *Caraqueños* as *La Araña* (the Spider).

In spite of this truly remarkable series of modernization projects, the transportation situation appears to grow worse each year. It has been estimated that 65 per cent of all passenger transportation is by private automobile, the almost exclusive travel media of the upper middle and upper income groups. Middle-income groups rely heavily on *carros por puersto* (jitneys) that most enterprisingly serve all parts of the city with some sixty established lines, and adapted readily to new outlying developments as soon as they appear. The lower-income groups use the not-too-reliable and greatly overburdened seventy bus lines that impatiently make their way through the massive traffic jams that have become a way of life and a major topic of conversation in Caracas.

The almost completely decentralized, yet relatively compact structure of Metropolitan Caracas, has brought about patterns of movement, unique among cities generally and in Latin America especially. It is normal elsewhere that peak hours are clearly distinguished by considerably increased traffic flow at certain times of the day; yet in Caracas, the fluctuation at what should normally be peak hours is relatively small.[18]

It is obvious that a rapid transit system is not only urgently needed to break the hold of *los pulpos* and *las arañas* brought by motorization, but would have great promise in effectively competing with such travel habits. The marked lineal structure of the metropolitan area, dictated by topography and limited building space that for so many years has been an obstacle to efficient spatial organization and communication, is a decided advantage for mass rapid transit system design and operation. Assuming an attractive, economic and time-saving system will be built, a much wider range of passengers could be attracted than do the present mass transportation media. An integrated pattern of transportation could have significant social implications. A rapid transit system can provide low-income families, many of whom still live a somewhat rural life style in the midst of an urban environment, with improved access to jobs, to education and health facilities. These can contribute in more basic ways to their social betterment than the mere provision of shelter which has been the predominant public policy in Caracas for several decades.

It is fortunate the Caraqueños have taken the first step toward the construction of a transit system that would ultimately serve the entire metropolitan area. In 1964, the Oficina Ministerial de Transporte (OMT) was established under the Ministry of Public Works for the purpose of studying the feasibility of and developing plans for a rapid transit system. By 1970, these plans were well advanced on a system of thirty miles in length with a total of forty-eight stations in locations that will serve to reinforce the present lineal pattern of the city as well as to ultimately serve some outlying districts. The main trunkline—from Pro Patria in the west to Petare in the east—had a tentative completion date of 1974 and would make the trip between those two points in a half-hour; the present bus system requires one hour or more.

THE URBAN PLANNING PROCESS IN CARACAS

The National Government and Urban Planning

To understand the organizational framework for urban planning in Caracas it is essential to review the three major phases in the evolution of this field in Venezuela: the period from the early forties when reorganization after the dictatorship of Gómez became fully effective, the period of the 1950s, and the years after the fall of Pérez Jiménez from 1958 to the present.

In the mid-1940s, a renaissance in thinking took place among the younger men especially those in the fields of architecture and engineering who were identified with the new government. Some of these men had endured years of repression and were eager to demonstrate their unused capacities; some had studied abroad and others in the new professional schools that had been recently established in the university. They relished the opportunity to make a civic contribution to national development. Social and economic reform was a major concern, particularly since greatly increased royalties on oil concessions held by foreign companies brought forth images of unlimited design projects and building programs. With a highly limited private building industry at that time and with income essentially flowing to public sectors of the economy rather than into private enterprise, it was logical that the focal point of investment should be in public works.

These were originally intended to stimulate agricultural and industrial development by providing a national system of highways, airports, shipping terminals and other infrastructures serving the various regions of the country. During this period, basic legislation for urban planning was in an elementary form and systematic methods of budget co-ordination to provide an orderly framework for development programs were only beginning. Work was centered in the ministries of Public Works, Agriculture and Development and in the Banco Obrero, the national housing agency. Unfortunately, during the late 1940s, with the shift to the Pérez Jiménez dictatorship which lasted until 1957, a more arbitrary, laissez-faire policy broke these earlier beginnings of rational planning. A great amount of indiscriminate energy was unleashed. Major programs of public works centered on Caracas, with a compulsive motivation to make visible to a maximum number of Venezuelans the benefits of that particular regime. A National Urban Planning Commission (Comisión Nacional de Urbanismo—CNU) had been established in 1945 in the Ministry of Public Works of the earlier government. Although it was intended to distribute planning efforts throughout the country at various levels, its loosely stated authorization provided opportunities in the early 1950s for politically oriented intervention in programming. For example, although the CNU had been given the duty to prepare development plans for all of the cities in the country for the purpose of guiding the location of new highways, airports and public buildings, much of the focus was toward immediate, detailed projects, often lacking realistic consideration for ultimate urban spatial patterns.

During the early 1950s, the large professional staff located on the two top floors of the Torre Sur of the recently finished Centro Bolívar took on the planning of the fifteen major cities. However, the magnitude of the problem of Caracas itself, visible from the panoramic windows of the work space, brought great attention to the capital. Steps taken in the early 1950s to provide local planning offices for the several jurisdictions in Caracas were frustrated by the awkward division of the capital—one which to this day has not yet been corrected—into two major administrative units, the Federal District and a group of municipalities, politically linked to the state of Miranda. This was further complicated by the fact that most of the decentralization by private builders was taking place in the adjacent state where local authorities were unlikely to abide by restrictions established by the central government. However, this experience was valuable for it led to renewed and deep-seated concern for urban planning related to broad regional planning and to social and economic purposes that were the major theme of the third major period since 1958.

Thus, with the reorganization of the late 1950s, a second period of evolution came with greater focus on economic and social planning, interagency co-ordination and, to a degree, decentralization of decision making. A National Co-ordinating and Planning Board, known as CORDIPLAN, was created; included in the legislation was the authority to establish a properly constructed base for urban planning throughout the country, and especially to meet the needs of the capital. The work of this agency throughout the 1960s has been of greatest importance in improving the decision-making process with relation to development. However, for whatever classic reasons may be assumed, the urban planning function remained in the Ministry of Public Works and the CNU was replaced with the National Office of Urban Planning, with increased facilities and even more direct supervision of the Ministry itself.

With the planning agency serving in an executive role, there has been, during this past decade, little opportunity to allow for the necessary participation of each of the municipalities themselves in the planning process. An important exception is the case of Caracas, one of the only five cities in the country in which local planning offices had been established by 1972. The others are the Ciudad Guayana, the new city near the mouth of the Orinoco, Barquisimeto, Maracay and Valencia. The latter was created by pressure from the municipality which in 1966 rejected the Ministry's plan after an evaluation financed with municipal funds. Other important cities such as Maracaibo and San Cristóbal have vigorously sought their right of involvement in the planning of the future of their communities, even to the point of resisting nationally prepared planning programs. In general, it would appear that at the national level Venezuela is due for a new period in which the urban planning process will be completely restructured to reflect realistically the vitality of urban growth when linked with local participation in decision making.

Local and Government Responsibilities

At the present time, responsibility for over-all planning for the Caracas Metropolitan Area is lodged in the municipal office of Urban Planning of the Federal District (OMPU), created in 1960 to replace a small planning office that had been formed in the municipal Department of Public Works in the 1950s. OMPU, directly under the Municipal Council of the Federal District, is charged with the full range of planning tasks, basic research, long-range planning, certain phases of implementation, the details of zoning and similar administrative matters. While officially the agency's work is restricted to the Federal District, in practice it has functioned since about 1965 as a metropolitan agency, covering both the inner urbanized area in and contiguous to the valley of Caracas and the outer region, including the more distant valleys.

While this metropolitan area functions as a total physical entity, it falls into many parts for administrative purposes. The inner urban area itself divides into two distinct districts: the Federal District and the District of Sucre of the state of Miranda, whose boundary cuts between the newer eastern area and the older western portions of the valley. The Federal District also has its Office of Urban Planning, although it operates on a much more modest scale than OMPU, whose amply budgeted program and large staff reflect its informally assigned responsibilities of metropolitan and national significance.

Moreover, the number of ministries and semipublic authorities at the national level charged with development planning of many types within both the Federal District and the Greater Metropolitan Area form a complex web. These include —to name some of the principal ones—the Ministry of Public Works, responsible for the massive highway projects; the special office set up by the Ministry to plan the rapid transit system; the Banco Obrero, representing the greatest investor in public building in the area; an agency of special social interest, the redevelopment corporation of the Centro Bolívar, whose operation covers a critical portion of the downtown area; and, finally, the National Institute for Sanitation (INOS), responsible for water supply and sewerage.

Furthermore, in 1969, an official decree established for the first time in Venezuela a pattern of regions for the country as a whole, to serve as a basis for the partial decentralization of the work of CORDIPLAN. This incorporated the previously established regions, constituted as development authorities in four areas, including the Guayana and Andes regions. A farsighted decision was made to create, as one of these, a Capital Region, delineated to comprise the urbanized centers and all of the immediate area of influence of Caracas (see Fig. 1). This newly formed planning unit was expected to have its own planning office and, when staffed and budgeted, serve as a greater metropolitan regional planning office, closely related to national authority, yet functioning as a co-ordinating element with OMPU and other local planning bodies.

During these years of growth of the capital that we have reviewed, the extensive amount of effort that has gone into urban planning by these various agencies has been without the institutional mechanism envisioned in the mid-forties that would clarify the roles of agencies at national, regional and local levels and relate them to the increasingly dynamic role of private capital. This most recent step in forming a Capital Region provides a new and intermediate level for planning that could serve to co-ordinate these various efforts and at the same time focus on the full scale of the Greater Metropolitan Area. It is this scale that promises to be the target for the growth to come during the next several decades. If this regional approach is carried out effectively, the method might well serve as a model for developing urban planning procedures needed in other metropolitan capitals in Latin America.

Until the urban planning process for the capital has been fully institutionalized, viable guidance cannot be given to urban growth. Indeed, in order to accomplish this, similar reforms in the urban planning system in Venezuela as a whole need to be made. Since the mid-forties, when the national level of government was given the authority to establish standards and procedures for physical planning, this duality of effort has persisted with no equable distribution of responsibility between national, regional and local levels.

Fresh study was given to this problem in the late 1960s, and a revised structure was set up to overcome some of these deficiencies. Accordingly, at the national level, an urban and regional planning body lodged in CORDIPLAN and directly related to the office of the President was designed to collaborate with a primarily executive authority in the Ministry of Public Works. CORDIPLAN thus proposed: "the broad guidelines for physical and spatial planning at the national scale. . . . to coordinate planning to be done at the regional and local scales . . ."[19]

At the regional scale, the regionalization of the country that took place early in 1969 would provide the framework for the planning function through subcentral CORDIPLAN offices, each focusing on development of the regions, including the new Capital Region. At this regional scale, the research and training function is provided by the Center for Development Studies (CENDES), established within the framework of the university. Its work, since its creation in 1960, has focused on the development of techniques for guiding regional growth within a national urbanization framework.

At the urban scale, municipalities, at least the major ones, would have their own planning offices fortified by technical assistance from the national level. An important agency in advancing the local planning and urban development function is the Foundation for Community and Municipal Development (FUNDACOMUN), established in the early 1960s to strengthen the municipality as a development resource throughout Venezuela. Urban planning is a critical element in its work and the agency has lent effective support to increasing the number of local planning offices. Formed only as recently as 1968, the Instituto de Urbanismo (IU), like CENDES also a part of the university, is developing a new teaching and research program focusing on the need for both methods and trained personnel at the municipal and local urban level using only Venezuelan resources.

Present Development Policies and Programs

In general, planning as practiced in Latin America does not provide for a clear distinction between what are general development goals and policies and what are the implementing measures to be used in objectively seeking their achievement. While the urban planners of Caracas are moving in this direction with increasing conviction as they acquire more knowledge of planning method, the process of *ad hoc* decision making by public and private bodies moves along at a much faster rate than does the formation of rational planning systems. Opportunities to evaluate planning experience have been hampered by a lack of continuity over the past two decades, a failure that present programs are attempting to correct.

The two most serious efforts at establishing a comprehensive development policy for Caracas occurred during the period of 1951 under the CNU, and at the present time in OMPU. With a population of seven hundred thousand in the early 1950s and over two million today, it is obvious that the city has outgrown the earlier stage of planning, making the work of today almost a fresh start.

Toward this end, a highly competent study of the basic condition in the metropolitan area was completed in 1968, entitled *Caracas 1990, Plan de Desarrollo Urbano, Primera Etapa del Estudio.*[20] Essentially, it is organized as a study of the supply and demand for urban development space and facilities for the entire range of activities. These include residential, educational, welfare, recreational open space, commerce and storage, manufacturing, public and private offices, police, fire protection and cemeteries; the major issue of transportation and such miscellaneous activities as religious, cultural and military.

These are studied against the underlying characteristics of population make-up, the economy and the physical setting. A general set of alternative policies was presented for discussion prior to a second stage, begun in 1970, which will include the setting of specific social-economic goals and the detailing of a selected alternative. Most importantly, this stage included the designing of the institutional processes to implement the plan in recognition of the necessity for continuity in the urban planning process, so conspicuously lacking in the past.

The study proposes a concept for constant review of the development process as a basis for later evaluation of an operational program specifying interagency relationships. The process would make use of three time scales: twenty years, six years and one year. The first twenty-year target is the present work looking to 1990. Within this long-range period goals and directives for the operational periods of six years and of one year are set up. This concept, if adopted and detailed, would serve to fill a virtual void by providing continuity among the operational agencies and their respective staffs, in spite of political changes.

A significant innovation of the study is the recognition of the reality of metropolitan growth by shifting to a new and larger geographic frame of reference than the 1951 plan. Thus, the study has been carried out at two spatial scales: one, the Metropolitan Region, corresponding to the area including the outlying valleys described earlier and roughly covering the same territory as the recently decreed Capital Region. The spatial organization of this total area will be structured around the second smaller geographic scale, the principal focal point of the region, the Urban Area of Caracas.

The urban planners responsible for the official study, *Caracas 1990,* consider that the possibility of controlling growth at these two scales will depend on two kinds of measures: the general application of policies of regional development in Venezuela and the building of the new city in the Tuy Valley. It is estimated that if the broad national policy of regional planning is adopted as a single measure, migration into the Metropolitan Region and the Urban Area of Caracas would be reduced from the present 6 per cent to 3.9 per cent by 1990 and the population of the Urban Area of Caracas could be held to 4,500,000. If development policies were limited only to the building of the new city, migration into the Metropolitan Region would increase, but would decrease within the Urban Area to 4.4 per cent annually; the 1990 population would then be 5,000,000.

The significance of these two approaches can be evaluated when compared with the third possible position: that is, to allow present tendencies to continue. According to this alternative in the study, Caracas would reduce its immigration rate only slightly, that is, to 4.7 per cent, resulting in a 1990 population of 5,450,000. If this straight-line projection were to be the case, the consequences would be even more difficult for the institutional structure to handle, requiring a far more comprehensive type of urban planning than in the past.

For example, the study estimates that urban facilities would need to be provided for 3,500,000 persons during the next twenty years. Jobs would have to be created for 1,500,000 additional members of the labor force. Assuming the continuation of present trends toward a reduction in number of persons per dwelling of 4.9 in 1961 to 4.2 in 1990, a total of 818,000 dwellings would be needed to be built in the next two decades, not taking into account the massive number of substandard dwellings now being used and that will need to be replaced. Assuming—in the interests of maximum reality—that the present trend in rancho construction would continue, the urban planners of OMPU estimate that 30 per cent of these dwellings would be ranchos. Services would be needed on an enormous scale; assuming 100 per cent primary school attendance—the only reasonable aspiration—816,000 classroom places would have to be added to the present 235,000. The urbanized area of Caracas would triple, from 11,500 hectares to 32,000, including even more intensive use of the hilly terrain, with all the implications of increased costs of construction and services.

During the year 1970, this was the complex and alarming picture presented to the officialdom of Caracas by the municipal Office of Urban Planning. There is no question but that this has been an effective strategy for stimulating debate and new and significant thought with regard to the consequences of any of the three alternatives. Fortunately, the emphasis has been placed, not on the choice among patterns of spatial relationships, but rather on the underlying forces affecting the form of urban growth. The question is, however, whether or not the urban planners of Caracas will be able to bring about the institutional structure and the planning processes that will make these choices a reality and not merely paper decisions.

AN APPROACH TO PLANNING FOR THE CARACAS METROPOLITAN AREA

The Choice of an Approach

The dilemma before the urban planners of Caracas, over the past several decades, has been the question of a conceptual approach on which to base the institutional processes. A latter-day Beaux Arts movement inspired the late 1930s, and a social orientation, the mid-1940s, only to give way in the early 1950s to a functional approach drawing on North American techniques. National planning with special attention to economic questions became the theme of the latter part of that decade, accompanied with a renewed social ingredient added to housing activities. The 1960s saw the first experience with comprehensive regional planning in the work of the Guayana area with inputs from recent North American thinking.† Present work in Caracas tends to a basic analytical emphasis, and

† Prominent in this was the Harvard-MIT Joint Center for Urban Studies advisory team. (Editor.)

only most hesitatingly is beginning to move in the direction of the creative policy making that Caracas needs.

The urban planners of Caracas, of course, have inherited a little of all of these schools of thought and have made their own contributions as well. Yet, these have not been synthesized into a clear concept to provide an effective basis for coordinating the individual technical work that has been undertaken in the various agencies. In developing such a concept, there are those who contend that this technical work should be applied only to the individual elements of the urban area, and not to the system as a whole, allowing growth forces to have relatively free sway and an organic form to come about. However, this is what has produced the Caracas of today, replete with fine, though unrelated, accomplishments and problems that grow out of discontinuity among these elements.

There are others who believe that until the entire social and economic system within which Caracas operates is brought within a more rational and comprehensive decision-making order no meaningful urban planning can be done. It is questionable, however, that the scale of the task of restructuring the institutional frameworks of an habitually free-wheeling enterprise like Venezuela's capital would allow the institutional upheaval needed.

The choice between these two extremes is limited to one which works with maximum clarity and social purpose within present frameworks. The goal is a pragmatic one—truly to influence the lives of the population through the urban planning field here and now. With the firm application of an action and process-oriented approach, realistically looking toward the evolutionary changes in such structures, it should be possible to guide to a maximum degree possible the dynamics of development at work in Caracas. An approach along these lines also holds the potential for speeding evolutionary change in Latin America.

Land, Community Patterns and Integration

As yet little study has been given to the environmental changes that have taken place with the urbanization of the valley of Caracas. However, there is evidence of pollution of the waterways, erosion of the hillsides, loss of natural vegetation, increase of temperature and the beginnings of smog. Systematic study of the intrinsic geographic character of the natural landscape into which Caracas has been built, taking into account some measurement of the impact of development on ecological relationships, should offer a rational basis for determining more precisely what policies should prevail in future development.

The Caraqueños have always had a strong sense of identity with their landscape. The move to the hills, both on the part of those who can afford the fantastic dwelling sites in *urbanizaciones* overlooking the valleys, and on the part of the rancho family, reflects this attraction. By working with the residents of the various physical areas into which Caracas readily breaks down, this sense of identity can be enhanced through making decisions that sensitively reflect their values. This would relate to location and design of circulation routes, community focal points and residential character, for example. A more human scale for Caracas can be emphasized to offset the increasingly massive and impersonal scale of such public projects as the *superbloques* and some of the new private apartment towers, to name but two examples.

Running through Latin American culture is a marked sense of identity with the land, especially urban land, as evidenced by the *plaza* and the *calle* (local street) as focal points of urban life. The difficulty in attempting to dislodge the rancho dweller from land he has invaded is a contemporary example, highly pertinent to Caracas. Although the sites selected in this spontaneous process may not be entirely desirable in planning terms, there are social advantages in accepting the more appropriately located of these areas in the interest of deepening this sense of identity and building toward greater community structure and stability. The often irrational mixture of urban land types in Caracas as opposed to the overly zoned land uses of U.S. cities—once accepted as a reality—may in the long run have desirable effect on the underlying processes of social mobility that permeate the transformation of this capital.

Urban Planning as an Agent of Social Change

In making the choice of an approach to urban planning, the planners of Caracas would want to accept a conceptual definition of urban planning that would be a socially dynamic force in advancing and guiding the physical framework of the capital. Indeed, it may be that—in view of the compelling transformation taking place in all Latin American capitals—only such a definition can lead to the survival of the field, let alone its meaningful evolution. In this sense, the limits of physical planning as presently practiced can be pushed considerably beyond those that appear to confine its scope. Goals for the future development of Caracas should be taken to be nonphysical—that is, in the social and economic realm—while physical planning and related institutional programming are both no more than means to achieve goals. Thus, literacy is a goal, while the favorable location and timing of school buildings and grounds with relation to other services are physical means; improved health is a social goal, while hospitals and clinics contribute to achieving that goal. The urban planner can maximize and facilitate their use, in his role as co-ordinator of both the spatial location and the timing of a host of needed facilities at the metropolitan, municipal, community or *barrio* (neighborhood) level.

Such goals need to be systematically formulated to reflect the wide range of purposes and diverse sets of values of a metropolis in fluid transformation like Caracas; thus far these kinds of underlying goals are not specifically set forth in the urban planning process there. Nor has this been done in Latin America generally, where—with the notable exception of Chile—the emphasis has been technical and physical. The urban planners of Latin America will be working in the direction of changes now under way if they turn from middle- and upper-class values and reflect all segments of the community in formulating the broad end purposes of urban planning. These goals will need to be spelled out comprehensively with relation to all of the deeply interrelated components of the social, political and economic systems, even if the present institutional framework only permits urban planning, decision making essentially in the physical realm. From this position the Latin American urban planner can still wield major influence with those agencies who are responsible for making social policy and can offer them as well a more comprehensive and objective framework within which to relate both physical planning and the management of services.

An overlooked concern in urban planning in Latin America is projecting into the future the quality of urban life, as against the sheer numbers of people to be dealt with. The patterns and levels of social development of today are not those of Caracas twenty years ago, and further changes are now taking place. When policies for the future are being set in physical form, it is necessary to project what these changes in life styles are likely to be in the light of the decisions made now.

In view of the unusual resources available, the planners of Caracas especially will have to ask: To what extent will the urban planning process be able to advance these changes? The children in the statistical columns of present population studies of Caracas are the persons who will be the young adults of the 1980s and 1990s. Their aspirations and capacities are going to be quite different from those of their parents who were children in the Venezuela of the 1930s and 1940s. Any straight-line projection—frequently common practice in statistically oriented Latin American urban planning—will unconsciously do no more than project into the future the problems of today, rather than actively solve them. Urban Latin America is confronted at present with the accumulative results of this approach over the past decades.

Problem Solving as a Basis for Urban Planning in Caracas

The urgency of the urban situation in Caracas, and in Latin America in general, requires that the degree to which planning is comprehensive must be compatible with real issues and cannot be determined on the basis of what is theoretically more rational in concept or method. To assure this compatibility, urban planning for a rapidly changing city like Caracas should be based on commitments to solve identified problems as a basis for sustained action, and secondly on the degree of comprehensiveness.

Governmental planning agencies in Latin America are prone toward seemingly endless fact-finding in a form that is often more comprehensive than relevant to a particular problem on which action needs to be taken. Although the urban planning process in Caracas has greatly advanced in sophistication, the encyclopedic tendency is still evident. Long-range planning has yet to come to focus on the reality of timetables for short-range increments in the implementation process. This is due to the failure to be selective in dealing with well-identified problems and the tendency to build conceptual frameworks of growth that are overly broad. It also results from a tendency prevalent among urban planners everywhere to look at problems from the view of the planner rather than from the view of the consumer of his services, the citizen. By involving the people of Caracas in the process of problem selection, the citizen can become engaged in the urban planning process and give the urban planning process relevance. Similarly, if called upon to participate in the process of problem identification, the many diverse and frequently individualistic agencies of government can be drawn into the planning process. Through this approach the groundwork can be laid for the planner better to play the role of co-ordinator rather than that of bold knight on a white charger.

The imposition of elite values, often prevalent practice in Latin American urban planning, has brought about a focus on problems out of context with the concerns of the *real* community at large, most of whose members stand outside the decision-making process in a state of distrustful apathy. It is more important to gain the confidence of the community, to engage it in the day-to-day planning process and thus to release the latent dynamics of the development process, than to prepare perfectly articulated long-range plans.

A Process Orientation for Urban Planning in Caracas

Urban planning as applied to the rapidly growing capitals of Latin America is deeply dependent upon the understanding of two kinds of processes: the natural processes of urban growth and the continuous and comprehensive process of planning and co-ordination among the many agencies involved in decision making related to urban development.

The first kind of process has its special kind of dynamic character in Latin America and in almost no other capital is it so epitomized as in Caracas. When one looks back twenty-five years and sees in perspective the changes that have taken place there in the scale and quality of urban life, the impressive and demanding nature of these dynamic forces can be better understood. It is also possible to see more clearly the urgency for establishing institutional processes by which the natural growth processes can be channeled during the oncoming twenty-five years.

To have done this twenty-five years ago, when planning was first introduced in Caracas, may not have been possible, since the urban planning field—in Latin America, Europe and the United States—was in a much more primitive state than at present. Today, the knowledge gained in the field of urban studies in general and in urban and regional planning in particular, together with new technologies for use in urban development, make it possible—at least in theory—not only to understand natural growth processes and their causes and effects, but to design specific urban planning processes by which institutions can systematically guide urban growth.

It is especially critical to apply these potentials in Latin America, where institutional patterns inherited from the past lend support to a preoccupation with physical development plans unidentified with social goals and without a clear relationship to the means for their implementation. In Caracas, for example, too much attention has been given to the static end product—the plan itself—without relevance to a logical sequence of steps for both preparation and realization of the plan (the so-called "delivery system").

A first and basic step, for example, is the determination of the authority to plan and the scope to be allowed. Who is or are the client(s) of the urban planner and what are the planner's constraints? How far can the planning go into social, political, and economic questions intimately related to physical planning? Does the present institutional structure within which planning is to take place permit a broad outlook compatible with aspirations of the coming generation? The failure of many attempts at urban planning in Latin America and much of the weakness in the urban planning process in Caracas has been due to not having posed, nor thought through, the answers to such questions.

Other steps in the planning process need elaboration: review of relevance of data collection to avoid encyclopedic fact-finding, more systematic identification in the full range of social and political administrative, economic, physical and institutional problems; goal formulation—a step almost entirely omitted from Latin American urban planning; and realistic determination of constraints and alternative directions to be taken. Rarely in Latin American urban planning are alternatives objectively and quantitatively weighed; political and personal opinions carry great weight. Finally, with the selection of a single alternative, the plan can be built in detail for the Caracas Metropolitan Region, for example, and for the urban areas, sector by sector and barrio by barrio.

Perhaps the weakest element in the series of planning steps as practiced in Caracas is in the general area of development strategies. Metropolitan Caracas needs a cohesive over-all policy for plan implementation and project development giving an appropriate role to each governmental level involved—national, regional and local—and more comprehensive and balanced programming of public investments among each of the development sectors. These policies need to be exposed to the community to open the door for debate and involvement, time-consuming as it may be.

The adoption of this kind of urban planning system for the capital city would set the model for the remainder of the country. Yet, it is questionable that this can be achieved in Venezuela in view of the striking contrast between the dynamic nature of urban growth and the static and rigid nature of the institutional system. Nevertheless, a way must be found, for the quality of urban life to be experienced in Caracas and the other Latin American capitals by 1975, 1980 and 1990 depends on the planning processes that are institutionalized and the action taken today.

Models from the United States, from Great Britain, Yugoslavia or Sweden cannot be relied upon. The Venezuelans and the Latin Americans themselves in each of their countries only can take meaningful leadership in thinking through their own appropriate urban planning system. By focusing the urban planning process on the solution of the more profound of the massive urban problems, the path can be created by which institutional change—and therefore deeper cultural change—will take place. Urban history is the record of change, and to review the changes that have already taken place in Latin America's urban areas is sufficient indication that history will be on the side of the urban planners who work with social perspective and approaches relevant to the present and the future.

NOTES

[1] For a vivid description of the implications of the massive urbanization taking place in Latin America, see Miller and Gakenheimer (eds.), *Latin American Urban Policies and the Social Sciences.* Beverly Hills, Cal., Sage Publishers, 1972.

[2] For a discussion of the pros and cons of these two points of view, see *The Urban Explosion in Latin America: A Continent in Process of Modernization,* edited by Glenn Beyer, Cornell University Press, Ithaca, N.Y., 1967.

[3] These figures and others in this portion of the chapter are taken from a monograph in preparation by the author on "Metropolitan Urban Areas in Latin America," for the Institute for Governmental Studies, University of California, Berkeley.

[4] Ibid.

[5] Cf. *Community Development and the Urban Planning Process in Latin America,* by F. Violich and J. Astica. Latin American Center, University of California, Los Angeles, 1967.

[6] Source of these and preceding figures: Direccion General de Estadisticas y Censos Nacionales, Ministerio de Fomento, in Fernando Travieso, "El Caso de Venezuela," *Journal of the Inter-American Planning Society,* 1969.

[7] For a nostalgic, though factual, look back into the urban character and life of Caracas in this period, see Guillermo Jose Schael, *Caracas—La Ciudad Que No Vuelve,* Graficas Edicion de Arte, Caracas, 1968. The book effectively uses collections of postal cards of the period as a basis for reconstructing an image of what was then a town of 90,000 almost totally liquidated by the metropolis of today.

[8] "Caracas, 1990," Alberto Morales Tucker in *El Farol,* April–May–June 1969, Caracas.

[9] *Caracas 1990, Plan de Desarrollo Urbano, Primera Etapa del Estudio,* Consejo Municipal del Distrito Federal, Oficina Municipal de Planeamiento Urbano, Caracas, 1968.

[10] See Talton F. Ray, *The Politics of the Barrios of Venezuela,* University of California Press, Berkeley and Los Angeles, 1969.

[11] Tucker, op. cit.

[12] Carlos Acedo Mendoza, *La Vivienda en el Area Metropolitana de Caracas,* Fondo Editorial Comun, Caracas, 1969.

[13] Ibid.

[14] Tucker, op. cit.

[15] Mendoza, op. cit.

[16] Tucker, op. cit.

[17] Lander, "El Problema del Transporte en Caracas," in *El Farol,* No. 221, April–May–June 1967.

[18] Anthony Penfold, "Caracas: Urban Growth and Transportation," *Town Planning Review,* University of Liverpool Press, Liverpool, England, April 1970.

[19] *Caracas 1990, Plan de Desarrollo Urbano, Primera Etapa del Estudio,* op. cit.

[20] Ibid.

PART III

Non-Western Cities

CHAPTER 8

Moscow: The Socialist Alternative

B. Michael Frolic*

I would like to live and die in Paris,
if there were no such city as Moscow.
Mayakovsky

Moscow, with a population of 7,500,000 and the economic-cultural center of a region containing over 30,000,000 inhabitants, may have done the best job of physical planning and urban reconstruction of all the world's great capitals. According to William Robson, the British urbanologist, "Moscow is the best

* Associate professor of political science, York University, Toronto; a specialist on Soviet and Chinese urban development; author of the forthcoming book *Soviet Cities in Transition,* and many articles in scholarly journals; he has twice visited the Soviet Union and China. He is currently on leave in Peking, as first secretary in the Canadian Embassy. Professor Frolic, a Canadian, attended the University of Toronto, receiving his Ph.D. from Cornell in 1970. In 1964–65 he studied at Moscow State University; in 1971–72 he was a research fellow at the Harvard Russian Research Center, where this article, part of a larger study of Moscow, was written.

For the convenience of readers, English language sources are cited wherever possible. Interviews that are referred to in the text were conducted by the author in Moscow in 1965 and 1969, and by Dan Dimancescu and Crocker Snow, Jr., in 1971. The author thanks Dan Dimancescu, H. Wentworth Eldredge, Jane Mosher, Hans Blumenfeld and Lev Kogan for their advice and assistance; and his special thanks to the Russian Research Center of Harvard University for their generous support of his project.

FIG. 1 Stalinist "wedding cake" versus "socialist realism."

planned of all the world's great cities, and we should study the development of Moscow more closely to see what we can learn from her." When walking along Moscow's streets, one is struck by the absence of overhanging wires and signs, the cleanliness, free-flowing traffic, low noise level, spaciousness, and the small amount of air pollution, in comparison with other cities of similar size, such as Tokyo, New York, London or Paris. Moscow has an excellent public transportation system, with one hundred miles of spotless, efficient subways and a network of squares, which co-ordinates the exchange of above- and below-ground traffic effectively. Moscow has carried out one of the most extensive programs of urban renewal of any major old city (founded in 1147). Since the Revolution of 1917, and especially since the Moscow Plan of 1935, the city center has been transformed from a tangle of two-story wooden houses on narrow, crooked streets into a modern cultural-administrative central core. Whole sections of the city have been demolished to make way for new construction. Other buildings were painstakingly rolled back forty feet or more to widen downtown streets. Gorky Street, Moscow's showpiece thoroughfare, is now one hundred and twenty to one hundred and fifty feet wide; in 1930, it was a cramped street forty to sixty feet in width (Fig. 1).

Western tourists and town planners may notice other attractive features of Moscow. They can walk around Moscow or ride the subway at night without worrying about being mugged, raped or murdered. There are numerous parks and trees, and the amount of public green space per capita is thirty-three square yards, compared with approximately twenty-two square yards per capita in New York City. Industrial and residential areas have been reasonably separated from each other. Thus, the southwest part of Moscow is basically residential and is the main area of Moscow in which massive blocks of new apartments are currently being built. The northeast and eastern parts of Moscow tend to be areas of heavy industrial concentration. Moscow's population size has officially been restricted for years, since the Plan of 1935, in order to minimize the consequences of overurbanization. Promyslov, Moscow's mayor, recently said in a personal interview "While Moscow has her problems, she fortunately does not suffer from Tokyo's problem of uncontrollable population growth." New industrial development has officially been prohibited for years, and entire factories have been relocated outside the city limits to slow down the city's growth while drawing upon the manpower resources of the suburban area and the Moscow region. "These and other policies make our city the most advanced metropolis in the world," says Promyslov. "In the new Moscow Plan, our goal is stated quite clearly: Moscow will be *the* model communist city—the model for the Soviet Union and for the world."

Yet for all its achievements in physical planning and in urban redevelopment since the adoption of the first Moscow Plan in 1935, Moscow falls short of being a planner's paradise or a city in which many Western citizens would care to live. Despite the great changes which have taken place in socialist Moscow, the city's life style seems drab and spartan by Western standards. Moscow is a city of cramped apartment dwellers and apparently lacks the diversity and excitement of other metropolitan centers. Foreigners claim that after 6 P.M., downtown Moscow becomes a city without people, color and activity. "Even during the daytime," reports one disgruntled foreign resident, "there is no place to sit and watch the city go by. No cafés, no places to meet people. The planners were so busy creating new streets and buildings that they forgot about the people." Too many well-intentioned policies have not been carried out because the Soviet Union lacks the social and economic resources to do the job properly. Too many policies also have suffered from an overzealous commitment to ideology and to politics at the expense of daily urban needs. The famous Stalinist "wedding-cake" buildings are an example of this. These relics of a costly attempt to combine monumentalism, Russian tradition and socialist values tower above the city. Soviet city planners have provided the physical shell in which to house a modern, socialist supercity, but now they must try to make socialist planning ideals mesh with the realities of Moscow's life and politics.

Despite a remarkable program of housing construction, with a total of 37,000,000 square yards of housing space having been built between 1957 and 1970, Moscow nevertheless continues to suffer from an acute housing shortage. The pace of new housing construction has meant that in the past ten years over two and one-half million Muscovites received new apartments, but still, in 1971, the average apartment dweller had only sixty-five square feet of housing space, enough for a room approximately seven feet by nine feet, and many Muscovite families have to share their apartment with other families. Most of the newer housing has been built too quickly with minimal regard either to quality or to aesthetics, and Moscow officials freely admit that housing remains one of Moscow's (and the Soviet Union's) main problems. The blame is not laid upon past and present Soviet policies, however, but upon the Czarist legacies of wretched urban housing conditions and upon the devastating effects of World War II.

Moscow's planners and politicians admit that service facilities have lagged far behind everything else, including housing, and that today Moscow's service facilities are markedly inferior to those of most of the world's large cities. "We could not afford to invest in consumer-oriented facilities in the past," said one planner, "and we continue to be plagued by poor service facilities today." For example, Moscow has only a half dozen functioning laundromats; less than 10 per cent of Muscovites have their own telephone, for which there is an average waiting time of over four years; in the entire city in 1970 there were only five automobile service and repair stations to accommodate the 150,000 private cars in the city. Long line-ups characterize most shopping trips; a recent Soviet survey showed that the average Muscovite spends one to two hours every day shopping, and that the majority of shoppers are dissatisfied with Moscow's shopping facilities.

Has Moscow paid too great a social and political price for its centralized planning system? This is a criticism regularly raised by Western observers. While Muscovites insist that there is a high degree of citizen participation in Moscow's planning and administration, citing the election of over 1,000 municipal deputies to the city Soviet, and approximately 8,500 deputies to Moscow's twenty-nine borough Soviets every two years, in fact citizens make almost no impact on Moscow's decision making. There are no organized citizen's groups in Moscow to compare with the neighborhood groups and other formalized interest groups active in North American cities. Aside from the voting ritual, when over 99 per cent of Moscow's eligible voters go to the polls, citizens apparently only get involved in municipal politics and administration when being informed of a decision already made. Citizens "tag along," and decisions such as the limiting of Moscow's population, the choice of urban redevelopment sites, urban spending priorities, the location of parks and service areas are invariably handed down from above, for information and approval only. Promyslov defends this kind of citizen participation as being "perfectly consistent with the principles of socialism. We are a government acting purely in the interests of the people, and no decision is made by us without taking these interests fully into account."

Actually, key policy and planning decisions are not made by the mayor and the elected city Soviet of 1,140 deputies. The person who really runs Moscow is Grishin, the current first secretary of the Moscow City Communist Party Committee. It is the city Party Committee which calls the shots and Mayor Promyslov, though he is one of the Party's higher ranking members, functions as the Party's administrator by carrying out Party instructions. The city Party organization, in turn, takes its policy-making cues from another, higher authority, the national Party organization. Grishin, the Moscow City Party leader, cannot pursue policies which might contradict or be independent of national Party policy. The fusion between Moscow and the central government is so tight that Moscow's plans and policies are, in effect, national plans and policies. "This is logical enough, isn't it?" asked one Moscow planner. "After all, Moscow is our model city; it is our greatest city; it produces 8 per cent of the Soviet gross national product; it has a current budget of 1.6 billion dollars; its top leaders regularly consult with the national government on all matters [Grishin is even a member of the Politburo of the Party Central Committee]; Moscow is part and symbol of our national heritage, so it has to be closely tied to the national government." Western critics will contend that this argument for national direction of Moscow's politics is unacceptable to them because, by their standards, Moscow suffers adversely from overcentralization, serious limitations upon the autonomy and credibility of its government, and almost meaningless citizen participation (from the Western democratic point of view), since citizens do not elect any of the Party officials who run Moscow.

Is Moscow overplanned? Surprisingly, some Moscow planners might be tempted to agree with this view. Some of them now feel that certain socialist policies have to be altered to conform to the realities of daily life in a modern, urban environment. It may be that Soviet planners have too rigidly, for too long, tried to apply inflexible planning techniques and solutions to urban problems which now require new concepts and more flexible policies. "What this means," remarked a top official of Moscow's Town Planning and Architectural Main Administration (the organization responsible for the technical execution of the Moscow City Plan), "is that we have to pay greater attention now to the urban nature of our environment, *to accept the fact that urbanism is a universal process with universal features, similar problems, and quite possibly, similar solutions to most of these problems in all the world's major cities.*"† If all large cities in industrializing societies throughout the world tend to develop in a similar fashion and exhibit the same urban culture and urban values, regardless of ideology, then some of the Soviet Union's socialist urban policies need to be altered or even abandoned because they apparently are in conflict with universal urban processes. Which of these socialist policies need changing or alteration?

"There are five," noted one Moscow sociologist. (1) "We now realize, for example, that it is almost impossible to limit the population of Moscow. The city has grown and grown, no matter what measures we have taken to try to halt its growth first at five million, then six million, and seven million. Soon we will have eight million inhabitants. Furthermore, some of our economists, sociologists and geographers no longer agree that big cities are necessarily bad and all small cities, good. We are gathering data to show that actually life in large cities may be more enjoyable and more socially and economically productive. Many of these specialists now say that big cities and regional agglomerations are an inescapable, productive and positive feature of industrialization. So we are thinking of revising our present policy of limiting the size of Soviet cities which now have over a million inhabitants."

† (Editor's italics.)

(2) Moscow planners have also significantly changed their concept of the *mikrorayon,* a neighborhood social and planning unit which was stressed in the 1950s and early 1960s. The mikrorayon was to unite from between 4,000 to 18,-000 inhabitants into thousands of decentralized subcommunities within Moscow. Everyday services were to be located within walking distance from one's apartment; residents would rarely have to leave these decentralized communities except to go to work and, perhaps, to the Bolshoi. But two things happened. First, because of a scarcity of resources, service facilities were never built in time nor on the scale originally envisaged by the planners. Because of Moscow's rapid population growth, it became necessary to raise residential population densities far beyond the intended capacities of the neighborhood units and of the meager service facilities which were temporarily provided. Second, Soviet researchers discovered that Muscovites did not really care to live in these semi-isolated urban subcommunities. They did not want to orient their lives exclusively around their apartments. According to one Soviet sociological study, "Based upon our research, inhabitants of urban apartment complexes in neighborhood units know only five or ten of their neighbors by sight, three to five by name, and almost nothing about where they work, or about their character."[1] The idea of a self-contained neighborhood unit has been more or less forgotten, the size of the current mikrorayons is some 50,000 inhabitants, planned population densities have more than tripled, and full service integration has been long abandoned.

(3) Stalinist "wedding-cake" style buildings (see Fig. 1) are also no longer being built in Moscow. They are an example of another policy that failed; the seven skyscrapers are expensive monuments to the last in a series of ill-fated attempts to develop in Moscow a uniquely "socialist architecture" which would be different from, and superior to, the constructivist architecture found in bourgeois cities. In the words of one architect, "Buildings of this type, like Moscow State University on the Lenin Hills, mistakenly tried to combine the greatness of Russia's past [the towers of the Kremlin are an example of this] with the techniques of modern construction. But these buildings were failures, aesthetically and economically. They are excessive in all respects, and they are ugly." Khrushchev ordered a halt in their construction in the mid-1950s; they now squat like seven ersatz castles upon the Moscow horizon.

(4) Another socialist policy which has been tried but never successfully implemented is the communal kitchen. From the debates of the 1920s and early 1930s up to the present time, Moscow architects, planners and social scientists have been pondering the efficacy of the communal kitchen.‡ The kitchens would save space, promote collective values and liberate women from the tyranny of cooking. Yet Muscovites never willingly turned to them; only as a last resort when no other facilities were available. Most Muscovites prefer to cook meals in their own apartments, a fact confirmed by a number of recent sociological surveys, but the ideological compulsion to build communal facilities remains, and planners continue to experiment with them. Recently, a few "houses of the New Type," experimental fourteen-story apartment buildings supplied with communal eating facilities, were built in Moscow. Moscow State University was asked to administer two of these buildings located near the university, as a social experiment, to see just how well selected families and individuals would adjust to this "new way of

‡ Carried further in Maoist China to "communal living." (Editor's note.)

life" with its communal facilities. But the university filled the buildings up with students to alleviate an acute shortage of dormitory space. Finally, after some public criticism, they grudgingly agreed to resume the experiment.

(5) Observed one Moscow official,

> We have become far less rigid today and are beginning to adjust to the demands of the large, modern city. This means accepting the inevitable spread of automobiles, planning for increased traffic congestion, greater population mobility, more urban noise and pollution. It is our contention that Moscow possesses the most suitable means of any of the world's major modern cities to solve these problems. With central planning and public ownership of all land we should be able to accomplish anything. Maybe we will have to change some of our older socialist policies in keeping with the imperatives of urbanization and of urbanism. But a suitable compromise can work out, and Moscow will emerge as a far better place in which to live than New York, London, Tokyo, Rome or any of the bourgeois giant cities.

Perhaps he is right, but so many of Moscow's achievements are expressed in the future tense, that is, they *will be* (*budyet*). "Moscow *will be* the best place in which to live; Moscow *will build* so many million units of new housing; Moscow *will have* the best leisure and recreational facilities of any modern city," and so forth. These future-oriented judgments make it difficult to evaluate the successes and failures of Moscow's development, since there is a sizable gap between Soviet planning ideals and performance.

This gap may be due to several factors. Moscow planners may have been too impatient in trying to speed up a developmental process which has its own logic and rhythm. They may have been too ambitious in assuming that they could easily bend this process radically in a socialist direction. They may have been too optimistic in thinking that man can readily predict and shape the future. They may also have been too idealistic, since even in the Soviet Union, the planner must defer to the politician, and long-range city planning ideals have been repeatedly sacrificed to the immediate needs of the economic planners, i.e., production has always had first priority in Moscow.

In examining how Moscow has changed and grown since the Revolution of 1917 and in analyzing the urban policies carried out by Moscow's leaders in the past half century, we can acquire some understanding of the various factors, economic, political and cultural which, taken all together, have produced the present metropolis of 7,500,000 inhabitants. We must go back briefly into Czarist Russia, to examine Moscow's spatial development, her sociocultural significance for the contemporary capital and her way of life and level of productivity prior to the twentieth century. The main emphasis is on modern socialist Moscow, whose development will be treated chronologically as follows: (1) before the Great Plan of 1935; (2) the Great Plan to the death of Stalin in 1953; (3) Moscow after Stalin; (4) the new Plan and the future of Moscow. The dominant themes in each of these four periods are analyzed and their linkage to the key processes of urbanization and urbanism, and to the specific policies of the regime's leaders is examined. The analysis raises a number of questions. How well did the needs, capacities and perceptions of Moscow's politicians, planners and citizens mesh? Can a pragmatic shift from socialist to more universal urban policies and programs be detected over the years?

BEFORE THE GREAT PLAN

The official founding of Moscow is accepted as 1147. Actually settlements existed earlier, standing at the junction of the Moscow and Neglinnaya rivers, the crossroads of several major water routes going from the Caspian to the Baltic, from Smolensk to Vladimir and from Novgorod to Ryazan. Prince Dolguruky in 1156 converted one of the higher parts of his estate at the river junction into a *kreml* (a fortress, or Kremlin) by building a strong timber wall around it. This first Kremlin, the dominant political, economic and cultural center of Moscow over the years, became the nucleus of a small town which emerged in the fourteenth century as the center of medieval Russia. The Kremlin was enlarged and strengthened with oak walls, and artisans, traders, princes and merchants sought protection beside it. A century later the princes of Moscow had extended their control over a considerable part of northeast Russia. The city had expanded in size to over three square miles, the Kremlin was refortified with brick and powerful towers, large buildings already surrounded the Kremlin, villages sprang up around the city, and radial streets connected them to the concentric central fortifications of the city. Many of these fourteenth- and fifteenth-century roads are twentieth-century Moscow thoroughfares: the road to Novgorod is now Herzen Street; the road to Tver is Gorky Street; the road to Smolensk has now become Kalinin Street. Moscow's present concentric-radial city pattern had thus been firmly established by the fifteenth century.

The city also established itself as the economic and cultural center of northeast Russia. After the fall of Constantinople in 1453, Moscow, already the home of the Russian Metropolitan, now became "the third Rome," last bastion of the beleaguered Orthodox Church. Over a two-hundred-year period, the city sprouted churches like mushrooms, including the famous Cathedral of the Assumption (Uspensky Sobor), St. Basil's Cathedral in Red Square, and the Cathedral of the Archangel. It also developed as a key trade and transportation point, linking the major parts of Russia. Furs, wax and honey went through Moscow to the Crimea and then on to Istanbul (then Constantinople) in exchange for silk, paper and weapons. Goods from the Mediterranean and the Orient were transshipped through Moscow to Novgorod, in exchange for cloth from the Hanseatic towns. The Moscow region's population grew rapidly, the city's economy prospered, and wealth flowed easily into the hands of Muscovite merchants and princes. Diplomatic ties were established with several nations, and immigrants came from Greece, Italy, Germany, Poland and other parts of Europe.

In the sixteenth century new fortifications were erected to protect the growing city. The settlement area around the Kremlin, which was called the Chinese City (Kitai Gorod), was enclosed in a stone wall and incorporated into the Kremlin system. A third ring of fortifications was built around the White City (Bely Gorod) which lay beyond the Kremlin and Kitai Gorod. Beyond this, still another wall was constructed, a ten-mile earth and timber fortification with numerous towers, enclosing an area called the Earthen City (Zemlyanoi Gorod). The boundary line of Zemlyanoi Gorod eventually became the Garden Circle (Sadovoye Koltso), which today is considered the central city area of Moscow. Moscow's size increased four times to twelve square miles with a population of over 100,000. The city was beginning to grow in onionlike layers, in a northward direction toward the sources of raw materials needed for its developing handicraft industries. By the seventeenth century, Moscow had become the center of an all Russian market, which amalgamated smaller markets from the surrounding localities (Fig. 2). One Soviet source offers this description of the city at that time:

> . . . there were more than 120 trade streets or alleys in Moscow, each selling a specific amount of merchandise or food; bread, lard, butter, cabbage, onions, mushrooms, apples, cucumbers, vodka, vinegar, fur coats, cloth, lace, linen, furs, sable, footwear, bast sandals, saddles, raw hides, boilers, cutlery, bells, needles, soap, icons, books, pottery, lanterns, mirrors, etc. . . .[2]

Out of this tangle of commercial activities emerged eighteenth-century Moscow. Taking advantage of the nearby skilled labor of artisans, continuing capital ac-

FIG. 2 Moscow in the seventeenth century with the Kremlin in the center. *From Historic Urban Plans facsimile of an engraving in the Library of Congress*

cumulations and the excellent communications/transportation network of which Moscow was the key element, the city developed a diversified range of manufactured goods, including textiles, gunpowder, bricks, glass, paper and metal products. The population had jumped to 200,000 by 1700 helping to stimulate this economic growth, though it then shrunk to 140,000 after Peter the Great in 1713 transferred the Russian capital to St. Petersburg (now Leningrad) where it remained until the 1917 Revolution. It was a measure of Moscow's economic-geographic resiliency and cultural significance for "Mother Russia" that the city survived the loss of her political-administrative powers, and still remained Russia's great city for the next two centuries.

Eighteenth-century Moscow had already developed an architecture and style that bound it inseparably to the history and culture of Russia, regardless of its sudden political-administrative misfortune. "The big village," as Moscow was called by its residents, was just that—a mélange of peasants, merchants, artisans and princes wandering about muddy streets, a step away from the countryside. Following foreign invasions, fires and plagues, many Muscovites melted back into the countryside, to reappear when the dangers had subsided. Fires took their toll of the wooden buildings: two thirds of Moscow's buildings were destroyed in the Great Fire of 1812. Enough remained to preserve the architecture of Moscow, which is uniquely Russian in its blend of East and West. "Liberated by Byzantine traditions, but not yet overpowered by Western influences . . . a vivid illustration of two streams of world art, Eastern and Western, infiltrating, modifying, complementing one another and forming a complete synthesis of world architecture."[3] At the center of this spider's web of old and new was the Kremlin with its high towers and tightly packed cupolas, stuccoed palaces, red brick walls, and striking golds, silvers and yellows, with St. Basil's and Red Square off to one side. Moving away from this central core, this city within a city, one could encounter Rastrelli-influenced buildings designed by the architects Bazhenov and Kazakov. Or two-story wooden buildings hidden behind the squares, with fretted woodwork around their windows, each one different from the other. There were the buildings which had survived the fires from older periods, reflecting traditional Russian architecture; the structures later put up by invited foreign architects; and the various Russian copies of Byzantine and other foreign architecture. "There is not one Moscow, but a thousand. The eternal city of the Slavs seems to change its innermost temper with every shift of the weather. Every turn in its zigzag streets flashes a new facet of the city and no skyline ever looks exactly the same twice. Its jumble of fantastic architecture, squalor and splendors . . . other capitals can be photographed and described, but the quality of Moscow is kaleidoscopic."[4]

In the nineteenth century, after the Great Fire, the city was rebuilt. Its population began to increase steadily, and it developed into a major industrial center. In 1830, Moscow's population was 306,000 and its area was thirty square miles. After 1860, its population leaped rapidly upward: between 1860–85, Moscow's population grew by 122 per cent; between 1885–1907, it rose again by 68 per cent, an absolute increase of 546,000 inhabitants in less than twenty years; by 1917, at the time of the Revolution, the city contained 1,854,000 people, a further increase of nearly 38 per cent. This tremendous growth characterized Moscow's first wave of urbanization (it later experienced two other major surges of urbanization in the twentieth century, between 1926–39, and again between 1950–70). Moscow also expanded spatially in this period, into a sprawling city the size of Paris. By 1917, Moscow occupied some ninety square miles, and had expanded from the central area bounded by the Sadovoye Koltso mainly northward and to the southeast, toward water basins, transportation facilities and factory, warehouse and transshipment sites.

In less than a century, the city tripled in area and increased tenfold in population. In 1871, nearly half of the city's population were former peasants, and by 1897 this had risen to 70 per cent. The 1882 census showed that only 26 per cent of Moscow's population had been born there; in 1902, the figure was still 28 per cent. At the turn of the century, the average Muscovite was a male (60 per cent of the population was male); probably illiterate (over 50 per cent of Muscovites could not read or write); of peasant background (85 per cent came from the provinces adjoining the city). Forty per cent of Moscow's working force was employed in the city's rapidly expanding industries; Moscow had over 20,000 commercial establishments, with textiles and metallurgy the most prominent industries. Moscow's development as the key Russian railway and water transport junction greatly enhanced the city's industrial growth. Freight turnover increased rapidly, and raw materials, fuel, and semifinished goods poured into the city along Moscow's nine radial railway lines and waterways, to be exchanged for manufactured goods and industrial products.

The city had undergone a remarkable transformation. A. N. Ostrovsky, the nineteenth-century Russian playwright, observed, "Moscow's public of 40 or 50 years ago consisted mostly of the gentry; landowners from *gubernias* [provinces] far and near came to Moscow for the winter to parade their daughters at the Elite Club. . . . As a result of exceptionally favorable conditions for trade and manufacture since the twenties of the century, enterprising craftsmen and various factory owners from the industrial *gubernias* have flooded Moscow's suburbs and outskirts and vicinity with factories, and all sorts of industrial enterprises."[5]

The social costs of this rapid change were tremendous. The city lacked the fiscal authority, administrative powers and social infrastructure to deal with the many problems of accelerated urbanization and industrialization. It could not house, educate or provide basic services for its exploding population. Living conditions rapidly deteriorated into some of the uglier portraits of humanity in despair. Nineteenth-century Moscow may have been a city of progress, color and an unusual blend of Eastern and Western architecture and style, but it was squalid, with narrow streets full of wretched men and women, thieves, beggars, pickpockets and prostitutes. Leo Tolstoy recoiled in terror from his visit to the Khitrovka market, where vodka was czar and men played out useless lives in pursuit of just a gram of vodka to deaden the pain for a moment. Khitrovka was the setting for Gorky's *Lower Depths* which conveyed the horror of this new urban environment, where 10 per cent of the population lived in cellars. Many more lived there psychologically, cut off from their families (over 50 per cent of Muscovites were not living in their normal family groups); squeezed into inadequate housing, lacking sewage, running water and ravaged by periodic epidemics of typhus and cholera. It is estimated in 1900 almost one third of the population lived in some form of institutionalized housing such as military barracks, almshouses, hotels, factory housing and hospitals, and in rooming houses or workers' co-operatives (*artels*).

Faced with inadequate finances and a swelling population, the city could not significantly ease the burdens of urbanization. Water was in such short supply that it had to be rationed to institutions. Not until the end of the nineteenth century was central Moscow finally provided with a sewage system to replace the traditional night-soil collecting brigades. Moscow could not educate its semi-literate population quickly enough. While Vienna, Paris and Berlin were spending roughly ten francs per inhabitant on municipal schools, Moscow could only afford one tenth this sum. In 1893, Moscow had one fifth the revenues of Paris and one third of London's. In order to raise revenues, Moscow municipalized a number of its basic services, forming municipal enterprises to administer water supply, sewage, and refuse collection, printing, the stockyards and slaughter-houses, drafting offices and bakeries. At the beginning of the twentieth century these municipal "socialist" enterprises produced 25 per cent of Moscow's revenues and by 1916, 55 per cent of the city's income. Conditions in Moscow were primitive by Western European standards. In 1914, Moscow possessed one asphalted street, the rest were cobblestones. Seventy-five per cent of the housing supply was of wood; over 50 per cent were one-story buildings; another 41 per cent were two-story buildings; 5 per cent of urban dwellers had gas stoves; 11 per cent, baths; 22 per cent, central heating; 30 per cent, sewage; 40 per cent, running water; 30 per cent, electricity.

The majority of Moscow's citizens were disenfranchised and a small elite dominated the life and politics of the city. The 1917 Revolution thus came to an urban population that had ample social and economic reasons to rebel. On the night of November 2, 1917, following the seizure of St. Petersburg, the Kremlin was taken and Soviet power was proclaimed in Moscow. A new social experiment was in the making, and Moscow would become its model, a precious jewel to be displayed in the socialist diadem. Could the Bolsheviks transform this eight-hundred-year-old city into a modern metropolis? It was to be an imposing challenge to a succession of Soviet politicians and planners.

The immediate consequences of the Revolution were threefold. The capital was moved back from Leningrad to Moscow after two hundred years. All urban land became public in 1918 after a series of decrees permanently abolishing private ownership of land. Because of food shortages and wartime conditions, the city's population shrunk to only a million inhabitants by 1920 (a loss of 800,000 in three years). Because of the population loss and the redistribution of surplus housing, Moscow suddenly had the largest per capita housing space in its history. In 1920, Moscow residents had almost twelve square yards of housing per capita, a figure which was to decline steadily over the years to reach a low of four square yards by 1950. For those who remained in postrevolutionary Moscow, life improved immeasurably. During the New Economic Policy period, 1921–28, the city's uncontrollable urbanization temporarily slowed down, though the old problems of illiteracy, family dislocation, massive rural-urban migration and lack of urban amenities, services and other facilities were still unsolved. In 1926, two thirds of Moscow's population were not born in Moscow and, of these, two thirds were peasants. Average housing space had plummeted to six square yards per capita, illiteracy still remained at a high level, and the city continued to lack sewage, water and other utilities. But it was hoped that the Bolsheviks, having in their hands control over all urban land, as well as the administrative, fiscal and planning powers of a centralized hierarchical state, would respond to this urban challenge in a pioneering fashion.

The Bolsheviks wanted to make Moscow a model socialist city, and permitted in those early years open and lively discussion of the various planning and architectural alternatives which might transform Moscow, and other Soviet cities into the best environment for modern industrial Soviet man. Soviet architects and planners were encouraged to submit their blueprints and visions for a new socialist city to the appropriate Party and government officials, and for a decade, Moscow became an architect's laboratory. All kinds of experiments were tried and rejected. Foreign architects streamed to the capital to be consulted and to volunteer their services in this great opportunity to make utopia work. Competitions were held, journals were founded, arguments among opposing planning and architectural schools raged into print. The chance to remake an entire city of two million, let alone a nation the size of the Soviet Union, was an exciting challenge. One foreign city planner, in recalling how he came to Moscow, said, "There I was, sitting in Vienna, working as a draftsman, drawing conventional designs and buildings for conventional cities. Suddenly came this unbelievable opportunity to break away from the traditional system and to design something I had always wanted to create. This time there was a chance that my visions would become reality. And the Soviet Government was willing to pay me for putting my dreams down on paper."

So they put their dreams down on paper, Soviet and foreign architects, and what emerged covered all directions: constructivism, futurism, and socialism. Russian traditionalism and combinations of all these. A few of the new buildings were actually approved and constructed, and still stand in Moscow today, testaments to a time of great creativity and experimentation. Contemporary Moscow is still dotted with examples of postrevolutionary architecture, such as the Lenin Mausoleum in Red Square, the Central Telegraph Building on Gorky Street, the Izvestiya and Pravda buildings, the Palace of Culture at the Likhachyov Automobile Plant, the Narkomfin apartment block on Chaikovsky Street and others. Soviet architects such as the Vesnin brothers, Melnikov, Barkhin, Ginsburg, Shchusev, and Leonidov were joined by Le Corbusier, Ernst May, Bruno Taut, Frank Lloyd Wright, Hans Schmidt, Hannes Meyer and others. Many of the most innovative designs never left the blueprint stage, but even their paper existence symbolized the potential of the new revolutionary architecture.

The search for a new revolutionary architecture was important, but, even more so, was the search for new concepts in city planning. Soviet planners and architects spent the twenties trying to solve the dilemmas of urbanization in modern industrial society. Some tried to break the city into tiny pieces and, in effect, fling it into the countryside. Others dreamed of three-hundred-foot-high cities similar to Le Corbusier's *La Ville Radieuse.* Between these extremes lay a wide range of city planning proposals which sought to transform urban life in "a socialist direction," utilizing the new Soviet planning technology.

Attempts were made to plan for socialist institutions within new and rebuilt cities. One Western architect recalls that "The arguments about what was 'socialist' went on forever. Should we put in kitchens? Why not only communal facilities? How many workers' clubs? How much privacy was necessary in a collectivist society? What about the children? The planners were trying to provide for the New Soviet Man in an urban environment that was not ready to receive him."

Le Corbusier, whose "urbanist" ideas inspired several Soviet architects, and whose plan for the construction of a vertical Moscow was rejected by the Soviet authorities, criticized many of the Soviet planners and architects for their fantasies. Le Corbusier wrote that it was folly to try to stop urban growth and decentralize cities: that Soviet planners would have to accept the inevitability of urbanism and not run and hide from it. He wrote an appropriate epitaph to this decade of extraordinary architectural and planning experimentation[6]:

> People were encouraged to entertain an idle dream; "The cities will be part of the country; I shall live 30 miles from my office under a pine tree; my secretary will live 30 miles away from it too, in the other direction, under another pine tree. We shall both have our own car. . . ."
>
> Then one day authority, which is the door of reason against which all dreams—just and chimerical ones alike—must eventually knock, authority in the USSR said: "Enough, it's all over! And stop that laughing!"

The Party Central Committee had enough and complained that "highly unsound, semifantastical and hence extremely harmful attempts are being made by certain comrades to surmount 'in one leap' the obstacles that lie along the path to a socialist transformation of the way of life, obstacles rooted, on the one hand, in the economic and cultural backwardness of the country, and, on the other, in the need in our present stage of development, to concentrate most of our resources on *the rapid industrialization which alone will create the necessary basis for a radical transformation of the way of life*" (my italics). The Party resolution attacked "recently published projects for the reorganization of existing cities and construction of new ones," and condemned as "harmful" and "utopian" those who advocated "the immediate and complete collectivization of every aspect of the worker's life: feeding, housing, education of the children in isolation from their parents, abolition of normal family life, and administrative bans on private preparation of meals." In 1931, Lazar Kaganovich, first secretary of the Moscow city and regional Party Committee, and specialist on the reconstruction and planning of Moscow, announced it was time to establish basic principles of urban development, to develop an appropriate Moscow city plan, and put an end to the irresponsible experimentation of the past decade. He attacked those who had not been progressive enough: "It is high time to get rid of the amateur methods and habits and the limited outlook inherited from the prerevolutionary city governments." Yet, at the same time, he said, "We must reject every harmful and useless attempt to run too far ahead."[7] Citing Stalin, Kaganovich spelled out the new parameters between which Soviet city planners would henceforth be confined: (1) Economic and political criteria would be the main factors affecting future city planning (production over planning, and politics over ideology); (2) cities were naturally good: "Eliminating the differences between town and country" meant turning peasants into town dwellers, and not worshiping garden cities, noble savages, or rural idylls; (3) radical transformation of social life was out of the question for the moment, since the Soviet Union could not afford it.

Meanwhile, living conditions in the city had rapidly deteriorated. People were pouring in from everywhere; Moscow's population doubled from two million to four million in only ten years. Having decided to give first priority to industrialization and to the needs of production, the Party had almost nothing to spare for capital investment in housing, transportation, public utilities. As soon as a room was built, five or six persons squeezed into it. People got married and divorced to gain an extra square yard of housing space. Bread, sugar and tea were rationed, and the long line-ups for scarce goods were unbelievable. A foreign architect noted, "I remember my first impression of Moscow in the thirties. Old wooden houses, terribly overcrowded. Narrow crooked streets and jammed buses and streetcars. Primitive facilities. An incredible influx of peasants clutching loaves of bread and picking at guitars. The smells of cabbage and of alcohol. People smelled. They lined up. They waited for something to happen. How on earth would we be able to help them?" The Party decided that the problems of Moscow had to be solved quickly, because the social costs of uncontrolled urbanization were beginning to affect labor productivity adversely. Moscow was the Soviet showpiece, and if it was allowed to degenerate, then the whole socialist experiment might be in doubt. Ten years of "free planning" had produced many choices, but few answers and no grand plan. The Party, having decided against radical changes in the urban setting, now needed a realistic blueprint to deal with immediate, pragmatic problems of population concentration and rapid urbanization. The decision was made to prepare a ten-year general plan for Moscow's development. An international competition was held; thousands of Soviet architects, planners, engineers, economists, and Party and state officials participated. The Party hoped that the Plan would be finished by 1933; but after several delays, the Great Plan was finally approved in July 1935.

FROM THE GREAT PLAN TO THE DEATH OF STALIN

The enactment of the 1935 Plan marked the symbolic end of the "old" Moscow and produced the master blueprint for a modern, industrial "socialist" city (Fig. 3). Not only did the Plan describe how Moscow was to be reconstructed and developed as a new capital city, but it also established the basic principles of future urban development in the whole Soviet Union. Whatever was to be done in Moscow would henceforth serve as a model for other Soviet cities. A pragmatic response to the immediate needs of the Soviet state and of the city of Moscow, it was also a piece of propaganda designed to show how progressive the Soviet Union could be, at the very time when Soviet urban conditions were pitiable and showed little likelihood of immediate improvement. The decree approving the Great Plan spoke of "low decrepit houses huddled together," "haphazard distribution of industrial enterprises, railroads, and other branches of the economy," "a city . . . reflecting the barbaric character of Russian capitalism," "making imperative a radical and planned reconstruction."[8]

Moscow was to be permanently limited in its population size to no more than five million inhabitants; population growth would be controlled by the future re-

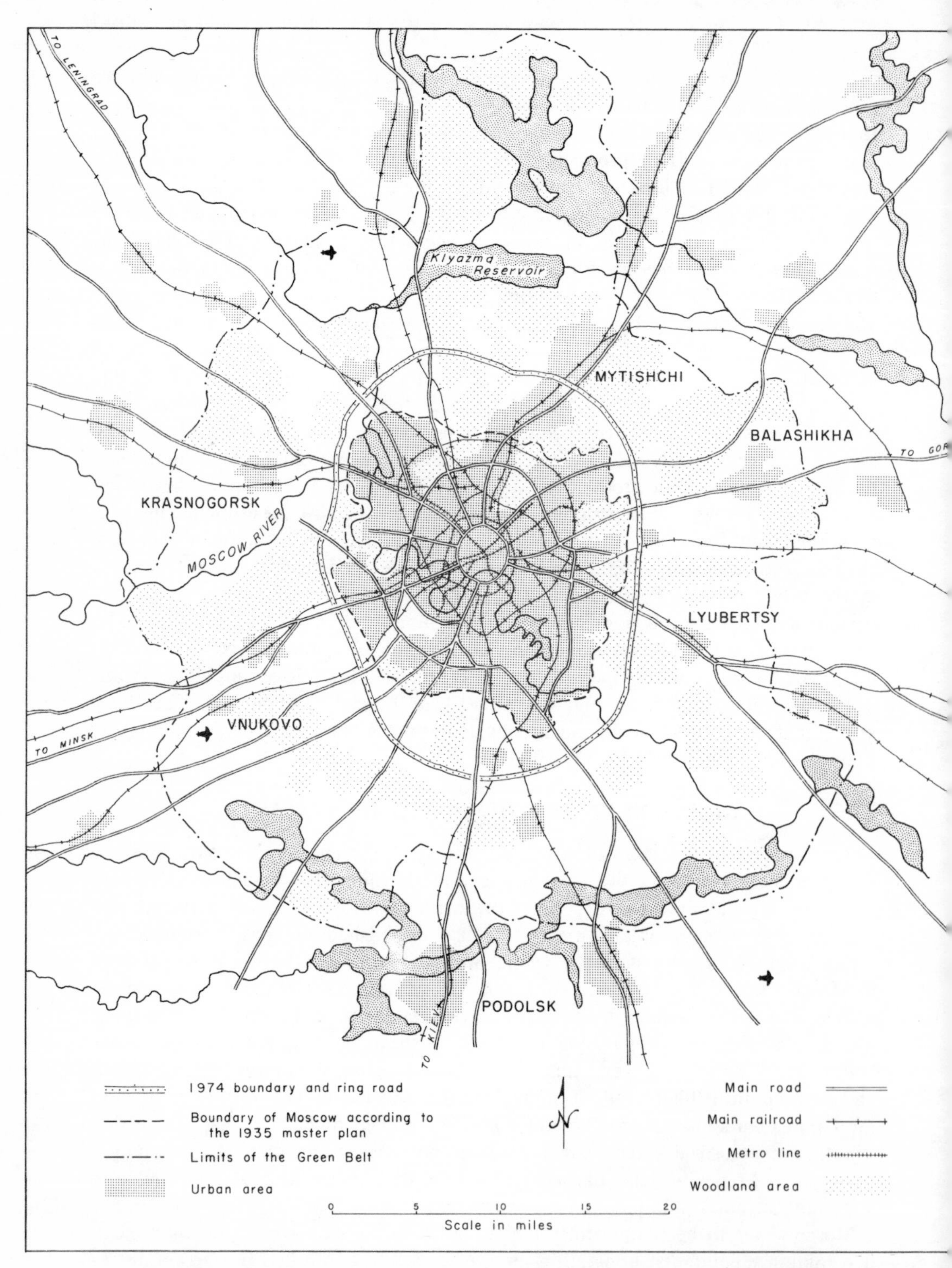

FIG. 3 Stalin's Great Plan of 1935 and the present boundaries of Moscow and its Green Belt. *Cartography by Van English, based on various Soviet and other maps*

striction of industrial expansion within the city boundaries, and a rigid system of internal passport controls (special permission was needed to live permanently in Moscow). The city's area was increased from 111 square miles to 219 square miles, thus decongesting the city and providing a planned density of 160–200 persons per acre. Two thirds of the new territory was in the southwest part of Moscow, where the future campus of Moscow State University would be built, and where the bulk of Moscow's massive new housing construction would eventually be concentrated. The city was ringed with a Green Belt, six miles wide, serving as Moscow's "lungs," for recreation, and as a link between the region and the central city.

The Plan did not disturb the traditional concentric-radial pattern of Moscow. It supplemented this pattern, by developing large radial streets such as Leninsky Prospect, to relieve congestion in the central core of the city, and by widening and paving the existing circular thoroughfares. The Kremlin area remained the heart of the city. It would not be a museum piece, as had been suggested by some Soviet city planners, but would remain Moscow's administrative-cultural center. Red Square was to double in size and the surrounding squares were enlarged and rebuilt mainly with government structures.

In deciding to preserve and extend the central radial-ring system, the planners committed themselves to a major restructuring of the municipal transportation network to let people, goods and services move easily in, and through the central ring. The first prerequisite was the continuation of Moscow's subway, its first stage already begun in 1931 by Kaganovich, and later completed by Nikita Khrushchev (Kaganovich's successor as first Party secretary of Moscow). The decision had been made to move people *under* the city center, the most rational means for moving traffic. Moscow's railways were reorganized to relocate the central freight yards, electrify the rail network and eliminate level crossings within the city. "Freight sorting stations and railway depots as well as inner city warehouses near the railway lines shall be gradually removed beyond the limits of the city. . . . All the lines of the Moscow railway junction shall be electrified, starting with the electrification of the suburban lines." The city's waterways were also radically transformed. Work had already started on the Moscow-Volga Canal in 1932 joining the two rivers and providing quicker access to the Caspian, Baltic and the White seas. As a result, the water level of the Moscow and Yauza rivers was raised, requiring reconstruction of the river banks inside Moscow. The Plan determined that "the embankments along the Moscow River shall become the main thoroughfare of the city; the banks of the river shall be faced with granite, and broad avenues shall be constructed, permitting the passage of through traffic along the embankments . . . along the banks of the Yauza River . . . asphalted thoroughfares, 25–30 meters wide . . ." Eleven bridges were to be completed immediately to span these rivers, and more bridges would be built in the future. The river embankments would become "the most favorable part of the city for residential quarters, they shall be reserved exclusively for the construction of dwelling houses and public buildings."

Having established the desired size, density of population, spatial development and transportation network, the planners turned to problems of housing, municipal services and sociocultural amenities. The Plan stated that Moscow's housing space would double in the next ten years. The central area was to be reconstructed, and the old wooden houses pulled down. In the surrounding area, residential neighborhoods would be built in *rayony* (districts) designed to decentralize the city's population and provide integrated sociocultural and educational facilities for 100,000 to 600,000 inhabitants per district. Each district would have its own administrative center, though the Kremlin and its surrounding area would remain the administrative center of the city. The *kvartal* (superblock or residential neighborhood) would contain from 4,000–15,000 inhabitants, depending on its area and location. Kindergartens, elementary schools, clubs, play areas, shops and similar facilities would be provided for each neighborhood. The heights of individual buildings were to rise from the three- or four-story dwellings then being constructed to more economical heights. "Dwelling houses of not less than six stories shall be constructed in Moscow, while on the main thoroughfares and at such points in the city as call for the most effective and imposing architecture (embankments, squares and broad streets), dwelling houses of seven, ten, and fourteen stories shall be built." The Plan also committed Soviet builders to put cultural and service institutions on the ground floor of some apartment buildings, a policy which has met criticism in the Soviet Union over the years for the failure to provide better and cheaper services.

In 1935, Moscow authorities were faced with a chronic lack of basic municipal services. The Plan dealt with such problems of water supply, central heating, gas, sewage and other utilities. Kaganovich had pointed out that only 73 per cent of Moscow's streets and 42 per cent of the city's houses were connected to water mains, and while the average consumption of water per head had risen to thirty gallons, Moscow needed twice that in 1935, just to keep up with industrial and individual requirements, even if the population would not increase any further. The Plan recommended building canals, deepening river beds, and adding pumping stations, reservoirs and filtration plants. "The Stalin Waterworks, using Volga water, shall be begun immediately. . . . The total capacity of the Moscow water supply system shall be increased to 280,000,000 gallons daily by 1939 and to 450,000,000 by 1945." Kaganovich had complained that 57 per cent of Moscow's streets and over 60 per cent of her houses were still not connected to water mains. In some areas of the city, less than 10 per cent of the dwellings had sewage disposal facilities; there were only four hundred miles of sewage pipes and only two effective sewage treatment beds. The Plan recommended the construction of additional sewage treatment plants and more pipelines.

In its thirst for energy, Moscow turned to gas as the long-range source of fuel, heat and power (gas now accounts for three quarters of Moscow's heat and power supply). The supply of gas in the 1930s, however, was only 10 per cent of demand. The pipeline from Saratov had not yet been started, and Moscow was desperately short of energy. The Plan recommended immediate construction of stop-gap additional gasworks which, together with the new supply from Saratov, would produce twelve times the 1935 capacity by 1945. The Plan also recommended expanded development of the Moscow TET system which provided central heating by utilizing the steam from turbines at steam-electric power generating plants. All utilities were to be placed underground in one container. Moscow officials were encouraged "to proceed in 1936 with the reconstruction of the underground pipe and cable system of the city of Moscow by placing the telephone, telegraph, light and power cables, and gas and water mains into one collector, which shall permit the control, regulation, and repair of these conduits without tearing up the pavements."

The 1935 Plan thus provided a concrete program for the development and reconstruction of a modern metropolis during a period of rapid urbanization. While many of its provisions responded to acute urban problems, it was also an *a priori* document which tried to anticipate future urban problems. For example, the Plan's emphasis on cheap and fast public transportation was forward-looking. So was the decision to convert to gas, a more economical and cleaner fuel than coal. The decisions to convert to central heating by using steam from power-generating plants, and to put all public utilities underground in master conduits, were significant steps forward. The emphasis on green space, although hardly novel, was not misplaced, particularly the creation of an outer Green Belt; the decision to expand toward the southwest for future residential development seems to have been a wise step. So was the decision not to tear down the central core nor preserve it as a sterile historical museum relic, but to develop the administrative-cultural (and commercial) center as the active capital.

In other respects the Plan contained well-meaning but unrealistic proposals. The decision to limit Moscow's size to five million inhabitants is the clearest example of this. As long as politicians and economic planners decided that increased productivity had to have first priority, it was impossible to limit population. Additional labor was needed by factories to meet plan requirements, so factories were allowed to continue expanding inside Moscow boundaries, and the passport control system was not strictly enforced. Too many people and too little money also added to the housing crisis. In 1936–38, housing construction was 40 per cent less than stipulated in the Plan; by 1940, the housing plan was 80 per cent behind schedule. Not only was it impossible to build enough housing, but sociocultural and municipal service construction in the residential neighborhoods lagged far behind. The Plan had too optimistically set unrealistic goals to double Moscow's housing space in only a decade. The ten-year-plan concept was well meaning, since it provided continuity and long-range goals, but it also resulted in the annual postponement of many planned projects for another year when resources might hopefully be found.

Many of the Plan's failings were due to prosaic breakdowns in administration and planning. The Moscow Party and government could not cope with all the problems of co-ordination, nor with the technical execution of planning details. Parkins provides a list of some of the immediate "mechanical" shortcomings, citing Soviet sources:

> Many completed plans for public buildings (clubs, hotels, stores) were awaiting a location plan. Often an accurate topographic map of a specific area was lacking, resulting in poor site plans . . . architects often limited themselves to facades of individual buildings, disregarding orientation to the interior plan and appearance of the streets and the background . . . tall buildings were built in the outskirts of the city contrary to construction zoning rules. . . . Specific problems (squares, streets) were often designed for twenty-five and more years in advance while current construction projects were ignored; many plans were inflexible and unrealistic as applied to the immediate tasks . . . the City Soviet neglected to adhere

> to the General Plan. Temporary permits were often issued by the Moscow Soviet for the construction of industrial buildings in areas not intended by the General Plan. These temporary structures were soon expanded and made permanent . . . at many street crossings new structures obstructed clear vision . . . little practical planning work was accomplished in the Moscow suburbs.[9]

What role did Stalin play in the Great Plan? While it is not clear just how much he personally contributed to the shaping and execution of the specific details in this Plan, his priorities for Moscow and for the Soviet Union certainly determined what was built in Moscow. A Soviet source of that time noted, "Comrade Stalin during the preparation of the Plan repeatedly convened sessions to discuss the reconstruction of the capital . . . personally gave a number of key directives on the basic and decisive questions of the reconstruction of the capital . . . carefully checked on the work of reconstruction. Repeatedly after a walk through the city Iosif Vissarionovich would note a number of defects and mistakes, pointing out the most immediate tasks."[10] By deciding that the Soviet Union had to industrialize rapidly and that Moscow would serve as a model for the Soviet Union and for the world, Stalin made the Great Plan into a political document which he utilized for his own purposes. If the grand boulevards and wide streets made good (monumental) city planning sense, they could also serve to move troops in and out of the city center quickly and easily. If the widening of Red Square and other central squares provided more space in the heart of the city, it was also space in which crowds of people could be gathered to listen to Party officials. If keeping the historic unity of the city center was good planning policy, it also preserved the Kremlin as a viable central, walled, political nerve center. If the subway proved to be a great planning achievement, it was also a spectacular political success, a paean to Stalin, with its lavish stations and facilities. The great buildings on the Moscow embankments may have been a logical planning solution to the problems of the thirties, but they also were an expression, in their costly, ornate Stalinesque architecture, of the power and glory of Iosif Vissarionovich Stalin.

World War II intervened before the Plan could be completed. Even though Moscow was not occupied or damaged during the fighting, nevertheless most of the construction stopped and scarce resources were diverted for the war effort. Strategic construction, such as the completion of a subway line to the industrial south of the city in 1943, and the beginning of the Saratov gas line in 1941, did not stop. By the end of the war Moscow had become a badly run-down city. "Gaunt, as forbidding in their rawness as the skeletons of the burned out city of London, the frames of unfinished apartment houses lined the main roads that radiate from Moscow to the ancient cities of central Russia."[11] In 1947, Moscow had its 800th anniversary but there was not much to celebrate, aside from the end of the war. Something had to be done at once about housing and an immediate increase of 500,000 square yards of space was ordered with 3,000,000 square yards to be completed by 1950 (almost twice that built in 1936–40).

The 1946–50 Plan for Moscow retained all the main features of the 1935 Plan, promising hopefully to carry out those tasks that had not been fulfilled "within the next three or four years." The subway was extended to eighteen miles; large expenditures were made on public utilities, the continuation of TET construction, provision of gas, water and sewage facilities; bridges were built, roads asphalted and thousands of trees planted. In March 1948, the decision was made to relocate Moscow State University (MGU) in the southwest part of the city on the Lenin Hills. The new university was to be thirty-two stories high, and together with its spire would become the tallest building in Europe at that time. It was one of the last of the Stalin "wedding-cake" structures with lavish architectural superfluities, costly ornaments and massive stolidity.[12]

MGU was completed in 1953, but Stalin had already died and a new era was beginning. The Great Plan of 1935 had not been fulfilled, though a decisive start had been made on the physical restructuring of the city. The war had seriously interrupted the development and reconstruction of Moscow, but the war was only one factor among many explaining why so much of the Plan remained in the realm of utopia. The Party had not allocated enough money to carry out its planning goals, which were, in effect, too ambitious, and Moscow lacked the human resources to execute the envisaged projects successfully. The Plan was subject to the whims of a powerful dictator, who chose expensive monumentalism and totalitarian architecture, which cut still further into scarce resources. Finally, as the city's population zoomed past five million, it became clear that urbanization and population movement could not be effectively controlled even in a totalitarian society. No one could stop the growth of Moscow and apparently no one wanted to. The social costs of rapid urbanization were more than canceled out in the minds of Soviet citizens, planners and politicians by the immediate economic and cultural benefits of living in the great metropolis.

MOSCOW AFTER STALIN

While Stalin's successors did not fundamentally change the physical structure laid down in the 1935 Plan, nor seriously alter the basic policies established in the thirties, they nevertheless added flesh to the gaunt socialist skeleton they inherited, giving to Moscow more housing, better services and a faster pace of urban development. Khrushchev, who began his climb to power in Moscow while completing the first subway in the thirties, now found it prudent to become the city's patron in the fifties by sponsoring its massive postwar housing construction program. According to one Moscow official, "Nikita Sergeyevich became the champion of housing in Moscow. He promised better, faster and bigger housing. And he delivered it, too. This may have been his greatest achievement." Anyone who has seen the rows of new housing going up throughout the city, hundreds of giant cranes hoisting prefabricated sections into place, the empty spaces of the city filling up almost overnight, has to be impressed by the scale and speed of Moscow's housing construction program. While this new housing was not just due to the efforts of Nikita Sergeyevich (indeed, already from 1951 on, under Stalin, the rate of housing construction had begun to rise appreciably), Khrushchev did make it *his* policy by going from construction site to site, talking incessantly with workers, planners and architects, waving his hard hat, cajoling, haranguing and trying to squeeze out more speed and greater productivity in construction.

Between 1952 and 1958, over 10,000,000 square yards of housing space were constructed. From 1959–66, approximately 20,000,000 square yards were constructed, more than all the housing existing in Moscow in 1950. In the last five years, an additional 21,000,000 square yards have been completed, which means that a total of 51,000,000 square yards of new housing was built in twenty years. Soviet officials like to mention that every day in Moscow, on the average, more than three hundred and fifty new apartments are completed. Since 1953, per capita housing space has risen from less than 4 square yards to a more respectable 7.5 square yards in 1971, still less than the current Soviet standard of 9 square yards, but a tremendous gain under the circumstances. Most of the new housing construction is comprised of high-rise apartments built with prefabricated panels inserted into place by giant cranes. This method has become the model for housing construction in the Soviet Union and has proved successful enough to attract much foreign attention. After visiting construction sites in 1969, a group of American specialists concluded, in a U. S. Department of Commerce publication, "The Soviet construction industry . . . is generally recognized as preeminent in the extent to which building industrialization has been accomplished."[13]

The massive housing construction effort has not been without its problems: Plans were consistently underfulfilled. In the sixties, the construction of new housing consistently fell 10–20 per cent short of planned goals. Early postwar housing was frequently of poor quality; facades crumbled and required wire nets to catch debris cascading down on pedestrians; builders had not properly learned the new construction techniques; maintenance costs for recently completed buildings soared and many became economic liabilities. The city lacked the funds to provide occupants of new apartments with everyday services and utilities when they moved in. One Moscow acquaintance noted, "Often the building is opened to tenants before there is a decent road from the construction site 'back to civilization' so to speak. The water mains may not have been connected, and there are no shops for miles around. It usually takes at least four years to get a telephone." To keep producing new housing in the face of rising costs and higher production norms, Moscow planners upped residential densities, raised the minimum height of new apartment buildings from five to nine stories, lowered ceilings and accelerated prefabrication. Large areas of Moscow soon acquired the surrealistic bleakness and monotony of the new standardized architecture: row upon row of naked concrete blocks, often lacking landscaping or any distinguishing features, moving up and down the seven hills.

The defects in housing stem to a large extent from a continued uncontrollable surge in Moscow's population. Once again the planners were confounded by population dynamics, and the realities of urbanization. The city's population leaped from 5 million in 1950 to 6 million in 1960, and, in 1972, the population was approaching 7.5 million. Besides providing improved housing for five million (no simple task in itself), the authorities have had to find space for an additional 2.5 million persons. "This tremendous rise in Moscow's population put a great burden on our housing construction program," remarked a Moscow official. "It meant that 20,000,000 square yards of additional housing space had to be built beyond the amount originally calculated in the early 1950s." Once they were publicly committed to providing new housing for Moscow's citizens, Khrushchev and his successors could not renege on this all-important issue. So they built quickly and ruthlessly, sacrificing quality and aesthetics for speed, somehow trying to narrow the gap between two generations of promises and Soviet reality. And today, despite the tremendous amount of space which has been built, the construction cranes seem barely a step ahead of the increasing population.

While new housing was, and still remains, the dominant issue for most Muscovites, other important planning decisions and policies of the post-Stalin era have affected the life style and appearance of the capital. In 1960, to accommodate the extra population, and to provide more space for Moscow's future development, the city's area was increased over three and one-half times to 338 square miles. For planning and administrative purposes, the city was divided into four inner boroughs within the Sadovoye Koltso, and seventeen outer boroughs radiating to the new Moscow city limits. A sixty-six mile, four-lane Moscow Belt Highway now encircles the city, serving as Moscow's new boundary. Beyond this highway is the seven-hundred-square-mile Green Belt containing almost a million inhabitants. According to Demichev, first secretary of the Moscow City Party Committee in 1960, this extension of Moscow's boundaries

> was an event of great political significance and a brilliant manifestation of the indubitable advantages of the Soviet social system. . . . The extension of Moscow's boundaries will make it possible to build up additional areas. It will be possible to create big municipal parks and gardens, stadiums and cultural and trade centers. Satellite cities will be built . . . along with what is being done in Moscow this will help to decongest the city and to disperse the population . . . our task is to make Moscow the most beautiful and modern city in the world.[14]

The enlargement of Moscow was an important planning decision because of its concrete move toward a metropolitan or regional concept of development. It extended Moscow's city limits, providing for a larger, decentralized city population; emphasized that the Green Belt was fully under the city's jurisdiction, to be used "for the mass recreation of Muscovites"; deconcentrated some of Moscow's population in satellite cities in the suburban zone beyond the Green Belt. By doing these things, the 1960 decree bound Moscow politicians and planners to a program of integrated city and regional planning as the way to cope with future population increases in Moscow. The impossibility of controlling the population size of Moscow was accepted. The only solution for Moscow lay in the regional dispersion of urban dwellers, who still remained focused on the central city. For commuters, this necessitated a well-developed transportation system inside the city limits and between suburbs and the city.

To cope with this more widely dispersed population, the subway system was developed substantially. Over-all mileage in 1971 totaled eighty-five miles compared with eighteen in 1950. Additional lines were built outward from the city center, to link areas of new housing construction with the industrial, commercial and administrative sectors. New lines were built through the Lenin Hills in the southwest to Yugozapad station and through Novye Cheremushki to Kaluzhskaya; the line to the northeast was extended to Shchyolkovskaya in 1963. The subway system has faithfully replicated the city's geographical layout, with an inner circular route, serving the Sadovoye Koltso, and long spidery radial lines stretching outward toward the city limits. In 1970, the subway carried over four million passengers a day (four times the number carried by New York's subways) at a cost of five kopecks (pennies) a ride. It has eighty-six stations, and seventeen hundred subway cars in operation. Waiting time between trains is short: no more than two to three minutes during regular hours and less than a minute during rush hours. Service is excellent; the trains are fast, clean and punctual. The first stations were built in pseudoclassical style with marble floors, mosaics, magnificent statues, stained glass, bronze and crystal chandeliers. Even so, investment in these ornate lines was actually recouped, according to Soviet sources, in two decades. Today's plainer and cheaper subways apparently repay their initial investment more quickly.

Only 35 per cent of Moscow's fifteen million daily passengers on public transport use the subway; the rest use buses (37 per cent), trolley buses (16 per cent), and streetcars (12 per cent). In 1970, Moscow had 285 miles of streetcar lines, 1,712 miles of bus routes, and 386 miles of trolley buses. Most of the streetcars have been removed from central Moscow and replaced by trolley buses. It was originally planned to eliminate all streetcars, but in recent years Moscow planners discovered that trams were economical, particularly in the outlying areas, where their operation does not directly affect traffic flow. Buses, trams and trolleys are not as efficient as the subway, but they generally provide good, cheap public transportation for Muscovites, except to the outlying areas, where buses are often slow and overcrowded. In the opinion of most foreigners who have lived and traveled in Moscow, the public transportation system is one of the best of any major city. Traffic flow has been speeded up by reducing the number of intersections on the main arteries, particularly those which run through the Sadovoye Koltso (i.e., the Gorky Street-Leningradsky Prospekt artery). These radial routes are connected to the circular Belt Highway which has no level crossings and can carry a one-way stream of 3,000 vehicles an hour around the entire city. Public vehicles move relatively quickly through most parts of the city, even during rush hour traffic. It is estimated there are 600,000 cars in Moscow, of which 150,000 are privately owned. By restricting the supply of private cars until now, Moscow so far has avoided the capitalist problem of private cars choking off public transportation, although this situation may change as the number of private cars rises sharply.

The growth of the Moscow metropolis, with a population of twelve million to fifteen million living within forty miles of the city, and with a regional population of close to thirty million, has necessitated improved transportation ties between the city and the region. Not only has the region's population increased substantially, but its inhabitants are more mobile, stretching transportation facilities almost to the breaking point. Five hundred thousand persons commute daily into Moscow to work, returning nightly to their respective satellite town, village or cottage. With the introduction of the five-day work week in Moscow in the 1960s, Muscovites had acquired enough leisure time to want to travel to the Green Belt and beyond; today, on normal weekends, 25 to 30 per cent of Moscow's population leaves the city. Suburban railway lines have been electrified and carry a large volume of traffic. While the linkages between the subway and the railway are not as well developed as, for example, in London, "much has been done to reduce the distance separating the underground railway stations from the suburban railway stations, to make change-over transfers at lively junctions like Elektrozavodskaya more convenient, and to increase the number of daily two-way suburban trains."[15] Greater use has been made of the Moscow River system to move people in and out of the city. It is estimated that over ten million persons used the Moscow River ferries in 1971 to travel to recreation areas in and around the city.

While increased housing, expansion of Moscow's boundaries, the move to a regional concept of development, and the growth of Moscow's transportation system were the four most important planning decisions made in the post-Stalin period, several other policies and experiments are worth mentioning. The mikrorayon (neighborhood unit) represented a genuine attempt to decentralize Moscow in a socialist fashion.** The neighborhood unit had its antecedents in experiments briefly carried out in Moscow in the twenties and thirties, resembled the kvartal described in the 1935 Plan, and was based on the assumption that urban alienation can be eliminated through the deliberate creation of urban residential subcommunities. Khrushchev and his planners in the first flush of their massive housing construction program propagandized the neighborhood unit as the most sensible way to integrate housing and everyday services. The concept was a logical one: build new housing in units of four thousand to eighteen thousand inhabitants, keeping densities low, with plenty of green space, and providing a hierarchy of nearby services to residents. Each residential unit would have its own identity, like an urban village, and its residents would develop attachments to this "community." Since Moscow had just expanded its boundaries, there should have been ample room for thousands of these communities scattered throughout the city, thus minimizing the sterility of the new prefabricated architecture. But two Soviet realities intervened to force the mikrorayon as it was conceived in the late fifties into the realm of utopia by the end of the sixties. First it was uneconomical to build low density units with an elaborate range of services. Land quickly became scarce in Moscow: heights of buildings were raised to nine stories; densities increased; the minimum size of a unit rose to fifty thousand inhabitants. They could not provide the integrated service facilities required to give the neighborhood unit its village identity. Second, Moscow social scientists belatedly discovered, through the use of surveys, that Muscovites did not want to live in "urban villages" far from the Bolshoi or from the Kremlin. They want to ride the subway and shop at the GUM store off Red Square. According to one Soviet sociologist, "The neighborhood unit came into conflict with the fundamental principles of urbanism. One of the characteristics of the modern urban way of life is the desire for information, and for the mobility to go and seek that information. People came to Moscow to get this information and to free themselves from the fetters of village life. They want to be mobile. They don't want to be forced to be part of a community and forced to make friends. For these reasons, in the new Plan formulated in 1968 the small neighborhood unit concept has been effectively eliminated as a planning goal."

A similar fate befell the satellite (*sputnik*) city concept, which was advanced with gusto in the late fifties as one solution to Moscow's pressing population problems. The city of Kryukovo (renamed Zelenograd) was to have been an example of the satellite concept in practice. The prospective satellite city was located twenty miles from Moscow, to contain seventy thousand people and to be a self-contained settlement (not a dormitory town) with its own industries. According to Saushkin, Kryukovo was one of "several projects submitted a few years ago to

** The neighborhood unit idea was well known in European and American planning in the early thirties. (Editor's note.)

limit the growth of Moscow's population and remove a number of industrial establishments, institutions of higher learning and tens of thousands of people to satellite towns." He concluded that the success of this experiment "will show whether it pays to go on with the building of other similar towns. . . . Now that Moscow has great reserves and possibilities for building large-scale housing, the decision to build satellites must be thoroughly warranted and based on a sound, long-term calculation."[16] Discussions with Moscow planners indicated that Kryukovo's construction had gone badly, and that the satellite concept was being restudied. Today the autonomous satellite city has been rejected†† in favor of large-scale housing construction within the city boundaries, and a few dormitory towns in the suburban area beyond the Green Belt.

Co-operative housing has made a significant comeback in Moscow. The co-operative concept was originally advanced and partially applied in the 1920s, but was phased out in the 1930s, apparently for ideological and political reasons. Today co-operative housing has become an important element in Moscow's housing construction program. Fifteen per cent of Moscow's housing is now co-operative housing; this type of housing differs from the conventional state housing in the following respects: Co-operative housing is built for a specific group, by the state; the group secures a down payment from each member equal to 30–40 per cent of the total cost of an apartment. The state then builds the apartment building for the co-operative group; members of the co-operative pay a monthly charge after they move in to pay off their mortgage over a fifteen- to twenty-year period; with the co-operative's permission, they may sell their share in their apartment at any time to anyone else, even for a profit. Co-operative housing (which is the dominant form of housing in Eastern Europe) encourages the use of private funds to build scarce housing. It has helped to ease Moscow's housing shortage. At the same time it poses certain ideological problems. Invariably co-operative housing is of better quality than regular state housing, since members of co-operatives are usually comparatively well off and are able to persuade builders to put in more amenities. There is the danger that this can accentuate differences among income groups, especially since one can make a profit when selling one's share in a co-operative. As one Soviet planner put it, "The best housing in Moscow either belongs to the Party officials or to other privileged groups, such as artists. Those who live in co-operatives also have better housing than the average Muscovite because they can pay for it." The future of co-operatives is a matter of concern to Moscow politicians and planners, many of whom see the co-operatives as a long-run political liability, though a short-term economic necessity.

A 180-degree turn in Soviet architecture has occurred in the post-Stalin period, away from the pseudoclassicism of the earlier "wedding-cake" buildings and from the lavish monumentalism and facades of the Stalinist period. In a 1955 decree, "On Eliminating Excesses in Design and Construction," the new Soviet leaders explicitly rejected "huge artless structures patterned after Moscow State University," and "the exaggerated ornamentalism of the early postwar years." Soviet writers and scholars added their criticism: "The appearance of the New York skyscrapers was dictated by the high cost of land. There was logic in this. But to erect a building with an enormous tower along flower beds and lanes (like Moscow State University, for example) with the sole purpose of making it visible

†† Approximately one thousand Soviet new towns have been built. (Editor's note.)

from a distance of tens of kilometers is at best illogical."[17] Moscow's skyline soon changed to more conventional modern architecture, shaped by the cost of construction and by construction technology. While occasional successful designs have managed to avoid "constructivism" (the Palace of Congresses next to the Kremlin, the Rossiya Cinema), most of Moscow's new buildings tend to look like modern buildings in other world cities, and there is nothing very "socialist" about them. So far, it seems, Moscow architects have not found this "socialist" synthesis of Russian tradition and modern design despite the use of color, new shapes and forms, though they have managed in some areas to moderate the starkness of the prefabricated large-scale projects.

One of the more successful central city projects has been the Kalinin Street redevelopment in downtown Moscow, a fifteen-minute walk from the Kremlin. Modern twenty-six-story office and apartment buildings stand on both sides of a wide street. The structures set off a major new shopping and service area with cafés, a supermarket and the best bakery in Moscow. Foreigners are taken to Kalinin with some pride, because it is a Moscow showpiece—modern, gleaming, bustling and *very urban.* Kalinin symbolizes a new Moscow, not that much different in appearance from any other big city (unless one looks off to one side and sees a tiny Russian church with golden onion cupolas nestled between the glass and concrete, or turns around to glimpse the walls of the Kremlin [Fig. 4]). Kalinin Street and its surroundings juxtapose the old and the new, what is Russian and Soviet, socialist and urban.

Statistics concerning social composition, employment and the provision of amenities help to fill out this brief portrait of contemporary Moscow. There are still more women (56 per cent) than men, a legacy from the last war. Approximately 50 per cent of the population is thirty years or under; 15 per cent, sixty years or older; an estimated 40 per cent was born in Moscow. Over 99 per cent are now literate! Every fifth working Muscovite has a higher education, and every third working person has a specialized or technical education. There are currently 950,000 students in Moscow. The great majority of Muscovites are Russians (89.2 per cent); the two other significant national groups are Jews (4.1 per cent) and Ukrainians (2.3 per cent); 58.2 per cent of Moscow's total population is employed; 15.7 per cent are pensioners and other persons receiving government assistance; 25.9 per cent are dependents of various people (children, students receiving grants-in-aid, the aged and others involved solely with housekeeping and child rearing). Fifty-eight per cent of the working population is employed in industry, construction and transportation; 18 per cent, in scientific work; 10 per cent, in education, public health, housing and communal services; 8 per cent, in trade and food supply; 4.1 per cent, in the administrative apparatus of the state and economic organizations; the remaining 2 per cent, in communications, art and technical supply fields. Moscow, with 2.8 per cent of the Soviet population, produces 8 per cent of the country's gross national product. More than half of Moscow's working population are women (54.4 per cent) and 70 per cent of all women are employed. While women constitute only 40 per cent of employees in machine building and metalworking, they total over 80 per cent in Moscow's textile industries. Women comprise 88.9 per cent of public health workers, 81 per cent of those in trade, and 71 per cent in the field of education. The majority of Moscow's doctors, teachers and economists are women.

The city has seventy-five doctors for every ten thousand people, a high ratio

FIG. 4 Historic preservation: An old church saved by popular action, Kalinim Allée. *Photograph by Michael Putnam*

compared to other countries. There are 1,200 schools, including 150 specialized secondary and 156 vocational schools. More than two thirds of Moscow's preschool-age children attend kindergartens and day-care centers operating on weekly and daily bases. Some 600,000 students attend seventy-six institutions of higher learning (this includes night school and correspondence course registration). The most important is Moscow State University which has 30,000 students, including 3,000 foreign students from seventy nations. The faculty of Moscow's higher educational institutes totals 27,000 of which 2,000 have Ph.D.s and 12,000 have M.A.s. Thirty-seven per cent of the Soviet Union's scientific establishments, 20 per cent of her scientific personnel, 42 per cent of her graduate students, and 20 per cent of her college students are in Moscow. All college students receive full state tuition and a stipend for living expenses.

Compared with the rest of the Soviet Union, Moscow has a high proportion of married people and a lower family size; Moscow's families average 3.3 persons against a Soviet average of 3.7. Family size in Moscow is declining as the local birth rate plummets downward. The city has one of the lowest birth rates of any large Soviet city. At the present time Moscow's population would decline if there were no continuing migration into the city, because the death rate is greater than the birth rate. A recent survey of 1,462 married working women in four Moscow factories revealed that the average number of children desired by married working women was 1.66, a figure below the mechanical population replacement requirement.[18] Moscow working women cited inadequate housing space as the chief reason for not wanting many children, though lack of income and insufficient day-care centers were also cited as factors. Another sociological survey concluded that women with high educational qualifications also wanted small families, but these women wanted to give up their jobs to stay home with their young children (unlike female factory workers). This attitude could intensify Moscow's increasing labor shortage though it might lead to an eventual increase in the birth rate. Forty per cent of Moscow families live in their own apartments; the rest still have to share apartment space with other families or individuals. There is no privately built or individually owned housing in Moscow. Apartments are fairly functional and simply furnished. Rent and utilities (heat, gas, electricity, water) can total 10 per cent of income. Ninety-six per cent of Moscow dwellings have running water; 75 per cent have gas; over 80 per cent have central heating; all have electricity. Less than 10 per cent of families have telephones. Rent is calculated according to the amount of housing space which a family occupies, and the quality and location of the building. Tenants are responsible for simple maintenance such as painting and plastering. Waiting lists for new housing are long; it may take several years to get improved space. Housing allocation priorities are based upon a list of factors which take need and occupational importance into account. On the whole, the allocation system appears equitable, and in many buildings one finds professors, factory workers and secretaries living next to each other. Unlike most North American cities, Moscow has no "ethnic ghettos." Moscow's population is distributed fairly heterogeneously throughout the city. Still there are special areas in which the Party elite, writers, artists and other privileged groups tend to live.

The average Muscovite works a five-day week, and spends one and one-half to two hours a day traveling to and from his or her job. Shopping for food is a tiresome daily task, also taking up from one and one-half to two hours. *Babushkas* (grandmothers) clutch their net bags and sally out to battle the clerks in the stores all day long. Working men and women stop off at the various shops on their way home to see what's available for supper.

Leisure activities are becoming increasingly important to Muscovites. Many of them attend evening courses and extramural study programs; others take advantage of the subsidized public theatre and ballet (a ticket to the Bolshoi can cost as little as a dollar), movies, clubs and libraries. Television sets have spread into many Moscow apartments. The head of the Moscow police force noted that crime in Moscow (which is insignificant by New York standards) has decreased at night now that Muscovites stay at home to watch television. With the shortened five-day work week Muscovites now have two days in which to get away from cramped apartments and to head for the countryside, either to private and co-operative cottages (*dachas*) or to recreation areas. The dachas, whose construction has now been restricted, vary in quality from small huts with vegetable gardens to fancy homes reserved for Party officials or members of the Moscow intelligentsia. What Muscovites do with their *veekend* is of great concern to Soviet planners, because they have to provide the transportation network to move people in and out of the city, and to build adequate recreational facilities in the Green Belt and suburban area as well as central city. One Moscow planner said, "The demand on existing leisure facilities is staggering. Just try to get into the Aragvy or the Pechora Café on a Saturday night! The extra time for leisure together with more spending money has rapidly increased the mobility of the population, affecting Moscow's life style, changing behavior patterns (why bother visiting your parents when you can fly to Leningrad for the weekend?) and increasing the city's diversity."

How is this increasingly complex city administered? The basic principles of Moscow politics and administration have not changed much in thirty years (Fig. 5). The Party still runs the city and is responsible for policy making. *Moscow's priorities are determined at the national level, in the Party Central Committee and the USSR Council of Ministers.*‡‡ The most powerful central Party organ in the USSR, the Politburo, contains one former Moscow Party leader (Demichev) and the current Moscow first secretary (Grishin) among its members. The 885,000 member Moscow City Party organization is the largest city Party organization in the USSR. An additional 320,000 communists, members of Moscow regional, USSR and other Party organizations also live in Moscow, giving the city a ratio of seventeen communists per 1,000, against a national average of six per 1,000. Moscow's top communists are first-rate administrators and specialists in various branches of the municipal economy. Most of them have endured a long apprenticeship in Moscow politics and administration, at the factory and borough level. All the top Moscow Party leaders have a higher specialized degree, and many of them are experts in housing construction and in branches of the municipal economy.

The Moscow Party organization is a smaller version of the national Party structure. The first secretary, Grishin, is appointed by the Politburo, and is the head of the Moscow Party organization. The main governing organs are the bureau (the most important, since it contains the eighteen key Party officials) and the *gorkom* (Party committee) of one hundred twenty-nine members, which contains the leading Party members in Moscow. Party organizations in Moscow are each responsible to a higher Party unit within a carefully determined hierarchy. This system includes twenty-nine city borough Party organizations, the city of Zelenograd, several subborough units, and over 8,500 primary Party organizations

‡‡ (Editor's italics.)

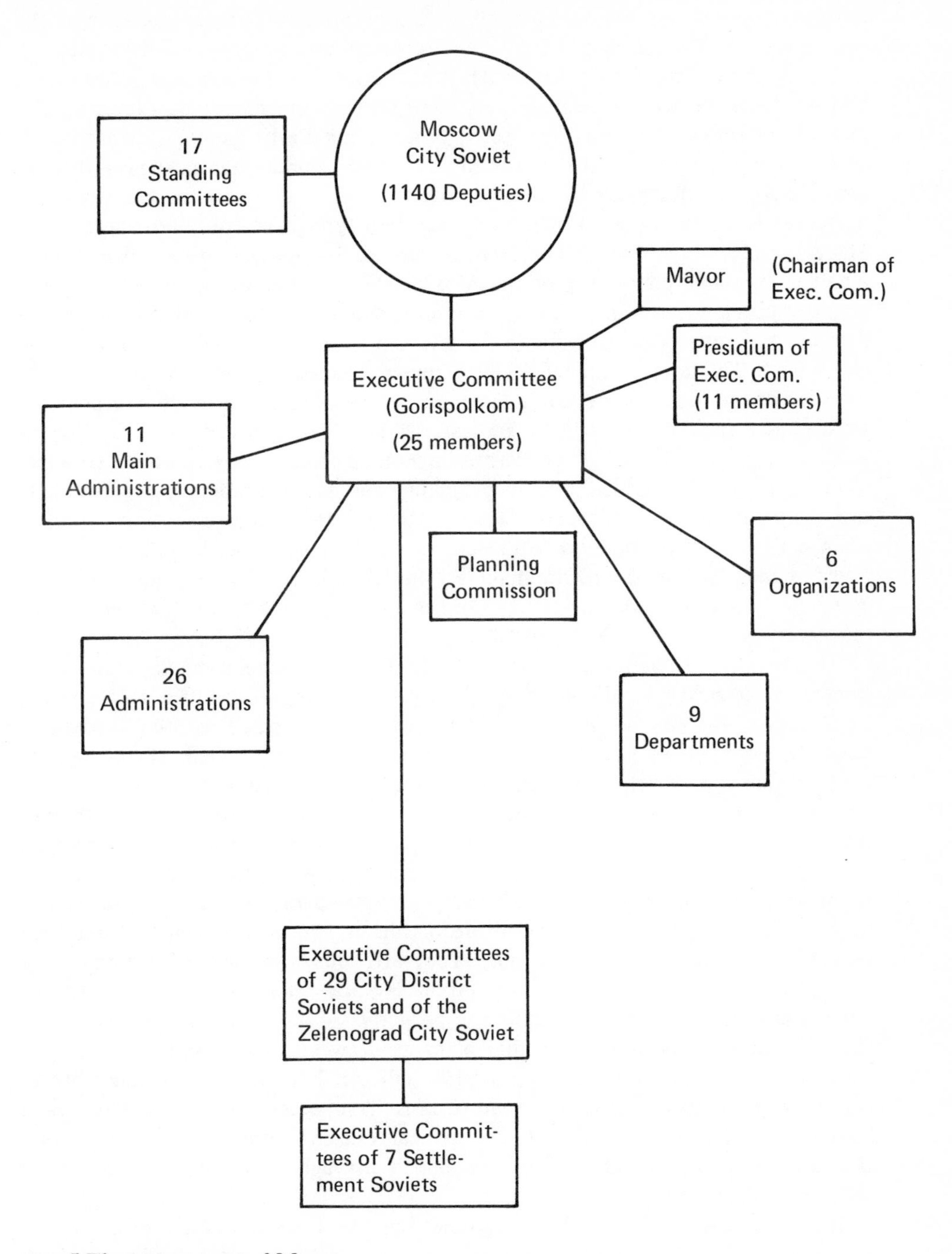

FIG. 5 The government of Moscow.

which direct and organize economic and cultural life at the factory level. The municipal Party organization directs the day-to-day work of municipal government through an apparatus of Party departments, divided into three categories: political-ideological, economic-productive, and Party-administrative. These Party departments co-ordinate the administration of Moscow and provide guidance to the city Soviet, which is the administrative and representative arm of the Soviet state.

The Moscow City Soviet (council) is the ostensible government of Moscow, and its chairman, who is elected every two years, is the mayor of Moscow. The current chairman, Vladimir Promyslov, is a leading Party member, specialist on housing construction, and sits on the Moscow Party bureau, its most powerful organ. He is sixty-four years old and has been mayor of Moscow for ten years. As mayor he is the titular head of the city, receives foreign visitors and functions as Moscow's chief executive at conferences abroad. He is head of the twenty-five-member executive committee of the Moscow Soviet, and of the smaller eleven-member presidium within it. The presidium conducts the daily affairs of administration and reports back to the larger executive committee and to the overlarge city Soviet. The latter contains 1,140 deputies, elected for two-year terms. Fifty per cent of the deputies are Party members; 46 per cent are women; 50 per cent were elected for the first time in the last election. The deputies meet together in sessions four times a year and participate in various committees in between sessions. Their main function is neither policy making nor administration, but representation. They are the link between authority and citizens. They send down and explain policies and information to the masses, and transmit the latter's complaints and demands back to the policy makers. These deputies essentially are amateurs: They do not stay on as deputies for more than a couple of terms, and they maintain their regular jobs while serving as deputies.

"Professional" deputies usually head the fifty-three departments, administrations and commissions of the Moscow City Soviet. These deputies are full-time employees of the city Soviet and are automatically re-elected to their posts. For example, Konovalov, head of the Organization-Instruction Department (which trains deputies and helps to organize mass campaigns), has been head of this department for more than a decade. These deputies perform administrative, rather than executive, functions, and together with their top assistants could be said to constitute the municipal civil service, Moscow's permanent staff of administrators. On the whole, this is a competent group of bureaucrats, usually experts in their respective fields by virtue of higher educational degrees and long tenure in a specialized municipal post. They are, almost without exception, Party members. These administrators are responsible for seeing to it that Moscow's current annual budget of $1.6 billion is properly spent; that housing gets put in the right place at the right time; that planners draw up their designs and execute them in conformity with the current plan indices; that there are enough buses, shops, roads, baths, restaurants; that citizens have access to bureaucrats (each administrator has weekly office hours to hear citizen complaints and requests); that the city's cultural life is well developed through a municipal network of schools, clubs, theatres, movies, etc.

The list of responsibilities is large, reflecting the absence of private enterprise and management in Moscow. The municipality, together with other administrative levels, is responsible for activities such as housing trade, utilities and production, which in capitalist cities would, in whole or in part, be performed by individual enterprise and corporations—the private sector. Some of Moscow's administrations resemble North American corporations in the grand scale of their work. The Main Administration of Construction (*Glavmosstroy*) currently builds 85 per cent of Moscow's housing, has 250,000 employees and an annual payroll of $350 million, an impressive organization by any standard. Glavmosstroy was created in 1954, by amalgamating hundreds of small construction organizations, to facilitate Khrushchev's impending industrialization of the city's housing construction. Its first head was Promyslov, now Moscow's mayor, and many of its top officials have been appointed to high posts in the USSR, reflecting the importance of the Glavmosstroy's work.

The apartments and buildings which Glavmosstroy builds are designed by the Moscow Town Planning and Architecture Main Administration which has over 10,000 employees and operates several institutes, factories and design workshops. The Main Administration of Construction Materials provides building supplies to Glavmosstroy. The latter has to wait for approval from the Main Administration of Capital Construction in order to get paid for the finished building. Once the building is completed, then the Administration for the Allocation of Housing takes charge of the distribution of new housing and the Main Administration of Housing assumes responsibility for housing operation and repairs. It is estimated that this process involves hundreds of thousands of Muscovites working in various aspects of the housing economy. The scale, complexity and importance of this work put a great burden on the shoulders of Moscow's municipal administrators who are under constant pressure to deliver scarce housing to anxious citizens.

The Party directs and controls the work of the city Soviet in several key ways. The most important municipal officials are Party members; the mayor and other members of the presidium are appointed on the advice of the Party, which also staffs other key economic and state posts in the municipality; the city Soviet makes no policy—this is the exclusive right of the Party; parallel Party organs supervise the work of municipal administrators. For example, the Construction Department of the Moscow City Party Committee supervises the work of the Main Administration of Construction Materials of the city Soviet. One Moscow official remarked, "All that the Party needs is a telephone. Then the phone rings all day and it is the Party checking up on something, to nag, to co-ordinate, to give or to get information." Aside from directly supervising the work of municipal administration, the Party mobilizes Moscow's population in support of its policies, through a network of thousands of activists propagandizing Party policies in the media and in face-to-face meetings with citizens. At the lower levels, the Party organizes groups of citizens to do voluntary public tasks (tree planting on Sundays, militia work, housing repair work), informs citizens about the meaning and content of Party policies, and seeks citizen commitment by presenting candidates for elections to Soviets every other year. The Party performs perhaps its most important task in supervising production. This is not directly a "municipal" responsibility since over 90 per cent of the production of industries located on Moscow's territory is under the jurisdiction of higher governmental levels (the Russian Republic or the USSR level). But increased productivity of these enterprises brings greater tax revenues to the Republic and central coffers, eventually producing more revenues for Moscow.

In addition to the municipal Party and Soviet organizations, there are twenty-nine borough Soviets and borough Party organizations. They are smaller versions of their municipal parents, fully under the latter's jurisdiction. Moscow's boroughs average approximately 250,000–300,000 inhabitants, and their Soviets each contain about 250 deputies. The borough Soviets also have fewer administrations and departments, in keeping with their more limited range of functions. According to one Moscow official, "The borough organizations decentralize the administration of Moscow and bring government and people closer together. We are trying to give more responsibilities to the boroughs, to give local administration more control over local matters." Those officials and Party members who perform well on this level will eventually be rewarded with a promotion to the municipal level of politics and administration.

How does the average citizen participate in the administration of Moscow? Municipal officials note that every two years, over 99 per cent of Moscow's eligible voters turn out to vote for borough and city deputies. They state that every person's claims and demands can be heard by a responsible official, "because," according to the head of Moscow's Organization-Instruction Administration, "we have a veritable army of politically conscious activists, deputies, the media and other channels through which a citizen can make his opinion known." Soviet officials point out to Western visitors that there is more citizen involvement in Moscow than in any comparable capital city in the West. "Everybody has a duty to participate in everything, from helping to fix his own apartment, to directing traffic, fighting against alcoholism, beautifying the city and so on." The official handbook on Moscow converts this "participation" into statistics: "During the past year the city was enriched by the planting of 140,000 trees, 700,000 bushes, the opening of over 7,000 children's playgrounds and sportsgrounds. Almost 900 libraries, 390 bookstores and counters, 20 kindergartens, 70 clubs, 480 polyclinics and first aid quarters, over 2,000 various amateur groups were created . . ."[19] All this, according to this source, was done because of public, "voluntary" participation.

Despite these impressive claims and statistics, some Moscow sociologists feel that Muscovites are becoming alienated within their city. "Our surveys show," said one sociologist, "that Muscovites don't want to spend their time in these voluntary civic duties, and that most of the work is done by a few activists. The majority of Muscovites find in big city life a chance to be autonomous and to cut group ties. Tree planting and activities like that increasingly act as an intrusion on this life style. This is a serious problem and we have to try to counteract such antisocial tendencies." While citizens do not seem to relate well enough to Party-sponsored attempts to enlist strong civic solidarity and support through mass projects or routine elections, citizens are beginning to "get involved" in municipal affairs in a different direction. Brief citizen protests over particular issues have occurred. A group of citizens complains about a problem and manages to get media space to air a complaint. Then official action is taken. The complaint is never directed against the Party or against a particular Party policy: The criticism is of failures in policy execution by administrators. For example, the fuss over Moscow State University converting two experimental housing units into dormitories precipitated a lengthy exchange of views in the Moscow press. The university and those who had permitted the university to do this had to back down and resume the experiment. Citizen pressure took place when the small church wedged in between the twenty-six-story skyscrapers on Kalinin Street was scheduled to be torn down (see Fig. 4). Insistent complaining by various groups of architects, planners and other citizens finally forced the authorities to build around the church.

To those who are used to the comparative anarchy of life and politics in cities such as New York, these examples of citizen participation may seem rather forced. But in the Soviet context they represent a step forward; Muscovites who want to air their views on issues may find it easier to do so in the future. On the other hand, it appears that the majority prefer to enjoy the improved life style of Moscow without getting involved in its politics or administration. "As long as things keep getting better for us each year," said one Muscovite, "why complain? Most of us have been waiting for years for new housing; now we want to enjoy our apartments, our extra leisure time and life in general." A Soviet sociologist, well read on the literature of urbanization and urbanism, suggested that the above view may be a short-run reaction to prosperity, and that in the long run the nature of citizen participation will change from passivity to action. "When people become more mobile, have more leisure time, more access to information, and are more articulate, it is inevitable that they will have something to say about the issues and policies affecting their lives. The Party and the government have to anticipate this shift and provide adequate channels for active citizen participation in the future. We must use the lessons of urban development elsewhere to avoid the mistakes of Paris, Tokyo and New York, and make the socialist city socially and psychologically satisfying as well as functionally sound and physically attractive."

THE NEW 1971 PLAN AND THE FUTURE OF MOSCOW

For more than a decade Moscow planners and officials have been working on a new Plan for Moscow. In 1963, the Moscow City Party organization and the executive committee of the Moscow City Soviet submitted the basic outlines of the prospective plan to the Soviet Party and government for approval. By 1965, the Plan's basic outlines had not yet been approved, apparently because of a debate over restrictions on industrial expansion within Moscow's boundaries. Moscow's planners had submitted a document limiting the size of Moscow to 6.6–6.8 million inhabitants, which forcefully restricted future industrial expansion and asked that $250 million of previously approved, though still unbuilt, industrial construction be halted. This apparently was strongly opposed by *Gosstroy, Gosplan* and other top USSR ministries who argued that without the continued Moscow industrial expansion, productivity would decline. The Central Committee of the Party apparently stepped in to support the Moscow planners and permitted public criticism of Gosstroy and the ministries' position. A 1965 decree of the USSR Council of Ministers stated that excessive concentration of industrial enterprise was not permissible. Finally, a 1966 draft Plan was published, though the draft after several changes was not approved until 1971 (see Fig. 3).[20] In the interim, some compromises were made. The population limit had to be raised from 6.6–6.8 million to a more realistic 7.5–8.0 million, and much of the disputed new industrial construction did manage to get built.

In 1968, Moscow was administratively reorganized when the existing seventeen boroughs were replaced by twenty-nine smaller boroughs. This had the effect of more rationally distributing Moscow's population among its administrative subunits. Now the largest borough contained 300,000 inhabitants, whereas before the change over 700,000 inhabitants lived in several large boroughs. For planners and politicians the administrative reform may have been a necessary prerequisite for the final approval of Moscow's Plan; it may also have been that controversy over the administrative reform had delayed approval of the Plan. Many Muscovites were upset at the prospect of redrawing borough boundaries.

The Plan in its present form reaffirms basic principles established in 1935 and in subsequent planning practices. It is a future-oriented document, pointed to the year 1980, when every Muscovite will have twelve to fifteen square yards of housing space and hopefully even a separate apartment for each family; the growing city will be decentralized into eight semiautonomous planning zones; the transportation system will be so well developed that citizens can travel to any point in the city in under forty minutes; citizens will have telephones, laundromats, cars, and fresh vegetables and fruits twelve months of the year. According to Mayor Promyslov, the new Plan will be fulfilled.

The Plan assumes that the Moscow region will continue to grow to over fifty million by the year 2000. Ties between the city and the region will intensify and transportation facilities will expand greatly. The city will have to be prepared to receive up to two million travelers of all kinds daily, and this means further development of the railways, airports, waterways and high capacity expressways. Eight million inhabitants will reside within the city boundaries; an additional one million will live in the Green Belt to be further developed as a recreation area. Within the central city, all industrial expansion will cease. New industries must locate in the suburban zone beyond the Green Belt, and it should be impossible for heavy industries within the city to expand. The city's industries will become more specialized: "Moscow will develop, first of all, industry requiring highly skilled labor—precision machine building, instrument manufacturing, machine tool manufacturing, radio engineering, electronic and electrical engineering industries, as well as high quality consumer goods." Moscow's service industries will increase their volume of production, and by 1980, the majority of Moscow's working force will be employed in the service sector (present ratio is 57 per cent for industry/ manufacturing, and 43 per cent for service).

Moscow will now be constructed and planned "polycentrically." The traditional monocentric planning structure of the city has been replaced by eight complex planning zones, each having a population of a million inhabitants. "The central hub concept is no longer valid in a city of eight million spread over a large area," says N. Ullas, one of Moscow's top planners. "By decentralizing the planning of Moscow, we can minimize the problems of metropolitan growth. . . . Apart from the Sadovoye Koltso, we will develop other subcenters to help decentralize the city." The eight planning zones will be broken down into planning districts (*rayony*) with population ranging from 250,000 to 400,000 each. These rayony in turn will be comprised of a number of residential districts of 30,000–70,000 residents each, with all the required everyday services, sports and cultural facilities. Population in Sadovoye Koltso will be reduced from 600,000 to 250,000–300,000 to lower population density in the city center. The planners expect to remove from the Sadovoye Koltso all small and unnecessary factories and administrative buildings. The number of employees in institutions and enterprises in this area will decrease from 500,000 to 250,000. "Thus," according to Ullas, "the city center will become a real cultural-administrative focal point, along with the main Moscow shops and some residential housing such as we have in Kalinin Street. We will build new parks, widen streets, provide more facilities for residents, pedestrians and shoppers."

The provision of adequate housing is a key element in the new Plan. "Every year we have to relocate 500,000 people in Moscow," observed Promyslov. "So in the current twenty-year period (1961–80) we plan to build 2.2 million apartment units. As of 1970, we had already built 1.3 million apartment units." Yearly housing construction will average 3,500,000 square yards, almost all of it prefabricated, large panel construction. The minimum heights of buildings will be raised to nine stories, and, in some areas, residential buildings will be twenty-five stories high. "The main factor in the future," says Promyslov, "is better distribution of land use. By raising the heights of individual buildings we can reduce their per unit cost. The density of the residential area will not increase because the buildings will be spread out farther from each other." By 1980, only a small percentage of Moscow's total housing space will be in buildings below nine stories, the old two-story and one-story houses will have vanished from sight, and Moscow will have become a city comprised of high-rise apartments and office buildings.

Rapid housing construction is to be accompanied by large-scale development of public utilities, sociocultural services and trade facilities. Industrial and personal water consumption will almost double, from 140 gallons per capita per day to 240 in 1980. Large capital investments are being made in the sewage system, and planners expect that by 1980 they will have built enough treatment facilities so that they will no longer have to dump raw sewage in the Moscow River. The supply of electricity will quadruple, and the central heat supply which is derived from the generation of electricity will reach 95–98 per cent in the housing sector, and 80–85 per cent in industry. Gas will increase 3.5 times over 1960. According to the Plan, "Gas will practically displace all other kinds of fuel, with the exception of those necessary to special technological needs and an emergency reserve." Gas will be piped to Moscow from Western Siberia and Central Asia and stored in huge underground storage tanks with a capacity of five to six million cubic yards. An attempt will be made to provide Muscovites with more telephones and to put an end to the long waiting period.

Moscow's planners recommend converting wastes which are presently buried in dumps into secondary raw material suitable for reusage and also into organic fertilizer. Moscow's green space will increase per capita, from the current per capita average of thirty-three square yards to over forty square yards (including the Green Belt). Green space will be distributed more evenly throughout the city, by building and enlarging parks in the central area. The city is developing its "green wedges"—strips of park land radiating outward to the Belt Highway and to the Green Belt—and expanding the banks of the Moscow River system for park land and natural forests. Since the Green Belt has become so important to Muscovites for their recreation, private dacha construction has been controlled, and only a small increase in the permanent population of the Green Belt will be permitted. Market gardening facilities will be expanded, and hostels, camping grounds and other recreational facilities are to be developed close to transportation facilities.

Transportation is a key element. Public transportation has to be greatly expanded since the number of passengers will double by 1980. The subway will be lengthened to two hundred miles, and construction may begin on a second circle linking up the new radial lines now being built. Streetcar, trolley bus and bus line mileage will be doubled. The share of passengers carried by the subway will rise to 38 per cent. Subway and suburban railway lines will connect to each other wherever possible, so that traffic can move easily into the region. The Plan notes, "It is also necessary to pay attention to the construction of new kinds of transport such as monorail and the rapid streetcar to connect the peripheral districts of the city and places of mass recreation." Other possibilities would be the conversion of the circular railway line now used for freight traffic for passenger service; or constructing a central railway station, so that "through" passengers don't have to change stations inside Moscow. The planners have established guidelines that Muscovites should spend no more than thirty to forty minutes on any trip inside the city; one and one-half hours to reach any recreation area within the Green Belt, and not more than two and one-half hours to places located within the Region.

"In five years," says Promyslov, "Moscow will have over a million cars"; there may be 1,500,000 cars in 1980, three times the number currently in Moscow. Radial routes are being widened and extended through the city center to the Belt Highway; work is already under way on a number of these projects. Proposals are being discussed for roads joining the radial routes to each other farther out from the inner circle, so that traffic will not always have to go through the center. Another proposal suggests the immediate construction of high speed freeways for buses and cars across the city. Planning for cars will not be easy, but Moscow planners have done their best to control their use. First, they have created a public transportation system that is as good as any existing public transportation system. Second, they have provided wide roads well geared to motor traffic, to reduce congestion and pollution. Third, cars are being introduced fairly slowly—it takes up to five years to get a car after application through normal channels. Inner city parking and service facilities are being developed gradually so as not to make downtown automobile transportation too attractive. Efforts are being made to direct automobile flow from Moscow to the suburban area and beyond by improving roads, by constructing service areas on the Belt Highway and by building motels.

The projected increase in automobiles has evoked concern over pollution. Despite past claims to the contrary, Moscow is not pollution free, though it has suffered less than most modern cities. Saushkin already noted a decade ago "a haze, consisting of smoke, ash, dust, the exhaust fumes of cars and aeroplanes and various industrial particles. Like a gigantic grayish umbrella that can usually be seen from a great distance, this pall hangs over large industrial cities, including Moscow."[21] "The greenery and birds have been permanently driven out by an endless cavalcade of noisy vehicles," complained a Soviet citizen; his criticism is too harsh. This writer found the city cleaner, quieter and less polluted than any other large modern city, with the exception of Peking, which has practically no motor traffic and no comparable industry. But Soviet planners and citizens are trying to keep it that way by taking immediate action. The Plan calls for removing polluting industries; continuing to convert to gas; and facilitating rapid movement of traffic through the city center.

There are other forward-looking points covered in the Plan: the anticipated tenfold increase in Moscow's air traffic volume; the necessary increased quality of housing maintenance and repair; provision of improved trade and consumer service facilities; construction of hotels and tourist facilities for Soviet travelers as well as foreign guests; more sports facilities, schools, day-care centers, movies, clubs and libraries; twenty thousand taxicabs (which will carry 5 per cent of passenger traffic); strong efforts to make Moscow more attractive architecturally. Concerning the latter, many Moscow architects and planners wonder how they can make a city of prefabricated concrete high-rise apartments attractive to occupants. Landscaping may be a partial answer to the bleakness of the new Moscow constructivism, but it is difficult to provide year-round landscaping in a northern climate. Beyond that there is little hope. In a recent article in *Kommunist,* Promyslov complains about "the monotony of the houses, the architectural monotony, and the faceless development of some new city districts."[22] Hopefully future builders and architects can vary their designs through a "Standard Catalogue for Unified Industrial Goods" (modular housing components) now being tested in Moscow.

Compared with its 1935 predecessor, the new Plan is more modest and, therefore, more likely to succeed in its goals. Much will depend on whether the Soviet Government can find the resources to build the necessary housing and provide new occupants with the promised full range of sociocultural services at the same time. If the development of the expanded transportation network lags, the Plan will be in serious trouble. More importantly, can the planners, after forty years of trying, finally manage to control the size and the movements of Moscow's population? There is already talk of enlarging the current boundaries in order to reduce rising population densities. In the thirties and forties, Plan fulfillment was hampered by inexperienced planners and administrators. Has Moscow at least been able to develop a competent corps of administrators and planners? Mayor Promyslov is quick to reply. "Yes," he says, "we have money. We have authority. We have everything. . . . All the designing is in the hands of the Moscow Soviet and Moscow has its own construction industry. The Moscow Soviet is master of this city."

CONCLUSION

Moscow of the twenty-first century is already a topic of discussion. A recent conference examined Moscow in the year 2070 with these conclusions: (a) the family will definitely still be the basic social unit; (b) apartments will be the dominant housing unit, and housing complexes will provide all essential services (a twenty-first century mikrorayon?); (c) Moscow will not become a skyscraper city (planners rejected a proposal that a population of 54,000,000 be contained in cone-shaped megastructures; (d) nor would they accept the concept of endless cities stretched along the Moscow region's main transport arteries. They earnestly spoke of eliminating differences between town and country in a service-oriented totally urban society; they expect that the USSR will have 550 million city dwellers (95 per cent of the population) by the middle of the twenty-first century. Their socialist vision for Moscow seems quiet and conservative, removed from the raging battles over utopia which once took place in the past.

In tracing the history of Moscow's development since the Revolution, and in looking at planners' visions for Moscow a hundred years hence, one is impressed by the way in which the physical structure of the city from a Czarist "big village" has been reshaped into a modern metropolis. Yet the bigness of Moscow, the complexity of her technology and the massive scale of her physical transformation have produced a city which tends to diminish the human element, the original primary concern. What seems to be missing in the 1971 Plan is the intense social concern which characterized the twenties in Moscow, and which was to be the main criterion for urban life under socialism. Gone are the fanciful attempts to restructure human life in industrial cities, the communal kitchens, the search for a revolutionary architecture, the attempts to develop small "urban villages" inside Moscow. Rather the current Plan is designed to cope with the problems of managing bigness; it is an administrative document rather than a guide to revolutionary city and social planning. The key to the development of Moscow now is *management,* as Promyslov clearly notes in discussing the future municipal economy of Moscow[23]:

> The extensive use of mathematical methods and computers is a major trend in the development of the city. . . . [We] will create a Main Scientific Research Computer Center to manage the work of the branch automated management systems. The center will deal with current and long-range planning tasks, capital construction and the development of all sectors of the city economy; it will provide forecasts in all fields.

Soviet planners and politicians contend that it is possible to manage a big urban agglomeration and still provide the humanized sociopsychological setting that Marx sought a century ago. "To compare Moscow today with our post-1917 expectations is unfair," observed one sociologist. "The proper comparison ought to be with nineteenth-century Russia on the one hand, and with capitalist cities such as New York and Tokyo on the other hand." This statement serves as a focal point for six conclusions about the significance of socialist Moscow's planning and development experience.

First, it is fair to conclude that Soviet performance has not measured up to the stated goals. This should not necessarily be taken as an adverse criticism, but as an acknowledgment that Moscow planners and politicians were always too impatient to transform society overnight; they set impossible goals which could not be met because of inadequate economic and human resources. The 1971 Plan is more realistic. Planning goals are more likely to be realized if they involve the physical, rather than the social restructuring of Moscow.

Second, the process of urbanization once set into motion is difficult to control and almost impossible to direct. No matter how progressive their values and goals, and despite possessing the best resources of the Soviet state, Moscow planners and politicians were powerless to alter the basic thrust of urbanization. They did manage to apply cosmetic surgery to this process, but were unable *in the short run* to stop population growth and provide adequate housing, consumer services and public utilities. *In the long run,* they may have created the basis of a better human environment, but it has already taken several generations to get to this point, despite central planning, strong powers and an ambitious master plan. Ullas admits that "urbanization is a nonreversible process." Moscow's planning experience has been one of attempting to regulate, but being unable to control, urbanization. "Urbanism is a type of culture, a social psychology intimately tied to conditions of life in all modern urban agglomerations. . . . The city has its distinctive social problems . . ."[24] Moscow social scientists are now conducting surveys and research to see why there is a gap between their social planning ideals and the realities of urban life. These Soviet social scientists con-

FIG. 6 Industrialized housing in suburban Yugo-Zapadnāya, a Metro stop. *Photograph by Michael Putnam*

clude that the increased individual mobility, heterogeneity and anonymity of modern big city life basically contradict the group norms of socialism. Socialist policies may have failed because it is the nature of urbanism to make them fail.

Third, central planning does not solve everything and that Soviet planners have made their share of mistakes. Planning is not enough when funds are lacking to carry out the Plan, or when administrators and technical experts are unable to execute the Plan properly. As long as economic and political considerations have first priority, socialist city planners cannot function "successfully." Planners are also fallible; they made mistakes in predicting population growth and in several construction projects (by facing the Moscow River embankments with granite they rendered them useless for beaches and park lands; the Belt Highway was practically obsolete from the time it was built). Planners make mistakes because, among other reasons, no one can predict the future accurately, even under socialism.

Fourth, while Moscow is the Soviet capital and a "model for all Soviet cities," one must not assume that the rest of the more than two thousand Soviet cities are smaller replicas of Moscow. Moscow is a special model, representing the very best achievements of Soviet urban development. Per capita capital investment is lower in almost every other Soviet city. No other cities have built as much new housing or possess such a well-developed transportation system (Fig. 6). Just thirty miles outside Moscow are relatively primitive towns and cities, with muddy streets, wooden houses, limited facilities and empty shelves in small shops. Moscow is the Soviet Union's "Potemkin Village," behind whose walls stand the less privileged, less developed cities of the Soviet Union. Almost every social and planning experiment is first applied in Moscow; the city's planners also draw up plans for other cities based on their experience in Moscow. No other Soviet city has Moscow's resources or Moscow's powers. No other city has Moscow's unique relationship to the central Party and government. A succession of Soviet leaders from Lenin through Stalin, Khrushchev and Brezhnev have emphasized this special status. At the recently 24th Party Congress Brezhnev again announced that "We must strive to make Moscow a model city for communism." Moscow is the example of what other Soviet cities might be like in the future.

Fifth, Moscow's experience has limited relevance for the developed "capitalist cities" of the world because Moscow's planning is based on public ownership of land and on central planning, two concepts which are seemingly an anathema to the ideology of capitalism. The West cannot conceive of giving so much power to the Plan and to the planners to regulate our lives; it would be folly to try to convert to 100 per cent public land ownership in capitalist society. Nor would the fundamental political, administrative and economic changes required to make central planning effective be permitted. Adequate financing for metropolitan development would not be available. Apparently, the West does not care for Moscow's concept of citizen participation—involvement in the administration of policies, but not in their formulation. But once fundamental "systemic" differences are pushed aside, there are at least three lessons to learn from specific features of Moscow's physical reconstruction: Moscow's experience in the industrialization of high-rise apartment construction; Moscow's public transport for commuters from the suburbs and the distant areas of the city into the city center, by extending radial subway lines over long distances and establishing a single fare subway system with monthly unlimited travel passes; and Moscow's centralized municipal financing without the property tax as a municipal revenue source. Moscow's example of reliance on centralized revenues and budgeting is also relevant for us.

Sixth, it appears that Moscow's experiment in urban development is more suited to large cities in developing nations, with strong central governments and limited traditions of Western democracy. The Soviet Union was a developing nation itself when it initiated Moscow's urban redevelopment scheme, and rapid urbanization and industrialization have transformed the face of Moscow in this century.

Moscow evokes strong attachments from those who have lived there. This jumble of architecture, wide empty streets and crowded stores is a beautiful, fascinating combination of old and new; Moscow has a charm that buries itself in your heart. It also contains a promise of a better life to come for its inhabitants. There is optimism in Moscow that man can control his urban environment through centrally planned socialist urban development. Only fifty years ago Moscow was a big village full of illiterate peasants; today the city is one of the world's great capitals. So, judgment of Moscow's planning experiment should be suspended a while longer to give Moscow planners, politicians and citizens more time to catch up with their ideals.

NOTES

[1] A. V. Baranov, "Sotsiologicheskiye problemy" (Sociological Problems), *Stroitelstvo i arkhitektura Leningrada,* #6 (June 1967), p. 13.

[2] Yu. G. Saushkin, *Moscow,* Progress, Moscow, 1966, p. 49.

[3] A. Voyce, *The Moscow Kremlin.* Berkeley, University of California, 1954, p. 3.

[4] E. Lyons, *Modern Moscow.* London, Hurst and Blackett Ltd., 1935, p. 22.

[5] Saushkin, op. cit., p. 53.

[6] A. Kopp, *Town and Revolution: Soviet Architecture and City Planning 1917–1935.* New York, Braziller, 1970, p. 172.

[7] L. M. Kaganovich, *Socialist Reconstruction of Moscow and Other Cities in the USSR.* Moscow, Cooperative Publishing Society of Foreign Workers in the USSR, 1931, p. 86.

[8] Sir E. D. Simon, *Moscow in the Making.* London, Longmans, Green & Co., 1937, p. 184. This book contains an abbreviated translation of *O generalnom plane rekonstruktsii goroda Moskvy* (The 1935 General Plan of Moscow). Moscow, Moskovsky Rabochy, 1936.

[9] M. Parkins, *City Planning in Soviet Russia, with an Interpretive Bibliography.* Chicago, University of Chicago Press, 1953, pp. 45–46.

[10] *Moskva sotsialisticheskaya.* Moscow, Moskovsky Rabochy, 1940, p. 33.

[11] Ralph Parker, *Moscow Correspondent.* London, F. Muller, 1949, p. 213.

[12] Cf. A. Vlasov, *Moscow's Multi-Story Buildings* (Moscow Foreign Language Publishing House, 1954), p. 54; and B. Svetlichny, "The City Awaits a Reply," *Oktyabr,* #10 (1966), translated in *Current Digest of the Soviet Press,* XVIII, 48 (December 1966), pp. 15–17.

[13] U. S. Department of Commerce, *Industrialized Building in the Soviet Union.* Washington, National Bureau of Standards Special Publication 334, May 1971, p. 1.

[14] V. Demichev, *"Novy etap razvitti sovetskoy stolitsii"* (New Step in the Development of the Soviet Capital), *Izvestiya,* August 19, 1960, p. 1.

[15] Saushkin, op. cit., p. 140.

[16] Ibid., p. 179.

[17] V. Nekrasov, "About the Past, the Present and a Little of the Future," *Literaturnaya gazeta* (Literary Gazette), February 20, 1960, translated in *Current Digest of the Soviet Press,* XII, 11, p. 4.

[18] V. A. Belova and Le. Darsky, "The Survey of Attitudes as a Method of Studying Family Planning," in A. G. Volkov (ed.), *Izucheniye vosproizvodstva naseleniya* (The Study of Population Reproduction). Moscow, Nauka, 1968, pp. 285–95.

[19] *Moscow, A Brief Outline,* n.p. (1967), p. 85.

[20] Cf. *"O generalnom plane Moskvy"* (On Moscow's General Plan), *Stroitelstvo i arkhitektura Moskvy,* #11 (November 1966); *"Generalny plan razvitii Moskvy"* (The General Plan for Moscow), *Pravda,* June 10, 1971, translated in *JPRS,* 166, 53732, August 1971; V. Promyslov, "A Matter of Honor for the Entire Soviet People," *Kommunist,* #4, March 1972, pp. 26–39.

[21] Saushkin, op. cit., p. 38.

[22] *Kommunist,* op. cit., p. 31.

[23] Ibid., p. 38.

[24] *Institut konkretnykh sotsialnykh issledovanii AN SSSR, i sovetskaya sotsiologicheskaya assotsiatsiya, Sotsiologicheskiye issledovaniya goroda* (Urban Sociological Research), *Informatsionny byulleten 16,* Moscow 1969, p. 1.

CHAPTER 9

Tokyo: Giant Metropolis of the Orient

Masahiko Honjo*

TOKYO TODAY

In 1969, the population in Tokyo-to (Tokyo Special Prefecture) reached 11.5 million; the size is comparable to the populations of Austria with 11.5 million and the Netherlands with 12.5 million. The total income earned by residents in Tokyo-to, which amounted to around $18 billion, also equals approximately that of the Netherlands as a whole, which is $18.6 billion.[1] Thus, Tokyo is an administrative unit which can compete with some nations not only in terms of population, but also in terms of economic activities.

The commuting areas of Tokyo extend beyond this administrative boundary. The Densely Impacted District in census terms[2] surrounding Tokyo reaches out twenty to thirty miles from the center of the city and is clustered along the rail-

* Acting director of the United Nations Center for Regional Development at Nagoya, Japan, and professor of housing and planning, University of Tokyo. A Ph.D. from Tokyo, he has served in several offices of the Japanese Government and in the Japan Housing Corporation as architect and planner, as well as the Bank of Construction of Iran as adviser. Considered the leading student of Japanese housing and planning, he serves as a member of various ministerial commissions and represented his country in the United Nations Committee on Housing, Building and Planning. He is the author of journal articles and various planning and housing reports in Japan.

road lines. Within a twenty-mile zone from the center, 30 per cent of the working population commutes to Tokyo and even within the thirty-mile zone, the percentage does not fall below 10 per cent.

It is a wonder that such a huge mass of people as Tokyo with virtually *laissez-faire* planning and *laissez-passer* administrative competence can manage somehow to maintain its daily activities.

A Historical Perspective

Only five hundred years have passed since Tokyo started its development as a tiny hamlet. During the fifteenth century when the feudal system was forming, Dokan Ota, a lord of the powerful local clan, built a castle around an eleventh-century fort on the site now occupied by the Imperial Palace. Thus was Edo, the former name of Tokyo, founded; the site overlooked a wharf on the shores of Tokyo Bay.

The first feudal Shogun, Ieyasu Tokugawa, made the fateful decision upon which the future course of the town was based. In 1590, he entered the castle-town as the new lord and, after succeeding in securing national dominance by the decisive victory of Sekigahara in 1600, decided to govern the entire country from Edo.

Edo was located in the center of Kanto Plain—east of the guard station at the mountain barrier at Hakone—distant from the former political and economic centers of Kyoto and Osaka. The Kanto area, which so far had had the status of a mere colony to Kansai—the area west of the Hakone barrier—now acquired a superior position and Edo became the capital in reality while Kyoto faded gently away as a symbolic capital where the imperial court resided. The centralized feudal age of the Tokugawa Shogunate lasted three hundred years; Edo was once a local center in the underdeveloped Kanto area with little prestige in traditional culture compared to the ancient cities of Kyoto and Osaka. The Shogunate, however, tried hard to bring prosperity to the town. In order to prevent revolts by the *daimyos* (nobles), heads of the other clans, their wives and children were forced to stay at Edo and the lords themselves were ordered to go back and forth between Edo and their home territories, spending half of each year at Edo. This Shogunate court resulted in the growth of Edo as a market and promoted the development of commercial and manufacturing activities there. On the other hand, its population structure was distorted with a heavy concentration of such unproductive people as warriors, monks, professional entertainers and prostitutes (Fig. 1). The population concentration continued and by 1800 reached 1.2 million—one of the largest cities in the world at that time.

With the Meiji Restoration of the Emperor in 1868, Japan was reborn as a modern nation out of the feudal confederation. Under the flags of the imperial court at Kyoto, revolutionary factions (mainly composed of the Western clan lords and their retainers) destroyed the dominance of the Tokugawa Shogunate. However, when the new regime decided on the location of its capital, it chose Edo over Kyoto and renamed it Tokyo. By that time Edo had acquired enough significance to be selected as more dynamic than traditional Kyoto. Tokyo became the unique capital by name, as well as by substance, and its development accelerated.

FIG. 1 Old map of Edo in 1716; castle in the center surrounded by the moat. Compare with Figure 3. *From Koban-EdoZu Shūsei (Collection of Old Maps of Edo), Vol. 17, by Chūō Kōron Bijutsu Shuppan & Co., Tokyo*

The Exploding Metropolis

When the new Meiji Government was first established, there was a sharp decline in Tokyo's population. In 1868, just after the Restoration, it amounted to only 87,000, composing a mere 2.5 per cent of the national total. But it grew rapidly thereafter with an average annual increase of 4 to 5 per cent and by the turn of the century it had already exceeded two million, 5 per cent of the national total. In 1920, when the first formal national census was taken, Tokyo had grown to 3.69 million and comprised 6.7 per cent of the Japanese population.

World War I promoted the modernization of Japan's industrial structure and, parallel with it, urbanization proceeded. Tokyo continued to gain more and more population after the war; the great Kanto earthquake and fire in 1923 seriously damaged central Tokyo, but all through the reconstruction period population spread into the suburbs and enlarged the functional metropolitan area. All through the 1930s with Japan involved in war in China, national intervention in the economy was stepped up to develop war industry. In the process, Tokyo bore a more and more important role leading to further population concentration. The population of Tokyo annually gained 150,000 throughout the 1920s and 1930s, and, in 1942, it reached 7.36 million. Its share of the national total now exceeded 10 per cent.

During World War II, Tokyo was one of the major targets for air attack and suffered heavy damage. Its inhabitants were relocated voluntarily, as well as forcefully, to the countryside. The Tokyo population declined sharply as a result and by 1945 it was half that of before the war, 3.5 million.

As soon as the hostilities ceased, people commenced to return. Furthermore, Tokyo began absorbing a great number of in-migrants. By 1955, ten years after the war, its population had already exceeded the prewar level amounting to eight million. This growth was accelerated by the remarkably rapid economic development of the entire nation which started about that time. Tokyo absorbed an annual in-migration of three hundred thousand and by 1962 the total had passed ten million.

It should be noted that notwithstanding this considerable increase, the *growth rate* commenced to fall during the past decade; recently the total population of central Tokyo has started to decline. In contrast to this fact, population growth on the outer fringes of Tokyo is now quite remarkable, resulting in the so-called doughnut phenomenon—similar in fact to the U.S. metropolitan area pattern. In other words, in-migrants head toward suburbs in the Tokyo metropolitan region, which continues to act as a population magnet and the urbanized area is continuing to expand.

TOKYOITES

Influx of a Younger Population

Tokyo is visibly a developing city; this fact should be viewed against the background of the present remarkable urbanization of Japan in toto. The speed of urbanization is so rapid that Japan has achieved as much urbanization in fifty years as Britain or the United States experienced in the past hundred years.[3]

A considerable portion of this sharp increase in population is composed of the influx of young workers. Rapid economic growth obviously means an expanded employment capacity in metropolitan cities. On the other side of the coin, this implies the draining of the young from rural areas, leaving an increasingly aging population behind. These two aspects of rapid urbanization are viewed as a serious social problem and Tokyo is the focus of the drama with its abundant opportunities acting as a magnet for mass in-migration from every part of the nation. Thus, Tokyo has comparatively few native born and its age structure remains remarkably young; this has contributed a great deal to its incessant energy and its rapid, as well as chaotic and anarchic, growth. It would be no exaggeration to say that Tokyo does not now have an established and hereditary elite society. It reflects no established culture; instead, it is a "stout stomach" that devours whatever is new from all over the country and the world as well.

The in-migrated young population after World War II has now reached child-bearing age and has begun to contribute to Tokyo's future potentially large natural growth.

Slowing Down of Population Increase and Its Aging Composition

The above described situation, however, has recently come to a turning point. Population is now decreasing in the older parts of Tokyo-to—the central twenty-three wards. Migration into Tokyo attained its highest peak of an annual 700,000 in the latter half of the 1960s and has maintained that level without much fluctuation since then, while emigration from Tokyo has been ever increasing from the level of the annual 400,000 in the latter half of the 1950s to an annual rate of more than 700,000 in the latter half of the 1960s. Thus since 1966, emigration exceeds in-migration in central Tokyo, resulting in a net population decrease from this cause.

Natural increase has been growing steadily from an annual level of 100,000 in the latter half of the 1950s to 200,000 in the latter half of the 1960s. The birth rate in Tokyo in 1967 was 20.5 per 1,000, surpassing the national birth rate of 19.3. Together with Osaka and Aichi prefectures in which two other of the largest metropolitan cities are located, the rates are highest among all the prefectures. Summing up these trends in social and natural growth, Tokyo-to is still gaining about 150,000 annually, although natural increase is now taking over the major part of the growth and Tokyo has entered into the stage of growth from within (Table A).

Emigrants from Tokyo-to are also mainly composed of the younger generation. This does not mean that they return to their native rural land; instead of going back to farming villages in a U-turn curve, they move to surrounding areas in a J-turn curve as their families grow. Their destinations become farther and farther from the center of Tokyo as the urbanized area is expanded. In the latter half of the 1950s, this migration was to a six-mile zone around central Tokyo, but in the first half of the 1960s they moved to a six- to fifteen-mile zone and in the latter half to a fifteen- to twenty-mile zone. In general, the earlier migrants were absorbed in the west to southwest suburbs with good road access, but recently there has been remarkable shift to the northern and eastern suburbs where comparatively more space is available. Thus, all surrounding areas of Tokyo are now witnessing a tremendous urbanization regardless of direction.

The younger generation is highly mobile. According to a survey made in 1969[4] in an industrial area of Tokyo, 50 per cent of the in-migrants were under age twenty-five, while 33 per cent of the emigrants were under that age; 43 per cent of the total emigrants moved out before the lapse of three years. The major reason for this mobility is undoubtedly due to the ever-growing housing problem; the housing inventory in Tokyo simply cannot accommodate the increasing population. Throughout the period of rapid economic growth in the 1950s and the 1960s, the young population suffered most from the housing shortage. They were forced to move outward as they married and had children; as a result the age structure of Tokyo, which has contributed so much to its dynamism, is now

TABLE A Population structure by marital status, age in five-year groups, and by sex, for Tokyo-to (1965).

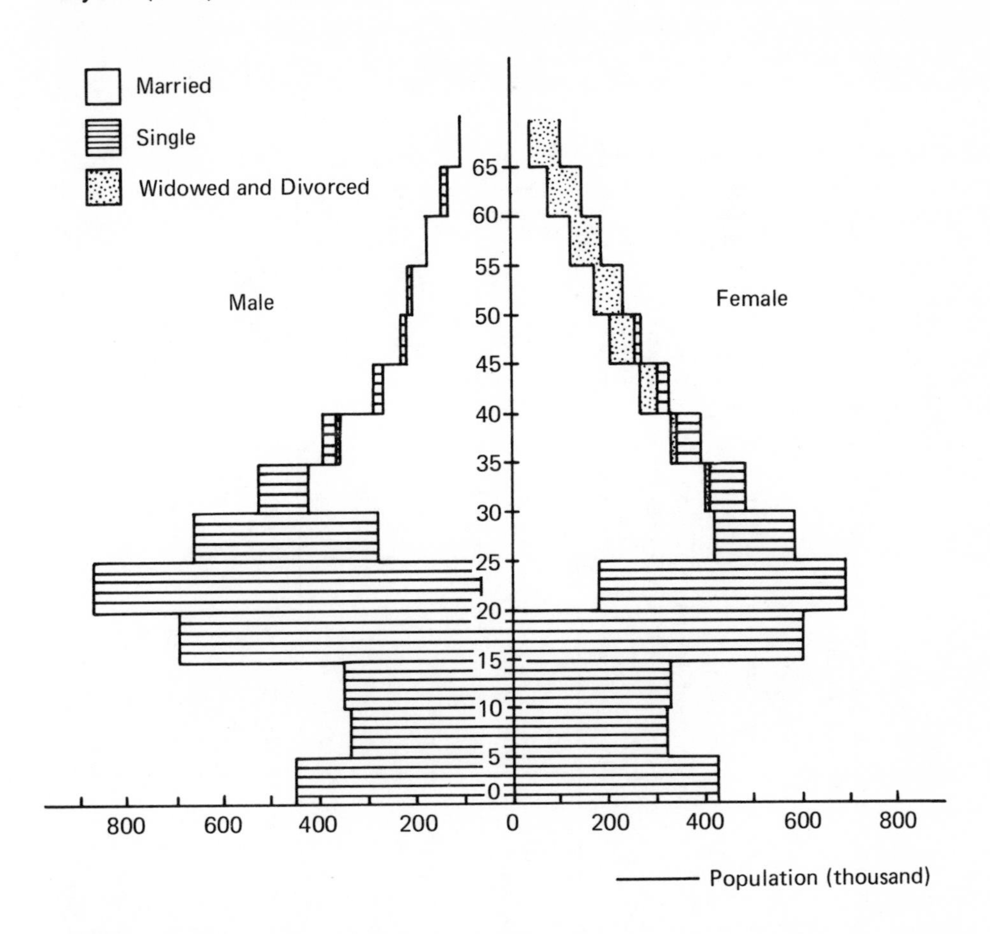

changing toward a more aged one, which will become increasingly pronounced in the next twenty years.

Daily Fluctuation of Population: Commuting

As a result of suburbanization, there is a vast gap between the daytime and nighttime populations of inner Tokyo. Added to Tokyo's resident population of 11 million, some 1.1 million commuters arrive each morning from the neighboring prefectures. The amount of the incoming daytime population has increased by half a million since the beginning of 1960. As the outflow of daytime population from Tokyo is about 200,000, there is a gap of 900,000 between day and night.

A more remarkable gap can be seen in the central business district (CBD); the influx of daytime population into the central three wards amounts to about 1.5 million including the daily commuters from other wards, mostly from western Tokyo-to. Take, for example, Chiyoda Ward, which comprises the core of the CBD itself: the daytime population exceeds 700,000 with a population density of 270 persons per acre, whereas at night the population falls to 80,000, creating a true ghost town.

TABLE B

IMPORTANCE OF THE TOKYO AND THE OSAKA REGIONS TO JAPAN AS A WHOLE IN PERCENTAGES

Tokyo's Share (Approx.)	Index	Time	Tokyo-to (Special prefecture)	Tokyo Region (Tokyo-to and 3 neighboring prefectures)	Osaka-fu (Special prefecture)	Osaka-Kyoto Region (Two special prefectures and neighboring 4 prefectures
1%	Habitable area	1960	1	8	1	5
	Primary industrial	1962	1	8	1	5
	Population income of primary ind.	1961	1	8	1	5
10%	Social overhead capital	1960	11	18	6	14
	Housing stock	1960	12	21	6	14
	Population	1964	11	21	6	14
	No. of government employees	1962	12	22	5	13
	Transportation & communication workers	1962	12	23	6	15
15%	Service industry	1962	14	22	5	13
	Workers. Labor force of 15-29 age	1960	14	23	7	15
	Wholesale & retail workers	1962	16	21	8	15
	Tertiary industrial population	1962	15	25	7	15
	Population of cities	1964	15	26	9	18
	Over 30,000 industrial capital	1960	16	26	10	17
	Secondary industrial pop.	1962	15	26	10	19
	Manufacturing product output	1962	15	30	13	23

20%	Gross prefectural product	1961	18	28	9	17
	Amount of retail sales	1962	19	28	9	17
	Income of tertiary industry	1961	21	29	10	17
	Income of secondary and tertiary industry	1961	21	31	11	18
	Undertakings with more than 100 workers	1963	21	29	13	20
	Population of cities over 100,000	1964	21	33	11	21
	Consumptive purchase power index	1963	23	30	11	18
	No. of telephones	1964	23	31	11	20
30%	No. of pieces of mail accepted	1963	28	34	10	18
	Sales of theatre tickets	1963	27	33	13	22
	Retail and wholesale amount of sales	1962	27	32	24	28
	Deposits in banks	1964	29	36	13	20
	Purchase of economic publications	1962	31	38	12	21
						2 special prefectures and 4 pre-fectures
	No. of university graduates	1960	33	45	9	19
40%	Loans from banks	1964	42	45	19	24
50%	University students	1964	49	53	9	20
	Invested capital of firms	1962	49	54	16	23
	Top business leaders	1962	59	64	8	23

Source: Saburo Okita, Jiro Sakamoto, *et al. Nijunengo-no Tokyo* (Tokyo after 20 Years), *Nihon Keizai Center*, Tokyo, 1967, p. 26.

The commuting problem has become more and more severe; improvement in mass transit has supported this suburbanization with the resultant pressures on daily movements.

TOKYO'S FUNCTIONS AND ACTIVITIES

Multifunctional City

Tokyo is very diversified in its functions; it is simultaneously the nation's political center, the administrative and managerial center for business, the chief commercial center and the chief cultural center. It still contains a large amount of manufacturing activities. There was a time in the twentieth century when Tokyo was considered the political center while Osaka remained the center of commerce, but as the economic intervention of the central government was intensified through World War II and after, Tokyo's supremacy in trade and commerce became clear. The preceding table shows the dominance in diversified functions of Tokyo within the national framework (Table B).

In the Tokyo region which occupies only about 1 per cent of the surface area of the nation with only 11 per cent of the population, over 60 per cent of the top business leaders and of the total invested capital, one third of the deposited banking accounts and one third of university graduates are concentrated. This illustrates clearly how intensely administrative and managerial functions converge in this city. With a 15 per cent share of the working population in tertiary industry, it earns 21 per cent of the tertiary industry income of the nation while retail and wholesale sales amount to 27 per cent. In regard to secondary industry, it contributes about 15 per cent in all aspects, either in the weight of shares of private capital stock, of working population, or of sales of manufactured products. About half of the university students gather in Tokyo, demonstrating the cultural dominance of this metropolis.

Administrative and Managerial Functions and Accumulated Information

Among the various concentrated activities, the most noteworthy are the administrative and managerial functions. In Japan's politicoeconomic setting, the fact that Tokyo is the capital has been the cause for most of this concentration. Historically, even in the process of national growth following the Meiji Restoration the Kansai (Osaka-Kyoto) area, which preceded Tokyo in its economic as well as cultural development, maintained enough accumulated functions to rival Tokyo. The commercial business function has gradually been reversed and Tokyo came to preponderance. The share of top national business leaders in Tokyo and its vicinity in 1930 was already 48 per cent compared to 36 per cent for Osaka and its surrounding four prefectures; by 1960 the ratio had further changed to 64 per cent to 23 per cent in Tokyo's favor.

The most obvious cause for this changing ratio can be attributed to the intensified control of the national economy before and during the Second World War, and the following reconstruction period when the central government played a crucial role in the economic recovery of the nation. The relative decline in the importance of light industries, such as textiles, compared to the growing heavy and chemical industries through these periods also helped to degrade the Kansai area with its flourishing light industries. In the controlled economy of this period, where most of the important decisions (such as the allocation of capital and raw materials to specific enterprises) were made by the central government, it was vital for an important corporation to station top management close to political power in Tokyo. Although the present economy of Japan has returned to a free enterprise and collaborative planning one, the growing share of national finance and banking has made Tokyo's role ever more important.

Moreover, the significance of accumulated administrative and managerial functions in Tokyo should be recognized now, under the new insights into present society, as information oriented. Private enterprises have grown colossal and more complicated in structure, while the internal and external linkages among big businesses (and with the central government) have further intensified, demanding more and better information for decision making. This accumulation of business enterprise has provided more opportunities for contact and wider availability of information.

In such an environment, the very accumulation of functions in Tokyo yields externalities; by locating their offices in Tokyo, business firms can secure far better access to information concerning the other firms of the same genre and the availability of financial resources and technical/professional services. Tokyo as the central node in the national information network is an incomparable place for collecting and collating information.

Parallel to information accumulation, there is a growing centralization of cultural activities. The concentration of universities (one half the national student population) exemplifies this quite clearly. Such a quasi-monopolistic situation has been furthered by Tokyo's supremacy in information accumulation. Journalism, television and publishing firms and the information media also locate in Tokyo for the same reasons. All of the big newspaper enterprises with a national circulation have their main offices in Tokyo where they build their networks for circulation as well as for information gathering. Almost all news is sent to the main offices in Tokyo and then redistributed to the local branches covering the nation. The circulation of the five major newspapers in Tokyo totals 52 per cent of the entire national circulation. In television, the National Broadcasting and Television Corporation (NHK) with its fifty local branches dominates and 90 per cent of the programs on the main channel of NHK are produced in Tokyo. Tokyo's dominance is even more remarkable in book publication, covering 86 per cent of the total sales of books. It seems inevitable that the full utilization of the recently developed computer- and electro-communication technology in Japan will speed up the current trend of concentration. Tokyo's social structure as a whole will change from industrial to postindustrial society with emphasis on the tertiary industries, and this information orientation will be strengthened.

Manufacturing Industries

Primary industry, of course, is almost negligible with a 1 per cent working population in 1967.[5] Tertiary industry is increasing its share and in that same year it reached 58 per cent. The remaining 41 per cent of the working population was engaged in secondary industry. Among the total employed population, 2.2 million were in secondary industry and 3.2 million in tertiary industry.

The pyramidal industrial structure is characterized by a vast base with numerous small industries contrasting with the towering administrative and managerial functions of the top.

The most important feature of Tokyo's manufacturing industries is to serve this busy population agglomeration. Although Tokyo is often viewed as a typical modern industrial zone, there are few heavy industries. It is true that big steel factories and petrochemical complexes exist in Kawasaki and Chiba along the Tokyo Bay industrial belt, centered around Tokyo. But the leading sector of Tokyo's industry is the production of consumption goods, such as medicines, cosmetics, soaps, films, ink and dyeing materials, radios, television sets, cameras, binoculars, with automobiles being added recently. One of the most important sectors is printing and publishing. All sectors have been developed utilizing the huge consuming hinterland of Tokyo as a stepping stone for occupying a central place in production for the national market. These consumption goods industries now aim at meeting the demands from abroad as well.

At the same time, the installation of heavy and petrochemical industries, handling bulky raw materials, that had been located here in the past are now moving out of the area because of the deterioration of locational conditions.

The production of daily consumption goods and durable consumption goods occupy 47 per cent and 44 per cent, respectively, whereas heavy industry now occupies only 8 per cent of the total output in price.[6]

Industries in Tokyo are run mostly by numerous smaller firms, as are the manufacturing industries of Japan as a whole. Japanese statistics classify the size of firms by the number of employees; factories with 30 employees and less as "small," 30 to 299 as "medium," and 300 and over as "large." Small firms made up 90 per cent of the national number of firms in 1969. The number of total employees in each class is about one third, respectively. In terms of sales, the small occupies only 17 per cent, the medium, 34 per cent and the large, a share of 49 per cent. In the case of Tokyo, this pattern is somewhat distorted because of a larger share by small- and medium-sized firms; the number of employees in large industries amounts to only one fourth, leaving the rest divided between small- and medium-sized ones in equal proportion. The small accounts for 23 per cent of sales; the medium, 40 per cent; and the large, 37 per cent; although the distribution pattern of the number of firms is quite similar to that of the nation as a whole.[7] Thus, the major elements of Tokyo's industrial structure are composed of small- and medium-sized factories.

All these firms are closely interrelated and form a complicated production system. Two major components of the system are groups of smaller manufacturers centered around wholesalers, and groups of smaller subcontractors gathered around parent manufacturers. The former arrangement is popular among firms producing daily consumption goods, while firms manufacturing finished products subcontract a great many parts and, as they grow, systematization of subcontractors and their specialization proceeds. This interwoven industrial complex results in favorable conditions for such firms producing consumption goods which constantly must adapt to ever-changing market conditions.

In some cases parent firms try to transfer their own risks to subcontractors; difficulties to the parent firms rising from shrinking demand tend to be handed down to the subcontractors. But in other cases, subcontractors have benefits: They may use the brand of their parent firm when they develop a new product for which it would be difficult to find a market using their own unknown brand. Or, they are sometimes rescued from the bankruptcy of their parent firm by rearranging their relationships connecting them to other subcontractors in the intermediate stage or even to other parent firms. It is the very existence of this accumulated industrial complex of numerous smaller firms, with adequate flexibility to cope rapidly with changing situations, that supports Tokyo as the pre-eminent production center for highly developed consumption goods.

Retail and Wholesale Activities

The same type of dual structure also prevails in Tokyo's commercial activities. From first impressions, the outward appearance of its retailing activities appears to be quite modern as represented by the large and luxurious CBD department stores. Actually, most retail trade is carried on by traditional small businesses in a polarized dual structure. Downtown department stores in Japan are still prosperous and with their scale offer comprehensive facilities for shoppers, including the provision of unique opportunities for urban recreation. The floor area of the largest ones such as Mitsukoshi or Isetan amounts to 600,000 square feet with average annual sales of $150 million. On the other hand, there are in Tokyo numerous small stores connected with residences that are run by family labor; in Japan as a whole, retailing tends to be carried on by tiny businesses offering personalized services.

Out of a total of 125,000 retail stores in Tokyo in 1966, 80 per cent, or 104,000 stores, employed less than four persons, while only 0.2 per cent of the stores employed more than fifty. This situation does not differ much even in the case of wholesalers, for a little less than 40 per cent of the firms employ less than four and those larger units that employ more than fifty amount to less than 0.3 per cent.[8]

As a result, Tokyo's commercial activities assume a somewhat bazaarlike character and the distribution system of goods is multilayered. For example, only 40 per cent of the so-called wholesalers buy their goods directly from the manufacturers; the rest buy from other wholesalers. Recently, an innovation in the distribution system has appeared: Both department stores and supermarkets are increasing. In the case of both retailing and wholesaling, there is a considerable increase in the number of firms with more than fifty employees, whereas the number of tiny shops does not show any remarkable change. This dual structure of old and new will remain for some time in the retailing system of Tokyo.

LAND USE PATTERN

Old Mold

Tokyo's land use has developed following the pattern of the Edo period (see Fig. 1). The castle occupied the center; the city was composed of the area encircled by the outer moat of the castle, which lay in a 1.5-mile radius from the castle center, and the adjoining commercial downtown district with handicrafts industry located in the northeastern part of the city. The former hill area was inhabited by the retainers of the Tokugawa Shogunate clan and local feudal lords, whereas the merchants and craftsmen resided in the downtown area forming a commercial-industrial-residential combination. The wholesale district was located at Nihonbashi northeast of the castle, an area reclaimed from the sea, which has survived as a central part of the CBD until now. Civilian towns also developed along the major highways radiating from Edo (Figs. 2a, 2b). At the city gates on these highways, two to three miles from the center of the castle, amusement quarters (including brothel areas) developed, traces of which still remain even now although completely engulfed by urban development.

The towns on the east bank of the Sumida River assumed a totally different character from those on the west bank. Edo was largely built of wood and frequently suffered from great fires, which necessitated a large amount of lumber. The east bank developed as the place for handling this huge demand. There, a rectangular system of small and large canals created town blocks, which suggests that limited town planning was carried on even in the Tokugawa feudal age. This area was converted into industrial land after Edo was renamed Tokyo.

FIG. 2A Nihonbashi area: wholesale stores and barges, 1800.

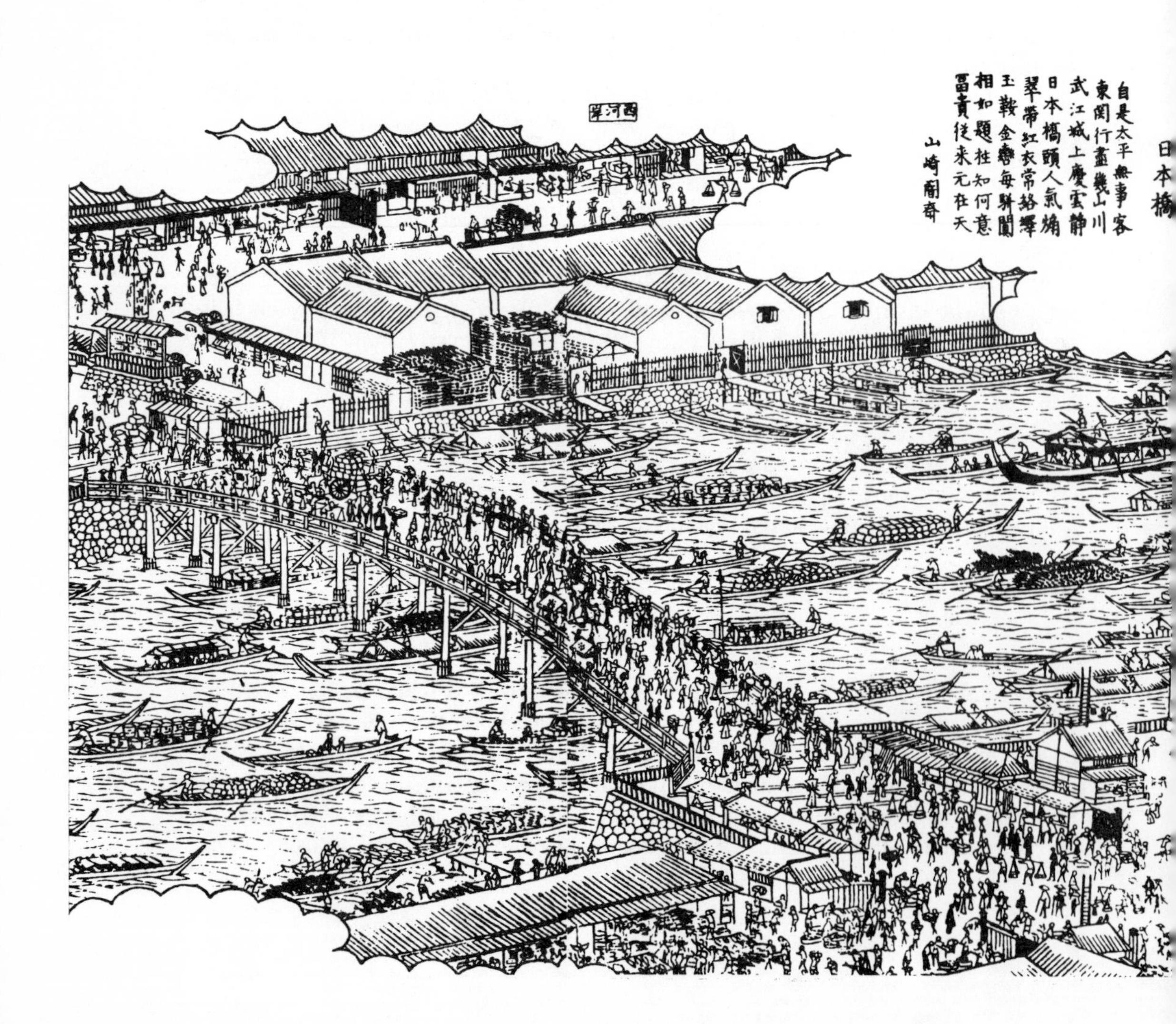

FIG. 2B Nihonbashi area: the ancestral shop of the Mitsukoshi department store in the foreground, 1800. *From EdoMeishi Zukai* (*Famous Places of Edo Illustrated*), *prepared in 1800 and published in 1832; reprinted by Jinbutsu-Orai-sha, Tokyo*

The old feudal mold can clearly be seen today in the structure of the central part of Tokyo. The former site of Edo Castle, the present site of the Imperial Palace, provides a huge open space right in the middle of the metropolis (Fig. 3). Surrounded by the moat, the palace garden gives serenity and charm to the bustling town. The Imperial Palace woods are the favorite habitat of wild life, and the moat is visited by an enormous number of migratory birds during wintertime.

Each of the radial sectors around the Imperial Palace are characterized by different functions: the south, Kasumigaseki Central Government district; the east, Marunouchi and Ginza central business and amusement district; from the east to north, Nihonbashi and Kanda wholesale commercial district; and the west, former high-class residential districts. The ancient pattern has determined the land use that followed.

Open green space left over in Tokyo is mostly the former or present sites of important temples, shrines and palaces. The most remarkable aspect is the green wedge penetrating from the southwest into the center, consisting of Akasaka Detached Palace, Meiji Shrine and its Sports Park, Shinjuku Imperial Garden, and Yoyogi Sports Center, most of which are either used by or devoted to the memory of the Imperial household, and have been gradually opened to the public through the years. In fact, open space in Tokyo has been retained by the sovereignty of the Imperial regime or by the devotion to religion. After World War II, the Imperial government changed to a democratic one, and the many assets of open space were handed over to our contemporary society. It is most important to establish a new feeling of the value among all the citizens of preservation of this precious heritage.

Needless to say the competition for land in inner Tokyo is very intense. There have been several discussions as to whether all the Imperial Palace grounds should be opened for public use. Even relocation of the Palace has been suggested. Fortunately nothing drastic has yet been done leaving enough time for further deliberation. There is now a growing consensus on keeping the Imperial Palace in the same place, and utilize the surrounding area increasingly for cultural and recreational use. As a matter of fact, the Imperial Palace was extensively rebuilt in 1968, while the northern part of the palace gardens, including the former base of the grenadier regiment, has been opened up to the public as a park with many cultural facilities.

Creation of a New CBD and Suburban Development

Expanding the CBD to areas adjoining the castle to the south and east was the most remarkable development at the turn of the century; the CBD now spread over the entire old area. Edo Castle as the headquarters of the Imperial regime following Restoration was surrounded with vast military areas for the purpose of defense. But as the regime became stabilized, such land was subdivided and converted for government as well as private offices. The revision of the "unequal international treaties," giving concessions and capitulations obtained by threat of superior arms when opening the doors of our nation, was one of the major political issues for the newly established government to solve. In order to create a favorable atmosphere for the revision, construction of urbanized areas following Western patterns was planned. Rows of brick buildings in the central areas emerged from the reconstruction of the Ginza district after the big fire of 1872. New central government offices were constructed in the area directly to the south of the castle. In 1890, the Marunouchi district was sold to the Mitsubishi *zaibatsu* (financial clique) and has since been developed into the most important office area of present Japan. By 1910, the CBD took shape more or less, followed by an accelerated development after the opening of Tokyo Central Station in 1915.

As the CBD grew, housing developments for white-collar commuters expanded from the previous residential sites of ousted feudal retainers to the western and southern suburbs.

In pace with the already described rapid influx of population, the metropolitan area of Tokyo continued to expand rapidly. Figure 4 illustrates how the built-up areas have expanded. Tokyo's urban area in 1910 could be encircled by a 2.5- to 4-mile radius and was well served by the streetcar system. The Yamate Railroad Loop, which later became one of the most important networks, was laid down around the fringe of the circle. With the impact of the Kanto earthquake and fire in 1923, the expansion gained momentum and, as suburban railway lines were extended toward the west and south, built-up areas stretched westward and southward across the Loop to a distance of four to five miles. This set the pattern for later suburban development. The post-World War II flood of immigrants

FIG. 3 The Imperial Palace and the downtown area.

formed a tentacle-like development of DIDs (Densely Impacted Districts) along the western and southern suburban railways and reached to thirty miles and even along the northern and eastern lines, twenty to twenty-five miles. Thus the built-up area has expanded approximately ten times during the sixty years since 1910.

The western and southern suburban development took the form of white-collar towns, while in the north and east of the river delta and across it a completely different type of mixed area containing blue-collar housing emerged among the small and scattered commercial and industrial facilities. Blue-collar workers are bound to live quite close to their jobs because they cannot afford commuting long distances from the suburban residential areas with high amenities (Fig. 5).

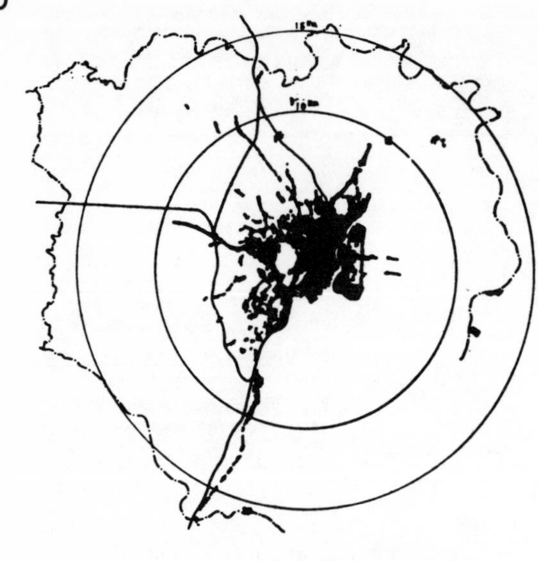

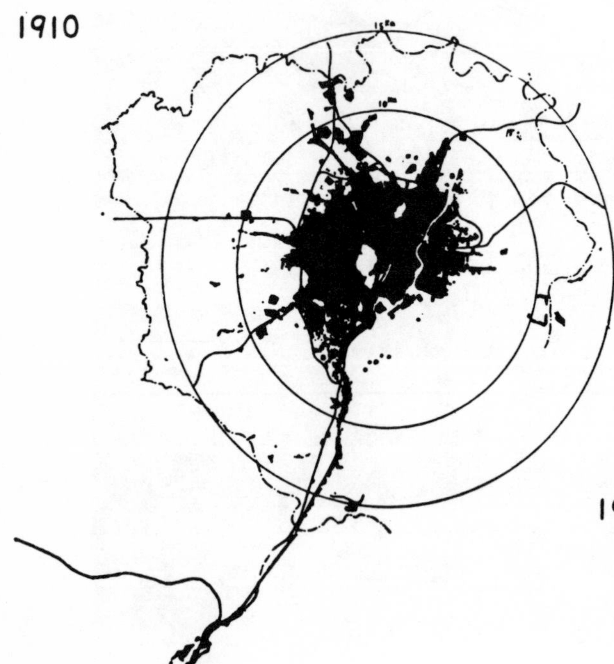

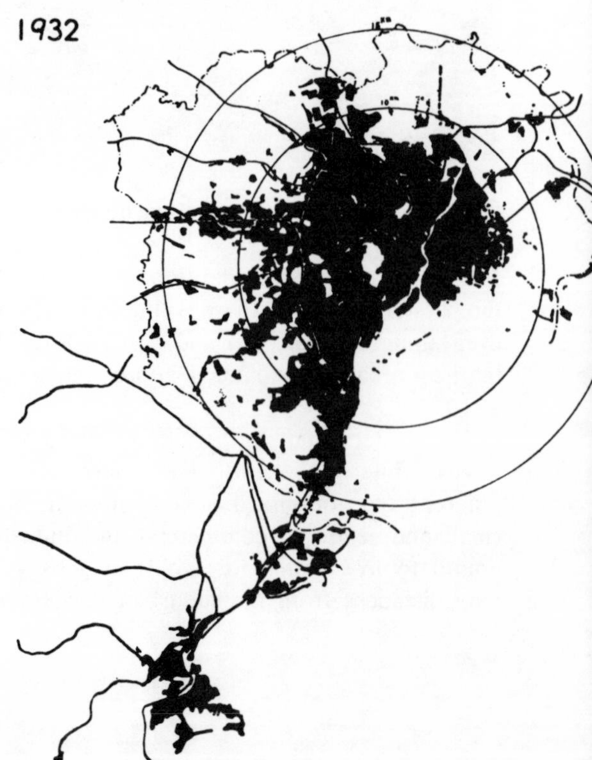

FIG. 4 The expansion of Tokyo, 1880–1965.

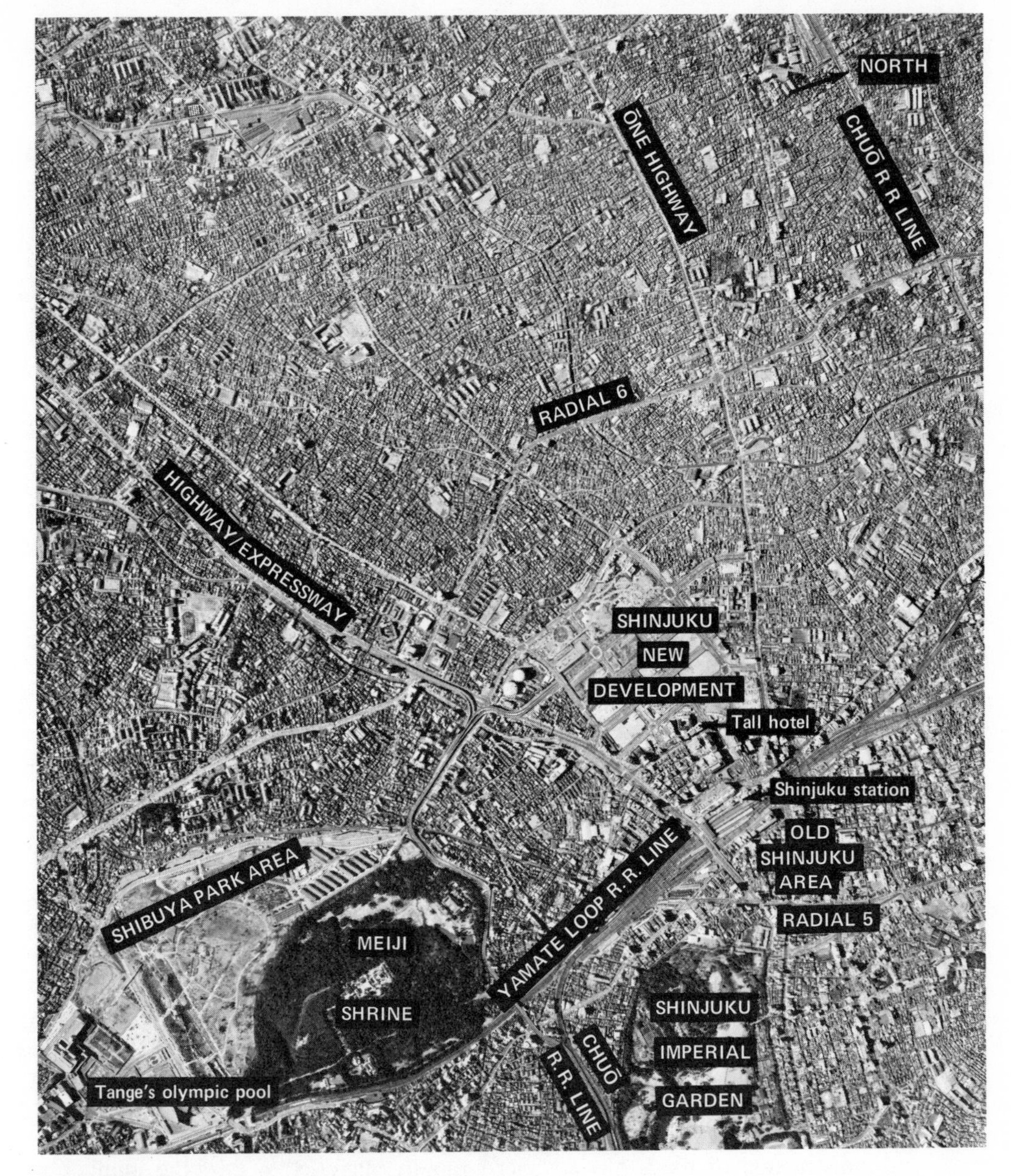

FIG. 5 Shinjuku, white-collar subcenter to the west.

They are attached to their job at the sacrifice of a better living environment, but also with the benefits of convenience and lower living expenses.

These two zones have clearly different qualities. On the hills of the western and southern residential zones, white-collar workers with higher income and better education are accommodated in a fairly good environment; while in the lower and damp zones in the north and east, blue-collar workers with less income and less education are crowded together in a disorderly fashion.

Tokyo's Industrial Areas

The industrial areas developed according to the pattern which has been previously explained. The first industrial zone was built along both sides of the southern part of the Sumida River. In that area, which has become today's CBD, many factories appeared along with household industries. Before long, industry grew larger in scale and, seeking to take advantage of water transportation, moved along the eastern canals of the Sumida. With the growth in business activity, the original industrial area in the CBD gradually moved out of the southern part. The continuing growth of industry caused a new industrial region to come into existence outside the CBD. From 1910 on, construction began of large-scale industries on reclaimed land in Kawasaki, which lies between Tokyo and Yokohama. In the 1930s, a total of 750 acres of land in the adjoining areas was reclaimed from the bay. Industries such as steel, shipbuilding and milling (which were dependent on imported raw materials) developed in this area.

The expanded World War II industries caused a further growth of industrial areas. Farther inland, in the western suburbs, new industrial acreage was opened up for the manufacture of airplanes and electrical equipment. These new manufacturing locations were twenty to twenty-five miles away from the center of Tokyo and widely separated from the built-up sectors. They were chosen because the land could be easily obtained and factories had to be widely dispersed for purposes of defense against air attack.

Economic growth after the last war caused a phenomenal expansion in the industrial areas in and around Tokyo; the expansion of coastal industries and the development of truck transportation were the fundamental causes for this growth. For Japan, which is poor in natural resources and whose economy is based on industrial trade, growth in productive capacity means an ever larger exportation of finished products. This has made the location of coastal industries all the more important. Rapid advances in the technology of land reclamation from the sea make possible a cheap supply of land for industrial use. In the Tokyo area along the shores of Tokyo Bay, land has been rapidly reclaimed and areas for large-scale industry developed. The most outstanding of these areas is in Chiba, about twenty-five to thirty miles east of Tokyo. With the steel and petrochemical industries leading, eight thousand acres of land with modern industries have been developed since 1951, with expansion still continuing. In Kashima, fifty miles northeast of Tokyo and facing the Pacific Ocean, the development of five thousand acres of land for industrial use has been going on since 1963 and is almost completed.

Truck freighting has also developed rapidly. From the 1950s, the improvement and construction of roads has advanced rapidly. Parallel to this, the number of vehicles has also greatly increased, bringing about considerable change in the conditions of industrial location. Industries, whose transportation conditions were previously limited by the railroad, have been given new possibilities with heavy road transport. Opportunities for industrial location in the entire Tokyo area have thus been greatly widened.

On the other hand, the condition of industrial location in inner Tokyo has markedly deteriorated. The worsening transportation problem due to highway congestion, the difficulties of plant expansion due to high land prices, the increase of public nuisance created by industry including air pollution, the sinking of land caused by excessive use of underground water, not to mention the expansion of all business activities, have caused a great deal of damage. It has become economical, following world trends, to have large, flat, spread-out factories for streamlined, large-scale production. The rise in land prices made it possible for outmoded factories to be scrapped and modern ones outside the existing city area constructed at the cost of selling the land at the old location.

The number of plants wishing to move out of the central city is increasing. According to an investigation of the Tokyo Chamber of Commerce and Industry, 42 per cent of all plants surveyed, covering all scales of production activity, wish to move.[9] As a matter of fact, the movement of factories out of Tokyo has generally followed the main highways. This dispersal extends forty to sixty miles to the northwest, twenty to forty miles to the west, and forty to one hundred miles to the southwest along the highway connecting Tokyo and Osaka and increases each year. In the first half of the 1950s, the greatest increase in factories took place around six miles from the center of Tokyo, but was gradually overtaken by increases at distances of about fifteen to twenty miles. After 1960, development at a six-mile distance decreased, and the greatest expansion took place twenty to twenty-five miles from the center of Tokyo.[10]

It can be expected that the new ring highway, which will encircle the city at a distance of twenty miles from the center, will have a great impact on industrial dispersal into the inner area of the Tokyo region. On the other hand, large-scale reclamation projects are going on in Tokyo Bay, and a 330-foot-wide express-highway along the bay will link these newly created areas with express highways going to western Japan. Part of this area is already developed as an extensive transportation base with container harbors and truck terminals. Its completion will further add to the development of the regional structure of Japan.

Each of the sections of the industrial area of Tokyo tends to be rather specialized. For example, in the center, consumer goods are produced, especially printed and published materials. In the eastern section, there are subcontractors producing daily consumer goods for wholesalers. In the southern section, there are parent manufacturers producing durable consumer goods together with their associated subcontractors. In the northern section, there are factories producing durable and daily consumer goods coexisting in the same area. As stated before, these various plants are closely bound together in contractor-subcontractor relationships, so that it is not at all advantageous for any one plant to transfer its operations to another area alone, resulting in obvious external diseconomies. In many cases, these plants tend to move out farther along the same principal roads extending from the sections where they existed. Small- and medium-sized factories of the same or associated kind of manufacturing move as a group to a new industrial tract. However, as the scale of the factory decreases, transfer to another location becomes increasingly difficult. Therefore, although the investigation cited earlier showed that all types and scales of factories wished to transfer elsewhere, there are very few small-scale factories which have concrete plans to that effect.

Despite the tendency for industries to move out of the old industrial areas, those with special characteristics such as printing and top-quality consumption goods will remain, and also the tiny subsistence ones will be left over for the above reasons. The latter are like sediment, and the problems they create are also related to those of old people, already touched upon. All those circumstances will limit the development of industrial areas inside the city in the future.

THE PHYSICAL ASSETS OF TOKYO

Railroads and the Meaning of Mass Transit

The railroad has made Tokyo's huge and widespread agglomeration possible and is truly Tokyo's skeleton. The city expanded along the railway lines, and the subcenters developed in relation to the Yamate Railroad Loop. One must not forget that until very recently motorization had little meaning for the Japanese. According to the Ministry of Transportation, in 1967, in the area extending thirty miles around Tokyo, there were, on the average, thirty-five million people carried daily by all means of transportation. Fifty-eight per cent of these were carried by subways and surface trains, 5 per cent by street trolleys, 19 per cent by bus, 8 per cent by taxis and 11 per cent by private automobiles. Roughly half of these were commuters using long-term discount tickets or passes. The largest percentage of all commuters was dependent on trains and subways (Fig. 6).[11]

This massive movement creates a tremendous rush-hour jam at all Tokyo stations. At the Central Station, each train line is identified by orange, yellow or blue paint; the different lines stand parallel to one another, with the normal train being over seven hundred feet in length. During the peak hours of the day, trains run at two-minute intervals, carrying two to three times their normal capacity of passengers. This is really a "nightmare of modern times." Adding to this passenger capacity is the rapidly developing subway system, so that roughly one and a half million people are said to be transported to the CBD during rush hours. It is said to be, despite the overcrowding, "a very sophisticated system showing magnificent foresight and planning in its conception and realization."

But the truth of the matter is quite another story! Tokyo's railroad network is completely a product of chance. It was built in frantic response to the pressures of overwhelming demand. Gradually, it has grown into a sophisticated system.

The development of the Japanese National Railroad System (JNR), one of the first things attempted when the new government was formed in 1868, was to provide a national rail transportation network. Since Tokyo was the capital, it naturally followed that railroads were constructed to radiate from Tokyo in all directions. Between 1870 and 1890, the Tokaido Line between Tokyo and Kobe, the Tohoku Line serving northern Honshu (the main island), the Shin'etsu Line serving northwestern Honshu, and the Chūō Line, running through the mountainous region to the west of Tokyo, were built, with Shimbashi, Ueno and Iidabashi as their terminal stations. These main lines were at first not linked together, but to permit the routing of freight trains from one line to another, the Yamate Loop was later built beyond the city limits. It was only in 1915 that Tokyo Central Station was completed, with a view to making it the focal terminal for long-distance lines emanating from the capital. However, with the increase in commuter traffic carried by the local electric coaches on the Keihin, Yamate and Chūō lines, this station eventually also became the key depot serving the most important business center of Tokyo, namely, the Marunouchi area, and later became the hub of the Japanese National Railroad system which has borne the brunt of the commuter traffic.

From about the time of the Kanto Earthquake and Fire of 1923, the role of the railroad network of Tokyo became increasingly important as the principal carrier of commuter traffic. The fire caused the loss of a tremendous number of

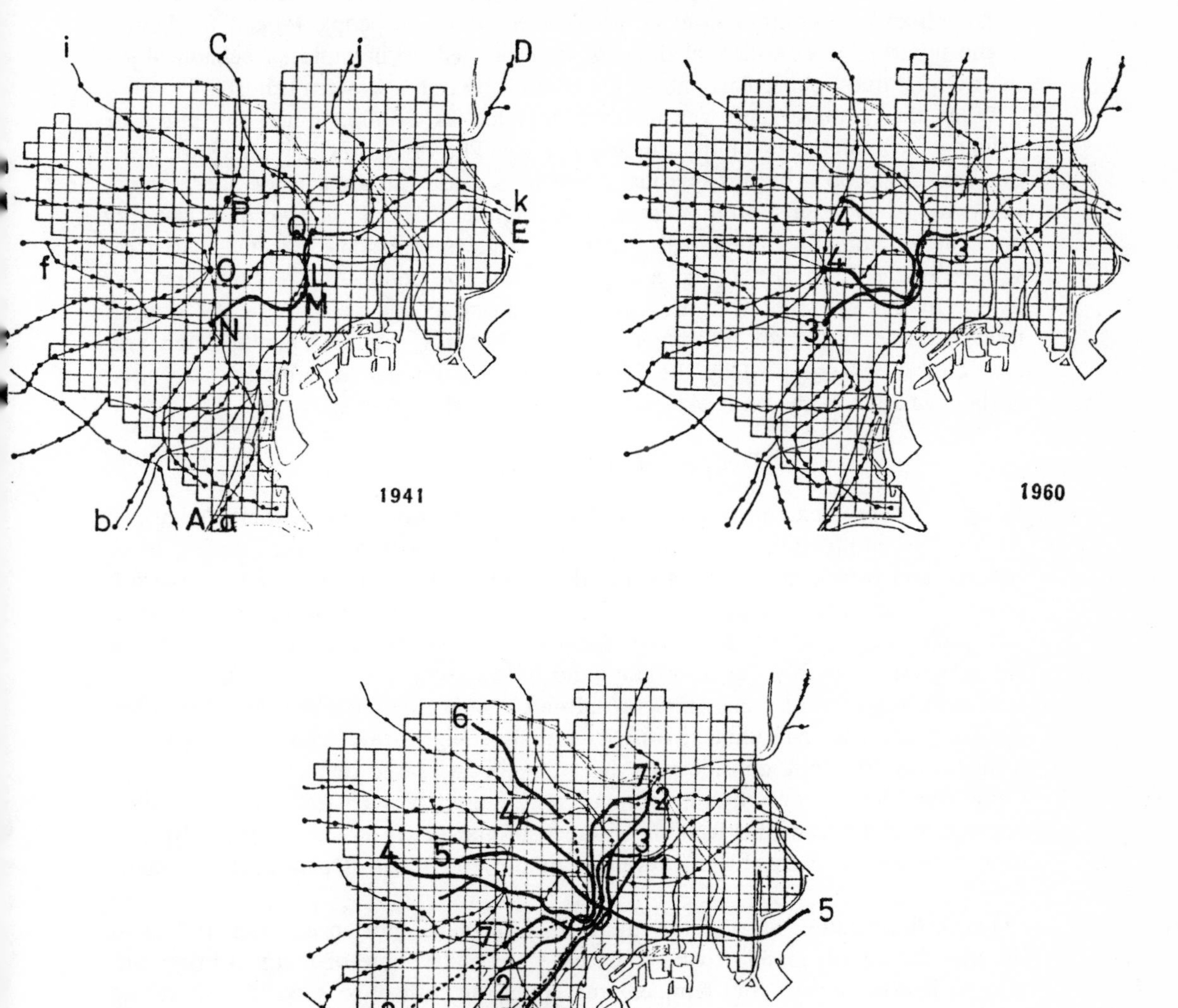

Railroads
Subways
Subways under construction

FIG. 6 Railway network and subway construction, 1969.

dwellings inside the old Tokyo city area with population concentration in the outer metropolitan area continuing at an accelerated pace. As people looked for homes in the suburbs, new residential districts were opened up in rapid succession along the railroad lines, particularly along the Chūō Line in the western suburbs.

When the Yamate Line was finally completed as a loop, it had the effect of defining the boundaries of the municipal area. The government, hoping to make the Yamate Loop grow prosperous, decided to close the area inside the Yamate Loop to private transportation enterprises. Until 1950, mass transit in the city area, apart from the municipally operated trolleys and some bus lines, was restricted to the JNR system and a single subway line connecting Shibuya and Asakusa. In this way, the JNR was assured a monopolistic position in the arterial transportation system of the municipal area. The ring of the Yamate Loop and the connections provided by the Chūō, Keihin, Tohoku and Sobu lines resulted in the formation of the basic skeletal framework of the city area.

Effect of the Railroad System

What of the problems arising out of this rigid framework? First, there is sprawl. As the JNR improved its commuter service with the operation of expresses, more coaches and trains, and better timing, the residential areas continued to expand, up to an hour's commuting distance. The increased volume of commuter traffic in turn prompted improvement of JNR facilities and services, and the sprawl of the city progressed notably westward along the JNR system.

Second, supported by this efficient railroad system, the CBD developed into the relatively compact Marunouchi district and its neighboring areas. The development of this area took considerable time, but the increased demand for commuter traffic could be met only by dumping a large amount of such traffic into a limited number of stations within walking distance of the newly erected offices. By this means the district was able to develop without too much dependence on motor vehicles.

Third, the creation of city subcenters is of special importance. After 1920 and through the 1930s, many private railroads were built, some of them to bring citizens to famous shrines and temples, and some, of course, to serve the sprawling suburbs. But, because of the transportation policy explained above, none of these private lines penetrated inside the Yamate Loop with which they were connected. The junction points where they connected with the JNR on the loop were destined to develop as subcenters of the city. Shinjuku, Shibuya and Ikebukuro are the examples (see Fig. 5). In those days, it was the wisest thing to create such a system of railroads, since the over-all social cost of municipal transportation could thus be minimized. Subsequently, however, Tokyo's population began overflowing into the areas along the private railroad lines, and with this trend the subcenters prospered enormously. After the earthquake of 1923, buses were also introduced into commuter traffic and began servicing the suburban population with those subcenters as terminals, thus further accelerating their growth.

The development of the urban subcenters became conspicuous from the 1930s onward. Places of recreation and consumption for the masses such as restaurants, bars, cinemas began to cluster at these places. Downtown department stores established branches, and later the private railway companies terminating in those subcenters entered the department store business. The subcenters became popular gathering places.

This development greatly increased the amount of traffic into the subcenters. Commuters who reached these points on private railroads from the suburbs had to change to the JNR or trolleys. The congestion which came about as the result of the development of these subcenters and the necessity for changing trains became a very serious problem. Gradually it was necessary to increase both the size of the terminals and the plazas in front of them where buses would load and unload their passengers. However, such changes required large-scale municipal reconstruction and were not easy or inexpensive to make. It was necessary to wait for the end of World War II before these problems could be tackled.

Efforts to Improve the Transport Capacity of the Railroads After World War II

As has already been pointed out, there was an increasing concentration of population in Tokyo following the end of hostilities. The number of commuters entering the city increased constantly and rapidly—even more sharply during the second half of the 1950s. The number of workers in the three CBD wards doubled from 660,000 in 1954 to 1,113,000 by 1963. By 1969, the figure reached 1,575,000. Recently, an increase in the traffic in areas surrounding the CBD has also become noticeable.

The already overloaded transport facilities have had to carry more passengers. The problem of increasing the transport capacity of these facilities has, therefore, become very serious. The first measure taken was the improvement and enlargement of the already existing facilities. The number of tracks on the main lines of JNR were increased, and sections with multidual tracks were extended. The construction of the epoch-making, high-speed New Tokaido Line connecting Tokyo and Osaka also contributed to the expansion of this system. The burden of the long-distance express service on the old Tokaido Line was transferred to the new one, thus giving more room for the old line to increase its commuter services.

In keeping with the increase in JNR transport capacity, operation on the existing private railroad commuter lines was intensified, showing an increase in the number of coaches and in the speed-up of trains. Most of the existing road crossings were level crossings which had to be reconstructed as overpasses or underpasses. Terminal facilities were improved, together with the building of huge terminal buildings, often including department stores. There was very little construction of new railroad lines with the exception of the extension of the Tokyū Line, referred to below.

Subway Construction

The congestion which resulted from the recent increase in automobile traffic has paralyzed the city streets. The transport of passengers within the Yamate Loop by trolley as a result has become extremely inefficient; bus transportation is fast becoming so. In response to this situation, the problem of transport capacity within the city had to be re-evaluated. Since World War II, subway construction has advanced rapidly as a means of coping with this problem (see

Fig. 6). The first subway constructed since the war was the Marunouchi Line, which goes from Ikebukuro to Shinjuku, passing through the CBD, in a large U-shaped route. Construction began in 1951, was completed in 1959, and then extended farther to the west beyond the Yamate Loop to relieve the heavily overloaded Chūō Line. Since that time subway construction has progressed continuously. As of 1969, there were six subway lines with a total trackage of eighty-six miles. Teito Rapid Transit Authority (TRTA) operated sixty-eight miles of lines, Tokyo Metropolitan Government operated eighteen miles of lines. The subways' share of commuter traffic rose from 3.7 per cent in 1955 to 10.5 per cent by 1966. Construction is continuing; construction has been authorized of eleven new lines with a total of forty-nine miles.

There are several unique characteristics of the Tokyo subway system. The first is the mutual use of tracks by TRTA and the private lines which service the suburbs. The former government policy of keeping the area within the Yamate Loop free of private lines has been discontinued in response to the increase in traffic. Now the acute problem is how to deal with the traffic jam at the subcenter transfer points. The solution to this problem has been the mutual track-usage system. For example, the Hibiya Line links the private Tokyū Line (which runs between Tokyo and Yokohama) with the Tobu Line (which serves Tokyo's northern suburbs). The Tozai Line connects JNR's Chūō Line with the Sobu Line which services Chiba Prefecture, east of Tokyo, acting at the same time as the bypass for both. In many cases, including the above, the terminals of the subcenters have been bypassed. The lines are diverted from the existing lines at points outside the Yamate Loop and enter the city across the Loop at stations other than the subcenters.

This has finally provided a successful solution to the subway tangle despite the exceedingly high costs involved. It connects the two ends of a huge passenger flow already created by the suburban railroads, thus ensuring a very high volume of passengers. The historic policy of the Transportation Ministry of severely limiting the entrance of large-scale transportation inside the Yamate Loop has consequently brought about the unique development of the transportation system as well as the city subcenters of Tokyo, and has eventually resulted in bringing considerable advantages to the city. First, the new system of bypassing the city subcenters has given increased possibilities for development to places other than the already overgrown subcenters.

Second, these new lines have been constructed to service the very limited existing CBD only. They are concentrated in the active and attractive Marunouchi and Ginza areas. Arguments have been advanced to construct lines that would bypass the CBD and guide development elsewhere, but no such construction has taken place to date. This decision was made, it appears, solely because of the considerations of profit in the CBD; it has resulted in the further intensification of already accumulated business activities there.

Third, there is a question as to who should construct and operate the subway lines. It was necessary to establish a body to construct and operate the "tunnel-and-track"; the Teito Road Transit Authority, established in 1941 to operate the first subway, was developed to take charge of this. The TRTA is financed by the JNR and the Tokyo Metropolitan Government, but it also issues bonds and raises capital from the private railroad companies and other sources with which it constructs Tokyo's subways. In actual operation, the TRTA uses its own commuter cars but at the same time on certain sections of the track system, JNR and the private lines can use a set number of their own cars. They pay TRTA for this operation.

The fourth and most urgent problem facing the subway system is that of management, which is also true of all other railroad operations. The upping of public fares causes a great deal of political resistance—especially apparent at the present, when the nation is faced with inflation caused by an expanding economy. The Japanese commuter, by using long-term discount tickets, shoulders only a small part of the traffic costs. The JNR, with its highly efficient metropolitan transport operations and the use of its already amortized assets, runs in the black as far as the Tokyo area is concerned. However, these profits must be used to cover the losses of the local tributary lines, most of which operate in the red.

At the present time, improvement or construction of railroad lines is enormously costly. In 1964, the JNR sold 2,680,000 long-term tickets per day. The book value of the total assets which serviced these commuters was $390,000,000 or $145 per individual. In JNR's third extension plan, a $1,200,000,000 investment will be necessary to increase transport capacity by 1,240,000 people, or, in other terms, $970 per individual. Thus, to increase carrying capacity by 50 per cent, investment must be increased sevenfold.[12]

This fact is especially important for the subways. Construction costs rise rapidly each year: one mile on the Marunouchi Line (completed in 1959) was $17.6 million and one mile on the Tozai Line (completed in 1967) was $15.6 million; one mile on the No. 1 Line of the Tokyo Metropolitan Government (1968) cost $19 million. The TRTA, because it operates the already amortized prewar line, uses the profits from this line for the operation of its new lines, thus avoiding serious financial problems. As of 1964, seven years after the opening of all the Marunouchi Line to traffic, the line was completely amortized and commenced making a profit. In 1968, the TRTA had a profit of $5.6 million from the new line and made up the losses incurred on the Tozai Line.[13] However, for the Tokyo Metropolitan Government lines, which do not possess such already existing facilities, the present fare system keeps the operation very unprofitable.

Future Problems

As far as mass transportation is concerned, Tokyo is completely dependent on the railroads and subways. This is especially true for white-collar workers, who have come to regard long-distance commuting as quite natural to their way of life. This is the mechanism by which the activities of this huge agglomeration of eleven and one-half million people are sustained in the face of its relatively poor road network. Unfortunately the sense of resentment of the average citizens to the wastage of human time and energy merely for the sake of commuting seems to have become atrophied—until very recently when there have been several commuter riots.

From the point of view of integrating home and work, which was sought in the planning of New Towns in England, such long-distance commuting is quite shocking. Dr. William Robson (London University), who visited Tokyo in 1967 and 1969 in response to the governor's invitation, severely criticized this aspect of Japanese land use "planning."

Ryohei Kakumoto, a transportation expert in the Ministry of Transportation, has proposed a plan to build a network of commuter express lines like the high speed new Tokaido Line to cope with the excessive price of land and concentration of people in Tokyo due to the shortage of residential land. Using 120-miles-per-hour railroads would greatly enlarge the one-hour-time-distance commuting area around Tokyo. It would be possible to build new towns in places where land is cheap and to house in a human fashion those who must commute to Tokyo. The main point of this proposal is that the construction costs of the new railroads would be covered by levying taxes on the expected considerable rise in the price of land in the new towns resulting from this development. In order to meet the transportation needs of an additional future population increase of ten million in the Tokyo region, it is proposed to construct twenty-three such high-speed railroad lines.† Backed up by the increased confidence in the technology of the JNR as the result of the successful accomplishments of the New Tokaido Line, this proposal has been hailed as a great breakthrough in solving the seemingly insoluble land problem. However, it is far from the idea of homework linkage.

Assuming that Tokyo's white-collar population will continue to increase, the railways radiating out from Tokyo will perform an ever more important function. Therefore, Kakumoto's idea will most likely be carried out, though on a more modest scale. It will be important to examine what kind of new regional structure may appear as a result of this reality.

ROAD TRANSPORTATION

The Weak Road System of Japanese Cities

The road system of Tokyo is very poor. Not only is there no adequate system, but traffic capacity is insufficient. The roads and streets make up only 11.6 per cent[14] of the ward area of the inner sector of the city, and much less than 10 per cent in many suburban areas. This is considerably less than in other major cities of the world.

The reason comes partly from the fact that Japanese cities did not depend on vehicular traffic in the past; transportation was either by ship or on foot. Even today, 95 per cent of the streets have no separation of vehicular from pedestrian traffic.

The other reason is, of course, Tokyo's rapid expansion; planning could not keep pace with the sprawling growth. In suburban areas dwellings were built on former farm land with little change in the pattern of the rice paddies and fields; narrow lanes and footpaths meandered through the gaps between the houses. City planning came rather as an afterthought, often with futile attempts at zoning and land reallotment by legislative or administrative action.

However, major disasters like the Kanto Earthquake and Fire of 1923 did provide a chance for correcting past shortcomings. The fact that the old city areas, centering around the downtown district, possess a relatively orderly network of avenues and streets is because the areas have been completely burned to the

† Similar to the Paris Réseau Express Régional (RER) system. (Editor.)

ground several times, thus offering opportunity for a more sophisticated replanning of the street patterns.

The suburban areas, on the other hand, present a picture of utter chaos because of the overwhelmingly rapid and uncontrollable growth. In 1932, the administrative area of Tokyo had already expanded through the incorporation of adjacent towns and villages to extend beyond the Yamate Loop of the JNR, which had more or less defined the old city limits. The present urban section of Tokyo-to, comprising thirty-five autonomous wards, thus came into being only fairly recently. Prior to that, the administration of the suburban areas surrounding the old city (Tokyo-shi), the areas in which population growth was most pronounced, was in the hands of relatively naive and weak local autonomous bodies. This accounts for the fact that city planning remains backward or seemingly nonexistent in the newer suburban city areas.

Trends in the Motorization of Tokyo

One of the main characteristics of the city's road traffic is the dominance of trucks. As already mentioned, the industrial sector is composed of groups of smaller manufacturers centered around wholesalers and the group of small- and medium-sized manufacturers centered around the parent manufacturers, thus creating a very complicated flow of goods and resultant traffic pattern. The transportation of raw, half-finished and finished products between manufacturers and wholesalers has created a huge traffic volume passing through the center of Tokyo. Also, in order to meet the daily needs of the citizens, a vast volume of goods is transported into Tokyo. Most of the foodstuffs formerly brought in by railroad and ship—now partly by truck—are delivered by local trucks to all parts of the city from markets near the center, causing an ever increasing amount of congestion, especially in the central area.

The motorization of Tokyo has advanced very rapidly in the past few years. The number of private passenger cars has also spurted. There were 608,000 vehicles in Tokyo in 1960; by 1968, the number had almost tripled to 1,749,000. The ratio of passenger cars to trucks in 1963 was 1:1.5; by 1968, it had reversed and become 1:07.[15] Passenger cars (including taxis) are playing an increasingly important role in downtown business activities and have added a new element to the total traffic volume. Due to the heavy concentration of office buildings in the CBD, the traffic situation has become even more hopeless.

Of course, this development was anticipated. But Tokyo and indeed all the cities of Japan have not had sufficient resources to catch up with their explosive expansion. Efforts were absorbed in coping with mass commuter transportation (contrary to American cities) and less attention was paid the street and road system. At this stage of accelerated motorization, Tokyo is faced with the need to take drastic measures, at least to meliorate the urgent traffic problem; it should be noted that the resultant air pollution in central Tokyo is as acute as any place in the world (traffic police are given regular doses of oxygen when on duty).

City Planning and Road Construction

In Japan, city planning was the synonym for infrastructure construction. When the nation came suddenly into the modern age after the Meiji Restoration, it was at once necessary to proceed with the construction of basic urban services such as roads, harbors, water supply and sewage, parks, etc., so as to develop the city from its feudal form. Road construction was especially urgent; land reallotment measures were widely applied to create necessary land for this purpose. Thus, this measure alone has often been understood as city planning itself.

As explained above, city planning has made great advances with the opportunities afforded by each major fire. The reconstruction after the Kanto Earthquake and Fire of 1923 was especially meaningful. Almost all of the downtown area was destroyed by fire; one million people out of a total of four and one-half million were victims of the catastrophe. Reconstruction was under the direct control of the central government in the form of the Imperial Capital Reconstruction Agency, first headed by the then Minister of the Interior Shimpei Gotō. Under his imaginative leadership, basic principles for rebuilding were formulated. Roads received special emphasis in planning. First, a modern ring and radial system of some fifteen hundred-foot square blocks was laid out for the city. Shōwa Avenue was constructed as a major artery to run north–south on the eastern side of the city center, which greatly alleviated congestion. National Highway 1, running between Tokyo and Yokohama, was improved by the central government and linked to Shōwa Avenue. Another important step was the building of ten incombustible bridges over the Sumida River, which flows through Tokyo. Elementary schools located in each of the fifteen-hundred foot blocks were rebuilt with fireproof material. Nevertheless, most of the dwellings were rebuilt with wood. When Tokyo was again heavily damaged by the fire raids of World War II, these schools served as emergency bases for relief and aid. The reconstruction after the 1923 Earthquake was the first large-scale planning operation fundamentally reorganizing the central area of Tokyo.

The second great opportunity for modern city planning came with the rebuilding activities following World War II. By this time the dispersal of population to new areas outside the Yamate Loop had already taken place, so that an enlarged ring and radial road system was obviously necessary. As already described, the need for reorganization of the subcenters was recognized. Efforts were made to this effect during the war; but as all resources were mobilized for military purposes, little could be actualized in city planning. As a defense measure, the combustible wooden houses were cleared around important installations such as railway stations, along major roads and railroad lines in order to make fire prevention zones. This was, in reality, planned destruction; however, the fire raids burned out most of the city area.

The confusion—both social and physical—experienced by Japanese cities after the war was a desperate one. Black markets quickly came into existence, illegally occupying the plazas and burned-out areas around the railway stations, and conducting business in brazen disregard of the law. However, as established institutions returned to normality, city planning was once again initiated.

Unfortunately, owing to the necessity of economic recovery, the first planning steps were devoted to reconstructing basic production activities. Investment capital was concentrated in this sector. The cities, still reeling from the destruction of the war, did not have enough financial resources to make badly needed

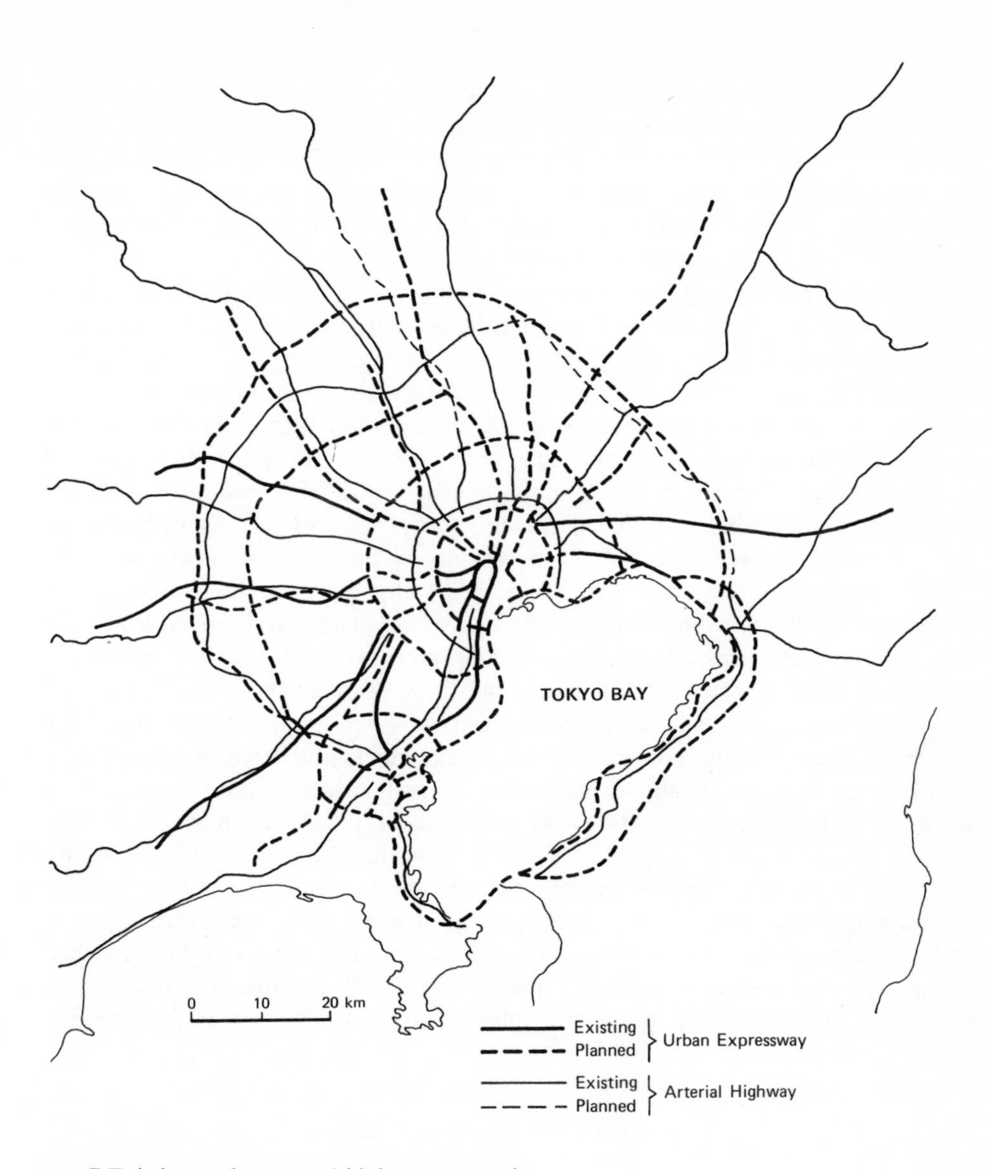

FIG. 7 Existing and proposed highway network.

infrastructure investments. In this initial period, city planning was concentrated on developing the main station plazas along the Yamate Loop and on the construction of the Ring Highway No. 7, running at a six-mile radius from the city center, while other activities were necessarily postponed (Fig. 7).

The next great opportunity was the 1964 Tokyo Olympic Games. The then Governor of Tokyo Ryutaro Azuma seized this occasion as a means of advancing city planning. Using the Olympics as a spur to greater efforts, all of the conspicuous problems such as (a) the expansion of the road system to cope with motorization, (b) the construction of parks and recreational facilities, (c) securing of an adequate water supply and (d) the construction of major transportation facilities of national importance (such as the new Tokaido Line) were worked out with increased financial resources available for this special event.

The American Forces' dependent housing at the former Yoyogi Parade Ground was cleared away and Kenzo Tangé's magnificent Olympic pool was constructed. In the relatively new Komazawa area, a series of stadia were built. These, plus those which already existed in the Meiji Memorial Park (Meiji Shrine's Outer Gardens), became the principal Olympic Centers.

The expressway linking Tokyo International (Haneda) Airport and the downtown area was also completed and an interesting, if largely nonfunctional, monorail constructed parallel to it. The expressway system was considered to be an absolute necessity for dealing with Tokyo's traffic congestion. The expressway system was built by the Tokyo Expressway Public Corporation. Established in 1959 as a toll road, the expressway consists of a loop encircling the Imperial Palace and a series of radial routes going in all directions which are connected with the original ring and radial pattern. At present, thirty miles of the planned seventy-five-mile system have been completed. Owing to the lack of vacant space in Tokyo, the inner city system was constructed sadly by filling in unused canals, destroying green space and building elevated roads. This has been criticized for putting even more pressure on the dwindling green space by placing monstrous scale structures in the middle of the miniature gardenlike urban texture of Tokyo. However, one must clearly recognize that this road system was absolutely necessary; traffic, despite public transport development, just keeps increasing. The four-lane freeway is already overcrowded at rush hours although planned to meet the traffic volumes of 1985. As might be expected, the new roads have already generated an even greater volume of traffic. The exact effects of this reciprocal relationship cannot yet be forecast, but it seems that the expressway system may indeed lead to new contradictions. Undoubtedly, the construction of this expressway/freeway system has taught the lesson that when a city has reached a stage of overloading its physical assets, there still remains a possibility of mobilizing resources for a pragmatic solution, even at the cost of inviting still further problems.

Improvement of Industrial Location

The construction of the expressway was very striking, but note also should be taken of the construction of the highway network promoted at the same period which extends to the areas around Tokyo. Since the 1960s, road construction and improvement have been accelerated to keep pace with motorization. The freeway linking Tokyo and Osaka-Kobe was opened to traffic with the completion of the Tokyo-Nagoya section in 1969. The Chūō expressway from Tokyo to the mountainous region of central Japan is now under construction. Including the No. 3 Keihin Highway connecting Tokyo and Yokohama, various new high standard roads servicing the areas around Tokyo have been built. Their most pronounced effect on the capital area has been to improve industrial location with probable gains in efficiency. As already related, the dispersal of industry into the areas around the city has been made possible by these new roads.

The Dichotomy between Old Streets and the New Trunk Roads

It is not sufficient to discuss only the striking development of Tokyo's main roads. Road construction up to the present has simply paved the basic city pattern inherited from feudal times. As soon as one gets off the main roads, one enters into the old urban precincts of small irregular streets without sidewalks. City planning up to now has simply cut up the city area by a grid of major roads leaving the old precincts as they were and expecting them to modernize by themselves. This has not happened; the new trunk roads, symbol of modernity, and the old urban pattern, symbol of traditional ways, have not blended into one another. They both remain as dichotomized as ever. Motorcars are invading the old capillary veins of the precincts, filling up the narrow streets. People complain about this congestion (calling it a public nuisance) but no concrete citizens' movement to alleviate this condition has yet appeared. This kind of dichotomy and its attendant problems can be solved only by the citizens themselves. These difficulties and their solution will become the arena for Tokyo's next age of urban renewal as more attention is paid to the quality of the deteriorating domestic environment.

HOUSING

The Home Consciousness of the Japanese People

Housing is one of the most critical problems in the city. The low housing standards are indicated by the fact that 28 per cent of the families in Tokyo live in substandard, overcongested houses or in dilapidated housing, and that 34 per cent complain about housing difficulties. Moreover, 32 per cent of the employed citizens must spend more than one hour in badly crowded trains to commute to their places of work. Land prices are fantastically high: $15 per square foot in the residential areas near the city center; $7.50 to $10 per square foot in the suburbs twenty miles from the city center. The average size of a dwelling is only 550 square feet; when this is compared with housing indices in Western countries, one cannot help but be shocked at the low standard of our housing.[16]

Historically, the Japanese people have not attached much importance to housing. There is a proverbial saying, "Half a mat for standing, one mat for sleeping." Little space has been traditionally sufficient for our living. Such is the attitude toward housing of the Japanese people whose ancestors lived in warm, Southeast Asia. It is an attitude partly influenced by Zen Buddhism, introduced into Japan in the Kamakura period (1192–1333), of indifference to the outer world. It is indicative of what modest demands the Japanese people make on housing.

The Japanese consciousness of community is also said to be low. Generally speaking, traditional Japanese houses are surrounded by fences, and the space thus enclosed is used exclusively by the household; interest in the space within the fence is very high, but attention paid to the community outside is not necessarily high.

The majority of housing in Japanese cities are wooden structures, and streets designed for pedestrians are narrow and irregularly laid out. Residential areas are flat and extend horizontally, but dwelling density is very high. The customs of the past have contributed to the extremely low standard of housing.

TABLE C Distribution of housing in Tokyo by tenure and by income, 1968.

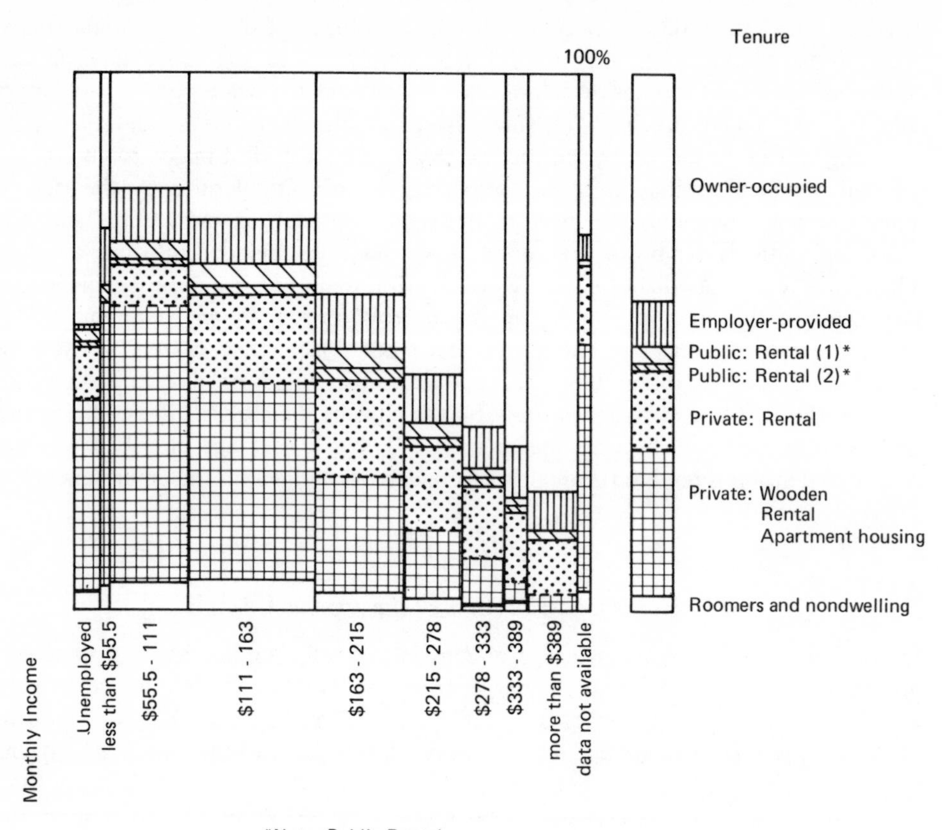

*Note: Public Rental
(1) Subsidized public housing by local government
(2) Japan Housing Corporation, Local Housing Association

The Housing Supply in Tokyo

The most serious housing problem in the capital is the housing shortage; the housing supply has not been able to catch up with the demand created by the concentration of population. To deal only with the mean averages in the housing demand-supply situation, however, is to ignore the crux of the problem. It was pointed out above that the northeastern part and the southwestern part of Tokyo differ considerably in their occupational and income structure, and that the age structure of the population is characterized by the dominance of youth. Therefore, different strata of people with different occupational, income and age characteristics are faced with differing housing problems.

Here are the results of a survey of housing demands conducted in Tokyo in 1968.[17] In Table C, the horizontal axis indicates the level of household income, with the width of a column indicating the distribution of households within the corresponding income level; the vertical axis indicates housing by type of tenure, with the height of the column indicating the distribution of each kind of housing;

thus, the area of each rectangle represents the proportion of housing by income and tenure to the total housing stock.

Slightly less than half of the total housing stock is owner occupied, and also slightly less than half are dwellings for rent, while about 8 per cent is employer-provided housing and about 6 per cent is public housing for certain income levels, which is further divided into those built by local governments and those built by the Japan Housing Corporation and housing-supply associations. A majority of dwellings for rent are wooden-structure apartment houses, and their physical standards are extremely low. This low-quality housing accounts for 28 per cent of the total housing stock in the city. The ratio of those who live in low-quality wooden structure apartment houses is highest among low income people, but, as is expected, the ratios of those who live in housing for rent and those who live in owner-occupied housing are reversed as the income level rises. It is surprising to find that public housing and employer-provided housing,‡ which are aimed primarily at low-income people, are actually widespread in all income strata.

A similar trend was detected in the national housing survey conducted in 1965. In the past few years, the floor space of newly built dwellings for rent has not increased but has remained at the level of 330 to 440 square feet, while the average size of owner-occupied housing has increased from 820 to 980 square feet, while that of employer-provided housing has ranged between 650 and 760 square feet. The proportion of new housing to the total housing stock in Tokyo is very large, with houses built since 1960 accounting for 45 per cent.

Rental Housing

In the past, the most common type of urban housing in Japan was rental housing. A survey, made in 1941,[18] indicated that 73 per cent of all citizens in Tokyo lived in rented dwellings. Taking this as a prewar model, the decrease in the ratio of those who live in dwellings for rent, from 73 per cent in 1941 to 47 per cent today, is a significant change. The reasons for the change are: the great loss of housing during the war, the decline of the landlord class, and a reduction in investment in rental housing as rent control and other measures designed to protect the rights of tenants have been enforced. As a result of inflation, the rents for old dwellings are remarkably low, with the mean being about $20 per month in 1969. Since the construction cost of a dwelling for rent is now at least $3,000 (excluding the cost for land), investment in rental housing is only marginally profitable at the present level of rent.

The results of the rents being kept at a low level is twofold. First, the average household's ability to pay for housing costs is very low, and thus the standard of newly supplied housing must be kept extremely low in order to meet the affordable rents. (However, rents for new dwellings are considerably higher than the average rents.) Second, the liquidity or fluidity of housing is very low; this is especially the case with old construction. Tenants, who have lived in the same rental housing or public housing for many years at very low rent, simply do not move to other more appropriate housing even when their present abodes are no longer adequate and convenient due to changes in their family structure and from the standpoint of commuting to their places of work.

‡ Widespread in Asia. (Editor's note.)

The situation is further aggravated by the extremely high price of land. In Japan, the pressure on land is so high, and its price has been pushed to such a point, that it is far in excess of the reasonable capital value against the profit it will produce in proportion to its utility. As a result, when one plans to build a house one needs resources as much as or more than the cost of the housing to pay for the land alone.

Wooden-structure apartment houses have been one answer to a mounting housing demand under such circumstances. The construction of these apartment houses began to be accelerated in the late 1950s and, as stated, they now account for 28 per cent of the total housing stock of the city. In 1968, the average size of units in these apartment houses was 150 square feet, and most of the units were one-room apartments.[19] In the early 1960s, facilities such as lavatories, kitchens and bathrooms were jointly used by households in such multiple dwellings, but today the general standard has been raised to that of private dwellings of this general level with *private* facilities, as above.

Wooden-structure apartment houses are to be found in highly concentrated areas convenient for intraurban commuting. Their tenants are low-income people who are forced to place a higher priority on convenience in commuting than on housing standards. Thus their location is necessarily limited to the areas that can meet the needs of such people. In the early 1960s, these areas were old residential areas within a six-mile radius of the city center, and landlords often made use of their gardens to build such low-quality apartment houses. This kind of housing supply has aggravated further the concentration of population in the city center at the sacrifice of filling up scarce open space.

The housing crisis, which was anticipated, has been overcome by the supply of the most undesirable form of housing; the "solution" of the problem may be compared to that of squatter settlements in developing nations.

Owner-occupied Dwellings

The government expected the construction of owner-occupied houses to go a long way toward solving the housing shortage. As shown in Table C, owner-occupied dwellings account for about a half of the housing stock. In Japan, the system of housing financing, a precondition for owning a house, has not been well developed. Until recently, loans from the government-established Japan Housing Loan Corporation have served as the main resource for financing a private house. In the Japanese economy, whose activity has been focused on investment in industrial equipment to accelerate economic growth, housing financing has been a rather neglected sector. The situation is, however, changing as the economy reaches maturity. One reason for the recent increase in the volume of construction of owner-occupied dwellings is that households have been able to allocate an increasingly large proportion of income to housing investment due to the rise of the general income level. At the same time, the system of supplying housing in the private sector has also developed to a considerable degree. Until recently, the main builders of housing in the private sector have been limited to small-scale real estate developers or home builders; economies of scale by larger entrepreneurs now seem to be emerging.

The pattern of housing supply for sale is determined by basic income levels and the need for economy by individual families. It is estimated that three to four

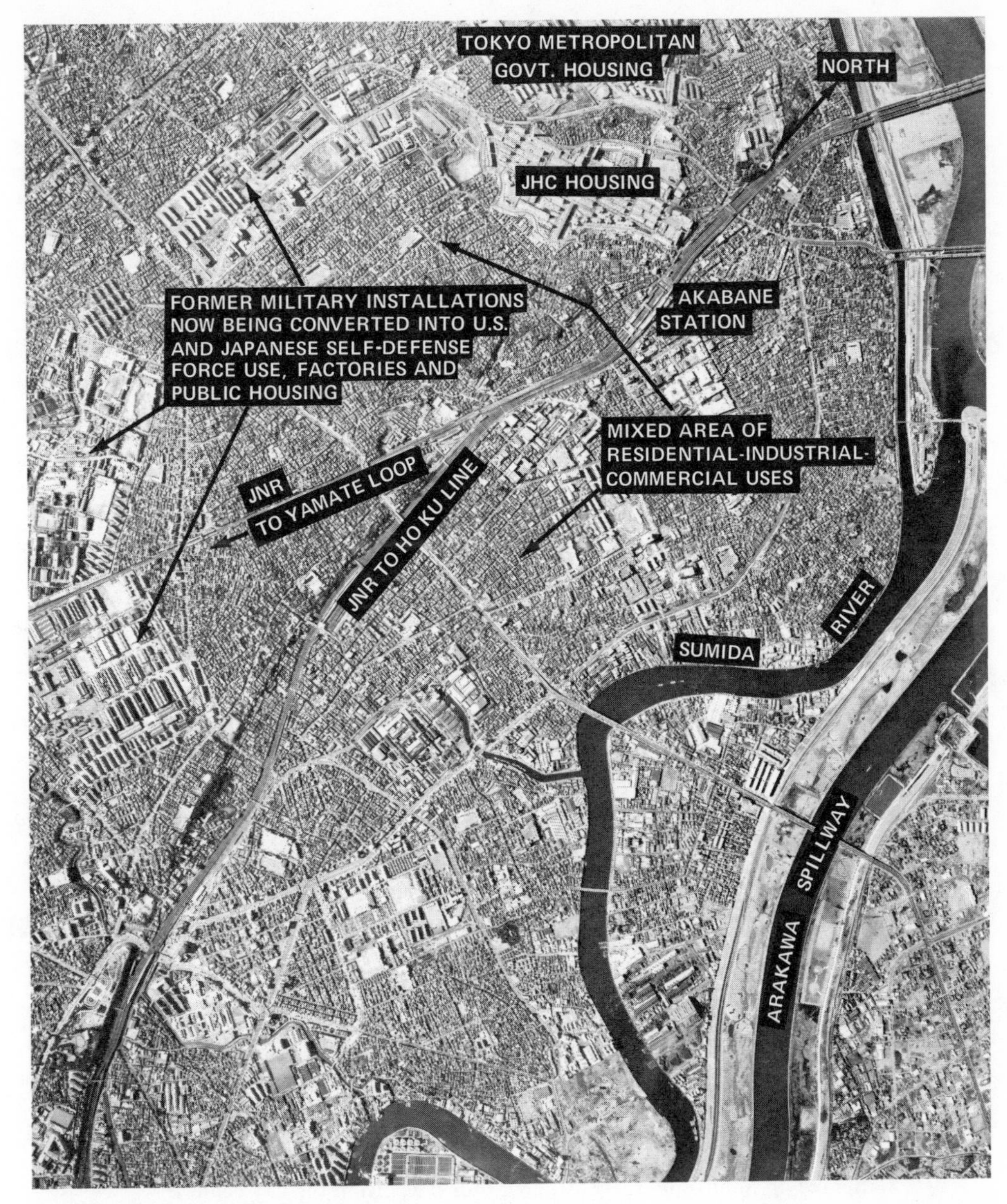

FIG. 8A Eastern residential-industrial zone: Former military area converted into public housing estate, four miles from the city center.

years of household income is needed to purchase a house and land at the market price. The land must be accessible by mass transit and will be developed at as low a cost as possible, provided with minimal infrastructure on a plot of land for one house averaging between 1,000 and 1,700 square feet. The price of such a plot of land is about equal to the construction costs of a house. As large a house is built on the plot as the zoning code permits, but its size is, in most cases, between 360 and 550 square feet.[20] Houses of this order are springing up in large numbers in the rural areas to twenty miles away from the city center.

It is not difficult to see that housing supplied in such a manner is very inadequate in physical terms. However, since these houses do match the minimum needs of

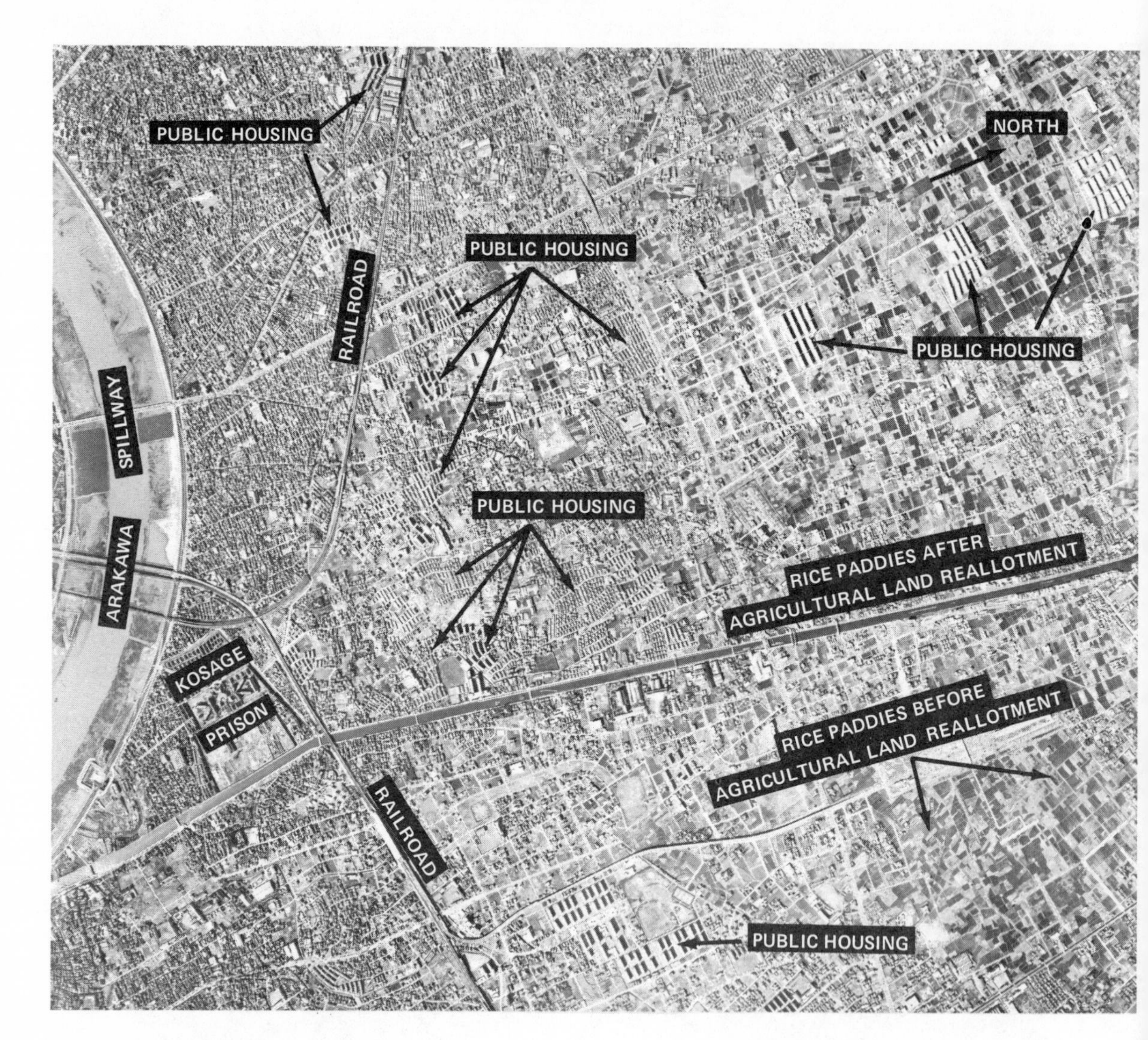

FIG. 8B Sprawling suburbs on the East Side, four miles from the city center.

citizens looking for homes, people have spread to the suburbs of Tokyo in tremendous numbers. The suburban areas have thus become extensions of unattractive, congested, built-up areas. The provision of urban infrastructure, which should precede suburban development, always lags behind. Moreover, such a sprawl contributes to the rise of land prices. In this way, uncontrollable waves of urban scatteration are submerging the Tokyo suburbs.

Public Housing

How, under such high cost circumstances, has public housing been provided? There are two noteworthy general characteristics of it in Japan. First, public housing began as emergency housing for war-damage sufferers in the winter of

1946. The *Dojunkai,* the forerunner of the present *Jutaku Eidan* (Housing Authority), which played an important role before and during World War II, was originally established to provide housing for sufferers of the 1923 Earthquake. Public housing policy in Japan has tended to provide a large quantity of housing in crises at the expense of quality. The second characteristic is the tendency toward building incombustible, multistory apartment houses, (Figs. 8a, 8b), resulting from the hard lessons brought to the Japanese people by both the 1923 Earthquake and by World War II incendiary bombing that houses made of paper and wood are extremely vulnerable to fire.[21] It is also an expression of the intention to change the characteristic flat, sprawling urban structure into a more modern, more compact form.

The postwar public housing policy in Japan was invigorated by turning over the responsibility for the low-rent housing supply to the local governments with the central government providing housing subsidies to help reduce rents. In 1950, the Japan Housing Loan Corporation was established to extend long-term, low-interest loans to middle-income people who wanted to build homes of their own. The construction of public housing mentioned above, however, created new problems in large metropolitan areas. Many people whose lives are closely related to Tokyo have overflowed into neighboring prefectures, and it has become necessary to provide housing for such people. The Tokyo Metropolitan Government, however, cannot provide public housing in areas outside its administrative boundaries. Neither can the neighboring prefectures afford to provide large-scale public housing for people who have overflowed from Tokyo. In such circumstances, an authority that could provide public housing on a regional scale had to be created.

The establishment of the Japan Housing Corporation (JHC) in 1955 was in response to such demands. Among the many tasks assigned to the JHC are the construction of incombustible, multistory apartment houses, the construction of new residential cities and the development of residential and industrial land. The JHC has also been given the role of providing housing based on revolving funds, in contrast to public housing based on central government subsidies. From the very beginning, the amount of construction by the JHC has been very large; in the first year of its operation it built 20,000 units. Now the number of units built in a year is about 81,000. By 1970, the JHC had built 700,000 units. Thus the JHC has become one of the main suppliers of public housing together with subsidized public housing by the local governments and has played, in the past fifteen years, the role of pioneer in public housing construction.

The JHC was faced with many problems at its inception. The first was the types of units to be built. Being an enterprise using revolving funds, rents for JHC apartments were considerably higher than those for other public housing. In order not to raise rents, the size of housing units had to be reduced; as a result, the JHC started building very small-size housing units, with the standard type being two rooms and a dining-kitchen, with a total floor space of 470 square feet.

Inadequate as they were, supplies of housing by the JHC contributed in some measure toward solving the housing shortage under the prevailing social and economic circumstances. Small-sized housing units built by the JHC matched the postwar tendency toward nuclear, or conjugal, rather than extended families and met the demand of an increasing number of new households while the feeling that the rents were high was gradually lost in the midst of the growing inflation. Rather, the JHC housing units helped instill in the Japanese people a sense of a new life style represented by such phrases as "vertically piled-up dwelling" and "privacy provided by lock, steel door, and private bath." The JHC apartments paved the way for private developers to build similar new types.

The second problem was the power of the JHC to provide public housing regardless of the boundaries of local governments. Constructing a large number of housing units in one place was in effect equal to creating a new community, and it involved a great deal of work with local government. This problem grew in importance as JHC projects increased.

When the JHC built large housing estates (*danchi*), it also had to build the minimum amount of community facilities, including schools and shopping centers. By doing so, the JHC created self-contained communities (without jobs). On the other hand, the land price continued to soar, and the JHC was forced to build new *danchi* in more and more distant suburbs where land was available at cheaper prices and in larger quantities. These far-out suburbs were the places where the existing community facilities were most inadequate and where the construction of new facilities was absolutely necessary if new estates were to be built and function successfully. To provide housing on a large scale, the JHC was forced to build larger and larger danchi. This meant that the scale of community facilities became larger and larger and the danchi more self-contained. Large-scale danchi made it possible to improve the existing transportation facilities by opening new bus routes and railway stations and thereby to overcome locational disadvantages.

The growth of danchi in scale went hand-in-hand with their location at a greater distance from the city center; the first contained about 1,000 dwelling units and were located within a distance of six miles from the city center. Today, large impersonal danchi comprise 4,000 to 8,000 units and are located at a distance of twenty to thirty miles.

These phenomena could not help but trigger reactions. One of the reactions concerned the loss of the green areas in Tokyo which were wedges between railway lines radiating from the city center to the suburbs. Such wedgelike green areas could remain because bus and other transportation services had not developed serving the interstices between railway stations. Since the construction of large danchi made it possible for bus services to operate in hitherto inaccessible areas, the sprawl of private housing began in green areas, taking advantage of new transportation services to the danchi, and rapid urbanization resulted. The construction of danchi by the JHC helped accelerate the encroachment on the remaining green areas and urban sprawl—functions it had not quite expected to play.

The second reaction was the great social confusion experienced by weak local governments as the result of rapid urbanization. New danchi dwellers were commuters to Tokyo and had very little to do with rural villagers; being middle-class people, the danchi dwellers demanded high-level community facilities and social services, but local governments could afford to meet such demands only halfway. The JHC provided minimum amounts of community facilities, but these facilities merely served as further incentives to attract more people to the areas surrounding large housing estates. The local municipalities were expected to build schools and to improve roads for the population thus attracted. Being forced to defray expenditures for the development of community facilities beyond their fiscal capability, the local municipalities began to oppose the construction of danchi by the JHC in their areas. The opposition grew intense around 1960 when JHC construction activity became brisk, and in subsequent years the JHC experienced many difficulties with the local authorities.

Thus, the building of danchi by the JHC, on one hand, helped instill in citizens a new modern life style and, on the other, contributed toward widening the gap between housing supply and over-all city planning and local administration.

The Construction of New Cities or New Towns

The area within a thirty-mile radius of the city center, the Tokyo metropolitan area, has a present population 15.6 million and is expected to increase to 25.9 million by 1985.[22] The problem faced is whether the expected further population increase of 10.3 million in the metropolitan area should be accommodated by construction of new cities or by urban redevelopment, and if both approaches are to be pursued, what will be the proportion between them? The construction of new cities has two major aspects:

First is the construction of new cities by public authorities. As was mentioned earlier, the construction of danchi by the JHC has encountered many difficult problems and yet it has provided an opportunity to start creating so-called New Towns in connection with residential land development. The first new town development in Japan commenced in the 1950s in the western suburbs of Osaka; local governments, the JHC and other organizations have collaborated to develop this new town into a city of 200,000 population today. The growing trend of urbanization convinced the Tokyo Metropolitan Government of the need to undertake a similar new town development. In co-operation with the JHC at both the planning and the implementation stages, the Tokyo Metropolitan Government is now building a new city with a projected population of 400,000 in the Tama Hills in the western suburbs of the capital.

Tama New Town is being planned as a commuter city. It may be said that reliance on mass transit for commuting in the past construction of danchi and the pressing need to supply a large amount of residential land engendered the scheme. The new city will be created in the last large rural area remaining in Tokyo-to, linked with the city center by extensions of the existing two railway lines. Professor William Robson of the London School of Economics criticizes the new city plans as follows:

> In my opinion the Tama New Town project is fundamentally misconceived. It should never have been planned as a mainly residential town for commuters. Its location is not far enough from the central area for a satellite and is not near enough to achieve a reasonably short journey to work. It is therefore unsatisfactory from both points of view.[23]

The move to build new cities is seen in the private sector, too. Large demands for housing and the possibility of urban development have drawn the keen attention of private enterprise (Fig. 9). Skyrocketing land prices have served as the great incentive for large enterprises to enter into the real estate business. But profit from land value increase does not lead to a healthy development of sound business; increasingly private enterprise is more and more interested in comprehensive urban development projects. Among the large-scale urban development projects in Tokyo is another New Town development in the Tama

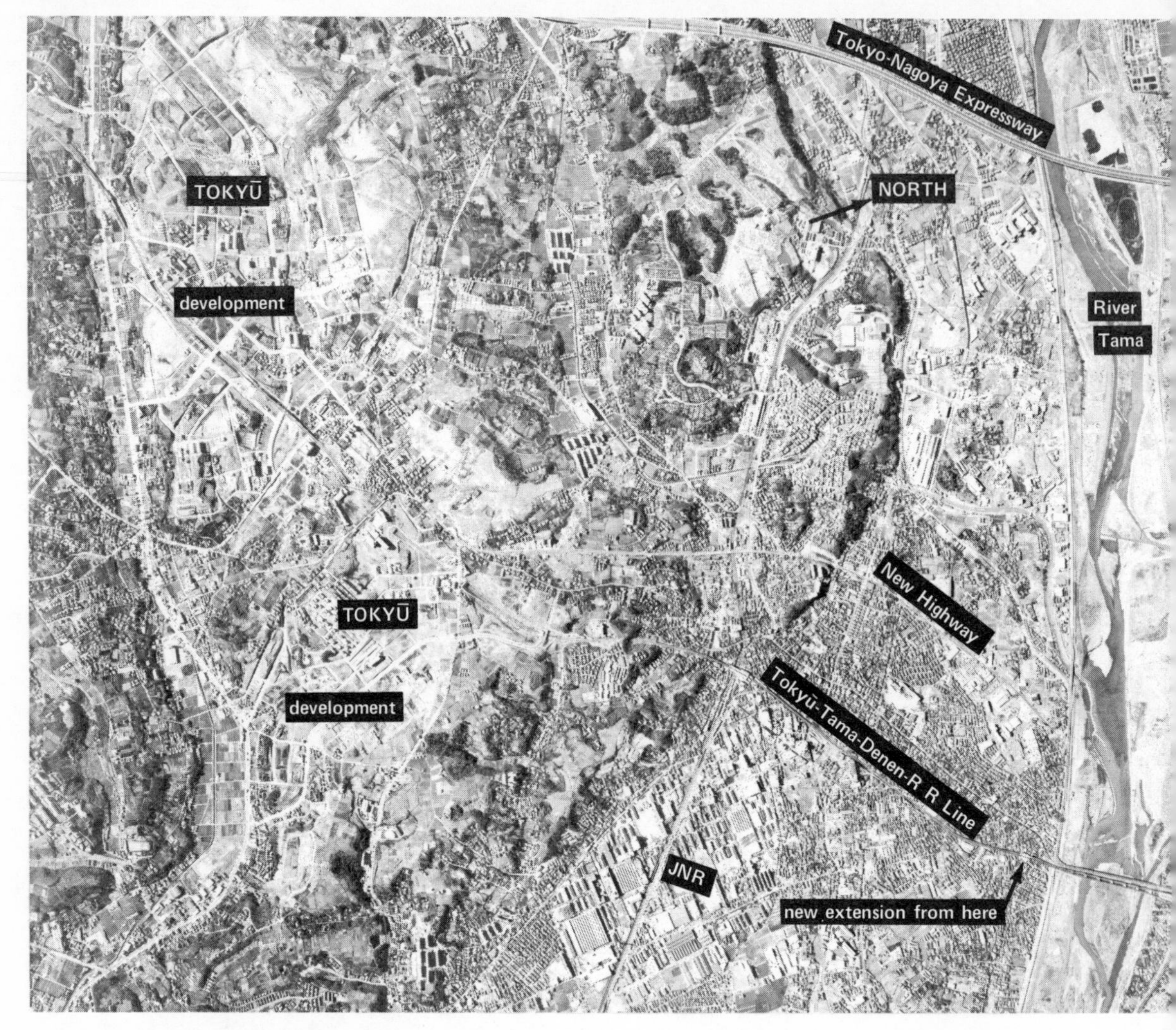

FIG. 9 Sprawling suburbs on the West Side; large-scale development by the Tokyū Railroad Company.

Hills by the Tokyū Railways Company. Tokyū bought an extensive area of land in the southwest suburbs of Tokyo, extended one of its branch lines six miles to the area, developed residential compounds along the new railway line, and sold it for housing in collaboration with land reallotment operations of the local government. The line, built as a subway, connecting to downtown forms an integral part of the project planning. Tokyū also is building apartment houses as part of its development projects.

Since railway fares are controlled at a rather low level by the government in Japan, it is extremely difficult to finance the construction of new railway lines on a commercial basis. It is possible, however, to recover railway construction costs leading to deficits in the railway department, with profits from the real estate department. The New Town development by Tokyū is expected to bring an increased population of 300,000 to the area.

The success of projects like Tokyū's have encouraged the Japanese National Railways; the Kakumoto plan mentioned earlier is a proposal linking residential land development with the construction of express commuter railway lines. Significant new forces have joined the old ones in shaping the Tokyo region. These powerful new forces are likely to develop urban structures of a higher level of amenity, different from the ones so far developed by small-scale real estate entrepreneurs.

Urban Redevelopment

While Tokyo expands horizontally, interest in the redevelopment of old parts of the city is also rising. The meaning of urban redevelopment in Japan is quite different from that in American cities. Certainly, brisk new construction is going on in the centers of Japanese cities; accelerated by the expansion of CBDs, urban real estate values are increasing. But there is little motivation to redevelop older urban areas because they are blighted; redevelopment in Japan has been pushed primarily as a means for creating urban public spaces such as widening streets and development of station plazas and only rarely has it been employed to improve the residential environment.

Recently, the transformation of sites vacated by industrial factories into residential land has attracted much attention in the name of urban redevelopment. This interest has been spurred by the realization that the construction of new cities designed primarily for long-distance commuters is not serving the need of low-income, blue-collar workers. There are now many cases where the JHC and other public organizations have bought former factory sites and built high density public housing. Unfortunately, since the rents for such public housing built on expensive land tend to be high and beyond the means of blue-collar families, higher income people are likely to move into the areas formerly inhabited by low-income population.

Private developers are also becoming interested in urban redevelopment. Their interest has crystallized in the construction of apartment houses that are popularly called "mansions" in Japan. In the past few years, elegant apartment houses aimed at high income consumers have been built in large numbers on sites very near mass transit in the city.[24] Old upper class residential areas have been chosen as the sites of such apartment houses because of their high prestige value and also because large plots of land are available there. High-class apartment houses in the city are highly competitive with dwellings in suburban areas, for the land price in the latter has soared. The popularization of apartment houses by public enterprise has changed the "home consciousness" of citizens; more people now feel at ease with high-rise apartment life. As many as ten thousand units of private mansions a year are now being built.

City Dwellers and Their Homes

As noted earlier, Tokyo has continued to expand with the influx of a young, working-age population added to the older residents. Young people migrate to Tokyo in large numbers every year; they settle in dormitories provided by employers and rooming houses near their places of work or find live-in jobs. They set up independent households by moving to wooden-structure apartment houses conveniently located or, if fortunate, to public housing when they get married. They then move to public housing or single-family houses in the suburbs when their babies are born. Such is the basic pattern of life for migrants to this dynamic capital. It applies reasonably well to white-collar workers, who can endure long-distance commuting from suburban areas twenty to thirty miles away from the city center. But it does not apply to blue-collar workers for whom long distance commuting is financially impossible. In fact, blue-collar workers must endure high density living in wooden-structure apartment houses or rooming houses near their places of work. New housing created by urban redevelopment cannot be homes for low-income, blue-collar workers because of the high rents, and there is little prospect for the improvement of the deleterious housing conditions in the northeastern part of Tokyo, for example.

A solution must be sought in a change in regional structure. In the section on industry, it was noted that the industrial areas of Tokyo are expanding far and wide. At newly located factories, locally recruited workers are greater in number than those who moved out from Tokyo. Workers from the countryside are accommodated at newly constructed company dormitories. On the other hand, farmers are becoming part-time farmers and get a second job at the factories. With the expansion of residential areas, urban-type settlements are spreading in rural communities, accompanied by new schools and shops. The diffusion of such settlements helps rural people to familiarize themselves with urban life styles and prepares them psychologically for urban occupations. The newly located factories will attract research institutes and organize new hierarchies of subcontract factories, thus creating new agglomerations of functions and people which in turn bring about new agglomerations of commercial and business activities. Around the stations of suburban railways there are already developing small-town centers.

It may be said that this *laissez-faire* urbanization in Tokyo is already at work creating a new regional structure. The compact, mononuclear urban structure with a twenty-mile radius is now changing rapidly to a more dispersed network-type structure, spurred by the dispersal of industry. National Highway No. 16, a ring road running at a distance of about twenty miles from the city center, has been attracting many factories to the areas along it. Right inside this ring highway are the areas where the population increase is highest in Tokyo; this population increase will spread inevitably outside the ring highway as industry is further dispersed.

Looking at these realities, a new perspective on new cities emerges. The mononuclear city expands, a real differentiation takes place, and new linkages are formed, which demands new multinucleated plans for coping with the process of change taking place in the urban structure as megalopolis takes shape in the Pacific Belt stretching two hundred and sixty miles from Kobe through Osaka, Kyoto, Nagoya, Yokohama and Tokyo.

EPILOGUE

The preceding analysis has examined how various human activities were performed within the historical and geographic mold called Tokyo, and how these activities in turn have shaped Tokyo as it is today. The present is the result of all the past developmental processes, and all the developmental processes now at work will determine the next present, the future. Planning is to predict accurately what will happen at the next stage and to work out an appropriate program of action to meet it.

This, however, is more easily said than done, because contemporary society consists of many varied sectorial frameworks whose specific behavior contains elements that often contradict each other. What is favorable for one sector is not necessarily favorable for another. An action taken at one time may cause an entirely unanticipated result at an unanticipated time and at an unanticipated place. Our prediction often lacks reliable insights of true sophistication. Our society consists of sectorial frameworks and each sector is deeply concerned with solving its problems according to its limited scope.

Tokyo has now reached the point when public investment could be undertaken on an enlarged scale. The impact it will generate will become larger and larger, and this in turn involves us in further investment. Just as in the case of improving highways, the more they improve, the more traffic is generated, and we are thus obliged to construct in an ever enlarged scale with more sophisticated means. Sometimes it may even lead to ever enlarging difficulties as unexpected effects occur; in fact we are being pushed around by the inhuman power which we ourselves have created.

The description of the past development of Tokyo may sound fairly optimistic about the possibility of coping with these problems. Tokyo with its agglomeration of 11.5 million people does continue to perform its vigorous activities in spite of *laissez-faire* planning and *laissez-passer* administration. One striking example is that of the initial national railway policy of prohibiting private railway companies from extending their suburban lines to the area inside the JNR's Yamate Loop Line. This policy was originally adopted to maintain the profitability of the National Railway's operations, but it has contributed toward the happy development of lively and viable subcenters at the points where suburban railway lines and the Yamate Loop Line meet. There are other unexpected external economies.

Through all the stages of development until the present, Tokyo was always short of resources as well as administrative machinery to cope with the tremendous expansion of the metropolis. The measures taken were always piecemeal; each sector tried to employ as many resources as available within its means to meet the need posed in the most pragmatic fashion. The accumulation of such piecemeal efforts is what Tokyo is now: a huge village full of confusion, but still working. It seems that such flexible measures, rather than rigid comprehensive planning, have been better suited to our case in this constant process of trial and error.

From such a viewpoint, the growing present dispersal or urban functions in Tokyo and the reorganization of the metropolitan area into a much larger regional or megalopolitan area have been described with a perspective toward possible planning solutions based on this emerging large-scale reality.

Looking into the future, however, I must express my serious concern over negative possibilities quite contrary to my optimistic observations. My main concern is with the problem of environmental disruption which is becoming ever more serious. The extraordinary concentration and agglomeration of function and population in the Tokyo region have brought about serious imbalance between the productive activity, human living and the natural eco-system. The very mechanisms which have expedited the development of Tokyo up to now are working to aggravate the present problems. The rapid development so far was promoted by converting the internal diseconomy of specific sectors to an external economy, thus maximizing the economic gain of prominent sectors. Tokyo's urban structure was formulated on this behavioral pattern of economy, and prominent sectors developed within the old mold neglecting the sectors concerned especially with the daily life of the citizenry. The natural environment was seriously exploited during this process. The resultant urban structure cannot carry out the drastic reorganization of land use which Tokyo should have if it is to continue its existence.

At this stage, when urban functions have become so massive and combined together in such complex ways, any new improvement needs holistic planning. Environmental problems are the most striking examples. In the early stage, the causes of environmental disruption were relatively simple, and the sufferers of the damage were identifiable. Now various environmental disruptions are caused by the complex combination of living and industrial activities, and damage unspecified groups of people and industries. Piecemeal measures can no longer provide solutions in such a situation.

The problem is further aggravated as Tokyo has become much more regionalized. It is sprawling into the wide hinterland in a limitless manner, pushed ahead by new and intensified technological and capital forces. These same mechanisms that have promoted the development of Tokyo are working with accelerated powers in the regions around Tokyo where the capability to cope with this expansion is still very limited. The confusion which Tokyo suffered for almost a century is now being repeated on an enlarged scale. Once again the old philosophy is evident: Help the productive sector and the citizens can take care of themselves.

The fundamental problem is that of the eco-system. We should look into the "capacity" of the natural environment of the region as a whole. Expansion of urban areas has decreased the green and open spaces in Tokyo-to (administrative area of Tokyo's government) into half in forty years, or down to 7.7 per cent by 1969.[25] In the surrounding regions the same devastation is proceeding. The air of Tokyo-to is polluted by the 800,000 tons of sulphur oxidant (in 1970, by combustion of crude oil alone) and by the exhaust from four million automobiles.[26] The photo chemical smog phenomenon which is caused by the combination of several exhaust gases can be observed in many places. Control measures against exhaust have been taken up with some success in cutting off the peak, but with the negative result of expanding the pollution into a wider region.

The water pollution in Tokyo Bay, which is the terminal of all the human and industrial pollutants discharged as the result of the activity of this gigantic metropolis, has been further aggravated and now surpasses the natural purification capability of the bay. Against the BOD of 644,000 tons poured into Tokyo Bay in 1969 alone, only some 50,000 tons of dissolved oxygen were supplied by natural purification, thus resulting in the annual addition to BOD accumulation of 600,000 tons.[27] The favorable topography of Tokyo Bay as a natural port with its comparatively narrow mouth has now turned into a drawback, making it easy for the pollutants to stay in the harbor as well as hindering the traffic of vessels which are not only increasing enormously in number but also becoming larger in size. Deposits on the sea bottom are increasing. Already fishery production is badly damaged, and it is feared that the nocuous elements which these deposits are producing will bring serious nuisances to the life of the ordinary citizen and to the seafront industries facing the bay.

The problems of water resources are also serious. Available water supplies are limited, but the demand is rapidly increasing; a tremendous shortage of water is anticipated. It should be noted, moreover, that the intensive use of river water cuts off and decreases the flow of water in the river itself, thus lessening its capacity to dilute and purify the pollutants flowing into it, aggravating further the pollution.

The expansion and concentration of Tokyo Region has thus come to the point where it is destroying its ecological system in an irreversible manner. The problem now is how we could change this very mechanism of imbalanced growth. Here I would hope that the reaction of citizens against this environmental disruption will bring about a breakthrough for change. So far the citizens' movement to protect the environment has been weak. However, since 1970 the social atmosphere has changed into a very radical one. Serious cases of environmental disruption as the result of industrial pollution have triggered a wide citizens' movement of protest. The case of Minamata in which fishermen were afflicted by mercury in the disposal water from a fertilizer factory; the case of Toyama in which farmers were poisoned by the cadmium component in the waste water from a mine; the case of Yokkaichi in which air pollution by petrochemical industries caused many citizens to suffer from asthma, and several other similar cases have been brought to light. In all these cases, the vociferous accusations by the citizenry were the most essential force that forced the enterprises to accept responsibility.

Through such experiences more and more active citizens groups are joining the attack. The United Nations Conference on the Human Environment in Stockholm in 1972 made "the only one earth" a world-wide appeal. Now protection of environment has become one of the most sensitive political problems in Japan. Progressive parties are, of course, taking the lead in this campaign, but conservative parties no longer can neglect these problems. In the meantime, the progressive parties are winning in most of the metropolitan areas in Japan in the election campaigns of governors and mayors. One of the first to win by the support of the progressive parties is Dr. Ryokichi Minobe, the present governor of Tokyo.

This new trend appears to be the most important factor forcing change. The benefits and costs of development can only be made clear through the outspoken complaints of those who suffer. This is the beginning of the search for a more holistic solution. Planners are now faced with the challenge to make a new start on this basis and find out ways to make plans for the betterment of the quality of life with intelligence and creativity. All this facing the overwhelming reality that approximately 90 per cent of Japan's energy is supplied by imported oil!

NOTES

[1] *United Nations Statistical Yearbook.*

[2] Densely Impacted District (DID): agglomerations with five thousand and over population, and with densities of at least sixteen persons per acre.

[3] Kinglsey Davis, "The Urbanization of the Human Population," *Scientific American,* September 1965.

[4] Masahiko Honjo et al., *Kita-Shinagawa Hōkoku* (North-Shinagawa Report), unpublished, 1969.

[5] Tokyo Metropolitan Government, *Tokyo Tosei Gaiyo* (Tokyo Metropolitan Government Handbook), 1969 edition, p. 12.

[6] Sumiya Mikio (ed.), *Keihin Kogyo-Chitai* (Keihin Industrial Area), Tōyō Keizai Shimpō-sha, Tokyo, 1965, p. 14.

[7] *Tokyo Tosei Yoran,* (Tokyo Metropolitan Government Handbook), 1967 edition, p. 18.

[8] *Tokyo Tosei Gaiyo,* op. cit., p. 19.

[9] Ibid., p. 15.

[10] Data from the Science and Technology Agency (mimeograph), 1969, p. 187. Hitoshi Sasao, *Kyodai-Toshi ni okeru kōgyō shuseki. Bunsan ni tsuite* (On the Concentration and Dispersal of Industry in Big Cities).

[11] Ministry of Transportation, *Toshi Kōtsū Nenpō* (Urban Traffic Annual), 1967, p. 72.

[12] Shigeto Tsuru, *Tokyo-e-no Teiah* (Proposals for Tokyo), p. 126.

[13] Ibid.

[14] Tokyo Metropolitan Government, *Sizing Up Tokyo: A Report on Tokyo under the Administration of Governor Ryokichi Minobe,* May 1969, p. 61.

[15] Ministry of Transportation, *Toshi Kōtsū Nenpō* (Urban Traffic Annual), 1968.

[16] *Tokyo-to Jutaku Juyo Jittai Chosa* (Survey of Housing Demands in Tokyo), 1968. The official definition of *substandard, overcongested houses* is "houses with less than nine mats where more than two persons live, or houses with less than twelve mats where more than four persons live." One *tatami* mat, 3'×6', is the basic unit of housing in Japan. *Sorifu Jutaku Chosa* (Housing Survey), Office of the Prime Minister, 1968; *Kensetsu-sho Chika Chosa* (Survey of the Land Price), Ministry of Construction, 1968; *Tokyu Fudosan Chika Chosa* (Survey of Land Prices), Tokyu Real Estate Co., 1968.

[17] Ibid. (Survey of Housing Demands).

[18] *Daitoshi Jutaku Chosa* (Survey of Housing in Big Cities), Ministry of Health and Welfare, 1941.

[19] *Sorifu Jutaku Chosa* (Housing Survey), Office of the Prime Minister, 1968.

[20] These figures are estimated from the Housing Bureau, Ministry of Construction, *Minkan Jiriki Kensetsu Jutaku Jittai Chosa* (Survey of Housing Construction in the Private Sector), 1967.

[21] Cf. "Tokyo Earthquake Countermeasure," *Tokyo Municipal News,* Vol. 23, No. 9, November/December 1973. An eightfold disaster prevention scheme has been drafted to combat earthquake-induced fire. (Editor)

[22] *Shutoken Seibi Linkai Jimukyoku Hōkoku* (Report of the Secretariat), National Capital Region Development Commission, 1969.

[23] William A. Robson, *Second Report on Tokyo Metropolitan Government* (mimeo), Tokyo Metropolitan Government, 1969, p. 35.

[24] Masahiko Honjo et al., *Kōsō-jūtaku Kaihatsu no Visiou* (Vision of Middle and High-Rise Housing), Chūkōsō Kenchiku Kaihatsu Kyokai, Tokyo, 1968.

[25] *Keizai-Shingikai Kankyo-Kenkyu Iinkai* (Environmental Research Committee of the Economic Council, Japanese Government) ed.: *Nihon-no Kankyo Mondai* (Problems of Environment in Japan), Table 13, p. 69. Shiseido, Tokyo, 1962.

[26] *Nihon-Kaihatsu-Koso-Kenkyusho* (Research Institute for Urban and Environmental Development Planning) ed.: *Tokyo-Wan Sosei Keikaku* (Revitalization Plan of Tokyo Bay), p. 12. *Nihon-Kaihatsu-Koso-Kenkyusho,* Tokyo, 1972.

[27] Ministry of Construction: *Kensetsu-Hakusho* (White Paper on Construction) *for 1971,* p. 55. Government Printing Office, Tokyo, 1971.

PART IV

Developing Nations

CHAPTER 10

Chandigarh: Monumental Sculpture

Norma Evenson*

The city of Chandigarh was conceived amid the crisis and confusion accompanying the birth of the new Indian republic. Freed of British colonial rule, the country was torn within by religious and political conflict, and it seemed problematic that the newly formed nation, foundering in a sea of instability and disunity, would survive at all. When the bitter conflict between Hindus and Moslems was finally resolved in partition in 1947, the province of Punjab was split

* Professor of architectural history, Department of Architecture, University of California (Berkeley). Trained at Yale University, receiving a Ph.D. in the history of art in 1963. Special areas of research have centered on modern architecture and urban design; field work on Chandigarh was carried out during 1961–63, and on the architecture and urban design of Rio de Janeiro and Brasilia during 1966–67. Her publications include *Chandigarh* (Berkeley: University of California Press, 1966), *Le Corbusier: the Machine and the Grand Design* (New York: George Braziller, 1969) and *Two Brazilian Capitals* (New Haven: Yale University Press, 1973), a study of the architecture and urban design of Rio de Janeiro and Brasilia. Awards and fellowships include the Monticello and John Addison Porter prizes at Yale University; a Fulbright grant to India, 1961–62; and American Philosophical Society grants for study in India and Brazil, 1963 and 1966; in addition, research in Brazil during 1966–67 was also supported by the Social Science Research Council, together with the University of California Center for Latin American Study, Professional Schools Program and Humanities Institute. Current research centers on a history of the planning of Paris in the past one hundred years.

between India and the new state of Pakistan. Lying disorganized amid the debris of bloody rioting, the Indian province of Punjab was faced with the problem of resettling the hordes of refugees who had poured across the border having abandoned homes, land and possessions in what was now Pakistan. Among the dispossessed was the government itself, uprooted from the ancient provincial capital of Lahore now enclosed within the borders of the new Moslem state. Meeting in Simla, the old Himalayan summer capital of British India, the rulers of Punjab began their attempts to create order from the chaotic conditions on the plain below and to establish a permanent government headquarters. In spite of economic difficulties and political uncertainty, the government decided not to attempt a makeshift relocation in any existing town; but to build a new provincial capital city.

Significant in influencing the decision to build a new town was the need at this time for such a symbolic gesture. India, filled with new national pride, needed focal points for unity; the Punjabis needed a lift for their morale. Chandigarh, coming into existence in a time of disorder and uncertainty, could stand as a tangible embodiment of the will to maintain a stable society. The colonial yoke had been thrown off, and the moment had arrived for India to show the world that she could stand alone, that she could command her own destiny and govern her own house, and that against the brutality of nature and the vastness of her continent she could impress an ordered yet viable pattern of human life—proof that Indian civilization, though ancient, was still vigorous and creative.

Much of the impetus for the project came from the enthusiastic support of Prime Minister Nehru who said of Chandigarh,† "Let this be a new town, symbolic of the freedom of India, unfettered by the traditions of the past . . . an expression of the nation's faith in the future."[1]

Although the city was to be symbolic of the vigor and creativity of the new, independent Indian state, it was taken for granted that the planners must be obtained abroad. During the British tenure in India, a large body of trained Indian civil servants had been built up, able to take over the administration of the new government, but there was no comparable group of technically trained Indians. Good architectural schools were nonexistent, the old native building tradition was debilitated, and even local craft skills were disappearing.

The first master plan for Chandigarh was devised by the New York firm of Mayer, Whittlesey and Glass, who had received a contract for the work in 1950. Included in the work of this group was a general layout for the city, and also a series of excellent architectural studies by Matthew Nowicki, a much admired young Polish architect who died in a plane crash while engaged in the Chandigarh project.

Following the death of Nowicki, a new team of designers was assembled. Le Corbusier, a long-time leader of the modern movement and one of the most influential of contemporary architects, was engaged as architectural adviser for the project. In this capacity, he outlined a new master plan and designed the major architectural monuments of the city. Working with Le Corbusier on the planning of Chandigarh was his cousin, Pierre Jeanneret, and also the British architects Maxwell Fry and Jane Drew. This group resided in Chandigarh for the first three years of the project, supervising construction, developing the resi-

† New Delhi was pretty much frozen in the British Imperial mode. (Editor's note.)

dential sectors and designing government housing, shops, schools, etc. When his British colleagues returned to their London practice in 1954, Pierre Jeanneret remained in Chandigarh directing the Capital Project Office until his retirement in 1965.

Although the chief architects initially were foreign, administrative direction of the new city rested in the hands of two Indians, P. L. Varma, the chief engineer of Punjab, and P. N. Thapar, a former member of the British Indian Civil Service who became administrative head of the project in 1949.

The site of Chandigarh, chosen from airplane reconnaissance, was in the submountainous area of the Ambala district about one hundred and fifty miles north of New Delhi, the capital of the republic. The area was a flat, gently sloping plain of agricultural land dotted with groves of mango trees which marked the sites of twenty-four villages. From one of these villages, the site of a temple to the goddess Chandi, the new capital city was to take its name.[2] (*Garh* in Hindi means "town," and is used like the suffixes "burg" or "ville." *Chandi,* the Hindi word for silver, in this case refers to the goddess of power.) The building of the city would involve the dislocation of about nine thousand people for whom compensation was arranged and land set aside for resettlement.

The general ground level of the site ranges from between one thousand to twelve hundred feet with a 1 per cent grade giving generally adequate drainage. To the northeast are foothills standing below the Himalayas which rise abruptly to about five thousand feet, forming the most striking natural feature of the site and creating a dramatic backdrop to the city.

The city is bounded by two river beds about five miles apart, the Patiali Rao to the west and the Sukhna Choe to the east. For most of the year the river beds would be dry, until the monsoon in July and August sends great quantities of water rushing down from the Himalayas. A subsidiary stream bed, heavily eroded, runs irregularly through the city area. Although the Sukhna Choe has been dammed to create an artificial lake and a permanent source of irrigation, the primary water supply of the city is obtained from artesian wells.

The climate is one of extremes. The most agreeable season is the winter consisting of about five months of crisp, clear weather during which temperatures may go down almost to freezing. The summer brings dry heat accompanied by dust storms and hot winds with temperatures often reaching as high as 115° F. before the breaking of the monsoon in July, after which the weather continues hot and humid until winter nears again.

Although some visitors have found the spreading plain of Chandigarh monotonous, the architects of the city were unanimous in praising the dramatic beauty of the site. Jane Drew found there "a quality of beauty hinted at in the paintings of Giotto—a quality due to the light, producing at the same time olive and tender pale greens against the vast cyclorama of the intense blue sky of the north Indian plains. The slope of the site is toward the south and thus the eye is led up to, and is always roving over the background of the endless ranges of the Himalayas, where sometimes, even when the plains are hottest, snowcaps may be seen."[3] Le Corbusier stated, "The site is marvelous."[4]

The planning of Chandigarh was purely physical; one might say, in fact, that the city was designed rather than planned. Land was acquired, money was appropriated, streets and building sites were laid out, and construction was begun. The capital function was assumed sufficient to ensure the life of the city and also to attract industrial and commercial enterprises, although their exact nature was not specifically foreseen.

It is easy, therefore, to see in the shortcomings of Chandigarh the reflection of a too limited approach to city planning, one which from the beginning conceived of the task of founding a new community only in terms of site layout and architecture.

Although the site might have been selected with a view to more immediate economic potential, it is difficult to assess what could have been attempted along the lines of regional planning. At the time, conditions in India were chaotic, especially in the province of Punjab which had been physically dismembered, shorn in the process of its best arable land, disrupted socially and burdened with refugees. The economy was prostrate, the future uncertain, and although the government may have had some sort of general aims regarding future industrial development or economic improvements, nothing specific in the nature of comprehensive planning was under way. Economists were scarce, and provisions for economic investigation and analysis, together with the large amounts of statistical information so readily available in other countries, were nonexistent. Had the builders of Chandigarh been compelled to wait until the city could become part of a coherent and viable program of regional economic planning, it is doubtful that the city would have been built at all.

The social situation of the new province was also understandably confused. India as a whole is divided into a multitude of linguistic, religious and caste groups, with a variety of social customs and usages, so that to an Indian of one group, an Indian of another community may seem virtually a foreigner. Moreover, India has devoted relatively little systematic and objective study to her own social structure, and in the period immediately following independence was undergoing a time of almost overwhelming social disorganization. The long-present tension between Hindus and Moslems, exploding with unforeseen violence, had brought about partition and left a residue of bitterness and insecurity.

The old province of Punjab had been populated largely by Moslems, Hindus and Sikhs, but with partition the Indian province had lost most of the Moslem population, while receiving an influx of Hindu refugees from Pakistan. In this part of India Moslem custom had long been a pervading influence. The two dominant communities were now the Hindus and Sikhs, the two official languages being Hindi and Punjabi, and throughout the development of the new capital, the unity of the province itself would be continually threatened by pressures from the more militant Sikh groups for a separate Punjabi-speaking state.

It was obvious that India was about to undergo social changes as she attempted to move from a disunited and backward agricultural colony of Britain to a democratic, industrialized, unified and independent nation. Yet just how or at what speed these changes might come was, and still is, difficult to predict. An increased movement of people from villages to cities, a modification of the ancient custom of *purdah,* an increase in national and political unity with a decrease in the strength of caste and local linguistic groups, together with a raising of educational standards—all might be considered part of the predictable future; yet the precise implications of these for a given urban plan might be difficult to ascertain. Should a new city be built in accordance with local custom insofar as it was understood, should it attempt to anticipate certain changes, or should it be designed in some way to help bring about desired social changes?

In the case of Chandigarh, the program of the city as a government center carried with it certain definite social implications. The specialized community of civil servants forming the dominant element of the population would be accommodated according to rank in government houses, following the established custom, and in this way an occupational hierarchy would underlie the over-all building pattern of the city. This system, inherited from the British, was followed consistently throughout India in all types of government housing. The built-in social structure of the provincial civil service was part of the physical program of the city presented by the Indian officials to the planners. Although in designing government housing some efforts were made to lessen the wide disparity between upper and lower echelons, and also to provide general low-cost housing, Chandigarh was never intended by its founders as a social experiment.

The city as planned, therefore, was essentially a physical creation, representing the individual judgments of a group of architects and planners dominated by the vision of Le Corbusier. Although other designers have subsequently come to be associated with Chandigarh, the visual quality of the city remains strongly influenced by the initial architects, and the pattern of urban expansion continues to be governed by the original master plan.

Chandigarh, at the time of its inception, was highly controversial, and its justification rested more on psychological than utilitarian grounds. The city existed because it was made to exist; yet, as time wore on, Chandigarh became a legitimate focus of pride. In the years following independence, India produced a welter of projects and ambitious plans, many of which failed to be effectively realized. Chandigarh, by contrast, whatever faults might be found with the details of its planning, has continued to grow and thrive—a visible tribute to the determination of its founders.

THE MASTER PLAN

At the time Le Corbusier became associated with the Chandigarh project he was not only firmly established as a leader of modern architecture, but was also famed for his innovative theoretical urban designs. Beginning in 1922 with his exhibition project, a City for Three Million People, Le Corbusier had been prolific in polemical writing and visionary design aimed at renovating the modern city. Incorporating extensive high-rise building with systems of motor freeways and wide areas of greenery, Le Corbusier's early schemes combined futurist conceptions of speed, movement and mechanization with a garden city emphasis on open space. Although the conception was keyed to advanced technology, the design was unified by a geometric formalism reminiscent of the classical Beaux-Arts tradition. Le Corbusier's urban schemes were frequently criticized for their failure to come to grips with the social and functional complexities of real city life. Nevertheless, they excited the imagination with their audacity and established one of the most pervasive urban images of our time, an image still dominating the vision of many planners and most comprehensively realized in the new capital of Brazil.

It was ironic that after a lifetime of seeking to master the demands of the machine age, Le Corbusier should have been given his only chance to realize a city plan in an environment still largely untouched by industrialization.

Although plunged into an unfamiliar ambience, and compelled to work in conditions contrary to his previous predilections, Le Corbusier found in India perhaps the most receptive patronage he had ever known. His unwavering confidence was reassuring to the Indians, while the largeness of his vision and the grandness of his concepts seemed to harmonize appropriately with their aspirations for the new capital. Although Le Corbusier had frequently found government officials less than sympathetic, his personal relations with the Indian administrators of Chandigarh seem altogether successful, and Prime Minister Nehru, who took great interest in the project, became a warm friend. It was once observed that "India understands idea men and treats them well—perhaps better than any other country—and Le Corbusier benefits from this."[5]

The plan which the Mayer firm had produced for Chandigarh assumed a fan-shaped outline, spreading between the two river beds which defined the site. The provincial government buildings were located within a single complex at the upper edge of the city, while the central business district occupied an area near the center. A curving network of main roads surrounded a system of residential superblocks, each of which contained a central area of parkland. Two larger parks extended through the city, one of them following the path of an eroded stream bed. To the east of the city was an area set aside for industry. Initial development of the city was to take place in the northerly portion of the site, with future expansion projected toward the south.

Although retaining many features of the Mayer plan, Le Corbusier began his modifications by classicizing and geometricizing the design, straightening major streets and transforming the slightly irregular superblocks into rectangles. He sought to give the city a large-scale unified design appropriate to its monumental character, linking together major focal points within a single configuration.

The city was conceived in its essential form as a square containing a cross axis, with the capitol complex culminating the northeastern axis toward the mountains (Fig. 1). This simple diagram derives from one of the oldest traditions of urban design. What is believed to be the oldest symbolic representation of a city is an Egyptian hieroglyph consisting of a circle containing a cross, and the rectilinear shape embodying a cross axis of principal streets was later the customary form of Roman settlement.

More significantly, perhaps, this is the gesture by which all Indian towns were laid out according to the rituals codified in the Mānasāra Silpa-sāstras. Once cardinal points were established, the two main streets were laid out in what was termed the "cosmic cross" and the so-called magic square representing the four quarters of the universe. The two streets forming the arms of the cosmic cross were broad avenues and believed to have been planted with shade trees. The center of the town at the intersection of the cross was the recognized meeting place for the Council of Elders who regulated local affairs, and the center, according to Mānasāra, was the auspicious place for an assembly hall or for a temple of Brahma, which had four entrances. At Chandigarh, the crossing of the two main streets, one of which leads into the city from the province, and the other which forms a monumental avenue of approach to the capitol complex, marks the

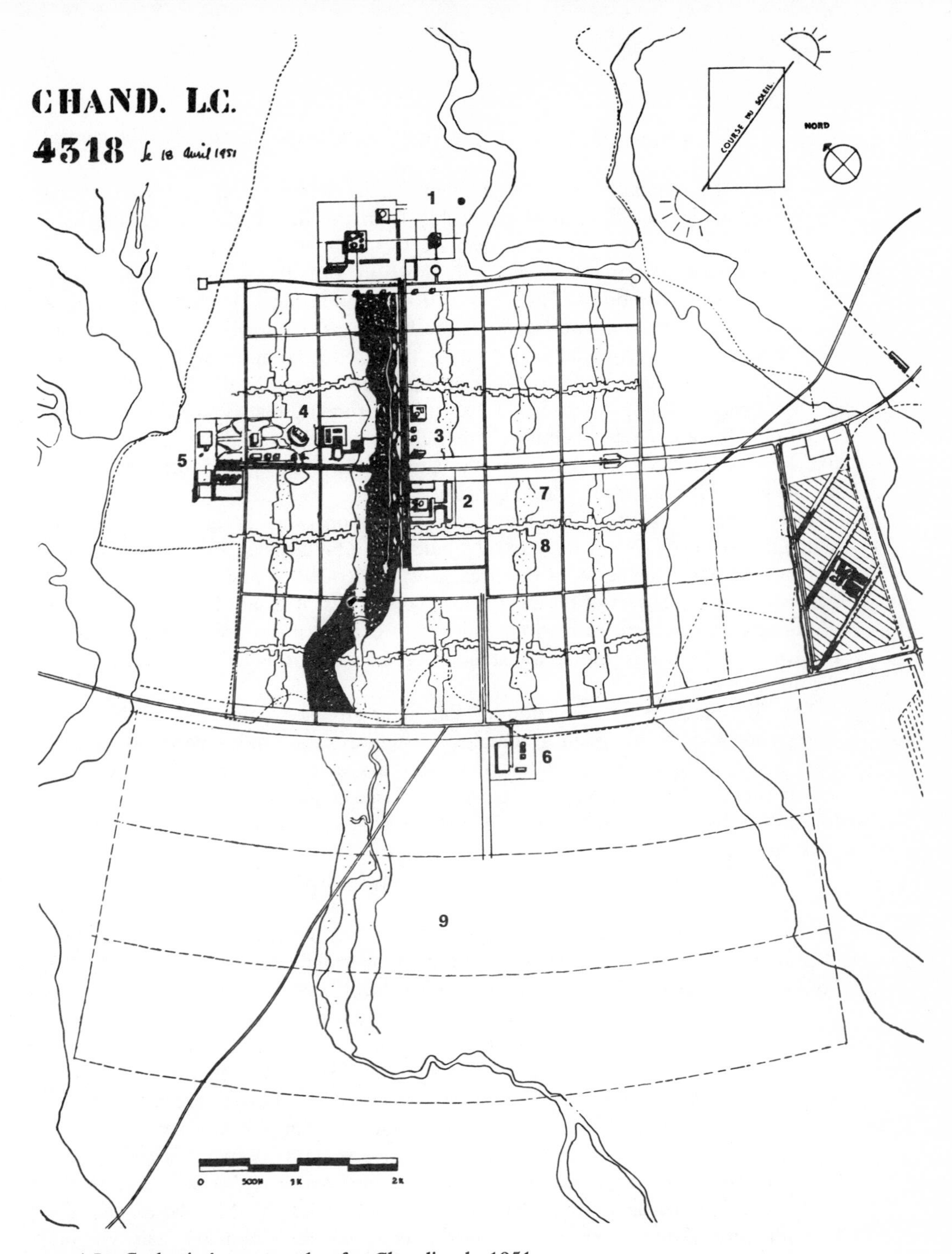

FIG. 1 Le Corbusier's master plan for Chandigarh, 1951:
1. Capitol complex
2. Central business district
3. Hotels, restaurants and visitors' center
4. Museums and stadium
5. University
6. Wholesale market
7. Park bands extending through residential areas
8. Shopping street (V4)
9. Area below the market to contain expansion of the city to a population of 500,000.
Photograph by Charles Edward Jeanneret-Gris, from Le Corbusier Oeuvre complète 1946–52, *Zurich: Girsberger, 1953. Reprinted by permission of George Wittenborn, New York, 1964*

location of the civic center containing the local administration and also the central business district.

It is in the emphasis on a monumental axial composition that the second plan of Chandigarh differs most noticeably from the initial scheme. Although in both designs the capitol area was planned to stand against the mountains, only in Le Corbusier's plan was there an effort to provide a single monumental approach linking the body of the city to its symbolic head and relating along a single axis the two main public areas of the city, the capitol complex and the civic center. The ceremonial approach to the capitol complex was projected as a wide tree-lined boulevard, bounded on one side by parkland and on the other by multistory buildings—important banks, government offices and large hotels. According to Jane Drew, the aim of this scheme would be to produce "something like Princes Street of Edinburgh or the Champs Elysées of Paris and it will be the subject of special architectural control."[6]

The other main street, leading from the station, was designed to alter its character when it crossed the capitol boulevard. On the east side, extending toward the station and the industrial area, it was intended as a street of commercial depots and headquarters of business firms. To the west it would become the center of higher education and recreation, and was to contain in an area of parkland the theatre, civic museums and sports stadium. Terminating this axial street would be the university.

The city center at the junction of the main streets would contain the large stores and office buildings in a complex of squares and piazzas designed to lead from one to another and intended to create "a spacious intimacy reminiscent in layout (but not in character) of Venice."[7] A large center area would be restricted to pedestrians and the sector would contain a system of arcading and planned parking areas.

In general, the conception of Chandigarh represented a relaxation of the rigid geometry which had dominated Le Corbusier's earlier designs, embodying an interweaving of geometric and picturesquely ordered elements. The determination of proportions in the civic design as well as in the architecture involved use of the Modulor (a system of proportioning which Le Corbusier had evolved during World War II and patented as an invention in 1947), but related also to traditional classical ordering. The basic unit of the city, the residential sector, was formed on the golden rectangle, with dimensions of 800 by 1,200 meters (½ by ¾ mile). The measurement of 800 meters, which recurs in the planning of the capitol complex and elsewhere, may be found also in the monumental composition which Le Corbusier admired in his native Paris. In Paris, it is 800 meters from the Louvre to the Place de la Concorde, and another 800 meters from the Place de la Concorde to the Place Clemenceau, while the Madeleine and the Chambre des Députés terminate opposite ends of an 800-meter axis passing through the Place de la Concorde. In Chandigarh, the distance along the monumental avenue between the commercial center and the capitol complex duplicates that between the Étoile and the Place de la Concorde.

Incorporating elements of the scale of Paris and employing the proportioning of the Modulor, Le Corbusier apparently sought to give Chandigarh a suitably monumental character through the establishment of a large-scale unifying order.

Essential to the plan of the city is the system of traffic separation based on a scheme of organization which Le Corbusier termed "les Sept Voies" (the Seven V's) and which he projected in his postwar planning schemes for Bogotá and Marseille Sud. Although some degree of traffic differentiation was always present in Le Corbusier's urban designs, the Seven V system represents the architect's attempt to develop a fully organized, universally applicable system, establishing a breakdown of traffic into a series of seven categories containing every level of circulation from arterial roads to apartment house corridors.

The specific organization of the Seven V system in Chandigarh is as follows: The V1 represents regional roads leading into the city from the outside, while the V2 designation refers to the two major cross axial boulevards of the city. One of these provides the ceremonial avenue linking the central district with the capitol complex, while the other forms the cultural-commercial axis. Surrounding the residential sectors and establishing the grid pattern of the city are the V3 streets intended for fast motor traffic. Frontage development along these streets is prohibited, the sectors being designed to focus inward. Bisecting the long side of each sector is a bazaar street, the V4, following a slightly irregular path and permitting a variety of slow-moving traffic. This street, intended to provide for neighborhood shopping needs, carries shops only on the south side, to ensure shade for pedestrians and also to eliminate excessive street crossing. The V5 is a loop road intersecting the V4 and serving as the main distributor of traffic within the sector, while V6 lanes give additional access to houses. A strip of parkland containing schools extends through each sector, providing continuous bands of open space throughout the city, and including the V7 pedestrian paths (Fig. 2).

Applying his favored biological analogy to the road system, Le Corbusier stated, "The 7V's act in the town plan as the blood stream, the lymph system and the respiratory system act in biology. In biology these systems are quite rational, they are different from each other, there is no confusion between them, yet they are in harmony. They create order."[8]

The abundant provisions for motor traffic in Chandigarh represent an anticipation of future mechanization, rather than a system adapted to present conditions, although the wide mixture of traffic characteristic of Indian cities, ranging from trucks and automobiles to bicycles and bullock carts, justifies an elaborate system of separation. The success of the Chandigarh system, however, can only be evaluated when traffic volume, especially of motor traffic, has risen sufficiently to justify its design.

Both technical and social conditions determined that Chandigarh be predominantly a low-rise city, although in preliminary drawings, Le Corbusier indicated a desire for the inclusion of some high rise building both in the capitol complex and the central business district. In general, the architectural composition of the city reflected Le Corbusier's long-term preference for a controlled environment, for a simplification of building types and a disciplined unity of building form. Government housing followed a pattern of standardized designs, while private housing was architecturally controlled. Neighborhood shops were built to specified designs, and in the central business district, a potentially competitive and varied architecture was forestalled by Le Corbusier's predetermined plan.

The most important park area in the city is that developed in the eroded stream

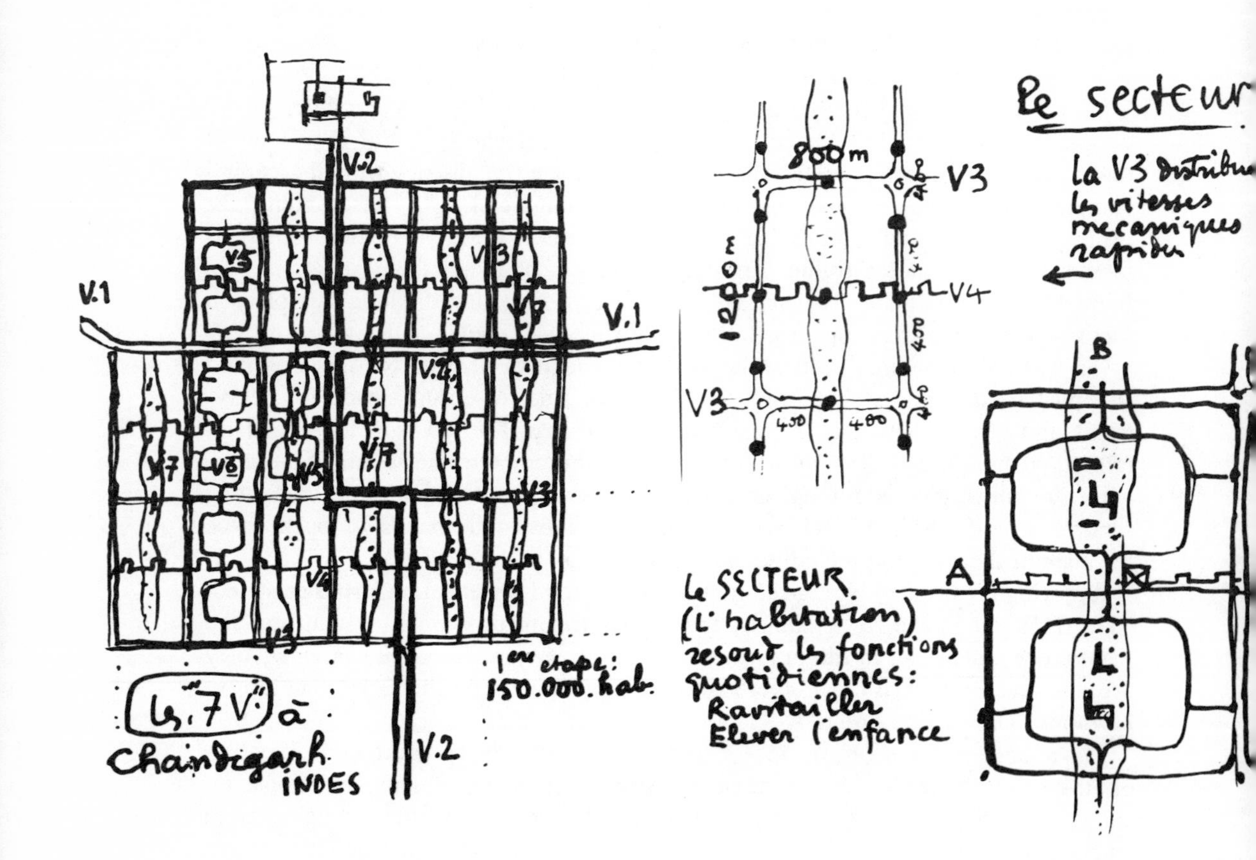

FIG. 2 Studies by Le Corbusier in 1951 for Chandigarh showing the 7V system. Schematic design of a residential sector to be surrounded by streets carrying through traffic (V3) and bisected by a neighborhood shopping street (V4 and A). Loop roads would distribute local traffic, while a band of park land (B) would extend through the sector providing a site for schools. *Photograph by Charles Edward Jeanneret-Gris from* Le Corbusier, Modulor 2, Harvard University Press, 1958

bed running through the city. This area, termed by Le Corbusier the Valley of Leisure, contains a gorge five to six meters deep which varies in width from one hundred to three hundred meters. To Le Corbusier, "six meters below the ground is enough to create an atmosphere of solitude and complete isolation."[9]

Water would be canalized through the valley and made into "glyptic forms where the pedestrian will be invited to take part in . . . pleasures of an intimate kind." Projected also was a small open-air theatre and a "little lido for boating and swimming, etc."[10]

An additional civic recreation area was developed as a result of damming the Sukhna Choe to create an artificial lake in the area to the east of the capitol complex. This dam formed an extension of the capitol boulevard. In order to preserve this area as a quiet retreat, Le Corbusier insisted that the lake be forbidden to motorboats and the top of the dam prohibited to bicycles, cars and buses. Le Corbusier also forbade the introduction of any lighting in the evening except for a low lamp of his own design. The intention was to produce a city park where "it is possible to see the stars in the sky and the stars in the water, the mountains, too, in the water—and all in absolute silence." The commemoration stone carries in Hindi, Punjabi, Urdu and English the following text: "The founders of Chandigarh have offered this lake and dam to the citizens of the new city so that they may escape the humdrum of city life and enjoy the beauty of nature in peace and silence."[11] In addition to the major park areas, there are park belts running through the residential sectors, furnishing local recreation areas and sites for schools and community buildings.

A 580-acre tract was set aside for industry of which 336 acres were to be developed during the first phase of the city, the location to the east of the city near the railroad terminus permitting easy transfer of raw materials and finished goods without the need of transport through the city. In the event of the city expanding southward, Le Corbusier suggested the creation of an additional industrial area in the southern part of the city where a second railroad station could then be established.

One of the first problems to be met in mapping out the definitive plan of Chandigarh was the distribution of population throughout the city. The Mayer plan had proposed three groupings of income as a classification of neighborhood units, an idea which was incorporated in the final plan, producing density patterns ranging from twenty-five persons per acre in the upper class districts to fifty persons per acre in middle-class sectors and seventy-five persons per acre in the lower class areas. The most desirable building sites were assumed to be those on the upper edge of the city, nearest the capitol complex and commanding the finest view of the mountains. It was here that the houses of the ministers and high court judges were located and the largest private building plots laid out. Provision was made occasionally in these areas for the inclusion of servant-class villages in order to enable these people to reside near their employers, and some attempt was made generally to mix income levels in order to avoid too rigid a stratification. By and large, however, the economic class of a neighborhood was determined by its distance from the upper edge of the city, giving the city a somewhat hierarchic pattern and also compelling the poorest government employees to travel the longest distance to work each day.

In addition to controls established for development within the borders of the city, the Periphery Control Act of 1952 gave the planners of Chandigarh the power to regulate development within a five-mile limit beyond the city. The purpose of such control was "to prevent the creation of bad semi-urban conditions on city boundaries. . . . To protect the rural community from degeneration by contact with urban life, and to lead it towards a harmonious partnership in which, without loss of rural status, it may improve living conditions by supplying the city with milk, eggs, chickens, vegetables, etc."[12] The establishment of additional towns and villages in the area around Chandigarh was prohibited, and although specific areas were established where brick fields and lime kilns were permitted, no other commercial or industrial development of the adjoining areas was to be allowed. Thus, the new city would be surrounded by a permanent green belt.

In its over-all conception, the master plan of Chandigarh provided for the integration of two orderings and two scales: first, a large geometric framework linking the monumental elements of the city, providing for rapid traffic and defining the residential sectors; and second, within these sectors, opportunity for the establishment of more varied, informal elements appropriate for a pedestrian-dominated domestic environment. Unfortunately, however, the implications of the dual scale of the Chandigarh plan seem not to have been fully grasped in its initial execution, and as the city began to take form, its most disappointing aspect lay in the internal development of the residential sectors.

As a simple diagrammatic outline of the city and as a guide for future, more intensive planning, the master plan had much to recommend it. Although not precluding the creation of variety and flexibility within the sectors, the basic layout of Chandigarh established a clear and logical framework within which the more intricate drama of the city might subsequently unfold (Fig. 3).[13]

Getting Under Way—the "Three Disciplines"

Shortly after Le Corbusier's group assumed command, a schedule for construction of the city was established, with the first year to see the completion of the master plan and preparation of the site, including the paving of roads, installation of water mains and sewers, etc. By the end of six months the initial projects for the buildings of the capitol complex were accepted, and by the eighteenth month construction on the High Court and Secretariat was under way. Development proceeded at a pace which permitted the shift of nearly all departments of the Punjab Government from Simla to Chandigarh in limited strength by the end of 1952, and by September 1953, the entire government staff could be accommodated. On October 7, 1953, the city was formally declared open by the President of India, Dr. Rajendra Prasad. The Punjab High Court and Bar did not move to Chandigarh, however, until January 1955. By July 1954, over twenty thousand people were living in government housing, and with this housing went shops and schools, a health center, a hotel, a government press and a cinema.

Administration of the Chandigarh project was under the control of the Capital Project Organization, a body similar to the Development Corporation in England, which controls the establishment of new towns. Commenting on the administrative organization governing the construction of Chandigarh, Maxwell Fry observed:

> This great work was done, and is being done, as the result of very great pressure and against the machinery of a Public Works Department for which I can find little good to say. In the best interests of Indian development plans this out-of-date system should be drastically reorganized. . . .

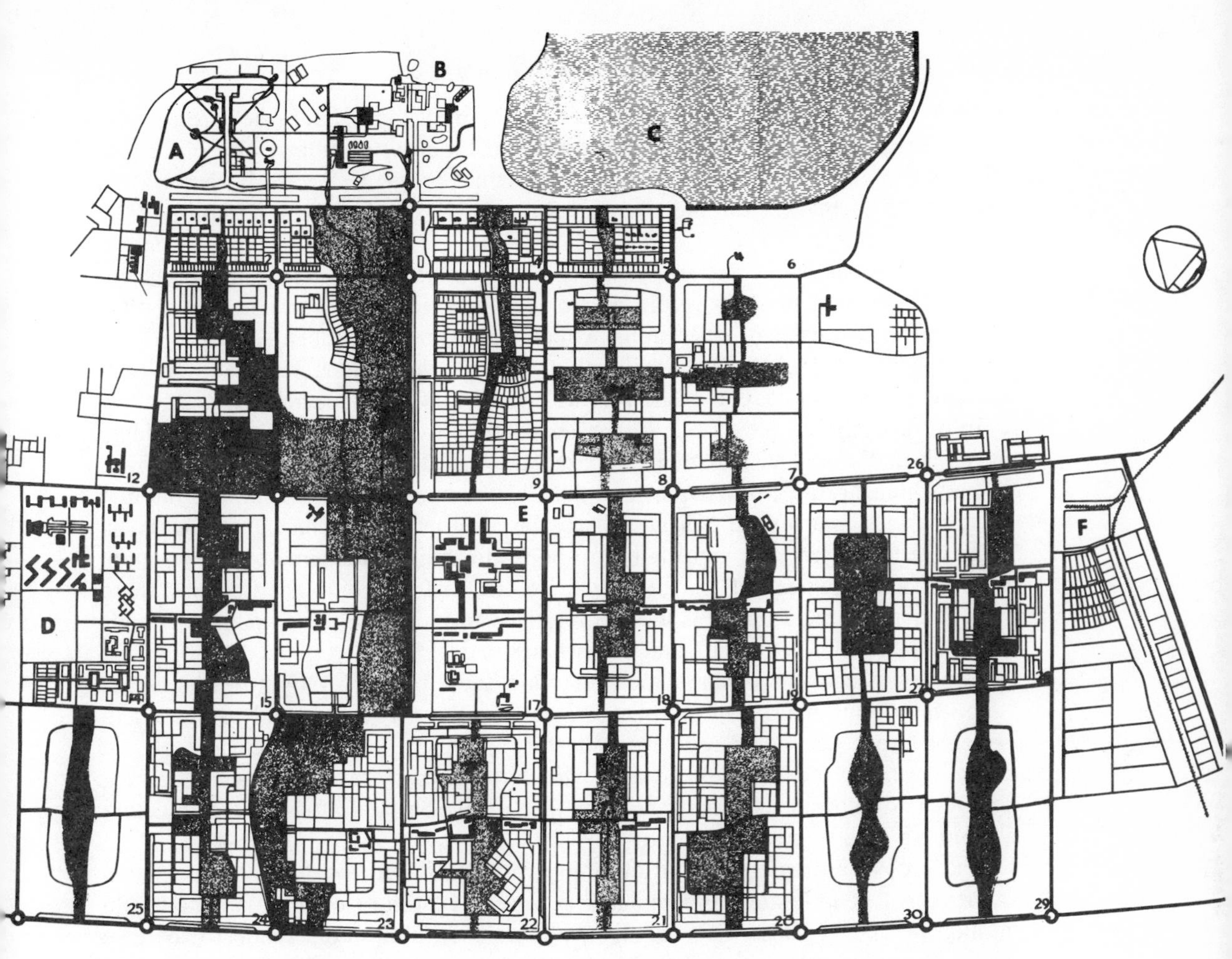

FIG. 3 Chandigarh plan as developed by 1962. The design incorporates the master plan of Le Corbusier with detailed sector layouts by the Capital Project Office. Le Corbusier's 7V system of traffic separation provides a large-scale grid in which rapid motor vehicles are restricted to the V3 streets surrounding the residential sectors, while a variety of irregular streets serves the needs of local traffic. Each sector is bisected by a V4 shopping street which, in turn, is intersected by a loop road, the V5, serving as the principal internal distributor. A central band of park land containing V7 pedestrian paths is provided within each sector. A. Rajendra Park, a recreational area adjacent to the capitol complex. B. Capitol complex. C. Lake (an artificial lake created by damming a river bed adjacent to the site), D. University (Sector 14). E. Central business district and civic center (Sector 17). F. Industrial area. *Chandigarh, Department of Architecture*

> The lot of the Indian architect in public service is indeed unenviable, but the engineer is no less crippled by the lack of faith reposed in him by the ridiculously small powers of financial sanction and by the tedious administration that deprives him of his power to act, and in the long run, to think. A fine body of talent and energy goes half-wasted until these reforms are carried out.[14]

Although much freedom was given by the Indian officials to Le Corbusier at Chandigarh, the design of the project was subject to what he once termed the "three disciplines"—money, technology and climate. "India has the treasures of a proud culture; but her coffers are empty,"[15] and throughout the project the desire for grandness was hampered by the need for strict economy. The procedure for imposing budgetary restrictions on designs, according to Le Corbusier, was as follows: "The budget for the construction of the city has been established by the Administrator (Thapar) and the Chief Engineer (Varma) in an impeccable manner. It consists of an enormous mimeographed volume containing an explanation of the total expenditures to be engaged, and consequently everything to be constructed. Everything, street, palace or house betokens a rigorous program, detailed piece by piece with the exact dimensions required for each element and the application of the various prices of different coefficients."[16]

In working up his designs, Le Corbusier consulted the program for each building as given in the budget and then prepared the initial project. In giving approval, "The Administrator, Mr. Thapar, and the Chief Engineer, Mr. Varma, are the first judges, then come several delegates from the Ministers or interested commissions. Only one thing was ever argued: the response to the requirements of the program and the absolute respect for the price, to the last rupee! If he satisfies these requirements, Le Corbusier is left entirely free to create his own architecture, his own methods of construction and his own aesthetic."[17]

The architects of the mass housing found their budget even more restricted. "You may bring me a house design," Chief Engineer Tharpar used to say, "and if it is a rupee over the estimate you know you will have to go back and plan it away. I will not consider cost because what is in the project estimate must be kept to. But I will consider livability because that is my job; and after that architecture is your job, and we may both enjoy it."[18]

The project estimate covering the initial plan provided for 150,000 people on 8,919 acres of land and contemplated a total expenditure of approximately $36 million in its first phase. Of this, slightly more than half would relate to the cost of development and of civic amenities, while the balance would represent the cost of government building and water supply, with recoupable items bringing the gross expenditure to about $39 million.

It was hoped that development costs would be recovered from the sale of plots to the public, and taking into account rents paid for government buildings in the first phase, the net expenditure was estimated at about $18 million. At Chandigarh, a general reliance on local materials would be essential. The scarcity of steel in India made steel-frame construction impossible, and even steel sufficient for reinforcing would be so expensive that it could be employed for only relatively large and important buildings. Seasoned wood was also scarce, so that in much of the housing brick would be used for shelves, balustrades, sunbreakers, etc.

Available in quantity, however, was good clay, stone, sand and, above all, human labor. The materials of which Chandigarh has been constructed are rough concrete in the capitol complex and the central business district, and for most of the city, especially in housing, locally produced brick. Describing the construction, Le Corbusier reported, "Things were done *à l'indienne,* that is to say with an innumerable labor force and very few machines. . . . One does not 'Taylorize' the design to economize on labor since the population is innumerable. Everyone sleeps on the spot under a rush mat carried on four stakes (there is no rain during six months). . . . The gangs of workmen come from afar with their families."[19]

An account of the scene during the early days of construction is given by correspondent Achal Rangaswami as follows:

> The new capital is the scene of intense activity. Thirty thousand workers—men wearing dhotis and women clad in multicolored saris work seven days a week. Machinery is limited to a few bulldozers and concrete mixers. Women pour liquid concrete in wooden molds. After setting, a slab is removed and carried by hand to the house nearby. Bricks are carried from trucks to building sites in baskets delicately balanced on the heads of erect women, while men mix mortar with their feet. Boys carry water in big leather bags of buffalo hide. Hundreds of men are busy smashing huge boulders into gravel with hammers. There are some road machines, but molten tar is poured and spread on the roads by men who wrap their hands and feet in jute sacking to protect them from being scalded. Roads are scooped out by bulldozers, but donkeys remove the mud to artificial hillocks being raised nearby.[20]

The crudeness of the workmanship at Chandigarh appears to have been no handicap to Le Corbusier: "For fifty years concrete has been treated as a poor material, but here it is treated as noble. Here we leave it rough. It is like the stone of the mountains."[21]

The Punjab Government before partition was, like the British central government, a migratory organization, which had moved annually from Lahore to Simla to escape the summer heat. Chandigarh, however, was intended from its inception to function as a year-round capital, and it was hoped that the architects could evolve a type of building which, lacking the mechanical aids of the West, would be habitable during the extreme seasonal variations of temperature and precipitation in the city.[22] As Le Corbusier expressed it:

> Besides the administrative and financial regulations there was the Law of the Sun in India: a calendar of sensational temperatures, extraordinary heat, dry or humid according to the season or the location. The architectural problem consists first to make shade, second to make a current of air (to ventilate), third to control hydraulics (to evacuate rainwater). This necessitated a real apprenticeship and an unprecedented adaptation of modern methods.[23]

In citing the general aspects of the architecture at Chandigarh, Jane Drew has written, "Here a house is essentially a shade and shelter from the elements. No vast glass areas to create interpenetration of exterior and interior. The extraordinary climatic variety, cold in winter and both hot-dry and hot-wet heat in summer, dust storms and monsoons—the sun is an enemy more often than a friend."[24]

In attempting to design livable housing, Fry reports that he gradually found himself

> paying less attention to the needs of cross ventilation, which in the critically hot period is of no avail, and more to the creation of cool interiors, as large as possible, and as amply protected from the southwest sun as ingenuity and exiguous funds permitted. . . . With temperatures up to 115 F., and high night temperatures, the only defense is to retreat behind massive walls or their equivalent, with every aperture closed . . .[25]

Particularly noticeable throughout the city is the use of the *brise-soleil,* or sunbreaker, a device favored by Le Corbusier for controlling the admission of direct sunlight into an interior. The brise-soleil forms an exterior cladding of horizontal or vertical projections which block the rays of the sun to prevent them from striking the surface behind. Aesthetically the use of sunbreakers gives a plastic quality to the building surface, and in intense sunlight creates a dramatic pattern of shadows. In the High Court building, an additional cooling device was attempted in the parasol roof raised above the true roof and open at both sides to permit a flow of air between the two.

Approaching the situation in Chandigarh, Le Corbusier stated, "The symphonic problem of climate has not yet been understood. Modern architecture, foraging through manuals and magazines from all over the world, blindly absorbs French, American, Indian, German, English or Scandinavian discoveries and shapes. Confronted with this inconsistency, we felt the need for a climatic screen, and we have created it."[26]

THE RESIDENTIAL SECTOR

At the time Chandigarh was planned, the neighborhood unit was a widely accepted concept of residential design. Essentially the neighborhood idea was developed from an attempt to create within the large modern city physical and social units of relatively small and manageable size, providing for the systematic distribution of educational, recreational, cultural and commercial facilities, enabling inhabitants to find most of the needs of daily life within easy reach of home.

In addition to physical convenience, the neighborhood unit has been considered desirable by many planners as a means of providing a greater degree of social interaction. To a certain extent, the social concept of the neighborhood unit is based on an ideal of small-town rural life with its presumably strong sense of community. The neighborhood may also relate to the local political unit, the ward, or, in India, the *mahalla.* In India there has been a long tradition of caste quarters in cities, in which a social identity of religion, custom and occupation would be reinforced by physical containment, creating, in a sense, small homogeneous towns within cities.

In Chandigarh, however, the neighborhood unit would have no social base other than a general similarity of income. As a government city, Chandigarh would draw its population from many parts of the province and from varied social groups, housing being assigned according to occupational rank. Thus, Chandigarh would of necessity provide for a greater juxtaposition of caste, language and religion than might be found in a typical Indian town, a factor which might mitigate against the development of a strong community sense within the sectors, but which could also help to break down many of the traditional barriers which for centuries have isolated Indians from one another.

Although no two sectors in Chandigarh are identical, all follow the same basic plan: Each contains a central park band and is bisected by the bazaar street (see Fig. 2). Intersecting the bazaar street is an interior loop road serving as the principal distributer of traffic within the block, and from this other streets branch, giving access to housing groups. Within the somewhat irregular street pattern of the sector, groups of building plots are laid out. In the division of labor among the designers of Chandigarh, Le Corbusier was responsible for the general outlines of the master plan and the creation of the monumental buildings, while Pierre Jeanneret, Maxwell Fry and Jane Drew were charged with the task of developing the neighborhood sectors with their schools, shopping bazaars and tracts of government housing. As Chandigarh would have as its primary means of existence the functioning of a provincial administration, the necessarily large areas of government housing would have great visual dominance, and although Le Corbusier was able to reserve for himself all major commissions, it would be his colleagues who, through the sheer amount of building for which they would be responsible, could establish and control the prevailing architectural aspect of the city. It is the government housing which gives Chandigarh its definitive character, not only because of its extent, but also through the effect it has had on private building.

In Chandigarh, each government employee would be assigned to a subsidized housing unit, for which he would pay in rent, according to Indian custom, 10 per cent of his salary (Figs. 4a, 4b). In the program presented to the architects, thirteen categories of houses were specified, each corresponding to a level of government employment. In addition to providing for the thirteen ranks of government employees, the architects also designed a house cheaper than the lowest government category to provide for the poorer people of the city, the *tonga* drivers, laundrymen, sweepers, cobblers, etc. This type of house, furnishing minimal accommodation, was designated simply as "cheap houses" or sometimes as type 14.

There were, needless to say, levels of population in Chandigarh which even the cheap houses could not accommodate. Large numbers of construction workers of Chandigarh, for example, had no housing except small shelters which they put up near the building sites. Eventually, so-called Labour Colonies were established in outlying sectors, where for a nominal rental nine-by-six-foot plots were made available upon which small huts could be erected. Many people, however, remained on the site with no shelter at all.

In designing housing in Chandigarh, the architects encountered, in addition to difficulties of climate, budget and technology, the problem of design for an unfamiliar way of life. This problem was complicated, moreover, by the fact that Indian society is currently undergoing many changes and it would be necessary to foresee the directions of change in order to create an architectural framework of long-range appropriateness. Jane Drew once commented: "The clerk's houses in Sector 22 were built in two patterns. Originally, they were built to a plan which strictly followed the established customs and taboos, and later to a more modern form which had less passage way and where sweepers‡ would cross the living room, and where balconies had no purdah verandas. It became clear very early that tradition was not important except where it followed the climate and habits of living."[27]

In many cases the traditions and customs of India derive directly from a rural rather than an urban situation and must, of necessity, be modified by urbanization. The architects of Chandigarh, therefore, may have been justified in attempting to derive their basic schemes from what seemed the practical aspects of the program, rather than from catering to local tradition. According to Fry, "The housing in

‡ Outcastes. (Editor's note.)

FIG. 4A Type II government housing by Pierre Jeanneret. *Photograph by Norma Evenson*

Chandigarh offered a character derived very directly from the new urban way of life in India, from the climate, and from the economics of the particular situation." The dominating factor would be the climate. As Fry put it, ". . . for it is climate that dictates agriculture, moulds customs and affects even religion. Climate is a great element in India. To discover its laws and obey them is to create architectural character as directly as possible."[28]

In the villages of Punjab, houses are built of mud-clay, with thick walls and very few openings. The resulting interior, although cool, is in most cases so dark that the house functions not as a dwelling but as a storage place. The living activities of the household—cooking, eating, sleeping and so on—all take place in the walled courtyard. Larger and more prosperous houses might be of brick or stone, but the courtyard would retain high importance as a living area, often augmented by roof terraces. Among the well to do the bungalow type has been popular, taking the form of a large detached house surrounded on all sides by a wide shady veranda. This type of house was considered too costly for extensive use in Chandigarh, where the veranda has been largely replaced by the more economical brise-soleil. Some effort was also made to keep main rooms on the north or northeast and service rooms and circulation on the hottest sides. A limited veranda was often employed on the exposed side, having the effect of blocking the vertical summer sun but permitting the low winter sun to enter the house.

Common to all local housing, however, and considered essential in Chandigarh would be the provision for some outdoor area for sleeping. During the hot season in Chandigarh every solid object absorbs heat during the day, and by nightfall walls, floors and ceilings all radiate heat. In order to sleep at all, one must move away from surrounding building surfaces into the open air, and for this reason all houses in Chandigarh provide the inhabitants with either a walled courtyard or a roof terrace. In two-family dwellings, the ground floor flat would have access to a rear courtyard, while the family on the upper floor would have the roof for its use. In addition, open verandas were provided wherever possible. It is this need for outdoor area which, among other factors, has tended to limit building height in the city and which has prevented apartment living from becoming customary in India.

The climate of Chandigarh varies to such a degree throughout the year, however, that the task of designing for year-round comfort becomes almost impossible. Mrs. U. E. Chowdhury, a Capital Project Office architect, has observed that to meet all the requirements of the Chandigarh climate one would need three separate interconnected houses.[29] During the dry, cold winter, one requires a compact house with ample fireplaces or other heating devices and large window areas to admit the sun. The hot dry season demands high ceilings and small openings which can be sealed to keep out the sun and heated air during the day. During the monsoon season, however, when the rain prevents outdoor sleeping and when the air is somewhat cooler, the house needs large openings to ensure extensive air

FIG. 4B Central Scientific Instruments Organization housing by M. N. Sharma. *Chandigarh Department of Architecture*

circulation. All the houses in Chandigarh represent to some degree a compromise solution oriented toward the hottest season.

The design idiom of Chandigarh was established at the beginning as an architecture of one- or two-story brick houses, the smallest of the government houses providing two rooms, cooking and bathing areas, and a small rear courtyard. For reasons of economy, most housing was built in terrace formation, the repetitive use of basic housing types necessitating the development of individual units capable of harmonious extension into a street facade. For upper ranks, however, free-standing bungalows were provided.

Pierre Jeanneret, in contrast to his colleagues Maxwell Fry and Jane Drew, preferred to work largely with exposed brick, although his larger houses often incorporated a variety of materials including brick, plaster and local stone. His search for varied surface treatments led him to enliven wall surfaces with numerous decorative window openings, patterns of projecting bricks or perforated brick screens. Much of his design was characterized by exposed brick contrasted with white plastered details such as projecting cornices and window trim. Jeanneret had a dominant influence on the prevailing architectural character of Chandigarh, not only because of his long association with the city and the large amount of building for which he was responsible, but because his stylistic mannerisms were frequently adopted by other architects working in the city.

Chandigarh became a heavily controlled environment in terms of design. The large tracts of government housing reflected a standardization which was soon extended to many aspects of private building. Private houses constructed along the V4 bazaar street were required to be built according to government-designed facades in order to assure uniformity of appearance. Private row houses became subject to a law of "frame control" which regulated roof lines, prohibited extensions and overhangs and instituted controls on sizes and types of door and window openings. Commercial building in the neighborhood bazaar areas, although privately owned, was required to follow government designs. These buildings were planned as "shops-cum-flats," with two floors of living quarters above ground-level shops. All shops were set behind a continuous veranda providing a shaded walkway for customers. The concept of architectural uniformity for private commercial building was applied also in the area projected as the central business district. Here, the basic building type consisted of a four-story concrete framed structure carrying a pattern of exterior verandas.

Although the architects of Chandigarh claimed to have been mindful of local conditions in developing housing designs, the over-all conception of the sectors appears to have been developed from currently fashionable Western ideas of hygienic building placement rather than from an observation and understanding of the existing Indian townscape. However admirable their intentions, the architects seem to have lacked an eye for intimate scale and for the subtle aesthetics of the nonmotorized environment. As the city developed it became evident that the widely spaced and monotonous pattern of building placement, large tracts of unsheltered open area and overscaled streets accorded poorly with the prevailing lack of automobiles, and a climate characterized by dust storms, searing hot winds and scorching sun.

Chandigarh appears to have been based on an unimaginative application of design formula, rather than on a sensitive awareness of the lively qualities of Indian town life. Traditional vernacular building, employing narrow streets and a relatively dense pattern of inward-oriented courtyard houses, represents a far more sophisticated method of coming to terms with a tropical climate, a predominantly pedestrian environment and a preference for privacy than is evidenced in the misplaced garden city ambience of Chandigarh.

Life Within the Sector—Three Surveys

Although the program of Chandigarh was not developed with specific social intent, the city in its social make-up embodied conditions rather different from those of a typical Punjab town. The citizens of Chandigarh represented a mixture of people from throughout the province brought together by the circumstance of being in government service, and the housing provisions of the city have established groupings of people based on a system of occupational rank without regard for traditional groupings. To this extent, the program of Chandigarh, although somewhat hierarchic, could be considered as aiding a trend, generally advocated by most progressive elements in India, toward the breaking down of old barriers and the creation of a new sense of national integration.

Chandigarh, of course, was not unique in India in offering its citizens possibilities for a new degree of social mixture. India's large commercial cities and industrial centers have also served to pull people away from the villages and, in offering a new range of employment, have begun to help minimize caste barriers formerly embodied in a rigid hierarchy of traditional occupations. In many cases, however, the unifying potential of physical proximity is more apparent than real, and many of India's larger communities have lost the social organization and cohesiveness of the village without gaining any of the benefits of broader social interaction. Many of India's present-day city dwellers are rootless and confused, torn away from their ancient homes and the security and stability of traditional life, and yet unable to create effective social unities within the strange new urban environment. To a certain extent this appears to be borne out in Chandigarh.

Although the development of the physical plan of Chandigarh was not accompanied by any systematic efforts at sociological study, in May 1957, six years after Le Corbusier and his colleagues began work, the Economic and Statistical Organization of the Punjab Government undertook a socioeconomic survey of the city. In addition to assembling demographic statistics, the survey also dealt with housing, stating that "A very bold departure has been made in Chandigarh in the realm of house designing and the people put in these houses have had to adapt themselves in certain respects to the new type of accommodation. It would, therefore, be interesting and instructive to record their opinions in this respect."[30] To achieve this end, every tenth household was questioned regarding the relative merits of the Chandigarh houses compared with those of their previous residence. Of those residing in government houses, 76 per cent preferred their Chandigarh houses, citing such amenities as shower baths, convenient water taps, water closets, courtyards and general good planning. Of the inhabitants of private houses, only 61 per cent preferred their new residences, a circumstance partly attributable to the chronic housing shortage with its resultant overcrowding and high rents.

When asked to indicate specific defects in government houses, 49 per cent of the tenants complained of lack of safety, objecting, for example, to windows and ventilators which lacked iron bars or wire gauze.

An additional criticism was made by 35 per cent of the households regarding the adequacy of living space, a complaint naturally more frequent in the low-income groups whose houses are extremely small and whose families may be sizable. A lack of privacy in government houses was found objectionable by 30 per cent of those questioned, mainly the inhabitants of house types 9 to 13, the cheap houses and the university area. For the sake of economy, many houses had unwalled backyards, and this, it was said, precluded the full use of backyards for daytime sitting or sleeping at night. About one fifth of the households, chiefly those of type 13 and cheap houses, objected to their bathrooms which lacked both roof and doors, while 14 per cent, mostly residents of cheap houses, complained of the inadequate rain protection of the veranda-kitchens.

Roofs were often found to leak, and poor street drainage resulted in water collecting both in front and in back of houses. It was also found that the small size of the verandas in government houses made them inadequate for sleeping purposes, although in private houses 33 per cent were employed for this purpose. Many expressed a desire to have the veranda converted into an extra room.

In India, cooking is usually done over a solid-fuel fire burning in a masonry hearth called a *chuhlla*. Traditionally, the preparation of food is done at floor level, with the floor serving as a work surface. As it was felt in Chandigarh that the poor would prefer continuing their old customs, the chuhlla was placed at floor level in all houses up through type 11, and at counter height in higher income houses. It was found that of those given the traditional type of chuhlla, 94 per cent were satisfied with it, while among those given the raised chuhlla, only 51 per cent preferred it.[31] A similar preference for the Asian water closet was shown. Houses in the upper categories down to type 9 have either Western-style commodes or both Indian and Western types, while houses in the lower categories have only the Asian-type toilet at floor level. Of those given the Asian toilet, 95 per cent were satisfied with it, while of those given the Western type, only 64 per cent were satisfied. Naturally, no one objected to having both. Generally speaking, in spite of its variance with some traditional patterns, the government housing of Chandigarh was considered satisfactory by its occupants.

Beginning in 1961, some attempts at investigating social conditions in Chandigarh were initiated through a series of individual studies by students of the Department of Sociology at the University of Punjab. By the time the students began their work, population had risen to almost 100,000 and building activity was under way in almost all of the planned sectors. The neighborhood unit was taken as the basis for most of the investigations and interviews were directed primarily toward discovering the kind of social relations existing among neighbors, attempting to ascertain the effect of physical proximity on personal contact. In general, the questions asked by the students concerned the frequency of entertaining among neighbors, problems of neighbor relations, intimacy of relationships, etc., and the results obtained, by and large, indicated a striking lack of community life within the sectors.

It was found by the students that *purdah* was still an observable factor in social life, one paper noting that "The ladies are mostly uneducated and suffer from an inferiority complex, and have a notion of being cheap in too much mixing."[32] The investigators encountered certain difficulties in interviewing women, who were reported as "hesitant in imparting information," and as a result most interviewers were compelled to work between seven to nine o'clock in the morning and six to nine o'clock in the evening when the male members of the households were home.

It was found that few people in Chandigarh had any personal relations with their neighbors and also that "only with very few neighbors can the respondents meet regularly at places like clubs, offices, religious places or *mahalla* committee."[33] Of Sector 20, among the clerks it was reported that "people in the locality have a very limited circle of acquaintances with whom they may be said to have some sort of relations. . . . Mostly people know their neighbors by subcaste and not by name. . . . People are very much self-centered, and they do not want to come in close contact with the neighbors."[34]

In the middle-class Sector 8 it was noted, "Only a few invite their neighbors to tea or dinner, but only on some special occasion."[35] Among the white-collar workers in Sector 27, "The habit of extending invitations among the residents is in a very low ebb. If at all there are invitations, they are on formal occasions which are celebrated under social compulsion. Very few invite their neighbors for tea or dinner. People cannot afford to give dinner. . . . People seem to lack confidence in one another. . . . The fear arising of any complication out of such real relationships is predominant in their minds. . . . The question of visiting the neighbors does not arise at all. . . . So it may be said that the neighborhood relations in the present unit are superficial and formal."[36]

It was found also that the rigid classification of housing in Chandigarh affected social relations, and in the upper middle-class Sector 16 it was noted that "the allotment of houses on the basis of income and occupation creates a sense of superiority among the government servants and their wives and children. Consequently higher officers and their wives find it below their dignity to visit a neighbor who is subordinate to them in occupational status. According to one respondent, this segregation even extends to schools and colleges, because the children of one socioeconomic category form one group and are averse to talking to the children of the business men."[37] The objection to the differentiation of house types was felt most strongly among the lower categories and among the clerks: "The majority of cases have expressed strongly against the 'categorization' of the houses. They do not like it as it creates discrimination between the residents in the houses of different types. . . . Many respondents suggested a lesser number of types."[38]

In considering social relations, it should be borne in mind that in India the traditional joint family long provided its members with a wide range of companionship within the home, and there was little incentive to seek intimate relationships elsewhere. In Chandigarh, however, as in many other parts of modern India, the joint family is disappearing. The average family size in Chandigarh was found to be 3.9 persons, the majority of families consisting, as in the West, of single conjugal units. Studies have indicated that only 36 per cent of households in Chandigarh have any relatives living in the city, and people seem generally to be well adjusted to the absence of kin. Surveys have recorded that "Most of the persons who did not have relatives in Chandigarh did not experience any feeling of isolation because if it."[39]

In the opinion of one Indian, however, "The newcomer to Chandigarh is acutely confronted with its so-called 'soullessness.' He finds no ready made social groups into one or the other of which he can comfortably fit, no focal points in the form of rendezvous places or community centres where the people of the neighborhood are accustomed to gather of an evening, and little offered to him by way of social diversion. . . . Even the market area where 90 per cent of the social life in any city is concentrated is clean and neat and well-planned but totally lacking in the colour, gaiety and charm of the traditional 'bazaar.'"[40]

A comprehensive social survey in Chandigarh was directed by Dr. Victor S. D'Souza, head of the Department of Sociology, University of Punjab, and published in 1968. The survey was based on a study of 10 per cent of the built-on residential plots of Chandigarh, producing a sample group of 2,091 households, or 8,192 people. In general the results of this survey corroborated the conclusions of previous studies.

In terms of religion, the city was found to be 70 per cent Hindu and 27 per cent Sikh, with small numbers of Jains and Christians. Hindi was found to be the mother tongue of 54 per cent, and Punjabi the mother tongue of 43 per cent. Most people were multilingual, however; 86 per cent speaking languages in addition to the mother tongue. In general, Hindus and Sikhs were mixed throughout the city, although Sector 11 was found to have a large number of Sikhs, and Sectors 16, 14 and 12, disproportionate numbers of Hindus.

Government service accounted for the livelihood of 70 per cent of the population, the preponderance of white-collar employment making Chandigarh an unusually well-educated town for India. The sample population was found to be 72 per cent literate, while 12 per cent had been educated to the level of a college degree, and 5 per cent had equivalent professional or technical training.

The survey attempted to analyze the functioning of the sector as a neighborhood unit, considering the use patterns of local facilities, and the social relations among the inhabitants. It was found that generally the sectors did not function as social units, and only 15 per cent indicated that they felt the inhabitants had a sense of belonging to the sector community more than to the outside. Although in many sectors shopping facilities were well patronized, the local schools were frequently not used by neighborhood residents. It was found that even for primary education, 42 per cent used schools in other sectors, the reason being that although such schools were provided in all sectors, quality of education was not uniform. People would often send their children outside when seeking a more desirable school.

Although when asked to compare Chandigarh housing with their previous residence, 79 per cent of the respondents declared themselves satisfied, it was clear from the survey that housing in the city suffered from serious overcrowding. From the beginning, the pace of building had not equaled the need for dwelling space, and it was found that 62 per cent of the people in the sample lived in shared quarters.

The chronic housing shortage affected both private and government housing, but was more severe in the former. The average number of households per private plot was 2.4, while that in government housing, 1.3. In contemplating the effect of such congestion on living conditions it should be borne in mind that 72 per cent of all households were living in either one or two rooms.

Complaints with regard to housing centered mostly on the effects of overcrowding, lack of space, absence of a kitchen, need for sharing bathrooms and lavatories, lack of privacy and access to private open space. Placing two or more families in units designed for one produced inevitable tensions and animosities regarding joint use of facilities, and such points of contention as shared utility bills.

In spite of such problems, however, when asked to compare Chandigarh with their previous place of residence, people seemed generally satisfied with the new town. Areas of satisfaction in descending order were sanitation, 90 per cent satisfied, educational facilities (80 per cent), housing (79 per cent), shopping facilities (72 per cent), medical facilities (67 per cent), public transport (61 per cent), street lighting (60 per cent), recreational facilities (55 per cent), economic opportunities (34 per cent), cost of living (10 per cent). All in all, 76 per cent of the respondents reported themselves satisfied with general living conditions in Chandigarh.

The lack of community life which was observed in the sectors also characterized the city as a whole. In general, people recognized no community leaders, and there was little evidence of voluntary association within the city. Part of this lack of community feeling resulted from the absence of local government. Because of the desire of the planners of Chandigarh to keep the development of the plan free from local interference, no municipal government had been permitted. Commenting on this, Dr. D'Souza noted:

> While a complete control by the local public might have smothered the process of planning, a limited authority granted to a locally elected body might have gone a long way towards the development of local leadership and the generation of local interest in community problems. As it happened not only did the community lose the opportunity of hastening the process of integration, the planners too did not exercise the powers at their disposal to strengthen the process of planning.[41]

THE CAPITOL COMPLEX

The focal point of the city, both visually and symbolically, is that area which gives the city its reason for being and the majority of the inhabitants their livelihood—the complex of government buildings standing against the mountains at the upper edge of the city (Figs. 5a, 5b). The importance given to these buildings may be seen to embody something of the excitement of newly acquired self-government on the part of the Indians. It might be wholly suitable, therefore, that this center be a place where state functions were not merely housed, but celebrated, and where an architectural statement could be created strong enough to embody a sense of power and permanence, of seriousness and exaltation.

The design commenced with a visual consciousness of the site:

> We are in a plain [began Le Corbusier]. The chain of the Himalayas locks the landscape magnificently to the north. The smallest building appears tall and commanding. The government buildings are conjugated

FIG. 5A The Secretariat and Legislative Assembly viewed from the High Court. *Photograph by Norma Evenson*

> with one another in a strict ratio of heights and sizes. . . . There was anxiety and anguish in taking decisions on that vast, limitless ground. A pathetic soliloquy! I had to appreciate and to decide alone. The problem was no longer one of reasoning but of sensation. Chandigarh is not a city of lords, princes or kings confined within walls, crowded in by neighbors. It was a matter of occupying the plain. The geometrical event was, in truth, a sculpture of the intellect. No potter's clay in your hands to experiment with. No maquette that could ever have served as a genuine aid to a decision. It was a tension, mathematical in nature, which would bear fruit only when the buildings were completed. The right point. The right distance. Appreciation. . . . It was a battle of space, fought within the mind. Arithmetic, texturique, geometrics: it would all be there when the whole was finished. For the moment, oxen, cows and goats, driven by peasants, crossed the sun-scorched fields.[42]

Le Corbusier had observed that "in contrast to all contemporary problems, the town of Chandigarh has a freedom which is in itself a dangerous difficulty. The space devoted to the capitol is vast, the buildings occupying a fabulous ground area. How could sufficient visual cohesion be given to such a huge conception? This was one of the most difficult problems which was solved by Le Corbusier."[43] The problem, of course, was of the architect's own devising, as it was he himself who established the scale of the complex.

In its final conception, the capitol complex appeared as a grandly scaled ensemble basically ordered by a plan involving 800 and 400 meter squares, but depending for visual cohesion on an interplay of massive building forms seen against the distant mountains, and within a configuration of excavated earth mounds and reflecting pools. The scale of the complex is vast, in keeping with the surrounding landscape, an area designed for sweeping visual impact, rather than ease of physical communication.

The capitol area as a whole was conceived as a pedestrian plaza, motor traffic being channeled into sunken trenches leading to parking areas. The generating motif of the complex was a slightly asymmetrical cross axis, one arm of which comprises a pedestrian promenade penetrating the area and extending the line of the monumental boulevard leading from the commercial center. The long slab of the Secretariat bounds the space to the left, and stands adjacent to the Legislative Assembly, while the High Court and Legislature terminate the cross axis on either side of a 450-meter esplanade. The center of the area is marked by a series of monuments devised to illustrate Le Corbusier's theories of city planning, while outlined against the hills at the outer edge of the complex was projected the Governor's Palace (the site later designated for a Museum of Knowledge). Also defining the outer edge of the complex would be a symbolic sculptural monument in the form of a great open hand.

In the relatively brief period of its existence, the capitol complex, like the Taj Mahal, seems to have afforded a constant challenge to the descriptive powers of

FIG. 5B The High Court in the capitol complex. *Photograph by Norma Evenson*

its admiring visitors, typical of whom is the American architect Paul Rudolph who visited the area in 1960. As he commented:

> The first sight of the buildings is the Secretariat on the left hand, sitting at right angles to the mountain range. In every way it opposes the mountains: the angled stairway, the ramp on the roof, the projecting viewing stand—all of these angles are obviously and carefully conceived to oppose the receding angles of the land masses.
>
> Slowly one becomes aware of what appear to be foothills among the buildings themselves, but these subsequently prove to be man-made hills rising out of the plain. Their scale is immense; this is sculpture. These man-made hills are as important to the siting as the buildings, and are indeed an integral part of the whole complex. One is not aware that the buildings are still on the plain. The artificial hills obscure the view at first of the High Court building, and they also define the limits of the entire site as well as shutting off the major part of the city of Chandigarh when one is in the governmental complex. Indeed the relation of the buildings to the site—also the manipulation of the site in terms of the various levels of both the geometric depressions and irregular hills—is unsurpassed anywhere at any time. You think you are on the face of the moon. In a sense it becomes one great horizontal plaque. Most of the sunken automobile accesses are not yet there, but the intent is clear.
>
> As time goes on I am sure that every man will understand the importance of Chandigarh: people will go there as they now go to the Piazza San Marco. They will go not because of any individual building but because of the relationship of buildings to site, the environment created, the aspirations of man realized. It is the only grouping of the 20th century of which I know that makes any sense whatsoever, undoubtedly the century's greatest.[44]

As the capitol complex began to be realized, it was apparent that the new structures taking form under the scorching sun of Chandigarh were an epoch-making culmination of all the recent directions in Le Corbusier's work. Disciplined by a limited budget, a primitive technology and a brutal climate, yet given a sympathy and freedom unusual in his career, he had been able to create in India an architectural expression surpassing in power any of his previous efforts. Neither specifically Indian nor European, these buildings seem to present a creation which is both the product of a particular time, place, and set of conditions and yet peculiarly ageless and unlimited in concept.

The program of the High Court building specified provision for eight law courts and a high court, together with necessary office space. In plan the building took the form of an abbreviated L-shape with the long facade facing the capitol plaza to contain the courtrooms and the small rear extension to accommodate offices. Essentially, the building is a rectilinear frame within which interior functions are defined, the eight courtrooms identically expressed on the main facade and separated from the larger high court by a monumental columned entrance rising the height of the building.

On the main facade the deep (4 feet 7 inches), fixed concrete brise-soleil gives a strong and scaleless pattern to the building, and only human beings and the unobtrusive courtroom doors can be used as visual keys for reading the dimensions of the surface. Commented the architect, "Here the brise-soleils take the place of the weather-drips on a classical facade, but they cover not only the windows but the entire facade, and influence the whole structure."[45] It is the concrete screen which gives the main facade its over-all unity, so that it is perceived not as an assemblage of floor levels and courtroom chambers, but as a single entity of plastically interwoven elements, in which the horizontal ground line, repeated in the two roof levels, is countered by the powerful upward thrust of the entrance piers and the pillars between the courtrooms, whose vertical line is echoed in the roof supports.

The rough concrete of the building is treated in a variety of manners. For much of the surface, including the underside of the parasol roof and the exterior side walls, the marks of sheet metal formwork characterize the surface. In portions of the interior and on the ramps, wooden boards have been inserted within the metal forms to give the concrete surface the impress of their jointed pattern, while other surfaces, including those of the massive entrance piers, are finished with gunnite cement.

When the High Court was dedicated, the gunnite-coated entrance piers were painted white, producing a surface closely harmonizing with the light gray concrete, and reminding some visitors of the pristine clarity of Greek temple columns. Later, however, Le Corbusier decided to paint the columns in bright polychrome, a transformation which was effected in 1962. The inside wall to the left of the piers was painted black, and the adjacent pillar painted green. The center pier became yellow, the right-hand pillar red, and the remaining portico wall primary blue. The High Court stands alone on one side of the capitol complex, and Le Corbusier may have felt that in order to balance more effectively the large Secretariat and sculpturally assertive Assembly building opposite, this relatively small rectilinear structure should be given the added visual weight of a vibrant color scheme. Although justifiable criticism has been directed at the functional aspects of the High Court, there is no doubt about its visual impressiveness.

Le Corbusier had long maintained a predilection for high-rise construction and it was evident from his early designs for the capitol complex, that he hoped to house the Secretariat in a high-rise building. This would not have been feasible within the circumstances of Chandigarh, however, and the design which was accepted established the building form as a long, horizontal concrete slab, the great size of the building (254 meters long and 42 meters high) giving it the aspect of a massive wall enclosing the capitol complex on one side. The building is composed of six eight-story blocks separated by expansion joints, and in its length the structure presents almost the appearance of a street facade composed of separate, but architecturally related, units. The central pavilion, Block 4, contains the offices of the ministers, defined on the facade by a distinctive brise-soleil of deeply sculptural two-story porticoes.

The principal approach to the Secretariat is by means of a roadway leading below ground level to a parking area in front of the central block in which a floor is left open to provide an entrance hall. As individual automobiles are rare in Chandigarh, it was estimated that most of the employees would arrive by bus, bicycle or on foot.

In addition to the plasticity of the concrete sunbreaker which masks the entire facade, sculptural emphasis is given the building by free-standing exterior ramps enclosed in rough concrete perforated by small square windows. As mass elevator service would be too costly and unreliable for Chandigarh, it is these ramps which provide the principal vertical circulation for the bulk of employees.

Le Corbusier's design for the government complex attempted to contain all the Secretariat functions in one large structure which by its placement co-ordinates with, but does not dominate, the more symbolically important buildings of the area. The Secretariat serves compositionally as a space definer, bounding the capitol area to the left as one approaches along the entrance axis. Together with the earth mound at right angles to its facade, it delineates a corner of the great compound, in its vast size becoming almost like some large natural barrier—a cliff forming part of the setting of the remaining structures. These smaller structures, moreover, are connected by a large pedestrian plaza augmented by water basins, landscaping and monuments. The Secretariat, by contrast, is approached only by a utilitarian roadway terminating in a parking excavation.

The High Court was put into use in March 1956. It was not until six years later, however, in 1962, that the Assembly building facing it across the capitol complex would be dedicated, completing a balance of monumental structures and complementing the simplicity of the High Court with a more active, complex and intricate system of elements. Across the expansive plaza two great porticoes acknowledge one another, one high, massive, vibrant with color, the other horizontal, monochromatic, fragmented into a series of planar supports for the heavily curving canopy.

Of all the buildings of the capitol complex, the Legislative Assembly embodies the greatest richness and complexity of design. Primarily the building was designed to house the legislative assembly of one hundred eight members and a smaller governor's council, together with auxiliary offices. Le Corbusier evolved a design in which the legislature would be contained in a hyperbolic structure similar in shape to an industrial cooling tower. Enclosed within the rectilinear frame of the office block, this tower rises 124 feet, breaking through the roof line, creating an external sculptural element visually responsive to the jagged forms of the distant hills. Also projecting above the roof line is a pyramidal skylight initially illuminating the governor's council chamber.

Within the Assembly building, the central space is left open from the level of the plaza to the roof, providing an extensive area for circulation and meeting which Le Corbusier termed the forum. Within this open space the hyperbolic tower of the assembly chamber stands free.

It is for the members of the Legislative Assembly that the majestic sequence of spatial experiences created by the forum is provided. The delegates enter the Assembly building through a small reception hall at basement level and proceed upward by means of a concrete ramp. As one ascends into the great hall, the space suddenly expands both vertically and laterally. To the right rises a three-storied block of offices faced with concrete balcony corridors which bound the interior space on three sides. To the left spreads the forum comprising an area about two hundred feet square, within which looms the vast and compelling form of the Assembly chamber. A forest of slender concrete columns rises forty-five feet to the black ceiling, its darkness evoking a dimensionless void overhead. Sudden shafts of light stream from deep-set occuli in the roof and from a band of clerestory windows set between the wall and roof planes. Lofty, dramatically illuminated, seemingly scaleless in visual dimension, this space is one of the noblest in modern architecture, infusing some of the serenity and exaltation of a cathedral with the excitement of a great concourse. The soaring columns punctuate the verticality, while the great cylindrical tower tends to create a flow of movement, inviting circumambulation almost like a *stupa.***

Although relatively small, the governor's palace occupied in the plan of the capitol complex a position of considerable importance—that of defining the outer limits of the complex as it opened toward the panorama of distant hills. As designed, the building would have embodied the most dramatically sculptural profile of all the capitol structures, reflecting some of the jaggedness of the mountain range behind it and also, in its horizontal divisions, giving physical identity to the varied functions within. It was to serve not only as a private residence for the governor but as a headquarters for the governor's office staff, as a guest house for state visitors, and as a place for official receptions and entertainments.

When it was subsequently decided not to house the governor in the capitol complex, Le Corbusier produced a simpler design for what he termed a "Museum of Knowledge" to be built in the same place. As yet, nothing has been constructed on this site.

The buildings of the Chandigarh capitol complex, through their massive plasticity of form and bold use of exposed concrete, were influential in liberating postwar architecture from the formal restrictions of the international style, reinforcing Le Corbusier's position as an innovative leader of modern design. For devotees of architecture, the Chandigarh capitol complex has become a place of pilgrimage, as much a part of the Indian itinerary as more ancient monuments.

More importantly, Le Corbusier's efforts served to revitalize the modern concept of monumental building. As Le Corbusier had sought to redefine the master plan of the city to achieve a suitably monumental scale, so he struggled to give the capitol complex the imprint of unity and power appropriate to its symbolic function.

Disciplined by climate, poverty and primitive technology, the buildings of the capitol complex rise from the earth, asserting the presence of man against the vast sweep of plain and the distant mountains. There is no shelter here. Battered by rains and dust storms, scorched by a brutal sun and buffeted by winds, these structures have been laboriously built by the toil of many men. They are meant to last.

However impressive the Chandigarh capitol complex might be architecturally, it could be criticized as an unsuitably extravagant gesture for a relatively small provincial capital. The justification for such a project lay in the circumstances of its creation. In a country newly independent and in the process of organizing functioning institutions of its own, attaching a powerful symbolism to government buildings would not be inappropriate. When Chandigarh was founded, self-government was not yet something taken for granted, but the culmination of a long period of struggle and sacrifice. The importance given to the governing function in Chandigarh was not, therefore, an artificial grafting, but a reflection of existing reality.

Moreover, it may be remembered that India comprises a society in which a

** A Buddhist mound or tower shrine. (Editor's note.)

modern civic sense is only being developed. For centuries Indian society has evolved in a fragmented manner, with social unities based on the family, the caste or the religious community, but without a correspondingly strong sense of national consciousness. The qualities of citizenship, of identification with and loyalty to the state are only being learned. For this reason it may have seemed important that the functions of government be surrounded by whatever symbolic grandeur and pageantry could be achieved. It may be remembered also that, as many Indians are illiterate, physical symbols must do the work of verbal communication, and as the cathedral of the Middle Ages served to communicate a conception of the strength and permanence of the Church, so the civic buildings of Chandigarh may convey something of the importance and dignity of government and of the continuity of the state.

CHANDIGARH—THE SECOND PHASE

For more than fifteen years the development of Chandigarh remained under the direction of its initial planners, with Pierre Jeanneret heading the Capitol Project Office, and Le Corbusier continuing as architectural adviser. Following the death of Le Corbusier in August 1965, and the retirement of Pierre Jeanneret in December of the same year, the planning of the city was taken over entirely by the Indians. Primary responsibility for directing the planning effort was assumed by the chief architect of Chandigarh, Mohan N. Sharma.

The initial plan of Chandigarh was projected for 150,000 people. By 1968, the population was estimated to have risen to 170,000, and to accommodate the increase, two rows of new sectors were added to the southern portion of the city.

The expansion of the city has generally maintained the design principles of the master plan, and new sectors reflect the basic layout of existing neighborhoods. Under Sharma's direction, however, some attempts were instituted at improving the internal design of the sectors, with the aim of remedying some of the deficiencies of the city. With regard to housing, it was stated that "there is going to be a change in the grouping of buildings to provide more feeling for community."[46] New designs by Sharma included a three-story scheme in which a system of setbacks provided each level with open veranda space. His projected housing schemes tended to avoid the repetitive straight rows and uniform roof lines of earlier designs, replacing them with a more varied pattern of building composition, and he sought to modify the somewhat amorphous pattern of open space to produce more small and usable enclosures within the housing groups. In order to make the government housing somewhat less rigidly stratified, the number of house types was reduced from thirteen to six.

In addition to receiving changes in planning personnel, Chandigarh was also subject to a dramatic political reorganization. Punjab, it may be recalled, contained two dominant groups, Punjabi-speaking Sikhs and Hindi-speaking Hindus. For many years, the more militant Sikhs had agitated for a separate state, and although Pandit Nehru had opposed such a split, Indira Gandhi, in 1966, granted the request. Punjab, previously divided between India and Pakistan, was reapportioned into the Sikh province of Punjab and the smaller Hindu province of Haryana. The problem of the disposition of the capital was temporarily solved by converting Chandigarh into a federal Union Territory serving as a joint capital for both provinces.

Thus government buildings designed for a single administration came to be shared by two political establishments. In the capitol complex, office space in the Secretariat was divided between the two provincial bureaucracies, while the High Court was given joint use. Within the Legislative Assembly building, the larger chamber served Punjab, while the smaller (formerly the governor's council) accommodated the Haryana legislature. Although the two government establishments were separate, there was no physical division of the residents of the city into discrete Hindu and Sikh enclaves.

Meanwhile, the Sikhs continued to put pressure on the national government to be given exclusive possession of Chandigarh, while similar efforts were made by the Hindus to obtain the city for Haryana. In January 1970, having been faced with threats of suicide from leaders of both groups, the government awarded the city to the Sikh province of Punjab. In order to give Haryana time to build a new capital of its own, however, Chandigarh was to continue serving both provinces for a period not to exceed five years. Whatever its success or failure in terms of design, Chandigarh had clearly become a symbolic prize which neither Sikhs nor Hindus would willingly relinquish.

At the time of its creation, the plan of Chandigarh embodied many of the current principles of physical town planning as it had been developing in the West—the separation of urban functions, the establishment of differentiated traffic patterns, the maintenance of architectural controls, the regulation of peripheral development and the employment of the neighborhood unit. Chandigarh is a city where the rules were obeyed, too well perhaps, and with so little imagination and sensitivity that the resulting environment has impressed many as deficient in both visual appeal and functional practicality.

In terms of aesthetics, Chandigarh provides an essay in the weaknesses of thoroughgoing architectural control. The planners of the city, perhaps understandably, wished to avoid visual chaos and to create a sense of serenity and order throughout. Yet to many observers, Chandigarh seems a bland and monotonous expression of a single uninspired vision. The design controls of Chandigarh have succeeded in making even the bazaar areas, usually the most colorful and exciting part of any Indian town, as orderly and dull as any American suburban shopping center. Confident in the good taste of their own conceptions, the government architects dominated the visual character of the city. Their efforts were often creditable, yet upon exposure to the seemingly endless tracts of grimly virtuous government housing, even the most vulgar and inept individual design refreshes the eye like a welcome taste of sin.

It is undeniable that by Indian standards, Chandigarh is a triumph of hygiene. The city is well supplied with modern utilities, and any foreign visitor would be reassured by the general cleanliness, the ample supplies of electricity and running water, and abundance of flush toilets. What was lacking in the creation of the town, however, was an eye for the intimate texture of a pedestrian-scale environment, and this neglect in creating an appropriate physical ambience in the residential sectors forms the most legitimate basis for the accusation that the city is not sufficiently "Indian." It is true that the Indians administering the Chandigarh project were not seeking a traditional solution to the problem of civic design but rather one which would grow from the circumstances of the project. How these circumstances might be interpreted, however, would depend on the sensibilities of the designers.

Although at the inception of Chandigarh there was in India no contemporary school of town planning theory, there were vernacular traditions of town building which could have provided excellent points of reference for planners. A recognition of the virtues present in much traditional Indian town building should not be confused with a sentimental desire for medieval quaintness or a misguided longing for the past. The vernacular building tradition of India is defensible because it frequently evidences a more practical grasp of the realities of the Indian climate and way of life than may be found in the work of many trained Indian planners. The reason for this seems to lie in the fact that most contemporary standards of physical planning were developed in Europe and America for a given climate, technology and way of life, and these principles have been frequently applied throughout the world regardless of appropriateness, even as they were being modified in their places of origin. Modern Indian planners often work according to standards of building placement developed for cold and cloudy northern Europe at a time when, in reaction to the congestion of nineteenth-century industrial cities, an ideal was established in which every ray of sun was courted and large window areas invited the creation of long vistas. With a local building type specifically designed to exclude the sun, oriented toward an inner courtyard and having very small exterior windows, wide separation of buildings becomes senseless, and the desirable shade produced by narrow streets is lost.

Anyone who has walked about in the intense Indian summer sun is aware that distances which may seem quite small on paper become agonizing in terms of fatigue and discomfort when one attempts to traverse them on foot. Le Corbusier once stated, "A city made for speed is made for success."[47] In India, it might be more appropriate to say that a city made for shade is made for success.

Much of the physical inconvenience of Chandigarh, especially in the early period of development, stemmed from the circumstance that the city was designed primarily for motor transport, rather than for existing facilities. Although the planners may have been justified in anticipating eventual mechanization, it soon became clear that some provision should have been made for the period when nonmechanized transport would predominate. Difficulties in communication and transport were accentuated by the sequence of development initially established in Chandigarh. The planners chose not to begin construction with a concentrated settlement designed to expand outward. Instead, a series of small nuclei were established in widely scattered sectors, leaving the inhabitants with long distances to travel through unbuilt areas.

Although Chandigarh was in many ways intended as a model town for the nation, the city in its over-all conception, bore little relevance to India's immediate requirements in housing and planning. At the beginning, the construction of the city was accompanied by much talk about stringent finance, yet in viewing the miles of wide paved streets, often bordering unbuilt areas, and in contemplating the extended water, sewer and electrical lines serving isolated settlements strung over the vast expanse of the city, one might have found it difficult to believe that Chandigarh represented a truly economical solution to the problem of urban planning in an impoverished country. Chandigarh represented an attempt virtually to duplicate the public utilities and civic amenities of a modern Western city, and in doing so made housing for really poor people impossible to provide. The serious overcrowding of both government and private dwellings suggests that housing standards may generally have been set beyond the resources of the city. In addition, the extravagant provisions for parkland if fully developed and maintained, may prove a heavy drain on urban finances.

It is true, of course, that Chandigarh would have failed in its symbolic purpose if it had not attempted to embody a high standard of physical amenity, one which would represent a technical improvement over many older towns and which would satisfy the desire to create a truly modern city. Chandigarh was meant to serve as a monument, and it was to this purpose that the central government of India provided generous financial support. The importance of such symbolic showpieces in an undeveloped country should not be underestimated. But the result is that the planners of Chandigarh work in a somewhat sheltered position, isolated from many of the primary problems of Indian planning. Chandigarh, from the beginning, represented an atypical and somewhat exhibitionistic project rather than an example of how to cope with the major realities of Indian urbanization. In presenting fundamental solutions to India's pressing housing needs, and in demonstrating town planning solutions consistent with the Indian economy, climate and way of life, Chandigarh, unfortunately, has had little to offer.

All in all, the initial planning of Chandigarh represented a well-intended effort in which, working within a difficult set of circumstances and an unfamiliar environment, a group of Western architect planners sought to create a long-range framework for the development of an Asian city. Conditions required that many decisions be made intuitively, with the designers compelled to draw on their accumulated knowledge and their own observations. Although in terms of current theory the design approach would satisfy neither the advocates of "scientific" planning nor those favoring over-all spontaneity of urban development, Chandigarh in its inception reflected an urban vision common to many planners and visible in many other postward projects. While it is not difficult to find fault with many aspects of the plan, it represents the almost inevitable product of its time.

A master plan, however, should be regarded as a guide for future growth, rather than a detailed blueprint for the ultimate development of every aspect of the city. There was nothing in the over-all plan of Chandigarh to preclude experimentation, change and improvement as the city evolved, and it is to be hoped that the expansion of the city will be accompanied with a continuously creative planning effort.

Judging the failure or success of a city is rather like judging the failure or success of the human race. In a sense its very existence is its success. It is possible that both physically and socially Chandigarh may fall short of the most optimistic dreams of its founders. Chandigarh, like all cities, is far from ideal, yet it remains and grows, the fruit of a courageous gesture and a hard-won victory at a time of confusion and political opposition. The realization of the city as it stands today has embodied a difficult accomplishment in the face of severe financial restrictions, unskilled labor, scarcity of materials, inadequate legal powers and an often hampering bureaucracy.

In the beginning Chandigarh was essentially the creation of its planners; eventually it will be the creation of its people through time. Already the city has been embroiled in political events unforeseen by its designers, and is becoming, like all cities, part of a continuum of change. Chandigarh represents a generous investment of courage and hope, of talent and devoted effort, and it will continue to require such investments. When Chandigarh becomes a true city, however, it will be when its people have given it a history, when it has become free of its planners to acquire a destiny of its own. Ultimately the people of Chandigarh must achieve the city they deserve.

NOTES

[1] Quoted in L. R. Nair, *Why Chandigarh?* Simla, Publicity Department, Punjab Government, 1950, p. 6.

[2] Maxwell Fry, "Chandigarh: the Capital of the Punjab," *Journal of the Royal Institute of British Architects,* Ser. 3, 62:87–94 (January 1955), p. 90.

[3] Jane Drew, "Chandigarh Capital City Project," *Architects' Year Book* 5. London, Elek Books Ltd., 1953, p. 56.

[4] Quoted in Christopher Rand, "City on a Tilting Plain," *The New Yorker,* 31:35–62 (April 30, 1955), p. 70.

[5] Ibid., p. 42.

[6] Drew, op. cit., p. 57.

[7] Ibid.

[8] Le Corbusier, *Oeuvre complète 1946–52.* Zurich, H. Girsberger, 1955, p. 99.

[9] Quoted by J. Tyrwhitt, J. L. Sert, E. N. Rogers, *The Heart of the City.* London, Lund Humphries, 1952, p. 51.

[10] Drew, op. cit., p. 56.

[11] Le Corbusier, *Creation Is a Patient Search.* New York, Frederick Praeger, 1960, p. 277.

[12] *Project Estimate of the New Capital of Punjab, Chandigarh,* Government of the Punjab, p. 42. Difficulties resulting from a lack of such peripheral controls may be seen on the outskirts of many Indian cities where squatter colonies of shanty-town bazaars and commercial districts spring up just outside the taxable area of the city but close enough to reap all the advantages of the city location. In Chandigarh itself some difficulty has arisen over the expansion of the nearby village of Manimajra. (Periphery control can prevent the establishment of new villages, but not the expansion of old ones.) Because of its nearness to Chandigarh, this village has tended

to attract residents who may build there because of its low land values and still be able to take advantage of many of the civic amenities of Chandigarh such as schools, hospitals and theatres.

[13] Le Corbusier, *City of Tomorrow*. New York, Payson and Clark, 1929, p. xxi.

[14] Fry, op. cit., p. 92.

[15] Le Corbusier, *Oeuvre complète 1952–57*. Zurich, Girsberger, 1958, p. 51.

[16] Le Corbusier press conference, op. cit.

[17] Ibid.

[18] Fry, op. cit.

[19] Le Corbusier paper delivered at a press conference at the Palais de la Découverte, March 18, 1953. (Author's translation.)

[20] Quoted in "What Corbu Has Been Up To," *Architectural Forum* (September 1953), p. 146.

[21] Quoted by Christopher Rand, op. cit., p. 58.

[22] The Mayer firm, in preparing the initial plan of Chandigarh, employed the climatologist H. E. Landsberg as a consultant. After presenting a detailed report on the region of Chandigarh, Landsberg made the general observation that the "climatic handicaps of the region are such that the margin of improvement that can be achieved by site planning, orientation of buildings and detailed landscaping and house construction are exceedingly small." (Unpublished report from files of Mayer, Whittlesey and Glass.)

[23] Le Corbusier press conference, op. cit.

[24] Drew, op. cit., p. 65.

[25] Fry, op. cit., p. 91.

[26] Quoted in "What Corbu Has Been Up To," op. cit., p. 144.

[27] Jane Drew, "Sector 22," *Marg,* Vol. 15, No. 1 (December 1961), p. 25.

[28] Fry, "Problems of Chandigarh Architecture," *Marg,* Vol. 15, No. 1 (December 1961), p. 20.

[29] Mrs. U. E. Chowdhury, "High Cost Housing and Interiors," *Marg,* Vol. 15, No. 1 (December 1961), p. 27.

[30] *Chandigarh Socio-Economic Survey*. Government of the Punjab Economic and Statistical Organization. Pub. No. 13 (1958), Preface, p. 34.

[31] Household equipment is generally simple in India, especially that involved with the preparation of food. The smallest kitchens in Chandigarh are provided with a small *chuhlla* at floor level and a single water tap, while in larger houses, the *chuhlla* is expanded and a sink added. Food-storage provisions are usually minimal, although a few relatively well-to-do people provide themselves with refrigerators.

[32] Santosh Veina Mahta, "Neighborhood Relations in Sector 22-A" (unpublished thesis, Department of Sociology, University of Punjab, 1962).

[33] Ibid.

[34] Surendra Dutt, "Neighborhood Relations Among Clerks in Sector 20" (unpublished thesis, Department of Sociology, University of Punjab, 1962).

[35] Pushpa Malik, "Neighborhood Relations in Sector 8" (unpublished thesis, Department of Sociology, University of Punjab, 1962).

[36] Har Gopal Singh, "White Collar Workers—a Study in Neighborhood Relations, Sector 27" (unpublished thesis, Department of Sociology, University of Punjab, 1962).

[37] Raksha Bhalla, "Neighborhood Relations in Sector 16" (unpublished thesis, Department of Sociology, University of Punjab, 1962).

[38] Hridesh Dhody, "Socioeconomic Conditions of Clerks" (unpublished thesis, Department of Sociology, University of Punjab, 1962).

[39] Victor S. D'Souza, *Social Structure of a Planned City: Chandigarh.* Bombay, Orient Longmans Ltd., 1968, p. 63.

[40] Sneh Pandit, "Social and Cultural Life in Chandigarh," *Chandigarh Festival Souvenir,* pp. 32–34. (Chandigarh, Festival Committee, 1967), p. 32.

[41] D'Souza, op. cit., p. 278.

[42] Le Corbusier, *Modulor II.* Cambridge, Harvard University Press, 1958, pp. 214–15.

[43] Le Corbusier, *Oeuvre complète 1946–52,* op. cit., p. 119.

[44] Paul Rudolph, "The Contribution of Le Corbusier," *Architectural Forum,* pp. 83–102 (April 1961), p. 99.

[45] Le Corbusier, *Oeuvre complète 1946–52,* op. cit., p. 118.

[46] Dr. M. S. Randhawa, chief commissioner, Chandigarh, *A Brief Review of Work Done in Chandigarh Since November 1st, 1966.* Chandigarh, Government Press, no date, p. 2.

[47] Le Corbusier, *City of Tomorrow,* op. cit., p. 179.

CHAPTER 11

Dakar: Postcolonial Crisis

John W. Sommer*

THE EARLY DEVELOPMENT OF FRENCH WEST AFRICA

Euphoric was the spirit in the majority of decolonizing countries in the first days of independence in the early 1960s; high resolve, expansive plans and seemingly limitless energy characterized the newly unshackled of Africa and Asia. Superpower and minipower played court to the urban elites of the capital cities in the Third World, and assurances of massive transfers of largesse from the wealthy nations for an indeterminate transition period flowed as easily as chief's wine and sultan's robes. Urban centers, particularly the former colonial capitals, bloomed as new buildings outstripped tropic vegetation in rapid growth.

Within five years this budding flower of quasi-Western urbanism in the non-Western world was nipped as foreign economic assistance programs were pruned back sharply. The transition period came to an end more abruptly than antici-

* Ph.D. in geography from Boston University; at Dartmouth College since 1964 where he recently headed the Urban Studies and City Planning Program. Having lived in the Middle East and Africa for almost a decade, he has had a sustained interest in urbanization in the Third World. During 1968 he carried out research in Senegal and Gambia under the National Academy of Sciences-National Research Council; in 1970 he participated in the Rehovoth Conference on Urbanization and Development in Developing Countries and returned again to Africa to gather materials for a study of African urbanization.

pated by host governments. Expansive plans, including urban plans, turned out to be just too expensive; high spirits evaporated; the energy levels of the urban systems of these countries could not sustain themselves and they resettled at new, lower plateaus. In short, the initial euphoria evaporated.

The effect of colonial withdrawal on African capital cities was less than on those towns subordinate in the urban hierarchies; the capital cities remain the national repositories of skill and wealth. The collapse of the secondary towns of many developing urban systems has, however, thrust an added burden on the capitals, a burden of urban refugees from the small towns, and of new city folk who might have been absorbed in the smaller towns had these towns retained their vitality.

Dakar, capital of the Republic of Senegal, fits this scenario to an unhappy degree: It is a developing city in an undeveloping country. The growth of Dakar is, in some measure, at the expense of the rest of the Senegalese urban system; as the interdependence of the system is diminished one can observe "hollow towns" (towns with growing population and stagnating functions) where active urban centers had stood before. This malaise, which has been termed "over-urbanization," is creeping up the urban hierarchy toward the capital city. What are the manifestations of this ominous circumstance in tropical Africa's most urbanized state? Will the end of this process be a single, dominant center for Senegal? What are the implications of this for past plans and future planning?

Dakar

Dakar rests on Cap Vert, a polished product of Western colonialism on Africa's western most protuberance (Fig. 1). Location and archetypical colonial ties with France have produced a unique set of relationships between Dakar and its hinterland and with the rest of the world. These relationships have helped to define Dakar's functions as a port and as a place of governance. Location and the sequence of events, colonial and postcolonial, have also intertwined to affect the development of the internal structure and spatial layout of the city.

The settlement sequence of the area within which Dakar is located is traced from much earlier times than the nineteenth-century European scramble for Africa. From archaeological evidence it is clear that man has inhabited Cap Vert since paleolithic times. Later historical references define the character of this early society.[1] At least one document suggests that a half millenia before Christ, Carthaginian colonists set forth in galleys from what is now Tunisia, went through the Pillars of Hercules (Gibraltar) and, sailing southwest, passed by Cap Vert.[2] The Carthaginians described the area as "inhabited by savage men, clothed in skins of wild beasts, who drove us away by throwing stones and hindered us from landing."[3]

These early peoples of the peninsula were fishermen, whose descendants, the Lebous, still ply the same trade. They did not develop the dense village clusters so characteristic of the forest area of western Nigeria. Indeed, there is nothing to suggest that the average density figure of about thirty persons per square mile, characteristic of rural Senegal today, was surpassed on Cap Vert until the twentieth century.[4]

European contacts with this coastal area began in the mid-fifteenth century.

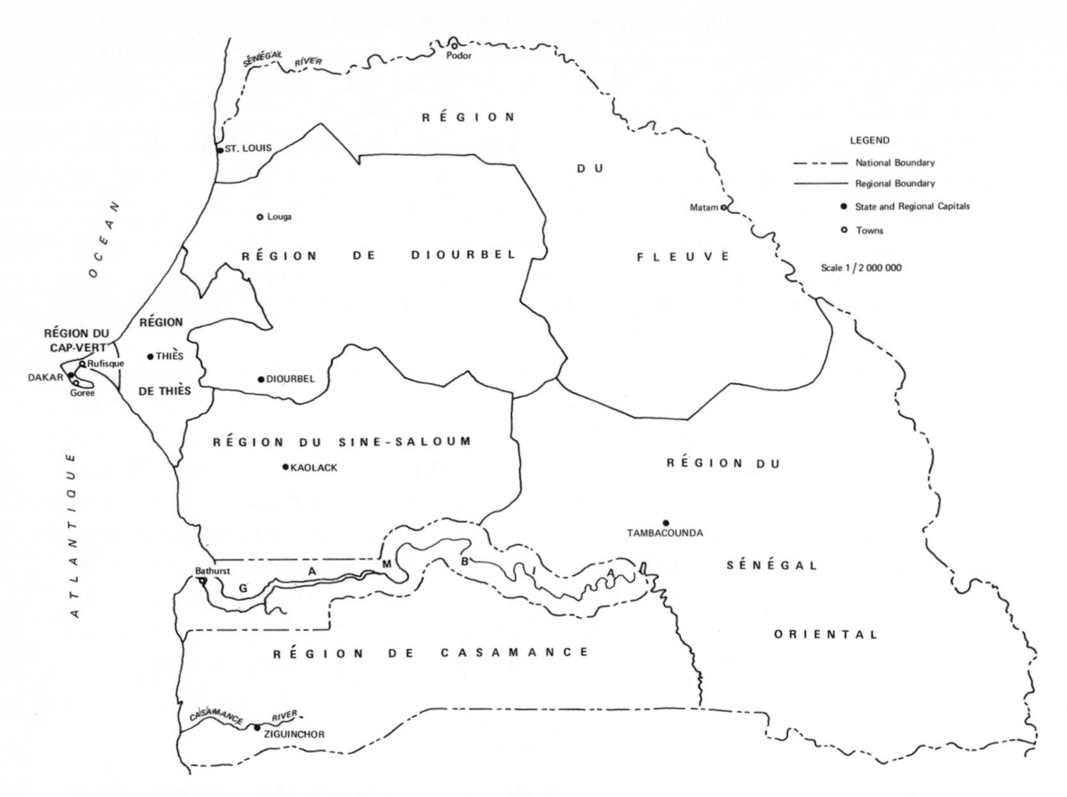

FIG. 1 Republic of Senegal. Dakar in the 1860s.

The Sahara barrier had shielded the large, inland African kingdoms of the western Sudan from all but peripatetic contacts with the Mediterranean and European before then, but these contacts were enough to stimulate some trade with fifteenth-century Europe. Tales of Timbuktu and other centers were filtered through Sijilmassa and Fez, each step of the filtration process seeming to embellish the image of these African cities. Gold, ostrich feathers and slaves were supplied to European cities from the great bend of the Niger via the tortuous desert routes.

At the beginning of the fifteenth century the Portuguese developed a better sailing technology and reached Cap Vert in 1444.[5] This maritime outflanking of the Sahara trade routes ultimately spelled the doom of the interior cities as well as of the camel caravans: Gao, Segou, Djenne, and Timbuktu faded as the stage was being set for city growth along Africa's coasts. Future urban sites were generally at river mouths revealing potential routes of easy access to the lands behind the coast.

St. Louis

The mouth of the Senegal River north of Cap Vert, provided the site for the settlement of St. Louis—one of the first colonial outposts south of the Sahara. An abortive attempt to establish a settlement here began in 1488 when the Portuguese conspired with Bemoy, who claimed to be the leader of a large empire of Wolof people and who was killed in a quarrel with his Portuguese escorts.[6] The town was not established then and it was left to the French trading companies in the early seventeenth century to create the settlement that later became St. Louis. The town was, in reality, a fortified trading post which was christened St. Louis du Senegal (after Louis XIV) in 1659. The French factories (warehouses) were important in the development of a number of Senegalese urban centers, but of these St. Louis remained the most important until this century.[7] Thus the *développement St. Louisien* on the Senegal River became the chief commercial location for the western Sudan, as well as a key administrative center for France's West African empire. But the town at the mouth of the Senegal was not to remain unchallenged as a settlement site in this region. Competition from Gorée Island (and later Dakar), in the area of Cap Vert, made inroads on the position of St. Louis during the late eighteenth century and throughout the nineteenth.

Gorée

The growth of French contact with the Cap Vert area increased rapidly from 1677, after the Dutch (who had been there since 1629) had been defeated and as trade developed with the Africans. Slaves became the chief item of commerce once it appeared that gold supplies were smaller than first anticipated. So lucrative was the trade in human beings, and so intense was the competition that European powers fought for fortified trading places such as Gorée. Indeed, Gorée changed ownership many times from the seventeeth to the nineteenth centuries; through these changes from Dutch to French and then back and forth between English and French, and through these slaving activities, a kind of cosmopolitanism was imparted to the settlement. People from different nations, African and European, slave and slaver, melded to create a distinct cultural group.

The Gorée settlement at its height in the early nineteenth century had a population of five thousand, and of those who worked, almost all were engaged in commerce or administration.[8] The architecture reflected the functions: Large stone warehouses with numerous chambers were constructed, many with sea-level doors for direct access to the holds of the slaving vessels. A prison and other fortified buildings were complemented by residences and a church built in the style of southern France.

Gorée had a good harbor and rapidly became an *entrepôt* of importance. At a macroscale Gorée and Cap Vert offered much in terms of location. To the traders going from Europe around the Horn to the Orient, this point was important for victualing their ships; for those coming from the north, it was the first green place beyond the dun-colored Saharan and Sahelian regions; for those coming from the south it was a welcome harbor compared to treacherous sites in the Bight of Benin. For the Atlantic trade the Gorée-Cap Vert area was the springboard for the Americas, and many of the original black population of Brazil and the Caribbean passed through the stone halls of Goree before this trade was suppressed early in the nineteenth century.

With its insular position Gorée also was secure from surprise attack, and until the French military presence became important in the nineteenth century this was an important factor. Once the effect of French arms had been felt other trading centers developed. Gorée was ideally situated as a nodal point through which trade was funneled, but Gorée traders felt that their base for trade could be widened by the development of trading outposts on the mainland; penetration and pacification of the hinterland were prescribed and performed. New towns were given impetus by the military operations of Captain (and Governor) Louis Faidherbe. Dakar was formally established in 1857. Rufisque, on the coast south of Dakar, gained permanent commercial installations in 1860, although it had been a small trading port for nearly two hundred years. At Thiès, in the interior, a post office was established in 1864.[9] Further south, in the Sine-Saloum river area, Kaolack was founded by soldiers on the site of a Serere village.[10]

The establishment of these towns came at the end of the trade in slaves and at the beginning of the peanut trade, a commodity much in favor in Europe for making soap. France actively encouraged the growth of oil seeds in its empire to meet the demand for vegetable oils at home. Nowhere did the leguminous roots take firmer hold than in the soils between Louga, Kaolack and Thiès. From this triangular region the main support base grew, and except for a perceptible southward shift in the intensity of peanut cultivation within the triangle, this region continued to sustain the Senegalese economy until the postcolonial era.

Given the economies of peanut production new lines of penetration were extended into the interior: From the Cap Vert settlement a rail line was run through the peanut region, thereby stimulating the greater growth of that crop, and also the growth of various inland towns. To the north, St. Louis still commanded the seasonal water route to Kayes on the upper Senegal, while the river ports of Matam and Bakel developed new institutions and installations unlike those of the precolonial era. In the south, British influence in the Gambia River cut into French West African imperial ambitions.

In rapid sequence around the turn of the century the interior settlements developed from villages with a European store into towns with varied functions. This growth was especially vigorous with the coming of Levantine traders (mostly Christians from Lebanon escaping Turkish repression) who manned many of the stores of the big French commercial houses. The Lebanese have played an especially important role in the urban development of Senegal. In 1897, there were only ten Lebanese in Senegal, but by 1929 there were well over two thousand.[11] By the end of the colonial period there were few settlements of any size that did not have at least one Lebanese merchant acting as both importer and exporter of goods and products.

With the establishment of the French naval base at Gorée, and with the successful expansion of the peanut trade, the island could no longer cope with its own activities. It became obvious that a move to the mainland was both feasible and desirable. The colonial period began in 1857 when Dakar was officially founded by J.M.F. Pinet-Laprade, the commandant of the Gorée garrison. Laprade, who became governor of Senegal in 1865, viewed Dakar and the Cap Vert region as something more than a place for overspill from Gorée. He believed that Dakar was an excellent location from which to consolidate France's position in Senegal. He and two fellow commissioners reported to Governor Faidherbe in 1863:

> In sum, the harbor of Gorée and Dakar, by its geographical position, by the fortifications which protect it, and as we will soon see, by the commercial interests which it represents, is the most important port in all of

> West Africa. That is why we must focus our naval operations there and organize it as an important maritime establishment. This is the unanimous belief of the Commission.
>
> If we now look at the question only from the point of view of our interests on the West African coast we shall demonstrate that in the near future we must establish the seat of government of the colony on the peninsula of Cap Vert.[12]

By 1865, the main trade passed through Cap Vert rather than through St. Louis giving Dakar the economic push needed for subsequent growth.[13] Since that time Dakar has continued to acquire functions at a relatively greater rate than St. Louis.

The official founding of Dakar was preceded by a build-up of relationships between Gorée and the mainland, beginning with the actual ceding of much of the Cap Vert peninsula to the French by the local African leader between 1764 and 1787. France did not relinquish legal authority until 1960, the termination date of the colonial period. As has already been mentioned, Goréen commercial houses had been established at the village of Dakar and at Rufisque, but it is also true that the French had attempted to gain a foothold on the peninsula by the 1840s. In 1817, a private colonial society tried, and failed, to establish a commercial agricultural community on Cap Vert.[14] A Catholic mission, a cemetery (the dead had also overpopulated Gorée), and some extensive defensive installations were created by 1845–46 (Fig. 2).[15]

Much of the direction of Dakar's early growth came by virtue of policies developed in France; in 1857, new postal lines were established between France and South America and sound bunkering facilities were decided upon for Dakar.[16] By 1862, at the behest of the Minister for the Colonies, heavy construction was begun on Dakar port. Further development of the town occurred with the completion of the Dakar-St. Louis railway in 1885, but, as Peterec observes, Dakar faced continuous commercial competition from Rufisque (which had become an outlet for peanuts) until the turn of the century.[17] Gorée too, was still important, because it retained its governmental functions for the administration of the southern half of Senegal.

The turning point of this century was also a turning point for Dakar. In 1895, a decision to co-ordinate the policies of the diverse colonial entities within the French West African empire was implemented, and St. Louis (then capital for Senegal) became the seat for this expanded governmental activity. This choice of a governmental seat was short-lived however, and in 1902 Dakar was selected as the permanent capital for Afrique Occidentale Française. This decision in turn, stimulated the local Chamber of Commerce of Dakar to develop a new commercial port to complement the construction of a new French naval base, begun in 1898. By 1910, there were new wharves, warehouses and open stores for private trade as well as a rapidly increasing number of French military personnel.

Thus, by the end of the first decade of this century Dakar had managed to eliminate Gorée and St. Louis (and, in a commercial sense, Rufisque) from a competitive position in the developing system of Senegalese towns. Gorée was too limited in size; St. Louis had always been plagued by the necessity of dredging sand bars in the Senegal River and, too, the completion of the rail link to Dakar

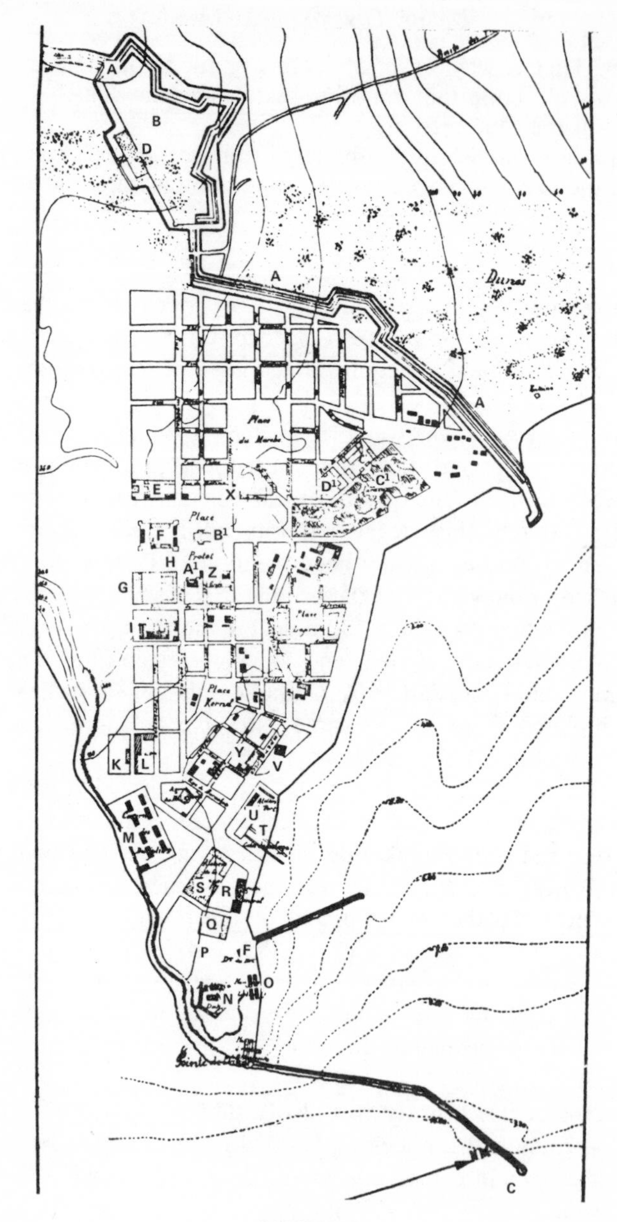

LEGEND

A. Fortifications*
B. Fort*
C. Lighthouse*
D. Troop Quarters*
E. Troop Quarters*
F. Old Fort
G. Official Guest Quarters*
H. Church*
I. Prison
K. Artillery*
L. Arsenal
M. Military Prison
N. Battery
O. Cool Sheds
P. Port Offices*
Q. Port Offices*
R. General Warehouse
S. Shipworks*
T. Shipworks*
U. Shipworks
V. Customs*
X. Chamber of Commerce*
Y. Warehouses
Z. School
A^1. Police Station
B^1. Church*
C^1. Government House*
D^1. Administration*

*Planned but not constructed.

FIG. 2 Dakar, 1870. Scale, 1:5,000. *Adapted from J. Charpy's* La Fondation de Dakar

in 1885 rechanneled some of the flow of goods away from St. Louis toward Dakar's new port facilities. The port at Rufisque was physically not capable of handling large-scale operations. Dakar had been named as the center for the West African empire and from 1910 forward the town developed into a true colonial capital, setting the frame of reference for the contemporary city.

THE COLONIAL CITY OF DAKAR

Dakar's status as a colonial capital city was firmly established at the beginning of this century; and continued to develop within the context of colonialism until the late 1950s when Senegal, by then an autonomous, self-governing unit in the French African communauté ruptured most of its formal linkages with the French state. During the half century or so of colonial tutelage, Dakar grew in the image of colonial cities everywhere, and prospered by its ties to the *métropole* Paris. These ties led to the articulation of new functional relationships between Dakar and the rest of Africa, and within Senegal itself. These ties also led to the growth of new local functions expressed in the physical development of the city.

It is a convenient artifice to assert that cities exist as points and areas at the same time—but not at the same scale. At a macroscale one can view a city as a bundle of energy, ideas and aspirations focused at a point, interacting with other similar modes in different places. At the same time, but at a microscale, a city can be seen as an array of land uses, ethnic neighborhoods, transportation lines and more, comprising a holistic functional structure. One refers to the microscale as the *site* characteristics, and to the macroscale as the *situational* characteristics. Such distinctions are useful to make in treating colonial Dakar. Some point or situational characteristics of the city have already been touched on in the previous section, for example, Dakar's placement on that part of Africa closest to the Western Hemisphere. The purpose of this section is to fill out these point characteristics and to introduce the area or site characteristics.

Dakar as a Point of Colonial Attachment

Colonial cities are points of attachment between the agencies, public and private, of the "mother country" and a vast hinterland of producers and consumers in the colony. The colonial city is a commercial *entrepôt* and a mediator in bureaucratic relationships. The colonial city is the point, when "looking into" the colonial region, through which trade goods are funneled (rather than a point at which they are produced), and through which authority is passed (rather than generated). "Looking out" from the region provides an inverse view of the role of the colonial city, wherein primary products are directed at the entrepôt capital, and obeisance tends to flow in the same direction. Succinctly, the colonial city is *dominated* by conditions and decisions made in places removed from the city itself largely because it lacks a strong economic base from which authority may be asserted.

Dakar became, in the half century of French development, an archetypical representative of a colonial city, and by the end of that era it had almost assumed a *métropole* status of its own for French West Africa. No city in French West Africa grew as rapidly or to such size and grace as Dakar. In 1921, Dakar had a population of thirty-three thousand, while its major French West African competitors, Abidjan and Bamako, were only half its size. Dakar sat at the top of a reasonably well-developed urban hierarchy spread over nearly two million square miles.[18] As such it proved to be a major pole of attraction for many intra-African migrants. With 375,000 inhabitants in 1961. Dakar remained at the pinnacle.

Naturally, Dakar was also dominant at the national scale, yet it was supported by a surprisingly strong secondary urban system, which suggests the generative capabilities of strong "growth poles" (Table A). By 1964, there were six towns with populations between thirty thousand and eighty thousand. This secondary tier was itself supported at the next level by fifteen towns with populations between five thousand and thirty thousand. Each of these towns at the lower levels showed remarkable growth between 1949 and 1964 (a period for which general records are available); it is not surprising that much of this growth may be attributed

TABLE A
Towns of Senegal, 1964*

Level	*Town*	*Population*	
I	Dakar	374,700	(1961)
II	Thiès	77,000	
	Kaolack	69,200	(1961)
	St. Louis	53,000	
	Rufisque	49,700	(1961)
	Ziguinchor	31,600	
	Diourbel	31,000	
III	M'Bour	18,700	
	Louga	17,600	
	Tambacounda	12,700	
	Tivaouane	9,200	
	M'Backé	9,100	
	Fatick	8,700	
	Bambey	8,000	
	Kolda	8,000	
	Guinguineo	8,000	
	Bignona	7,000	
	Matam	7,000	
	Podor	5,700	
	Gossas	5,500	
	Meckhe	5,500	
	Dagana	5,400	

* *Source:* République du Sénégal, *Le Peuplement du Sénégal,* Tome II, Dakar, 1966.

to Dakar's colonial functions. Each of the towns listed under II in Fig. 3 were administrative subcenters in their own right.

Dakar, then, developed as an extension of Parisian authority and rested at the crest of a colonial hierarchy that included the state capitals of Afrique Occidentale Française (A.O.F.), the regional capitals of Senegal and a host of lower order settlements.[19] From this vantage point it oversaw the workings of empire and responded with a major growth of functions.

Population has been used here as a crude indicator of hierarchy, but other, more refined, indicators such as variety and density of functions, lend even greater credence to Dakar's primary role in French West Africa. Additional important functions illustrate Dakar's paramount position; government, transportation, education, commerce and industry are good examples that lend themselves to a scalar view.

Government activity is crucial to the colonial city, and Dakar exhibited an accretion of bureaucratic functions during the colonial era that was unparalleled in any West African city. From 1902 onward, the offices of the French West African territories were located there. It was a major center for the processing of messages from France to the territories and those returning from the colonies. Military units, naval, land and later air, were dispatched from Dakar to points of friction in other colonies. Inspection teams for public health, justice or commercial research went from Dakar to the interior towns of West Africa. In any number of colonial functions Dakar served as the base camp for Paris. Within Senegal, Dakar functioned as the territorial capital too. Here again was found a bureaucracy associated with a lower order organization, the state of Senegal, carrying out many of the same functions that were played on a larger scale for French West Africa.

Below this level were the headquarters for the Région de Cap Vert (one of seven in Senegal), and those of the city of Dakar.[20] Table B, p. 448, is a simple model which indicates these surrounding areas.

Much of the same scalar model could be applied to Dakar's role as a major node in the *transportation* hierarchy because it served as an international center unsurpassed by any of the other French West African cities, or for that matter by any in Africa south of the Sahara until recently. Air-route connectivity, sea freight tonnage unloaded, passengers per rail mile carried are only three measures of Dakar's prime nodal role. On a territorial scale, Dakar is the base for most of Senegal's bus and trucking companies, not to mention taxis. Curiously, Dakar is also the hub of inland waterways traffic, in terms of tonnage shipped on the rivers Casamance and Senegal even though neither river mouth is within a hundred miles of Dakar's port: River traffic leaves from Dakar.

Educational hierarchies were much the same; Dakar's facilities were far superior to the other territories. From the top level down Dakar dominated the scene: It had, during the last years of the colonial period, the only university in French West Africa and this a completely integrated member of the French university system. This fact, along with its array of good technical institutes and secondary schools, attracted many Africans from the other French colonial territories. This phenomenon operated at the territorial and regional scales as well. Dr. Schacter, for example, writes of the role that the Lycée William Ponty (located in the metropolitan area rather than Dakar proper) played in the development of French West African elites and national leadership:

> The high political, civil service, and commercial posts which graduates of Ponty occupied after 1945 demonstrate that calling that institution the prewar Oxford of French West Africa is no exaggeration.[21]

In the case of *commerce,* most of the large firms of Paris, Bordeaux and Marseille that became established in Africa had their headquarters in Dakar.

From there, branch offices were placed in the interior of Senegal, in the Gambia and in Soudan. Some of these firms used Dakar as a home base for retail outlets in Guinea and in the French states of the Benin Coast, but, in general, the commercial circuits were established with branch offices in places like Abidjan or Lomé reporting directly to France. Dakar was the most important of these bases even though the offices in the other territories were not directly dependent on Dakar.

In Senegal itself most of the imports came through Dakar's fine port where they were repackaged into units consonant with the scale of internal trade, and then shipped to the interior. In some rare instances goods were shipped directly from France to the interior, but these shipments were minimal compared to those directed to Dakar. Rail shipment of bulk goods to the north and the upper Senegal went through St. Louis; in the latter part of the colonial era trucking became more important than rail shipment.

The bulk-breaking function of Dakar occurred mostly in the warehouses of the major French firms and in a few of Lebanese management. Most of the trucking, however, was in Lebanese hands, as were the shops of the interior. The Lebanese often employed African traveling salesmen who completed the distribution function.

Normally one would not expect a colonial city to develop an *industrial structure,* but Dakar, because of its location and its wide web of authority, did develop a relatively large number of manufacturing firms, particularly those of an assembly or processing nature. For instance, petroleum refining facilities were established at Dakar to service the heavy bunkering needs of ships. This was truly an entrepôt function because Senegal (and French West Africa) had no petroleum resources of its own, and consumed little of the total tonnage off-loaded.

Some regionally oriented plants did develop such as truck and passenger vehicle assembly, matches, Bata shoes, wine bottling, a phosphate and a cement processing plant, and cloth printing. These were located at Dakar (or between Dakar and Rufisque). Products of these plants were shipped to other parts of the French West African community, and the industries were indirectly subsidized by guaranteed governmental protection through tariffs for these products and for industrial products from France.

These regional industries distributed their goods within Senegal too and were complemented by a host of territorially oriented secondary producer firms. Processed foods such as beer and yogurt are typical of industries with a territorial orientation, and almost all of these were concentrated in Dakar. Naturally Dakar has its measure of purely locally oriented industries like bakeries and newspapers, and it has them in quantities far disproportionate to the per capita average for the Senegalese urban population. In per capita as well as in absolute terms Dakar had a much higher proportion of the population engaged in industry than at any other point on the colonial hierarchical scale.

In summary for all of these *point* characteristics, Dakar was relatively and absolutely dominant at every level of the hierarchy. This roughshod dominance in government, transportation, education and commerce that showed up on a macroscale is also revealed at the microscale when points expand into areas and land use patterns emerge. The examination of the *area* characteristics that follows serves as a good springboard for a discussion of changes wrought on both scales as Senegal shifted from colonial to postcolonial existence.

The Colonial Impress on Land Use

City-forming processes are a series of intricate sets of interactions between men, and between man and his physical environment. The discussion of the development of French colonial influence in Senegal in the preceding section showed Dakar to be a node in the colonial system, and it is not surprising that the colonial impress is evident in the patterns of land use within the city. From the first colonial settlement at the port to the indigenous residential fringes, land uses evolved largely in response to French needs. It would be callously ethnocentric and patently wrong to minimize the important influences of other peoples than the French on the development of the internal spatial structure of Dakar, but it would be equally wrong not to make clear the overriding French role. Flags of all stripes and colors over Dakar seemed to have flapped in time to the "Marseillaise"!

Since 1964, Dakar has been circumscribed by a boundary reaching nearly twenty miles east of the built-up area, but for most of this discussion the land boundary is taken to be the edge of the built-up area, appropriately defined by the route Front de Terre. In its broad definition Dakar encompasses virtually all of the peninsula of Cap Vert, an area of two hundred square miles.[22] The central built-up area is approximately ten square miles.

The configuration of the land is that of a series of scallops between headlands. These scallops, for the most part, are thin sandy beaches backed by rocky cliffs up to one hundred and fifty feet high. Three exceptions to this regularity are the wide beaches of Hann and Soumbedioune, and the port of Dakar itself; these two beaches are loci for fishing villages, and the port is the center of Dakar's economic activity.

North of the coastal promontory of Cap Manuel is the high point of the city proper and it is from here that Dakar begins to slope to a virtual plain approximately twenty-five feet above sea level. This higher Plateau area enjoys the full benefit of Dakar's fine climate, especially the healthful sea breezes and better drainage—two factors of importance in tropical cities. Conversely, the flat interior, extending northward from a line between Pointe de Dakar and the beach at Soumbedioune does not have the advantages of the Plateau. The heavy rains of July through September cascade down the streets of the Plateau, but lay stagnant, unruffled by the wind, in the interior. Other elevated points, such as Bel-Air and Fann are localized areas, like the Plateau, that escape the unpleasant conditions of the interior.

The harbor of Dakar is a gem in West Africa—it is deep and it faces east, thereby avoiding the direct onslaught of the Atlantic waves.[23] There are large portions of the harbor with usable depths to forty feet and, in all, the port covers more than five hundred acres studded with numerous piers.[24]

Dakar is divided into six major areas, each having its own internal divisions and some degree of cohesion. Figure 3 shows downtown Dakar, Medina, Grand Dakar, Fann-Pointe E, S.I.C.A.P., and an assemblage of peripheral areas.[25] Except

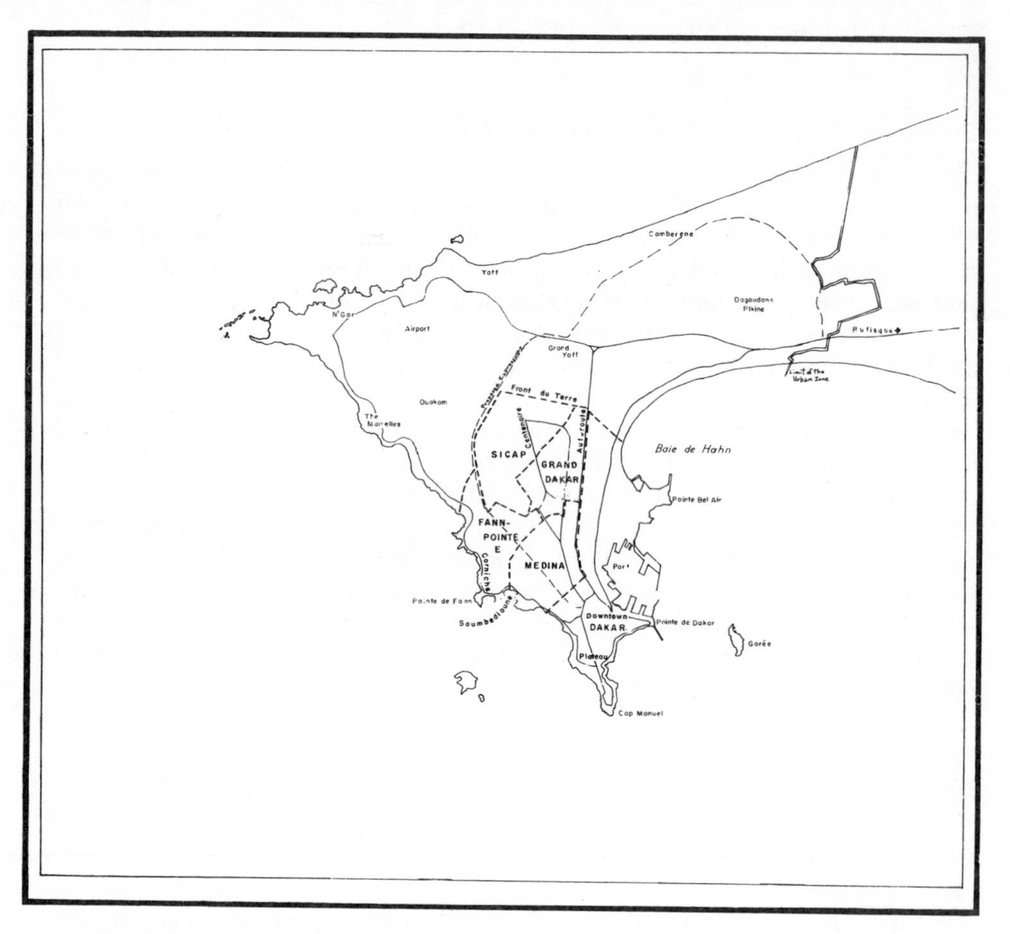

FIG. 3 Cap Vert, 1967. Scale, 1:50,000.

for the last category the other areas are within the built-up area. Each of them reflects some attempts to guide urbanism over more than a century of growth.

Downtown Dakar

Downtown Dakar is the original core of settlement of the town and the *port* is the economic hinge for the whole city. During the colonial era the port accreted functions and physical structures. Peterec has mapped the changes in the port from 1900 to 1950, showing especially the jetty and pier development in the earlier years and more recently, warehousing and bunkering facilities.[26] Permanent population in the port area is very limited (chiefly French small businessmen) but there are some small hotels and bars on the periphery of the area. The heart of the port is the assortment of port facilities themselves, offices of shipping firms and some government offices. Here too is found the main station and headquarters of the Dakar-Niger railway which played so important a role in tying together the colonial web. The northern edge of this zone includes a number of bulk-processing industries.

Immediately south of the port zone is a triangular area whose apex points at Gorée. This is the CBD, or European commercial core. It is a modern sector of high-rise apartments and hotels, banks, department stores, company head offices, cafés and boutiques. Most of these facilities are either occupied or run by the French. Exceptions to this commercially oriented zone are some government buildings and a military installation overlooking the southern coast.

The obvious focal point of this sector is the Place de l'Indépendance (Fig. 4), a large, manicured square surrounded by some of the city's most luxurious buildings. There is also an important secondary core at the Kermel Market a few blocks to the east. This market for fresh produce and meats is unusual for an African city in that many of the stalls are manned by French nationals, a fact that reveals the existence of a white *petit-bourgeois,* a result of long-standing French influence in the area. The clientele too is mostly French, or the African household employees of the French and other Europeans. Another interesting cultural characteristic is evident in the market and in nearby shops and restaurants: There is a great demand for Vietnamese food items by African veterans of the Indochina conflict and their Indochinese wives.

South of the European commercial sector, is the Plateau, a prestigious area that is sharply divided between national government buildings (ministries, hospitals, military areas, National Assembly and the Hall of Justice) and élite residential dwellings. Virtually all of the coastal land and the tip of the peninsula is reserved for public buildings, but the northern and central portions of the sector are covered with single-family villas punctuated with an occasional modern high-rise apartment. This is an extremely attractive area of radial streets and impressive round points. During the colonial era most of the population here was French, but now it is inhabited by high Senegalese officials and by the international diplomatic corps (Fig. 5).

This high-class residential area grades into an area of *Lebanese commerce* and apartment dwellings to the north and into some dismal African residences to the northwest. For many years the busiest section of the city has been the area around Sandaga Market, where Levantine cloth and hardware merchants lent vitality to an already colorful street life. Down the side streets are found Lebanese wholesaling houses and trucking companies. Seck estimates that this area has over half of the personal service and business service establishments of the city and fully two thirds of the wholesale houses.[27] Many of the resident population of the area are Lebanese who live above their stores, but here too are very crowded African apartments, called *barraques.* The population in this zone is heterogeneous, having attracted Cap Verdians, Mauritanians and a number of migrants from the economically depressed region of the Senegal River.

Directly west of this area is one of poor and unsanitary African housing lined up on unpaved streets. The population density is very high and there are many unemployed who seek work in the adjacent business center. This area, called Rebeuss, is now scheduled for renovation.

Downtown Dakar is heterogeneous in virtually every way—mixed land uses, public and private ownership, architecture, street patterns, radial in some parts, checkerboard in others, ethnic groups, population density to mention a few. Downtown Dakar gains what unity it may be said to have through its modern commercial

FIG. 4 The Chamber of Commerce, long-time symbol of French influence, dominates the magnificent Place de l'Indépendance. *Photograph by John Sommer*

and governmental functions, through its focus on the port and through its concentration of decision making.

The basic grid plan of Pinet-Laprade certainly was the guiding force in the layout of Downtown Dakar, but this did not prevent adaptations to enhance the attractiveness of the city. In typical French baroque style, squares and round points were strategically placed; the main commercial arteries of William Ponty, Avenue Roume, and Avenue de la République are tree lined, and a handsome twisting coastal boulevard runs along most of the peninsula.

Probably the greatest anomaly in the existing land use pattern of Downtown Dakar is a residual effect from the colonial era. A substantial portion of the most attractive and salubrious ocean-front land is reserved for military camps. This is true in other parts of Dakar as well, chiefly in Fann-Pointe E and further

FIG. 5 The exclusive Plateau area has more green space than other parts of Dakar. *Photograph by John Sommer*

to the northwest near the Mamelles. This situation is recognized by the present government and the latest city plan outlines the transition of this land to residential use.[28] What is not clear is whether most of the residences along the shore front will be inhabited by military personnel or the general citizenry.

The Medina

For the first half century of Dakar's existence there was little formal ethnic segregation, but after 1914–15 when the city suffered a serious outbreak of bubonic plague latent European desires to separate the African residences from their own led to the creation of an indigenous town: the Medina. The Medina was separated from the built-up area by a "hygienic zone" roughly a half-mile wide, and Africans were encouraged (but not forced) to take up residence therein. A grid plan of small blocks and wide streets was laid out, first in the eastern portion near the industrial zone, and later to the west toward the Bay of Soumbedioune. The Medina was bounded on the north initially by the canal of Gueule Tapée, but later by an immense drainage ditch called Canal IV.

In its original conception 56 per cent of the land was allocated for residences, 36 per cent for transportation, and the remaining 8 per cent for public uses.[29] Buildings were to be created in durable materials rather than wood or straw, primarily for sanitary purposes, but this particular condition for development was honored in the breach. The effect of the building material provision was inhibitory to the resident Lebou villagers who had inhabited this area for centuries, but who were now threatened with displacement by the enfranchised Africans coming from the city of Dakar.[30] Their response was simply to rebuild straw homes in the courtyards of the newly constructed cement buildings, which were often owned by someone in their extended family. The obvious result was ever greater crowding.

This result was particularly unfortunate because public services of water, electricity and sewage were slow to be installed, thus making the Medina even less attractive to the African inhabitants of the city of Dakar who were not inclined to move there anyway because of the increased journey-to-work distance. In the late 1920s, the Medina's population was eight thousand, while twenty thousand Africans remained in the city. The initial flurry of planning in 1914 subsided and the Medina was left to stagnate for twenty years. At first the Medina grew slowly and unattended. Slum conditions also remained in the city of Dakar and continued to be a source of aggravation and concern to French officials. To their credit there were many efforts made to create low-cost public housing.[31] Between 1935 and 1938 some model housing projects were begun in the Medina, but their impact was nil.

In 1931, Toussaint, an architect, provided a visionary, and costly, plan for Dakar and the Medina, but it was so impractical that it was never implemented. Full public services (water, electricity and sewage disposal) were proposed for every house. One historian has pointed out that Toussaint's monumental fountains, full of allegorical reliefs derived from his conception of Africa's past, was a classic example of imposed European urbanism rather than an effort to meld diverse cultures into a true Eurafrican urban context.[32]

Much of that which was lacking in Toussaint's plan was promoted in the formal planning proposals of Lopez and his associates in the *Plan Directeur of 1945–1946*. Chief among these was zoning, previously eschewed in Dakar's development, and the establishment of "neighborhoods," each with its own public facilities. Some serious anthropological studies led Lopez to conclude that attention should be paid to African forms of residential layout and neighborhood divisions, but these plans were set aside in favor of driving a *grand boulevard* through the Medina, the Allées du Centenaire.

Throughout most of the period between the wars the Medina grew, largely unplanned, on its basic grid layout and dividing itself into five recognizable zones: Medina West (a), Medina East (b), Colobane (c), Fas (d) and Gueule Tapée (e). Medina West is the most attractive, and the best kept portion of the

Medina. The majority of the dwellings are cement, set on tree-lined streets and provided with water. On the seaside is a colorful government-inspired artisans' village and a small cluster of personal service establishments, but Medina West, like most of the Medina and adjacent Grand Dakar, lacks strict functional differentiation. Residences are mixed with small shops and here and there are limited medical and educational facilities.

Medina East extends to the autoroute and is bounded on the south by the remnants of the hygienic zone of 1914. This hygienic zone is now given over to some extensive sport stadia and an Institute for Hygiene! Most of this sector, except for extensive renewal in the form of modern apartments and stores along Allées du Centenaire, has small houses of wood and straw. The streets are not paved and it appears to be more crowded than Medina West.

Separating Medina East from Colobane on the north is a large area devoted to the public waterworks. Colobane is pinched in between the autoroute and a new secondary school complex. This small, but densely packed area houses many of the original Lebou population who were pushed out of the Medina. Colobane is cohesive as a neighborhood even though it is more poorly developed physically than Medina East. Directly west of Colobane is Fas, an area that has abandoned the earlier grid plan in favor of a more helter-skelter placement of dwellings (most of which are straw or wood) due to the marshy character of the area where houses had to be placed carefully to avoid flooding. Lacking most public facilities it is easily understood how Fas could become a very unhealthy area; still there remains considerable open land used for garden agriculture. Farther west is Gueule Tapée with Lebou inhabitants who are fishermen with boats kept at Soumbedioune.

The Medina as a whole has been a catchment area for many tribes from all over Senegal, but it has caught mainly those who have "made it" in the city. There are other areas, more closely approaching the classic *bidonvilles* (squatter shack areas) where migrants live a temporary existence. The Medina is crowded to be sure: There are more than seventy thousand people in an area of one square mile, or to put this figure in more comprehensible terms, there are slightly more than two and one-quarter persons per room in the Medina.[33] Almost all of the Medina (Gueule Tapée excluded) is scheduled for extensive renovation under the latest *Plan Directeur,* but it can be postulated that this proposed renovation will meet with serious resistance from the residents who fear increased housing controls and possible raises in rents to finance change.[34] This fear is not unwarranted because the families displaced by the development of modern low-rise apartments on Allées du Centenaire discovered that even with government subsidies living costs there were too high. For the student of housing problems in developed areas too, this situation is all too familiar.

Whereas Downtown Dakar is functionally distinct, the Medina is not. It is unfortunate that more of the Lopez plan could not have been instituted so that greater cohesion could be brought to some of the subsectors. The Medina presents a face of general uniformity, punctuated by three focal points and two barriers to interchange. The activity at Soumbedioune, at the Thilene Market on the border between the east and west parts of the Medina, and the Allées du Centenaire pull the population apart, while the barriers of the canal at Gueule Tapée and the waterworks reduce effective movement of people and goods. The challenge of

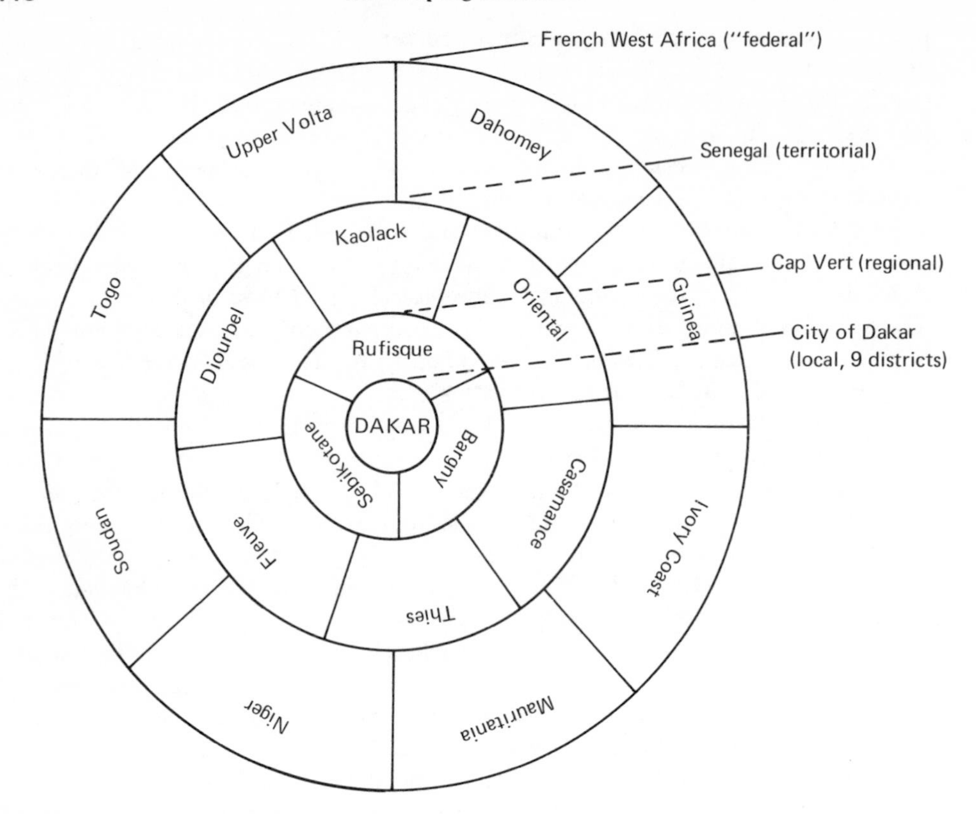

TABLE B. Scale model for the Dakar region and French West Africa.

the Medina to the planners is how to provide better public services, including transportation, and to create more cohesive nodes for local internal development.

Grand Dakar

Formerly Grand Dakar was considered to include all of the land north of Canal IV and west of the autoroute, but more recently the term has been applied to the area bounded by Rue 10 on the west, Avenue Bourguiba on the north, and the Fann-Bel-Air route on the south. Grand Dakar thus straddles the central axis of the extension of the Allées du Centenaire and is flanked by the largely uninhabited industrial zone on the east, and the luxurious, but relatively sparsely inhabited Fann-Pointe E to the west. To the north is Societé Immobilière du Cap Vert, with all of its modern structures.

Luxurious, modern, and lightly inhabited, Grand Dakar is not! This part of the city offers a variety of house types and neighborhood formations—and it offers some of the worst shack villages in the whole city. Here are very crowded conditions, especially in Mbode and Nimjat, where Seck estimates that 29,000 persons live on 110 acres.[35]

Grand Dakar has subsectors which are more easily identifiable than those of the Medina. This identifiability is probably due to the planned housing developments abutting areas of squatter homes, where the substantial differences in income levels are strikingly evident. In the squatter category one would place Mbode and Nimjat, while in the category of systematically developed residences one can group Zone A, Bop, Ouagou Niaye, Cité Port du Commerce and Cité de la Douane.

Except for marked differentiation in land use and house types along the main arteries the rest of the sector may be thought of as the "true" Grand Dakar. What is the character of this residual sector which we may refer to as Grand Dakar proper?

Grand Dakar proper is located between routes 10 and 13, and covers approximately 220 acres. More than thirty thousand persons live there. Many of the residents were there prior to Independence so it is not a transient community, yet this portion of the city receives many Africans directly from the "bush." The population is extraordinarily heterogeneous and the street life is made especially colorful by the different styles of dress and the various languages spoken.

This sector has a grid plan—often ignored—and plots are unofficially subdivided by the local inhabitants who occasionally place a lumberyard, a charcoal pile, or an animal stockade where an intersection should be. Land uses are highly mixed as residences vie with tiny food stores for space. Perhaps the chief perceived regularity in the land use pattern is the inevitable Mauritanian trader's shop on each corner of virtually every intersection. The Mauritanians are shrewd traders and they seem to have appropriated the optimum traffic locations for their businesses.

Some artisans such as carpenters and mattress makers are located throughout the subsector, and there is a small industrial clustering at the northern edge near a large cookie and biscuit factory. Among these establishments are metalworks, electrical repair shops and other small business operations run mostly by Senegalese.

The small dwellings are constructed of wood or of rattan covered with a lime plaster and both kinds sport tile roofs. There are also more durable houses, located chiefly near the main routes. Often several houses together surround an interior courtyard; contrary to the generally filthy streets, the interiors of the houses and the courtyards are immaculately swept and cleaned. The streets are unpaved sand and dirt and there is usually a mire around the public water facility located at the ends of most blocks. There are some public toilets, but much of the sewage is captured in latrines in the compounds. This area desperately needs better public facilities, but it has escaped renovation thus far.

Such is not the case with Mbode and Nimjat which have, since Independence, begun to undergo extensive redevelopment. During the colonial era these two areas grew into classic bidonvilles (Fig. 6). Shanty houses were placed anywhere space could be obtained and there were virtually no controls exerted over this growth. These areas were unsanitary and, it was alleged, socially disorganized to the point of interpersonal violence—unheard of elsewhere in Dakar. As a natural target for the urban planners, a great many new publicly financed apartments have steadily replaced the tin-roofed huts. Most of this work has been conducted by the Office of Low Rent Housing but the result, so far, has been to displace many of the slum dwellers to Dagoudane Pikine (a kind of "refugee-from-the-city" town several miles north of the built-up area) and to replace them with middle-income families.

As the names suggest, Cité de la Douane and Cité du Port de Commerce were constructed largely for the public officials who had positions in the port and customs agencies. Much of this construction was carried out during and shortly after World War II. The homes here, as in the rest of this zone, are mostly single-family, whose architectural form is characteristically block or "bubble," and they are tightly packed. These residential areas are now served by a full range of urban amenities;

there is an abundance of trees and some public play areas. Many of the houses, however, are beginning to show the stress of a quarter century of tropical sun and rain. At the southern and western limits of this subsector is a huge open area called Cerf-Volant, which has been reserved for future public development, but presently it is used for recreation and agriculture. In a cone-shaped area north of Cerf-Volant are found public medical and education facilities. Most of the population in this subsector are middle-level salaried employees in government (more than half of Senegal's salaried employees are on government payrolls). Some of them have private vehicles but only a few are of high enough status to command a government vehicle. The population here is even more stable than in Grand Dakar proper because of their positions in the middle-level bureaucracy, and one can sense an identifiable bourgeois neighborhood character to the area.

Grand Dakar is an area of contrast between Western planned urbanism in some subsectors and uncontrolled shanty-town development in other subsectors. Middle- and lower middle-class Africans rub elbows with the desperately poor and although some of the resulting friction may have tribal overtones, most of the discord comes from the adjacency of the urbanized and the not-yet-urbanized African. Thus far the planning programs, such as the housing developments in Mbode, have done more to remove (to Dagoudane Pikine) the problem than to solve it. Although the solution by displacement may be only a short-run answer, it may be the only one available to the Senegalese.

Fann-Pointe E

Fann-Pointe E presents no fewer, nor less striking differences than exist in Grand Dakar, but the social and economic scales are significantly higher. Whereas the modern sections of Grand Dakar housed the middle-level and lower-level officialdom and the middle to lower income salaried persons, the upper end of the Senegalese social and economic scale, as well as a significant portion of the wealthy foreign population live in Fann-Pointe E. It is a spacious and attractively designed suburb with substantial modern villas occupied by a mixture of diplomats and high Senegalese ministry officials. During the colonial era this sector was almost completely European, the most exclusive homes are located on the extreme west, facing the sea.

Fann-Pointe E also contains some of the earliest examples of the housing developed by the Société Immobilière du Cap Vert (S.I.C.A.P.), a quasi-governmental organization discussed in detail below. This sector has some major public services which occupy about half of the total area: the University of Dakar, Fann Medical Center and a military camp buffer the elite areas of Cité de Fann, and, to some extent, Pointe E, from the less prestigious subsector of Fann Hock. Many other services, particularly educational and governmental, are scattered throughout this sector. Curiously, Fann-Pointe E also harbors a large number of industrial establishments. Most of these establishments are private, universally French, and usually have their own housing for French employees attached to the firm. These industries have also been made inconspicuous by elaborate and attractive gardens, and by dense vine-covered fences and hedges. To a certain extent the development of personal goods and services, particularly food stores, reflects the economic standing of the population. Instead of the typical pattern of

FIG. 6 Women draw water from a public spigot in Dakar. *Photograph by John Sommer*

many tiny stalls scattered among the residences there are a few larger, modern specialized shops, for meats, pastries or bread.

Nowhere in Dakar, not even on the Plateau are there such chic, modern residences, as one finds here in Cité de Fann and along the Corniche to the north. Immediately north of the university grounds are found some of Dakar's most expensive homes and rental properties; there are about two hundred in this area. It is not uncommon for rents to exceed one thousand dollars a month. The streets are shaded by overhanging trees and brightened by brilliant tropical flowers in the gardens of virtually every home. This luxurious *quartier* is isolated from other residential areas by the large open spaces of the university and the hospital. Naturally there are a number of students and patients in residence in these facilities, but they are concentrated along the border of Pointe E.

In the center of Pointe E is an enormous egg-shaped park with recreational facilities and some vegetable gardens. Facing this park are some of Dakar's few charming homes made of stone. This subsector contains most of the industries of the whole sector and they are located in a peculiar way: ringing the zone. Mostly construction firms, there are also a Lebanese bakery, an African tanning and dyeing operation, and a French metal awning assembly plant. On the whole, this subsector comes the closest of any part of Dakar to the notion of a Eurafrican city. The population is mixed and living harmoniously at roughly the same economic levels. Several private kindergartens are filled with a heterogeneous population—children of all colors and mixtures are taught by a multihued set of teachers.

Located on a knob of land facing the Bay of Soumbedioune and Pointe de Fann, there are attractive villas along the Corniche (similar to those of Cité de Fann), backed by mixed housing and bordered on the east by low-income residences. Adjacent to the military camp on the north are some miserable two- and three-story apartments that house military dependents. This zone is purely African and there is a marked declining income gradient as one moves inland from the sea. A recent addition to Fann Hock has been the construction of a magnificent museum of African history overlooking Soumbedioune. Together with the artisans' village across the bay and the colorful fishing boats on the beach, this area is fast becoming an important tourist center. In 1952, about four hundred residences were constructed by S.I.C.A.P. in Fann Hock but they are much less attractive than those developed later.

Fann-Pointe E is an attractive and spaciously laid out area with considerable internal diversity in terms of population and land use. Current plans call for the continued development of luxury villas in the northern portion of Fann, which should help to expand the neighborhood contacts of foreigners and upper class Senegalese. At the present time there seems to be no threat to the ample public lands around the university and the hospital, nor are there plans to remove the military camp from its present location.

Most of the planned developments of Fann-Pointe E were constructed with Europeans, chiefly Frenchmen, in mind. Since Independence, with its attendant removal of many colonial authorities and the departure of a number of French businessmen, the pre-existing structures are being filled with other foreigners and increasingly with Africans. With this changed population one might expect some alterations in the structures to satisfy different tastes. For example, some Vietnamese restaurants and some specialized stores that catered to the French have already closed. Structural change, however, has been minimized because many of the Senegalese elite have, themselves, been reared in the context of western urbanism (in Paris as well as in Dakar) and are imbued with modern urban values. It is doubtful that this area will change its character significantly in the near future.

Before turning to a consideration of the sectors of S.I.C.A.P. and the outlying areas, to be treated in terms of the postcolonial period, it is useful to summarize some aspects of the impact of colonial authority on the internal spatial structure of Dakar.

Clearly the colonial impact on Dakar has been great. Port development in response to global French naval and commercial ambitions fixed a central focal point for the city, with a "spin-off" of adjacent industrial and commercial land uses. The placement of all levels of region-wide governance in Dakar brought large numbers of Frenchmen to the city and much of the residential and commercial structure that subsequently developed was attuned to their preferences. The takeover of high land overlooking the coastline for the development of military bases to support French global and regional policy presents an independent Senegalese government and the citizens of Dakar with gross anomalies in the land-use pattern. The economic vortex created by the various commercial and governmental functions attributable to the French sucked into Dakar large numbers of African migrants who were then compressed into such areas as the Medina and Grand Dakar. French prestige alone was probably a major contributing factor in Dakar's areal spread: It is alleged that De Gaulle, upon hearing that Churchill had designs to build Accra (then capital of the Gold Coast) into West Africa's greatest city, decreed that Dakar should not be surpassed.[36] The Lopez *Plan Directeur of 1945–1946* followed shortly thereafter.

Planned urbanism however seemed to be more of a reactionary force prior to 1950, but at mid-century, and especially with the turnover of the government in 1960 to the Senegalese, more long-range attention has been given to the direction and dimension of Dakar's future growth. It is only fair to add too that this greater attention may have been focused on urban problems in Dakar in these recent times because the problems themselves were greater and information about them more complete.

Two agencies of government have had an especially important role in directing the course of urbanism in Dakar. The Office des Habitations à Loyer Moderé (O.H.L.M.), office for Moderate Income Housing, and the Société Immobilière du Cap Vert (S.I.C.A.P.) made important advances in the Medina, Grand Dakar and Fann Hock during the colonial era, but since Independence there has been an enormous growth of new housing at the northern edge of Dakar, in the sector called S.I.C.A.P. (each subsector having its own name). Because much of what has transpired in S.I.C.A.P. during the last decade mirrors other aspects of urban planning in Dakar the remaining areas will be described along with the role of the two agencies mentioned above in their development.

S.I.C.A.P.

As the colonial era entered its last decade it was fast becoming obvious that Dakar had begun to mushroom upward and outward. The intense stimulation from wartime activity and the building momentum of the aggregation of functions at Dakar transformed the colonial capital city into a whirlpool whose outermost effects extended deeply into the African countryside. The 1955 census showed that there were two and one-quarter million Senegalese, of whom about one-half million were living in towns, half of them in Dakar. Urban population had jumped from less than 5 per cent of the total Senegalese in 1910 to more than 20 per cent by 1955 and to 27 per cent by 1964.[37] Likewise, Dakar grew from 25,000 in 1910 to 231,000 in 1955 and 375,000 in 1961.[38] The 1961 census confirmed many of the suspicions raised in 1955 and ominous predictions of a total urban population of two million or more by 1980 (representing more than 40 per cent of the Senegalese population), and a population for Dakar of about 1.1 million sent the planners hurrying to their conference rooms to decide on a feasible course of action.[39] It was clear that Dakar was growing and it seemed likely that it would continue to grow. Burgeoning bidonvilles were everywhere, and increasingly vocal, educated young Senegalese were without individual shelter. Two agencies, O.H.L.M. (public) and S.I.C.A.P. (quasi-public), played large roles in the attempt to meet the housing crisis and in guiding the urban thrust both vertically and horizontally (Fig. 7a, 7b).

Much of the vertical vector was stimulated by public housing programs under O.H.L.M. This office developed low-rise apartments focused on the axis of Allées du Centenaire and on the eastern margins of Grand Dakar, rather than on the new areas north of Avenue Bourguiba.

FIG. 7A O.H.L.M.'s earlier apartment buildings with ground-floor shopping facilities were developed for families. *Photograph by John Sommer*

The outward sprawl has been provided by S.I.C.A.P. with its extensive suburban development along the northern edge of Avenue Bourguiba, where more than three hundred acres have been covered with stylish single-family dwelling units (Fig. 8). S.I.C.A.P. is charged under the new plan to continue to develop land between Avenue Bourguiba and Front du Terre, and to fill in a large open area south of Avenue Bourguiba between Grand Dakar and Pointe E as well as in "the outlying areas."

O.H.L.M.

The Office of Low Cost Housing (O.H.L.M.) was established on the eve of Independence in 1959, heir to the activities of the Office of Economic Housing (O.H.E.) which had been in operation since 1926. O.H.L.M. under the Ministry of Public Works had the expressed purpose of "providing each citizen with healthy and comfortable shelter at a low rent"—a slogan expressing more good intentions than concrete projections.[40] The complexity of the task of housing everyone under these proposed conditions is simply too great and the staff and funds of the organization too small. An idea of the magnitude of the problem may be gained from the waiting list of persons desiring to rent dwellings—more than seven thousand in 1968! Urban housing demands have become so great that an Office of Rural Housing (previously within O.H.L.M.) had to

FIG. 7B Avenue Bourguiba sets highly modern S.I.C.A.P. (left) apart from Grand Dakar (right).

split off to meet nonurban problems while O.H.L.M. was left to confront the heavy urban housing demand.

O.H.L.M. has responsibility for all urban Senegal and it has developed low-rent housing for other major towns of the country, but it is fair to say that the preponderance of work carried out by the Office has been in the capital city. Of the roughly five thousand dwellings built between 1960 and 1970, three quarters were constructed in Dakar. Most of these flank the Allées du Centenaire or are in the redevelopment areas of Nimjat and M'Bode.[41] Within route Front de Terre, O.H.L.M. has built approximately three thousand units and has plans to build another three thousand in the triangle formed by the auto route, Avenue Bourguiba and the Nimjat housing project of H.L.M. to the south. Current work is focused in the Fas section of the Medina.

Beyond Front du Terre the principal target for O.H.L.M. (three thousand units built, three thousand planned) is Grand Yoff, where about two thousand units will be built. O.H.L.M. "is in the building business," to quote Roger Bocandé, director of O.H.L.M., but it has also been an overseer of some other urban renewal efforts such as the Medina Renovation of 1966 in Gueule Tapée. At first, O.H.L.M. was interested in housing families but now its desire is to provide housing for low-income single persons (mostly male migrants) as well.

Believing "that modern life makes vertical development imperative," O.H.L.M. has concentrated on multifamily dwellings, most of which have been two-story,

FIG. 8 Recent villa developments along Avenue Bourguiba are particularly valuable property. *Photograph by John Sommer*

four-room apartments. These apartments are attractively mixed in with single-story duplexes. Each concentration of O.H.L.M. housing also has a small complement of shops and personal service establishments, as well as play areas for children. The average four-room apartment has seven-hundred-plus square feet of living surface and rents for about forty dollars a month. This sum, while not large, is out of reach of many Senegalese whose monthly income is less than one hundred dollars. Nevertheless, the waiting list is long and a priority system has been established based on the family situation of the applicant, his present condition of lodging, the permanency of his employment and the length of time he has been applying for space. Rental fees may be applied toward the purchase of the property, a process that takes fifteen years to complete.

In the first decade of its operation O.H.L.M. has tried to alleviate some of Dakar's housing problems, and it has accomplished much in providing adequate shelter for low salaried families. It has not met the problem of the truly poor who cannot afford even the most meager rents (fifteen dollars a month) in O.H.L.M. housing. If the new in-migrant does not have relatives upon whom he can depend, and if he does not qualify (and most do not) for O.H.L.M. housing, he must squeeze into the bidonvilles, move to Pikine or return to his village. There is no truly low-cost, sanitary and comfortable shelter in Dakar!

Peripheral Areas

But what of the operations of S.I.C.A.P. in its extensive development of residential and commercial properties on the expanding perimeter of the city? Do these developments offer a solution to urban crowding? Answered tersely, no! The major thrust of S.I.C.A.P. in the last decade has been to provide housing for middle and upper income salaried families in an attractive suburban setting. Stated matter-of-factly by one high official at S.I.C.A.P., "We build for the richer clients; O.H.L.M. for the proletariat."

S.I.C.A.P. was founded in 1949 during the colonial period by the Grand Council of French West Africa to help meet the crisis of lodging and urban amelioration in all of the associated states, but in practice its operations were focused on Dakar.[42] The organization was founded as a "mixed society," meaning a joint public and private venture; the reality of the situation has been that S.I.C.A.P. is very closely identified with the government since private capital never exceeded 10 per cent of the total funding of its approximately twenty million dollars. Financing for the operation of S.I.C.A.P. comes from loans from the central bank and from French foreign aid.

Twenty years have passed since the first dwellings were constructed under the auspices of S.I.C.A.P.; these two decades lend a time perspective not offered by the operations of O.H.L.M. The scale of S.I.C.A.P. is much greater than that of O.H.L.M., and, apparently, more in favor with the government; S.I.C.A.P., for example, has almost five times the number of employees of O.H.L.M.

The earliest developments of S.I.C.A.P. were on the edge of Grand Dakar in 1951 and in Fann Hock in 1952, both within the limits of Avenue Bourguiba. This early housing was of a low-cost, low-rent quality. From 1952 until 1966, S.I.C.A.P. concentrated on the area north of Avenue Bourguiba, filling in a vast terrain with beautifully laid out row houses and single-family dwelling units. Since 1966, S.I.C.A.P. has engaged in filling in vacant land south of Avenue Bourguiba, and in expansion toward Front de Terre. S.I.C.A.P. constructed over 13,700 dwellings between 1951 and 1968; 6,200, north of Avenue Bourguiba and 7,400, south, thus providing lodging for nearly 50,000 people. The present goal of the organization is to develop about seven hundred dwellings a year, which, if one accepts the density figure for the previous 7,400 units, would mean new shelter for 5,000 persons per year. This rate of development is impressive in the context of the problems faced in mobilizing large-scale construction, but it is not impressive relative to the growing need for shelter. S.I.C.A.P.'s effort can meet only one third of the new demands each year. Together with O.H.L.M., no more than one half of new housing needs are being met, and the few private real estate corporations operating in Dakar are not operating on a scale that will satisfy the remaining need, especially since most of the dwellings constructed by these firms are very expensive.

S.I.C.A.P. provides the option of rental or rental with intent to buy. In the first case about 2,500 units rent for about twenty dollars a month. These are small, mostly older houses or apartments with electricity, running water and a garden. The second category, most of which are row houses or free standing units, permits ownership to pass from S.I.C.A.P. to the individual after ten years. Monthly rents for these dwellings are about fifty dollars. Since 1970, some very expensive rental villas also have been built.

The majority of the older, less expensive housing of S.I.C.A.P. is south of Avenue Bourguiba, while the newer areas to the north of this route house a uniformly wealthier population. Villas have dominated the most recent type of construction by the Society and it appears that future construction is aimed at this spatially extensive residential use. S.I.C.A.P. made one venture into high-rise apartments at a round point located at the junction of Avenue Bourguiba and Allées du Centenaire. Apartments in these buildings rent for nearly one hundred dollars a month and it is not surprising that racial segregation has followed income segregation, even within one of the wealthier sections of Dakar. According to Society authorities, the single-family residences in their suburb are about 95 per cent African, while the families in the apartments are about 80 per cent European, or are families of mixed marriages.[43] The better incomes of Europeans and the pressure of French wives of Senegalese men have helped to set this complex apart from the rest of the suburb.

The ground floors of these apartment buildings are given over to commercial uses—shops, banks, grocers, and a variety of services occupy some of the most modern commercial quarters in Dakar presenting a form of vertical zoning. In fact, in the initial conception of these chic suburbs it was determined that commerce would be limited and clustered in three places on the edge of the development.

S.I.C.A.P. has developed, in addition to residential and commercial properties, a fine sports complex, school areas and small parks. There has been, from the late 1950s to the present, a heavy emphasis within S.I.C.A.P. (and within the government) to develop suburbs in the image of a modern Western city. A brochure of the organization printed about 1961 reports:

> S.I.C.A.P. is definitely a true, modern agglomeration provided with all necessary amenities—lights, water, good roads, a commercial center, schools, parks, playgrounds, green spaces and flower gardens. This social infrastructure provides the whole with a human character unlike the soulless barragues.[44]

President Senghor, speaking publicly in 1962, was quoted as saying:

> The betterment of Man's habitat is called "the effort of civilization." This fact is manifest in the S.I.C.A.P. developments where the people spend less on frivolous things and more on furniture and on works of art . . . and they are creating a new civilization there, Negro African, and modern.[45]

In the effort to meet the image of a modern city, S.I.C.A.P. harked back to the old French colonial emphasis on sanitation in urban policy. The Society has imposed severe constraints on those who take up residence in the suburbs; the reverse side of S.I.C.A.P.'s rental agreement lists seventeen articles, many of them designed to maintain the appearance of the neighborhoods. There are strict rules regarding additions to houses, on refuse disposal and on the conduct of noisy activities, to cite a few. The rules applied in the S.I.C.A.P. suburb, however, are not generally applicable in Dakar, nor could they be applied without severe difficulty and conflict. In S.I.C.A.P.'s suburb, in fact, there have been gross breaches of the rental codes; for example, the location of commerce has been a sore issue that highlights the dilemma of trying to transfer a modern Western urban model to a different milieu.

Shopping facilities in the S.I.C.A.P. developments north of Avenue Bourguiba are limited to three locations, equally spaced along the avenue. The largest facilities are at the round point mentioned above and the other two are at one-half mile intervals southwest along the route. Each commercial facility, although located along the edge of the development, was expected to serve a substantial sector of the suburb. The stores are large, modern, relatively impersonal and not functional in the local context. Much of the space set aside for commercial activities has seen a procession of failing businesses. In 1968 and 1970, many store areas were unrented. Why could this be if the firms locating in these facilities were handed a virtual monopoly? The African resident's answer to legal monopoly has been to transfer purchase support to illicit shops that sprouted up in garages and in back yards, even though these minifirms are unsanctioned, and lacked the variety, cleanliness and attractiveness of the modern stores. Two chief factors accounted for this shopping orientation: traditional preference for neighborhood stores and low physical mobility.

Most of the shopping for family needs is done by the wife of the household and shopping for her is not a mere economic transaction, it is also a social event. Friends may be found at the store; the shopkeeper knows the woman and her family; and there is ample time for chatter and bargaining if she is not far from home. The larger stores, often run by French or Lebanese, do not provide a comfortable setting for traditional shopping behavior. It is true too that even though the S.I.C.A.P. developments have the facade of a modern society, modernization is only partial—a man may be well educated and hold a high position in the government, but his wife often lacks formal education and may not be far removed in life style from her rural relatives.

The inaccessibility of modern shops is a second factor that inhibits their use. The suburbs are spread out, automobile ownership is not widespread (and most women do not drive), bus service is inadequate and expensive, and the layout of the suburb does not allow for path development away from the roads. Virtually all movement for convenience shopping is done on foot, yet many of the residences in the S.I.C.A.P. development are a half mile or more from the nearest sanctioned commercial site. With the rise of illicit stores, this distance factor has shrunk so that no residence is removed from a shop by more than one sixth of a mile. On the other side of Avenue Bourguiba, in Grand Dakar, no residence is more than one hundred yards from a shop. It was the original desire of S.I.C.A.P. to break up this localized, traditional shopping pattern, typical of Grand Dakar, and to replace it with one of more "modern" dimensions—with little success to date.

This thirst for modernization permeates most aspects of Senegalese society, not merely its urban phase. Agricultural modernization, industrial development, international recognition are also urgent issues to the Senegalese leaders who wish to rush the nation into the pattern of a mid-twentieth century technocratic life style. In this drive many difficult factors of adjustment have been overlooked. Often more attention has been paid to the adoption of the structural concomitants of modernization, modeled on Western society, than has been paid to the functional bases within Senegalese society which may (or may not) provide the foundation for facilitating change (not necessarily toward a Western model).

During the first decade of independence Senegal has, by Africa's standards, been blessed with conditions of relative stability. Internal disorder has not threatened the state, nor have there been any serious external threats. Senegal has built up its industry, it has pushed for modernization in agriculture, and it has done much to make its capital city a gem of modern urbanism. These changes do not, however, make Senegal a modern society, nor do they imply that the state and its capital have begun an unretraceable march up the slope of an economic growth curve. The opposite effect is closer to the truth. The Senegalese economy began to slow down during decolonialization process of the late 1960s.

POSTCOLONIAL CRISIS

Virtually every former colonial territory has undertaken to reassert its politico-economic independence from its departed suzerain in the immediate years following the formal granting of independence. This exorcising of colonial devils may be viewed as a kind of "inoculation against neocolonialism," and the potions employed are as varied as the reactions they produce in these tropical states. The treatments generally share one overriding characteristic: They have been very costly for the new nation.

After the granting of autonomy to the former French West African states under the *loi-cadre* of 1956, followed swiftly by the granting of independence in 1960, these states arrayed themselves in a spectrum of independence from France. While Guinea broke completely with Paris and the Ivory Coast remained closely allied, Senegal sought the middle ground. The other states fitted into the interstices. Guinea's bid for absolute political independence was accepted, and Guinea in turn accepted the condition of absolute economic independence, a condition that included the termination of all French aid. The result in Guinea has been severe economic depression, internal conflict and heavy emigration. Ivory Coast politicians, instead, chose to devalue political independence in favor of continued French presence, public and private. French investment has crowded into the Ivory Coast, making it one of Africa's most active growth centers, and making Abidjan one of Africa's most rapidly developing cities.

The Senegalese tried to make the best of balancing tough anticolonial (and anticapitalist) talk with moderate practices. Unfortunately for Senegal this policy soon cost them the confidence of the business community (a part of which migrated to the Ivory Coast), and has reduced France's willingness to support Senegal's economy. The postcolonial crisis for Senegal, therefore, has been the accelerating depression of its economic system, brought on by the unwillingness of private investors to participate in the making of "African socialism," and by the unwillingness of France to continue to subsidize Senegalese peanut farmers through direct price support.[46] The characteristics of this crisis have been a drop in national output, especially in agriculture, a reduction in money circulating in the economy as the French and Levantine community have withdrawn, and incipient violence in rural areas as farmers have rebelled against supporting the urban elite. Naturally there are other consequences, but these are singled out here for special consideration.

The postcolonial crisis for Dakar is a reflection of economic conditions in Senegal, but there exists a lag effect that has allowed the capital city to retain an outward appearance of prosperity while other towns in the national urban system have subsided. The characteristics of the crisis in Dakar have been reflected in its functions; specifically, the volume of trade through Dakar's port is beginning to decline and the port is losing its relative position in Africa. Dakar's role as a regional capital for former French West Africa has also declined as more and more of the functions that were previously pegged at a regional level (and were located at Dakar) have now been reorganized at a national level and dispersed to the capital cities of the other postcolonial states. However, on the national scale, that is, within Senegal, there has been a reversal of this general trend toward diminishing Dakar's importance; *in fact there is a definite shift toward a primate capital.* As the rural areas of Senegal have suffered agriculturally, and as the towns in these areas have also declined, there has been a migration of the wealthier individuals, chiefly merchants, away from the interior to Dakar. Many of these people have resettled in Dakar, at least temporarily. This migration has resulted in the maintenance of the facade of Dakar as a bustling city with active boutiques, restaurants and small grocery stores. The shops continue to function and apartments remain occupied as the migrants from the interior have filled the places of those departing from Dakar and emigrating from Senegal to find better opportunities elsewhere. Another result of this selective migration has been the creation of "hollow towns" in the interior. These hollow towns, so symptomatic of overurbanization, as noted above, are places of population concentration, but whose economic functions are so severely diminished that support for the remaining population is precarious.

The impact of these processes of change and succession on the land-use pattern of Dakar has been minimal so far, yet there have been economic and social indicators such as the disappearance of Vietnamese restaurants mentioned earlier that point to a more austere future. One or two streets in Downtown Dakar that had bustled with commerce in 1960 had many empty store fronts in 1970.[47] This change reflects the departure of many French, particularly the military and their dependents, and it also points to changes in the French way of life in Dakar. Now that transportation is much cheaper than before, the French technical assistant and his family return to France for their vacation where they stock up on goods that would have been purchased in Dakar in former times. Still another modest indicator of the changed circumstances of Dakar is the unwillingness on the part of shopkeepers and realty companies to invest in building maintenance, repairs or decorations; this unwillingness to make even minor investment is beginning to promote a tawdry tinge to the CBD. It will be useful in the remaining pages to document the factors that have led to the "undevelopment" of Senegal and the effect of this process on Dakar, and to see what the planning authorities are doing to cope with this change.

Departure of the French

In the early postcolonial years Senegalese politicians strongly voiced the need to become politically and psychologically free of France. Some of these political discussions spilled over into economic considerations as the case for African socialism was promoted. Early responses by the Senegalese to the perceived threat of neocolonialism took the form of pressure on France to withdraw its forces from Senegal, and for foreign merchants to liquidate their businesses. Both pressure policies met with success.

Between 1960 and 1970, there were many thousand French military personnel withdrawn from Senegal. This precipitous outflow of a relatively wealthy group created eddies of diseconomy in Dakar and in the interior towns. Simultaneously, the Senegalese put heavy pressure on the existing marketing structure by setting up agricultural and consumer co-operatives to compete with the foreign traders who had organized and carried out trade for half a century. These traders were limited to selected lists of items they could sell, many of these bearing the highest import taxes, and they were restricted by price ceilings established by the government. Strong, and economically troubling though these purgative measures may have been, the truly hard economic problems of Senegal lay in its agricultural base.

The economic stagnation of Senegal may be directly attributed to its position as a one-crop country whose single crop, peanuts, is not competitive on the world market. Peanuts accounted for about two thirds of Senegal's income from agriculture and about three quarters of the total value of Senegalese exports in 1968. Until 1963–64, France guaranteed a price for Senegalese peanuts about 20 per cent above that of the world market, but by 1967–68 this support was removed. France maintained the price supports as long as it did to help ease Senegal's economic transition and to keep Senegal aligned with French foreign policy. Thus, for almost a decade the Senegalese farmers and the Senegalese government did not have to face many of the realities of the world economy. When France removed its support the government responded to the new economic situation by reducing the prices paid to producers through the government agricultural co-operative system. Soon thereafter the government devalued the currency of the country, the effect of which was a 15 per cent drop in agricultural producer income, and withheld 5 per cent of producer payments for 1968 until an investigation of mismanaged co-ops could be completed. Meanwhile, the government paid the producers in scrip instead of currency, a decision which promoted the greatest loss in confidence in the government by the farmers.

The farmers responded to government policy by reducing the land under peanut cultivation, smuggled some of their peanuts into Gambia (where cash could be obtained) and sold the government scrip for less than its face value. In some parts of the country the farmers refused to turn their production over to the co-ops and also refused to take delivery on equipment purchased on their behalf by the co-operative system. Sometimes these refusals were accompanied by violence. The 1969 peanut crop was the smallest since 1956. Grave consequences for Senegal's economy have resulted from the withdrawal of French personnel and price supports and this has been reflected in Senegal's towns.

To sustain a viable urban system in which there is more than a single, giant city it is necessary to have a strong base (or bases) of support for other cities as well. Lacking this economic strength and the economic goad of competing growth poles, there is a constant threat that the capital, the primate city, will be transformed from a "motor for economic development," as Sheldon Gellar has portrayed it, into a "parasitic city."[48] This suggestion is more than idle musing with respect to Senegal and many other African countries. As the economy of Senegal has shrunk through the diminishment of the country's ability to export anything of major value, so too has its ability to support several thriving urban centers diminished. Like a plant that has expended itself to produce one flower while the others wither, the postcolonial urban system of Senegal has channeled its effort into Dakar. An occasional shower of good luck, such as the energizing effect the closing of the Suez Canal has had on Dakar's port, may be only a temporary reprieve from collapse. The desperate search for a resource base has yet to yield solid evidence of great riches beneath the sea or the soil. Petroleum prospecting, particularly off shore, has shown promise, but there have been no hard indications for its economic exploitation in the near future. Efforts to improve Senegal's small fishing industry have been moderately successful, but this success ranks very low in the context of the total sustaining need of Senegalese society. Senegalese fishing can be only marginally competitive in the world market, and most of its product will probably go for internal consumption in heavily protected markets. The plight of Senegalese industrial production is typified in the example of Senegal's cement industry, whose product is still more costly in neighboring Bathurst (Gambia) than cement shipped from England. Agricultural diversification, particularly rice and sugar projects, is aimed at import substitution rather than export, and in both cases imported commodities are less expensive than those grown at home. Senegal was accustomed to an imbalance in imports over exports when France was willing to pay for "political services," such as military bases, but the condition of postcolonialism requires that new support be sought.[49]

It is paradoxical, perhaps, that Senegal's most promising resource is not its agricultural base or industrial structure, but once again it is its location and its people: the country, and especially Dakar, can render services to a clientele of international tourists who would vacation in one of black Africa's most elegant and certainly its nearest cultural center. The Senegalese have been slow to realize this resource, but economic realities are now pressing for change and new luxury hotels are beginning to rise on Cap Vert.

Should tourism, or possibly petroleum or fishing provide a brighter economic future for Senegal, what will this mean for Dakar and the rest of Senegal's towns? Curiously enough, the existing tendency to move toward a primate city condition will probably be reinforced: Both off-shore petroleum operations and fishing are likely to find their base of operations in Dakar. Tourism will also be focused on Cap Vert.

In addition to these factors for concentration working on Dakar is the circumstance that the agricultural system upon which most of the interior towns found their *raison d'être* is dying. Thus, under the best circumstances one can posit intensified growth of the capital and a static or declining future for most of the interior towns. If, however, there is no discovery of a resource base to replace the "clientship" of colonialism then one may expect a dramatic decline of the urban system of Senegal, including Dakar. It is entirely possible that as enterprising Senegalese emigrate (as many do now to France and to other, wealthier, African countries like Gabon), and as the inflated bureaucracy grows, Dakar will be crushed under the weight of its own debt to its hinterland. In effect, the government services provided by the capital, which represent so great a proportion of the salaried labor of the country, are valued less and less by the hinterland agriculturist who is being asked to pay for them. The African peasant has demonstrated in the past that payment for government may be terminated simply by failing to drop a seed to be germinated, and that classic process is beginning to take place in Senegal today. The haunting possibility of a descent into what Gerald Breese has called "subsistence urbanization" is a real and grave possibility.[50]

This general decline has thrust additional uncertainty on those concerned with planning for Senegal's future. The four-year plans for the economy have had to be revised in light of diminished income, and it has been necessary to seek more, and broader, foreign economic assistance. One might expect that these perturbations in national planning would be reflected at the local level, but it is too soon to suggest what modifications will have to be made, if any, in Dakar's *Plan Directeur.* It is possible that the plan might be accelerated because of the increased concentration of growth in Dakar relative to the rest of Senegal's urban system. In any case consideration of the plan is essential for a prognosis of Dakar.

PLAN DIRECTEUR: 1967

The 1967 *Plan Directeur* prepared by M. Ecochard is an imaginative document, reflecting the period in which it was formulated and considerably more realistic than previous plans. It is also one of the most comprehensive urban plans for a tropical African city, and has the virtue of special attention to the entire urban region of Dakar as well as to the built-up central city. The plan is flawed, however, particularly in use of space, which is discussed at the end of this section. Although the full plan has not been made public, a highly informative *Rapport Interprétatif* and some of the planning and zoning maps are generally available for scrutiny.[51] In particular, the zoning plan, which was approved in mid-1967, provides insight into official designs for Dakar.[52] Similarly, the *Rapport* provides a feeling for the general philosophy behind the plan and shows clearly that the plan had been built on current development vectors rather than seriously rupturing the existing use of space.

It has not been the actual growth of Dakar up to this time that has upset its planners; it is that the rapid rate of population growth in Dakar seems to be increasing rather than leveling off. Add to this dynamic situation the fact that youth predominates in this growth and that youth demands more public facilities to care for its needs than it has the ability to pay for. The growing population comes from a wide variety of ethnic and social backgrounds and the stress of integration into a national, urban life style provides an ever present threat of social disruption. Such disruptions have occurred in Dakar and they have had a national impact because of Dakar's superordinate influence.

The health of the population of the city is another realm of concern for many of the same reasons mentioned: The population is young, growing, mixed and of national importance. The cadre of planning technicians believe that it is absolutely imperative that the public health of Dakar be given priority treatment.[53] This priority treatment is seen in the heavy emphasis on public health facilities and plans to ensure adequate water supplies, and to assure better and more sanitary housing for the population.

Population density regulation and the provision of open space are regarded as important concomitants of the two previous considerations, the growth of population and its qualities. Planning officials argue that for financial, sanitary and social reasons the density of population for the whole city area should not exceed eighty per acre.[54] Yet these constraints must operate within the context of others such as the reservation of large areas of land for very low density uses, be they green spaces, villas or transportation routes. In the case of transportation it is also understood that the heavily traveled routes must not impinge on residential areas, nor on the areas set aside for public enjoyment. Obviously, some portions of the city will be more densely populated than others. The current density of the built-up area as a whole is about sixty per acre, while the bidonvilles are closer to three hundred and twenty per acre.

Some of the major goals of the plan may be seen in what the Senegalese planners call the *politique nouvelle d'urbanisme*. These goals include renovation in the core, the full linking of the city of Dakar with suburban Pikine (and development of Pikine as an integral part of the city), and solving of technical problems of the transport system, water supply and sanitation.[55] The time context for the realization of these goals is fifteen years, but involved with the development of urban structures is also a hoped-for growth in adaptability of the plan to the people and of the people to the plan—"we declare ourselves for an evolutionary urbanism which progressively adapts itself to the evolution of living standards, thereby creating a habitat."[56] This is a particularly brave declaration when so many of the city's inhabitants are new migrants.

The *Plan Directeur* recognizes and encourages the continued renovation of four parts of the city and one part of Pikine that were being worked on prior to the adoption of the plan.[57] These areas are: 1) the projects of O.H.L.M. in the area of Allées du Centenaire; 2) S.I.C.A.P. renovation south of Avenue Bourguiba; 3) the Medina; 4) Rebeuss; and 5) the northeast part of Pikine. The plans of these areas are being kept in general harmony with the *Plan Directeur.*

But more than this concession to past trends and pre-existing agencies, the *Plan Directeur* proposes some specific goals for the Dakar metropolitan area hopefully to be realized by the early 1980s. Specifically, the total integration of Cap Vert through a vastly articulated expressway system is envisioned. The major route in this system will proceed from the downtown north westward toward the airport along the edges of the extended S.I.C.A.P. developments, ultimately linking up with the existing airport expressway. Branching from this new route will be another that ties Pikine into the main arterials.

An extensive series of public water outlets (one for every five hundred inhabitants) is projected, which will require the tapping of source waters farther and farther away from the city. This is an ambitious goal, but one that can be realized now that foreign aid donors are contributing to its completion. Intimately tied to water availability are the public health plans, which are also extensive and which call for general solid waste disposal.

Serious evaluation of the *Plan Directeur* must await its full disclosure, but some tentative comments may be made, especially with respect to residential density and the route system. Although many details of the plan are admirable, it must be stressed that Dakar's planners have made a choice for space extensiveness in a country that can ill-afford the luxury of a dispersed urban settlement pattern. In their attempt to look broadly at the total urban complex of Dakar, M. Ecochard and his associates have struck a blow for amenities in the urban environment at the risk of increased transport cost. According to the plan, in the Dakar of the near future the presently crowded bidonville population will be spread over virtually all of the surface of Cap Vert and there will be few multiple-family dwelling units. The working population will be tied to the downtown and the industrial areas to the east by an improved transport network. Such a spatial structure requires an extensive (and expensive) public transport system, and/or widespread automobile ownership. The only condition that now obtains is expensive mass transportation in the form of buses and minibuses.

It is very difficult to imagine that the outer-fringe inhabitants of Dakar will, by the beginning of the next decade, have the personal mobility to cope with this settlement pattern. Economically more rational than this dispersion, would be a greater investment in more centrally located multistoried residential structures and better orientation programs for new migrants to the city. Certainly the spatial extensiveness of the population militates against cost cutting. This is regrettable, but perhaps "higher" values of calm and uncrowded neighborhoods are more important than sheer economics!

CONCLUSION

Dakar was implanted by French imperialists, nourished at the fount of colonialism, and it grew to dimensions defined and described by overarching processes largely foreign to its native population. Efforts to plan the course of urbanization in Senegal succeeded in grafting small elements of native stock to the main branches of French urbanism. These efforts were rewarded by town growth throughout Senegal, but this growth proved to be fragile when the sustaining effect of French capital was withdrawn. Now the larger drama of Senegal's search for an economic base is being replayed in small urban theatres throughout the country, but it is being played to empty houses. At Dakar the episode is heightened by its scale, and while the audience remains large, there is still a forbidding echo reverberating from the wings.

Dakar's problem is classic—it is following the path of its subordinate towns toward overurbanization, a path that leads migrants into the city and the supporting functions out. Dakar's problem *is* the problem of Senegal—the Senegalese population is growing, perhaps to seven and one-half million by the year 2000, but its economic functions are in decline. If Dakar could be given one line to speak in the drama of its threatening decline, it might choose the words of Louis XIV, under whose reign France first arrived in Senegal, *"l'État, c'est moi."* Unfortunately, the lines may ring too true for those African elites who had hoped to cultivate a new kind of urbanism on Africa's shores.

NOTES

[1] Hubert Deschamps, *Le Sénégal et la Gambie.* Paris, Presses Universitaires de France, 1964, p. 41.

[2] H. R. Palmer, *The Carthaginian Voyage to West Africa in 500 B.C.* Bathurst, Government Printer, 1931, pp. 15–16.

[3] This is a portion of the account of Hanno, the Carthaginian commander, cited in Palmer, op. cit., p. 2.

[4] *République de Sénégal, Ministère du Plan et du Developpment. Aménagement du Territoire. Le Peuplement du Sénégal,* Tome 1, Dakar, 1966.

[5] John D. Hargreaves, *West Africa: The Former French States.* Englewood Cliffs, N.J., Prentice-Hall, 1967, p. 33.

[6] Hargreaves, op. cit., p. 37.

[7] For a fascinating account of this early history one should read André Delcourt, *La France et les Établissements Français au Sénégal Entre 1731 et 1763.* Dakar, 1952; and Léonce Jore, *Les Etablissements Français sur la Côte Occidentale d'Afrique de 1758 à 1809.* Paris, 1965.

[8] Hargreaves, op. cit., p. 79.

[9] G. Savonnet, *La Ville de Thiès: Étude de Géographie Urbaine.* St. Louis, Sénégal: Centre d' Institut Française d'Afrique Noire, 1955, p. 19. Published as *Études Sénégalaises,* No. 6.

[10] A. Dessertine, *Un Port Secondaire de la Côte Occidentale d'Afrique: Kaolack.* Kaolack, Senegal: Chambre du Commerce, 1959 (?), p. 31. See also Martin A. Klein, *Islam and Imperialism in Senegal, Sine-Saloum, 1847–1914,* Stanford, California, 1968, pp. 8–9.

[11] Jean et René Charbonneau, *Marchés et Marchands d'Afrique Noire.* Paris, La Colombe, 1961, pp. 94–95.

[12] Afrique Occidentale Française. *Rapport d'une commission composée de M. M. Pinet-Laprade, Revin et Rocomaure, sur divers points relatifs à l'importance militaire, politique et commerciale de Dakar, le 23 Aout, 1863.* Cited in Jacques Charpy, *La Fondation de Dakar (1845–1857–1869)*. Paris, Larose, 1958, p. 416 (translation by the author).

[13] Klein, op. cit., p. 37.

[14] Richard J. Peterec, *Dakar and West African Economic Development.* New York, Columbia University Press, 1967, p. 37.

[15] Charpy, op. cit., p. 10.

[16] Peterec, op. cit., p. 39.

[17] Ibid., p. 42.

[18] Assane Seck, "Dakar," in *Notes et Études Documentaires.* Nos. 3505–06 (6 Juillet, 1968), p. 50.

[19] The capitals and countries (in parentheses) of A.O.F. are as follows: Abidjan (Ivory Coast); Bamako (Soudan, now Mali); Conakry (Guinea); Cotonou (Dahomey); Dakar (Senegal); Niamey (Niger); Nouakchott (Mauritania); Ouagadougou (Upper Volta); and, included here, Lomé (Togo).

[20] These *régions* formed the first tier of the administrative substructure. Below this level are *départements* and *arrondissements.*

[21] Ruth Schacter Morgenthau, *Political Parties in French-Speaking West Africa.* Oxford, England, Clarendon Press, 1964, p. 12.

[22] République du Sénégal, *Journal Officiel,* 112e Année, No. 3871 (30 Janvier, 1967). See reference to official Decret 61–060 of 3 February, 1961.

[23] Richard Peterec, op. cit., pp. 10–11.

[24] Ibid., p. 46. There are several good discussions of the port of Dakar. Peterec's is the best in English but one may also look at Joseph-Clément Chappex, *Le Port de Dakar.* Université de Dakar, Faculté de Droit et des Sciences Économiques, Thèse, 1967.

[25] Seck, a Senegalese geographer of extraordinary competence has made a major study of Dakar in which he presents much information on the various *quartiers* of the city. This chapter draws on Seck's work but finds some of his categories unworkable for this discussion.

[26] Peterec, op. cit., p. 41.

[27] A. Seck, op. cit., pp. 21–23.

[28] République du Sénégal, Direction de l'Urbanisme, *Plan Directeur du Cap Vert.* Dakar, 1967.

[29] Raymond Betts, "The Problem of the Medina in the Urban Planning of Dakar, Senegal," *African Urban Notes,* Vol. IV, No. 3. September 1969, p. 6. Cited with the author's permission.

[30] Dakar was one of the original communes of Senegal, wherein any person, African or European, with five years' residence, enjoyed the right to vote. It was, therefore, impossible to deal arbitrarily with much of Dakar's population.

[31] Betts, op. cit., pp. 8–9.

[32] Ibid., p. 9.

[33] Ibid., p. 12.

[34] While carrying out field research in this area, map in hand, I created some un-

easy moments for the local inhabitants who took me for a French urban planner with grave designs on their neighborhood.

[35] A. Seck, op. cit., p. 31.

[36] Betts, op. cit., p. 10.

[37] République du Sénégal, *Le Peuplement du Sénégal,* Tome II, Dakar, 1966, p. 100.

[38] Ibid., p. 123. The 1961 census area was larger than that of 1955 so the figures are not strictly comparable, but growth during this six-year period was spectacular.

[39] Ibid., p. 198; and *République du Sénégal, Ministère des Travaux Publics de l'Urbanisme et des Transports. Directeur de l'Urbanism et de l'Habitat. Plan Director de Dakar, 1967: Rapport Interprétatif,* Dakar, 1967, p. 6.

[40] République du Sénégal. Office des Habitations à Loyer Moderé. O.H.L.M. Dakar (?), 1966 (?), p. 1.

[41] Information on O.H.L.M. was obtained through interviews with Roger Bocandé, director of the organization, in January 1968 and August 1970.

[42] Seck, op. cit., p. 66.

[43] This separation phenomenon may not be entirely income determined; O.H.L.M. officials have observed reluctance on the part of some African families to take apartments above the ground level, a reluctance they attribute to "traditionalism."

[44] Mimeograph flyer from the head office of S.I.C.A.P., in 1961.

[45] Quoted from the cover of a S.I.C.A.P. brochure. President Senghor's statement was made in Thiès in February 1962.

[46] Leopold S. Senghor, *On African Socialism.* New York, Frederick A. Praeger, 1964.

[47] John W. Sommer, *Urban Market Systems and Internal Trade in Senegal: A Prologue.* Report to the National Academy of Sciences, National Research Council, 1971, mimeographed, p. 51.

[48] Sheldon Gellar, "West African Capital Cities as Motors for Development," *Civilizations,* Vol. XVII, No. 3 (1967), pp. 1–9.

[49] Banque Centrale des États de l'Afrique de l'Quest. "Indicateurs Économiques," No. 169 (January 1970), p. 10.

[50] Gerald Breese. *Urbanization in Newly Developing Countries.* Englewood Cliffs, N.J., Prentice-Hall, 1966, pp. 133–36.

[51] République du Sénégal. *Rapport Interprétatif,* op. cit.

[52] République du Sénégal. Ministère des Travaux Publics et Ministère du Plan. Direction de l'Urbanisme. "Plan de zoning. No. 402 D.U." *Plan Directeur du Cap Vert.* Dakar, 1968.

[53] *Rapport Interprétatif,* op. cit., p. 15.

[54] Ibid., p. 33.

[55] Ibid., pp. 4–6.

[56] Ibid., p. 5.

[57] Ibid., pp. 27–28.

CHAPTER 12

Brasilia: "Yesterday's City of Tomorrow"

Norma Evenson*

In the course of an expedition through South America in 1913, Theodore Roosevelt had crossed the western edge of the Planalto, the high central plain of Brazil. Describing this "healthy land of dry air, of cool nights, of clear, running brooks," he stated,

> The air was wonderful; the vast open spaces gave a sense of abounding vigor and freedom . . . the sky was brilliant; far and wide we looked over a landscape that seemed limitless; the breeze that blew in our faces might have come from our own northern plains. The midday sun was very hot; but it was hard to realize that we were in the torrid zone. . . . Surely in the future this region will be the home of a healthy, highly civilized population. . . . Any sound northern race could live here; and in such a land, with such a climate, there would be much joy of living.[1]

These interior uplands, which inspired such enthusiasm in the former President, had long been regarded by Brazilians not only as an area for potential settlement, but also as a desirable site for a new national capital. The latter goal was finally

* For a biographical sketch see first page of Chapter 10. "Yesterday's City of Tomorrow" is a phrase of Lewis Mumford's.

achieved through the creation of the city of Brasilia begun in 1956 and dedicated in 1960. Dependent initially on the strong sponsorship of President Juscelino Kubitschek da Oliviera, the new capital may be considered one of the most audacious urban projects of our time, a controversial planned city forced into existence like a costly hothouse bloom.

Although Brasilia in its present stage may function primarily as a symbolic monument, the foundation of the city was accompanied by the expectation that it would be instrumental in aiding the long-term development of the interior, serving as a magnet for population and economic enterprise. Brasilia was also planned as the focal point of a new system of interior highways linking the north and south of Brazil, providing, for the first time, a ground transportation system uniting the country from within.

One of the peculiarities of Brazil is that in spite of a prevailing mythology of boundless resources and untapped wealth, Brazilians have yet to take possession of their own land. The great spontaneous migration which populated the United States had no Brazilian counterpart, and today one might consider Brazil the world's oldest land of the future. Brazil has promised much, but the fulfillment of the promise is yet to be seen.

For all the optimism which has surrounded Brazil, this vast territory (equal to the United States plus another Texas) has remained in many ways unchanged since the days of colonialism—a string of coastal settlements, frequently more closely tied to the outside world than to one another. In spite of many pioneering efforts at exploration and exploitation of the interior, viable and lasting settlement somehow failed to thrive. Discussing the achievements of the Brazilian pioneers or *bandierantes,* Israel Pinheiro, who administered the initial construction of Brasilia, observed,

> Once the gold mines were exhausted . . . and the alluvial soils used up, and the mineral soils abandoned as being unsuitable for agriculture and too distant from the population centers forming along the seaboard, we found ourselves back at the point of departure: we returned to the coast and never again left it. Between our cities and the distant outposts of those heroic standard bearers, there remained only a few sparse settlements, without sufficient means of subsistence and beyond aid of any kind. Along the coast, from which we could communicate east with the Mother country and maintain our close dependent relationship, we built an industrial civilization utterly unrelated to the Interior.
>
> We divided Brazil into two disproportionate parts—the coast and the Interior—and that unbalance daily grew more marked. In the final analysis, Brazil's present crisis is the result of this disgraceful state of affairs, in which the most primitive agricultural development and the most progressive industrial expansion are neighbors, and the inflationary centers of our coastal cities border vast areas of depression in the hinterlands. Beyond doubt, the inflationary spiral annihilates fixed income and impoverishes nations, but far worse than inflation is the inadequate distribution of wealth characteristic of the Brazilian case, thanks to which the Interior is deprived of good working conditions and stripped of its reserve capacity, while the coast progresses towards the mirage of isolated prosperity.[2]

The current economic and social problems of Brazil are many and complex, and considering the unstable and unbalanced economy, the depressed and feudal agricultural system, together with the general illiteracy, abysmal health standards and grinding poverty of the people, the establishment of a grandiose new capital may seem a questionable enterprise. In spite of the optimistic hopes that Brasilia would contribute substantially to the settlement of the interior, the establishment of the city could hardly be considered a substitute for thorough regional and national planning.

Brasilia has been subject to both sweeping condemnation and extravagant praise although clearly the project does not lend itself to easy judgment. It is only the future which can decide the success or failure of the city, especially as it may relate to over-all national development. At present Brasilia stands as a massive effort, the focus of the greatest organizational achievement in Brazil's history. Although internationally the postwar period produced a number of new town projects, the scope and intensity of the accomplishment in Brasilia remains such that it has no contemporary parallel.

THE EVOLUTION OF AN IDEA

Former President Juscelino Kubitschek once observed, "Brasilia is not an improvisation: it is a maturation."[3] He wished to stress that the creation of the new capital was not an arbitrary or precipitous decision on his part, but the fruition of many years of preparation. Concurring, Israel Pinheiro pointed out, "No other national problem has been debated and analyzed over so long a period of our history—from colonial times up to the present day."[4]

The first recorded advocacy of a new capital appeared in 1789 in a statement by a group of political revolutionaries in the state of Minas Gerais, who called themselves the *"Inconfidentes Mineiros."* Pioneers in the movement for independence from Portugal, they incorporated in their program the concept of a new governing center free of the symbolic associations of the colonial regime.

The desire for a new capital appears to have been embodied in much of Brazil's revolutionary political activity. One of the principal figures of the republican revolution of 1817, Father João Ribeiro urged that a central city be raised, "at least 30 to 40 leagues away from the sea-coast, as a residence for the Congress and the Government . . ."[5] To the patriarch of Brazilian independence, José Bonifacio de Andrada e Silva, the foundation of a new capital seemed a natural accompaniment to the creation of a new nation, and in 1821, the instructions prepared for the Brazilian delegates to the Portuguese Côrtes included recommendations for such a city.

Although no immediate action was taken to establish the new capital, the idea remained alive, forming a recurring theme of nineteenth-century political rhetoric. It was not until after the proclamation of the republic in 1889, however, that the groundwork for the move would actually begin. Specific provision for the establishment of the new capital was contained in the Constitution of 1891, in which Article 3 stated, "From now on, an area of 14,400 square kilometers will belong to the Government for the location of the New Capital." To reinforce this provision, a bill was passed to "authorize the exploration and demarcation of the area intended for the new capital on the central plateau of the territory of the Republic."[6]

In specifying a location within the central plateau, the Brazilian legislators were adhering to the generally held view that this part of Brazil provided the most reasonable site for the new capital. Although the concept of centrality was important in moving the capital away from the coast, to have placed the city in the geographic center of Brazil would have put it in the northeastern corner of the state of Mato Grosso in an area of impenetrable wilderness, impossibly remote from any centers of population or directions of population growth. In 1890, the national population center was in the northern part of the state of Minas Gerais, with trends of movement toward the south. The placement of the new city was designed to combine a symbolic centrality of siting with a realistic relation to actual patterns of settlement. In terms of climate, resources and relative accessibility, the plains of the central highlands could be seen as a suitable area into which population movement might be deflected.

The initial attempt to find a specific site for the new Brazilian capital was made by a government commission formed in 1891 under the leadership of Dr. Luiz Cruls, director of the Federal Observatory. The result of their investigations was the delineation of a 160 by 90 kilometer rectilinear area which, in accordance with the requirements of the 1891 Constitution provided an area of 14,400 square kilometers (5,500 square miles). Henceforth, the area selected by the Commission would appear on many maps as "Future Federal District," but no steps were taken to develop it as a capital site.

Further specific action was not taken until 1946, during the administration of Eurico Caspar Dutra. A commission consisting of twelve members headed by General Djalma Polli Coelho was selected to conduct studies for the location of the "New Capital."[7] The new commission disregarded the studies done by the Cruls Commission, and attempted to begin selection of the general area of the capital all over again. They chose an area larger than one million square kilometers for initial study, and within this, selected eight separate zones for more intensive examination. Unable to come to an agreement regarding a specific site, they proposed two solutions for the consideration of Congress.

The matter was subsequently debated in Congress for almost five years; Getulio Vargas had been re-elected President. On January 5, 1953, a law was passed providing for a final demarcation of the Federal District. An area of approximately 52,000 square kilometers was defined by the legislative group which included almost all of the Cruls Rectangle and some of the areas suggested by the Coelho Commission.

A Brazilian photogrammetric company, Aerofoto, a subsidiary of the airline Cruzeiro do Sul, was asked to survey the study area through aerial photography; this was accomplished in August and September of 1953, at which time it was decided to seek foreign assistance for the final site studies. A contract for this work was concluded with the firm of Donald J. Belcher & Associates of Ithaca, New York, on April 20, 1954, whose task it was to study the quadrangle established in 1953, and to select five alternate city sites, each with the capacity of supporting an urban population of five hundred thousand. A Federal District comprising an additional four thousand square kilometers would then be delineated surrounding the site chosen.

Following the completion of the site studies, an expedition was organized to permit members of a government commission to visit the five locations selected.

Because of difficult landing conditions, however, only two of the sites were actually seen from the ground. Major responsibility for the final decision appears to have rested with the head of the commission, Marechal José Pessôa, and although two members resigned from the group on grounds that the decision was achieved too hastily, a final official judgment was made in the second week in April 1955.

The present Federal District of 5,814 square kilometers (approximately 20,000 square miles) lies between the parallels of 15°30′ and 16°03′, and is bounded on the east and west by the rivers Descoberto and Prêto. The terrain is gently undulating, with a type of vegetation called *campo cerrado,* or tree savanna, characterized by large tracts of short grasses and occasional clumps of shrubs and low scrubby trees. The altitude ranges from 2,953 to 3,609 feet. The climate of the district is relatively mild, the lowest recorded temperature being 39.2° F., and the highest recorded temperature 98.6° F. Relative humidity ranges between 55 per cent and 86 per cent, and the seasons consist of a dry winter lasting from April to September, and a rainy summer lasting from October to March.

Within the Federal District, the city itself occupies a roughly triangular site originally bounded by two rivers, the Bananal and Gamma which converged to form the Paranoá. Subsequently the Paranoá was dammed, creating a fifteen square-mile artificial lake surrounding the site of the city. The water table of the site ranges from 164 to 328 feet, and the soil presents no obstacles to construction other than a hardness, which eventually necessitated a type of building supported by concrete stakes.

While efforts to establish a site for the new capital had been proceeding quietly, Brazilian political life had been exhibiting its characteristic complexity and theatricality. In 1954, following charges of corruption and pressures by some members of the military establishment for his resignation, Vargas committed suicide. A somewhat chaotic period followed, with Presidents Café Filho, Carlos Luz and Nereu Ramos following in rapid succession. By 1955, a complicated four-sided contest for the presidency was underway, with the governor of Minas Gerais, Juscelino Kubitschek da Oliviera appearing as a compromise candidate.

President Kubitschek's Dream

Kubitschek won a narrow victory with approximately one third of the vote. Some contended that his failure to achieve a majority made it unconstitutional for him to assume office, and it required considerable pressure from War Minister General Lott to enable Kubitschek to be inaugurated in 1956. Although he had arrived in office with a somewhat doubtful mandate, Kubitschek's administration was characterized by remarkable dynamism and self-confidence. With the slogan of providing "Fifty Years of Progress in Five Years," he made strenuous efforts to stimulate economic development of the still backward economy. His methods were sometimes controversial, and he is often credited with promoting Brazil's disastrous monetary inflation. The most notable achievement of his administration, however, is the construction of the new capital.

Kubitschek's initial support for the city seems to have come about somewhat by accident. During a political rally in Goiás during the 1955 campaign, someone in the audience called out to Kubitschek, "What about Brasilia?" The candidate impulsively shouted back, "I will implement the constitution." He later admitted, "I had hardly considered Brasilia before then."[8]

From this moment onward, the new city became virtually a compulsion with the President who placed behind the project all his political skill and personal enthusiasm. Some felt the project was undertaken with undue haste, but speed was necessary in the circumstances. Once Kubitschek had determined to build Brasilia, the task had to be accomplished within his single five-year term of office. By law he could not succeed himself, and he knew that Brazilian politicians are loathe to continue any project begun by a previous administration. In order for Brasilia to endure, therefore, it would have to be sufficiently complete before Kubitschek left office so that the project could not with reason be abandoned.

In August 1956, as the initial step in developing the new capital, the Brazilian Congress authorized the creation of NOVACAP (Companhia Urbanizadora da Nova Capital), a government corporation charged with directing the construction of Brasilia.

For Kubitschek, Brasilia was a focus of intense pride, and it is inevitable that to many the city would appear as primarily one man's monument to himself. The city has never been free of criticism. To Kubitschek's political enemies Brasilia was a waste of labor, time and money, ruinous to the Brazilian economy, and as costs rose, a frequently hostile press dubbed the President a "Brazilian Pharaoh." Rio's *Correio da Manha* once termed the project "The limit of insanity! A dictatorship in the desert!," while *O Globo* pronounced the verdict of "Madness."[9]

To the opponents of Brasilia, the time was not yet ripe; Brazil had no need for a new capital and lacked the resources to construct one. To the city's supporters, Brasilia was long overdue. As Kubitschek phrased it, "I am not the founder of Brasilia, but in my soul came the realization that the hour had come for this act . . . that a new era for our land has begun!"[10]

Among the factors working in favor of the Brasilia project was the increasing population pressure within the old capital, Rio, where shortages of housing, inadequacies in services and problems of transport and communication were becoming acute. The topography of the city made expansion difficult; building sites were at a premium, and the government establishment was scattered somewhat chaotically throughout the teeming commercial metropolis.

By 1956, one could convincingly argue that the old crowded capital was inadequate to meet the future needs of government. Then too, Rio, with all its beauty and ease of living could be seen as symbolically inappropriate as an administrative center. As J. O. de Meira Penna argued, "Tens of thousands of government employees live in the impressive row of modern buildings along the bay, but for many of them serving the state seems merely an easy way of life, a peculiar but congenial form of social welfare. Rio breeds a parasitical bureaucracy, and there is neither the physical nor mental climate for a small and efficient civil service, capable of coping with the urgent problems of a growing colossus. A resort town, surrounded by all the seductions of nature and steeped in a luxurious atmosphere, a Cythera where one basks in the sun, swims in the cool waters and enjoys the pleasures of life with nonchalance is not the proper site for a capital. . . . A large city. . . . is not the proper seat for a federal government."[11]

The new capital could thus be justified as an effort to free the government from what had become a cumbersome and frequently corrupt bureaucracy, and to bring a more efficient and dedicated administration in closer touch with the problems of Brazil as a whole. In place of the part-time multiple employment common in Rio, the civil servant of the new capital would presumably bring full-time concentration to his government job, and government offices, in Rio generally operating only half time, would work on a full schedule.

Also important in making Brasilia possible was the circumstance that Brazilian technical capacity was, perhaps for the first time, equal to such a project. Of great importance in this respect was the development of the aviation industry. Before highway and rail links could be constructed, an efficient air service kept lines of communication open to the new capital, even assisting initially in the transport of building supplies.

In the long run, however, the most important factor in keeping Brasilia alive may have been the popular support the project eventually received. With what now seems shrewd political insight, Kubitschek seems to have sensed that the Brazilian people were ready for an adventure, and that popular imagination would respond to such a grand gesture more readily than to pedestrian and "practical" enterprises. By 1960, Kubitschek was able to proclaim confidently, "The capital is moving, and anybody who tries to stop it will be lynched by the people."[12]

The Competition

The first administrative steps for the construction of the new capital having been made, Kubitschek approached an old friend, the architect Oscar Niemeyer, for assistance in developing a plan for the city. It would not be the first collaboration between the two. In 1942, while mayor of Belo Horizonte in Minas Gerais, Kubitschek had promoted development of a suburban lakefront district called Pampulha, for which Niemeyer had been commissioned to design several buildings. At a time when modern architecture in Brazil was already attracting international notice, Niemeyer's work in Pampulha, which included a gambling casino, yacht club, restaurant and church, had given further evidence of the freedom, imagination and lyrical creativity for which Brazilian designers were noted. Niemeyer's career had prospered and at the initiation of the Brasilia project, Niemeyer could, with reason, be considered the nation's pre-eminent architect.

It was clear from the beginning that Brasilia was to be an architect's city, a circumstance which has drawn repeated criticism. As currently conceived, the creation of a city should involve many considerations other than physical design, and to many, the faults of Brasilia lie in the limitations of its initial conception as an architectural scheme, rather than as the product of collaborative effort including ecologists, economists and sociologists. According to currently accepted tenets of modern planning, a city is not a piece of architectural sculpture to be arbitrarily placed in a landscape, but a living organism whose existence depends on a complex interworking of geographic, economic and social factors. Among those most consistent in attacking the basic conception of Brasilia has been the Brazilian sociologist Gilberto Freyre who once demanded, "Doesn't Brazil also possess economists, ecologists and social scientists ranking in the same category as her architects?"[13]

Regarding the situation realistically, however, one can see justification for placing the creation of Brasilia in the hands of an architect. Kubitschek did not want to plan a city; he wanted to build a city. Within a brief period of time, he had to give Brasilia physical reality, and only the indisputable presence of a sufficient investment of asphalt, concrete and steel on site could guarantee the continuation of the project. Had Kubitschek sought to begin with a series of lengthy and very likely inconclusive social and economic studies, it is more than likely that the city would never have come into existence.

Although Niemeyer agreed to begin designing some buildings for Brasilia, it was decided that the city plan be determined by a competition. In September 1956, NOVACAP announced a contest for the design of Brasilia to be open to all architects, engineers and urbanists licensed in Brazil. The program has been termed "perhaps the simplest ever issued for a competition of this size."[14] Entrants were requested to submit two essential documents, (a) "A basic layout of the city, indicating the position of the main items of the urban structure, the location and interconnection of the various sectors, centers, installations and services, the distribution of the open spaces and lines of communication, to the scale of 1:25,000, and (b) A supporting report."[15] The program also indicated additional areas of planning to which reference might be made, depending on the special capacities of the entrants. These included agricultural economics, land tenure, water and power supply, employment opportunities, and the planning and investment required at various stages of development.

It was stated that the projects would be judged initially on the functional elements, and secondly from the standpoint of architectural synthesis. The "functional elements" were cited as 1, Consideration of topographical data; 2, Size of the city projected in relation to population density (human scale); 3, Integration of urban elements within the city and 4, Relation of the city and surrounding region. "Architectural synthesis" would include general composition and specific expression of the government site. The projected city was to accommodate a population of 500,000.[16]

NOVACAP made available to the contestants detailed maps and aerophoto mosaics of the topography of the site, plus information on soil conditions and climate. The government also facilitated visits to the site for the competitors. The closing date of the competition was March 11, 1957, providing a period of six months for the entrants to complete their presentations.

The jury included Oscar Niemeyer, who had become director of the Department of Architecture of NOVACAP, Paulo Antunes Ribeiro, representing the Institute of Brazilian Architects, and Horta Barbosa of the Society of Engineers. Three foreigners were also invited, Stamo Papadaki from the United States, André Sive from France and William Holford from England. The president of NOVACAP, Israel Pinheiro, served as nonvoting chairman.

The competition attracted twenty-six entrants, among them some of the most distinguished architects in Brazil. In view of the limited time available, and in spite of the fact that only a physical plan had been requested, many of the competition projects were remarkably thorough. Some entries included not only elaborately detailed drawings for the master plan, but also lengthy studies relating to the regional economy, projected population analyses and statistical presentations of future growth patterns of the district. Included among the plans were outlines for systems of local government, educational and social programs, proposals for the financial organization of the city and the development of varied transportation systems.

In terms of physical planning, the Brasilia competition provided a synthesis of generally prevailing principles of urban design. Almost all were based on the idea of functional zoning, with a sharp segregation of major urban activities. Systems of traffic separation were included. The green belt as an urban divider was used extensively, while residential areas were based on the superblock and neighborhood unit concept.

Although many of the entries exhibited imagination and skill, they shared a common formality of design and a lack of intimacy with the site. Although the setting of the new capital included a lake, almost none of the designs were oriented in any way to this natural feature. The discrete zoning of most of the plans tended to produce a fragmentation of urban form, as well as an oversimplification of urban function, and none seemed designed to include the full range of a Brazilian urban population. The competition produced a series of generalized schemes, apparently based on ideas about urban design, rather than an applied knowledge of existing Brazilian cities. Although this may be seen as a weakness of the designs, the contestants were correct in anticipating that the jury was not looking for a typical Brazilian city. Brasilia was never meant to be an ordinary town.

From their evaluations of the competition entries, it was clear that the jury was seeking, above all, a monumental scheme, a design which would definitively embody the conception of a capital. There was an evident desire to place the national government within the sort of symbolic setting which Rio de Janeiro, for all its natural beauty, had never provided. In Rio, government buildings were more or less integrated with the commercial buildings of the city, and the consciousness of being in a capital was vitiated through lack of a ceremonial focus.

The jury stated that

> a Federal Capital, to express the grandeur of a nation-wide desire, should differ from other cities of half a million inhabitants. Then, too, the Capital, a functional city, should have its own personal architectural style. Its principal characteristic is the governmental function, and around this and converging upon it, all the other functions should be grouped. In all cities, housing units, work, commerce and rest centers are rationally integrated and related to each other; in a Capital city, these sections must in addition be slanted toward the central purpose of the city: the governmental function.[17]

In their deliberations, the jury had begun by eliminating all but ten of the entries, and from an examination of this group, five prizes were given. In awarding the first prize of 1,000,000 cruzeiros, the jury stated that they had been "seeking a well-knit project which would give the city grandeur through the clarity and proper ranking of its components; in the opinion of the members, the project which best integrates the monumental elements into the city's daily life as a Federal Capital, and which is presented as a rational, essentially urban composition—in fact a work of art—is number 22, submitted by Mr. Lúcio Costa."[18] (Fig. 1)

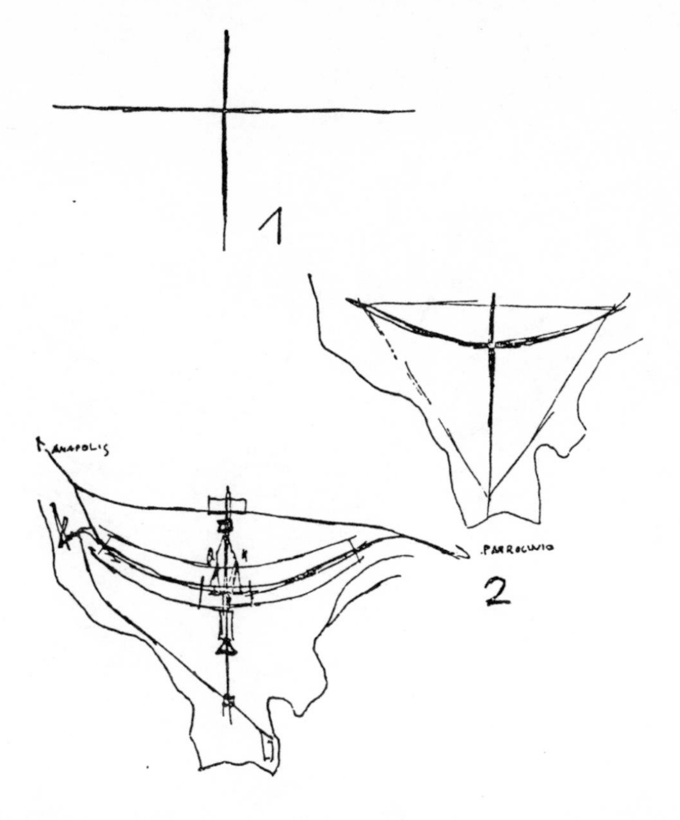

FIG. 1 Preliminary studies for Brasilia by Lúcio Costa, showing the evolution of the cross-axial concept.

The jury concluded that, in comparison with the other schemes, Costa's design was "the only plan which is for an administrative capital for Brazil. The elements of the plan can be seen at once: it is clear, direct and fundamentally simple, as exemplified by Pompeii, Nancy, Wren's London, Louis XV's Paris."[19]

In contrast with the other entries, Costa's presentation was minimal—five cards containing a few freehand sketches and a brief statement. He began with an apology, explaining that "It was not my intention to enter the competition—nor in fact am I really doing so. I am merely liberating my mind from a possible solution which sprang to it as a complete picture, but one which I had not sought."[20] (Fig. 2)

Although to base a major urban design on a sudden inspiration may seem a drastic violation of all currently accepted rational planning tenets, such an intuitive approach has a certain appropriateness in Brazil. Extemporization seems to accord with the Brazilian temperament, and in an undeveloped country, decisions in many areas must of necessity be made without recourse to elaborate information or preliminary study.

William Holford† described the judgment as the result of a "choice between breadth and depth."[21] At the first reading of Costa's report,

† Later Lord Holford, so singled out as Britain's most prestigious urban planner. (Editors' note.)

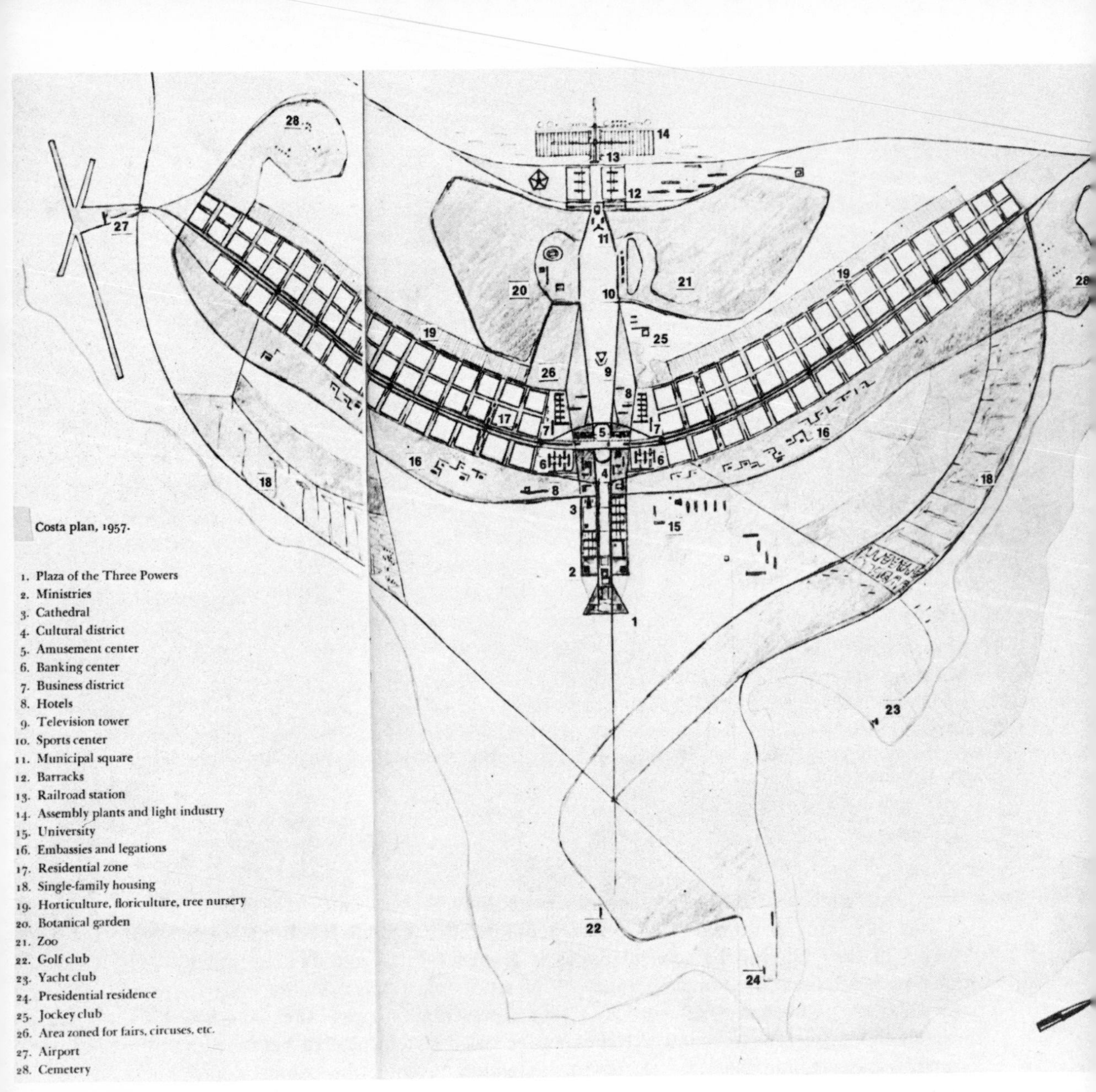

FIG. 2 Costa Plan of 1957. *Photograph by Norma Evenson, from* Two Brazilian Capitals, *Yale University Press, 1973*

one realized that here was a thinker, an urbanist, of the first order. On second reading, one realized that there was not a single unnecessary word in the report, and not a single unnecessary line in the sketch plan or diagrams: yet everything essential was said. And on further reading, this member of the jury, at least, became more and more convinced that the direction of advance for a great administrative capital had been indicated in a masterly way, and the fundamental problems of communication, urban residence, metropolitan character and richness of growth within a unity of artistic conception, had all been recognized and anticipated.[22]

The Costa Plan

With the acceptance of the Costa plan, the name of one of Brazil's pioneers of modern architecture was linked to the new city. Costa was among the small group of Brazilians who, in the early days of the modern movement, first attempted to interpret and adapt contemporary architectural developments in Europe to the Brazilian ambience. As director of the National School of Fine Arts in Rio from 1930 to 1931, he had sought to renovate the architecture curriculum previously modeled on that of the French École des Beaux Arts, and later had been influential in bringing Le Corbusier to Rio to consult on the now-famous Ministry of Education Building.

The young Oscar Niemeyer had entered the National School of Fine Arts in 1930, and following graduation went to work in Costa's office. According to Costa, "I tried to dissuade him from his intention of working with me in my office, because the turnover of work was small and would not give him sufficient remuneration. He promptly turned the tables on me and suggested compensating me for the right to take any part, whatsoever that might be, in my professional activities."[23]

While Niemeyer came to epitomize the virtuoso designer, intuitive, quick, exhibiting a flamboyant skill which led Walter Gropius to characterize him as a "Paradiesvogel" (bird of paradise), the older Costa, more intellectual and analytical, combined with his undoubted design talents, the reputation of a thoughtful and humane philosopher.

In introducing his plan, Costa noted that the city would be

> not the result of regional planning, but the cause; its foundation will be the starting point for the development of a regional plan. For this is a deliberate act of conquest, a gesture of pioneers acting in the spirit of their colonial traditions; and each competitor is, in effect, being asked how he conceives of such a city. It should be conceived, I believe, not as a mere organic entity, able to function effortlessly and vitally like any modern town; not as an "urbs," therefore, but as a "civitas," having the virtues and attributes appropriate to a true capital city. To achieve this, the town planner must be imbued with a certain dignity and nobility of purpose.[24]

In describing the origin of the design, he stated,

> It was born of that initial gesture which anyone would make when pointing to a given place, or taking possession of it: the drawing of two axes crossing each other at right angles, in the sign of the Cross. This sign was then adapted to the topography, the natural drainage of the land, and the best possible orientation: the extremities of one axial line were curved so as to make the sign fit into the equilateral triangle which outlines the area to be urbanized.
>
> Finally, it was decided to apply the free principles of highway engineering together with the elimination of road junctions to the technique of town planning. The curved axis, which corresponds to the natural approach road, was given the function of a through radial artery, with fast traffic lanes in the center and side lanes for local traffic. And the

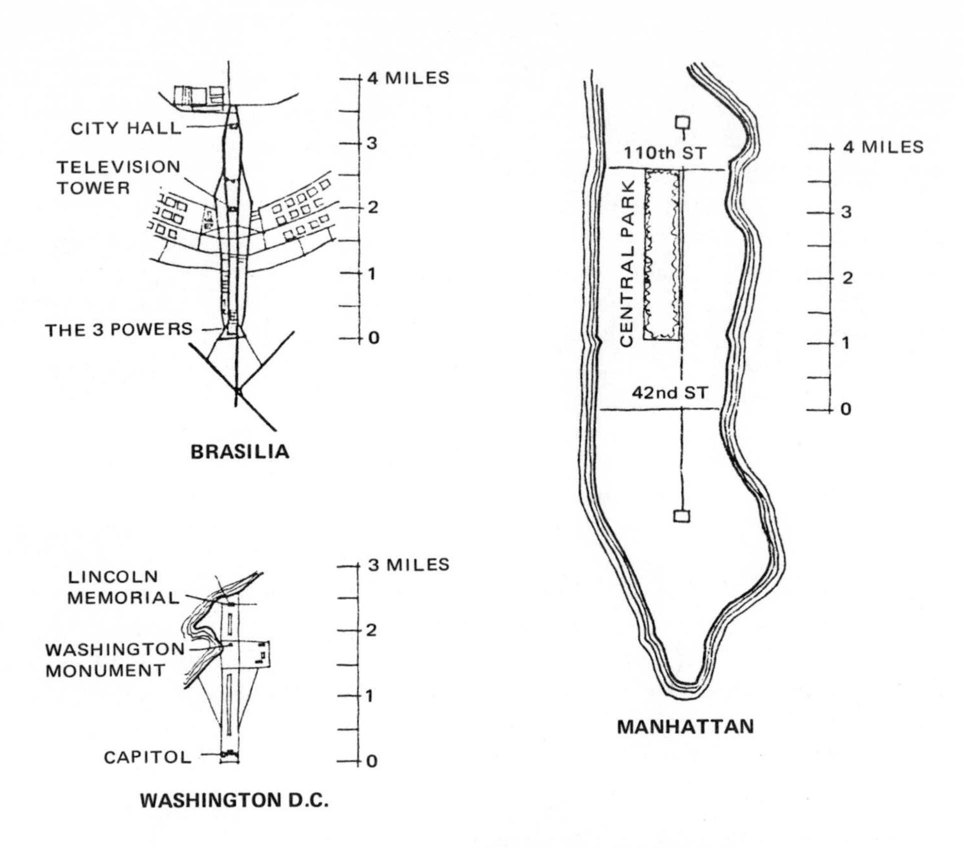

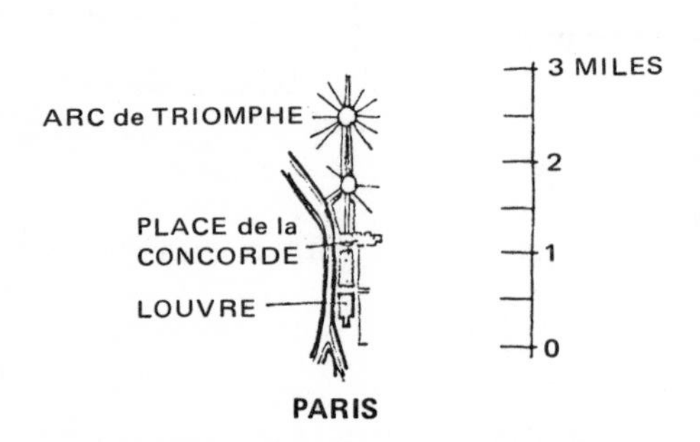

Capital malls at same scale:
Brasilia; below it Washington Mall and Champs-Élysées at Paris. Above: lower Manhattan; extending approximately 4 miles from its point to the railroad, Brasilia's mall is as long as New York's Fifth Avenue from 42nd Street to the head of Central Park at 110th Street. (Maps from a Harvard study.)

FIG. 3A Brasilia's mall seen comparatively. *From* The Architectural Forum, *November 1960, Whitney Publication, Inc.*

> residential district of the city was largely located along this radial artery.
>
> As a result of this concentration of the city's housing, it seemed logical to dispose the other important centers along the transverse radial artery, which thus came to be regarded as the monumental radial artery.[25]

The traffic system was of considerable importance to the plan, and seems, in fact, to have been essentially the generator of the design. Confronted with the example of Rio, where the hazardous and brutal invasion of motor traffic had made disastrous inroads in the existing urban fabric, it is natural that Costa would wish to forestall future difficulties by adapting the new capital to the circulation of automobiles. Although the plan incorporated a conception of traffic separation between motors and pedestrians, Costa felt that such a system "must not be taken to unnatural extremes, since it must not be forgotten that the car, today, is no longer Man's deadly enemy; it has been domesticated and is almost a member of the family."[26]

At the intersection of the two urban axes would be a multilevel traffic interchange accommodating the central transport terminal. Through traffic would be routed to lower levels, while the upper level would provide a broad platform serving as a site for the theatre and entertainment district. The area of the city adjacent to the intersection would provide sites for the banking and financial center and the central business district.

Projecting on both sides of the interchange, the monumental axis would be developed as a wide, landscaped mall (Fig. 3a). As it extended westward, the axis would be punctuated by a television tower and would provide sites for a hotel district, a sports center and a municipal headquarters. At the western terminus of the axis would be the railroad station, together with a warehousing and industrial area.

The axis as it extended from the interchange eastward toward the lake would be devoted to the headquarters of the national government. Although the residential axis was centered on a motor freeway giving the city an immediate image of mechanization and modernity, the monumental government axis remained essentially a traditional Beaux-Arts composition. A long grass mall would be flanked by uniform rows of federal office buildings and terminated by a triangular plaza containing the major government buildings. According to Costa, "the highlights in the outline plan of the city are the public buildings which house the fundamental powers. These are three, and they are autonomous: therefore the equilateral triangle—associated with the very earliest architecture in the world—is the elementary frame best suited to express them. . . . At each angle of the triangular plaza—the Plaza of the Three Powers, as it might be called—stands one of the three buildings: the Government Palace and the Supreme Court at the base; the Congress Building at the tip."[27]

The residential district of the city was planned in a series of square superblocks flanking the motor axis and containing apartment housing. Within these blocks, he stated, residential buildings could "be arranged in varying manners, though always in obedience to two general principles: uniform height regulations —perhaps a maximum of six stories above the pilotis—and segregation of motorized traffic and pedestrian transit, especially near the entrances to the Primary School and the urban amenities located in each superblock." Each block was to have been surrounded by a band of greenery planted with trees, and "each one will give pride of place to one species of tree; the ground will be carpeted with grass, and shrubs and foliage will screen the internal groupings of the superblock from the spectator, who will get a view of the layout through a haze of greenery."[28] (Fig. 3b)

Each group of four superblocks would be served by a shopping street in which

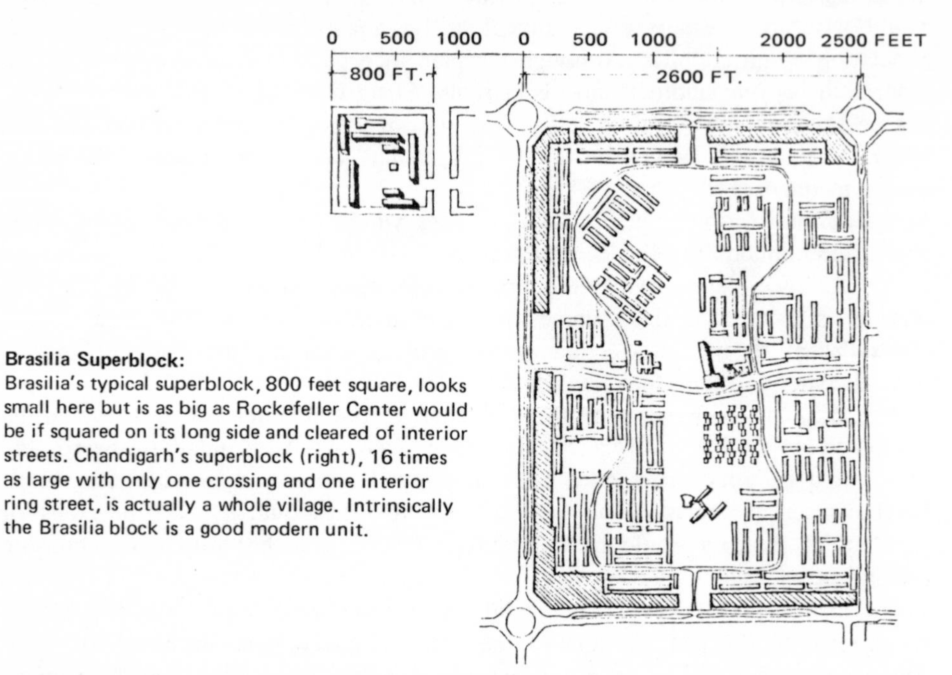

FIG. 3B Brasilia's superblock seen comparatively. *From* The Architectural Forum, *November 1960, Whitney Publication, Inc.*

shops would be oriented to face the interior of the pedestrian spaces of the blocks. In these neighborhood commercial areas the churches and secondary schools would be sited.

In addition to the apartment housing, two districts near the lake would be set aside for large detached houses. Within these areas, house sites would have access from cul-de-sac streets integrated with a system of continuous bands of parkland. In subsequent modifications of the plan, these districts of single-family houses would be shifted to two peninsulas extending into the lake. Most of the land along the lakefront was to be left as natural parkland providing sites for sport clubs, restaurants and playing fields.

Although the housing of the city would be generally unified in type, Costa observed that "The social structure of this housing zone can be graded by setting a greater value on specified superblocks, such as, for example, the single rows which adjoin the diplomatic quarter."[29]

It was expected that the "four-by-four grouping of the superblocks will, while favoring co-existence of social groups, avoid any undue and undesirable stratification of society. And, in any case, variations in the standard of living from one superblock to another will be offset by the organization of the urban scheme itself, and will not be of such a nature as to affect that degree of comfort to which all members of society have a right. Any differences in standard will spring from a greater or lesser density, a larger or smaller living space allocated to each individual or family, or from the quality of building materials selected and the degree of finish which these receive. And since such problems are being raised, the growth of slums, whether on the city outskirts or in the surrounding countryside, should at all costs be prevented. The Development Company should, within the scope of the proposed outline plan, make provision for decent and economical accommodation for the entire population."[30]

In terms of its origins, the Costa plan for Brasilia seems to have its roots in the visionary urban schemes which Le Corbusier produced beginning in the 1920s. In his attempts to create a conception of urban environment appropriate to the needs of the modern age, Le Corbusier developed a series of projects incorporating some of the technological romanticism of the Futurists with the landscape orientation of the Garden City advocates. To Le Corbusier, his imaginary cities provided a way to both have one's cake and eat it—to enjoy the benefits of a technically advanced, mechanized environment and at the same time have the advantages of suburban low-density living.

Le Corbusier viewed the modern city as a symbol of man's technical mastery of his environment.[31] In similar spirit was Costa's observation that Brasilia was "a deliberate act of conquest." Costa believed that Brasilia should appear to be clearly a deliberately planned man-made creation.

Costa once remarked, "We have to finish in five years or the forest will come back."[32] The forest was figurative, but the sense of threat was real. It is against a wilderness which still bears almost no imprint of human occupation that the image of Brasilia must be seen. There is nothing in the design of Brasilia which indicates a desire to harmonize the works of man with those of nature. But this is a country where nature is, in fact, dominant. Brasil has been considered a land that defies human effort to dominate it technologically; thus in Brasilia the symbolic image of the city is enhanced through its rather coarse facade of mechanization and technical mastery.

Brasilia tends to reflect a somewhat dated glorification of the machine; yet because Brazil is an unmechanized, relatively unindustrialized country, the facade of modern technology retains an appeal it may have lost elsewhere. The automobile in Brazil is not a commonplace possession; the romance of the machine is still a thrilling thing, and to have built an entire city to the scale of the motorcar is a source of great pride.

Brasilia shares with Le Corbusier's early schemes a similar conception of the residential superblock, comprising uniform-height apartment blocks raised on pilotis and set amid ample spaces of greenery. Common to Le Corbusier's schemes and the Costa plan is a vastly simplified conception of urban content, texture and function. Much of the initial appeal (and also the repellent quality) of Le Corbusier's early urban designs may have been the illusion they created of a brave new world, unnervingly clean, bright and swept clear of all disorder. This quality appears also in Brasilia, producing somewhat ambivalent reactions. As Costa concluded his plan, Brasilia was to be a "capital of the airplane and the freeway, city and park."[33]

Once the design of Brasilia was under way, Costa did not visit the site, freeing himself from the day-to-day vicissitudes of construction and from temptations to make changes vitiating the purity of the design.[34] Although Costa's pilot was in many ways admirable, the rigidity of the design failed to provide for either *planned expansion* or the *accommodation of new functions*.[35]‡ In the subsequent

‡ (Italics, editor.)

development of the city, therefore, the pristine order of the pilot plan has tended to be surrounded by an increasingly amorphous development. This may be seen, for example, in the new suburban districts being plotted for single-family houses.

Within the pilot plan itself, development has occasionally been at variance with the plan. Although neighborhood shops were intended to focus inward toward the superblocks rather than on the service road, in practice the merchants chose to orient their establishments to the street in the traditional manner. The master plan had provided for a wide street accommodating truck traffic to run parallel to the main radial artery, and on this road were to be wholesale and service establishments. The large, relatively low-priced lots along this street were taken up by retail commerce instead, however, with the result that this avenue (the W3), initially intended for service traffic, became Brasilia's downtown, main shopping street.

Although it had been Costa's intention that Brasilia accommodate all ranges of population, the eventual development of the city has been such that the pilot plan area is largely restricted to middle and upper class housing. The poorer classes have been accommodated in a series of outlying satellite towns lying between ten and twenty miles beyond the city (Fig. 4).

Whatever the virtues of the Costa plan as an over-all conception, there is no doubt that Brasilia has suffered from a lack of thoroughness in the development of the scheme. As the city began to attain reality, the grandeur of the large-scale design was not always balanced by a skill and sensitivity in detail.

THE REALIZATION OF A CITY

Pressures of time were such that work progressed in Brasilia even before the master plan had been selected. On October 2, 1956, Kubitschek began his first stay at the Brasilia site.

On November 1, Israel Pinheiro and Oscar Niemeyer arrived to begin studies for the first buildings of the city. Independent of any master plan, sites had already been selected for the President's Palace and a hotel, both to be placed near the lake. These structures, together with all major government buildings of Brasilia, were to be designed by Niemeyer who, as director of the Department of Architecture of NOVACAP, would supervise the architectural development of the city. Meanwhile, NOVACAP had established an office in the nearby town of Luziâna.

Brasilia, 584 air miles from Rio, was at this time 78 miles from the nearest railroad, 450 miles from the nearest paved roads, and 120 miles from the nearest airport. Among the first tasks of the city builders, therefore, was to start linking the site with the outside world. On October 9, 1956, a road was initiated between Brasilia and the nearby town of Anapolis, with projections for outside rail connections commencing a month later. The Brasilia airport was begun on December 2, to be inaugurated on April 2, 1957, its 3,300-meter runway making it the largest in Brazil. By the following month the initial studies were begun for a new national highway extending 1,300 miles between Belém, at the mouth of the Amazon, and Brasilia; the development of a system of interior highways paralleled the construction of Brasilia, and two months before the dedication of the city, a "Caravan of National Integration" traveled simultaneously by road from Belém, Cuiaba, Rio de Janeiro and Porto Alegre, meeting in Brasilia on February 2, 1960.

FIG. 4 Brasilia with satellite towns existing by 1967. *Photograph by Norma Evenson, from* Two Brazilian Capitals, *Yale University Press, 1973*

An American once described Brasilia under construction by stating, "It was as if the opening of the West had been delayed a hundred years and then done with bulldozers."[36] Simultaneously roads were built, apartments, houses and government buildings designed and erected, water mains, sewers and electrical installations prepared. As the land was graded and excavated, the dry red soil of the city hung over the site in a perpetual thick cloud, which one visitor noted, "soon dries the lips, clogs the nostrils, invades the ears and hair."[37]

During the final year of construction, activity continued around the clock, with building proceeding at night under floodlights. The creation of Brasilia represented a triumph of administration in a country never noted for efficient administration; it embodied adherence to a time schedule in a society where schedules are seldom met, and it demanded continuous hard work from a people reputedly reluctant to work either hard or continuously.

An almost wartime mentality applied to the financing of the city, in which the achievement of a desired goal overrode monetary caution. Cost figures given for Brasilia tend to vary, reflecting both a lack of detailed information and prejudice either for or against the city. William Holford once declared, "Nobody knows, least of all I think the New Town Corporation (NOVACAP), what this new town has cost. When I asked Dr. Pinheiro, the President of NOVACAP, whether he was bothered by accountants over capital expenditure, or by capital accounts committees and things of that kind, he said, 'No, no, no.' I said 'Do tell me the secret. How is it that you survive?' He said, 'It is quite simple. We have fixed a D-Day—April 21, 1960. The town must be ready then. I have said to Parliament, "'If you criticize me, you do not get your town.'"[38] A similar experience was reported by the British architect Max Lock, who observed, "I had the privilege of meeting Niemeyer, and I asked him how much his palace cost. He shrugged his shoulders, as I would like to be able to do, and said, 'I do not know. How should I know?'"[39]

The total cost of Brasilia from the initiation of construction to the dedication of the city has been calculated as six hundred million dollars, with estimates of additional expenditures up to 1966 of one billion dollars.[40]

An ex-minister of finance in Brazil once proclaimed that "construction of a new capital in a poor country . . . is a crime against the country's economy.[41] There is no doubt that the years of Brasilia's construction coincided with a sharp increase in inflation, and opponents of the city have frequently cited the project as having had a disastrous effect on an already shaky economic development. A pessimistic American businessman once predicted, "Brazilians will have to decide between Brazil and Brasilia."[42]

To the city's supporters, however, the long-term benefits of Brasilia would far outweigh the initial government investment. Moreover, part of the costs were balanced by the sale of land to private owners. Confidence in the new capital appeared to be such that there was no difficulty in disposing of land, and by 1960 NOVACAP reported the sale of 18,018 lots to private buyers. As the city developed, there was evidence of considerable speculation in land both within Brasilia and in the surrounding Federal District.

Oscar Niemeyer remained continuously on the site, directing construction. One visitor observed in 1960 that he "has a drafting table in a construction shack, a telephone, and apparently no secretary. There are perhaps two dozen draftsmen in an adjoining room. One of his chores is the making of hundreds of on-the-spot decisions in the course of a day. . . . Outside there were some 45,000 workmen who were doing, in effect, what Niemeyer had told them to do. 'Oscar isn't an organization type,' he replied. Suddenly he laughed. 'You know, if we had been organized we never could have done it.' "[43]

Although the construction was generally supervised by NOVACAP, the building of the city was by no means an exclusively government enterprise. Much of the building was carried out by large private contractors who provided their own engineering staff, specialized workers and construction experience.

Although such a large-scale project as Brasilia could have been a proving ground for experimental building techniques and new materials, the construction of the city followed conventional usages. The most important factor in governing building was the need for speed, and this, together with the large number of unskilled workers, prompted the employment of relatively simple designs and easily mastered techniques. With the exception of the Brasilia Palace Hotel and the government ministries, which used steel frame construction, all large buildings were of reinforced concrete. Gravel and sand were obtained at distances of six to thirty-seven miles around Brasilia, and bricks could be produced near the site. Other materials had to be brought over considerable distances. Timber came from the state of Parana, about 746 miles to the south, while steel had to be transported over 1,000 miles. Although, initially, airplanes were used for some supply transport, almost all materials were brought to Brasilia by truck.

In the early phases of construction, tank trucks supplied water for both building and drinking purposes. Each building site had a diesel-powered generator to furnish current for machinery, workshops and lodgings.

For the initial phase of construction, building activity was centered in the south axis of the city, the side nearest the highway approaches from Rio and Saõ Paulo. It was hoped that by the time of dedication, Brasilia would be sufficiently complete to provide housing for thirty thousand government employees.

As building progressed, Brasilia became a magnet for workers from all over Brazil. A pattern of migration from poverty-stricken rural areas which had already swollen the populations of most major cities was repeated in the new capital where the magnitude of the construction effort gave hopes for steady employment. Work camps, providing barracklike housing close to large building sites, accommodated some of the influx. In addition, outside the pilot plan area, a temporary settlement called Cidade Livre (Free Town) was established. Within this town land was made available free, with the understanding that, once Brasilia was completed, the town would be demolished.

Consisting largely of wooden shacklike buildings, Cidade Livre provided not only a place of residence, but the shopping, business and entertainment center for the area. By 1958, this settlement contained about 340 business establishments, including thirteen hotels, five banking agencies, four churches, four airline offices, and various enterprises such as restaurants, butcher shops, bakeries, drugstores, sawmills, a movie house and, as an inevitable accompaniment to a predominantly male population, an assortment of brothels.

Observing Cidade Livre, one visitor reported that "all sorts of riffraff and fugitives populate this wide-open shanty town," claiming that "it is not safe to venture far from the car."[44] Another witness concurred, stating that "Everyone carries a gun or knife, and life is cheap as in a mountain mining town. Police are not in evidence except for traffic."[45] Others, however, were attracted to Cidade Livre, finding it a lively and colorful contrast to the majestic but somewhat sterile city taking form nearby. In the opinion of one foreign observer, "The rip-roaring, blood-red life of the downtown Free City should have been placed bang in the center of the main city right from the word 'go.' "[46]

As construction progressed, and the dedication date neared, it became evident to the administrators of Brasilia that the city as planned was ill suited to accommodate the population which had actually accumulated around the site. As a national capital, Brasilia was designed to be inhabited by the administrative and white-collar class, and although the Costa plan had presupposed a certain range in income levels, the housing which was constructed was predominantly middle class. Neither the planners nor the administrators of the project had anticipated or made provision for the great influx of low-income people attracted to Brasilia, and obsessed with the urgent problems of construction, had tended to regard the large working-class populace as a temporary phenomenon. Eventually, however, they became aware that the large numbers of people drawn to the Federal District were not likely to leave and would require permanent accommodations.

When Kubitschek had made his first inspection of work camps in November 1956, there had been a total of 232 workers on the site. By January 1957, the number had risen to 2,500, and continued increasing rapidly. By 1959, the resident population of the Federal District was given as 64,314. Of these, 28,020 were living in work camps on the city site, 11,565 were in Cidade Livre, and 6,196 in another temporary settlement. Outlying towns contained 6,277 and 12,256 resided in the rural zone.

It was decided not to alter the planned character of Brasilia, but to accommodate lower income people in separate communities outside the pilot plan area. This involved the creation of a group of so-called satellite towns placed at distances ranging from about ten to twenty miles beyond the city. The siting of these communities initially related not to any comprehensive plan for the expansion of Brasilia, but to the rural development of the Federal District.

In an effort to encourage local sources of food supply, the Federal District had been planned with a series of rural centers (*Nucleos Rurais*), each consisting of a group of small family farms ranging from 60 to 150 acres in size. These farms, leased on a homestead system, were plotted as narrow strips extending from stream beds. Land laid out in this manner gave each farm part of the narrow forest belt lying on the valley bottoms and a larger area extending up the slope.

It had been projected that these rural settlements would eventually acquire small centers for local commerce, schools and co-operatives; thus when seeking new sites for low-cost residence, it seemed convenient to the planners of Brasilia to expand the rural centers into satellite towns. For this reason, the Brasilia satellites are frequently surrounded by farmsteads.

The town of Taguatinga was founded in 1958, with Sobradinho and Gama following in 1960. In 1961, Cidade Livre, originally intended as a temporary settlement, was made into a permanent satellite town and rechristened Nucleo Bandierantes (Pioneer Center).** Planaltina, which had been the oldest existing town in the Federal District, was declared a satellite in 1967. More recently cre-

** Now planned for a population of 40,000. (Editor.)

ated satellites include Guará and Jardim, while satellite status has been given to the existing settlements of Paranoá and Brazlândia.

The conception of a satellite grouping of communities derives from Ebenezer Howard's Garden City theory, in which the system would comprise a group of economically self-sufficient towns which might depend on a larger center for certain services. The Brasilia satellites, however, are not true satellites, but essentially dormitory towns for workers in Brasilia, and most of the residents are subjected to an inconvenient and expensive regimen of bus commuting. Neither Costa nor Niemeyer chose to associate himself with the design of the satellite towns, and their plans were produced by the NOVACAP staff.

Although land costs in the satellites are relatively low, urban amenities are rudimentary and far inferior to those provided the inhabitants of Brasilia. Schools and medical facilities are scarce, parks are absent, streets are frequently unpaved, and utilities are unreliable and unevenly distributed. By and large, the satellites present the appearance of ordinary unprosperous country towns, with housing ranging from wooden shacks to relatively comfortable brick bungalows, and commercial facilities consisting of small shops and outdoor markets. Because civic amenities are primitive, and so many of the houses little more than huts, some visitors have tended to confuse the satellites with squatter settlements or *favelas* (Fig. 5a).

Brasilia lacks the immediate juxtaposition of rich and poor which characterizes many Brazilian cities, where one may often find squatter slums next to expensive apartment houses. In Brasilia, the prevailing segregation of rich and poor is underlined by the pronounced physical separation of the poor in satellite towns.

The segregation of social groups has been one of the most disturbing aspects of Brasilia, especially to foreigners. To many Brazilians, however, it merely reflects prevailing social conditions. Even to Oscar Niemeyer, a self-styled Communist, the exclusion of the poor from the city seemed an inevitable result of circumstances. He once wrote,

> We were only saddened by the conviction that it would be unfeasible to insure the workers the standard of living assigned them by the Pilot Plan, which situated them, as would have been only fair, within the collective housing areas so as to allow their children to grow up with the other children of Brasilia in a friendly, impartial association designed to eliminate frustration and fit them for the new station which would be theirs when in time the just claims of humanity were fully granted. We realized to our regret that the social conditions in force conflicted at this point with the spirit of the Pilot Plan, creating problems it was impossible to solve on the drawing board and even demanding—as some of the more ingenuous suggested—a social architecture that would lead us nowhere without a socialist basis. Once again, it was brought home to us that all we could do was to support the progressive movements that envisage a better and a happier world.[47]

April 21, 1960, had been set for the formal inauguration of Brasilia, a date exactly three years, one month and five days following the selection of the master plan. As the time for dedication drew near, preparations reached a frantic pace, and NOVACAP director Israel Pinheiro was to be seen "running

FIG. 5A Housing in the satellite, Nucleo Bandierantes, formerly Cidade Livre, initially intended as a temporary workers' settlement. *Photograph by Norma Evenson*

madly from place to place on April 21st, shouting orders, terribly embarrassed and disappointed about so much not being thoroughly and completely finished, and saying all the time, in the most innocent good faith to whoever would listen: 'If I had only had another five days, another five days. . . .' "[48] In a final frenzied cleanup, 60,000 workers carted off debris, planted palm trees and scrubbed the red dust from the monumental buildings. In one day 2,000 steel light poles were installed, while overnight 722 houses were painted white.

In addition to a sizable infrastructure, the completed work included the Presidential Palace, the Brasilia Palace Hotel, and a government complex containing the Supreme Court, the Palace of the Planalto (the executive headquarters), and the National Congress. Eleven government ministry buildings bordered the monumental axis, although all were not yet ready for occupancy. Completed housing within the superblocks included 94 apartment blocks, 500 one-story and 222 two-story houses, accompanied by schools and shopping facilities.

The dedication of Brasilia was conducted with appropriate bravura. A reported 150,000 people converged on the site, where ceremonies included a special midnight mass, a joint session of Congress, a parade of 5,000 troops and 10,000 workers, and an evening pageant climaxed by thirty-eight tons of fireworks. Although the city was still unfinished, Kubitschek's triumph was complete!

By the date of dedication, most federal agencies in Rio had set up token offices in Brasilia, with a reported total of 975 employees. The bulk of the government establishment, however, continued to function in Rio. Although Brasilia had become the nominal capital, the question of how fast the transfer of capital functions would be realized remained open to considerable speculation. Once Kubitschek was out of office, the new president would strongly influence the fate of the new city.

For a time, progress in Brasilia seemed to stagnate. Jânio Quadros, who held the presidency briefly in 1961, had relatively little interest in the project, and his successor, João Goulart, who remained in office from 1961 to 1964 seemed similarly disinclined to promote the city. With the 1964 military coup, which placed Castelo Branco in power, however, presidential support for Brasilia revived, and Branco's successor, Costa e Silva, announced as he took office in 1967 that he was determined to complete the transfer of government to Brasilia during his administration. No one took this literally, needless to say, but it did indicate a degree of support for Brasilia. Following the incapacitating illness of Costa e Silva, Emílio Garrastazu Médici took office in October 1969 with reassurances of his intentions to promote the development of the capital. Although since 1964 the Brazilian Government has pledged support for Brasilia, no timetable has been established for the completion of the city, which is so heavily dependent on vagaries of presidential policy. While the idea of Brasilia seems to have become politically acceptable, the strong personal identification which Kubitschek felt for the project has been notably lacking in his successors.

Brasilia and its satellites have continued to attract immigrants, with the most rapid increase of population occurring in the satellites. By 1964, the population of the Federal District was reported as 268,315, of which 89,231 inhabited the Pilot Plan area.[49] By 1970, ten years after the founding of the new capital, the population of the Federal District had reached 538,351. Of this number 236,477 were living in the Pilot Plan area, and the remainder occupied the satellite communities.

In spite of the dire predictions of the city's initial opponents and the many people who still dislike the city, Brasilia appears to have evidenced a steady growth. Although many government officials have been loathe to leave Rio, and have made little effort to expedite transfer of their agencies, there is little doubt that sooner or later the move will be made. It is all a question of time, but in Brazil, this can mean quite a lot of time.

In 1966, the Brazilian Foreign Office announced the intention to transfer its entire staff and activities to Brasilia, providing impetus for the eventual transfer of all embassies, together with the diplomatic colony. The Itamarity Palace, the headquarters of the Foreign Office, designed by Oscar Niemeyer, was officially dedicated in 1967, and new housing for agency staff begun in the North Axis. The deadline for the move was set for April 1970. Foreign embassies were informed that after September 7, 1972 (Brazilian Independence Day), diplomatic accreditation, immunities and privileges would be granted only to those diplomats residing in Brasilia. Although it is not certain just how strictly this timetable will be observed, the shift to Brasilia of the diplomatic colony will doubtless enliven the social life of the city.††

The eventual quality of life within Brasilia is as yet difficult to assess, but compared to Rio, with its vigorous commercial activity, its abundant entertainment and cultural facilities, and its mixture of population, Brasilia will doubtless for a long time strike many as antiseptic and dull. Administrative capitals have seldom been among the most exciting of cities, and such planned bureaucratic centers as Canberra, New Delhi and Washington D.C. have often been derided for their lack of stimulation.

For many years, Brasilia was imbued with the excitement of the frontier, its citizens bouyed up through participation in a common adventure. A visitor to the city in 1959 observed, "I have never seen happier people—I mean naturally happy. They seem to have a definite purpose."[50] It remains to be seen how long this spirit can be maintained.

With regard to the present population of government workers, an American journalist noted, "The city is not only extraordinarily homogeneous in respect of class and income: it is also, as befits 'the most modern city in the world,' a city of young people."[51] Older government employees, with seniority in their positions, and with homes firmly established in Rio, have naturally been less likely to move than younger workers, for whom the transfer usually meant faster promotions and also subsidized housing far superior to what they could afford in Rio.

"Brasilia is, above all, a family town . . . overwhelmingly 'young married.'"[52] The superblocks, with their primary schools, lawns and playgrounds, seem clearly intended for the raising of small children, and the residential portions of the city exhibit much the same atmosphere as many North American suburbs. Observing this "close approximation of life in American suburbia," the journalist commented, "Apparently near-equality of incomes and ages, rootlessness, good public schools, space for outdoor games, and the ubiquitous car will produce the same pattern of society anywhere."[53]

THE ARCHITECTURE OF BRASILIA

Brasilia became known to the world primarily as an architectural image. Embodying one of the major trends in postwar design, the city initially appeared as the apotheosis of the glass box, the geometric clarity of the plan reflected in a pristine regimentation of building form. This consistency of form reflected architectural controls as well as a common vision apparently shared by the contributing architects. Because of the speed with which the city was designed, its building pattern tends to reflect a single moment in the history of architecture (Fig. 5b).

The stylistic idiom which first characterized Brasilia owed much to the visual qualities of the International Style. Such building was marked by a clear rectilinear frame, light external curtain walls, generous use of glass, and a preference for smoothly finished surfaces. Embodying what came to be termed the "machine aesthetic," this architecture attained wide acceptance during the 1920s as a symbol of modernity, and by the 1950s, continued to influence a large body of design.

†† Formal confirmation of Brasilia as diplomatic capital of Brazil took place in October 1972 when the transfer of all diplomatic missions, meeting stiff resistance, was finally completed. The New York *Times,* November 1972. (Editor's note.)

FIG. 5B Motor axis with superblock housing. *Photograph by Norma Evenson*

By and large, the architecture of Brasilia contained neither technical nor formal innovations, being based on existing concepts of design and methods of construction. Throughout the city, architecture was controlled and limited to standardized types. A single design sufficed for all of the government ministries bordering the central mall. Office buildings in the central business district were designed within a prescribed envelope of uniform height and orientation. Neighborhood shops adhered to a standardized two-story scheme, while those along the W3 maintained a consistent three-story pattern.

In the case of the apartment buildings within the residential superblocks, the master plan had provided restrictions of height combined with the requirement of an open ground level. This formula appears, like much of the urban plan, to relate to the prototypical apartment housing of Le Corbusier's early visionary cities.

The interior layouts of the 800-foot square superblocks have largely followed the example sketched in Costa's competition design, containing a series of apartment slabs placed at right angles to one another. The plan allowed for only a limited range of housing types, apartment blocks of six stories above the pilotis, or ground floor columns, less expensive apartment blocks of three stories above the columns, two-story and single-story row houses. Individually designed detached houses were permitted only in the upper-class residential peninsulas.

The housing developed for Brasilia was relatively conventional, including customary room layouts, together with the servants' quarters usually included in Brazilian middle-class dwellings. In a conventional Brazilian city block, the apartment buildings extend around the periphery, fronting on the surrounding street. Exposed to the interior of the block is a service area, usually containing an open balcony where laundry is done, and giving access to the kitchen and servants' quarters. Hidden within the center of the block, these service areas have seldom been of much architectural concern. The open placement of buildings within the Brasilia superblocks, eliminated the distinction between front and back, and presented a problem of concealment for the somewhat unsightly service areas. In Brasilia each apartment building has what might be termed an open and a closed facade. On one side are the large windows of the main living areas open to the view. On the other side are the service balconies which are closed behind various screening devices. A wall of open brickwork is frequently used for this purpose.

The presence of windows on only one side of the apartment buildings could have inspired a pattern of orientation with regard to the sun. There is no evidence anywhere in Brasilia of such considerations, however, and many of the ubiquitous glass walls receive massive doses of sunlight throughout the day. On some buildings, external sunbreakers have been employed, but in most, only curtains and blinds are available to control the glare. A serious problem with sun developed in the glass-walled government ministries, and vertical louvers of plastic were installed inside the glass.

Compared with many other places, Brasilia has an undemanding climate, and there is relatively little temperature variation throughout the year. The sun is frequently hot, but the air is dry and breezy, and the nights are usually cool. Presented with no extraordinary challenges, the architects of the city appear to have made no efforts at climatic adaptation. In addition to the failure to consider sun orientation, many buildings in Brasilia appear woefully lacking in natural ventilation, a circumstance which would be excusable if there were adequate air conditioning. This is used sparingly, however, in a few major buildings.

Although the mildness of the climate might warrant it, housing in Brasilia generally does not afford private open space. Apartments have no terraces or balconies other than the service areas, and houses contain no patios. In the case of the apartments, building regulations do not permit overhangs beyond the wall line, thus precluding balconies other than those recessed into the building block, and most designers evidently consider these a waste of interior space.

The housing areas do, however, provide ample communal areas in the form of lawns and playgrounds. The row houses are designed to front on common strips of greenery, with the service areas, containing garages and maids' rooms, having access from rear service lanes.

Although Brasilia as it now exists presents an image of architectural uniformity, some variations in facade treatment are appearing as the north axis develops. Some of the newer superblocks in this largely unbuilt section of the city have abandoned the glass wall for an extensive use of exposed brick and concrete. The most notable departure from what had been the prevailing architectural idiom may be seen in the housing for Foreign Office employees, which exhibits a massive use of rough concrete, and introduces six-story point blocks as a variation of the usual slab. It is reasonable to assume that as Brasilia grows, the architecture will reflect a degree of evolution of building styles.

Inherent in the architectural control of Brasilia was the maintenance of a visual hierarchy between the monumental architecture and the more utilitarian buildings of the city. The formal discipline governing the development of the Pilot Plan area underlined the symbolic role of the capital, attempting to assure the subordination of all other elements to the dominant monumental complex.

It was in the creation of the major government buildings that Oscar Niemeyer concentrated his own design efforts. Already known internationally for its formal innovations, Niemeyer's work in many ways epitomized the Brazilian contribution to modern design. While adopting many of the mannerisms of the International Style, he had infused them with a Baroque sense of curving free form and decoration. Although much of the doctrine of modern design had stressed an objective, impersonal, "rational" design adapted to mechanization and standardized methods of production, Brazilian designers frequently emphasized the personal, the intuitive, the emotionally expressive.

Niemeyer claimed to have felt himself frustrated by a social system in which the architect was "relegated only to wait upon the caprices of the rich,"[54] admitting that in these circumstances he had come to see architecture "as an exercise to be undertaken with a sportive spirit."[55] Motivated by clients "desirous of giving their buildings something showy and spectacular to be talked about,"[56] he had often executed projects hurriedly, relying on his originality and powers of improvisation rather than on meticulous attention to detail. For Niemeyer the "works in progress in Brasilia . . . mark a new stage in my professional activities. This step is characterized by a constant seeking for conciseness and purity, as well as greater attention to basic architectural problems. . . . I have become interested in compact solutions, simple and geometric: the fitness of unity and harmony amongst the buildings, and, further, that these no longer be expressed through their secondary elements, but rather through the structure itself, duly integrated within the original plastic conception."[57]

Niemeyer's monumental buildings in Brasilia represent in some degree a fusion of his new desire for a simplification of architectural form, seen in the rectilinear plans and essentially classical partie of the buildings, combined with his long-lived fondness for curving elements, evidenced in the extensive use of curvilinear columns.

Although the Brasilia commission coincided with a period in which Niemeyer had intended to devote increasing time and care to individual projects, the short deadline for the construction of the new city compelled him to rely once more on his talent for improvisation. He has claimed that each of the major government buildings of Brasilia consumed no more than fifteen days' design time, but, making a virtue of necessity, insisted that "it is just this pressure which is a favorable element in architecture, enabling the architect—once the architectonic solution has been settled—to avoid further modifications and thus preserve it in all its purity and spontaneity."[58]

The monumental complex of Brasilia as developed by Niemeyer followed the general layout of the Costa plan. The Plaza of the Three Powers, which terminated the ceremonial mall lined with government ministries, was based on a triangular plan with the National Congress Building marking the apex toward the mall. Beyond this, the Supreme Court Building and the Palace of the Planalto (housing the presidential staff) face each other across a wide paved plaza. Of the three, the most arresting visually is the National Assembly which provides the dominant focus of the government axis. This building was designed to create a wide horizontal platform carrying on its roof the two legislative chambers. The Senate of one hundred members is contained within a shallow dome, while the larger House of Representatives accommodates seven hundred members within a saucerlike inverted dome. Immediately adjacent, the administrative offices rise in the form of twin slabs sheathed in glass, the tallest buildings in Brasilia. Frequently photographed, the National Assembly ensemble quickly became the visual symbol of the city (Figs. 6a, 6b).

Niemeyer attempted to unify the architecture of the government complex by framing building exteriors with decorative tapering columns. Initially employed on the Palace of the Alvorado (Palace of the Dawn), the presidential residence, these columns appear in variations on the Supreme Court and Planalto Palace. This screen of curving elements was intended to add a delicate sculptural plasticity to basically simple boxlike building forms, providing also a conscious evocation of Baroque traditions. Supported by concrete, but sheathed in glass and a glistening veneer of white marble, the monumental building of Brasilia display variations on a theme of lightness and fragility.

Describing his over-all conception for the Plaza of the Three Powers, Niemeyer has stated,

> My special concern was to find—without functional limitations—a beautiful clear-cut structure that would define the characteristics of the main buildings—the palaces, strictly so-called—within the indispensable criterion of simplicity and nobility. But I was also concerned . . . with the desire that these buildings should turn out to be something new and different . . . so that they should strike future visitors to the capital with a sensation of surprise and emotion that would augment and engrave it on their memories. I called to mind the Piazza San Marco in Venice, the Palace of the Doges and the Cathedral of Chartres. . . . Plastic beauty alone is the guiding, dominating spirit, with its permanent message of grace and poetry.[59]

Niemeyer's intentions involved a notable departure from the traditional conception of monumental architecture. By long-term usage, monumental design has embodied a building type which is massive, plastically powerful and symbolically evocative of the strength, permanence and dignity of the institutions it represents. Although such imagery initially accompanied the constraints of mason construction, it has been maintained in some contemporary uses of reinforced concrete. The buildings of Le Corbusier's capitol complex in Chandigarh, for example, although modern in style, maintain many of the qualities of traditional monumentality. Massive, solidly rooted to the earth, they maintain a ponderous solemnity defiant of time and destruction.

The drama which Niemeyer sought to create in Brasilia was of a less traditional order—almost antimonumental in the customary sense, yet in its own way perhaps

FIG. 6A Government axis viewed from the television tower. *Photograph by Norma Evenson*

appropriate. Niemeyer's intentions were realized much as he described them, for the government complex does, frequently, convey an air of dreamlike unreality. For much of the year, the sky is filled with scudding clouds bathing the ensemble in shifting light and shadow, the floating formations of vapor often sustaining an illusion of greater substance than the man-made structures below. Appearing to rest but lightly on the tips of tapering supports, the buildings seem to have been placed by a magician's hand, rather than constructed by patient human labor, creating an apparition which strikes the vision with hallucinatory clarity. There is no emphatic and secure sense of possessing the site, of somehow marking it forever for human occupation. There is a poignant awareness of the ephemeral, a melancholy and sophisticated perception of how tenuous is man's grasp of the earth, and how transient are his works.

The ceremonial plaza marks an edge of settlement, defined by a retaining wall, above a stretch of rough open land. It is here that one becomes most conscious of the expansiveness of the site and the enormity of the wilderness seemingly waiting without to engulf the city. The insubstantiality of the architecture is accentuated against the image of the surrounding wasteland, and one senses what

FIG. 6B The Legislative Assembly and Secretariat. *Photograph by Norma Evenson*

an act of daring the creation of Brasilia was. The entire city reflects the bravado of a frontier town, and the gleam of marble and glass embodied in the decorative elegance of Niemeyer's designs defies the wilderness as gilt and plush once brought a breath of gentility and civilization to our own Western towns.

In a sense, the lightly framed pavilions of the ceremonial complex may not be altogether inappropriate as symbols of Brazilian governmental institutions. A Brazilian scholar, Aleu Amoroso Lima, once observed that "Brazil has no organic political structure, no political institutions which are characteristically Brazilian and participate in the native Brazilian humanism. . . . In matters of politics, Brazilians are conformistic. They are not partisan minded, or even very strongly public minded."[60] It is possible to see in Niemeyer's buildings a certain unconscious evocation of the very insecurity and shallowness of Brazilian political life.

It is possible also to see an underlying falseness in the symbolic placement of the major government buildings. It may be recalled that Costa introduced his plan for the complex by stating, "the highlights in the outline plan of the city are the public buildings which house the fundamental powers." He continued, "These are three, and they are autonomous: therefore the equilateral triangle."[61] Brazilian government does not in practice embody such a balance of power. Governmental authority is largely invested in the President who frequently writes his own constitution and to whom legislative and judicial functions tend to be subordinate. A more symbolically accurate architectural ensemble might well have focused on the executive building, as Lutyens' government complex in New Delhi focused on the Viceroy's palace. The visual dominance given to the legislature in Brasilia may be considered essentially a gesture to the ideal of parliamentary democracy.

Although Niemeyer's government complex was intended to provide a ceremonial focus to which the rest of the city would be architecturally subordinate, the visual impact of Brasilia lies in the whole, rather than in a single grouping of buildings. One may consider the city, in fact, as a *single unified work of art,*‡‡ planned as a totality, and controlled in execution.

It has been noted that Brasilia comprehensively realizes many concepts of urban design presented in Le Corbusier's early schemes. The postwar period, with its sudden increases in urban development, encouraged the creation of new towns, and permitted the application of many design concepts previously restricted to theory. Brasilia, with its rigid zoning of activities, its massive motorways and standardized building patterns is not unique, but a thoroughgoing embodiment of a type of environment becoming, in more fragmentary form, a universal experience. What Lewis Mumford once termed "yesterday's city of tomorrow" has in many other places been either wholly or partially achieved.

Inevitably, as the imperfections of planned perfection evidence themselves, some urban designers have rejected the ideal of the totally ordered city for a determined advocacy of variety, spontaneity and flexibility. The desire for functional zoning has been replaced by a tendency to regard close physical juxtaposition of housing, commerce and institutions as essential to liveliness and convenience within the city. Geometric, modular design and repetitive forms are frequently derided as sterile and monotonous, and to a new generation favoring complexity of form, the Italian hill town as a prototypical ideal has replaced the simplistic compositions of the 20s and 30s. Even in the short time of its existence, Brasilia has come to embody a somewhat outmoded conception of modernity.

The architecture of Brasilia is, like all architecture, the product of a given set of circumstances and a given moment in time. Although it may be assumed that nothing is preordained, once achieved, events tend to acquire an air of inevitability and rightness. Brasilia was a city of buildings before it was a city of people. It was architecture which gave Brasilia its existence, and architects who made a reality of the founders' dreams. Although the city is a conscious creation and could have been conceived otherwise, the reality of Brasilia now obliterates alternatives. The idea of the new capital is now inseparable from its realization.

BRASILIA AS SYMBOL

The symbolism of Brasilia rests on many levels, embracing both the reasons for the city's existence and the nature of its design. As a political concept, the idea of an inland capital is as old as the Brazilian nation itself. To the political revolutionaries of the eighteenth and nineteenth centuries, the new city was to have symbolized Brazilian independence, and to later statesmen it remained symbolic of a desired political unity. For many years the idea of Brasilia was embedded in the prevailing political rhetoric of Brazil, embodying a continuing dream of national greatness. Associated with the long-standing aim of populating the interior, the new capital, through the placement of institutional monuments on previously unsettled land, creates a symbolic possession anticipating actual development.

Although for practical reasons the city could not be placed in the geographic

‡‡(Editor's italics.)

center of Brazil, its present location was intended to represent a demographic centrality. No longer tied to the prosperous southern coast, Brasilia would, in the hopes of its advocates, bring the rulers of Brazil symbolically closer to the problems of the nation as a whole.

Conceived as a national monument, Brasilia in its physical realization embodies an interworking of symbolic images, appearing to some as less a viable city than a frigid and megalomaniacally scaled stage set. To those who, like Gilberto Freyre, would wish the new capital to present a thoroughgoing and easily recognizable summation of grass-roots Brazilian culture, Brasilia seems a disembodied abstraction unrelated to any local tradition. To the dismay of anyone with expectations that the city would provide a setting for social experimentation or amelioration of lower-class living conditions, Brasilia not only maintains prevailing class distinctions, but underlines them with a degree of physical separation not found elsewhere. Brasilia is not a city lover's city, and to observers accustomed to the visual complexity, variety and cohesion of older more "natural" towns, Brasilia will seem drastically oversimplified in urban form, architecturally regimented and socially fragmented.

To those who view Brasilia only in terms of what it is not, the city must appear a failure. Considered in its own symbolic terms, however, Brasilia seems in many ways a success. In Brazilian context, Brasilia is not a "real" city, but a city of aspiration. The motorized scale of the city, with its visual emphasis on freeways and traffic interchanges must be seen against the prevailing lack of technical advancement in Brazil as a whole.* Brasilia visually symbolizes a degree of mechanization which Brazil has not achieved, but seeks as a national goal. The residential districts within the Pilot Plan area present an image of prosperous middle-class living which is far above that enjoyed by most Brazilians. The fact that in order to preserve intact this vision of an atypical way of life, the poor were banished from the city has disturbed many visitors. For those who can accept the social segregation inherent in the city, the housing of Brasilia may effectively represent the achievement of an ideal environment.†

In terms of architecture, Brasilia embodies no real innovations, but maintains comprehensively a type of ambience seen elsewhere only in fragments. The predominant building pattern of Brasilia retains many characteristics of the International Style, and in this way reproduces what has been perhaps the most popularly accepted image of modern architecture. Thus with its automotive dominance and the glossy up-to-dateness of its buildings, Brasilia presents a facade which even the most unsophisticated can proudly identify as "modern." However superficial, the blatant modernity of Brasilia is relevant to its visual success.

It has been noted that in the Plaza of the Three Powers the symbolic placement of the major buildings provides a somewhat misleading representation of governmental authority. The relatively powerless National Assembly provides the com-

* ". . . vast traffic jam's, serious parking problems and the highest accident rate in the country are now features of a city that was built for the automobile." The New York *Times,* November 1972. (Editor's note.)

† See "Urban Growth and Public Policy in Brasília's Satellite Cities." Thomas G. Sanders, *American Universities Field Staff Report,* South America, Vol. XVII, No. 7 (1973). Brazil is now paying attention to Brasilia's satellite cities as filling a real need. (Editor's note.)

positional focus, while the dominant executive authority appears visually balanced by the Supreme Court. Just how many Brazilians ponder this discrepancy, however, is open to speculation. The government complex photographs effectively and is not without its own sense of poetic drama. The National Assembly, moreover, easily recognizable and frequently reproduced throughout the country, has provided Brazil with its first truly national architectural symbol.

William Holford once observed of Brasilia, "For the poor and illiterate this town building is a symbol which they can see and understand."[62] It is not only the unsophisticated who have responded to the city, however. For all its controversial aspects, Brasilia has increasingly become a focus of legitimate national pride.

To its opponents, Brasilia remains a ruinous extravagance, an act of political bravado irrelevant to practical problems. Brasilia represents more than a dictator's whim, however, and owes its existence to a genuinely enthusiastic common effort. It may be remembered that the achievements which throughout human history have inspired the most dedication have seldom been utilitarian, but more frequently those with strong symbolic meaning.

André Malraux once observed, "This Brasilia on its great plateau it is a bit like the Acropolis on its rock," and he added, "the forms of art destined to remain in the memory of men are invented forms."[63] As the Acropolis stood clear and sharp against the sky, so the less reassuringly rooted structures of Brasilia create an equally uncompromising affirmation of the human presence. The Acropolis was a civic extravagance, and the cathedrals of the Middle Ages were similarly wasteful of resources. Behind Brasilia may be seen an impulse akin to the irrational optimism which once prompted a group of thirteen bankrupt former British colonies to establish a capital so grandiose in its outlines as to provoke derisive comment for at least fifty years after its founding.

Brasilia is not a triumph of urban design, nor is its architecture universally admired. The city attempts to solve no social problems, and its economic contribution to the surrounding area is yet to be determined. But these factors are secondary to the essential purpose of the city, which is to exist where it is.

As our urban inheritance reminds us of the life and hope and folly of our ancestors, so Brasilia takes its place as a visible witness to the flawed, aspiring human spirit.

NOTES

[1] Theodore Roosevelt, *Through the Brazilian Wilderness.* New York, Charles Scribner's Sons, 1914, pp. 174–76. For this quotation, the author is indebted to Hollister Kent, who employed it in his doctoral dissertation, *Vera Cruz: Brazil's New Federal Capital,* Cornell University, 1956.

[2] Israel Pinheiro, "Uma Realidade: Brasília," *Modulo* 8:3–8 (June 1957). Quotation from English supplement, p. 12.

[3] Quoted by Raul de Sa Barbosa, "Brasília, Evolucão Historica de Una Ideia," *Modulo* 18:28–42 (June 1960). English supplement included.

[4] Pinheiro, op. cit., English supplement, p. 11.

[5] Barbosa, op. cit., p. 34. English supplement included.

[6] Ibid., p. 39.

[7] Hollister Kent dissertation, *Vera Cruz,* Cornell University, 1956, p. 18.

[8] "Kubitschek's Brasilia," *Time* 75:38–39 (April 25, 1960), p. 38.

[9] Ibid., p. 39.

[10] "A Historia da Construção de Brasília," *Brasília* 40:44–53 (April 21, 1960), p. 47. *Brasilia* is an official journal published by NOVACAP. The statement is reproduced from Kubitschek's New Year's message of 1957.

[11] J. O. de Meira Penna, "Brazil Builds a New Capital," *Landscape* 5:17–22 (Spring 1956), pp. 21–22.

[12] "Kubitschek's Brasilia," op. cit., p. 39.

[13] Gilberto Freyre, *Brasis, Brasil, Brasília.* Lisbon, Ediçao "Livros do Brasil," 1960, p. 156.

[14] William Holford, "Brasilia: A New Capital City for Brazil," *Architectural Review* 122:394–402 (December 1957), p. 397.

[15] Ibid. The complete program of the competition in Portuguese may be found reproduced in *Brasília* 3:19–20 (March 1957).

[16] "Concurso Para o Plano Piloto," *Brasília* 3:6–8 (March 1957), p. 7.

[17] Minutes of the Committee for Judging the Pilot Plan of Brasilia," published in the *Diário Oficial,* March 25, 1957, pp. 6.951–2. Reproduced in *Modulo,* 8:17–21 (July 1957). Quotation from English supplement, pp. 14–15.

[18] Ibid., p. 15.

[19] "Resumo das Apreciações do Júri," *Modulo* 8, pp. 13–16.

[20] Costa's competition report has been widely published, and appears in a number of English translations. The specific wording given is based on the report as published in *Modulo* 18 (June 1960). Pages not numbered.

[21] "Brasilia: A New Capital City for Brazil," op. cit., p. 397.

[22] Ibid., p. 398.

[23] Quoted in Stamo Papadaki, *The Work of Oscar Niemeyer.* New York, Reinhold, 1950, pp. 1–2.

[24] *Modulo* 18. Costa report.

[25] Ibid.

[26] Ibid.

[27] Ibid.

[28] Ibid.

[29] Ibid.

[30] Ibid.

[31] Le Corbusier, *City of Tomorrow.* New York, Payson and Clark, 1929, pp. xxi–xxii.

[32] Quoted in Douglass Haskell, "Brasilia: a New Type of National City," *Architectural Forum,* 113:126–33 (November 1960), p. 127.

[33] *Modulo* 18. Costa report.

[34] Ibid.

[35] Ibid.

[36] Douglass Haskell, op. cit., p. 126.

[37] "The 'Folly' Is a City," *Newsweek,* 54:45 (September 7, 1959).

[38] William Holford, "Brasilia," *Royal Institute of British Architects Journal.* 67:154–59 (March 1960), p. 158.

[39] Ibid., p. 157.

[40] These figures were provided in August 1966 to the Subcommittee for Appropriations of the United States House of Representatives by Lincoln Gordon, Under Secretary of State and former ambassador to Brazil. A Brazilian journalist, Maurício Vaitsman, in 1968 published a book purporting to disprove this estimate (*Quanto Custou Brasília,* Rio, Editôria Pôsto de Serviço, Ltda., Coleçao Livro-Verdade). Vaitsman provides an exaggerated transportation of Gordon's dollar figures into cruzeiros. It is always difficult to make such conversions because of the rapid inflation of the cruzeiro. At the commencement of Brasilia (December 1956), the cruzeiro was valued at 65 per dollar. At the approximate time of the dedication of Brasilia (June 1960), the rate was 187 per dollar. By 1966, when Gordon made his report, the rate of exchange was 2,220 per dollar. Vaitsman converted Gordon's estimate, which covered from 1956 to 1966, at the high 1966 rate, producing a total of three trillion, five hundred and thirty-six billion cruzeiros. Vaitsman's financial estimates are based on the results of a Brazilian Parliamentary Commission which assembled reports from all government agencies participating in the Brasilia

project. The total for construction costs up to December 1961 is given (page 88) as eighty-one billion, eight hundred and five million, eight hundred twenty-seven thousand, one hundred ninety-one cruzeiros (CR$ 81,805,-827,191). These figures cover a period when the cruzeiro ranged in value from 65 (December 1956) to 318 (December 1961) per dollar. If one were to use 200 as an average conversion rate for this period, the figure in dollars would be approximately four hundred million dollars ($409,029,140). The figure of six hundred million dollars for the initial construction period is given by Henrique Mindlin in *Brazilian Architecture,* p. 46. Mindlin at that time (1961) estimated subsequent completion costs for the city as one million dollars.

[41] "Brazil Builds a New Capital," *Fortune,* 59:108–13 (April 1959), p. 109.

[42] "Brazil Lavishes Money, Hopes on Dream City," *Business Week,* September 12, 1959, p. 133.

[43] George Nelson, "Out of the Trackless Bush, a National Capital," *Saturday Review of Literature,* 39–67 (March 12, 1960), p. 40.

[44] Wolf von Eckardt, "Brasilia: Symbol in the Mud," *American Institute of Architects Journal,* 36:37–42 (November 1961), p. 42.

[45] Walter McQuade, "Brasilia's Beginning," *Architectural Forum,* 110:97–99 (April 1959), p. 98. He was quoting from a report by Chicago architect Alfred Shaw.

[46] "Conversation in Brasilia Between Robert Harbinson and George Balcombe," *Royal Institute of British Architects Journal,* 68:490–94 (November 1961), p. 494.

[47] Oscar Niemeyer, "My Brasilia Experience," *Modulo,* 18:18–24 (June 1960), p. 26.

[48] Mindlin, op. cit., pp. 42–43.

[49] Statistics taken from *Brasília,* published by the Conselho Nacional de Estatistica of Brazil (IBGE), Coleção de Monografias No. 325.

[50] Ludwig Bemelmans, "Brasilia: the Capital and the Cardiogram," *Holiday,* 25:46+ (March 1959), p. 52.

[51] Gladys Delmas, "Brasilia Comes of Age," *The Reporter,* 36:25–33 (February 23, 1967), p. 32.

[52] Ibid.

[53] Ibid.

[54] Oscar Niemeyer, "Testimony," *Modulo,* 9:3–6 (February 1958), p. 3.

[55] Ibid.

[56] Ibid., p. 4.

[57] Ibid., pp. 3–5.

[58] Niemeyer, "My Brasilia Experience," op. cit., p. 23.

[59] Ibid., pp. 19–20.

[60] Aleu Amoroso Lima, "Men, Ideas and Institutions," *Atlantic Monthly,* 197: 117–21 (February 1956), p. 118.

[61] *Modulo* 18, Costa report.

[62] Holford, "Brasilia," op. cit., p. 154.

[63] André Malraux, *Brasília na Palavra de André Malraux.* Rio de Janeiro, Presidencia da República, Servico de Documentação, 1959.

PART V

Managing Urbanism

CHAPTER 13

The Urban Malaise

H. Wentworth Eldredge

LESSONS LEARNED FROM ELEVEN WORLD CAPITALS

Speaking generally, the chronicle of capital city planning, as evidenced by these case studies, has been the expected one of "too little too late." Inadequate grasp of the concomitant of *social-political-economic structure* as part and parcel of an underfinanced *physical design-oriented solution* pretty much tells the tale. Modern capital cities are neither efficient nor particularly handsome, nor do they all support a human life of warmth, style and quality. As a recent Czech quote has it, they tend to "lack a human face." However, faced with a general societal malaise, the reality of both extensive pollution as well as potential energy, food and space shortages on a global scale—not to mention the very gritty specifics of the startlingly inadequate urban scene—it is surprising that politicians, bureaucrats and planners have been able to accomplish as much as they have.

There are no pretensions here that the analysis of eleven world capitals can shed definitive wisdom on urban management, yet to repeat, much thought and treasure have been invested in the capital city as symbol and important reality. It should be admitted, though, that the multiple functions performed by a capital both entice population and make the task of *capital* planning more complex; being a "world capital" has both benefits and costs for those involved in its guidance.

Here is the planning record of the eleven test cases as seen by the reporting professional urbanists of quite divergent backgrounds. It would be difficult to find any great optimism among them about the future, i.e., the ability to carry out reasonable plans is clear in certain cities, but there is evidently no reliable capability for guiding civilization in a holistic fashion into the higher reaches of a style and quality worthy of man's Promethean dream. The synthesizing paragraphs that follow indicate the present stage of the art of urban guidance as evidenced by the relative successes and the relative failures in seven interlocking key areas of universal concern: city government; funds; economic development; physical versus social planning; housing and community; transportation; recreation, green space and the higher culture.

City Government

The functional city stretches far beyond the boundaries of the old political city. Moscow, Paris, London, Stockholm are all in varied ways reaching both territorially and functionally toward metropolitan government and even on to regional development, as is Tokyo with the amazing Tama New Town designed "to balance" the capital (not possible) with a population of over 400,000. Toronto has its metro government—good at physical planning, poor, it would seem, on societal development; Washington (merged with its suburbs in a feeble Council of Government), hampered by its curious federal district and past lack of local suffrage, has enormous difficulties in co-ordinating government action with Maryland and Virginia. New York's then Mayor Lindsay expressed in the autumn of 1972 in Tokyo at the meeting of big city mayors the pressing need to give great cities a special status equivalent to "states," "departments," "counties" just below the national government as a second-tier power. Evidence on metropolitan/city government from Dakar, Brasilia, Chandigarh is not so clear, although world sympathy is stirred by the challenges facing developing area cities with so very inadequate resources in skilled leaders, functioning bureaucracies, trained planners and especially funds.

Capital city governments appeared to chafe under inadequate power to manage their own affairs and despite national government interest (very clear in the case of Tokyo, Moscow, Washington, Paris, Dakar, for example) they have had to battle against *other national* priorities for the muscle to get physical things of local import actually carried out. From afar one envied communist bureaucrats as being "able to get on with the job" unencumbered by democratic dalliance; actually Moscow's planners (as creating partially a consumer product—as well as symbol) compete with heavy industry, military budgets, development areas (the Urals and Siberia). The general theories of territorial égalitarianism so clearly evident in the *métropoles d'equilibre* in France and the beefing up of the North and the Midlands in England also complicate the job of the capital city planner. Even Ciudad Guayana in Venezuela was conceived of as a foil to Caracas' wealth and Brasilia was, among other things, a lever to open up the interior. There was precious little hard evidence on national urban policies and plans in operation, although there was a certain amount of verbiage.

Funds

Resources are never sufficient and while capitals have undoubted priority, they also have very high pretensions and heavy investment in nondirect income-producing costly public works. There are large sectors of capital cities which bring no direct financial return: the renowned empty spaces—except for parked cars—of "Beautiful Paris" from the Étoile to the Place de la Concorde—even the decorative floodlighting—are most expensive. Handsome squares, elegant parks and plantings, cultural facilities from the Bolshoi to Kennedy Center pay no taxes and demand upkeep. The monumental sculpture of Brasilia and Chandigarh's quasi-functional key buildings and the startling emptiness of the former inflated costs and maintenance to the heavens. Presumably the upkeep of Tokyo's handsome Imperial Palace grounds come from the Imperial purse but Buckingham Palace, St. James's Palace in London and, in effect, the Washington Mall receive large national government subsidies. After all this, how do the citizens live? Is there sufficient funding to spruce up Tokyo's wooden inner city dwellings, Caracas' *ranchos,* Southwest Washington or the dull gray stretches of inner suburbs inhabited by working-class Paris? The industrial office building taxation base is not always solid enough for symbolic capitals. Where governmental urban funding rests on firm *income* taxation or a value-added tax rather than an uncertain property tax base the situation looks better.

Tokyo has a medieval lack of elementary human waste disposal[1] and a frightening excess of careless air pollution. Dakar, a simple Afro-Asian city, lacks physical infrastructure. Brasilia and Chandigarh are partially prepared since the nation-breaking initial construction costs were channeled into such facilities. Only now is the Thames recuperating from nineteenth-century London's callousness. Toronto suffers with the other Great Lakes/St. Lawrence dwellers and the Potomac reeks. But, finally, all cities in our survey and others are now alerted to the pressing needs to upgrade power, water and air inputs and clean up all human and industrial ordures. London with her amazing "smokeless" areas forced to use gas or coke for heating is staging a remarkable comeback; there are no longer flakes of soot in Central London and the birds in legion have returned to the parks (diesel fumes, however, are now quite overwhelming to one unaccustomed to that nasty stench).

Economic Development

Outside the capital cities of the developing nations, most Western capitals appear to be attempting to level off their size; Bruxelles, site of so many European functions, appears as an exception. If there are further jobs envisaged for capital cities, they are office type for the CBD or more importantly for high-rise subcenters in peripheral suburban regions. London and Toronto have succumbed to central area high-rise office buildings; Stockholm is flirting with such a development. Washington's unplanned high-rise office area across the chain bridge in Virginia, *La Défense* and other subcenters in Paris, and *Shinjuku* outside Tokyo set the mode of bowl-shaped high-rise development evident from Madrid to Belgrade in Europe. Stockholm's five massive office blocks in the perhaps dated Segelstorg development contradicts this. While the British New Towns were supposed to syphon off industrial and to a limited extent office jobs from Central London, they simply were inadequate in scale to do this. Both Washington and Moscow have been exporting government workers—the Veterans Administration to Philadelphia—and the CIA to McLean, Virginia, although one understands the K.G.B. still is housed near to the Kremlin.

World capitals are seldom great manufacturing centers, although this is not to gainsay the historic industrial roles played by London, Paris, Stockholm, Moscow, Tokyo, Dakar, Caracas and Toronto. Other than the occasional service or specialty industry, no capital planner for a sophisticated city foresees industrial development except perhaps outside the periphery. Without spinning out the rather evident conclusions gained from a study of these cases, it would appear reasonably clear that increased population density for developed capital cities is out and that *jobs* are generally under export pressure—certainly for industrial workers and pretty clearly for office types. National governments are under *national* pressures not to let the capital become top heavy; share the wealth even in bureaucratic jobs appears to be the slogan. Calcutta and Bombay tear at Delhi for a piece of the pie.

Physical Versus Social Planning

Physical planning antedates social/societal planning. Somehow the search for physical goals intuitively arrived at by design/engineering trained planners—a curious juxtaposition of aesthetics and technological/financial efficiency—has been the modal thinking. Somehow physical space and form are to mold the good life even though the good life is most assuredly not clear to anyone and especially to the traditionalist urban planners at work in world capitals. No doubt the aesthetics of traditional Paris, a Beaux-Arts creation that is the central "Beautiful City," are incredibly rewarding; London has a warm grandeur and despite its curious dated plans so has Washington to an extent. There is excitement in modern Tokyo, Toronto and Caracas; Moscow is a curious jumble except at dead center which was enlivened by the works of the Czars. Stockholm has a restrained elegance and profits by its watery surround. Dakar is hopelessly chaotic and, while opinions differ about the self-conscious physical forms of Brasilia and Chandigarh, backdropped by the Simla Hills, they do move the peasants as well as traveling aesthetes to marvel.

But are Parisians somehow ennobled by Bourbon and Napoleonic grandeur; there is no hard data to support this. Does the Kremlin "improve" Muscovites; one is tempted to inquire "how"? What precisely do Pennsylvania Avenue and the costly, if stolid, Mall buildings do for a Washington ghetto black? Frankly no one knows; reliable *bridges*[2] between behavioral/social science and design simply do not as yet exist.

Social planning, even in the narrow aspect of remedial welfare planning, is quite simply *not* included generally in the capital city plan. The editor explored this with each contributor at various times and none could report a carefully meshed sociophysical planning system in being. What liaison there was between physical and societal planning existed by habit in sophisticated countries and was limited to standard remedial family allowances, old-age care, child care, sickness insurance, community remedial services, etc. Developing countries (including Japan) have simply expected that older traditional practices of family and transplanted communal reinforcements would take care of such matters. Japan (especially Tokyo) appears to have been brought sharply of late to a realization that a twelve-million metropolitan area is not a rural community and that the city and the nation must go into welfare/social planning to prop up an uprooted citizenry smothered by numbers and smog in teaming wooden housing rabbit warrens—interspersed and surrounded by the new-fashioned concrete box barracks. Moscow is even more a sinner in this architectural direction.

Housing and Community

Adequate dwellings for urban (and rural) population are a priority world problem. World capitals in developed areas deserve little more than average marks both in quantity and quality. Paris has only recently started on a large-scale attempt to house the urban poor (often North Africans) adequately. London, after decades of assisted housing, still has square miles of dull, dirty, crowded dwellings; their public housing is hardly inspiring and the out-country estates, even if reasonably designed and spaced architecturally in "towers and blocks," are communityless. The British New Towns have played only a minor part in alleviating the central city population density; excellent as they are, the scale is just too small. Stockholm probably leads the eleven cases in the provision of adequate quantities and qualities of housing through the integrated *Tunnelbana*/semisatellite town system. However recently there has been noticeable unrest among imported South and Central European laborers unused to the Swedish disciplined way of life. Ample infrastructure for community development, both physical and societal (not under the city planner's auspices), is a traditional aspect of Swedish urban life. Washington is notoriously undersupplied with housing for the poor and there are acres of public housing, so unwisely designed, sited and managed, that they are falling derelict. The physical housing remedies remedied little. There is just beginning in Washington an increasing evidence of societal planning meeting the housing/community planning. The Fort Lincoln New-Town-in-Town finally got off the ground under private entrepreneurial leadership, which may turn out to be a good sign of progress in integrated housing, jobs and community furniture. Toronto, as a quasi-boomtown, has housed its population but hardly elegantly. There is in the usual North American tradition barely adequate provision of ancilliary physical/social community infrastructure. Caracas shows the rough juxtaposition of elegant apartments with a backdrop of free enterprise do-it-yourself *ranchos* as does Dakar with *bidonvilles*. Chandigarh in no way fits the traditional Indian living/shopping community patterns and Brasilia even less suits the local culture with the massive poor population of ordinary back-country laborers who are only belatedly accommodated in the rapid-fire upgrading of "frontier towns" or "free cities" used by construction workers. Nothing in Brasilia's sterile housing blocks remotely resembles Brazilian life of any class or region. Tokyo has a massive housing task including the protection by firebreaks for potential disaster areas of primitive wooden housing in the inner city. Social community services other than Shinto/Buddhist shrines are badly neglected and the simple lack of quantity of available dwellings makes it most difficult to upgrade space (less needed for Japanese culture) and amenity along community lines. Despite some excellent mass housing, there appears an increasing tendency toward higher densities with minimal communal facilities. Despite Herculean efforts since World War II, Moscow, as the probable leading exponent of systems building or industrialized housing in the world, suffers from an oppressive housing shortage and for the foreseeable future will continue to do so.

Transportation

Toronto, London, Paris, Stockholm and Moscow have all done reasonably well with public transport although the first four have had to face massive and unsettling increases in the automobile population. As noted many times, Stockholm's *Tunnelbana* is nicely integrated with central city business development and outer suburban housing (with a few jobs). But even the experienced Swedish planners were crossed up by auto love: With the increased mobility and the city population driving even farther to the second or summer home, traffic dislocation has been compounded during a large part of the year.

Tokyo's traffic in the inner city is in shambles despite a fantastic rail net; as central city congestion does not seem to improve the Japanese planners are now facing the problem via massive land-use shifts (jobs to the outer region). Washington's transport is primitive with middle-class (white) auto users from the suburbs holding urban working and lower-class blacks up for ransom by demanding Potomac vehicular bridges to get the so-needed subway finally under way.

The developing cities simply do not have any adequate mass transportation except for various decrepit trams, ancient buses and the ubiquitous microbus, freewheeling private entrepreneurial adjuncts to the ailing "public systems." In India's cities residents from outlying poor areas have been known to walk three to four hours to a poorly paying job in the morning and again back at night; but even if there were adequate public transportation they could not afford it. The splendid wide open avenues of Brasilia hardly make up a functioning transportation network if people lack private automobiles and cash; and the public transport is a disorganized shambles.

Recreation, Green Space and the Higher Culture

At a period of strong égalitarian leanings—at least in the sophisticated West—the style and quality of life are somewhat of a dirty phrase. Park space and simple recreational facilities (often badly mistreated by the people for whom they were designed, built and dedicated) are acceptable to the modern mood but sophisticated urban aesthetics or heavy funding of the dance, music, drama, plastic arts is looked at askance, especially in the United States. For the record, most of the great art produced by civilization in sculpture, architecture and music was developed by artists kept by rich patrons, be they theological, governmental or capitalist. The splendid Metropolitan Opera of New York ran on a much reduced schedule in 1973–74 due to lack of funds—it has a continuous yearly deficit. That city's multifunctional Lincoln Center operated at a $37 million loss in 1972–73 and is expected to lose $6.0 million net in 1973–74. The two finest ballet companies in the world, the Bolshoi of Moscow and the Royal Ballet of London, are socialist enterprises—for the people and as symbols of national cultural excellence.

As density hovers at the high mark, the necessity for green space (parks) and blue space (a Finnish phrase for urban water) has ever more become necessary. The parks are the lungs of the city (even though most urban parks now are cancerous from autombiles et al., air pollution and in some sad lands "people vandalism"). Paris has inherited magnificent open spaces in the Beautiful

City and on the flanks in the Bois de Boulogne and in the Bois de Vincennes; Moscow uses the Moscow Hills across the river and the banks of the Neva, now unfortunately granite paved, for recreational space. London with St. James's, Hyde and Green parks is now slowly recapturing the banks of the Thames; in passing, the attitude of Londoners toward their parks is very odd for Americans. Flowers are not torn out, trees not chopped down, furniture not destroyed and litter is held at a reasonably civilized level. Traditional aesthetics have been well maintained in both London and Paris—especially in the central city with poorer results in the inner suburbs. Washington spends a great deal in maintaining its valuable central open space quite well as a not-too-functional surrounding for the monolithic and costly building style—basically white marble. Stockholm has developed its beautiful island/hill/water site with great distinction. Tokyo lacks green space except for the small sector to date of the Imperial Palace grounds (the main area is reserved for the Imperial family) and the odd shrine here and there. Caracas seems not to be park oriented, while the classic amounts of space squandered on monumentalism in Kubitschek's Brasilia contributing to bankrupting the country, which had something to do undoubtedly with the appearance of the present military government. Interestingly enough, Brasilia's great national theatre has *not* been finished ($6 million plus is needed) which reminds us of the $72 million Kennedy Center in Washington, a "monument to both pop and sophisticated culture." Dakar has its beaches and harbor as a lively and spacious blue space.

Nations with a rich traditional culture such as Tokyo, London, Paris and Stockholm have equipped their capitals with the necessary physical facilities (often inherited) of theatres, concert halls and museums; capitals lacking such a background as Washington must buy such appurtenances. As an understanding of the higher culture goes more deeply into a more leisured population, aspirations for this culture also include expectations eventually of a more civilized life for increasing numbers. Cultural planning does not seem to be too evident in Chandigarh, although a tastefully dammed river (as in Brasilia) promises water recreation. Probably the most interesting aspects of the proletarian culture of Moscow are the magnificent levels for more or less apolitical music and ballet; modern visual art is true proletarian realism while urban design has sloughed off Stalinist wedding cake and now appears to worship factory modern. But in the apolitical world of dance and music the higher classical culture appears to be the word. The British Arts Council and André Malraux in France have contributed greatly to the quality of life in their respective capital (or noncapital) cities as a conscious attempt at artistic development planning; but only here and there are they firmly integrated with physical planning. Of the latter, the Royal Concert Hall on the renewing South Bank of the Thames near grimy and picturesque old Waterloo Station is the most startling example. The United States held its first Federal Design Assembly in April 1973 to upgrade design in all its agencies.

From this brief survey it should be crystal clear that there is still much to know about guiding urban society.

THE AGE OF DISCONTINUITY

In an uneasy world faced by "the triple revolution" of cybernation, nuclear power and human rights, it is hardly surprising that great capital cities cannot be managed well. There is little doubt that mankind is poised on one of the great watersheds of history as the industrial city, through an increase in societal scale,[3] develops into a wide-spreading information society.[4] This change rests on the intellectual, technical, biological, behavioral and societal technologies of our era which in turn are based on the ever growing proficiency of exact knowledge/science (not including apparently "wisdom"). Named earlier by Harold Lasswell as "the World Revolution of Our Time," Peter Drucker has dubbed this era "the age of discontinuity,"[5] and predicts that new skills will create an interdependent world society with multiple organizations in an elaborate pluralism leading to "the knowledge society," in effect a systems break with the present industrial city. Michael Harrington, from a socialist ideological stance at 180° variance with Drucker sees in the "decadence" of the national capitalist state, riven by the new technology, the emergence of a more "humane" and "democratic" world.[6] Herbert Gans, sociologist and urbanist, has written a persuasive tract[7] on "The New Egalitarianism" in which he drives the argument further and captures the present globe-encircling ethic of "all pigs are equal—and no pigs are more equal!"—by class, income, color, ethnic stock or region.

Donald Michael labels the West and specifically the United States as "the unprepared society"[8] facing "the crisis of industrial society" and "the crisis in American institutions" (to use the titles of two recent publications). No wonder Alvin Toffler has sold some five million copies—in English alone—of *Future Shock*[9] detailing the upsetting road ahead with the impermanence of practically everything! Various other soothsayers, both public and academic,[10] foresee trouble ahead for the remainder of the twentieth century and well on into the twenty-first. It would be foolhardy to ridicule their prognostications. And it would be equally foolhardy to believe we have even remotely entered into a period with co-operation, sufficient data, and skill in planning and in plan delivery to carry us along as rational men into a calm future.[11] The energy crisis and starvation in the winter of 1974–75 are earnests of the future.

Capping this parade of chaos et al. on a global scale is, of course, the Meadows' *The Limits to Growth*.[12] Admitting readily to the imperfections of their mathematical model, nevertheless the Meadows seems quite ready to go to the mat on the probability that the earth's finite resources will be exhausted, no matter what, through the exponential growth built into our technical technology and population. "Curtains" by the end of the twenty-first century, come what may!

If that be the approximate temperature reading for spaceship earth, what then is specifically the state of well being for that urban portion of society—the critical mass.

THE CITY IS THE CENTER OF THE VORTEX

There is a spate of recent books chronicling and/or predicting imminent urban disaster. Clearly, city problems are coming much faster than their solutions, especially in the United States. There is hardly a question in any concerned American's mind today that no one is capable of coping adequately with the present situation.

We are all witness to the trumpeted escape to the suburbs—pictured as ineffectual, bedroom, demicommunities increasingly stifled by their own success in luring both white-collar and blue-collar workers of above average affluence from the central city of *the exploding metropolis*.[13]

Bennett Berger has sharply questioned the accounts, especially in the United States, that one has received of homogenized *middle-class suburbia*—a derogatory term—and has pointed out that relatively few suburban communities have actually been researched, including precious few working-class examples. His own *Working Class Suburb*[14] indicates that there *are* divergent life styles extant even in suburbia. What variety one would witness if the scatteration of world suburbia were to be studied meticulously from the *bidonvilles* of Algiers and fringe *bustees* of Calcutta to Wimbledon and Neuilly-sur-Seine. With the septic tank, electric pump and four-wheel drive vehicle, no place is safe in the United States from the escapist affluent, or merely the escapist, as Vermont, Oregon and Montana already bear sad witness.[15] At the same time, spurred among other things by the further industrialization and general rationalization of agriculture, farmers and peasants all over the world rush hopefully to find—or not to find—jobs in the city. As a careful researcher of urban growth dynamics has noted:

> Without arguing the complexities of the mix of forces at work or the ramifications of their origins, we can now easily accept the fact of the great continuing drift toward an urban society. While the signs of urbanization are unmistakably clear, the implications to human thought, ways and behavior are not so well understood.[16]

Leonard Reissman searches hard for theory adequate to explain the dynamics of the urban process. "Only in that way is there any chance that we may learn enough to control our urban future, a future to which most of the world will very shortly be committed."[17] Charles Abrams from his wide experience—primarily in housing among developing countries—has made the point that *the city is the frontier* of human experience; it is here humanity will win or lose in its battle with nature—primarily itself.[18] Without continuous renewal, our cities will result only in *necropolis* (the city of the dead). *The Urban Condition* is examined by thirty multifaceted experts in a symposium edited by Leonard J. Duhl, M.D., and psychiatrist of the city. Duhl himself concludes that the almost universally accepted urban crisis is also a great challenge to find valid fresh answers[19] which bring us back to Arnold Toynbee's concept of challenge and response. Can our age meet this "urban challenge"?[20]

Lewis Mumford, as the sage of urbanism and leading student of the urban animal, in his collection, *The Urban Prospect*,[21] argues for regional planning, vast expenditures for public societal and physical infrastructure, and for the wisdom somehow to re-create human values in human communities replacing megalopolis. Mumford is hardly optimistic, but seemingly still has both faith in man and in the application of rational thought to the fantastically complex puzzle of urbanization/urbanism. Under present circumstances many contend that contemporary urban planning is little more than crisis or conflict management; it must appear that way certainly to most big city mayors.

URBAN MALAISE: ALIENATION, RHETORIC AND VIOLENCE

As a preliminary to planning the city, let us glance first at the contemporary urban

—especially American—societal fever chart. The exchange of reason for perfervid (if often extremely ill-informed) recommendations for anarchy, violence and revolution as has been evidenced recently. In effect, the abandonment of rational thought processes seemed to have gone further in modern America than in many lands. Lenin foresaw such a period of world (especially capitalist) chaos in our time. Writes Irving L. Horowitz:

> *Must it not be frankly admitted that anarchism is not so much a doctrine as a mood; and not a social and economic credo but an elaborate form of psychological therapy for the politically alienated and the intellectually disaffected . . . ?*[22]

Anarchistic qualities of the present scene are offered as the ultimate of "uncoerced individualization." There is little doubt that mankind over its entire life span on earth has been an extremely violent, warring creature. With the advent of the Age of Reason (the Enlightenment) in the eighteenth century, a rosy image of rational man married to older humanism and Newtonian precision was created. This is hardly in tune with reality, as history, Darwin, Freud, anthropology and perhaps ethology have clearly indicated in the nineteenth and twentieth centuries. Despite World War I and II, history's bloodiest in body count, man at least in the West had begun to cherish the illusion that progress was inevitable in a rational/planful way and that our cities had a very excellent chance of becoming civilized or, as David Riesman phrased it, "We are slowly growing less uncivilized."[23]

The United States was preparing after World War II to move reasonably and "legally" into the future in a state of benign euphoria without violence, crime and revolution. However, this dream was soon challenged, in particular by Lynne Iglitzin, a political scientist accepting the New Left philosophy and eschewing the value-free pose of social science, who concludes from a hard-nosed investigation of *Violent Conflict in American Society:*

> A new kind of American politics may be slowly emerging, a politics based on continuous struggle between the elites with power and the masses of the people without it. The peoples potential to resort to violence to achieve their goals is coming to be an integral part of the process in the United States.[24]

Hardly a happy portent for the development of long-term planning in the public sector, this age verbalizes varied *revolutions* both in developed and developing countries.[25] In addition there are the whole gamut of protorevolutionary and violent revolutionary movements now plaguing world society today with often ruralist theory—Chairman Mao and Che Guevara—mixed with older Marxist thought. However, these are now primarily urban centered. While some attention in thought and occasionally in practice has been paid to revolutionary nonviolence[26] with Gandhi and Martin Luther King as the patron saints, the tendency is to move toward direct action. Revolution has become *revolutionism* as a quasi-institutionalized political model. Possibly the seventies will be quieter. "Man cannot live by revolution alone, as so many national leaders have discovered."[27] But the contemporary urban scene reeks with violence both real and verbal. Careless, random violence—sometimes psychotic in spots and not unconnected with drugs and simple crime—is matched by coldly calculated violence, sometimes committed by regimes in power. Lewis Coser has informed us that conflict has the positive function of holding and preserving the in-group, especially in contesting for power over territory with out-groups. These competitive tensions produce a system, but:

> Our discussion of the distinction between types of conflict, and between types of social structures, leads us to conclude that conflict tends to be dysfunctional for a social structure in which there is no or insufficient toleration and institutionalization of conflict. The intensity of a conflict which threatens to "tear apart," which attacks the consensual basis of a social system is related to the rigidity of the structure. What threatens the equilibrium of such a structure is not conflict as such, *but the rigidity itself which permits hostilities to accumulate and to be channeled along one major line of cleavage once they break out in conflict.**[28]

To this observation must be added Hannah Arendt's recent reflections that violence is "normal" throughout history and that it occurs where there are clear evidences of the impotence of power both on the international scene and internally in a society.[29] Thus from a societal design viewpoint, a flexible societal structure must be designed and managed, ever cybernetic, and unafraid to utilize complex sets of powers to make the necessary adjustments to fit the continuously changing world.

Urban dwellers are frightened today as crime in the streets (and the home) is perceived as constantly escalating and the power (or the will to use power) seems to have evaporated. If Proudhon's edict that "property is theft" can be taken seriously, one can then understand that a ripoff from those that have is to be admired, if carried out by those who have not. Thus crime and revolution are joined together theoretically by certain black revolutionaries and members of the New Left.[30]

Statistics from the F.B.I.'s *Uniform Crime Statistics* strongly reinforce this as reality.[31] Between 1960 and 1968, the national rate of criminal homicides per 100,000 population increased 36 per cent, the rate of forcible rape, 65 per cent, of aggravated assault, 67 per cent and of robbery, 119 per cent. In the United States drugs peddled for profit seem to play an important part in funneling funds to crime and in expressing protorevolutionary behavior—contrary to the existing social norms—to disrupt the status quo. This they succeeded in doing by, among other things, corrupting the police.[32]

Echoes from Europe suggest that there, too, the urban world is being *coca-colanisé*. Japan appears to be only lightly threatened, but after a reputation for very harsh pre-World War II secret police action, it is afraid to be too tough and rioting/crime even there is on the slow increase.[33] Thus violence and revolutionary change are in the air and *on the city streets*. There is some evidence that the physical design and construction of the defensive city is already on the way piecemeal where middle-class urban dwellers wall themselves into secure enclaves.[34] On the other hand, as Richard Wade, the urban historian, has pointed out: "Violence is no stranger to American cities. Almost from the very beginning, cities have been the scenes of sporadic violence, of rioting and disorders, and occasionally virtual rebellion against established authority."[35]

* (Editor's italics.)

But is there not some better way to move into the twenty-first century? The analysis of revolutions indicates that "they never occur as a result of forces beyond human control. Creative political action is the specific antidote to revolutionary conditions, and the occurrence of a revolution is in a sense nothing more than testimony that this antidote was not recognized or not used."[36] Civil revolt is merely a sign of political/social incapacity. There are feasible political alternatives to violent revolutionary chaos—generally urban—and a considerable part of the remedial package is in holistic planning. This will be an integral part of an ever altering political system in a multigroup society which gladly accepts pluralistic values[37] as we shift on both a micro and macro scale from *ethnocentric* to *homocentric* behavior.[38]

The literature on revolution is itself escalating and indicating perhaps a fantasy desire to make a systems break with a society perceived as incapable, or at least unrewarding, for a rather considerable—and impatient—segment of the population. Aspirations have evolved into expectations and have been fanned by communications media with their astute product pushing; they have outraced the steady, if pedestrian, increase in the level of living. It is a well-accepted truism of revolutionary analysis that the truly downtrodden are too lost to revolt; it is only when some light is visible at the end of the long tunnel that the underdog truly becomes restive. The Black Power movement is clearly a case in point. Progress is perceived as dawdling. Let's advance it by total reorganization! "Power to the People" is the watchword as the sad sequential trilogy of frustration, tension and aggression—often displaced—makes the scene on the world stage and in the urban place.[39] A cataclysmic blowup is increasingly predicted as the majority of have-not nonwhites attempt to redistribute on a global scale worldly goods held generally by whites (and the Japanese!). There is in fact hard evidence that developing areas (the habitat of nonwhites) are continuously losing ground in per capita incomes vis-à-vis the West and their frustrations (due in fact to their own societal ineptitudes and initial poverty exacerbated by the "iron law" of compound interest) are in a sense "justified."

For purposes of analysis of the urban crisis, the vast outpouring of often half-baked ideas and erratic behavior accompanied by escalating aggressive rhetoric may be roughly classified under five headings with which American society and governments—and increasingly the rest of the globe—must cope.

These current five important nodes of alienation and violence, *all primarily urban,* can be readily identified; they have rather elaborate interlockings (clearly this is not a logic-tight classification): the *New Left;* the *Youth Revolt; Black Power;* the *Poverty Lobby,* and the *Paranoid Right. Fem-Lib*[40] and *Gay-Lib* will not be treated here as they are not yet of protorevolutionary significance, although the rhetoric is already understandably shrill.

The New Left

This is an international post-World War II development actually starting in the late 1950s and early 1960s. Disenchanted with the Union of Soviet Socialist Republics and its new class of neobourgeois bureaucrats and Russia-firstism (as evidenced in Hungary and Czechoslovakia), alienated by capitalist/nationalist selfishness and chicanery—and most especially in the United States by the Indochinese war and later the McGovern fiasco followed by Watergate—there is an amorphous minority ready to bust the status quo. Some literally intend to do so, as the Weathermen, using low technology bombs; others have resorted to communes, growing vegetables and handcrafting sandals/candles. These communes are general benign, but there are a few of startling evil (Charles Manson) and not unconnected with hard drugs. Alienated from the increasingly impersonal state of computer banks and IBM cards, assailed by dense urban populations (and often by the unfeeling police), they wish to revise America (the world)—whether the world is ready or not. There is predictably a whole pantheon of new heroes: Sartre, Frantz Fanon, Fidel, Herbert Marcuse, Malcolm X., Huey Newton, and Rudi Dutschke, Daniel and Gabriel Cohn-Benedit, Mark Rudd, etc.[41]

Mouthers of Mao and Che on the urban scene or on the "hash trail" to Nepal or on the beaches of the Mediterranean and the Aegean, they tend to preach a disorganized rejection of the status quo—a *systems break.* This group should not be treated too lightly for there are violent, well-trained New Left cadres using Marxist revisionist theories, Soviet weapons and Chinese training/tactics which could upset specifically the West by sporadic raiding of world air transport and established institutions (banks a natural!) for fun and funding. The "highly successful" Black September gang of Palestinian guerrillas are the leading exemplars. There is a wealth of do-it-yourself guerrilla manuals floating in printed and xeroxed/mimeo form about the globe. *The Urban Guerrilla* of Martin Oppenheimer brings it right down to the city level and moves toward action.[42] See the eminently practical listing in Abbie Hoffman's handbook[43] on such useful matters as growing marijuana, hashish cookery, boobytraps, explosives and homemade bombs, unconventional warfare, shoplifting, etc.

Patently the *New Left* is closely tied to the *Youth Revolt*—in fact one tends to regard the two as essentially synonymous although treated separately here. The American New Left hopes to be treated seriously by Black Power (admiring their forthright rhetoric and activities) who in turn tend to hold themselves aloof concentrating on black purposes and disdaining the often jejeune performances of those who would also don Afro wigs. But there are others besides the young who are recruited to the New Left; let us not forget the enthused academics. The ancient and benevolent Doctor Spock (who delivered at least spiritually so many of the American breed) and assorted aging child-clergy, oft inebriated writers and assorted bleeding hearts cry (or cried) the shibboleths no doubt partly to hold on to fast-fleeting youth. All wait for the promised utopia of hyper-freedom to be brought about by *The Greening of America*[44] which introduces us to youth's Consciousness III or better the "Third Reich."

Youth Revolt

In the collective search for identity in our troubled era, the adolescents are the most avid and the most confused seekers. The raucous voices of youth (and "honorary youth") have added a disturbing note to the already weary urban scene.[45] It is estimated that more than 50 per cent of the world's population is under twenty-five years of age—a most fertile recruiting ground.

The ethic of the youth culture pervades the West and seeps into both the socialist and developing worlds. It probably has reached its peak on the American scene where it has been centered in the "better" universities which so long have served as *crêches* for the "potential leaders of society." American students emerged comparatively late on the political scene contrary to the activities of their continental European counterparts, traditional political activists. The University of Milan, Berlin University and the London School of Economics had their brawling. The French Left Bank/Sorbonne disturbances in 1968, resulting in serious confrontation with the case-hardened French riot police, have been the prime exhibit.[46] Tokyo University had its problems too.

In Paris the students almost lured the workers to join with them to upset the overwhelming seniority imprint in the then Gaullist government and society[47]; the main result was some destruction of a handsome portion of Beautiful Paris and some far-reaching, long overdue, educational reforms in the generally stuffy and inadequate French university system.

In the United States the predominantly white Students for a Democratic Society (SDS) did not surface until after the predominantly Negro Student Nonviolent Coordinating Committee (SNCC)[48] on which it appeared to be modeled. The University of California at Berkeley in the fall of 1964 set the model for rhetoric and "trashing"[49] which was quickly followed across the country. Both prestigious Yale and Harvard had rather considerable troubles disrupting their particular city areas, while Columbia University, compounded by the fact that it was a generally white enclave in a black area of New York City, had still worse problems.[50] Campus power struggles became the norm resulting in only about ten deaths, which was surprising considering the level of violence (at least in rhetoric) that took place. It has been forcibly argued that the universities were stupidly gutless and maladroit in dealing with their youthful clients; there is little doubt that both education and the urban milieu initially suffered during the rioting that peaked in 1968. Urban universities as a result have been increasingly perceived as declining city assets, especially in the United States.

The miserable old, generally male, have always blocked the restless young since time immemorial; traditionally the old have held the power, the wealth and once the wisdom of the community. This is not unknown in prehuman society. In an era of accelerating social change, ancient wisdom and the wisdom of the ancients are no doubt rightfully held in generally low esteem; and youth now feels more than ever that it should be in the saddle to correct instantaneously the massive ills handed to them by past generations of incompetent oldsters. Thus the Children's Crusade, which appears to have fizzled so completely and wistfully—despite Watergate—in the sinking of that would-be standard bearer, Senator McGovern, in 1972. French youth, as noted, ran into La Garde Republicaine and Japanese youth ended up in prison—or so it would seem. Soviet youth and quasi-youth keep their mouths pretty shut. And generally speaking, Youth (with a capital Y) seems now to have been reduced to pot, dirty clothes, porno, loud music, loud mouths and cluttering up some once rather handsome squares, stairs, areas of once handsome cities. Junior-grade remittance persons struggle aimlessly about the globe, adding one more polluting aspect to the bedraggled cityscape.

And then, on quite the other hand, increasing numbers of the young are "boring from within" by learning all sorts of professions and advanced trades and shaking up the stuffiness of the not-too-successful-in-spots Western world (including the universities). Naked power still holds both the second (socialist) and third (developing nations) worlds pretty much in thralldom. Thus if the very considerable eternal idealism of youth should be harnessed to bring about a true systems break, the Western world especially may witness some quite startling institutional shifts in the next three decades. After all the shouting, many new clear voices of the young make good sense and suggest that man will continue trying to build a better world, an inevitably urban world at that.[51]

Black Power

Clearly the most serious and most justified disenchantment with the American system, as now constituted and managed, comes from black Americans who have become increasingly impacted in ever larger numbers into urban ghettos:

> The moderate growth of the Nation's central cities [1960 to 1970] was due almost entirely to black population increases: while blacks increased by 3.2 million and the population of other races by more than one-half a million, the white population of central cities declined over the decade by 600,000. The great population expansion in metropolitan areas outside central cities on the other hand was overwhelmingly the result of white growth; the large white population already established in the suburbs in 1960 increased over the decade by close to 30 per cent, or 15 and a half million persons. . . .
> As a result of these changes, blacks increased considerably as a proportion of the Nation's total central city population, from 16 per cent in 1960 to 21 per cent in 1970. But in the suburbs, their position did not change at all: in 1970 as in 1960, blacks comprised just under 5 per cent of all suburban residents.[52]

The American black community is becoming more politically sophisticated (there is some evidence that residential self-segregation in ghettos is partly a power move) and more insistent in demanding their constitutional rights. Black nationalism has proven a successful ploy. The blacks have also discovered that while the costs to them and to the cities of violence (and the threat of violence) are measurable and not inconsequential, the benefits *presently* appear to outweigh the costs.[53]

Violence, an ancient political ploy, unquestionably has focused attention on their plight and forced the Establishment system to give. Whether a white backlash will escalate the costs both to America's cities, badly mauled in the 1960s[54] by racial conflict, and to the black community remains yet to be seen. In 1969, one year after the initial report on civil disorders, the prestigious team from Urban America and the Urban Coalition concluded, "We are a year closer to being two societies, black and white, increasingly separate and scarcely less unequal,"[55] an American version of *apartheid*.

Closely linked with the Poverty lobby, blacks suffer from structured inequality and from, as is well known, a disproportionate percentage in the culture of the poor. Daniel Patrick Moynihan has shown that the black family suffers—among other things—from the nonsensical structuring of our welfare laws which tend to remove the unemployed father and perpetuate the slavery-induced pattern of instability and matriarchate.[56] Thus inadequate families produce inadequate offspring to spiral down to further degradation and upset the entire society both white and black. There seems little likelihood of decent American cities until black claims are answered and there is a viable urban black community or communities in metropolis.

Understandably, the Negro population of the United States has been meticulously studied by social scientists (primarily white) for the past seventy-five years.[57] Blacks now loudly proclaim that such work is biased and not remotely value free; presumably only a black can understand the black experience[58] and besides there is no such thing as value-free social science. Thus the flood of books pile up from black sources as part of the "search for identity," the search for a black cultural inheritance, and the building of black operational capabilities to achieve black goals—at least those goals defined by certain self-selected spokesmen.

Probably the most important tract used by the black community is Frantz Fanon's *The Wretched of the Earth: The Handbook for the Black Revolution That Is Changing the Shape of the World.*[59] He is a black psychiatrist from Martinique who confirmed his *négritude* as a French doctor assigned to a hospital in Algeria during the "War of Liberation" where he found his sympathies lay with the rebels. The tough militant voices of Malcolm X (assassinated black Muslim leader),[60] Eldridge Cleaver, Stokely Carmichael (SNCC), LeRoi Jones, H. Rap Brown, Floyd McKissick, Julius Lester (*Look Out Whitey, Black Power's Gon' Get Your Mama!*)[61] and the gentler voices of Bayard Rustin and Martin Luther King (assassinated) have fomented black revolt and black trashing of their own ghetto areas, assault on the police and firemen, and generally sharpened confrontation with the "motherfuckin Honkies." Both whites and blacks during the late sixties and early seventies foresaw further trouble—which fortunately has not yet materialized other than in quasi-mutinies on a small scale in the American Armed Forces.

The euphoria produced by Black Power may be ebbing except in sporadic war cries and mindless cruel violence from youngsters in the ghetto as a dual development takes place: on one hand, the shrewd politicizing of the black drive for a meaningful clout in the democratic process and, on the other, the increasing conservatism of large sections of white middle- and working-class Americans as they harden against Negro demands. George Wallace's following, the 1972 Nixon 61 per cent plurality, the growing antischool busing movement, the Governor Rockefeller drive in New York state for ultra stiff drug pusher sentences, agitation to revive capital punishment for heinous crimes, all drive home the point.

There seems no doubt that the countervailing power the white Establishment could generate to oppose even the best organized revolution of Black Power makes a Negro revolt doomed to failure. This rather obvious fact that a black revolution would be doomed from its inception does not guarantee that one will not be attempted.

Such is the poisoned ambience faced by urban America in the 1970s. There will never be "decent American cities" until the "Negro problem," compounded by Puerto Ricans and other Spanish Americans, can be solved and *no* solution can be predicted for the foreseeable future. No other society in the West faces such sharp ethnic/racial conflicts,† although the Walloon/Flemish strife in Belgium, the Union of South Africa, and the Quebec French minority echo such mindless hate situations. Japan mistreats its Eta or outcastes, but only in tribal Africa

† Save the religious war in Ulster.

(Nigeria, Uganda) or the Far Orient (India, Pakistan) does such internal strife equal the ferocity found in the communal interfaces of the United States. There are leading black voices still counseling nonviolent, legal political development—to the taunts of the extremists: Whitney M. Young has faith as he makes explicit the true open society and precisely how to move in that direction.[62] But America remains, in addition to having a multigroup society of ethnics, classes and religion, polarized in a caste society. Given economic collapse, a major war or both, it is not unlikely the urban front line would explode.

The Poverty Lobby

While hardly approaching the noise level and virulence of the New Left, Youth or Black Power struggles, the clear structural inequities of the American scene are starkly revealed by the Poverty Lobby's activities. "We've got rights, too!" claim the poor.[63] Since time immemorial human society has been structured unfortunately to keep the bumptious young in their place, and there have forever been disadvantaged economic classes and ethnic/racial subcastes held down. In a democratic society dedicated to *égalité* the large islands of grinding poverty provoke both those affected and the reformers dedicated to relieving injustice, continuously to attempt "to divide the pie more equally." The cybernetic lockstep of poverty marches through generations; social mobility—the essence of "the American dream"—is now effectively blocked for a large percentage of the population. Wealth, power and prestige—even decent living—are unreachable with the most profound effects on deprived lives especially in an era of recessions and galloping inflation.[64] Traditionally the "people of plenty"[65] have been incapable of grasping the fact that for some the theoretic cornucopia of abundance does not flow freely, quite contrary to the optimistic, comfortable assumptions on which traditional American life has appeared to rest.

With the rise of a powerful socialist humanitarian critique of the societal structure which produces *The Other America: Poverty in the United States*[66] and an examination of the seamy side of the affluent society, an attempt has been made toward politicizing the poor. Political action is seen as the one way to redress the structural distributional inequities existent in the late twentieth-century urban place. Rural poverty is no doubt more abject, but urban poverty is more dense, visible and potentially capable of political mobilization. While it may be possible under the existent system to reform the poor and make them good *petite bourgeoisie,*[67] the poor as protorevolutionary fodder are potentially a most valuable recruiting ground to be used by New Left, Youth and Black Power leaders for a societal ripoff. As yet this has not happened; only tiny segments of the poor have been politicized, radicalized and mobilized.[68]

The Poverty Lobby leaders are not the poor per se; they have identified with the poor and presume to speak for them. Up to the present the poor have *not* responded by an activist stance. They tend to have little aspiration—still less expectation. The proletariat, at least in the United States, are apparently marking time awaiting their late-model Lenin. So far neither the concerned Establishment governmental efforts nor the radical leadership have proven very efficacious in alleviating their plight.[69] Edward Banfield has stresssed the fact that our attitude toward the treatment of poverty is self-defeating since in effect we keep raising the poverty cutoff line making a built-in no-win policy.[70] It would be well to define this potentially explosive component—the poor—of the world's richest country's societal spectrum. The prestigious Committee for Economic Development has characterized the Urban Poor under eleven headings[71]; important among these are the conclusions that:

a) Poverty is more complex than mere lack of adequate income.
b) About 10 per cent of the metropolitan area population of the United States could be classified as poor and this per cent reaches 13 per cent in central city as compared to 7 per cent in the suburbs. Of the poor, two thirds were white and one third nonwhite.[72]
c) About 47 per cent of all metropolitan area poor are in households that cannot be expected to become economically self-sustaining at any time in the future—a large number of these are children (about 80 per cent) who will have future earning capabilities badly damaged by the experience since poverty is better understood as "a chronic state of failure, disability, dependency, defeat and inability to share in most of American society's major material and spiritual benefits."

As yet the tinder has not ignited, but the fire has been laid for the potentially most debilitating conflict of our era between the haves and the have-nots on the native urban scene—with echoes on a global scale. It gives credence to the opinion that the most important planning problem facing the United States in the late twentieth century is one of redistribution[73]—in an older phraseology, how better "to share the wealth." There are obvious global aspects of this problem too.

The Paranoid Right

This is a fine old American tradition going back to simplistic Know-Nothingism with its nasty head popping up again and again in the American saga. Starting with secessionists (not notably liberal), one can spot assorted Klan Kleagles, America Firsters, Gerald K. Smith, Lothrop Stoddard, Father Coughlin and the "Shrine of the Little Flower," Maddison Grant and other believers in the Yellow Peril, the John Birch Society, American Nazi John Rockwell, the late unlamented Senator Joseph McCarthy, George Wallace, the American Legion in spots, etc.[74]

Due credit should be awarded to German culture for Nazism, France for Poujadism, and Italy for *Fascismo* (even Norway had its Quislings); it is certainly not an American patent especially if the more startling dictators of Latin America, Africa, the Middle East and Asia are disinterred or exhibited in their more recent forms. Troglodyte "Big Daddy" Amin ousting Asians from Uganda is a splendid contemporary "third world" example. The possible cataclysm in the United States if there is ever a radical white-led *whitelash* to the *blacklash* revolt could be an incredible horror story. If the ignorant white lower classes of America were to vent their frustrations in counterrevolution on the 10 per cent black and other colored minorities—especially if aided and abetted by the military and police powers of the federal and more realistically the state governments—it would be a frightful blood bath. It has been guess-estimated that there are over one hundred million weapons in private hands in this country and the tolerance level of Americans is not notably high.[75]

As yet there are no private armies on a large scale (although sporadically such have existed). Working-class white Americans feel somewhat left out of the scene for concerned government action in the cities and the hard-hat "revolt" and ethnic mobilization are symbols of the underground fires below the surface. Goldwater was replaced by Wallace who was removed from serious political consideration by a would-be assassin's poor marksmanship, but there seems little doubt that there is the disturbing potential for armed counterrevolution on the American urban scene. If Black Power is perceived as a dangerous threat to the American dream by great masses of white Americans—still with faint tribal memories of "Judge Lynch" and "vigilante justice"—they may well attack. The "Right" revolution has happened elsewhere this century in presumably civilized nations and can happen here and in Western Europe once again.

THE LONG LAUNDRY LIST OF CITY PROBLEMS

The long laundry list of city problems is all too obvious. While it can be cogently argued and demonstrated in a quantifiable fashion based on relatively hard data that more people over the entire globe are better off than a century, even a decade ago, the perceived gap between what is expected in well-being (especially visible in urban places) and what is delivered appears to be as wide or even wider than ever. It is sobering to ponder briefly the imposing list of very familiar, unsolved late twentieth-century—mainly urban—problems (excluding, of course, the triple possibilities of *nuclear holocaust* escalating out of some minisquabble between—or within—nation states, of *overpopulation and starvation,* and of a *world revolution*). The main components of this catalogue of human failure to build a decent urban society can be sketched roughly under three major categories (with some evident overlapping): physical, sociopsychological and cultural.

Physical

too many people; too high density in urban areas,
atmospheric pollution and water pollution,
destruction of the earth's land surface,
noise pollution,
potential climatic damage,
destruction of flora and fauna,
too many poor and unskilled people migrating to central city and too many middle-class people migrating to the suburbs (population maldistribution),
ill health,
inadequate human food supplies and diet.

Sociopsychological

loss of community,
the identity crises: anomie and alienation,
interethnic and interracial dislike and even hatred,
crime, cruelty and violence,
drug addiction,
neuroses and psychoses,
totalitarian regimes,
decline of agreed-on religious and ethical standards,

irrational behavior,
nonfunctioning democracies,
loss of human sensitivity to human suffering,
decline of the need for achievement (foundation of human development both for good and evil),
lack of a widespread sense of public responsibility.

Cultural

(1) *Economic*
inadequate GNP,
unemployment and underemployment,
inadequate pay,
maldistribution of productive facilities both functionally and spatially,
maldistribution of national income,
too heavy a percentage of the GNP going to private disposable income,
irresponsible private corporations,
physically unrewarding occupations, both blue and white collar.[76]
(2) *Government*
war,
inadequate government between nations,
inadequate government within nations; especially for the region and in the metropolis,
inadequate and skewed taxing policies to finance the public sector,
inadequate public infrastructure for both physical and societal functions especially in urban places,
democratic vs. elitist or expert vs. totalitarian techniques of rule: an unsolved debate,
problems of bureaucratic forms and personnel,
lack of sophisticated delivery practices for agreed on policies and plans,
unsolved relations among the courts, legislatures, executive and bureaucratic parts of government,
criminal justice and the police,
solid and liquid waste disposal,
adequate transportation options,
urban renewal deserts,
slums and public housing.
(3) *Social*
disorganized families,
the "culture of poverty,"
inadequacies of education,
lost community structuring,
care of poor, aged, ill, young and deviant,
troubled adolescence,
drug culture,
crime, delinquency and vice,
inadequacies of health and social welfare delivery.
(4) *Recreational and the Higher Culture*
a) lack of adequate green space and ordered park areas; poor maintenance,
spectatorship instead of participation,
b) "the higher culture"

the great wasteland of (U.S.) television; other Western nations do better.
creation, production/display, consumption of the fine arts all inadequate,
starved theatre (commercial with little tradition of public financial support on the American scene),
starved ballet, opera and music,
c) starved, deteriorated urban aesthetics.

Such a list could be extended and refined indefinitely; there is already a difference of opinion as to what is a "problem" and their relative priorities; with further elaboration such differences would increase. In a multigroup society such as in the United States with its many class, color, religious, ethnic variants, divergence of values (or goals) should not only be expected but encouraged and designed for—even in a country such as Sweden with no major ethnic subgroups and less social distance between classes. While a unicultural solution is conceivable although hardly congruent with "the autonomous personality," there are already strong signs of divergent goal values, especially in the new Left, the young and blacks. All of these ills are interconnected—everything is related to everything else—and where to start moving this complex muddle faces the urban guidance expert with numerous dilemmas.

Having harshly criticized the metropolis, it should be noted that it is superior or is perceived so with respect to access to health, education, higher income, job options, variety of interest groups, cultural opportunities. The city is still the place where civilization develops and to which people flock.

VALUES AND GOALS FOR URBAN SOCIETY

What do we plan for? Social and behavioral scientists are reasonably adept at delineating through opinion surveys, employing clever sampling techniques, what it is people think they want. The intensity of these wants, too, can be measured and trade-offs of one value satisfaction versus another can be assessed; the results can be elaborately correlated and interrelated. Both profit-making and nonprofit-making organizations can be hired to engage in such activities. As is well known, the political pollsters have sharpened their skills in the real world of politics, where prior verbal statements of intention can be checked against the hard fact of behavior, i.e., voting! The precision of results is remarkable. In addition, behavioral market research for private business indicates trade-offs and preferences: How much is spent for beer and how much for classical recordings in a given market. Persons "vote" with dollars for their preferences. Thus existent values/goals can be approximated rather precisely for the whole society and more importantly today in a multigroup participatory democracy by age, sex, economic class, location, ethnic or racial group, etc. Two massive questions then obtrude: (a) how to effect trade-offs in satisfying the values/goals of subgroups such as outboard motorboat fans versus fishermen and canoeists in a smallish lake; between screaming rock singers and a chorale society and (b) are existent values no matter how puerile (a value judgment of course) to be catered to slavishly or do those responsible—even temporarily—for guiding the society have the obligation to search for "higher values" for the present and the future. It is more than likely in the 1970s that assiduous market researchers could prove that certain large segments of New York City's public show by their purchases preference for heroin over the Metropolitan Opera.

The obligation to establish a hierarchy of values for alternate value systems rests with each responsible planner, who is in effect a staff officer of a political person "in command." Society must wrestle with its collective soul, hammering out some sort of desired states or options for alternative possible futures. And as soon as the planning scheme becomes operationally airborne, feed-back loops will shift such values/goals. This is clearly a sophisticated political process that goes beyond one vote democratic nose counting and it may be possible eventually through two-way TV in "the wired city" and in the use of "educative" sampling technologies. Eventually there may be a way to develop scientifically "high values" to be attained as goals; as yet this is not remotely possible. But the necessity remains for all planners, especially on a national level, to make clear the assumptions about gross overriding values.

Certain marginal subgroups with or without a surfeit of butter could opt for more Beethoven (or even "to make" Beethoven in an orchestra). It is also conceivable that feedback over time could lead to such a happy result or something like it in a number of subgroups. From such values, explicit quantified goals can be set and by ingenious intellectual devices measurements can be made to indicate progress or lack of progress toward clearly expressed concrete and highly visible objectives nailed to the masthead of the plan.[77]

Value elucidation is simply not an ivory tower exercise; the more earthy of the American professional planning organizations, the American Society of Planning Officials (ASPO) who pride themselves on dealing with the "nitty gritty" facts of plan delivery, centered their 1973 annual conference on "Planning for Varied Life Styles."

Perhaps the best known—presumably global—hierarchy of human "needs" (values) is that of psychologist Abraham Maslow,[78] which to an anthropological/sociological eye looks somewhat culture bound in thrall to modern Western society. Here it is by levels from the simply physical to the "higher" intellectual/spiritual:

> Level 1. *physiological needs:* food, clothing, shelter, rest;
> Level 2. *safety or security needs:* "keep and protect";
> Level 3. *social needs:* "belonging, sharing and association, forgiving and receiving friendship and love";
> Level 4. *ego needs:* "self-confidence, independence, achievement, competence, knowledge" and "status, recognition, appreciation, deserved respect of one's peers";
> Level 5. *self-fulfillment needs:* "for growth, self-development, self-actualization—realization," full range of his individual potential as a human being.

One is tempted to inquire how well the modern urban place facilitates the attainment of such "needs" or goals; interesting trade-offs can be seen here in the way individuals and groups opt for more or less of Level 3 (*social needs*) versus Level 5 (*self-fulfillment*), or Level 2 (*safety or security*) versus Level 4 (*ego needs*).

Examining the complex of possible attitudinal and institutional shifts during the ensuing decade in the United States, Ian H. Wilson and his associates advised their noneleemosynary institution, the General Electric Company, on our "Future

Business Environment"[79] that these seventeen significant value shifts (including contradictory counterculture potential moves) seem likely:

1. war (military might) toward peace (economic development);
2. nationalism toward internationalism;
3. federal government toward state and local government;
4. public enterprise toward private enterprise;
5. organization toward individual;
6. uniformity (conformity) toward pluralism;
7. independence toward interdependence; sociability toward privacy (180° in conflict);
8. materialism toward quality of life;
9. status quo (permanence, routine) toward change (flexibility, innovation);
10. future toward immediacy;
11. work toward leisure;
12. authority toward participation;
13. centralization toward decentralization;
14. ideology (dogma) toward pragmatism (rationality);
15. moral absolutes toward situational morality;
16. economic efficiency toward social justice;
17. means toward ends (national goals!).

In the mercurial world of the present, it would appear that in the face of accelerating sociocultural change (1) the "war to peace" shift is not in question but (8) "materialism to quality of life" is hardly certain and even less so far as the foreseeable future is (2) "nationalism toward internationalism." There is ample evidence of a return to isolationism in the United States, for example. Despite such strictures, such value shifts, for which the empirical data is not as hard as one would like, a catalogue might be useful for the sociophysical planner to keep in the back of his head. Value forecasting is as important as it is as yet unreliable, and of terrific significance to both the public and private sector planners. It certainly is preferable to intuitive judgments. A concern with the quality of life (QOL) basic to self-realization (Maslow's Level 5, *self-fulfillment*), despite the noted adherence to materialistic interests, does seem to be emerging in the "information society" developing before our eyes. The United States Environmental Protection Agency produced a provocative anthology of readings for its symposium on QOL held in the summer of 1972.[80] Maslow's value hierarchy was extended to emphasize that various groups in a selective fashion adopt different levels in a continuously shifting value scene. The United States federal government has sponsored research (as has Japan) in goal setting over at least a dozen years, that is, if we accept President Eisenhower's Commission on National Goals which produced *Goals for Americans* in 1960 as a first official statement of the good life. August Heckscher argued therein for the higher culture and in a succinct piece Catherine Bauer Wooster presented the good urban society as "a rewarding home for man"; otherwise the product was a generally pedestrian effort.[81] This was followed in 1969 by the U. S. Department of Health, Education and Welfare, *Toward a Social Report*[82] which, although aiming at a societal indicator system, nevertheless implied the sort of national goals our society should be searching to attain by government action. This is evident in its readings of (a) the status of health and illness, (b) social mobility, (c) the physical environment, (d) income and poverty; (e) public order and safety, (f) learning, science and art, (g) participation and alienation. The National Goals Research Staff, appointed by President Nixon, raised high initial hopes in 1969, with the President's fivefold charge:

> 1. forecasting future developments and assessing the longer-range consequences of present social trends;
> 2. measuring the probable future impact of alternative courses of action, including measuring the degree to which change in one area would be likely to affect another;
> 3. estimating the actual range of social choice—that is, what alternative sets of goals might be attainable, in light of the availability of resources and possible rates of progress;
> 4. developing and monitoring social [societal] indicators that can reflect the present and future quality of American life, and the direction and rate of its change;
> 5. summarizing, integrating and correlating the results of related research activities being carried on within the various federal agencies, and by state and local governments and private organizations.

They reported back in 1970[83] merely posing issues of goal/values for debate by the American people. There was no expert "prescription." Attention was devoted to a spectrum of six issues: population, environment, education, basic natural science, technology assessment, consumerism. Despite a sophisticated and brilliant staff little of great import sifted through the guarding political net. And we remain nationally without explicit goals as the basis for a national internal policy and plan.

In the encyclopedic *Values and the Future,*[84] edited by Kurt Baier and Nicholas Rescher, the implications of sociotechnological change—very broadly interpreted—on American values are assessed, but the findings are not readily usable operationally in planning. "Value impact forecaster," a term coined by Alvin Toffler in his introduction to the volume, spells out the conundrum for all planners for they must plan not for "now," but for "then," when things will be different and today's "good" may become tomorrow's "bad" ("the voyage to the moon" and the American SST, for example, in 1975). Technology assessment now attempts to conceptualize and operationalize solutions to this dilemma.

The *Man and His Urban Environment Project*[85] brought such highly abstract and abstruse value systems down to the rural earth after a three-year study by stolidly cataloguing nine requirements for man in an urban system. This, as yet unweighted list, represents the consensus of a variety of social scientists and other urban specialists; it presumably defines "the good life." It should be noted that each "requirement" is relativistic to both culture and subculture, and with the revolution of rising expectations, tends to escalate in a climate of increasing shortages. Nevertheless this crude protocalculus does stake out what a city "ought to be like" in an understandable fashion. In short, what does man require in an urban system: (1) livable shelter, (2) effective urban services, (3) reasonable security, (4) hope for personal and community improvement, (5) a source of income, (6) reduction of waste, (7) effective cultural and recreational facilities, (8) transport that works and (9) a minimum of pollution and ecological disruption? It would be possible to quantify these criteria.

Finally let us hark to the Delphic voice of the National Planning Association's Center for Priority Analysis as it plots the *Changes in National Priorities During the 1960s: Their Implications for 1980*[86] in the five-part summary of their deliberations. This is an important study methodologically since the hard factual basis is how the United States, public and private, voted with dollars over the past decade—reflecting "private and public perceptions of the importance of different national needs and purposes." What comes first as a claim on the society's resources? They are not too different from Ian Wilson's prognostications for General Electric.

> 1. A significant shift in priorities, as indicated by expenditures, occurred in the public sector during the 1960s. Goals associated with domestic human welfare, such as education, health and social welfare, were assigned a higher priority; goals concerned with the nation's international posture, i.e., national defense and aid to developing nations, received a lesser priority.
> 2. Public and private outlays for urban development were accorded a low priority during the 1960s. Spending for urban development, including housing, diminished from 12.4 per cent of GNP in 1962 to 10.2 per cent in 1969.
> 3. The plant and equipment and transportation goals received the highest priority in the past decade among those goals pursued primarily through private expenditures.
> 4. Protection of environmental quality emerged as the major new goal during the 1960s. In 1969, over $6 billion was spent for environmental protection programs.
> 5. If the trends in expenditures of the 1960s were to continue during the 1970s there would be large gaps by 1980 between the levels of spending for many goals, i.e., social welfare or international aid, and the resources required to attain current aspiration standards in these areas. Spending for several other goals, such as transportation and national defense, would approximate or exceed the projected requirements for the goals standard.

This is precise enough and based on very hard data.

Much has been made of the counterculture of the young New Left; actual examination of their oft-proclaimed value systems indicates that they are generally complaining that the Establishment is simply not living up to its *liberté, égalité et fraternité* ideals to which it must return. This complaint, no matter how valid, is hardly a revolutionary stance! There seems little doubt that the remainder of this century will see egalitarian distributional problems and debate uppermost in everyone's mouths and minds[87] before we can get down to designing a societal and physical environment in which the *unequal* qualities of humans can be allowed to bloom. For the time being, equal opportunities must be opened up to each group in our pluralistic society; hopefully at the same time progress will take place for all to work up Maslow's value hierarchy to full self-realization. Thus modern planning attempts hopefully to offer rich options to *all* to *earn* "the good life" by "internal environmental planning" within themselves.

It would be rewarding to have in the United States such a clear pronouncement of goals and intentions as introduces Japan's *New Comprehensive National De-*

velopment Plan, May 1969, and feel relatively certain that both resources and adequate integrated government/private structuring stood behind the resolve to realize these goals. They are worth quoting[88]:

Objectives of the Plan

(1) The basic objective of this plan is to create an affluent environment for human beings by harmonizing the following four requirements with the aspiration for an advanced welfare society:
a. To maintain harmony between humanity and nature and to preserve and protect national environments permanently, to satisfy the people's desire for contact with nature which is expected to intensify as urbanization proceeds, and to conserve nature perpetually;
b. To modify the basic conditions of development and to provide proper balance in national development potentialities by the efficient utilization of all land areas to avoid lopsided utilization of particular regions;
c. To reorganize land utilization systems and improve efficiency by promoting independent regional development programs and modification to fit peculiar local conditions; and
d. To promote and conserve safe, pleasant and cultural environmental conditions throughout the urban and rural sectors and protect people from discomfort and peril as a result of increasing economic and social activities and the higher density of economic and social activity.
(2) There exist pending regional problems, overcongestion, oversparseness and regional differentials. Following are the basic approaches for tackling these problems.
a. In order to deal with overcongestion problems in large cities, social overhead capital should be improved in the fields of transportation, development of water resources and housing and living environment facilities. Simultaneously, industrial establishments unsuited for metropolitan areas because of (1) technological innovations, (2) a drastic expansion of production scale and (3) environmental changes will be completely decentralized. Various functions of metropolitan areas will be reorganized and measures will be taken to concentrate and strengthen the central management function. At the same time safe and functional city structures will have to be established by a complete remodelling of metropolitan areas so as to protect them from disasters and public nuisances.
In order to reorganize city functions, land utilization regulations and transportation regulations must be tightened on the one hand while various laws instituting user taxes and establishing the priority for public use of land must be enacted.
Public investment for industrialization alone has been relied upon in the past in sparsely populated regions to prevent the outflow of population. This approach must be re-evaluated. For areas where industrialization or the promotion of tourism are possible, active development programs to suit regional characteristics must be introduced and various measures must be taken to improve environment conditions, including the reorganization of communities.
For those regions where the introduction of effective development is difficult, however, various and over-all measures must be taken to pro-

vide social securities and to assist in settlement.

As to the problem of regional differentials, we take the stand that it is not so much a question of per capita productive income differentials but rather of the differentials in standards of living, particularly in the level of social living environments. While seeking to improve the social environment of the regional hub cities, the living environment of neighboring areas must also be improved to maintain a certain level in harmony with the regional hub cities.

A new task in relation to the problem of regional differentials is to provide new transportation and communication systems linking remote and less-developed regions with metropolitan areas to ensure the development potential for these regions and to create the basic conditions for balanced land development.

Whether all this can be accomplished with the present catastrophic energy situation in Japan—90 per cent dependent on foreign supplies, due to the Arab oil embargo and to the generally astronomical increase in crude petroleum costs—remains to be seen.

NOTES

[1] Only 30 per cent of the city is served by sewers.

[2] A happy phrase learned in personal conversation with Lawrence Mann, head, Department of City and Regional Planning, Harvard.

[3] "Today . . . it seems useful to conceive of urbanization, not as simply the multiplication of old-style cities, but as a characteristic of a total society. It is a characteristic that might be better described as *an increase in societal scale.*" Scott Greer, *The Emerging City*. Glencoe, Ill., The Free Press, 1962, p. 33.

[4] Cf. Daniel Bell, *The Coming of Post Industrial Society*. New York, Basic Books, 1973.

[5] Peter Drucker, *The Age of Discontinuity*. New York, Harper & Row, 1969.

[6] Michael Harrington, *The Accidental Century*. New York, Macmillan Company, 1965.

[7] Herbert Gans, "The New Egalitarianism," *Saturday Review,* May 6, 1972, pp. 43–46. "In a 'nation of equals' many are considerably less equal than others and have grown impatient about not getting their share", p. 43.

[8] Donald Michael, *The Unprepared Society: Planning for a Precarious Future*. New York, Harper Colophon Books, CN20, 1968.

[9] Alvin Toffler, *Future Shock*. New York, Random House, 1970.

[10] Including the editor: *The Second American Revolution*. New York, William Morrow and Son, 1964, which took an élitist meritocratic, future position rather than following the now current égalitarian mood.

[11] Daniel Bell, mistakenly, saw *The End of Ideology: On the Exhaustion of Political Ideas in the Fifties.* New York, Collier Books, BS43, 1961. Faced by an increasingly pragmatic USSR, the West had not yet been hit by that anarchic hurricane, the New Left of rather more heat than light, and Black Power.

[12] Dennis L. Meadows and Associates for the Club of Rome. Washington, D.C., a Potomac Associates book, Universe Books, 1972.

[13] Editors of *Fortune* (New York: Doubleday Anchor, 1957).

[14] Bennett Berger, *Working Class Suburb.* Berkeley, University of California Press, 1960.

[15] A. C. Spectorsky, *The Exurbanites* (New York, Berkeley Publishing Corp., 1955), early captured this flight to the bushes in a telling fashion.

[16] F. Stuart Chapin, Jr., and Shirley F. Weiss, *Urban Growth Dynamics.* New York, John Wiley and Sons, 1962, p. 1.

[17] Leonard Reissman, *The Urban Process.* Glencoe, Ill., The Free Press, 1964.

[18] Charles Abrams, *The Urban Condition.* New York, Harper & Row, 1965.

[19] Leonard J. Duhl (ed.), *The Urban Condition.* New York, a Clarion book, Simon and Schuster, 1963.

[20] New York state actually has issued a statewide plan for its cities with this title.

[21] Lewis Mumford, *The Urban Prospect.* New York, Harcourt, Brace & World, 1968.

[22] Irving L. Horowitz (ed.), *The Anarchists.* New York, Dell Publishing Co., 1964. In his "A Postscript to the Anarchists," this is one of the six fundamental questions on the subject posed by him (pp. 581–603).

[23] Michael McGiffert (ed.), *The Character of Americans* (rev. ed.). Homewood, Ill., The Dorsey Press, 1970, p. 400.

[24] Lynne Iglitzin, *Violent Conflict in American Society.* San Francisco, Chandler Publishing Co., 1972, p. 156.

[25] Carl Leiden and Karl M. Schmitt, *The Politics of Violence: Revolution in the Modern World.* Englewood Cliffs, N.J., Prentice-Hall, Inc., 1968, p. 3.

[26] Dave Dellinger, *Revolutionary Nonviolence.* New York, Doubleday Anchor, 1971. Dellinger is an unusual sort of "pacifist" New Left black.

[27] Abdul A. Said and Daniel M. Collier, *Revolutionism.* Boston, Allyn and Bacon, 1971, p. 153.

[28] Lewis Coser, *The Functions of Social Conflict.* Glencoe, Ill., The Free Press, 1956, p. 157.

[29] Hannah Arendt, *On Violence.* New York, Harcourt, Brace & World, Inc., 1970.

[30] See the puerile and explicit—also highly successful—do-it-yourself handbook on crime/revolution: Abbie Hoffman's *Steal This Book.* New York, Grove Press, 1971. "Liberate" both yourself and the property of the "oppressors!"

[31] The Report of the National Commission on the Causes and Prevention of Violence, *Violent Crime: Homicide, Assault, Rape, Robbery; The Challenge to Our Cities.* New York, George Braziller, 1969.

[32] The curious story of the "disappearing heroin" held as evidence by the New York police is one of the more startling examples of this. The New York *Times,* December 31, 1972.

[33] There is an unsubstantiated rumor that ten thousand students were arrested in the ugly revolts centering around Tokyo University in 1968. Of that number, it is said three thousand still remain in prison.

[34] Robert Gold, "Urban Violence and Contemporary Defensive Cities," *Journal of the American Institute of Planners,* May 1970.

[35] "Violence in the Cities: A Historical View," in Charles U. Daly (ed.), *Urban Violence*. Chicago, The University of Chicago Center for Policy Study, 1969, p. 7.

[36] Chalmers Johnson, *Revolutionary Change*. Boston, Little, Brown and Co., 1966, p. 166.

[37] Cf. the waspish little piece by Peter Schrag, formerly a clearly marginal man at Amherst College as an undergraduate, "The Decline of the Wasp," *Harper's Magazine,* Vol. 240, No. 1439 (1970), pp. 85–91.

[38] James P. Spradley and David W. McCurdy, *Conformity and Conflict: Reading in Cultural Anthropology*. Boston, Little, Brown and Co., 1971, p. 386.

[39] Cf. Part 4, "Some Mental and Social Antecedents of Revolution," primarily the material from John Dollard in the excellent reader: James C. Davies (ed.), *When Men Revolt and Why*. Glencoe, Ill., The Free Press, 1971, pp. 149–201.

[40] Cf. Robin Morgan (ed.), *Sisterhood Is Powerful; An Anthology of Writings from the Women's Liberation Movement* (New York: Vintage Books, 1970); Betty Roszak and Theodore Roszak, *Masculine/Feminine Readings in Sexual Mythology and the Liberation of Women;* and especially the balanced treatment in Jessie Bernard, *Women and the Public Interest* (Chicago: Aldine/Atherton, 1971). There are, of course, other items but these give the flavor of the movement.

[41] Carl Oglesby (ed.), *The New Left Reader* (New York, Grove Press, Inc., 1969), in short compass has a choice collection of relevant "theory."

[42] Martin Oppenheimer, *The Urban Guerrilla*. Chicago, Triangle Press, 1969.

[43] Op. cit.

[44] Charles Reich, *The Greening of America*. New York, Random House, 1970.

[45] David Cooper (ed.), *To Free a Generation: The Dialectics of Liberation* (New York, Collier Books, 09530, 1969), contains the predictable phraseology of "leaders" of this essentially New Left movement: Carmichael, Gerassi, Goodman, Marcuse, etc.

[46] South American university students were, however, old hands at "revolution."

[47] Allan Priaux and Sanford J. Ungar, *The Almost Revolution: France 1968* (New York, Dell Publishing Co., 1969), and Hervé Bourges (ed.), *The French Student Revolt: The Leaders Speak* (New York, Hill and Wang, 1968), including Jean-Paul Sartre (ancient) and Daniel Cohn-Bendit (German).

[48] Richard Peterson, "The Student Left in American Higher Education," *Daedalus* (Winter 1968), p. 293.

[49] Seymour Martin Lipset and Sheldon S. Wolin (eds.), *The Berkeley Student Revolt*. New York, Doubleday Anchor A486, 1965.

[50] Jerry L. Avorn, et al., *Up Against the Ivy Wall: A History of the Columbia Crisis*. New York, Atheneum Press, 1968.

[51] Maxwell H. Norman (ed.), *College Students Look at the 21st Century*. Cambridge, Mass., Winthrop Publishers, Inc., 1972.

[52] *1970 Census of Population and Housing,* U. S. Department of Commerce, Bureau of the Census, October, 1971, United States Summary PHC(2)-1, pp. 4–5.

[53] Ben Gilbert and staff of the Washington *Post, Ten Blocks from the White House*. New York, Praeger paperback, 1968.

[54] Cf. *Report of the National Advisory Commission on Civil Disorders*. New York, Bantam Books, 1968; copyright by the New York *Times*. According to Brandeis University's Lemberg Center for the Study of Violence, *The Long Hot Summer* (Waltham, Mass., 1972), the number of race-related disorders dropped from 176 in 1967 to 46 in 1971; in 1967, 80 per cent of the disorders were attributed to blacks, by 1971, the figure was 37 per cent.

[55] *One Year Later*. Washington, Urban America, Inc., and the Urban Coalition, 1969, p. 118.

[56] Incidentally, his conclusions infuriated the black community. *The Negro Family; The Case for National Action* (Washington, D.C., U. S. Department of Labor, Office of Policy Planning and Research, March 1965). Cf. Lee Rainwater and William L. Yancey, *The Moynihan Report and the Politics of Controversy*. Boston, M.I.T. Press, 1967. *The Black Family in Modern Society* by John H. Scanzoni (Boston, Allyn and Bacon, Inc., 1971) deplores the attention paid to abnormal Negro families and contends that 75 per cent do stay together and 50 per cent of all Negroes have made it to the middle class (p. 306).

[57] Examples of recent scholarship are Karl E. and Alma E. Taeuber, *Negroes in Cities: Residential Segregation and Neighborhood Change* (Chicago, Aldine Publishing Co., 1965), or that most sensitive community study by Elliot Liebow, *Tally's Corner: A Study of Negro Street Corner Men* (Boston, Little, Brown and Co., 1967).

[58] Logically no black could thus understand Plato, the Bible or Shakespeare, not to mention the U. S. Constitution.

[59] Frantz Fanon, *The Wretched of the Earth: The Handbook for the Black Revolution That Is Changing the Shape of the World. New York,* Grove Press, Inc., Evergreen Black Cat Edition, 1968, translated by Constance Farrington from *Les damnés de la terre* (Paris, 1961).

[60] Malcolm X, *The Autobiography of Malcolm X*. New York, Grove Press, 1964.

[61] *Look Out Whitey, Black Power's Gon' Get Your Mama!* New York, the Dial Press, 1968.

[62] Whitney M. Young, *Beyond Racism: Building an Open Society*. New York, McGraw-Hill, paperback edition, 1971.

[63] Richard A. Cloward and Frances Fox Piven, "We've Got Rights! The No Longer Silent Welfare Poor," *The New Republic* (August 5, 1967), pp. 23–37, reproduced in Max Birmbaum and John Mogey, *Serial Change in Urban America* (New York, Harper & Row, 1972).

[64] Cf. Cella S. Heller (ed.), *Structural Social Inequality*. New York, The Macmillan Company, 1969, esp. pp. 3–5.

[65] David M. Potter, *The People of Plenty: Economic Abundance and the American Character*. Chicago, University of Chicago Press, 1954.

[66] Michael Harrington, *The Other America: Poverty in the United States*. New York, Macmillan Company, 1962.

[67] Joel F. Handler, *Reforming the Poor*. New York, Basic Books, Inc., 1972. Cf. Gilbert V. Steiner, *The State of Welfare* (Washington, The Brookings In-

stitution, 1972), who makes clear that there are no possible public programs in the offing which could "clear up the poverty problem" in a few years.

[68] Stephen M. Rose, *The Betrayal of the Poor: The Transformation of Community* (Cambridge, Mass., Shenkman Publishing Company, 1972), for a mildly paranoid view of this attempt.

[69] Daniel P. Moynihan, *Maximum Feasible Misunderstanding* (New York, The Free Press, 1969, 1970), indicates the dimensions of the entire Office of Economic Opportunity (OEO) fiasco.

[70] Edward Banfield, *The Unheavenly City*. Boston, Little Brown, 1970.

[71] Anthony Downs, *Who Are the Urban Poor?*. New York, Committee for Economic Development, Supplementary Paper No. 26, rev. ed., 1970.

[72] Certain statistical quirks indicated that the percentage of persons suffering from poverty is lessening; this is simply not so, as rising welfare statistics surely indicate.

[73] Offered by Michael Tietz, head of the Department of City and Regional Planning, College of Environmental Design, University of California at Berkeley. Tietz made this remark at a seminar workshop on planning education at the AIP annual conference in Boston, October 1972.

[74] See Roland L. Delorme and Raymond G. McInnis (eds.), *Anti-Democratic Trends in Twentieth Century America.* Reading, Mass., Addison-Wesley Publishing Co., 1969.

[75] Herbert H. Hyman, "England and America: Climates of Tolerance and Intolerance (1962)," in Daniel Bell (ed.), *The Radical Right*. New York, Doubleday Anchor A-376, 1964.

[76] "A changing American work force is becoming pervasively dissatisfied with dull, unchallenging and repetitive jobs, and this discontent is sapping the economic and social strength of the nation." New York *Times* (December 22, 1972), commenting on *Work in America* (U. S. Department of Health, Education and Welfare, Washington, 1972).

[77] See Chapter 15 below, *Societal Indicators: a Necessary Calculus,* p. 600.

[78] Abraham Maslow, *Motivation and Personality*. New York, Harper & Row, 1970. A capsule summary of his value system is found in *The Futurist,* Vol. IV, No. 1 (1970), p. 6.

[79] Reported in *The Futurist,* February 1970, pp. 5–8.

[80] *The "Quality of Life" Concept: A Potential New Tool for Decision Makers.* Office of Research and Monitoring, Environmental Studies Division, the Environmental Protection Agency, Washington, August 1972.

[81] Administered by the American Assembly, Columbia University, Englewood Cliffs, N.J., Prentice-Hall, Spectrum Books, 1960.

[82] *Toward a Social Report,* U. S. Government Printing Office, 1969.

[83] *Toward Balanced "Growth": Quantity and Quality*. Washington, D.C., Superintendent of Documents, 1970.

[84] Kurt Baier and Nicholas Rescher (eds.), *Values and the Future*. New York, The Free Press, 1971. This is to date the foremost value-projection study.

[85] Fred Smith, *Man and His Urban Environment*. New York 10020, Room 5600, 30 Rockefeller Plaza, 1972. The focus of attention was the New Town or new community as part of a positive approach to a comprehensive urban system.

[86] Leonard A. Lecht, *Changes in National Priorities During the 1960s: Their Implications for 1980*. Washington, D.C., National Planning Association, Report No. 132, 1972.

[87] Robert S. Benson and Harold Wolman (eds.) for the National Urban Coalition, *Counterbudget: A Blueprint for Changing National Priorities, 1971–1976*. New York, Praeger, 1971. Goal one: full employment; Goal two: equal opportunity; Goal three: basic necessities, etc.

[88] Economic Planning Agency, Government of Japan (Tokyo, 1970?), English version, pp. 8–9.

CHAPTER 14

Alternative Possible Futures: A National Urban Policy

H. Wentworth Eldredge

ALTERNATIVE URBAN OPTIONS

The United States has a multigroup society with widely divergent value systems and an overriding democratic value system with heavy egalitarian overtones. This precludes any reductionism to *one national pattern* for planning societal/physical urbanism. This would apply to most societies in varying degrees. Such a naive, crude, cruel and simplistic perception of forcing "human nature" into one value pattern is not remotely feasible in any modern Western nation even though there is some tendency to approach it in totalitaria. The enormous powers of the intellectual, technical, even behavioral and organizational technologies make it possible for the first time in history to "have diversity, choice and to meet human needs."[1] Undoubtedly, we do have some options for our urban futures despite the present energy crunch.

In the postindustrial society with its heavy emphasis on the knowledge industry, there are bound to be many variants on the patterns common in the 1970s wherever. Paul Goodman sees *Seeds of Liberation*[2] in new thought patterns that free humanity for building, first, better societal futures, later, physical structures. The American Institute of Planners launched a massive enquiry in 1966, directed by

William R. Ewald, Jr., into the next fifty years, budgeting over one and a quarter million dollars from a great variety of public and private sources. This was a hefty attempt to illumine America's (and the world's) professional city planners as to the rich variety of the feasible roads ahead.[3] An amazing mishmash of contributors—many exceptionally perceptive—from an enormous spectrum of doers and thinkers adds up to the clear message that more of the same would be hopelessly inadequate. Urban design students, Kevin Lynch in "The Possible City"[4] stresses that "mobility, access and communication are indeed the essential qualities of an urbanized region—its reason for being." This has been echoed by transportation specialist Wilfred Owen, who hammers on the fact that access to activity nodes—jobs, dwellings and recreation—is the key to civilized community development and glimpses the developing interchangeability of communication (movement of ideas) with transportation (movement of people and goods), which is bound to affect life territory and life styles shortly.[5]

If market choices are to be largely replaced by designed options under a National Urban Policy (NUP), then widespread societal/physical alternate possibilities must be built for multiple life styles of the present and future. Minimum standards probably can be set; egalitarianism, heavily reinforced by increasingly scarce resources, will quite likely create iron maximums. However, within these very wide parameters a NUP can offer the citizenry a great variety of versions of an existence of "style and quality." There undoubtedly will be both monetary and possible societal costs for making available large numbers of available options, but the resultant stunting of society's rich fabric by dull sameness suggests immediate high societal costs and potential high monetary costs for the failure to provide such options. Inadequate life styles are "a shaped charge" aimed at urban viability; insistent frustration leads to tension resulting in the possibility of grim revolution (a most costly societal exercise).

Thus it would appear that one of the most overwhelming tasks of planners is to make readily available rewarding, feasible options in diverse physical and societal forms and combinations thereof.

Traditionally, planners have tended to think in terms of multipurpose or multifunctional cities; this seems a rather narrow conclusion to induce from a long human experience with governmental, religious, recreational, learning, trading, industrial types of cities. From this simple list, the future specialized cities could be derived: (a) the ceremonial city (Washington, Islamabad); (b) the university city (Oxford as it was); (c) the research city (Novo Sibirsk); (d) the artistic city (Aspen, Colorado); (e) the fun city or Hedonopolis (Cannes, Miami Beach); (f) the museum city (Bruges, Williamsburg, Nara), including museums of the future (Mesa City of Soleri); (g) the experimental city of varied types (health, new social relations, communal economic developments); (h) any combination of the above. In point of fact, each venture could be considered as an experiment,[6] and so treated. Actually, sharply differentiated satellite cities in a metropolitan area or sectors or communities within a city could offer rewarding variations.

Here is a realistic catalogue of feasible urban options ahead; these are relatively "surprise free" and assume that no major economic, military or ecological catastrophe will befall the world and its cities in the next three decades. Given multigroup society with divergent life styles and values, it is obligatory for holistic planners to offer a wide spectrum of choice. Despite both physical and societal utopianists, it is more than likely that in the year 2000 A.D. postindustrial society will be surprisingly like the present only—hopefully—"better." These fifteen options, are not mutually exclusive and much overlapping is implied; within options there are clearly suboptions which are not pursued. Further, the emphasis here is on the physical/spatial framework and on location (especially under Type A) which do not remotely determine societal structuring. Much social diversity is possible within similar man-made physical environments; the relationship between design and behavior is not one-to-one. These options are grouped under two categories: *Type A—Almost Certain to Continue;* and *Type B—Generally Far-out Potential Environments;* no attempt is made to weigh formally the importance of the various options. Certain options clearly occur within the territory of larger urban forms—others are relatively free standing entities or activity centers.

Type A: Almost Certain to Continue

Option 1. Megalopolis or urban region formed by interconnecting metropolitan areas. This is modern society's fate. Most of the postindustrial urban population will dwell in Options 1, 2 and 3: The Pacific Belt (Japan), Boswash, and Randstad (Hollard) are already here. Can such sprawling giantism be redeveloped by opening up "density breaks" (similar to "fire breaks" in a forest) and by the creation of varied activity nodes to restructure interaction and upgrade the Quality of Life (QOL) in these vast agglomerations?

Option 2. Metropolitan central city (500,000 and up) as a high activity area with cosmopolitan, sophisticated recreation, jobs, living: the French regional *métropoles d'équilibre* fit this pattern; high-rise, vertically zoned buildings as an experiment. Both "straight" and "counter" cultures can find room here. This is the locus of high pressure private and public development in the United States as "the city fights back" to lure middle-class population into returning from the suburbs. It means modern office buildings, pedestrian malls and pediment (or higher) walkways with interesting shops, recreational and cultural facilities—in short, the lure of the bazaar which has so importantly stoked urban fires. "New Towns in Town" (NTIT) belong here most certainly to divide the city, at least physically, into some semblance of meaningful service communities; social development planning will be a must in large sectors of central city.

Option 3. Smaller central city (50,000 to 500,000), similar qualities but on a less national and more regional scale. The possibility exists of creating an entire community spirit. Town housing; vertically zoned buildings with possible class and ethnic mixtures. Somewhere between a 250,000 and 500,000 population seems to be presently the critical mass for the full spectrum of city functions. QOL efforts would pay off richly here.

Option 4. Small central city or town (up to 50,000), still less national/regional interaction and scale. Local varieties adjusted more clearly to differing natural environments and with specific functions, such as the research city; shore city; recreation city; university/learning/information city; mountain city.

Option 5. Satellite cities for Options 2 and 3 to gain the putative benefits of Option 4; closely linked with new communities, but could be upgraded and expanded in existent towns or cities, similar to the British experiment under the Town Development Act of 1952.

Option 6. Inner suburbs for all three major city types (2,3,4) divided into "communities" (NTIT again) serving various life styles according to economic class, vocational and/or avocational interests, religion, ethnicity, race, etc.—high rise and low rise (town houses/cluster housing). There should be a great variety of suburban types to suit various life styles. The United States has its special problem in white/black antagonisms and unless adequate suburban space (both integrated and nonintegrated) is made available for blacks to leave the central city, the impacted ghetto poisoning American life for all will continue to fester. Some advanced nations and many developing countries face similar problems.

Option 7. Outer suburbs, similar but of a less "urban" character. Varied life styles are stressed by design both physical and societal; a greater attempt through cluster housing to create "community." Some high-rise buildings in open settings are inevitable; New Towns in Town again.

Option 8. Exurbia. Quasi-rural existence of a scattered grain, but due to improving transportation and communication it will be "urbanistic" in quality and not unrelated to "the wired city" and the four-day work week. Made possible by the electric pump, septic tank and four-wheel drive vehicle; haunt of hillbilly types and seclusive "intellectuals" and others. This is high-cost scatteration, but an immensely rewarding option for certain personality types—who may be either incompetent, truly creative, hiding from the horrid urban world or merely in search of peace.[7] Increasingly the haunt of the counterculture and very suitable for new experimental family/community variants. Alpine recreational resorts possibly fit this category.

Option 9. New Towns (or latterly New Communities). Building cities *de novo* has held a great attraction for mankind: "Leave the messy clutter behind and start afresh." This might even be traced back to mobile hunters striking the befouled encampment to move on to virgin areas. New towns imply dwellings, jobs, recreation, a wide spectrum of services and *controlled* size. Most certainly the current furor about new cities/towns/communities indicates a deep-seated dissatisfaction with existent urban forms. And unquestionably this is the option for widespread experimentation both with physical forms and with societal structure—and is a means of ascertaining and developing client desires or choices. Somewhat oversold everywhere as a universal panacea at the moment, the enormous costs for the needed infrastructure of a massive new cities program boggles the imagination. An example is the problem of coping with a significant per cent of the expected eighty to one hundred million new Americans (thirty-five million new households by 2000 A.D.). To build for 25 per cent only or twenty to twenty-five million would require two thousand towns each for one hundred thousand inhabitants and each costing between two and five billion in public and private investment, leading to an over-all expenditure of ten trillion dollars at least.[8]

While undoubtedly much will of necessity be spent in any case to house, amuse, service and provide jobs for the expected hordes, it is most unlikely that exploiting the vast existing urban infrastructure would even approach such costs. However, the possible benefits of thousands of new towns might be of extraordinary magnitude.

Before proceeding further it should be stressed that new towns can consist of:

(a) free-standing independent communities (Brasilia or Novosibirsk Academic City);
(b) groups of related free-standing functionally divergent communities (Lewis Mumford's ideal);
(c) satellite communities with high self-employment (London ring New Towns);
(d) extensions of cities; really glorified, quasi-independent suburbs (Long Island Levittowns and Stockholm's semisattelite cities);
(e) "New Towns in Town" (NTIT), lively tissue grafts to existing internal city structure (Fort Lincoln, Washington D.C.).[9]

Minnesota Experimental City (MXC), brainchild of oceanographer, physicist, meteorologist Athelstan Spilhaus, aided by assorted great brains (Buckminster Fuller, urbanologist Harvey Perloff, economist Walter Heller, etc.) was to have been built by private financing on 50,000 acres, 120 miles north of Minneapolis with a maximum population of 250,000.[10] This is perhaps the most obviously experimental effort to date both physically and societally: downtown to be roofed over; the municipal power plant to be partially fueled by garbage; cable TV to approximate "the wired city" (Option 15); farms and factories to be mixed together. People were to be housed in megastructures complete with waterless toilets, people movers and universal computer-managed charge accounts. New city Vaudreuil to house and provide jobs for 150,000 residents is to be built by the French Government in the Basse-Seine region outside Paris. It will have "the world's first urban center without noise or pollution and all green zones in the general area are to be preserved," proudly announced the late President of the Republic Pompidou. The city's traffic will flow underground; factory smoke is to be carried away by underground conduits—gases being burned off at the source; with all refuse moved through underground conduits to be used in adding to the city's requirements for central heating; apartments and business buildings to be soundproofed. These are merely the most "advanced" examples of a global movement of new communities (millennia old) which include the architecturally striking Brasilia and Chandigarh and the older Washington—all examined here. The thirty-odd British New Towns are world renowned and probably well over one thousand new towns of various shapes and sizes had been identified by 1963.[11] This has been capped by a recent announcement that forty million people live in over one thousand new towns in the USSR alone.[12] The best known U.S. examples: Columbia (Maryland), Reston (Virgina), Flower Mound (Texas), Jonathan (Minnesota) and Irvine (California), all privately financed, are in varying degrees innovative socially and physically—primarily in amenities. The semisatellite cities coupled to the public urban transit system of Stockholm (they do not provide jobs for more than half the population) have attracted universal attention. The design of these semisatellite cities concentrates especially on the town centers, so reminiscent of American shopping centers without that ugly, naked parking necklace of automobiles and on the functional connection with the metropolitan rapid transit system. The Dutch have done a splendid job in reclaiming the Zuider Zee for new town development. Tapiola, a tiny gem for only seventeen thousand persons in Finland, using adroitly both green and blue (water) space, has cheered the world with the realization that handsome urbanity can be possible. Japan with characteristic zeal plans to dot the hinterland of Tokyo with quasi-new towns composed of rather barren high-density dwellings of which Tama New Town, with a population of 410,000 on 7,500 acres, is the prime example (this is the same acreage as Reston, Virginia, which is planned to house 75,000 with high recreational amenities). India is planning a "New Bombay" for a potential population of two million[13]; whether it will be built is another question in that country's present unprecedented economic, political and social crisis.

As is well known, Israel has constructed a variety of new towns/new communities: larger ones for port or industrial purposes; smaller for agricultural development often connected with defense under an urban settlement hierarchy system based on Christaller.[14] Connected with the physical siting of population are the renowned versions of communal settlements, the *kibbutz* and *moshav*. Thus the twin experimental functions of new communities are exhibited: technological virtuosity and new social patterning. Noteworthy in new community development world-wide is the great variety of fresh governmental authorities or public corporations invented to get on with the job—where traditional government has been obviously too wooden to do so.

While, for example, the original or Mark I postwar British New Towns were aimed in the London region at decanting the central city population, new towns or massively developed old towns both in Britain and elsewhere are now perceived as potentially powerful development nodes furthering national urbanization policy with high technology, high education and population distribution.[15] Herbert Gans, égalitarian sociologist, believes that treated delicately new communities might possibly make positive contributions to the nasty desegregation muddle here,[16] as will perhaps Soul City, the black New Town in North Carolina near Raleigh-Durham under the leadership of Floyd B. McKissick, planned for an eventual population of fifty thousand.[17]

Finally, the United States Government is officially dedicated to sponsoring new communities in the Housing Acts of 1970 and 1972, but the action up to now has hardly been impressive; there is no remotely visible over-all strategy for siting or scale.

Option 10. Rural/agricultural setting could now be brought more easily into "urbanistic" living patterns by transportation and telecommunications. European agricultural life has long been town/village centered, contrary to the United States mode of isolated homesteads. Increasing humankind needs more and more food while a declining proportion of the population continue to opt for an agricultural life style. Of course, for some very considerable period there will be islands of "backward" rural culture preserved in Asia, Africa, Latin America and possibly portions of North America. Such areas could offer opportunity to increase food productions, a rewarding life style for the actual inhabitants and potential "museums for living" for the denizens of more urbanized habitats.

Type B: Far-Out Environments

These could be either physical or societal—or more likely some combination of both; they might serve as temporary experiences for the many or for the permanent life style of a few.

Option 11. Megastructures or "minicities" have fascinated man at least since the

Tower of Babel.[18] Characteristically, there is a Disneyland project, copyrighted in 1960, "The Community of Tomorrow" which will be a whole enclosed model town for twenty thousand persons on fifty acres *only,* to be part of the Florida Disney World. Paolo Soleri has had the greatest visibility recently as a highly successful youth guru with his concepts of giant supraterrestrial human hives housing up to hundreds of thousands of persons.[19] Soleri has fuzzy, complicated, intuitive, communalistic notions about group life joined to his often cantilevered bridgelike structures which ally him to far-out commune options as well.[20] It will be interesting to see the clients his constructions attract, once scale has been attained.

Apparently the term "mega"(giant)structure" was the invention of Fumihiko Maki of the Japanese Metabolist Group in 1964. *Habitat* by the Israeli architect Moshe Safdie, readied for Expo 1967 in Montreal, while financially an initial disaster, has become a much publicized example of this sort of "plug-in," "clip-on" structure.[21] For the record it is turning out to be both a financial and a societal success. Täby, satellite community outside Stockholm, houses five thousand people in one group of vast, curved structures, flanked by eight tower blocks containing another three thousand; while in Denmark "at Gladsaxe about 15 miles from Copenhagen, five 16-story slabs, each 300 feet long, extend in tandem." This latter construct seems to negate the usual warm humanism of Danish planning; the buildings are factory-made prefabs, site assembled: "These slabs are aligned with formal, rigid, relentless horizontality."[22]

Even megastructures (human hives) directly in town have been flirted with by responsible officials. In 1966, Governor Nelson Rockefeller of New York proposed a futuristic design for Battery Park City of massive towers for the lower tip of Manhattan: high connective bridges, dozens of apartments with a high pedestrian mall surrounded by other rabbit-warren dwellings on a large land fill, totaling ninety plus acres. After brisk and lengthy negotiations with the New York City fathers, the plan was realistically toned down into a less grandiose format[23] and is still being rethought.

In effect, though, vertically zoned buildings with garages below ground, retail trade at ground level rising to business offices, to schools and finally to varied dwellings topped by the inevitable penthouse (the higher you go the more it costs?) give promise of things to come. Many of these megastructures are theoretically capable of infinite expansion or contraction, an eternal Meccano set which might be one partial answer to an increasingly mobile society.

Option 12. The Water City. Scarcity of usable shore land and possibly usable shallow water (what happens to the ecological balance?) have led recently to large-scale "futuristic" designs for enormous activity nodes on made land or on stilts. Buckminster Fuller advocated this for Japan on the shallow waters of Tokyo Bay using his newly beloved tetrahedron shape as piles.[24] Given Oriental population densities and typical minimal family space, the water city/megastructure idea does not seem out of place now and may be a necessity in the future. Fuller carried his ideas further in the Triton Floating Community of thirty thousand persons with structures up to twenty stories; these ferroconcrete platforms could be built in shipyards and towed to usable places just off shore of existing coastal cities to be "anchored" in water up to twenty or thirty feet in depth.[25] This planning project was financed by the U. S. Department of

Housing and Urban Development; a trial construction nearly came to fruition in Baltimore Harbor. There is a present scheme to develop an artificial island off Tokyo; Kenzo Tangé had explored brilliantly the Tokyo Bay project earlier in his "Tokyo 1960" plan.[26] There have been, of course, precursor water cities: Swiss neolithic lake dwellings; Bangkok's *klongs* (canal life); Hong Kong's sampan colony at Victoria; Borneo and New Guinea stilt villages and even Fort Lauderdale. After all, most of the southern tip of Manhattan Island was once under water. Tangé's plan called for a reconstruction of the central city and for a huge expansion in megastructure form into Tokyo Bay—both linear in form—to take care of a 1980 estimated population of twenty million for the metropolitan area of the Japanese capital!

As a matter of fact, based on research conducted at the Athens Center of Ekistics on the "City of the Future Project," John G. Papaioannou concluded that "floating settlements on the oceans are expected to be considerably less costly than settlements on different land (mountains, swamps, deserts, frozen soil, etc.)."[27] Some seventy to one hundred years hence, if present trends continue, the earth may be one world city: Doxiadides' Ecumenopolis.

Option 13. Underwater, underground and space habitations on a scale large enough to be significant. Jacques Cousteau collaborated in the design of a floating island to be built off the coast of Monaco which would have undersea features. ". . . more comfortable dwelling quarters may be floating stably a hundred feet or so below the surface where any wave motion is so damped out as to be unnoticeable."[28]

The habitation-cum-fortress underground house is something new, although underground factories were well known in Nazi Germany and the United Kingdom during World War II as well as the ill-fated Maginot Line. The salubrious atmosphere of huge salt mine caverns could conceivably serve for community experimentation. *Sousterrain* dwellings could have temperature control and construction savings immediately applicable, especially in hot desert areas and possibly (?) in permafrost regions. Certainly in central city, burying certain structures and services below ground is already in progress with multistory underground parking garages in many cities (Paris, for example) and the increasing use of subsurface delivery roadways and shopping areas.

At least one group, *The Committee for the Future,* has as its avowed (and partially endowed) purpose the development of extraterrestrial space to ease the environmental burden and "the opening of the solar system for humanity beginning with the establishment of a lunar community available to people of all nations." Unlikely as some of this science fiction solutions may appear today at least they may offer recreational locations for future persons searching for new experience.[29]

Option 14. Communes and other societal innovations. Recent new societies in the United States with presumed behavioral innovations have been generally the efflorescence of the counterculture; they are usually consciously simplistic in technology and are the *nouvelle vague* in societal structuring. Chinese communist "communes" are obviously quite another thing! Even elementary contact with anthropology would suggest that middle-class, capitalist, nationalist, habitations/life styles with present Western economic, political, religious, familial, recreational institutions hardly exhaust the possibilities for human arrangements.

Nor does a minimal connection with the long story of Utopian schemes and real communities lead one to assume that it all began with *Walden Two*.[30]

Despite the often jejune aspects of such experimental communal Utopias and the relatively few persons involved in groups that approach a quasi-organized effort, the present impact is felt no matter how faintly—by a whole generation of American youth (and their foreign imitators) who see an appealing alternate life style to modern traditional Western civilization. In short, a counterpoint theme, no matter how unsubstantial, has been established; it is already "out there."

Physical communes are in a sense concrete expressions of Utopia, the no-place ideal world, to which the forefathers of most Americans emigrated from their assorted homelands. Once arrived, they and their descendants continued to pursue the dream across the wide and once beauteous continent until everything stopped in 1893 (the end of the frontier) on the shores of the Pacific. More extreme seekers for the perfect/ideal life probably founded more Utopian colonies in the New World than elsewhere (although Robert Owens was English and Charles Fourier was French). A catalogue of better known nineteenth-century ventures here would include the celibate New England Shakers (so-called because of their curious dancing/shuffling worship) who early preached "the careful craftsmen"; the Owenites at New Harmony in Indiana, a socialist/communist community; Brook Farm, a poetic phalanx with high-minded pretensions in almost anarchist interaction dedicated to "the honesty of a life of labor and the beauty of a life of humanity."[31] The Oneida community, believing in "Free Love and Bible Communism," started in 1847, still continues on in altered form as Oneida, Ltd.—successful silver manufacturers. The general theme running through such nineteenth-century experiments sounds familiar enough today in their search for "freedom," "love" and the escape from crude materialism to production "for use rather than profit." America's penchant for revivalist religious movements such as the Seventh-Day Adventists and the Mormons has produced somewhat similar far-out societal design. Patently, youth culture, unhappily extended well past sexual potency by the lumbering contemporary educational process (and the probable need to keep the masses of young off the job market in capitalist culture), has become enshrined in the whole counterculture movement of which the encyclopedic *Last Whole Earth Catalog* gives some clue of the myriad forms of this romantic reaction to industrialism and a search for a "new freedom."[32] The hippie communes both urban and rural (both benign and evil) possibly number some three thousand in the United States. If each group is comprised of a population of ten (a serious study for environmental purposes found in the Minneapolis metropolitan area that the twelve communes investigated there had a total of 116 members)[33] the total population of American communes would thus be 30,000 in a nation of 210,000,000, which hardly heralds the revolution! Even if there were 100,000 such communes, upset is not yet upon us.

Hippie core values as the extreme example of these minimum physical planning/maximum societal planning variants are an interesting summary of the counterculture: freedom, sensual expressiveness (anti-intellectual), immediacy, natural, colorful/baroque, spontaneous, primitive, mystical, égalitarian, communal.[34]

This largely societal option has been introduced here since it is clearly "innovative" and "revolutionary" (often in puerile ways) in its implications for standard society and in its messages to developing lands. It could be, moreover, only the tip of the iceberg of dissatisfaction with the mass culture of Western society. Minimal space seems to be the *only* physical planning expense involved; the commune people make their own societal plans. Such exotics must not be squelched—even if someone else has "to tend store." The affluent West affords millions of the idle rich, nonproducing youngsters and oldsters and millions of unemployed; it most certainly can afford a few tens of thousands experimenters seeking a better life on earth.[35] They might even have something!

Option 15. "The Wired City." With the phenomenal growth of cable television (capable of two-way transmission) added to the almost infinite potentialities of multichannel electronic interaction through "people's satellites,"[36] a nonterritorial, high-intensity participatory community fitted to the "postcivilized" or "information society," could await us.[37] Despite piecemeal research, considerable argument, a few limited experiments,[38] and a galloping electronic technology, it seems unlikely that the multiplicity of ordinary (and creative new) functions, potentially possible, will be much in operation in even the most sophisticated nations before the commencement of the twenty-first century. The bits of the picture puzzle are slowly being fitted together but they still do not form a whole. It appears that the basic scenario will be a national[39] cable/micro wave grid of metropolitan networks reinforced or supplanted with satellite connections and eventually lasers; computers serving both as storage facilities and as analysts with display capabilities will be at the center of this intellectual technology.[40] In the United Kingdom consideration is already being given to setting up a national computer grid. In the wired city every dwelling will have its typewriter-like keyboard with print-out capabilities and display screen in the home information/recreation/business center (additional home terminals are naturally possible). This equipment will not be cheap and some trained intelligence will be needed to operate such sophisticated gadgetry and thus bring up future questions of equity, égalitarianism and the massive financing and maintenance of such "public services."

Here are some of the bits yet to be assembled in a potential nonterritorial electronic society, partially substituting the transmission of ideas for the transportation of people and goods, and freed to a certain extent—from spatial considerations.[41] As transportation expert Wilfred Owen has pointed out:

> The significance of communications as a substitute for transport derives from the fact that while the unit costs of transportation continue to rise as quality declines, telecommunications tend to increase in quality and decline in cost. Distance is important in transportation, but with communication satellites distance is almost irrelevant.[42]

Here is what "the wired city" could provide:

Information storage available by computer/TV

national data bank on the total society (with all the safeguards to privacy);
national library;
national theatre/cinema library;
national health records and diagnostic information;
scientific information service;

crime information;
credit information.

Home service facilities

all banking and transactions ("the end of money");
shopping (plus delivery);
recreation (passive and active—"anyone for chess?");
crime prevention;
education in the home for children *and* adults;
automatized cooking;
visiting via video-phone;
print-out news (the New York *Times* nationwide);
"mail" delivery electronically.

Advanced societal innovations

public opinion surveys;
sampling to replace voting;
"participatory democracy"[43];
TV surveillance of public (and private!) places;
new industrial/business locations;
new employment patterns (four-day, three-day, even two-day work week in a *work place* away from the dwelling);
"home visits" by the doctor and specialists;
increased physical and societal design capabilities[44];
new and powerful techniques for mass behavior (control and surveillance);
national data systems.

The United States Department of Housing and Urban Development has commissioned a study of the impact of advanced telecommunications technology (TCT) on American cities during the next twelve years,[45] which concludes that:

(1) The advent of telecommunications technology, while highly beneficial to some segments of society, will prove detrimental to others.
(2) The positive impacts of TCT will be felt primarily in the middle-class suburbs, while the negative impacts will be concentrated in the central cities.
(3) TCT will not play a highly visible role in the major urban developments of the next twelve years. Unless specifically anticipated by federal and local planning, impacts will not be properly understood and regulated until considerable damage has been done.
(4) The primary urban impact of TCT will be to reduce the economic viability of the central city by accelerating (though not directly causing) the delocalization of business and commerce.
(5) The social impacts of TCT are to be found at least as much in the indirect effects of TCT on the fiscal strength of cities, as in the direct effects of new gadgets on the life styles of individuals.
(6) The sector most affected by TCT is the service sector, in which processes involving paper transactions are particularly sensitive to technological substitution.

(7) It is unlikely that the central city population will derive much benefit in the next twelve years from such "luxury" applications of TCT as shopping or working at home.
(8) The most important *positive* impacts of TCT in central cities will be in the areas of technical education (especially in programs designed to develop job skills among inner-city residents), and routine city services (especially in transit systems, police and fire protection, etc.), and remote medical or diagnostic services.

All is clearly not sweetness and light in this future city. If evil "philosopher kings" should occupy central positions in the national/international network? If "euphoria" characterized the initial "oh, wow" reaction to the two-way television, coaxial cable, computer, peoples satellite syndrome, one already sees signs of *alarm* prior hopefully to advanced *protective action* (including active *ombudsman* functions) before the need arises.[46] Finally for the loyal fans of central city as the place where the action is, the wired city is already posing quite a problem as "people stay away in droves" from downtown especially for evening recreation with simple-minded, one-way TV as one reason.

ELEMENTS OF A NATIONAL URBAN POLICY (NUP)

There is little question that a city is much too small a functioning entity to be managed/guided as a *closed* system with any remote idea of great success. External variables—decisions on a higher governmental level or international happenings of both an economic and political nature—can quite obviously upset the plans of micelike men at the city level. While it would be false to state that as Chevy Chase goes (restrictive zoning) so goes Washington or that a Yokohama happening (oil refinery) could upset Tokyo, there is an element of truth in the somewhat greater adequacy of scale for a metropolitan system regarded as a more independent whole. But then the metropolis forms only a part of megalopolis (which could be international as is the Ruhr). From a national planning position, the next smaller valid functional entity to the nation is the region which can serve as a realistic parameter for meaningful societal management. Clearly certain regions are greater than certain megalopolises (or great "conurbations" to use a deservedly ugly British term) and some are evidently smaller. The difficulty of defining a region is very real for planning purposes; there are now ten designated federal regions in the United States which presumably have validity for decentralized national government functions. These regions could conceivably serve as a second tier above metropolitan areas in a revised American governmental structure based on functionality. This leads us to the inevitable level of national policy and planning, the most solid need of this period in world history. Recapitulating, a more productive macrostructure for guiding urbanized society would consist of a first-tier government at the metropolitan level, a second at the regional and a third at the national. Of course, minigovernment at the local level could exist below the metropolitan government. There is mounting evidence on a global scale that just such a scaling of national governmental planning efforts may be gradually emerging.

However, as the European Economic Community (EEC) and the international business corporation assuredly indicate—not to mention the Union of Soviet Socialist Republics and the other subordinate nations of the "socialist world"—the reality of a macroterritory of the correct spatial dimensions for systems management is supranational, although not yet possible except in bits and pieces. Simple examples of protoplanning on an international, territorial, functional or sectoral scale are, of course, the World Health Organization (WHO), the Food and Agriculture Organization (FAO) and the United Nations Education and Scientific Community (UNESCO).

Be that as it may, for the present, the drive toward a national urban policy, plan and strategy as an integral portion of a national development plan conceived of both functionally and territorially, is the apogee of reasonable expectations. It is the only strategy for urban planning that might deliver today in an adequate fashion! National holistic planning (total environmental planning) is becoming the watchword in the last decades of the twentieth century for (a) the capitalist world, (b) the socialist world and (c) the developing world. Aspects of such planning are hardly new. With the inauguration of the first Soviet Five-Year Plan in October 1928, strong functional policy and planning under GOSPLAN (the State Planning Commission) became integral to the USSR. Even Nazi Germany prated about four-year plans (preceded by a useful rationalization policy during the Weimar Republic). While these were essentially military economic, functional or sector plans, there were of necessity territorial overtones of industrial locational decisions, as well as over-all societal dimensions in both Soviet and Nazi manipulations. The new India, formed following the 1947 partition, adopted a series of six-year plans (with no spectacular success) and the Chinese People's Republic has had a number of holistic development plans (with notable zigs and zags). Even England has elements of a national plan, with a growing regional planning capability[47] going back to a series of White Papers on the population/urbanization dimension at a national scale in the late 1930s[48] and such societal planning as the National Health System, various national education and social welfare programs—coupled with housing policy and a new towns policy (1946). Finally under the Tories in 1965, a national economic policy plan was haltingly cobbled together to go further than the feeble compensatory legislation, dating from the 1930s. This pre-World War II policy was a palliative to serve as a corrective of the gross territorial maldistribution of economic opportunities in the depressed areas.[49] "Neddy," as the national economic development policy/plan came to be nicknamed, is still not an integral part of any holistic English national plan combining territory, economics and social developments.

Symptomatic of world concern in the urbanization component of holistic national development planning are two important books taking a comparative stance that have emerged in this field in recent years—specifically, Lloyd Rodwin's *Nations and Cities, a Comparison of Strategies for Urban Growth*[50] and Ann Louise Strong's *Planned Urban Environments.*[51] One can also include a series of essays *Toward a National Urban Policy,* edited by Daniel P. Moynihan, just as he became President Nixon's urban specialist.[52] As the keynote speaker for the American Institute of Planners annual conference in 1968, I ventured a protoplan to commence the long process of building educational resources to develop the type of planners who could cope with national holistic planning.[53]

A preliminary grasp of European national development strategies to date could be helpful in appraising the NUP scheme that follows. A summary presented to the Subcommittee on Housing and Urban Affairs, Committee on Banking and Currency, U. S. House of Representatives in November 1972, cogently lists six fundamentals which appear to serve as the basis for a *national policy*[54]:

(a) *economic growth* is not questioned as the basic means to achieve social objectives;
(b) *balanced welfare,* "a more balanced distribution of income and social well-being among the various regions of the country";
(c) *centralization/decentralization,* local and national government structures to plan an implementation with particular care "to be accountable to local officials and the affected constituency";
(d) *environmental protection,* "channel future growth away from areas suffering from environmental overload" or to those worthy of special care and attention;
(e) *metropolitan development,* "promoting more satisfactory patterns of new area-wide governmental bodies";
(f) *nonmetropolitan development,* generally developing "growth centers" to enliven stultifying or as yet unusual natural regions.

"Total environmental planning" is the terminology used by the ecological movement with heavy emphasis on the *physical environment;* from a modern planning point of view, *holistic planning,* the term employed here, is more meaningful since it includes both the physical/environmental planning dimensions with a considerably heavier emphasis on societal planning both in structure and function. It would be difficult to conceive of any physical environmental aspect of our globe as untouched or unaltered by society; man has even managed to leave rubbish dumps on the moon and garbage in space. What then are the dimensions of holistic *national planning* preceded by an over-all policy—oriented toward a national system of feasible scale which could—given adequate data, wisdom, skill and resources—guide an urban world. It consists of five major components:

1. *Population policy;*
2. *Environmental/ecological management;*
3. *Land use and physical planning;*
4. *Multifunctional societal planning*
   (a) social, (b) governmental, (c) economic, (d) recreational and aesthetic;
5. *Time: cybernetic "rolling planning."*

It should be obvious that each of these five components is symbiotic and interpenetrated—that they are interdependent and interlocked. Global planning on this multifunctional macroscale is *not yet* remotely possible in the 1970s.[55] Thus the only system that practically might be planned and guided as a whole of sufficient scale in the proximate future is the national system.

What, then, is known, what might be known shortly, and what precisely can be done by *nations* to guide urbanization/urbanism under such a scheme?[56]

1. *Population Policy.* Death control through medical science is accepted worldwide and is highly successful; a balancing practice of birth control lags—in both its technological and especially its societal parameters. The reasons are very complex varying from *machismo* ("supermaleness") through religious taboo to simple ignorance. Urban planners have been known to snap that all they can do is "attempt to cope with too damn many people." Practically all of our contemporary

problems would be greatly mitigated if there were fewer humans crowding into densely impacted areas all over the earth. The destruction of amenities in advanced nations by too many people is linked closely to ecological/environmental problems and defeats traditional physical planning by outrunning urban infrastructure. Too many people lead to inadequate job opportunities in the central industrial city and to famine and death in developing areas.

Between 1960 and 1970, the U. S. Standard Metropolitan Statistical Areas (SMSA) grew by 15.1 per cent while the rest of America by only 5.1 per cent; but the true dynamics of the situation is reflected by the 25.6 per cent growth of the suburbs (a number of large central cities lost population, including Philadelphia and Detroit). This means that America is now over 73 per cent urban with 68 per cent in the SMSA compared to 66 per cent in 1960. For the picture of a truly urbanized nation, Great Britain is now the fourth most densely populated country in the world, exceeded only by Japan, Belgium and The Netherlands. It is nine times more crowded than the United States. By 1900, about 80 per cent of the people there were living in the larger towns, and aggregations of urban centers became the dominant type of British community. Today, about half of the country's population of almost sixty million live in seven urban centers (London, Manchester, Birmingham, Glasgow, Leeds, Liverpool and Newcastle).[57]

For developing nations excess population, as reflected in the phenomenon of overurbanization, is a disaster and flatly defeats the revolution of rising expectations and which can lead, as noted above, to global chaos. India is the leading exhibit. Thus Zero Population Growth (ZPG) has become more than a mere crackpot slogan. Both Meadows' *Limits to Growth*[58] and the widely used text *Population Resources and Environment*[59] have dramatized the world impact of too many people using too many things. Thus the first population question, the immediate question of course, is *quantity*. The second question is *geographic location/density*—how many, where.

The population problems that await just around the corner are of geometrically increased complexity. If competent molecular biologists and biochemists are to be believed, the cracking of the DNA double helix puzzle will shortly enable scientists by "gene surgery" to design human beings, first by sex and later by unit characteristics. Shortly man can be created in the form (physical and mental) desired. What precisely will be desired and who are to make such decisions about quality? As noted, presently it is even impossible to make simple quantity and locational decisions. By cell cloning (endless reproduction of identical beings),[60] individuals of "merit" can be infinitely repeated as is already possible with frogs and toads. Since only the slightest wisdom has been evident in the management of physical science to date as nuclear technology indicates, it would be foolhardy to expect much wisdom in the biological sciences' genetic manipulation. Not only are there practical problems of man's limitless self-modification but patently legal, moral and religious problems—what precisely will happen to the conception and practice of "parenthood" as a ready example of one potential startling complex of effects from artificial insemination and cloning.[61]

Before leaving the population keystone for national urbanization planning, two things must be recognized: that at another level behavior is increasingly being controlled by chemotherapy (both by professional and rank amateurs) and that a number of behavioral scientists believe that man can be designed by his social environment beyond and more quickly than through biological (gene) manipulation.[62]

Much of what has been mentioned briefly here is ahead of us—but not too far ahead to put off exploring what to do when the foreseeable results do arrive. Immediately national (and world) action must be taken in coping with population *quantity* and *geographic location.* Unless wise plans and effective action are taken at once all other human betterment schemes will be flatly negated. Not enough is known about even these initial steps of population planning in crude quantities and geographic location to date; government population policies are still primitive.[63] The lead time on mere quantity planning is at least thirty years before meaningful results can be recorded; at present there are few national successes other than in Sweden and Japan to record.

2. *Environmental/Ecological Management.* The latest battlecry of the instant reformers is ecology; the spoiled physical environment of our planet seems to have diverted attention for the nonce from the atrocious societal environment of our "civilized" (urban) life. As the Japanese New Comprehensive National Development Plan of May 1969 nicely phrases it, "A Human society is a part of the intricate subtly balanced natural order."[64] Be that as it may, the Stockholm world jamboree of June 1972 on the environment alerted all to global pollution, first signaled popularly by Rachel L. Carson's moving *The Silent Spring* of 1962.[65] Other environmentalists—both romantic and realistic from William Vogt[66] through Marion Clawson,[67] William H. Whyte,[68] Ian McHarg,[69] and Barry Commoner[70] have pleaded for attention to our wasting resources and the wanton despoiling of the globe's irreplaceable arable surface, subsurface and atmosphere along with the once fabulous richness of the flora and fauna of the land, sea and air. From "do-gooders" to strategic military planners (stockpilers of minerals, raw materials, etc. in short supply) all farsighted persons are now concerned.

Rooted in the conservation movement sired by President Teddy Roosevelt (1900) and Governor Gifford Pinchot of Pennsylvania (1910), which resulted in our (now far overpopulated) national park system, and in concern for the vanishing amenities and hard resources of the planet, public interest has exploded in recent years to stop the SST in the United States and make every manufacturer keep looking over his shoulder at the rapidly overtaking new values.[71] The 1972–73 and worse 1973–74 winter oil shortages in the United States, compounded by equal combinations of lacking resources and governmental muddle (not to mention Middle Eastern/North African predictable perversity), is merely a promise of things to come. Even the Atlantic Ocean in American waters atop the Continental Shelf has 665,000 square miles, found by Federal research teams, blighted by pollutants—littered by floating oil, tar and chunks of eternal plastic.[72]

In the broad sweep of holistic planning, one wonders how to get a "handle" on national planning—just where to start. For the countries with advanced industrialism it is very possible that the ecology/environmental concern may be just such a usable practicable handle capable of getting immediate action. The parameters of this situation are reasonably obvious: (a) broad public awareness of and annoyance with pollution—the political milieu thus is favorable; (b) measurable pollution levels, the possibility of setting precise quality standards despite expected hassles about trade-offs[73] (trouble with poverty needs, power shortages, wild life levels, "nature," etc.); (c) technological knowledge of how to manage pollution reasonably well; GNP growth would not be impossible despite higher costs for manufactured goods. Thus advanced countries seem almost ready to act effectively on water, air, natural resources, noise pollution and open land (which is disappearing in the United States at about one million acres a year to urbanization, although there are still over two billion acres left!). This is not so for developing countries, who tend to regard attempts to hold down their crude increases in industrial production ("needed" to realign their aspirations with expectations) as racist, capitalist, Western devices to hold them in thraldom. As is correct, they contend that the heavily industrialized West is the cause of present industrial pollution and destruction, not they. It is estimated that the United States gobbles up most of the world's raw materials; this percentage is likely to increase. The Japanese in their brilliant economic growth of the post-World War II era have polluted unbelievably their own environment (and damaged both their traditional high culture and their deep sense of community). They are already exporting their noxious industries to hungry, less developed lands and cleaning up at home. The military government of Brazil in the summer of 1972 loudly welcomed a Japanese filthy wood pulp operation, stating that interior Brazil still could take much pollution as a trade-off for economic growth, but by early 1973 they (the Brazilians) too reversed this position by enacting pollution curbs.

There are some very knotty value problems here not unconnected with what men want the postindustrial world to be like. The central operant question is "Can world expectations be met without cutting back the level of living of the advanced countries," which for the moment is patently impossible politically. This is not the least thorny issue delaying the widely perceived necessity to keep planet earth from turning into one large hungry cesspool filled with human and industrial waste. It is heartening to know that the United States has made at least a highly visible start with the Environmental Protection Agency (1969) by forcing the government and certain industries (atomic power reactors) to file environmental impact statements.[74] However, these have caused rather a storm and no over-all significant results as yet in protecting the threatened environment. Some sort of resource-conserving urbanism needs to be advanced very soon as a viable form for the promised world city or the world as a city! This is especially true now with the energy/food crisis already here.

3. *Land Use and Physical Planning.* Traditional "city planning" has been physical planning—the allocation of space and the design of areas for the work function in its varied forms, for dwellings, for recreation and green space, and for transportation arteries to connect such activity nodes.[75] Aided by useful and sometimes imperfect instruments such as zoning and subdivision regulations, building codes, the police power, general welfare concepts, general or comprehensive plans and urban renewal funds, the planning practitioners strove overtime for varied implicit societal goals (Beaux Arts beauty, economic or engineering "efficiency," amenity, possibly "fair shares for all") through physical constructs which would presumably influence individual and group behavior. That they attained no great success is understandable; it is surprising and praiseworthy that they did so much to keep the huge cities of the world from degenerating into complete chaos. It is easy with hindsight to ridicule the often naive assumptions about somehow bridging very inadequate social and behavioral science knowledge to the design of physical forms, aimed at attaining unclear social values. The training

of architect/planners (as they were and are named in Europe) simply was aesthetically and engineering efficiency/functionally oriented and in no way prepared them to understand society except by simplistic intuition; also, there was no reliable social/behavioral science knowledge even if the planners were intellectually sufficiently schooled to use it. The behavioral/social scientists, when first approached in the United States tentatively by urban planners in search of badly needed information following World War II, had little dependable knowledge of value to give. What they did know was hardly operationally relevant. They had only touched the surface in researching the problems meaningful to a planning framework; moreover there could be little communication because neither side, speaking different professional languages, truly understood the other. Further, it should be stressed that even today a careful empirical evaluation of the effects of physical forms on behavior has simply not been carried out in any remotely systematic fashion and whatever valid conclusions that have been obtained are simply not readily available in the tidy form that architects/planners are accustomed to use easily. Only very gradually is this bridging or linkage between the analyst researchers of society and the city planners being made.

But the groundwork has been laid and behavioral and social scientists are now commencing to provide more usable supports. Robert Sommer[76] has started a current respectable psychological bridging operation between microspace and behavior. William H. Michelson, sociologist, has listed twenty-four useful, if still imprecise, linkages between the physical/societal environment and social behavior on various spatial levels from micro to macro.[77] National/regional planning has little clear connection with behavioral science but does connect with regional science, economics and geography in the social sciences. Lowdon Wingo, director of Regional Studies for Resources for the Future, Inc., has indicated six conceptual issues, about which much more needs to be known in order to formulate operant national growth policies of merit[78]:

1) the general analytics of optimum city size;
2) private costs and benefits as a function of city size and economic composition;
3) negative and positive externalities as a function of city size and economic composition (and vice versa);
4) the distribution of city sizes in a national system as a function of the national economy, technology, incomes, consumer preferences and transport costs;
5) the current and capital costs of producing and distributing overhead services as a function of city size;
6) the welfare characteristics of internal migration.

While heavily economically oriented (patently a necessity) and weak on both social and political overtones, this is a good list and is indicative of the sort of things behavioral/social scientists must illumine for real world planners.

Stumped at the lack of spectacular success with simple spatial or land-use solutions, the planning professionals and their ever-questioning incubators (the planning graduate schools) switched to methodological consideration, aided and abetted by the glorious new computer technology to augment and clarify values, concepts and delivery systems. It would seem that this merely mechanized/quantified fog in its initial stages; but gradually, the sophisticated, analytical math models, gaming, information systems, system analysis, operations research, system dynamics have been introduced to handle the complex data and develop alternate planning solutions.[79]

Finally, on top of all the other approaches, the poor "planning technicians" (Swedish nomenclature) were dragged into "social policy" planning; if the city was truly to be managed/guided, why not plan institutional, not physical, structures to affect behavior and quality of life directly? Where then do we stand today on the question of land-use (spatial planning) and physical-design planning?

First, there can be no doubt that just as architects/engineers will continue to be essential in the construction of buildings and railroads so will physical planners be necessary to plan, construct and reconstruct cities, towns and nations! Physical planners now come in varied packages, for example: generalists; landscape architects doing site planning; transportation experts doing expressways and public mass transportation routing; regional science people designing larger areal schemes; but all appear to share a common skill of immense value. From long experience with varied urban functions and based on the ancient and somewhat weak concept of zoning as an operational tool, they have a most important available "handle" at command for national development planning. This is namely *land use* or the siting of activity nodes or activity centers on a micro- meso- and macroscale.[80]

Second, this skill can be reinforced—and this is widely understood in Europe—by the geographer and the economic geographer, who have conceptualized space in relation to purposeful activity.[81] Reinforced by ecological comparative studies of the city developed by sociologists (originating in the University of Chicago some fifty years ago), there is potentially an immediately applicable instrument to guide national developmental policies from the intricacies of neighborhood spatial design to a regionalism maximizing economic growth, environmental supportability and amenity in all its various ways.[82]

Perhaps an injustice is being done here to physical city planning, with all the skills of an art long in existence by its reductionism to land-use planning. But it is obvious today that locational expertise on a metropolitan scale appears to be the focal point of this profession. And it is in an increasingly sophisticated analytical and operational competence in this direction that the continuing key function of the city planner may rest. As he lifts the territorial scale of his skills up to the regional science approach and further on up to a national and international scale, he will be dependent on more and more reliable aid from the behavioral and social sciences (which are aided and abetted by the mathematical storage, retrieval and manipulation of data).[83] A further linkage of spatial design capabilities with the ecological/environmental model that is developing may turn out to be a much enriched core skill for an expanded physical planning on a national scale.

4. *Multifunctional Societal Planning.* There is little doubt that the center of gravity for modern urban planning has swung heavily away from the manipulation of the physical environment—with hopes for societal improvement—to the direct manipulation of societal structures themselves.

The watchword of contemporary architecture (at least until very recently) has been "form follows function." Whether this precept has actually been followed by an aesthetically oriented profession is quite another question. Social science, especially under the Jesuit-like ratiocinations of sociological thought, has been gripped by the Parsonian "structure/function concept" which is the social obverse of form follows function. Human social insititutions are thus shaped by time and design to perform certain functions deemed important and thus they must fit or eventually be cast aside. Unfortunately, only recently has sociological structure/function been shaken up to cope more adequately with the reality of eternal accelerating sociocultural change and the belated recognition that social sciences are hardly value free. One person's perceived function can be another person's perceived dysfunction.

Unarmed by any strikingly operant hard knowledge, anthropologists, sociologists, political scientists, economists, social psychologists and assorted hangers-on have leaped into the breach that is so evident in the nonresults, skewed results, or counterresults of physical planning. To technical-planning technology is being added behavioral/organizational technology. This new breed of behavioral/societal analysts turned prescribers/practitioners has hardly been more successful to date, but this in no way lessens the need for a rapid search for knowledge and some free wheeling (very expensive and humanly upsetting) world-wide experimentation in societal planning. The four major dimensions of societal planning sketched below indicate that only just now is the linkage of physical with societal planning taking place in the practice of urban planning, although the theorists in the discipline of planning have been on the theme for at least a decade.[84] We have already noted the work of Moynihan and Banfield,[85] which at least convinces them that we are probably more ignorant in societal planning than we have shown ourselves to be within the physical parameters—if anything, well-intentioned efforts have been even more counterproductive. Such reasoning is behind the "bomb shell" Nixonian budget sprung on the aghast welfare/social planning scene in January 1973 when he calmly axed some one hundred programs of the Departments of Housing and Urban Development and of Health, Education and Welfare for "throwing money at people," in his phraseology with precious little valid results.

At a meeting of thirty-four "experts" at Boulder, Colorado, for a forced draft, ten-day "think tank" in the summer of 1972, Harvey Perloff, student of future forms for our governments,[86] came up with a hard list of almost one hundred high priority research topics where valid, precise, societal knowledge is needed now or even sooner for planning purposes. At the Boulder meeting, two categories of priority were invented: "urgent urgent" and "merely urgent."

Having castigated societal planning as feeble, one must face the realistic and crushing fact that responsible governments, ignorant or not, face problems in social welfare, education, organization, economic well-being, health, leisure that must be solved *now* whether enough is known or not. It is frightening to deal with the rush of events remembering that the massive economic/social/political/physical urban renewal program in the United States over a twenty-year period at the cost of billions of public funds multiplied by private sector investments probably exacerbated central city problems. But mayors must act and nations must act and act they will, prepared adequately or not. However, there is a flood of bright ideas about in "good currency" today for the four major rubrics of societal planning. Societal is a more useful general term for our purposes than social (which tends to have negative welfare connotations only) and is employed here to include (a) social, (b) governmental, (c) economic and (d) recreational and "the higher culture" planning—clearly all interconnected but treated here separately merely for analytical convenience.

Social Planning

Traditionally, social planning has consisted primarily of the delivery of social welfare[87] generally after the event and hopefully as a curative. It has a hoary history of good intentions and unspectacular results. Social welfare planning was developed out of social work with sights raised from a primitive past when the poor were regarded as "sinners." Modern social policy planning and delivery are aimed (a) at curative action patently, (b) but more importantly at the erection of *preventive* societal structures and most importantly, although hardly under way at all, of (c) *raising the quality of life* (raising theoretical value problems immediately) or positive social planning. There are three layers for social planning structuring and delivery: the individual, the family and the community.

The first concern is the support and extension of the life chances and experiences of *the individual human being* which can be considered as the basic goal of any humanist-oriented planning. This means quite simply warm and complete medical service, full educational and occupational opportunities (especially for the disadvantaged in the United States).[88] European nations are not so égalitarian and certainly not "socialist" societies; they foster excellence. Is humanitarianism in the face of severely restricted resources enough?

> Since the days of Thomas Jefferson, we have believed that education is a means of achieving equality in our society. But in the last few years, social science has brought that assumption into question.[89]

Exhaustive hard data surveys tend to indicate that family is more important than school in motivation and accomplishment. Thus it is important to provide a secure/sturdy home environment in which one can develop and with which one can identify.[90] The "home" does not have to be a conjugal family nest as Bruno Bettelheim has shown with the Israeli Sabras, products of *kibbutz* living, who are seemingly so very competent.[91] The results incidentally of Chinese communist communal care of children are not nearly so clear, although scattered reports now suggest excellent "adjustment" to that society. Children require more nurture patently, but the three basics of *health care, self-development* and *economic well-being in a decent dwelling* apply to adults for the remaining four fifths of their lives! Finally, old age care, once earning capabilities have diminished and now that people live longer, is a special problem.

The second concern of a social policy program is *the family* (be it conjugal, extended or communal) in industrial society where there is a heavy psychological burden on this institution irrespective of over-all societal social supports. Clearly, good housing does not make good people but good people grow and live "better" it would seem within the supporting framework of adequate family space. Marvelous human beings emerge from the foulest dwellings; of this there is no question. Horatio Alger types from varied cultures do grow up in Harlem, *bustees, bidonvilles, favellas* or *barriadas,* but life starts are better and life is undoubtedly more rewarding in decent dwellings. As Charles Abrams has so well shown, based on a vast world-wide experience, *Man's Struggle for Shelter*[92] is humankind's most absorbing preoccupation beyond food. The gap between dwelling cost and income appears to be increasing. Housing costs especially in the United States are going through the roof with labor costs (wages, featherbedding), mortgage rates, escalating land values, and inefficient small-scale contractors—all of which lead to up to 35 per cent of the family income of the poor going into dwelling costs. Due to large governmental intrusion into housing production in European nations, the problem is not so overwhelming. Not so in the United States. President Johnson, as he left office, inaugurated a ten-year program in the 1968 Housing and Urban Development Act to construct twenty-six million new and rehabilitated dwellings including six million federally assisted units. Quite simply the federally assisted units were never funded and in 1973 President Nixon declared a moratorium on federally assisted housing in the United States. The provision of an adequate housing supply is an almost insurmountable task in backward nations. It is claimed that at least one half the population of New York City cannot afford decent housing without various levels of subsidy. Western Europe has, in general, done better than the rest of the world in providing adequate family living spaces—despite the two major wars of the twentieth century which destroyed so much of their housing stock. A more civilized ethic of responsibility, generally socialist-oriented municipal activities, industrialized building systems, farsighted land acquisition policies and complex subsidy systems, tending to subsidize the dweller rather than the dwelling, account for this relative success. Thus the societal planning of income maintenance programs and delivery systems as part of public welfare programming connected with education and public health are the key themes. European programs tend to separate production subsidy from family assistance.[93]

Socialist bloc countries, regarding housing as a consumer industry, with their relatively scarce capital resources that are better devoted to heavy industry (or armaments in some cases) lag in physical housing provision whatever income maintenance schemes (better full scale employment opportunities) there are. Experimentally in the United States there is a movement toward a guaranteed income or negative income tax (using the Internal Revenue Service as "welfare master") which has to date made small progress. Daniel P. Moynihan[94] as President Nixon's chief adviser on urban affairs had this as a primary task at which he "failed" for various complex reasons, despite the initial Nixon backing of a $1,600 minimum family income against the U.S. mean of approximately $10,500! The culture of poverty—basically family incompetence—perpetuates itself unquestionably from generation to generation due not to genes, but to impossible slum social environment—reinforced by inadequate physical environment.

On the other hand, while to middle-class eyes many sections of central city appear hopeless, this is quite simply not so as studies on both sides of the Atlantic clearly indicate; scruffy working-class districts (quasi-slums) harbor genuine reinforcing human community values.[95] The territorial component is strong for lower class life styles, which differ from the nonterritorial community of "cosmopolites" or professionals.[96]

The numerous assistance programs of urban services to poor families through neighborhood service centers[97] in housing blocks to "little city halls," ranging from prenatal care to legal assistance for life crises, are symptomatic of the enormous adult education job ahead for families who are societally inadequate. And these various types of family assistance have failed to prove themselves—at least in the eyes of those reorganizing welfare for President Nixon in 1973. Human benefits are estimated not to be commensurate with governmental costs; as yet the record is not clear on this.

We have all too briefly canvassed remedial social planning for individuals and families (lapping slightly into the community development level). What of efforts to develop positive individual capacities, aspirations and expectations with possibilities for fulfillment? This narrows down to providing both societal structures and physical forms for participation in the enormous cornucopia of civilization's psychic/intellectual/sensual fare. This assumes that there is sufficient native intelligence and that there are some shared values/goals variously interpreted which apparently tend to determine individual aspiration. Thus a self-civilizing motivation for all is one of the crucial problems for the postindustrial or information society already partially with us.

Community planning is the larger institutional shell for the nurture of individual and family life patterns. With both high vertical mobility (up and down the social scale) and horizontal mobility (back and forth across the country) it is difficult to conceive of strong community life developing in the United States. And Europe tends to regard this country as "the shape of things to come." Approximately 20 per cent of American families move each year. As Burnham Kelly has said, "Americans live in housing of limited liability [heavily mortgaged] as part of communities of marginal commitment." Thus while the bourgeois conjugal family feels capable in certain modern Western lands of an almost self-sufficient privatization; the age-old behavior of man (a social animal) suggests how needed is the physical and societal perception of reinforcing togetherness with other like (?) human beings. While *community* (shared perspectives), the perceived sense of in-group feeling, is patently lacking between the angry Protestant and Catholic denizens of Ulster, Northern Ireland, today, and between the American black and his white cocitizen, *generally speaking* Western peoples *within* nations have tended recently to get along with each other. This is simply not so in tribal and semitribal portions of Africa and Asia or in certain nonnations of Latin America. The naive conception of the American melting pot, which was conceived formerly as a rewarding process melding miscellaneous Europeans (not so Asiatics or blacks) into an homogenized Anglo-American style of society, has for the moment been laid aside here as ethnics and various "racial" subgroups search for group identity. This, of course, is not a bad augury for a potential multigroup society of multisubcultures (not necessarily along ethnic, racial, class lines) producing alternate urban futures of an interesting, rewarding variety. And this is in contradistinction to the gloomy prognostication of one dead level of mass culture/mass society made by radical American sociologists of the 1950s.[98] "Pop sociology" has phrased the current ambience as "a nation of strangers"[99] depicting the quasi-breakdown of community and the loss of a sense of national cohesiveness, foreseen over a decade ago by Maurice Stein in his review of American community studies.[100]

Scott Greer also glimpsed this in his emphasis on the "increase of societal scale" which has had the effect of releasing so many from closely held territorial/societal roots. In a striking study, which first appeared in 1953, Robert Nisbet has characterized "the quest for community—in whatever form, moral, social, political—so widespread in the world today and combined with an apparatus of political power, as the single most impressive (fateful) fact of the contemporary scene."[101]

Early concepts of the neighborhood community growing out of the work of Clarence A. Perry in *The Regional Survey of New York and Its Environs* of 1929 tended naively to see a physical neighborhood consisting of homes, park areas and basic service facilities grouped around a primary school as solving all our ills of anomie, frustration and alienation.[102] Accepted uncritically and woodenly, for example, in early 1950 Chicago planning, it led to naught except lines drawn in quadrangles on a map. Handled with more sophistication in Vällingby and Farsta, the Stockholm semisatellite towns, it turned out in practice that motorized Swedes did not interact in such spatially tight patterns. Plainly, physical neighborhoods were not communities; although with a slight modicum of social planning underpinning, a rich community life has developed in British New Towns that literally swarm with club/societies/organizations/activities—some two hundred and fifty in Harlow for example! Can the quest for community be structured by (a) the provision of adequate societal (and physical) structures provided by both the public and private sectors and more importantly by (b) the provision of social development officers? These specialists, a new breed, initially start up activities of promise from pottery making through nature studies to Bach chorale groups and a local "rep" theatre. It would appear self-realization through participation is only feasible by community-level societal/physical planning. The job is undeniably complex if everyone's horizon from the very top to the very bottom is to be reached. From active participation in the Metropolitan Museum of Art's varied programs to simplistic street theatre, the New York Department of Recreation and Culture is tending in just such a direction as did Parks of Culture and Rest attempted so long ago in the 1920 Union of Soviet Socialist Republics. Only now is society learning to touch on the wide, wide spectrum of repair and enhancement which makes up social planning.

There is an increasing literature on community development which boils down to a participatory planning effort by trained development officers egging people on to interact co-operatively for perceived goals.[103] It is a lengthy process needing outside organizational funds, physical infrastructure and the ability of such development officers to fade out of the picture. Training in group operational self-reliance —especially for the disadvantaged—remains an experimental operation as yet and so needed in the great impersonal urban "man heaps" of today.[104]

Governmental Structure Planning

A "correct" administrative framework could conceivably facilitate a meaningful holistic planning operation. "Bad" governmental structures can, of course, be made to work and are. As indicated throughout the preceding analysis, there is an important contradiction or tension between two seemingly 180° different tugs at contemporary governmental forms in Western society. These are namely the necessity, on one hand, of having national urban policy as part of an over-all national plan (macrogovernment) and the increasing and increasingly successful clamor for participatory democracy at the local level (minigovernment). A second controversial and related question is the possible creation of new interim levels of competent "functional/territorial" governments between the traditional political city and the nation. And a third major question is where to find the "adequate" financial resources and how to program them intelligently without which there can be *no* successful urban guidance. However, the mere allocation of resources in no way guarantees splendid results. Government—political management—is the crux of planning at all three levels of development, and government itself is in sore need of replanning. The complexities of successfully altering governmental structures that are in operation are somewhat similar to carrying out alterations on an aircraft in flight.

To a certain extent the macroscale problem has been analyzed above, but hard decisions based on values arrived at through the political process—be it totalitarian, authoritarian or democratic in form—must make difficult major distribution decisions on the location of people and activity nodes with both amenity and "development" ("growth" has become a dirty word today) kept in mind.

Five preconditions for even quasi-successful national development planning, essentially societal rather than physical in form, are fairly obvious: (1) skilled planners (both functional/sectional and territorial); (2) basic information or data systems; (3) adequate funding; (4) a capable (honest) administrative bureaucracy; and (5) some national political consensus or goals. The data system can initially be merely information storage and retrieval; later it can be upgraded to manipulation/modeling capabilities. Having stated that hard values or goals must be accepted as a precondition, it becomes clear that "rolling planning" with cybernetic feedback is in order; added inputs, resulting from initial planning, brings about change in both goals and capabilities. In essence, all national development planning—borrowing as it does from the experience of varied nations—remains still most tentative. We all are here exploring the capabilities of a new managerial/organizational technology only partly understood at present.[105] Certain functional sectors and territorial regions must be chosen to be the growth nodes for maximizing public investment returns on always limited capital funds to the predictable howls of neglected other sectors and territories.

People tend to impact in certain regions for a great variety of reasons. Presently in the United States there is a clearly evident rush toward water both to the East Coast and to California—and to a lesser degree toward the Gulf of Mexico and toward the Great Lakes. This is slowly denuding Middle America of people as the 1970 Census gave evidence (Fig. 1). In Canada, the population is surging, to their planners' considerable annoyance, to the United States border, neglecting their (admittedly unfriendly) North. This southward pressure is repeated in Finland, Norway and Sweden as the hardy inhabitants of the North drift down to the narrow more felicitous urban belts. All over Latin America, as also in India, the big cities are serving as magnets for rural peasants. In England, the Northeast and Northwest are neglected as hordes threaten to engulf the Greater London area and the Southeast. Siberia is not overly attractive to citizens of the USSR, who seemingly are shipped there in batches from time to time, and too many Italians wish to move away from the Mezzogiorno far south of Rome to the more industrialized North. But planful impacting is beginning to show up in some cases. France selected eight *métropoles d'équilibre* (equilibrium metropolises) by rigorous checking against a list of desired qualities from thirty cities in contention, while the "spectaculars" of Brasilia, Ankara (Turkey's capital), and to a lesser extent Chandigarh and Islamabad (Pakistan's new capital joined in converging parallel development with traditional Rawalpindi) were used to dramatize and energize regions in need of development for national purposes.

Besides these problems of regional and rural/urban maldistribution (overurbanization) which must be faced by allocation of government interest and governmental resources, a third distributional question remains: demanding solution or at least palliative treatment. It is the intrametropolitan problem of the emptying central city and the rush to the suburbs. This is especially true of the United States, which is deemed to prefigure in manifold ways the horrid fate in store for other Western lands.

At one pole, therefore, of political/administrative planning is the necessity for adequate prestigious national governmental structure and at the other pole, microgovernment or local structures are needed. The national planning structure must be close to the seat of power, able to lay down feasible goals growing out of the values of the society, to see that necessary information is available and to develop a series of policies, plans, funding and delivery systems as "rolling planning" goes into operation. Quite frankly, no NUP will work unless incorporated as part of a National Development Plan including territorial and functional dimensions. In past terminology, quite simply a National Plan is needed. This should be no news to the "socialist" world (*planification dirigée*) or even to the new nations comprising the Third World; in a real sense it still remains antithetical in its holistic/operational form to the more advanced nations. There are two possible exceptions of France and Japan where by elaborate gyrations and relatively cumbersome devices a *planification collaboratif* among governments and private sectoral interests is attained. In Japan's case this is furthered by the astute manipulation of centralized credit for "national purposes" (made somewhat easier by the Japanese propensity for consensual decision making).

During World War II, the British set up a limited cabinet group to guide/plan the crucial war effort in all its ramifications; this served as a partial model for the United States National Security Council (NSC) in 1947[106] which in continuously modified form still operates today (1974) serving as a vehicle for the study and construction of foreign policy under the remarkable Henry Kissinger. Using the NSC as a model, Nixon flirted with a similar National Urban Council, first under Daniel P. Moynihan (later in the spring of 1973 as the National Domestic Council under Henry Ehrlichman, a casualty of Watergate) to oversee over-all domestic policy. It was not an untenable model, but it has never received the needed unstinted support both spiritual and financial from the presidency. Somewhere near the top there must be a central "strategic" planning staff to guide presidential basic internal development policy in a realistic fashion mutually adjusted to foreign policy. The world is too complex, it would seem, now to depend 99 per cent nationally on "adhocracy." Practically every major and most minor nations of the world have some of the pieces, generally including a central planning group, for such an operation already in hand and slowly—all too slowly in most cases—these varied blocks are being fitted together.

The obvious territorial divisions to make for planning authorities within a nation are "regions." Actually this is a most difficult physical territory to delineate in the real world; but it is in fact accomplished by rule of thumb methods generally based on a fuzzy combination of natural or geographic and historical/cultural factors.[107] Patently an island is the easiest "region" to designate; the backward northern island of Hokkaido is an obvious target for Japanese development schemes.[108] Better perhaps than geographic or simple historical qualities as the basis for delimiting a region, would be *rational regions* searched for and discovered through elaborate analysis of operant potentialities. Areas can be selected as "depressed areas" to be beefed up with national funds regionally administered; boom areas impacted, tamped down or conversely driven at full horsepower to maximize GNP; or moderate growth areas pushed lightly so as to become "airborne."[109] This phraseology avoids the newest, most fashionable controversy, over "growth" as being, on one hand, environmentally/ecologically negative, but on the other imperative in meeting the aspiration/expectations of the common man both in developed and developing areas.

Unquestionably each region must have a growth node or activity center of some scale. This, in effect, means a viable metropolis or a city of at least 250,000, the present critical mass for a satisfactory urban place. A quarter of a million people seemingly are needed to ensure that a wide spectrum of urban services can be supported/used adequately. This appears to be the approximate target for Milton Keynes' New Town abuilding fifty miles from London, although Taby, eight miles north of Stockholm, has about 150,000 as its projected population. Tama New Town's population, forty miles out to the west of Tokyo, will rise to 410,000 by 1977; in Western eyes, at very high densities. Residential land values within a twelve-mile radius of central Tokyo have skyrocketed to a maximum of $500,000 per acre![110] High densities are almost imperative and even more imperative is an effective land-value control system which Japan lacks.

At the top tier of the NUP, as noted, must be a national planning body close to the chief executive; the next tier below national decision should be interpreted and administered regionally at some sort of combined headquarters with a certain degree of autonomy. Such regional planning bodies could be started in the United States by grouping a number of national or federal program outposts. In his proposal for a national plan for "Balanced Growth and Development," Senator Hubert Humphrey submitted to the Subcommittee on Economic Progress of the Joint Economic Committee of the United States Congress, February 26, 1973, a scheme to divide the country into "not less than eight or more than twelve" regions combining with and adjusting the boundaries of the six multistate regional development commissions authorized in 1965. In Humphrey's scheme, co-ordination is mandatory with the ten *Standard Federal Regions* (not followed at present by federal agencies in general). Eventually the jurisdictions of the multitude of local governments must be amalgamated and absorbed at the regional and the tier below, the metropolitan, levels. At the present time in the United States there are over 78,000 local units (15,700 of which are school districts).[111]

> Illinois is the most bureaucratic state, according to the survey with 6,385 governmental units. Hawaii had the fewest [which may account for its excellent start in state (regional?) planning]. Eight other states including New York had more than 3,000 local governments.

Such a morass makes reasonable long-range planning both a political and administrative impossibility. But no bureaucracy at any level in the history of man has ever given up power without some lusty screams after a battle to the last ditch. Whether in practice there has been much success, it is noteworthy that France tackled her seventy plus national *départements* (imposed in the early nineteenth century on the traditional provinces), reducing them in 1964 to twenty-one program regions. Actually the departments still hang on to considerable power. In the United Kingdom some hundreds of local planning jurisdictions were consolidated into approximately fifty in 1947 and Great Britain is now gradually moving toward regional development planning bodies and powers. Such a region may be realistically an *urban region* or megalopolis (what of that horror of linked megalopolises?). Again below the regional headquarters is the metropolitan governmental tier combining central city and suburbs. The embryonic system of Washington's Council of Governments (GOG) or the similar limited Stockholm system or, better, the Greater London Council are all cases in point. Undoubtedly more intellectual blood, sweat and tears—and practical political skills—have gone into the chase of that elusive mechanical rabbit, metro government, in the past two or three decades in the United States than almost any internal American political/administrative problem. There is a tidy statistical target in the useful census delimitation of 233 *standard metropolitan statistical areas* (SMSA) which could serve as the starting line. Of the dozens of monographs, papers and books, the Committee for Economic Development's allocation of functions in *Reshaping Government in Metropolitan Areas*[112] makes good sense and comes close to the Greater London Council system of area-wide functions assigned to the *metro* government and the basket of other functions to remain under local jurisdictions.[113]

This metropolitan government can be of the quasi-complete functional form of London's Greater London Council or, better, the Toronto Metro, or what all mayors talk about, the functioning metropolitan area as a "national city" reaching directly in the American model to the federal government as an equal of a state.[114] The Paris agglomeration is close to this, it would seem.

How to get a NUP off the ground? What feasible operational handles might be used to win political consensus even in fractious democracies for a national planning system? Four such operational handles have been suggested:

1. Population policy,
2. National land-use plan,
3. Ecology/environmental programs,
4. Social welfare.

Population policy. As stated, this is a *sine qua non* of any NUP but it is a tactic heavily charged with emotion and slow in showing results, at least as far as gross quantity and much more so as far as quality are concerned. However, operant locational decisions could be immediately possible, if linked with 2 and 3 above.

National land-use plan. This is still both the beloved skill of urban (physical) planners and on a larger territorial scale by geographers and regional scientists. It is well researched, and very useful societal technologies (if not remotely "engineering") capabilities have been developed. It is understandable to the layman and has roots in the widespread and long accepted (if not overly rewarding to date) practice of zoning at the local scale and is even in the United States a government-pushed program (with Congress still battling against it). This, too, has taken place in a period of a widely heralded drive to return powers to the states. It may be the most useful wedge for a NUP with minimum costs for maximum results, as actually such powers could be spun off with *appropriate national constraints* to the states and may well be, with appropriate national co-ordination.

Ecology/environmental programs. These have high public consensus and a rapidly increasing hard science knowledge base in the West at this point and as part of a multiple strategy seem everywhere slowly to be succeeding. But well-subsidized covert resistance is high and real costs in a competitive world could be very high—probably part of a rewarding national strategy especially if linked with No. 2. Use the "supporting power" of the land as a spearhead concept and both population and land use could form a mutually reinforcing triangle. With fuel shortages resource conservation becomes a key ploy.

Social welfare. Clearly welfare is in trouble in the United States. Men of good will from Franklin Roosevelt's New Deal period and earlier to the Great Society of Lyndon Johnson were out to help the common man and redress the disadvantages accruing to the poverty-crushed lower one quarter to one third of the population. In the eyes of many social scientists and practical politicians it has not accomplished much in its present form. Nixon's ruthless paring of such programs for the 1974 federal budget is sufficient evidence of popular conservative attitudes. Despite the very widespread waving of the banner of an égalitarian ethic, social welfare planning is quite simply not a feasible contemporary tactic in the United States. Wise men are well aware that during the remainder of the twentieth century there may well be a nasty world-wide distributional battle (possibly literally) between the haves and the have-nots.

Some weighing of operational handles behind us for the macroscale, an examination of that necessity of twentieth-century democracy, the micro/participatory government is in order. Minigovernments for communities of five hundred to fifty thousand below the metro-government level are much in the public eye today. Certain highly vocal, energetic, self-selected persons at the local level are unquestionably creating a most successful brush fire based on the tinder box reality of "the search for identity" in the great booming complex urban world which no one ever made—especially the ordinary citizen. Said citizens now "demand" the right to control their own destinies; and they are learning how, at least, to stop things from happening to them such as disruptive new roads or "different and difficult" neighbors moving in. They are also learning how to obtain government attention to and fragmentary funding of their perceived needs.

Citizen organizations in considerable numbers have fought the "good fight" savoring all the rich juices in the rewarding process of running oneself (aided and abetted by "expert" advocacy planners) and have seemingly extended as well democracy's incapacity by an endless proliferation of veto groups/veto powers. On the other hand, participatory democracy is an example of front-end loading in planning: It may be high on initial costs, the resultant plan may not be so sophisticated, but it does not blow up in everyone's face after theoretically going into operation.[115] Costs and benefits of participatory planning are as yet not precisely weighable.

A harsh series of questions must be faced: How in a closely interlocked world increasingly full of people, with an ever expanding industrial technology, undergoing accelerating social change, and exhausting its habitats, can little people gain the education, time, information and wisdom to run themselves at all well? It is hardly the province of this analysis to answer such questions. Hopefully men of talent, integrity and training will gravitate into internal political careers ready to accept high responsibilities and lead the development of understanding among the general population in new participatory organizational/governmental structures and styles.

The question of urban funding, a most complex one, must next be raised. Property taxation by individual cities is counterproductive. Where the national taxing policy either allows localities to collect *income* taxes directly on both corporate and individual incomes (in both capitalist and quasi-capitalist societies) or by law routinely allocates ample portions of national taxation income to urban places, urban financing can be adequate. Capital investment for urban infrastructure, both in physical forms and societal institutional devices, can be sticky in any case unless there is a clear urban-leaning quality to the central government (not rural dominated). In short, the political weighing of the urban versus rural must favor the first or no successful urban development will remotely succeed—after all, rural areas in modern states serve merely as city backyards! When a national (even a federal) government decides that "the city is the payoff," then both urban income accounts and capital accounts will be adequately funded—no matter by what ingenious fiscal gyration. The simpler the better! The United States under the most awkward system imaginable has some six hundred and fifty-six federal programs under sixty-four federal entities to ladle out (give back) income tax monies collected, to cities for both on-going expenses and capital investment; presumably there are better ways to do this.[116]

NOTES

[1] Leonard Duhl, "Teaching and Social Policy," *The Bulletin of the Association of Collegiate Schools of Planning,* Winter 1971, pp. 4–10.

[2] Paul Goodman (ed.), *Seeds of Liberation.* New York, George Braziller, 1964.

[3] *The Next Fifty Years* series commemorated the fiftieth anniversary of the founding of the American Institute of Planners. Published by the University of Indiana Press (Bloomington, Ill.), it consists of three volumes: Vol. 1, *Environment and Man* (1967), Vol. II, *Environment and Change* (1968), Vol. III, *Environment and Policy* (1968).

[4] Ibid., Vol. III, p. 145.

[5] Wilfred Owen, "Telecommunication and Life Styles," *The Accessible City.* Washington, D.C., The Brookings Institution, 1972, pp. 132–33.

[6] John McHale, *Future Cities: Notes on a Typology* (unpublished draft).

[7] Satirized some years ago by A. C. Spectorsky, *The Exurbanites.* New York, Berkeley Publishing Co., 1955.

[8] Extrapolated loosely from Walter K. Vinett, *Paper Number Three, the Scenario for Minnesota's Experimental City.* Minneapolis, University of Minnesota, Office for Applied Social Science and the Future, 1972.

[9] Harvey S. Perloff, *New Towns in Town.* Washington, D.C., Resources for the Future, 1966, reprint.

[10] *Time,* February 26, 1973. This project was canceled in the summer of 1973 as funds ran out.

[11] F. J. Osborn and Arnold Whittick, *The New Towns: The Answer to Megalopolis.* New York, McGraw-Hill, 1963, pp. 141–48. This listing is incomplete and already dated.

[12] The New York *Times,* April 26, 1973.

[13] Dena Kaye, "Across the Gateway and Into the Curry," *Saturday Review/World,* September 11, 1973.

[14] Ann Louise Strong, *Planned Urban Environments.* Baltimore, Md., the Johns Hopkins University Press, 1971, pp. 170–73.

[15] Cf. Lawrence Susskind and Gary Hack, "New Communities in a National Urban Growth Strategy," *Technology Review* (February 1972), pp. 30–42; also "New Communities," An American Institute of Planners Background Paper, No. 2, 1968.

[16] Revised version of a paper presented for the symposium on "The Human Dimensions of Planning," UCLA, June 1972.

[17] "The Planning Process for New Town Development: Soul City," A Planning Studio Course, Fall 1969, Department of City and Regional Planning, University of North Carolina, Chapel Hill.

[18] A visually striking book on megastructures is Justus Dahinden's *Urban Structures for the Future.* New York, Praeger, 1972. Dahinden's knowledge of societal reality is very slight.

[19] Paolo Soleri, *Arcology—The City in the Image of Man.* Cambridge, Mass., M.I.T. Press, 1969.

[20] See Ralph Wilcoxen, *Paolo Soleri: A Bibliography.* Monticello, Ill., Council of Planning Librarians Exchange Bibliography, #88, June 1969.

[21] Cf. William Zuk and Roger H. Clark, *Kinetic Architecture.* New York, Van Nostrand Reinhold, 1970. To quote the blurb, "Exciting open-ended planning: proposed and actual structures that are *replaceable, deformable, incremental, expandable, reversible*—even *disposable.*" Italics, the editor.

[22] The New York *Times,* December 2, 1965.

[23] The New York *Times,* November 22, 1970.

[24] *Playboy,* December 1967.

[25] The New York *Times,* November 3, 1968.

[26] Kenzo Tangé Team, "A Plan for Tokyo, 1960" (Tokyo), drawn largely from the April 1961 issue (in English) of the *Japanese Architect.*

[27] "Future Urbanization Patterns: A Long-Range World Wide View," paper prepared for presentation at the Second International Future Research Conference, Kyoto, Japan, 1970, p. 17.

[28] Congressional Record, November 15, 1965, "Extension of Remarks of Hon. Claiborne Pell, October 22, 1965."

[29] 130 Spruce Street, Philadelphia, Pa. 19106. See SYNCON, their elaborate physical and intellectual system to relate varied disciplines in a holistic effort to solve primarily urban problems. The American Anthropological Association planned a "Symposium on Extraterrestrial Communities" for their 1974 Conference, *The World Future Society Bulletin,* Vol. III, No. 7, July 1973. The concept of *Unibutz: Out of This World* (an international, interplanetary *kibbutz*) was explored at some length in the World Institute Council's *Field Within Fields* by varied intellectuals in 1971 (Vol. 40, No. 1).

[30] B. F. Skinner, *Walden Two.* New York, the Macmillan Company, 1948. cf. W. H. G. Armytage, *Yesterday's Tomorrows: A Historical Survey of Future Societies.* Toronto, University of Toronto Press, 1968.

[31] *The Complete Works of Ralph Waldo Emerson,* edited by E. W. Emerson.

Boston, Houghton Mifflin & Co., 1904, Vol. 10, pp. 359–60, quoted in Peyton E. Richter, ed., *Utopias: Social Ideals and Communal Experiments*. Boston, Holbrook Press, 1971, p. 129. The examples cited here were drawn from this work.

[32] *The Last Whole Earth Catalog*. New York, Random House, 1971.

[33] Michael Carr and Dan MacLeon, "Getting It Together," *Environment,* Vol. 14, No. 5 (November 1972). The study was conducted under the auspices of the American Association for the Advancement of Science.

[34] Drawn from Fred Davis, *On Youth Sub-Cultures: The Hippie Variant*. New York, General Learning Press, 1971—module.

[35] This most certainly is not to encourage elaborate planning provisions for odd groups searching for instant Nirvana through drug utopias—a not inconsiderable subset or variant of existent communal experimentation. Cf. Richard Blum, *Utopiates: The Use and Users of LSD-25*. New York, Dodd, Mead, & Company, 1963.

[36] For example, ANIK, the Canadian internal communications satellite.

[37] Sloan Commission on Cable Television, *On the Cable: The Television of Abundance* (New York, McGraw-Hill, 1971) is a fairly straight-line projection of more-of-the same TV pattern, only with more choice, up to the turn of the century. More imaginative alternative potentials could have been rewardingly explored; the societal planning lead time is shorter than one thinks to cope with *the wired city*.

[38] Jonathan New Town, Minneapolis, Minn., Tama New Town, Japan, and Washington New Town, County Durham, England.

[39] This, of course, could be international as Eurovision has already accomplished for one-way television.

[40] James Martin and Adrian R. D. Norman, *The Computerized Society*. Englewood Cliffs, N.J., Prentice-Hall, 1970, p. 66.

[41] Cf. Melvin M. Webber and Carolyn C. Webber, "Culture, Territoriality and the Elastic Mile," in H. Wentworth Eldredge, (ed.), *Taming Megalopolis*. New York, Anchor-Doubleday, 1967, Vol. I, pp. 35–54, which considers the existent professional nonterritorial community.

[42] Wilfred Owen, *The Accessible City*. Washington, D.C., the Brookings Institution, 1972, p. 132.

[43] *Project Minerva* (Electronic Town Hall Project) "has already carried out preliminary exercises in some 803 households of a middle-income high-rise housing complex in one of the nation's largest cities . . . in the comfort of their own homes recently, and aired their views about their security problems during an electronic town hall meeting." Amitai Etzioni, who is conducting this, believes he could do this out with forty thousand persons. Centers for Policy Research, Inc., 475 Riverside Drive, New York, *Newsletter* #8, January 1973, and *Behavior Today,* Vol. 4, No. 10, March 5, 1973.

[44] Robert Boguslaw, *The New Utopians: A Study of System Designs and Social Change*. Englewood Cliffs, N.J., Prentice-Hall, 1965. As well as explaining latent capabilities for powerful symbiotic man/machine interaction, Boguslaw wisely explores paranoid possibilities in Chap. 8, "The Power of Systems and Systems of Power."

[45] Marvin Cetron, *An Analysis of the Impact of Advanced Telecommunications Technology on the American City.* Washington, D.C./Arlington, Va., Forecasting International, Ltd., 1973, quoted from the "Executive Summary" p. lv.

[46] James Martin and Adrian R. D. Norman, *The Computerized Society,* op. cit. These terms are headings for portions of the Martin/Norman book.

[47] The epic *South East Study* started it going. (London: Her Majesty's Stationery Office, Ministry of Housing and Local Government, 1964.)

[48] The Barlow Report (Royal Commission on the Distribution of the Industrial Population), H.M.S.O., 1940; the Scott Report (Committee on the Utilization of Land in Rural Areas), H.M.S.O., 1942; and the Uthwatt Report (Expert Committee on Compensation and Betterment), H.M.S.O., 1942—the last named on a basic national land-use policy.

[49] *The National Plan,* London: H.M.S.O., 1965, Cmnd. 2764.

[50] Lloyd Rodwin, *Nations and Cities, a Comparison of Strategies for Urban Growth.* Boston, Houghton Mifflin, 1970. Rodwin heads the prestigious MIT Department of Urban Studies and Planning, which is increasingly concerned with national urban policies. His book deals with national planning in Venezuela, Turkey, Great Britain, France and the United States.

[51] Ann Louise Strong, op. cit. The national planning schemes of Sweden, Finland, Israel, the Netherlands and France are treated at considerable length with legal expertise in this volume.

[52] Daniel P. Moynihan (ed.), *Toward a National Urban Policy.* New York, Basic Books, 1970. Moynihan in his introduction lists ten fundamentals of a national urban policy.

[53] "Toward a National Policy for Planning the Environment" in Ernest Erber (ed. for the AIP), *Urban Planning in Transition.* New York, Grossman, 1970.

[54] *Urban Growth Strategies in Six European Countries,* Office of International Affairs, Department of Housing and Urban Development, A Report by the Urban Growth Policy Study Groups. Washington D.C., HUD, 1972, pp. 4–5.

[55] Regional blocs of nations (EEC?) may be able shortly to accomplish holistic planning.

[56] William Peterson, *The Politics of Population* (New York, Doubleday & Company, 1964), saw this clearly ten years ago. Cf. pp. 323ff.

[57] *HUD International Brief #18,* Washington D.C., Office of International Affairs, U. S. Department of Housing and Urban Development, June 1972, p. 1.

[58] Dennis Meadows and Associates. *The Limits to Growth.* New York Universe Books, 1972. H. S. D. Cole, et al., *Models of Doom: A Critique of the Limits of Growth.* New York, Universe Books, 1973.

[59] Paul R. Ehrlich and Anne H. Ehrlich, *Population Resources and Environment.* San Francisco, W. H. Freeman and Company, 1970.

[60] "Human Mass Production," Dr. James F. Bonner of California Institute of Technology terms it.

[61] Paul Ramsey, *Fabricated Man: The Ethics of Genetic Control.* New Haven, Yale University Press, 1970. Cf. Amitai Etzioni, *Genetic Fix* (New York, Macmillan, 1973), for an examination of the horrendous potentialities.

[62] B. F. Skinner, *Beyond Freedom and Dignity* (New York, Alfred Knopf, 1971), is the leading exponent of this position.

[63] David M. Heer, *Society and Population.* Englewood Cliffs, N.J., Prentice-Hall Foundation of Modern Sociology Series, 1968.

[64] Economic Planning Agency, Government of Japan, Tokyo, 1969 (?).

[65] Rachel Carson, *The Silent Spring.* Boston, Houghton Mifflin, 1962.

[66] William Vogt, *Road to Survival.* New York, William Sloane Associates, 1948.

[67] Marion Clawson, *Land for Americans* (Chicago, Rand McNally, 1963) based on the Resources for the Future Study of *Land for the Future* by Clawson, et al.

[68] William H. Whyte, *The Last Landscape.* New York, Doubleday & Company, 1968.

[69] Ian McHarg, *Design With Nature.* Garden City, N.Y., The Natural History Press, 1969.

[70] Barry Commoner, *The Closing Circle.* New York, Knopf, 1971.

[71] Cf. Harold Wolozin (ed.), *The Economics of Air Pollution.* New York, Norton, 1966.

[72] The New York *Times,* February 18, 1973.

[73] For a concrete example on a specific nuisance see Clifford R. Graydon, *Noise Pollution, The Unquiet Crisis.* Philadelphia, University of Pennsylvania Press, 1972.

[74] Frank Krieth, "Lack of Impact," *Environment,* Vol. 15, No. 1 (January/February 1973). The U. S. Department of Commerce has finally established an office of Technology Assessment and Forecast (July 1973).

[75] Lowden Wingo, Jr. (ed.), *Cities and Space: The Future Use of Urban Land* (Baltimore, the Johns Hopkins Press, for Resources of the Future, Inc., 1963), was certainly one of the milestones in a holistic view of land-use policy—see especially Catherine Bauer Wooster's "The Form and Structure of the Future Urban Complex," pp. 73–101. See also Joseph Passoneau on "The Emergence of City Form" in Werner Z. Hirsch (ed.), *Urban Life and Form* (New York, Holt, Rinehart and Winston, Inc., 1963), which approaches the problem from an urban design point of view on a total city scale.

[76] Robert Sommer, *Personal Space.* Englewood Cliffs, N.J., Prentice-Hall, Inc., a Spectrum Book, 1969.

[77] William H. Michelson, *Man and His Urban Environment: A Sociological Approach.* Reading, Mass., Addison-Wesley Publishing Company, 1970. Cf. also sociologist Robert Gutman's edited *People and Buildings.* New York, Basic Books, 1972.

[78] London Wingo, "Issues in a National Urban Development Strategy for the United States," *Urban Studies,* Vol. 9, No. 1 (February 1972), p. 16.

[79] Cf. Lloyd Rodwin, "Innovations for Urban Studies and Planning," *Journal of the American Institute of Planners* (September 1972), pp. 182–85.

[80] As an example of microscale physical planning, operationally oriented with a warm human touch including environmental/ecological overtones, some hard economic planning inputs as well as good aesthetic craftsmanship, see William H. Whyte, *Cluster Development.* New York, American Conservation Association, 1964. On the mesoscale, Martin Myerson and Jacqueline Tyrwhitt, Brian Falk and Patricia Sekler did an equally valid but more analytical than opera-

tional job for the entire city in *Face of the Metropolis,* sponsored by ACTION. New York, Random House, 1963.

[81] Dean S. Rugg, *Spatial Foundations of Urbanism* (Dubuque, Iowa, W. C. Brown Co., 1972), is a good illustration of this.

[82] Suzanne Keller, *The Urban Neighborhood: A Sociological Perspective.* New York, Random House, 1968. "The aims of this book are practical—to synthesize selected sociological evidence of relevance for physical planners in their work."

[83] See the work, for example, of Andrei Rogers and Michael Teitz at the University of California and of Britton Harris at the University of Pennsylvania.

[84] Henry Fagin makes this important difference clear between the practitioner facing the operational firing line and the necessarily fluid intellectual researchers in "the discipline of urban planning." See his "Advancing the State of the Art," in Ernest Erber (ed.), *Urban Planning in Transition.* New York, Grossman Publishing Company for the American Institute of Planners, 1970, pp. 125–41. See the social policy planning work of Melvin Webber at the University of California (Berkeley), Bernard Frieden at Massachusetts Institute of Technology, and Herbert Gans at Columbia University.

[85] Daniel P. Moynihan, *Maximum Feasible Misunderstanding* (New York, The Free Press, 1970), and Edward Banfield, *The Unheavenly City* (Boston, Little Brown, 1970).

[86] Editorial, "A Meeting in Boulder," *Planning, the ASPO Magazine* (September 1972), pp. 172–73. Cf. his edited *The Future of the United States Government.* New York, George Braziller, 1971.

[87] Harvey S. Perloff, "New Directions in Social Planning," in H. Wentworth Eldredge (ed.), *Taming Megalopolis,* Vol. II. New York, Doubleday Anchor, 1967, pp. 887–96.

[88] Further analysis of such prescriptions now is strongly recommended by the Committee for Economic Development, *Education for the Urban Disadvantaged: From Preschool to Employment* (New York, CED, 1971), on both delivery systems and the results obtainable.

[89] Godfrey Hodgson, "Do Schools Make A Difference," *Atlantic Monthly* (March 1973), pp. 35–46.

[90] Erik H. Erikson, *Identity: Youth and Crisis.* New York, W. W. Norton, Inc., 1968, Part III, The Life Cycle: Epigenesis of Identity."

[91] Bruno Bettelheim, *The Children of the Dream.* New York, Macmillan, 1969.

[92] Charles Abrams, *Man's Struggle for Shelter.*

[93] Irving H. Welfeld "European Housing Subsidy Systems" (U. S. Department of Housing and Urban Development, September 1972).

[94] Daniel P. Moynihan, *The Politics of a Guaranteed Income: The Nixon Administration and the Family Assistance Program.* New York, Random House, 1973.

[95] Michael Young and Peter Wilmott, *Family and Kinship in East London* (Baltimore, Md., Penguin Books, 1957); and Herbert J. Gans, *The Urban Villagers* (New York, Free Press, 1962). Slums as territorial groupings are explored by Gerald D. Suttles, *The Social Order of the Slum.* Chicago, University of Chicago Press, 1968.

[96] Melvin M. Webber and Carolyn C. Webber, "Culture, Territoriality, and the Elastic Mile," in H. Wentworth Eldredge (ed.), *Taming Megalopolis.* New York, Doubleday Anchor, 1967, Vol. I, pp. 35–53.

[97] The first such center built under the Neighborhood Facilities Program of the U. S. Department of Housing and Urban Development was opened at an Indian community fifty miles north of Seattle, Washington, serving the fifty-nine families living on the reservation as a headquarters for youth and adult activities.

[98] C. Wright Mills, *The Power Elite*. New York, Oxford University Press, 1956.

[99] Vance Packard, *A Nation of Strangers.* New York, McKay, 1972.

[100] Maurice Stein, *The Eclipse of Community.* Princeton, N.J., Princeton University Press, 1960.

[101] Robert Nisbet, *The Quest for Community.* New York, Oxford University Press, 1969, reissue, p. vii. Shades of Nazi Germany!

[102] James Dahir, *The Neighborhood Unit Plan* (New York: Russell Sage Foundation, 1947), and his excellent early operationally-oriented *Communities for Better Living* (New York: Harper & Bros., 1950).

[103] For example: Robert A. Mayer, *Social Planning and Social Change* (Englewood Cliffs, N.J., Prentice-Hall, 1972); Ralph M. Kramer and Harry Specht (eds.), *Readings in Community Organization Practice* (Englewood Cliffs, N.J., Prentice-Hall, 1969); and William W. Biddle with Loureide J. Biddle, *The Community Development Process: The Rediscovery of Local Initiative* (New York, Holt, Rinehart and Winston, Inc., 1965).

[104] Cf. "The Social Responsibility of the Planner" adopted in 1972 by the American Institute of Planners (Washington: 1776 Massachusetts Avenue, 1973), the official professional position.

[105] Interestingly enough, although the general world tendency is to utilize hierarchical, pyramidal (militarily derived command models?) systems, new managerial structures emphasize shifting task force "bureaucracies" of peer experts, coalescing and dissolving as the need arrives under a much looser framework (also similar to the task force military model). Cf. George E. Berkley, *The Administrative Revolution: Notes on the Passing of Organization Man* (Englewood Cliffs, N.J., Prentice-Hall, Inc., 1971) or the incisive pop sociology of Alvin Toffler's Chap. 7, "Organization: The Coming Ad-Hocracy" in *Future Shock* (New York, Random House, 1970), or the illuminating pop economics of Peter Drucker's *Age of Discontinuity* (New York, Harper & Row, 1969), Chap. 9, "Toward a Theory of Organizations."

[106] Senator Henry M. Jackson (ed.), *The National Security Council.* New York, Praeger, 1965.

[107] Cf. Chaps. 1 and 2 by Fulmer Mood and Vernon Carstenson in Merrill Jensen (ed.), *Regionalism in America.* Milwaukee, Wis., University of Wisconsin Press, 1951.

[108] The Winter Olympics of 1972 were held in Sapporo, the island capital, with heavy inputs of both public and private funds.

[109] W. W. Rostow, *The Stages of Economic Growth: A Non-Communist Manifesto.* Cambridge, England, Cambridge University Press, 1960.

[110] *Japan Information Bulletin,* May 1969, p. 182.

[111] The New York *Times,* March 4, 1972, commenting on Bureau of the Census figures.

[112] *Reshaping Government in Metropolitan Areas: A Statement by the Research and Policy Committee* (New York, February 1970).

[113] Ibid., pp. 19 and 20. In addition, community level minigovernments are suggested *below* the traditional existing local governments.

[114] John Lindsay, former mayor of New York, expressed this favorite theme of his eloquently at a conference on cities of NATO countries in June 1971, when he proposed that a "national city" status be given, obviously to New York, but also to cities like Houston, Detroit and Philadelphia which "are each larger than fifteen of the fifty states." New York *Times,* "For New National Cities," June 9, 1971. The U. S. Senate, of course, remains, similar with its emphasis on statehood, to a form of "rotten borough" system.

[115] See the detailed analysis series *Research on Conflict in Locational Decisions* carried out by the Regional Science Department at the Wharton School of Finance and Commerce, University of Pennsylvania. Specific cases explored include Germantown, Nashville, the Hudson River Expressway and New Orleans' waterfront expressway.

[116] Howard S. Rowland, *The New York Times Guide to Federal Aid for Cities and Towns.* New York, World Publishing Company, 1972. It was estimated that there was $43 billion in federal money available to cities during 1973.

CHAPTER 15

A National Urban Plan And Delivery System

H. Wentworth Eldredge

The city (or, better, metropolis) is a system which must export goods and services as well as provide goods and services for its own population; such activity must take place in order to import necessary goods and services from outside this limited system.

Economic Planning

Only recently have economists (other than economic geographers marginal to the economic social science mainstream) commenced to think in spatially limited urban systems. Traditionally oriented toward national functional analysis (or to a lesser extent toward the nation as a territorial system) they have begun to develop a new dimension to economic thought contributing valued research and needed insights to the urban scene. Preceded by work in regional analysis and accounts by "regional scientists,"[1] the past fifteen years have produced a number of publications and trained economists as urban specialists.[2] Without a favorable balance of accounts, the city will dwindle to a *nekropolis,* a city of the dead. The great cities of the world have grown over the millennia (in some few cases), the centuries (thousands) and decades (tens of thousands of smaller places) because in point of fact they have provided governmental functions (the eleven capitals treated here, for example); important commercial centers; basic manufacturing locations; as well as educational, intellectual and cultural hives of activity and creativity. Until very recently the urban place has had economic as well as non-economic comparative advantages or external economies. Quite generally cities have been able to provide higher levels of goods and services for their citizens than the relatively poorer rural places; most assuredly the wide availability of urban goods and services (both in the public and private sectors) is one of the primordial reasons for urban magnetism. The city has survived, increased, prospered because it has had a favorable balance of income accounts.

There is a second derived reason for urban economic magnetism; as is well known, the city has been traditionally "where the jobs are." The bountiful number and wide variety of city occupations is the attraction which brings in new population and holds those already there. However, the apogee of that development may soon be reached. There is undoubtedly an optimum city size for a certain socio-cultural milieu where optimal services and societal environment entail minimal costs; the 1960–70 pattern of medium-size SMSA growth in the United States suggests that a "city" with 100,000 to 1,000,000[3] population is rightly or wrongly perceived as a "good place" in which to live and work. But the loss of jobs in the New York (political) City for the third consecutive year—although at a decreasing pace—amounted to 73,300 evaporated jobs during 1972 or 2 per cent of the total, compared with a national gain of 2.8 per cent.[4] Noteworthy is the development in the four New York State suburban counties of 19,000 new jobs, but even with SMSA, New Jersey and Connecticut, New York suburban gains were not sufficient to offset the political city's losses. It should be evident that without sturdy productivity no city can provide the public services through an adequate tax income, however derived. Thus, central to the urban plan is the crucial necessity to maximize the efficient productivity of the urban area and to open up and maintain employment.

To recapitulate from an economic viewpoint the analysis of urban growth in Chapter 1, the comparative advantages of the early city in the rising industrial era can be catalogued easily: good banking facilities; often a transportation node or breakpoint; ready market; power (water and accessible fossil fuels often through cheap transport); labor supply; relative order and tranquility; comparatively better municipal services; an interesting style and quality of life. Industry and the city reinforced each other. That original city is now the old political city or central city (CC) or even the central business district (CBD) which has by now expanded to blanket the original city. The initial centripetal impulses have continued on a reduced scale, but within the large city or metropolis three centrifugal waves have made themselves felt in the entire Western world—with the full impact of the unsettling third wave yet to be felt outside the United States. The first centrifugal movement was the steam, later electric, suburban transit system which brought about the first ring of suburbs; around Western cities as upper class and middle class escaped to the then "rural" surroundings. The second wave commenced after World War I in the United States when the highway networks and, even more so after World War II, the superhighway networks pumped the citizenry even farther afield into the "slurbs" or huge sprawling agglomerations characteristic of today. Thus the sprawling metropolises tended to link up in the formless

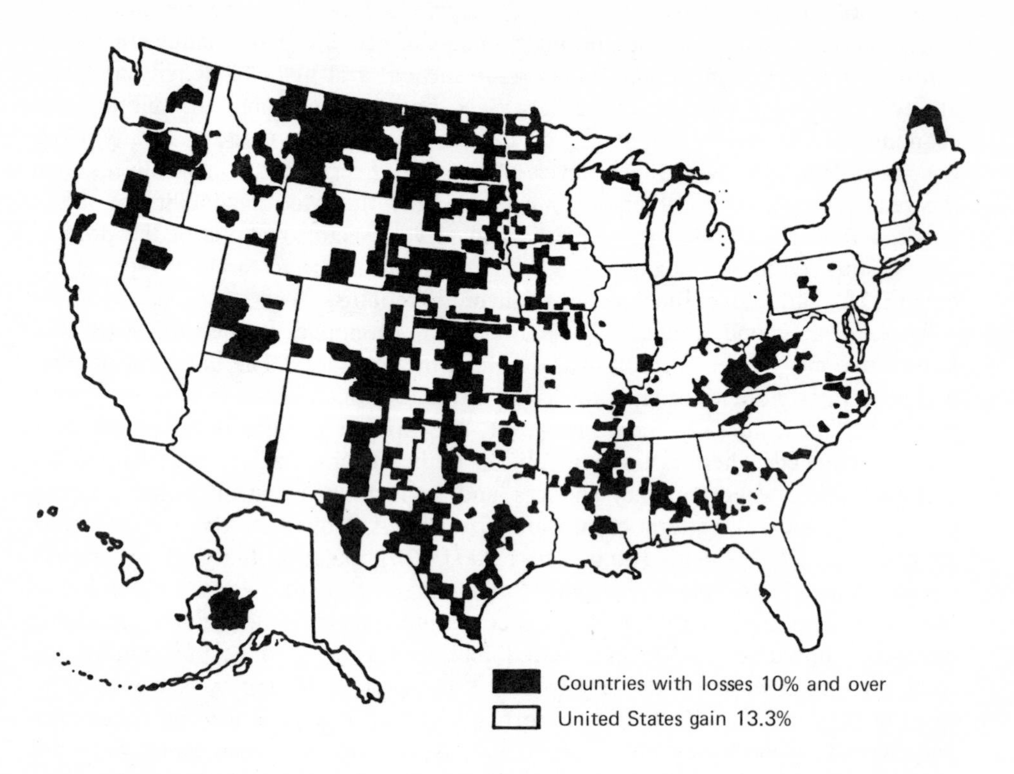

FIG. 1 Population changes, 1960 to 1970. *Based on "Percent of change in total population by Counties 1960 to 1970,"* United States Summary, Number of Inhabitants (*U. S. Department of Commerce Bureau of the Census*), *p. 28.*

awkward megalopolises: the third centrifugal wave. Muddles of conflicting, scrambled land use are characteristic of the entire industrialized world today with unrewarding chaos on the fringes and deadlock at the center. The original centripetal economic pulls have been largely reversed: banking now is nationwide, not local; truck transportation has pretty much broken the rail transportation nodes (at least in the United States); the market is increasingly national; power "strides on legs of steel across the countryside"; labor commutes by car (except the scarcely needed unskilled). In addition to economic factors, the style and quality of central city life have tended to evaporate because of pollution, crime in the streets and in unrewarding density. At the same time electronics have spread mass culture everywhere; the quality of public services has crept downward as costs mount with the spiraling value of usable central city land and the burdensome central city taxes. The comparative advantage for much of industry and business in the city has evaporated to the suburbs or even farther out to the hinterland of the Standard Metropolitan Statistical Areas.

Recent Western urban economic history is generally well known[5]; retail trade chased its relatively affluent suburban commuters to their lair; big industry starved for space to expand in central city decamped afield (literally); service bureaucracies were banished by governmental, industrial and business high commands; even the urban universities became too cramped and set up subcampuses on the urban fringe. Research institutes (think tanks) and business headquarters on the lookout for happier climes (near to executive and "expert" living areas) established their own green campuses away from central cities. What was left in the CBD? Most of the high command posts of big industry and big government—to hold the putative advantage of instant personal communication and of the good externalities of CC; department stores; specialty retail shops and service industries, not to mention the nonelectronic mass recreation business, remained. The rest of the economic mix has gone, leaving old office space in central city decaying, and aging dwellings filled irregularly in the United States by the poor, locked into a culture of poverty. To the existing poor, unfortunately, hordes of migrants from the even further impoverished rural areas have been added. The right jobs for those left in CC are not there, leading to awkward patterns of reverse commuting, exacerbating an already deficient commuter public transport system. The central city poor in the United States (all too generally minority group members) are not schooled or motivated to fill adequately the white-collar jobs now offered there. This is structural unemployment difficult to solve.[6] Briefly then, the city no longer affords the widest spectrum of industrial and office jobs to its present inhabitants and certain of its productive comparative advantages have melted away.

Why, then, economically, does it survive and can this pattern be expected to continue and, if so, for how long? These are hard and harsh questions to answer for the true believer in urban civilization at least in its traditional form. And its continued existence is further challenged by the developing technologies—see the analysis of "the wired city" for example—which make an open urbanism pattern prefigured in California, America's most populous state, by the SANSAN megalopolis from San Diego to San Francisco with Los Angeles, the prime exhibit. Are central cities really necessary?

There is no doubt that a great variety of economic/governmental interests are pushing a great variety of innovative attempts at central city rejuvenation. The entire United States urban renewal thrust costing over nine billion federal government dollars, multiplied by at least a factor of three for local and private investments for a total of over thirty-six billion since its inception in 1949, gives clear evidence that central city has still very heavy hostages to fate left. Actually this investment in grandiose new commercial structures[7] and above-average housing as well as Model Cities, O.E.O., etc., for more humble areas, gives evidence of high national concern with the danger of central city deserts—already tragically evident in ruined, empty, decayed sectors of major American metropolises. There is simply too much urban governmental infrastructure representing billions of dollars of public funds invested in the city and too much private capital, which cannot be either rapidly amortized or thrown away, to give up the central city soon. Deterioration is already becoming evident in both the inadequate inner and outer suburban areas of the giant urban complexes; it may turn out that cities of much smaller scale may be the benefiters in the decades ahead of the diseconomies of all territorial sectors of the great metropolis.

Jane Jacobs has ventured in *The Economy of Cities*[8] the thesis that the large city is a rapid breeder of innovational enterprises due to the externalities of the enormously rich spectrum of skills and facilities available. Present high city taxes, as we have indicated, are not urban faults per se but rather a maldistribution of tax receipts and an awkward governmental structuring. The general urban malaise could be a preliminary plateau to developing in the central city new fresh forms for both work and living—unlikely as that seems at the moment. The feverish growth of big central city office space can't all be losing money; although *La Défense* (Paris) and Shinjuku (Tokyo) indicate that fresh business/commercial activity centers may be grouped advantageously at the fringes rather than in the original CBD. There can be enough activity of varied sorts to be dispersed planfully and rewardingly throughout the metropolitan areas and the high density of the CC reduced. The economic benefits and costs of locating economic functions in the city are dependent on intergovernmental financial arrangements and on the over-all societal quality of the city, which alone can generate capable local administration and rewarding living to hold/develop competent populations to stand behind urban life rather than attempt to escape it. This seems presently not to be the case in many American cities but clearly is in large parts of Europe. The economic viability of the city depends on political-social-economic variables not on economic factors nakedly alone.

What about urban employment and the present distributive egalitarian economic concerns? Despite the failure of well-publicized, recent faulty job-training programs[9] where community action in the "war on poverty" spent considerable sums of money with precious little measurable results, the logic of structural unemployment demands two operant major quasi-economic strategies aimed at solution. *Stragey One* is to upgrade the skills of the existing inhabitants to hold onto the generally white-collar jobs already available without luring into the area hordes of unskilled migrants—a very hard order. This applies especially to developing nations where the *Green Revolution* is displacing the low-skilled, poor peasant tenants who stream into the underprepared urban places—Delhi, for instance.[10] And *Strategy Two* generates consciously new varied employment opportunities through complex public/private investment schemes and politico/economic structures.

There is theoretically a *Strategy Three,* namely "to decant" (Lewis Mumford's happy phrase) part of the existing CC urban population to the suburbs (New Towns in Town) or to new towns/new cities/new communities that are economically viable with built-in employment. The public infrastructure and private capital investment required for such a strategy on a meaningfully massive scale—not to mention the time lags—are patently very considerable. Some astute combination of the three strategies may be feasible.

The component parts of Strategy One include welfare policies so rigged throughout the nation and development policies so widespread that depressed regions (generally backward rural areas) have sufficient economic and other activities of their own *to hold* population rewardingly in place. A determined national public education system, harking back to Bismarck's technical schools in the 1880s or the Danish Folk High School movement of the early twentieth century, which gave evidence that simple people could be made to function well in the high industry of that day, might work.[11] Strategy Two suggests that constructive private capitalist enterprises (with or without government subvention) can locate as good neighbors in central city; these might be labor intensive (low capitalization per worker) at the outset and *could* become part of restoring a semblance of decent living to slum areas. While such created jobs could be both white and blue collar, the tendency appears to have been to create blue-collar employment at the outset. New York City through its Planning Commission initialed a city-financed industrial renewal operation. In that city, manufacturing, the second largest industrial sector, provides still about 800,000 jobs.[12] Some ten thousand industrial jobs have been created in four and one-half years, 75 per cent through an industrial park within the city limits; a second industrial park similar in scale is nearing completion. The astute assembly of suitable sites seems an important key to the economic revitalization process. The New York State Urban Development Corporation (a public authority) is just such a device which can assemble land, override parochial incompetence, tap large capital sources and build in central city (Welfare Island, New York). Similarly in Washington, D.C., on the fringe, adequate good new urban tissue is being formed in Fort Lincoln, the New-Town-in-Town which will hopefully generate considerable employment and living opportunities at the same time.[13] The Local Development Corporation (LDC),[14] apparently invented by McKinsey and Co., renowned management consultants, and the Harvard University Program on Science and Technology experts, is a device to enlist private, outside, local and various level government capital. The LDC is an example of an involved renewal operation using a seminal mixed economic structure, which could conceivably lead to more brisk upgrading of the urban scene and economy.

Various versions of the guaranteed income[15] or negative income tax—closely allied to the welfare function but clearly a version of employment income subsidy—should be noted as part of the unemployment/underemployment picture for CC. The failure to obtain the inadequate $1,600 minimal per annum proposed by President Nixon during the 1972–73 Congress was disheartening but it will come up again. To quote a Bedouin proverb: "The camel's nose is under the tent."[16] And seemingly further "employment income" at newly constructed CC factories will be available in the United States within a few years for unskilled segments of the population in central city, if present plans mature under various LDC guidance.

Finally, a most significant alteration in employment patterns—closely connected with all urban services, especially transport, and with recreational patterns—is the twofold demand by bored workers for meaningful jobs and flexible work day patterns. Increasingly "educated" populations (especially the young) are in fact revolting against the deadly monotony of the traditional assembly line or clerk's desk. The United States Department of Health, Education and Welfare (HEW) produced a massive and most controversial study, "Work in America," in December 1972, detailing widespread evidence of job dissatisfaction and even occupational despair. Expectations about "work" seemed far higher than reality! "Work-related problems are contributing to a decline in physical and mental health, decreased family stability and community cohesiveness and less 'balanced' political attitudes among workers"[17] not to mention productivity and profits! This showed itself in the production of the General Motors car, the Vega, where at a speedy new style plant high levels of unsatisfactory cars came off the line to face inspectors (and some to pass inspectors?). It was reported that beer drinking had been noted on the assembly line and that one whimsical chap welded his can to the inside of a fender. Workers claimed the speed and monotony of the process was deadly and inhuman. Turnover in "trained" workers was high. Senator Charles Percy of Illinois spoke to the National Conference on the Changing Work Ethic on March 27, 1973, stating that "the quality of work is an idea whose time has come"; that is, not only the product but the interface between man and his job.[18] Both Saab and Volvo manufacturers have faced this in Sweden by setting up team assemblies who produce "whole" cars demanding thought, varied skills and certainly the end of monotony. Work became "meaningful." It would appear on the surface (hard data is not yet at hand) that while initial production costs will rise, rejects, factory-financed repairs by dealers and callbacks (which have reached astounding levels on the American scene for this and other reasons) may quite possibly more than balance the obvious initial added expense. Probable retention of workers and potential lower absenteeism may be added to the benefit side; "work" may become "relevant," giving posteconomic psychic externalities. Much drudgery has been removed from many traditional white-collar tasks by use of the computer, emancipating drudges to become machine manipulators/masters or to shift to other jobs (what jobs?). There may be a new drudgery emergent in mere computer tending.

The second revolutionary concept in employment at all skill levels takes two forms: the sliding workday where the individual checks in and out at his or her convenience—even lengthening one day and shortening another slightly as long as a "full week," or forty to forty-five hours, is worked. This sliding workday is already well known in Germany and is being experimented with elsewhere. Obviously this scheme cannot be used for all levels in all office or factory work, but widespread application to increase job satisfaction *and* potential productivity (viewed holistically) is very possible. Even more spectacular is the four days, forty hours condensed work week with the days worked negotiated among the workers and the management.[19] The resultant long weekend (or midweek) break is reported to have much improved productivity in a variety of work situations (batch plants, for example), to have attracted topnotch personnel, and to have paid rich rewards to workers in family togetherness and leisure-time pursuits. If this became very widespread it could most certainly lead to varied settlement patterns, transportation oddities and recreational facility demands. The possible effects on central city at this moment are very hard to gauge.

Recreational and Aesthetic Planning

The age-old concern of traditional city planning has been aesthetics, an overriding concern with urban design. But it is certainly true that:

> Urban design, architecture, and landscape architecture are inescapable; *they are the only arts that cannot be avoided.* People can insulate themselves from painting, sculpture, literature, music, the dance. But they cannot avoid exposure to the design of buildings and open spaces or to the occasional but growing number of examples of urban design: the design of combinations of buildings and spaces.[20] (Italics, the editor.)

As oft repeated, the city planning profession has tended to consider itself as architecture on the grand scale and showed it through baroque grandeur, nineteenth-century pomposity (not excluding Stalinist "wedding cake" much later), right down to the casual cosmetics of certain marginal urban planning today. The "city beautiful" idea stemming from Daniel Burnham's "White City" of the 1893 World's Columbian Exposition and his Chicago Plan of 1909 lives with us yet; government legitimately still strives to put some aesthetic impress—or mere ornament—on the urban scene. But where is there empirical proof that the beautiful city of central Paris has actually ennobled the lives of Parisians or that the monumental buildings of Chandigarh or Brasilia will do the same for future Punjabis or Brasilians? Has Washington's imperial "magnificence" hindered black riots ten blocks from the White House or London's calm grandeur made contemporary British governmental action reflect inspirational wisdom? Or for that matter, has Toronto's handsome new city hall led to wiser administrative behavior there?

If we are true believers in the modern sense, that is, believers in the glories of nature and the ennobling effects of the natural environment, it ought to be argued equally vociferously that the man-made environment, the cityscape, is at least as personality rewarding/damaging as the natural environment. Most of us most of the time in most of the world have precious little contact (for most, none) with untouched-by-man nature. If our surroundings are to reward us they must be largely man made; modern man generally confronts man-made townscapes, not God-made landscapes. At this juncture the opinion seems warranted that no empirical evidence of a convincing sort will be forthcoming for some very considerable time, proving that scarce capital expended on urban aesthetics (under whatever definition of beauty) can be shown either by an economic or a trans-economic calculus to be worth the effort. But beyond, above—certainly outside—science or scientism is the judgment that urban aesthetics are one of the real or at least potential rewards of being a human being in "man's glorious cities." No Philistine can win against so old, rich and deep a human intuitive judgment, although most certainly the Philistine can make quite a case against the use of eternally scarce resources at a time of widely perceived human want for "artistic" urban expenditures.

Large segments of the ordinary public, unschooled in aesthetics, seem incapable of sharp reactions to the urban visual mess. They are just too accustomed to disorder. As Peter Blake in his profusely illustrated jeremiad at today's American city, *God's Own Junkyard,*[21] has shown, it would be possible to do much better than the truly revolting cities resulting from crass commercialism on this continent —and increasingly on the entire globe:

> ONE WORLD. The leading cities of the world are resembling each other more and more. They are being franchised into sameness. Holiday Inns, Sheraton and Hilton Hotels, McDonald's Hamburgers, Kentucky Fried Chicken, Shakey's Pizza Parlor, Pepsi, Coca-Cola, high-rise office buildings, supermarkets and shopping centers—all of these can be found outside the United States, the country of their origin.
> It is just a question of a few years before the Ginza in Tokyo will look like Broadway in New York which will look like Piccadilly in London which will look like the Champs-Elysées in Paris—at least from the franchise point of view.[22]

Even the somewhat naive "Beauty for America" theme, characteristic of the Texas' wide-open spaces viewpoint embraced by Lyndon Johnson with the full backing of the "Great Society" came to be focused on upgrading—generally at a simplistic cosmetic level—of the urban habitat.[23]

There is a surfeit of writing on the uglification and possible beautification of the city. Symptomatic of the traditional approach by excellent practicing architect/planners steeped in the older European tradition is the *Design in Town* issued by the British Ministry of Housing and Local Government. The national government wished to offer helpful assistance to those rebuilding the battered cities and at work in the New Towns after World War II.[24] Paul D. Spreiregen has done the same for the American scene, backed by the design-oriented American Institute of Architects in his *Urban Design: The Architecture of Towns and Cities*[25] "to foster creative design talent." This design ethic lies paraded starkly before us in Le Corbusier's Chandigarh planning and in the work of Costa/Niemeyer in Brasilia. Pushing a more wary practical aestheticism to larger, even regional dimensions, Christopher Tunnard and Boris Pushkarev, in *Man-Made America: Chaos or Control,*[26] move toward a happy union of cityscape and landscape as did Ian McHarg in *Design with Nature*[27] and William H. Whyte in his eminently convincing *Cluster Development*[28] on a domestic scale. Richard Dober has explored the relationship of human habitation to all space and has called for consultation between the actual user "clients" and professionals. He sees design as a servant of human needs (rapidly changing, too) and of the necessity to find a "home on earth"—even if temporary—and to create a sense of place to help in the search for identity so prated about today.[29]

Two promising developments need brief explanation. The first is the attempt to fix a hard metric or measurement of design excellence in the cityscape by Kevin Lynch and his followers, whose classic *The Image of the City,*[30] as viewed by a pedestrian, strives to identify the component part of the city image as a way to make that image rewarding. Does the city actually fix an image in the mind (and heart) of the observer? It appears to depend according to Lynch on four variable elements: *paths* (through the city); *edges* (to its districts and itself); *nodes* (activity centers); and *landmarks*. Could these not be quantified in due course? With John Appleyard and John R. Myer in *The View from the Road,*[31] he stretched the calculus by a shorthand note-taking form to record the impressions auto riders perceive moving into or out of urban places. Lynch has just added a fourth dimension time to his urban perception analysis in *What Time Is This?:*

> It is clear enough that space and time however conceived are the great framework within which we order our experience. We live in time-places.[32]

Here then could be the germ for the beginning of a quantified aesthetic to aid in battling the expert economic benefit/cost analysts on a dollar basis for a closer approximation to a true holistic benefit/cost analysis of urbanism.

A second most promising development is a slowly emerging social technology bridging the work of behavioral/social scientist with that of designers. Beyond Robert Sommer's *Personal Space*[33] there is a growing interest in the behavioral aspects of large-scale design, that is, how does urban design affect the behavior of groups of persons? If at the individual client or user level and also at the group-user level, a more meaningful relationship between physical form, societal structure and societal performance could be ascertained, a translation hopefully to a rewarding aesthetic might result in "paying off" with measurable increments of societal well-being. This would be a considerable gain beyond brilliant (if unreliable) intuitive insights about the effect of urban aesthetics on behavior.

Work and leisure have been increasingly dichotomized in the industrial city although now there is evidence that work, leisure and education are getting increasingly tangled up once again. The image of work as drudgery engaged in to earn leisure has increasingly overwhelmed the ordinary individual. There are a lucky few who seem still to enjoy work and find it "fun" such as: actors, painters, dancers, sculptors, musicians, salesmen reveling in the "selling game," professors (when not correcting papers), executives and politicians gaining power and honor through interesting manipulation, the occasional skilled craftsmen left in industrial society, racing car drivers, aircraft pilots. Even typists, it is reported.

A most pregnant analysis aimed at reforging into a unit this curious dichotomized modern man in industrial society is the attempt by the English writer Stanley Parker to make clear that *leisure* alone cannot be treated unless *work* too is rethought.[34] Actually many men *work* harder *at leisure* than they *relax at work;* it may be merely a question of definition and point of view where one activity ends and the other begins—actually the problem appears to be *living.* Possibly the *information* or *knowledge society* of the future as the Japanese term it contains the hidden answer.

No males in primitive society ever appeared unwilling to dump drudgery according to prevailing custom onto the backs of their women whenever possible. Males arrogated to themselves generally the embellishment of self and important objects, the exciting challenges of the hunt, rewarding fishing, while the fascinating arts of not-too-dangerous warfare paid high psychic rewards to men. Exhausting *labor* such as the all-night dance might be considered *work* (it was clearly fun) since such activities were engaged in for magico-religious "practical" purposes. Mass men and women today only grudgingly admit that exhausting efforts on the job sometimes pay psychic—as well as monetary—rewards. Admittedly the modern factory or office task can be regarded as dull! Such a value judgment on the other hand has been built into the culture; no doubt the gloomy Protestant work ethic played its significant part. Thus *work* today is largely discounted as rewarding and the period of time on the job has decreased until New York electricians are down to a minimal thirty-hour week at munificent pay scales. However, in this particular case the thirty-hour week is a ploy to skyrocket take-home pay by thus defining extra hours as overtime at time and one half or better. Over the past century the seventy-two-hour (or longer) work week has been shrunk to a normal forty- to forty-five-hour week with the addition of paid vacations and innumerable holidays variously honoring saints or national heroes, as the case may be. Pierre Dufau, chief architect of the Municipal Structures and National Palaces of Paris, estimates that shortly the year will be divided into 147 working days with 218 days off—away from the work place.[35] It would seem that the search for time off has been overwhelmingly successful. Time off each day, longer weekends, summer and winter vacations, late work career starts and early retirement in a longer life span —all this "awful" leisure is clearly a massive challenge![36] And all this with increasing affluence to "buy things to do"; the American family mean income is now $10,500 while some spectacular pay scales for simple workers suggest that there is possibly much unreported income. One of thirty-nine construction foremen at the World Trade Center in New York earned $94,000 in 1971, which indicates why domestic housing is priced beyond the means of half the local citizenry and why the World Trade Center costs have mounted to an estimated $700 million compared to the 1964 projected cost of $350 million.[37] Ordinary construction workers aided and abetted by their astute unions have annual incomes of this order[38]:

Indiana union workers average	$15,800
Southern California carpenters up to	$22,200
Cleveland common laborers up to	$27,000
New York electricians up to	$35,000

Compulsory mass education in the United States besides its nominal task of training youth appears to have three other covert functions: to keep them off the labor market, to train them to be superconsumers, and to afford splendid opportunities to *recreate* prior to *create!* World-wide youth culture (modified hippiedom) has in fact continued this leisured pattern "copping out" of the bourgeois work ethic.

Philosopher Sebastian de Grazia has pointed out in a mordant fashion that this modern free time has been in some cases literally "time to kill"; for others it has resulted in all sorts of subterfuge, second occupations or moonlighting which enable individuals to purchase the mindless, endless paraphernalia of consumer society and then to spend time taking care of the resultant gadgetry.[39] Unsurprisingly, De Grazia worships at the feet of the Greeks who regarded *leisure* as an important activity in which one engaged a 100 per cent of one's intellectual and physical self in upgrading the capacity to engage in sophisticated activities which in turn would further enhance one's resources. All this resulted in an ascending spiral which was no doubt as exhausting physically as it was rewarding. Several decades ago the hope was widespread that the ordinary human product of affluent society, faced theoretically by a legion of leisure choices, would increasingly opt for increasingly sophisticated time-off activities. This has simply not been so; recreation industries in the private sector especially in the United States have monopolized this free time by "spectatoritis" before the idiot box (TV), or in the cinema (now increasingly joined to it), or at great sport spectacles in enormous coliseums (bread and circus for the populace). In the United States today professional sports overlap each other in a year-long merry-go-round. Frenzied Europeans and Latin Americans kill each other at soccer (football) matches so they cannot be far behind. In the industrial society, the enormous capability of large-scale producers to *create markets* for their cornucopia of products[40] twists leisure activities. For example, such derived needs as outboard motors are besieging the globe and are undoubtedly *one* of the reasons for the world-wide search for water recreation areas. This leads to a skewed population distribution; as in the United States, and in Spanish resort areas, humans crowd the aqueous rims of the continents. With land in central city and transport to the outer reaches of usable open land/water so clogged, it is hardly surprising that the only solution is to cram one hundred thousand individuals in mammoth stadia to view some "world championship" or other. How many impossible acres would be needed for those one hundred thousand spectators to form two thousand teams (fifty to a side with adequate reserves) and actually participate directly in the sport! If the resident *aficionados* glued to a TV screen, beer in hand, numbering up to ten million were to be added to the potential players, it would take the Great Plains sodded with astroturf to support the milling hordes. It cannot happen here!

If the civilizations' great products are to be fostered, then the plastic, vocal, auditory, physical and intellectual *arts* and the three levels of the creation, the display/production and consumption of culture must all be planned (physically and societally) into the people place, the city.

There is no intention here to downgrade the essential simple rest (physical and psychic) so needed by urban man to counterbalance the hectic desired and not-desired interaction of urban society (mathematically, the potential daily meaningful and meaningless interaction of a small city of one hundred thousand inhabited by active individuals approaches infinity). Much of this, of course, can be tuned out—much cannot. Thus acres (even square miles) of quiet (hopefully green) must somehow be made available for the daily, weekly, yearly times off. Space, as indicated, is in short supply with resultant high costs. The denser the area the higher the need and, sadly enough, the higher the wear and tear on hard won public space for rest and refit. The high maintenance costs of overused central city parks is patent and to this, in the United States at least, must be added the costs of vicious, destructive vandalism. No one seems to identify with this public space except the paid keepers, who find their fractious charges almost impossible to guard. Americans view with envy the fragrant flower plantings of London, The Hague, Basel and Stockholm, to single out some notable cases; such public displays would not survive unguarded in an American city twenty-four hours. Even young trees are cut down or pulled out (in New York they are chained to a deeply buried concrete anchor to foil tree-nappers!). Unless the community itself has positive values of peace and quiet and unless the community identifies and supports simple recreation acreage it is hopeless to rely on fences and inadequate guards and continuous replacement of ripped-off furnishings. Thus societal structuring and individual responsibility must somehow be instilled in the mindless urbanite—especially the underoccupied, underemployed, undercivilized young.

To move to the higher reaches of sophisticated intellectual/artistic fare for the metropolis, it becomes clear that at least in capitalist society no profit is possible for performing or exhibiting "the higher culture." Production/distribution costs are too high and the limitation of space too great to bring in the level of mass participation that a society based on mass production must generate to show economic profit. It is completely clear that commercial activity has filled the profitable breach for "recreation" of a simple sort and that the fine fruits of civilization must be heavily *subsidized* at all three levels of creation, display/production and consumption. To concretize this briefly: Art is a lonesome creative act and there is no doubt that many artists have starved in learning how to produce some efflorescence of the divine spirit. Actually throughout history emperors, kings, popes, princes, tycoons, cities have commissioned/kept composers, musicians, painters and sculptors. Can the nation state (or a supranational government) do this, keeping clammy political paws off the entire creative process? The record of political interference and general ineptitude in totalitarian states is hardly encouraging. However, a guarded "yes" must be the answer. Search for talent (some "silent Milton," some "lost Leonardo") throughout the new crop of youth, facilities to learn in artistic directions, studios in which to paint, practice space for the dance are all needed. For example, in poor Finland, there are at least fifteen or twenty sculptors working hard in fine government-subsidized studios in greater Helsinki. After developing the drama, symphonies, books, sculpture, ballets or dancing ability, a market both public and private must somehow be made available in special galleries, markets, theatres, festivals so that the artist is rewarded with notice, prestige, honor and even a living wage. This costs government money too. It is noteworthy that probably the two finest ballet troupes in the world are socialist: the Bolshoi and the Royal Ballet of England—despite world-wide, jam-packed performances they are only made solvent by state subsidy.

Rolf Liebermann, lately intendant of the Hamburg State Opera and probably the most prestigious practicing operatic administrator in the world, has recently accepted the challenge of reinvigorating the Paris Opéra, which has in recent memory become "a byword for artistic obscurantism, technical backwardness and an administrative system of Byzantine complexity."[41] The French Government through the incumbent President has told him to make it into the world's finest with an annual subsidy of about $14 million. Composer and conductor Liebermann, a Swiss, has succinctly and importantly stated his position on government-supported art (in this case the opera):

> But from my point of view the problem of the Met [the Metropolitan Opera of New York] is that one is always dependent on the goodwill [contributions] of people who may or may not be willing to help, so that one can never plan on a really secure budget. That's one dangerous thing. The other is that if the budget is based on a 96 per cent box office, then that excludes every risk and anything modern. It excludes everything that makes it worthwhile being at the head of such a house. *I prefer an opera that is subsidized by the state.* Then you *have not merely the possibility, but the duty to be adventurous.*[42] (Italics, the editor's.)

Art only truly exists if consumed, which is a rather nice special sort of consumption, because the product (if well managed) does not wear out and conceivably could be improved, as in the repetitious study and production of a classic opera! But to consume, man must be educated to understand and must somehow come to feel that it is worth the effort to rise to the level of advanced creative activity—i.e., civilization.

Alvin Toffler, with a shrewd nose for emergent ideas, has catalogued the explosion of culture consumerism since the end of World War II. Affluent society is out to buy ART as any other consumption good and on the fringe fortunes have been made certainly in record pressing, pop music/art and by the exploratory mass media. Culture has become the latest status symbol for the striving middle class, but the mass society remains relatively untouched.[43]

It seems less and less likely in the crowded world of today and in the more crowded one of tomorrow that participation in the arts will ever be possible on a mass scale despite worthy/varied efforts to switch spectators into participants, an alternative more rewarding role. This would call for new and highly involved societal structuring (including financing) as well as physical planning (including financing) if man as *autonomous personality* is ever to develop his full presumed potential. This sadly may be a chimera for a packed mass society staring us in the face for the twenty-first century unless new hypertechnology of two-way cable TV is ever fully perfected and made available—a most unlikely event for a number of decades and probably longer. The use of leisure is perhaps the end value of all physical societal planning; it is the pay-off of civilized life. And the understanding and structuring for leisure are both only in their infancy.

This point of view in true egalitarian vein was cogently expressed in 1965 in that significant report of the Rockefeller Brothers Fund panel on the future of the theatre, dance, and music in America (the plastic arts were excluded but are most certainly of equal symbolic and real value)[44]:

> The panel is motivated by the conviction that the arts are not for a privileged few but for the many, that their place is not on the periphery of society but at its center, that they are not just a form of recreation but are of central importance to our well-being and happiness.

Despite the proposed 1974 federal United States budget for the National Foundation on the Arts and the Humanities of $120 million (with an increase of $60 million for generally pop-art activities in connection with the American Revolution Bicentennial) with reinforcement from the states and the private sector, this nation is not yet prepared to put the necessary financial muscle and thought behind this basic component of the *Quality of Life.* The furthering of creativity in the higher culture is most certainly worthy of better planning and more directive financing than a hit or miss system of income tax deduction. Western Europe is deeply involved and Japan characteristically is preparing to forge ahead; the socialist world already accepts its politicized version of the higher culture as a state obligation while developing nations generally lack the resources.

TIME: CYBERNETIC "ROLLING PLANNING"

The planning process has been conceptualized in six stages as (1) setting values or goals, (2) toting up available resources, (3) making alternate possible plans, (4) selecting "the" plan, (5) administering the plan, and (6) finally Utopia! The old watchword was "flexible planning," which caused certain wags to question the reality of such items as flexible highways, skyscrapers and housing developments. The new word in good currency is the feedback cybernetics system of Norbert Wiener[45] where loops keep returning from stage (5) to (1) altering *values* or *goals;* changing (2) *resources* quite obviously; (3) generating *new alternate plans;* thus resulting in (4) a *revised plan,* and patently (5) *new operant administrative patterns* once again. Stage (6), Utopia, now goes out the window in a never-ending system of proximate—or better ever-receding alternative Utopias —a suboptimization process.

This by no means is to negate Utopian thought which has been recognized by a number of American planning intellectuals as having a most legitimate function in mind stretching and in sketching alternative possible urban futures—useful both for stage (1) goals or values and (3) alternative possible plans. Without imaginative creativity[46] in which Utopian thought can play a part, there will be nothing worth while from which to choose.

One of the most puzzling problems in a cybernetic five- or six-stage planning process is that of value changes or shifts which come about for varied and complex reasons (not necessarily connected with the system that is being "planned"). Recent macroscale examples are the moratorium on the Alaska pipeline and the virtual cutoff the space program. Such shifts have complicated practically all productive processes in the developed world indicating altered priorities (not unconnected obviously with new environmental concerns) which have led among other things to the cancellation of the American SST after an exploratory research and development program amounting to at least $400 million. Value forecasting is a puzzling operation with as yet very little to merit even a quasi-scientific label. Since planning goals are to realize preferred values in the future, this brings the entire planning process into question. Progress toward agreed-on goals can be monitored by "evaluating" results; how "to figure" quantitatively benefits/costs under such a calculus is not yet possible. A preliminary attempt at a methodological framework for the predictive analysis of values has been worked out specifically to aid technological forecasting relevant to planning, but much remains still to be done.[47] No one seems to know what will be important in the future for sure.

No *future* planner pretends that long-range planning is as certain as short-range planning. But as has already been explored, short-range naive ad-hoc coping ends up with nations and cities in the soup, as America's Indochinese war and urban renewal give both external and internal evidence of the wages of sinful shortsightedness. Unquestionably though, unclarity ahead increases at a geometric rate with time. Certain American cities through capital budgeting over rolling five-year periods (Philadelphia, for example) give signs of growing up in fiscal backing for planning. The federal budget seems incapable of stretching beyond the next fiscal year except in certain narrow functions. The Port of New York and New Jersey Authority for many years reportedly has run "standard world" policy projections (no major changes expected) of up to fifteen or twenty years with firm *plans* for five and ten. This appears pretty much to be based on straight-line extrapolation of existent trends, although alternate societal scenarios are explored.

The complex world of *futurism, econometrics, systems analysis and systems dynamics, technological forecasting and technology assessment, environmental assessment, modeling* of national, regional and urban systems, and *gaming* is only just emerging, but it now seems reasonably certain that despite easily recognizable deficiencies in long-range planning (a Marxist "must" for at least one hundred years), it most assuredly is better than no long-range planning. This is especially so if the future-oriented schemes are *continuously, formally* and *astutely* modified by feedbacks from the changing real world, both *within* the system planned and *outside* it. While it seems unlikely that man can *invent the future*[48] afresh, he most certainly is playing a major role in making it right now and should be alerted to the distant (as well as the immediate) benefits and costs in his eternal plotting and planning.

French, Japanese and Swedish national planning with long-range and medium-range, as well as short-range, parameters is already a reality; within such systems the key urban nodes are the important considerations in structuring the national society for obvious reasons. But nobody appears to have convinced key decision makers that the energy catastrophe that arrived in late 1973 was a reality. A systems break?

Future studies, per se, are enjoying a considerable vogue throughout the world today especially in professional circles (where almost everyone is now alert enough to keep glancing over his shoulder at the on-rushing future). The popular mind, too, has been widely attracted by "futuristics" as an aftermath of Herman Kahn and Anthony Wiener's *The Year 2000: A Framework on Speculation for the Next Thirty-Three Years*[49] and, of course, Alvin Toffler's *Future Shock.*[50] An important contribution made by Kahn and Wiener was the plotting of an interacting thirteenfold, long-term trend, since revamped to fifteenfold, consisting of[51]:

1. Increasingly sensate (empirical, this-worldly, secular, humanistic, pragmatic, manipulative, explicitly rational, utilitarian, contractual, epicurean, hedonistic, etc.) cultures
2. Bourgeois, bureaucratic, and meritocratic elites
3. Centralization and concentration of economic and political power
4. Accumulation of scientific and technical knowledge
5. Institutionalization of technological change, especially research, development, innovation, and diffusion
6. Increasing military capability
7. Westernization, modernization and industrialization
8. Increasing affluence and (recently) leisure
9. Population growth
10. Urbanization, recently suburbanization and "urban sprawl"—soon the growth of megalopolises
11. Decreasing importance of primary and (recently) secondary and tertiary occupations; increasing importance of tertiary and (recently) quaternary occupations
12. Increasing literacy and education and (recently) "knowledge industry" and increasing role of intellectuals
13. Innovative and manipulative social engineering—i.e., rationality increasingly applied to social, political, cultural, and economic worlds as well as to shaping and exploiting the material world—increasing problem of ritualistic, incomplete, or pseudo rationality
14. Increasingly universality of the multifold trend
15. Increasing tempo of change in all the above.

The somewhat concealed factor of importance in these fifteen themes is their interrelatedness—each affects the others. Some are clearly intuitive judgments with little empirical backing but could lead the way to eventual mathematical modeling of society on computers. The unaided human brain simply cannot cope with cybernetic feedback from fifteen interacting variables. This, of course, is the theoretical basis for Jay Forrester's/Dennis Meadows' systems dynamics using fewer variables. Rachel L. Carson's devastating *The Silent Spring*[52] can be considered the send-off for the environmental pack baying at man's galloping ruination of his habitat by lack of foresight. The gloomy environmental prognostications in *The Limits to Growth*[53] and the world-wide success of *Future Shock,* as noted, on the impermanence of everything have further spread sensitivity over future implications. There are in the neighborhood of five hundred to one thousand future study courses taught at the undergraduate and graduate level in American and Canadian universities.[54] These courses employ the standard projective techniques: the codified expert prediction of the Delphi Method, straight-line extrapolations, scenarios of alternative possible futures, gaming, systems analysis with or without mathematical models. Urban/regional/national planning have shown signs of the use of systems analysis and mathematical modeling as well as the use of simplistic straight-line extrapolation and scenarios of alternate possible futures, with increasing interest and possible success. As Göran Sidenbladh, Stockholm's experienced planner, once remarked in stressing the need for long-range planning: "Everything lasts longer than one thinks." He could well have added, as all politicos, planners, bureaucrats are well aware, that "everything takes longer than one thinks," which stresses the enormous importance of operant delivery systems for results in the real world.

DELIVERY SYSTEMS: THE POLICY SCIENCES

Having explored at some length "goals for a good society," a rather considerable number of alternative possible urban futures and a National Urban Policy and Plan, one is driven to the realization that quite probably "more of the same" will be the lot of Western urbanism for the rest of this century and quite possibly well on into the next. This probably will be true for the socialist nations as well; a considerable degree of urban chaos is predictable for the developing countries. It is likely that there will be no urban systems break; far-out options will occur only here and there. The standard world projection of *one spread city*[55] slopping untidily into the next is all too likely for those nations incapable of the act of will, the intellectual effort, and the *Realpolitik* ability to direct their growth, as well as sufficient consensus and capital resources to bring about actively planned, alternate rewarding large-scale variations of the human condition. Superior "intentional societies and ordered environments" still seem just beyond our grasp.[56]

There is at hand a growing intellectual/expert disillusionment, already referred to above as the "Cambridge Syndrome," prevalent on the banks of the Charles River. This very critical point of view emanates from the questing research carried on at the MIT-Harvard Joint Center for Urban Studies. Typical published products of this group are Daniel P. Moynihan's *Maximum Feasible Misunderstanding*[57] (lambasting the Office of Economic Opportunity) and Edward Banfield's sour look at *The Unheavenly City,*[58] pointing out the counterproductive results of the national educational, poverty and crime prevention programs.

Bernard J. Frieden, present head of the Joint Center, studied housing programs in Boston to discover:

> In most of these programs, we estimate that between one-fourth and one-half the total federal subsidy does not reach the residents, but goes for federal and local administrative expenses and for tax benefits to investors. . . . In one instance . . . the city's administrative expenses during the past one and one-half years actually equaled two-thirds of the total value of loans and grants made to home owners.[59]

Lloyd Rodwin, former head of the MIT Department of Urban Studies and Planning, reached these somewhat jaundiced conclusions in his trail-breaking study of national urban growth strategies *Nations and Cities*[60]: ". . . there are many problems *in* cities and *of* cities which can be solved or ameliorated simply by giving people or cities more money" but others that clearly cannot. It would appear that in the United States and elsewhere too little is presently known to design correct programs "to better" the urban lot and even less about delivering/implementing programs—assuming they are "valid"—without counterproductive results. In effect, the existing ignorance of content and of application in planning tends often to exacerbate the situation.

The numerous bits and pieces of the elaborate jigsaw of wisdom, skills, resources and power needed to develop urbanism are still not in place. And only now and then in particular spots in particular countries do particularly rewarding clear interface connections give glimpses of the potential for guiding urban society into a rewarding civilization of style, quality and humanity. All this can take place only among peoples in harmonious international relationship with a renewed sympathetic contact with the natural environment of battered spaceship earth.

The so-called *policy sciences* (better, "policy studies") are a forthright attempt —if not yet remotely science—at marshaling existent capabilities for intelligent decision making and delivery (as well as building further capabilities) out of a mix of (a) the behavioral/social sciences, (b) the intellectual technology of systems analysis et al., (c) technological forecasting and assessment, long-range planning and futures studies and (d) the practical experience of real world politics—the "soft side of policy formation." This latter, largely intuitive wisdom, can be reinforced with profit by hard-data empirical research carried out by behavioral political scientist and political sociologists. Harold Lasswell[61] after a lifetime of work in studying and designing operationally oriented societal structures across cultures, Yehezkel Dror[62] of Hebrew University and the Rand Corporation, and the prolific and ingenious Amitai Etzioni are among the leading exponents of this new thrust[63] toward actually getting something significant *accomplished* rather than the mere *proliferation* of absolutely splendid ideas. John Friedman, an experienced urban and regional planner in both developed and developing areas, has applied this approach in "a theory of transactive planning": "This style—transactive planning—proceeds essentially by a process of mutual learning between expert and client groups, in which interpersonal relations acquire central importance. The dominant mode of communication in transactive planning is dialogue; it is through dialogue that knowledge becomes *morally engaged and embedded in a matrix of on-going actions.*"[64] (Italics, editor's.)

"During the twenty years which have passed [from Lasswell's 1951 proposal for founding policy sciences], many components of policy sciences were invented or significantly developed—such as operations research, systems analysis, theory of games, cybernetics, general systems theory, strategic analysis, systems engineering and various branches and aspects of applied social sciences."[65] Not only fine thoughts, glorious paper plans, but *measurable results in the real world* of people, institutions and things—including urban society as *the* activity node—is the object of the operation. Can democratic regimes accomplish this? Over the long sweep of history, it would appear that only tyrants or authoritarian regimes have been able to construct physically elegant cities. Democracies boast of their great people-enhancing skills, it remains to be seen whether this is in fact true beyond the reasonable accomplishments to date shown here in our test cases. Will it be necessary to perfect a version of "scientific Machiavellianism" in order to attain good ends and will the ends in turn be corrupted by such means? If, however, *inertia* or *stasis* is preferable, most certainly we in the Western world (with a few exceptions including that of "honorary Western nation" Japan) would have adequate means to rest immobile until the situation blows up in our collective faces. The socialist states are driving in tactical and strategic zigzags into the future, while the developing nations are stumbling into a world they never made and hardly understand. It is hard to predict Utopias for the First World and impossible for the Second and Third worlds for the foreseeable future.

Thus it behooves all concerned with building alternative urban societies for a better future to be acutely aware of the most recent developments in advanced delivery systems.[66] Four key components of the new complex mix of undertakings, which may promise in time a capability sufficient to develop and carry out national urbanization policies of merit, will be touched on briefly below. They are: symbiotic intellectual and technological technologies; societal indicators, a necessary calculus; behavioral and organizational technologies; and resource allocation for positive reinforcement.

Clearly there are other facets and varied interfaces in addition to those four—for example the mastery of legal forms in constitutional/parliamentary democracies is a must; nevertheless it is felt that both intellectually and operationally the four mutually reinforcing technologies and their subsets considered here have promise for eventual coping.

Symbiotic Intellectual and Technological Technologies

Massive amounts of reliable data carefully collected and collated, stored for easy retrieval, analyzed and eventually manipulated through yet-to-be-perfected mathematical models, offer the only firm basis for successful plan design and more importantly implementation. This arcane world rests on the electronic computer. Without adequate knowledge nothing works as Auguste Comte observed well over a century ago *savoir pour prévoir et prévoir pour pouvoir* (know in order to foresee and foresee in order to be capable of doing). It is even more so today as complexity escalates and change accelerates. There is a double envelopment attack possible in the problems of understanding and managing both complexities and change, consisting of first a symbiotic relationship among a whole bundle of operationally oriented, powerful operant intellectual technologies subsumed under the general heading of systems analysis/operations research[67] and, second, the technical technology of the computer plus its attendant softwear. The fruitful combination of these rapidly expanding technologies is probably the *only viable out* for actually guiding a NUP with any degree of wisdom and precision.

> General systems theory is a name which has come into use to describe a level of theoretical model-building which lies somewhere between the highly generalized constructions of pure mathematics and the specific theories of the specialized disciplines. . . . In recent years there has been an additional development of great interest in the form of "multisexual" interdisciplines. . . . Cybernetics for instance comes out of electrical engineering, neurophysiology, physics, biology, with even a dash of economics. Information theory, which originated in communications engineering, has important applications in many fields stretching from biology to the social sciences. Organization theory comes out of economics, sociology, engineering, physiology, and management science itself is an equally multidisciplinary product.[68]

All of which indicates that the "policy sciences" are in effect "management sciences" devoted to the nurture and delivery of future plans largely in the public sector.

To solve existent and emergent urban problems and to make the multitude of decisions that must be made by responsible elected officials and their advisers, a whole battery of analytic techniques[69] drawn from a great variety of fields/operations are increasingly available.

A combination of these skills put man on the moon, for better or worse, and could conceivably make it rewarding for him to remain on earth. Systems problem-solving and decision making leading to optimization and suboptimization of given values with minimal costs reach through the curricula of the graduate business, public administration and planning schools and they are beginning to be practiced increasingly both in business and in government.

Next in analytic techniques are *operations research*[70] and *game theory* followed by *systems analysis* and *general systems theory*[71] per se, which runs all the way from simplistic role playing exploring simulated real world situations to extensive computerized interactions employing sophisticated mathematical models. Much of the early theory here stems from military models and has antecedents in economics going back to World War II.[72] *Cybernetics* (communication theory), our old friend, is part of the bag of tricks drawn originally from feedback in electrical circuits, brilliantly applied by Karl Deutsch to governmental operations,[73] and by Richard Meier to urban society.[74] It is basic to the technique of "rolling planning" as a process. Finally these coping techniques move into *mathematical models and simulation* which is the pay-off dream of every macro-scale, holistic planner. Here "experimentation" with conceivable costs can be carried out on alternate feasible urban/national futures. Jay Wright Forrester's[75] work has been a powerful attention getter for a cybernetic mathematical model of urban processes far too complex for the unaided human intellectual capability to grasp. John Taylor,[76] an English planner and planning teacher, has collected nearly 500 models encompassing the fields of business and management studies, geography, teacher training, and urban studies. Karl Loewenstein[77] presents in a practical fashion some fifteen readily accessible games which could be a useful bridge between "systems analysis and public administration" as Allan G. Feldt has phrased it.[78] Finally, these analytic operant modeling techniques reach a crescendo in regional planning,[79] national planning and such global cybernetic systems (systems dynamics) as *World Dynamics*[80] and *The Limits to Growth*.[81] The French Government through DATAR is moving toward national planning simulation and it is understood that both the USSR and Japan are already so engaged.

The urban place has already been approached as a physical environmental system, a behavioral system, an economic system, a political system and a social system. It can be better viewed if examined as a subsystem to a whole national system, the concern here. Only a *cyborg,* half man and half computer, will be able to digest the masses of human transactions, order them, analyze them and manipulate them on a national scale to maximize decisions under *any* agreed on value system. No human being or group of human beings can manage a NUP without a warm relationship with the computer "machine."

The basis for valid empirical knowledge in the formation of urban policy are masses of transaction facts. Banked computers could store *all* needed human transactions (or samples thereof?) almost automatically in due course. Such data (collected through innumerable networks of urban data centers) would serve as the basis for models/simulations/gaming to create alternative possible future designs. These designs *would be tested* as models with minimum expense and human disruption rather than by the wild political assays, which have characterized heretofore so often the meanderings of urban planning and national urban policies everywhere. Such a hopeful situation seems still far ahead, but the bits are mounting into an already respectable and useful pile.

> Within the span of a few years the information systems field has become a major apostle industry in virtually every technologically developed country in the world. Although many manual systems were and are in operation, the development of high speed electronic computers [linked in nets] has brought about a virtual revolution in terms of the quantities of data that are being requested, collected, processed, disseminated and applied at every level of government, in business, in universities and so on.[82]

Problems have arisen and will continue to plague so essential and fundamental an operation, such as standardization compatability, transferability, coding and confidentiality. The last is already much discussed as a complex and important issue basic to the human value of privacy, which in any case is going to be most difficult to maintain in the crowded future world.[83]

Societal Indicators: a Necessary Calculus

Given the huge increased power of the growing intellectual technology which has been enhanced by the ever burgeoning computer capabilities to store and more especially to manipulate data, some broad calculus of both quantity and quality must be developed. This is needed to: monitor ongoing social change as an "early warning system," to weigh alternate possible planning solutions to physical and social problems, and to evaluate the success or lack of success in attaining stated goals of adopted plans.

In effect, various forms of "evaluative research: usable methods for assessing program effectiveness"[84] are very much in demand to find out actually what might be or is taking place. Among such methods are cost-benefit analysis (usually in monetary terms), programming-planning budgeting (largely economic considerations), experimental research designs and social statistics (social accounting) for basic data purposes, generally known as *social indicators* (SI). This latter promising value calculus is already attracting world-wide attention.

In the United States, inspired by the success since 1946 of a yearly economic report (economic indicators), expressed readily in monetary form, and since the founding of the Republic of demographic statistics (indicators), with a relatively simple number of variables (sex, age, location), thinkers have searched for a richer or "transeconomic" calculus for measuring society's changes, structure and adequacy of functioning. Early called "social indicators," it now seems preferable to look upon such statistics as holistic measuring devices for *all* aspects of society's well-being or "quality of life" (QOL). Thus a better term is *societal indicators*—under which existent economic and demographic indicators would have a crucial and honored position. There seems slight doubt that hard, but simplistic, economic indicators in monetary terms have skewed important national and local decision making. But just how does one weigh in with soft societal indicators? What does one include and how does one weigh symphonies played against the number of toilets per one hundred people in some sort of valid measurement system. And how can one weigh those gossamer things ("amenities" the English call them) not yet weighable—possibly never! Raymond Bauer of the prestigious operationally oriented School of Business Administration at Harvard, fired the first widely noticed, heavy salvo in 1966.[85] He collected a number of social scientists in an attempt to survey "the entire set of social indicators used in our society" and to block out areas of inadequate understanding and inadequate data. Probably the most informed contribution was by Bertram Gross, "The State of the Nation: Social Systems Accounting."[86] Gross examined both the adequacy of the system structure as well as how the system actually performed which he followed in 1969 with *Social Intelligence for America's Future.*[87] This is a wide-ranging symposium drawing on a variety of specialists to consider the collection of adequate data on the polity (participation, civil liberties); the cultural context (individual and group values, education and learning science and technology, mass media, the arts); social problems (poverty, inequality and conflict, unemployment, discrimination, crime, social breakdown, health and "well being"); and environments (natural, urban). The Russell Sage Foundation has been actively promoting similar research under Eleanor Sheldon and Wilbert E. Moore, which was packaged during 1968 in a holistic presentation[88] with the basic goal of monitoring social change by indicators, marching from (a) the *demographic base* through (b) *structural features:* measurement of economic growth; labor force trends; knowledge and technology; political changes; family change, religious change to (c) *distributive features:* consumption, leisure/culture; health; education and (d) *aggregative features:* social mobility; and welfare.

These quasi-catalogues have roused genuine qualms about the potential invasion of privacy on all aspects of an individual's life in massive detailed data banks and the enormous costs involved; this is indicated by the thrust of the topics on which detailed information would be required. However, the National Opinion Research Center at the University of Chicago, funded by the National Science Foundation, already appears to be by-passing both problems by collecting such information by a national probability sample of (only) nine thousand persons in five hundred neighborhoods, interviewing all the selected individuals in a rotating group fashion at least once a year. The idea is to give various federal agencies "guide fixes on a variety of community services, from housing loans to hospitals."[89] Does everyone have to be in the data bank, given the already existent sampling expertise?

It must be noted that governments other than the United States have not been unmindful of societal indicators. England is producing *Social Trends,* which made its bow in 1970 as "a new government statistical service publication from the Central Statistical Office about people and their environment."[90] Similar yearbooks are traditional in all Western nations. Our own Census Bureau has been at work for almost two hundred years actually with a rich fare of societal statistics as well as precise demographic ones; for example, the housing data collected is basic to all urban debate and plans. In Japan, a group of scientists and economists suggested recently a more meaningful "Gross National Satisfaction" index of broad humanitarian scope to replace the conventional GNP.

Thus it is not unexpected that *Toward a Social Report* was issued in 1969[91] by the Department of Health, Education and Welfare as a preliminary step toward regular social reporting. Lyndon Johnson had charged the Secretary of HEW in 1966 "to develop the necessary social statistics and indicators to supplant those prepared by the Bureau of Labor Statistics and the Council of Economic Advisers." A distinguished panel did the report on seven more meaningful bundles of societal concerns (beyond demography and hard economics). These points are worth noting as a tidy early summary of expressed official concern:

1. health and illness
2. social mobilities
3. our physical environment
4. income and poverty
5. public order and safety
6. learning, science and art
7. participation and alienation.

The connection with President Nixon's National Goals Staff and the evaluation of "progress" toward such goals is obvious.

The United Nations on a global scale has for some time done a periodic *Report on the World Social Structure,*[92] influenced by the 1954 *Report on International Definition and Measurement of Standards and Levels of Living Standards.*[93] "Standards" are, of course, values/goals and "level of living" societal indicators.

Thus there is a new evaluative planning expertise growing that is based on stored data, which uses fantastic computer memory banks, a most necessary tool for holistic planning. Each of the categories of social interest is capable of being broken down ingeniously into numerical terms—although not absolutely precise. Even in such a delicate area as art appreciation, some indication of interest and depth of penetration can be taken in classical record sales, symphony tickets, museum attendance, audiences for special programs on TV, etc. There is, of course, no guarantee of what transpires during, or as a result of, such exposures/transactions, but they certainly are *not* meaningless. It should be noted that quality often is a form of quantity—not in all cases—but, for example, the number of births/deaths of mother and child is a pretty clear indicator of prenatal and delivery of *"good* health care." The level of culture is "higher" it would appear if 90 per cent of a city's population partook of symphony concerts in the park than if only 10 per cent did. On the other hand, how is an "excellent" cityscape to be quantified as compared to a "poor" one despite Kevin Lynch—and how would excellent be "expressed" in percentages and weighted (the old question again) in dollars? Hardheaded and reliable *evaluation research* is still ahead both *before* and *after* the inauguration of an action program. Is there *no* way to trade X number of persons hungry versus Y number of persons enjoying a magnificent new waterside park or a handsome bit of sculpture? Do X deaths from sickle cells weigh more than Y symphonies? Societal indicators as yet cannot give preference—only increasingly precise data as to what is now, how are the data changing and what are likely to be the results of alternate possible plans viewed in a holistic, entire spectrum fashion. This would be a mighty step for man, if such ordered knowledge were at the fingertip of decision makers, and for the citizen on whom the decisions will impinge.

Finally, note should be taken of the biennial *Report on National Growth* required by the Housing and Urban Development Act of 1970; the first was issued by President Nixon in February 1972. Originally intended as a "Report on Urban Growth" based on *Toward Balanced Growth, Quantity with Quality,* it became obvious that "rural and urban community developments are inseparably linked."[94] This first report marks the beginning of a systematic effort to:

1. understand the forces that are shaping the communities in which we live and work;
2. articulate some of the challenges that must be confronted as the nation responds to the challenge of growth;
3. identify recent developments at the state and local level for coping more effectively with growth;
4. identify major actions of the federal government undertaken to deal with the problem of growth;
5. advance recommendations for federal action to strengthen the nation's ability to deal with the challenges of growth more effectively.

Each of these five objectives are addressed in a separate chapter of the Presidential summary.

This is a brave effort and a useful start, but it is nowhere remotely a thorough pulse-taking effort in firm quantitative terms of the American QOL, which is the *only hope* for an empirical way to plan and monitor a NUP. What is clearly needed is the *Social Report* called for by the Department of Health, Education and Welfare in 1969, listing hard information available and hard information not available. Bertram Gross has named this an important "Domestic Intelligence Gap" of *"one-sided, missing, distorted, misinterpreted, or unused information."*[95] There is much yet to be done even though *technology assessment* has come into the planning of all U.S. federal agencies through the Environment Protection Agency as an earnest contribution of the new sensitivity to holistic value accounting and in the U. S. Congressional Office of Technology Assessment which became operational in the winter of 1973–74.

Behavioral and Organizational Technologies

Men have been pushing men around for "good and sufficient" reasons since man was identifiably man. Animals educate their young and the intriguing, if inexact, findings of ethology show that there are most certainly hierarchies and "leaders" lead. The presumably innocent young are indoctrinated in human society both formally and informally with the going values and behavior patterns; neither sticks too well as recent evidence suggests. And the reactions to being pushed around during a lifetime by parents, teachers, policemen, officers, government officials and bosses occupy a considerable amount of the verbal activity of modern citizenry of, at least, the tolerant democratic societies. In at least two thirds of the world's cultures, *direction* appears to be more accepted—although not necessarily acceptable. A quantum jump will be made in this section to a heuristic position that physical/societal planning is "valid" and therefore should be put into operation. On the surface this is clearly untrue, since evidence indicates how shaky the whole planning operation is. On the other hand, plans are potentially moving toward a "better" society; despite Sorel and minor anarchistic prophets of the New Left, drift has never been spectacularly successful. It would be hard to conceive of a "no-plan" Greater Tokyo of twelve million or a future Calcutta metropolitan area with still no valid operational plans by the year 2000 containing upward of twenty million pullulating humans! Thus the question remains: How to manipulate humans by changing their behavior patterns directly as individuals and in groups and how to "crate" them in societal boxes, often physically outlined, which might make possible for them approximations of the "good life"—or better—alternative "good lives?"

There would be no great virtue here in developing learning theory at great length or exploring how individuals are socialized to a given culture or subculture. Society functions because of shared understandings in an invisible gossamer network in the minds and behavior patterns of the human participants. There will never be beautiful cities until there are beautiful people; no amount of physical infrastructure and societal institutional structure will make an urbanized world rewarding or even livable—unless warm group expectations are approximately shared. Although there is an initial infancy/childhood/youth indoctrination period, by the time adult status is reached individual behavior patterns are fairly well stabilized or set, nevertheless socialization (obedience training?) goes on until death. In today's rapidly changing cultural context under a situation of *quasi-directed* cultural change (i.e., piecemeal planning), it is perforce necessary "to educate" adult populations as to what is attainable and its benefits and costs and how to get there by operant structural design. In short, adult behavior too must change and cannot remain "set" in the modern world. "Elitist" experts have important roles in the clarification and weighing of values/goals and in developing methods for reaching varied options in the real world of always limited societal resources and finite human and societal capabilities.

Behavioral control has an ominous sound suggesting IBM cards and data banks at the mildest and the two-way unavoidable television screen of *1984* at the worst. Actually all education, including adult education, is behavior control, so it is hardly foreign to human existence, especially today in the high technology industrial city. Education in its richest sense is aimed at opening up possibilities and underlining potentialities for the autonomous person; most people simply are not aware of the physical options in design which are possible and much less aware of alternate complex sociopolitico-economic options congruent with such fresh physical forms. The ordinary citizen (and even the planning experts) know even less about *delivery systems,* as should be amply clear by now. Thus the planner, guided by his political master, must nurture a deep mutual understanding, trust and acquiescence to innovation in the population and in himself. There are slick ways to move people—from advertising through propaganda (government advertising) to brainwashing. This latter was (and still is) practiced with great enthusiasm and thoroughness in the Chinese Peoples' Republic.[96] There are newer possibilities, even fancier technical and behavioral technology devices at hand as *catalysts* of manipulated information: music (hard rock), rhythmic dancing (Shakers), mouthed slogans and songs, the pageantry of Red Square and the Nuremberg rallies, Mau Mau oath rituals.[97] Today these techniques are being "improved upon" by drugs—long known in primitive cultural rites—now much developed for use in psychotherapy, as well as the more traditional psychotherapy, and action-therapy.[98] Thus methods used to treat the mentally "sick" can be used to change the "normal" individual. Hypnosis, psychopharmacology, programmed learning, psychosurgery, direct electric controls,[99] mood drugs and chemically aided memory are all with us or not too far ahead. Out of this welter of often extreme technologies, planners will have to choose in facing the necessity to condition (in addition to themselves) both the young and adults to accept eternal change in physical and societal forms for a proximate future where society continuously adjusts both itself and its man-made environments without stop! Despite themselves, planners will be involved in planning human beings.

An important caveat should be brought out here at once; the spectrum of manipulative techniques touched on should not be overestimated. Very recent work at the Center for Policy Research at Columbia University is leading Amitai Etzioni to the uncomfortable conclusion that human beings are not very easily changed after all. Seat belts are much cheaper and more efficacious than driver training in cutting down highway casualties and other technological devices are more useful than "education" in "improving behavior."[100] In addition to such seemingly simplistic technological shortcuts in implementing social change, as a corollary it may be best to accept people as they are and change the circumstances in which they live "to solve" social problems. This is a new slant on the behavioral basis of design and vice versa (the design basis of behavior).

Going beyond essentially individual education, one moves into group dynamics (small group behavior)[101] and on to collective or organizational behavior. The recent history of American major election campaigns suggests that the expenditure of sufficient resources can cause latent drifts to be mobilized into voting activity to produce desired results. It is conceivable that if a national campaign with comparable resources were to be launched to build automobile-free central cities, such cities would be built. But no one has the available resources adequate for that purpose, or too many have the resources not to want it carried out, it would seem. Again on a macroscale, as indicated above, John K. Galbraith has shown massive productivity can create demand; the American automobile industry and its powerful allies are not prepared to allow auto-free cities to happen. The evidence is in that "follow the Fuehrer," "worship Mao Tse-tung" and "love that gutsy bus" can all be instilled into the mass mind in time, given sufficient resources. According to this line of thinking, when and if "big government" wants "big planning" strongly enough then there will be "big planning"; and that is not likely to occur until those who run big government perceive that their roles are in jeopardy by potential crisis/chaos engendered by an increasingly restive citizenry.

Structural inadequacy: It seems doubtful whether the modern democratic governments of industrial society are adequately organized to manage a NUP. They are astonishingly poorly structured in territory, function and time; few national political leaders seem to grasp (or wish to grasp) the big picture, and the governmental tools needed are not honed for use. Rigid bureaucracy[102] cannot cope with kaleidoscopic interaction, value shifts and increasing societal and technological complexity coupled with vast numbers of people. The demise of bureaucracy in its old form may be coming about in *task force government* (within reasonably rigid parameters), *central planning, cybernetic direction* and *participatory de-*

mocracy! As people take part in the challenge to build a better world, the process of doing so is perceived by many both as *rewarding* in and of itself and *highly educative*.[103] Demands for more individual autonomy under dated formalistic administrations in schools, factories and government offices were already heard a dozen years ago as it became clear that rigidity hardly leads to productivity in the *end* result especially when all this takes place under a demeaning *means*. Alvin Toffler has sketched popularly the *new ad-hocracy* of coequal task force experts beyond hierarchy in conjoint attack on problems. Who is boss if everyone is his own man? The "nonquestionable specialist" in a nonhierarchical bureaucracy of sideways relationship seems to be the planning pattern—especially for NUP holism—of tomorrow. *The Active Society* of Etzioni interacting as a complex whole in new forms of *societal guidance* basically through activist political mobilization techniques[104] and *planful consensus formation* seems to be the newest ploy for macrosocietal guidance. It is a thoroughly complicated time-consuming operation and is in effect the front-end loading discussed above. But it appears preferable to negative results for failing proper plan preparation through participation of the clients. Finally *new* societal structures can be invented to accomplish tasks decided on by the above slithery process—not only new levels of government but highly innovated hybrids of partial government/partial capitalist inspiration such as the already mentioned local development corporation, state development corporation, new town or community development corporation. This is a marriage of public and private government. Such "public" authorities outside of traditional government are now in the works in many places.[105] Beyond and outside of this is an empirical sort of behavioral Machiavellianism growing up to get worth-while plans operational in a world where veto powers and negativism reinforce inertia. How effective such political "con games" are remains to be seen, but they are clearly in the behavioral/social science research mills.[106] Lawrence D. Mann, head of Harvard University's Department of City and Regional Planning, states flatly, "To an important extent, American urban planning has become applied social science"[107] and as American planning *theory* goes so goes the world.

AN EARTHY CONCLUSION: RESOURCE ALLOCATION FOR POSITIVE REINFORCEMENT

"The cookie or the whip" nicely summarizes a simplistic bit of behavioral technology. B. F. Skinner, who symbolizes that psychological point of view, has taught us in his various analyses of behavioral control that positive reinforcements (rewards) rather than negative reinforcements (penalties) enhance the learning process.[108] Similarly nations have discovered, including those with strong centralized governments, that physical, financial and possibly honorific rewards to good "cities" and "good" regions get results. National capital investments lead local capital investments and generally exert a multiplier effect on private sector investments in capitalist countries. Charles M. Haar, lawyer/planner, while assistant secretary for Metropolitan Development at the U. S. Department of Housing and Urban Development, stated that "Capital programming is the primary tool available to planning agencies to translate their work into action."[109] Whatever the system of taxation and however it is turned back to or "owned" by local government, a certain important free residual amount of tax income tends to collect in the national treasury (more so even in such a federal system as the United States). This "free money" gives important real power to national government to carry out its will by "sharing" with local governments. If the borrowing power of the national government is added to this tax income, there is a very considerable leverage to direct the aims, extent and content of a national urban development policy—despite the predictable howls from functional sectors and territorial regions on which national beneficence fails to fall. One must report with considerable trepidation that in order to generate community-oriented "public works" of a sufficient magnitude that actually can mold the future, there will of necessity be *heavy* transfers from personal disposable income in "capitalist" society through taxation into government coffers and in socialist societies transfers away from dearly beloved and hard-won consumer purchasable goods (as well as armaments and heavy industry) to state granted services. Does either type of central government actually have the power or will to do this? Developing nations simply lack the resources to do much even with foreign aid except, of course, the new rich oil nations.

There seems little value in administering too much "whip" to force compliance, although the rather pragmatic list of "cookies" given below can be read in reverse as penalties to be used against public and private sector actors who fail "to go along" with the agreed-on, ever-shifting cybernetic national planning effort. "Salutory neglect" might be a simple summary of such penalizing tactics.

Here is a list, grouped under four rubrics, of positive reinforcements or governmental devices employed in one nation or another during the past decade, to direct a national urbanization policy/plan:

Psychic Rewards

designate a growth area,
publicize an "outstanding city,"
single out areas of "national importance" (historic, resources, special environmental quality).

Direct Infrastructure Investment

highways and streets,
railroad development,
harbor installations,
airports,
water supplies for industry,
cheap and plentiful power.

Indirect Infrastructure Investment

housing subsidies/low rentals,
housing crash-building programs,
educational facilities and subsidies,
cultural and recreational facilities and subsidies,
extended social services,
R & D aid,
domestic water supply/waste disposal systems.

Financial Inducements

grants to industries locating in area,
lower rents for business and industry in facilities built by government,
quick write-offs for factories, etc.,
travel bonus for workers to move to area,
extra wage payments to workers (government subsidy),
reduced taxation of various sorts,
differential power and transport rates,
government orders guaranteed.

Unquestionably, this is a very powerful battery of control mechanisms with innumerable ramifications and varied mixes. The crux of the matter is to get acquiescence under a territorial representational system to single out special areas (or functions?) for special favors—in fact, a whole bundle of favors. The sad fate in American cities of the Model Cities program—in effect the singling out of an inadequate neighborhood for a package delivery of federal government programs—is instructive on the microscale. All the other neighborhoods, furiously jealous, demanded equal shares—the egalitarian ethic—and finally forced the diversion of the funds to the mayor who parceled them out in driblets to all areas, thus having *no* appreciable impact. Similarly the eight *métropoles d'équilibre* designed to balance the magnetism of Paris are *not* exploding with new vigor, while the French capital continues to sop up national public and private capital, skilled people and the headquarters of all aspects of French life—not excluding the higher culture and possibly gastronomics!

The power of the fat purse held and continuously replenished in the hands of the national government as the taxing agent par excellence is tremendous, obviously too in socialist countries and through international aid (and oil revenues) in developing nations. Central government has "discretionary funds" (national disposable income) not unconnected with international relations functions which can hopefully be used: butter rather than guns and moon jaunts sacrificed to internal development. Unfortunately internationally generated variables can crash into the national system like wayward planets reversing human development decisions, as is the sad case in modern Israel.

A national urbanization policy and plan are an act of will. Too little is clearly known about society, about goals/values, about the relation of space to behavior, about the incredibly complex interrelationship of everything to everything else. Even less is known about galloping sociocultural change that threatens continuously to engulf us. Plans are often poor and tend to blow up in the faces of the all-too-ignorant "experts." But *no plans* will almost certainly lead to great trouble; man's life on earth is not an automatic progress machine. Decision making is unbelievably difficult and becomes more so. Human adjustment is sociocultural with ever new institutional structuring and technologies; there is no other way to survive. The stark question remains, however, can the adjustments made in macroplanning urban society on earth be efficacious enough soon enough? One wonders and yet in the great world capitals, as evidenced in our eleven test cases, millions and millions of humans do survive and some few already live well. Can't man spread the successes obtained and through hard thought and resolute action go still further?

A final note of warning on the two poles of disaster threatening modern society. The first is *revolution* or *anarchy* resulting from the fact that there is no legitimated authority enjoying a popular consensus based on a demonstrated "freedom" for the individual and a competence and economy in resource use.[110] The second pole is a *planned society under powerful centralized authority* that refuses to make any little mistakes, but waits to make truly major ones in societal misdirection. Witness the Japanese attack on Pearl Harbor and Adolf Hitler's early "splendid" Nazi victories and possibly America's Watergate on a smaller scale. Thus between the Scylla of *anarchy* and the Charybdis of *planned centralized macroincompetence* there may be something to be said for the fumbling intelligence of planning by democracies (it is at least cybernetic!) where decisions are made through mutual trade-offs in the market place of both ideas and political action.[111] Guiding assorted ships of state by variedly arranged NUPs into the information/service society of the Brave New World should keep urbanized man busy for sometime ahead. There remains a scarcity of knowledge and of skills. Well-planned cities in a well-planned society are still before us.

NOTES

[1] Cf. Walter Isard et al., *Methods of Regional Analysis: An Introduction to Regional Science*. New York, John Wiley and Sons, Inc., 1960.

[2] Cf. "Urban Economics" by Wilbur Thompson in H. Wentworth Eldredge (ed.), *Taming Megalopolis*. New York, Doubleday Anchor, 1967, Vol. I, Chap. 4, pp. 156–90. *The Journal of Urban Economics* made its bow with Vol. 1 in 1974, edited by a Princeton University economist.

[3] Bureau of the Census, *United States Summary, 1970, Census of Population and Housing,* PHC(2)-1, p. 11. Table D, "Percent Change in Population of 25 Fastest Growing SMSAs: 1960 to 1970."

[4] The New York *Times,* December 31, 1972.

[5] Raymond Vernon, *The Changing Economic Function of the Central City* (New York, Area Development Committee of Committee for Economic Development [CED], 1959), and David L. Birch, *The Economic Future of City and Suburb* (New York, CED Supplementary Paper, Number 30, 1970).

[6] Wilbur R. Thompson, "The Challenge of Structural Unemployment," *A Preface to Urban Economics*. Baltimore, Johns Hopkins Press for Resources for the Future, Inc., 1965, pp. 204–13.

[7] Cf. the Port of New York and New Jersey's World Trade Center in Lower New York City extravaganza with 10,000,000 square feet of rentable office space lodged in "the world's tallest building" (until Chicago's newest skyscraper), twin towers "soaring 110 stories and 1,350 feet into the air" and subsidiary buildings. It is more commodius than the Pentagon. What this will do to rental patterns in older New York office buildings is not yet clear.

[8] Jane Jacobs, *The Economy of Cities*. New York, Random House, 1969.

[9] Daniel P. Moynihan, *Maximum Feasible Misunderstanding*. New York, The Free Press, 1970.

[10] Marcus F. Franda, "Policy Responses to India's Green Revolution." Hanover,

N.H., American Universities Field Staff, South Asia Series, Vol. XVI, No. 9, 1972.

[11] For a competent, if somewhat optimistic, review of the component tactics for such a strategy, see "Training and Jobs for the Urban Poor" by the Research and Policy Committee of the Committee for Economic Development, July 1970. Denmark is considering such a strategy turning their entire land into a "green metropolis."

[12] Harvey W. Schultz, et al., *Planning for Jobs: New York City Attempts to Retain and Create Blue Collar Jobs.* Washington, D.C., A.I.P. *Planners Notebook,* Vol. 2, No. 1, February 1972.

[13] See Chapter 5 above.

[14] Richard S. Rosenbloom and Robin Marris (eds.), *Social Innovation in the City: New Enterprises for Community Development.* Cambridge, Mass., Harvard University Press, 1969, pp. 161–97. The Twentieth Century Fund produced an enthusiastic report on the Community Development Corporation's *CDCs: New Hope for the Inner City* (New York, 1971), reporting that seventy-five were already operating, largely in impoverished minority areas.

[15] Robert Theobald (ed.), *The Guaranteed Income.* New York, Doubleday, 1967.

[16] Daniel P. Moynihan, *The Politics of a Guaranteed Income: The Nixon Administration and Family Assistance Plan.* New York, Random House, 1973.

[17] The New York *Times,* December 22, 1972. Cf. Fred Best (ed.), *The Future of Work.* Englewood Cliffs, N.J., Prentice-Hall, Inc., 1973.

[18] The New York *Times,* March 28, 1973.

[19] Riva Poor (ed.), *4 Days, 40 Hours: Reporting a Revolution in Work and Leisure.* Cambridge, Mass., Bursk and Poor, 1970.

[20] Martin Meyerson with Jacqueline Tyrwhitt, Brian Falk, Patricia Sekler, *Face of the Metropolis.* Sponsored by ACTION, The National Council for Good Cities. New York, Random House, 1963, p. 7.

[21] Peter Blake, *God's Own Junkyard: The Planned Deterioration of America's Landscape.* New York, Holt, Rinehart and Winston, 1964.

[22] *Parade,* Boston Sunday *Globe,* February 4, 1973.

[23] Beauty for America, *Proceedings of the White House Conference on Natural Beauty,* May 24–25, 1965, Washington, D.C., U. S. Government Printing Office, 1965.

[24] HMSO, 1953.

[25] Paul D. Spreiregen, *Urban Design: The Architecture of Towns and Cities.* New York, McGraw-Hill Book Company, for the American Institute of Architects, 1965.

[26] Christopher Tunnard and Boris Pushkarev, *Man-Made America: Chaos or Control.* New Haven, Yale University Press, 1963.

[27] Ian McHarg, *Design with Nature.* Garden City, New York, The Natural History Press, 1969.

[28] William H. Whyte, *Cluster Development.* New York, American Conservation Foundation, 1964.

[29] Richard Dober, *Environmental Design.* New York, Van Nostrand, Reinhold, 1969.

[30] Kevin Lynch, et al., *The Image of the City.* Cambridge, Mass., The Technology Press and Harvard University Press, 1960. The sounds of music can be quantified.

[31] John Appleyard, Kevin Lynch, and John R. Myer, *The View from the Road.* Cambridge, Mass., The M.I.T. Press, 1965.

[32] Kevin Lynch, *What Time Is This?* Cambridge, Mass., The M.I.T. Press, 1973.

[33] Robert Sommer, *Personal Space* (Englewood Cliffs, N.J., Prentice-Hall, Inc., a Spectrum Book, 1969), and his later *Design Awareness* (San Francisco, Rinehart Press, 1972), which presses for at least that until stronger behavioral/social science support can be offered and stresses "client" input and feedback in physical planning at every level.

[34] Stanley Parker, *The Future of Work and Leisure.* New York, Praeger, 1971.

[35] "Housing in the Year 2000," *The MGIC Newsletter,* November 1971.

[36] Two serious little publications echo this concern. James C. Charlesworth (ed.), *Leisure in America: Blessing or Curse?* (monograph in a series sponsored by the American Academy of Political and Social Science, Philadelphia, 1964), and Charles K. Brighthill, *The Challenge of Leisure* (Englewood Cliffs, N.J., Prentice-Hall, Inc., 1960), with a religious twist.

[37] *Time,* September 18, 1972.

[38] *Time,* February 15, 1971.

[39] Sebastian de Grazia, *Of Time, Work and Leisure.* New York, The Twentieth Century Fund, 1962.

[40] John Galbraith, *The New Industrial State.* Boston, Houghton Mifflin, 1967.

[41] Peter Heyworth, "Will the Paris Opera Become the Greatest?" The New York *Times,* March 25, 1973.

[42] Ibid.

[43] Alvin Toffler, *The Culture Consumers.* Baltimore, Penguin, Inc. edition, 1965.

[44] Rockefeller Panel Report, *The Performing Arts.* New York, McGraw-Hill, 1965.

[45] Norbert Wiener, *Cybernetics* (New York, John Wiley, 1940), and *The Human Use of Human Beings* (Boston, Houghton Mifflin, 1950).

[46] "The Utopian Urge: You Make the Future Today," wraparound in *Harper's,* March 1973. This is a fresh hodgepodge of Utopian thinking which nicely illustrates the mind-stretching function in imagining novel "no places."

[47] Kurt Baier and Nicholas Rescher (eds.), *Values and the Future.* New York, The Free Press, 1969.

[48] Dennis Gabor, *Inventing the Future.* New York, Knopf, 1964.

[49] Herman Kahn and Anthony Wiener, *The Year 2000: A Framework on Speculation for the Next Thirty-Three Years.* New York, Macmillan, 1967. This grew out of the American Academy of Arts and Science's "Commission on the Year 2000," a prestigious panel of experts headed by Daniel Bell, the sociologist.

[50] Op. cit.

[51] Herman Kahn and B. Bruce-Briggs, *Things to Come: Thinking About the Seventies and Eighties.* New York, Macmillan, 1972.

[52] Rachel Carson, *The Silent Spring.* Boston, Houghton Mifflin, 1962.

[53] Dennis Meadows and Associates, *The Limits to Growth.* New York, Universe Books, 1972.

[54] H. Wentworth Eldredge, "A Mark II Survey and Critique of Future Research Teaching in North America," *Technological Forecasting and Social Change,* Vol. 4, No. 4 (1973). Later figures are now available.

[55] *Spread City: Projection of Development Trends and the Issues They Pose: The Tri-State New York Metropolitan Region, 1960–1985.* New York, Regional Plan Association, Bulletin 100, September 1962.

[56] Paul Reed, *Intentional Societies and Ordered Environments.* Monticello, Ill., Council of Planning Librarians Exchange Bibliography #320, 1972.

[57] Daniel P. Moynihan, *Maximun Feasible Misunderstanding.* New York, The Free Press, 1970.

[58] Edward Banfield, *The Unheavenly City Revisited.* Boston; Little Brown, 1974.

[59] Bernard J. Frieden, "Improving Federal Housing Subsidies," Summary Report Working Paper No. 1. Cambridge, Mass., Joint Center for Urban Studies, 1971, p. 1.

[60] Lloyd Rodwin, *Nations and Cities.* Boston, Houghton Mifflin, 1970, p. 267.

[61] Cf. "The Policy Orientation" in Daniel Lerner and Harold D. Lasswell (eds.), *The Policy Sciences: Recent Developments in Scope and Method.* Stanford, Calif., Stanford University Press, 1951, pp. 3ff.

[62] Yehezkel Dror, *Design for Policy Sciences.* New York, American Elsevier Publishing Co., 1971. Cf. also his *Ventures in Policy Sciences.* New York, American Elsevier Publishing Co., 1971.

[63] Amitai Etzioni, *The Active Society.* New York, The Free Press, 1968.

[64] John Friedman. *Retracking America: A Theory of Transactive Planning.* New York, Doubleday Anchor, AO-60, 1973, blurb. Italics editor.

[65] Yehezkel Dror, "Prolegomena to Policy Sciences," *Policy Sciences,* Vol. 1, No. 1 (1970), 10.

[66] The Rand Corporation think tank has been running a Ph.D. program in the policy sciences; it is not yet accredited.

[67] Robert Boguslaw, *The New Utopians.* Englewood Cliffs, N.J., Prentice-Hall, Inc., 1965.

[68] Kenneth Boulding, "General Systems Theory—The Skeleton of Science," in Walter Buckley (ed.), *Modern Systems Research for the Behavioral Scientist.* Chicago, Aldine Publishing Co., 1968.

[69] Roy F. Kenzie, *Urban General Systems: A Multidisciplinary Bibliography.* Monticello, Ill., Council of Planning Libraries Exchange Bibliography, #236, November 1971. This is an extremely useful organized breakdown of the numerous facets of the attack on the urban system, seen as a whole, which is followed here. Cf. C. West Churchman, *The Systems Approach.* New York, Dell Publishing Co., 1966.

[70] Cf. Russel L. Ackoff and Maurice Sa Sieni, *Fundamentals of Operations Research* (New York, John Wiley and Sons, 1968), with its journal *Operations Research* including varied materials and numerous esoteric activities: network planning, critical path analysis, suboptimization (in decision theory), linear programming, etc.

[71] For example, Guy Black, *The Application of Systems Analysis to Government Operations.* New York, Frederick A. Praeger, 1968.

[72] John Van Neuman and Oskar Morgenstern, *Theory of Games and Economic Behavior.* Princeton, N.J., Princeton University Press, 1955.

[73] Karl Deutsch, *The Nerves of Government.* New York, The Free Press, 1963.

[74] Richard Meier, *A Communication Theory of Urban Growth.* Cambridge, Mass., The M.I.T. Press, 1962.

[75] Jay Wright Forrester, *Urban Dynamics.* Cambridge, Mass., The M.I.T. Press, 1969.

[76] John Taylor, *Social Science Instructional Simulation Systems: A Selected Bibliography.* Sheffield, England, University of Sheffield, 1969. Cf. his *Instructional Planning Systems: A Gaming Simulation Approach to Urban Problems.* Cambridge, England, Cambridge University Press, 1971.

[77] Karl Loewenstein, *An Annotated Bibliography on Urban Games.* Monticello, Ill., Council of Planning Librarian Exchange Bibliography, July 1971.

[78] Allan G. Feldt, *Selected Papers in Operational Gaming,* Miscellaneous Paper No. 5, Center for Housing and Environmental Studies, Division of Urban Studies, Ithaca, Cornell University, 1966.

[79] H. R. Hamilton, et al., *Systems Simulation for Regional Analysis.* Cambridge, Mass., M.I.T. Press, 1969.

[80] Jay W. Forrester, *World Dynamics.* Cambridge, Mass., Wright-Allen Press, 1971.

[81] Dennis Meadows and Associates, *The Limits to Growth.* New York, Universe Books, 1972.

[82] Barry S. Weller and Thomas D. Graff, *Bibliography of Urban and Regional Information Systems.* Monticello, Ill., Council of Planning Librarians Exchange Bibliography, #316/317, September 1972.

[83] Jack D. Douglas has edited a concise little catalog: *The Technological Threat* (Englewood Cliffs, N.J., Prentice-Hall, 1971), which does point out that there are real and potential dangers to the individual in symbiotic intellectual/technological technologies.

[84] Carl H. Weiss, *Evaluative Research; Usable Methods for Assessing Program Effectiveness.* Englewood Cliffs, N.J., Prentice-Hall, 1972.

[85] Raymond A. Bauer (ed.), *Social Indicators.* Cambridge, Mass. The M.I.T. Press, 1966, p. 1.

[86] Ibid., Bertram Gross, "The State of the Nation, Social Systems Accounting," Chap. 3, pp. 154–271. See his earlier *The State of the Nation.* London: Social Science Paperbacks, SSP12, 1966.

[87] Bertram Gross, *Social Intelligence for America's Future.* Boston, Allyn and Bacon, 1969.

[88] Eleanor Sheldon and Wilbert E. Moore (eds.), *Indicators of Social Change.* New York, Russell Sage Foundation, 1968.

[89] *Behavior Today,* August 7, 1972, Vol. 3, No. 32.

[90] *Social Trends,* London, H.M.S.O. PL No. 29/1970.

[91] *Toward a Social Report,* U. S. Government Printing Office, 1969.

[92] *Report on the World Social Structure,* Committee of Experts (New York, United Nations).

[93] Report on *International Definition and Measurement of Standards and Levels of Living Standards,* United Nations Economic and Social Council, Commission for Social Development. New York, United Nations, 1954. A summary appears yearly. Cf. the excellent *Aggregate Data Analysis: Political and Social Indicators in Cross-National Research.* Paris, Mouton, 1968, edited by Charles L. Taylor.

[94] *Report on National Growth, 1972*. Washington, D.C., Superintendent of Documents, #1770-0156, 1972, p. ix.

[95] Bertram M. Gross in *Toward a Social Report*. Washington, D.C., U. S. Government Printing Office, 1969. Gross has an interesting series of tables detailing the evidence for this judgment, pp. 5–16.

[96] Robert Hunter, *Brain Washing in Red China*. New York, The Vanguard Press, 1951. Cf. the study of Joost A. M. Merloo (Dutch psychiatrist), *The Rape of the Mind* (Cleveland, World Publishing Co., 1956), which leans heavily on World War II Nazi activities.

[97] Perry London, *Behavior Control*. New York Perennial Library, Harper & Row, 1969, p. 30.

[98] Cf. H. Wentworth Eldredge, *The Second American Revolution*. New York, Wm. Morrow, 1964, Chap. X, "New Sources of Power: Thought Control from Education to Menticide."

[99] J. M. R. Delgado, *Evolution of Physical Growth of the Brain*. New York, The American Museum of Natural History, 1965. A "brave bull" was brought to a dead stop in a full charge through electrical impulses sent directly into his brain via electrodes.

[100] Amitai Etzioni, "Human Beings Are Not Very Easy to Change After All," *Saturday Review*, June 3, 1972, pp. 45–47. A book is forthcoming along these lines.

[101] Marvin E. Shaw, *Group Dynamics*. New York, McGraw-Hill Book Company, 1971. This too can be explored by mathematical model. Cf. Otomar J. Bartos, *Simple Models of Group Behavior*. New York, Columbia University Press, 1967, especially Part III: "Game-Theoretical Models."

[102] See Max Weber, "Bureaucracy" in Gerth and Mills, *From Max Weber* (New York, Oxford University Press, Inc., 1946), for the classic position.

[103] Fred E. Katz, *Autonomy and Organization*. New York, Random House, 1968.

[104] Sarajane Heidt and Amitai Etzioni (eds.), *Societal Guidance*. New York, Crowell, 1969.

[105] Richard S. Rosenbloom and Robin Marris, *Social Innovation in the City: New Enterprises for Community Development, a Collection of Working Papers*. Cambridge, Mass., Harvard University Program on Technology and Society, 1969. And symptomatic of the Business School (B-School) thrust on *delivery* is the McKinsey Staff Paper, *Managing Community Development: The Systems Approach in Columbia, Maryland,* by Mahlon Apgar IV, 1971.

[106] Cf. Guy Benveniste, *The Politics of Expertise* (Berkeley, Cal., The Glendersary Press, 1972), billed as a sociologist of planning he explores how the expert gets power to produce. Psychologists Richard Christie and Florence F. Geis have written forthrightly *Studies in Machiavellianism* (New York, Academic Press, 1970), examining "successful" ploys in more varied public and private operations.

[107] Lawrence D. Mann, "Social Science Advances and Planning Applications: 1900–1965," *Journal of the American Institute of Planners,* November 1972, pp. 346–58.

[108] As far back as 1953, *Science and Human Behavior* (New York, The Free Press, 1953), and more recently in *Beyond Freedom and Dignity* (New York, Knopf, 1971).

[109] "Remarks: Toward a National Policy for Planning the Environment," at the American Institute of Planners 1968 Conference, October 12, 1968, p. 1.

[110] Robert A. Dahl, *After the Revolution.* New Haven, Conn., Yale University Press, 1970, p. 56.

[111] This is a paraphrase of the wisdom contained in the not very well-known, little book by Charles E. Lindblom, *The Intelligence of Democracy: Decision Making through Mutual Adjustment.* New York, The Free Press, 1965.

Index